"This important update of *The Sustainable Enterprise Fieldbook* offers so much valuable and practical guidance for any manager to help his or her company become a sustainability leader. With its particular emphasis on people, their mental models, the development of new behaviors and expectations, and the metrics and feedback by which progress can be evaluated, this book goes to the core of how to motivate change in any organization and help us strive for, in the words of John Ehrenfeld, a flourishing and sustainable world."

Andrew J. Hoffman, Holcim (US) Professor of Sustainable Enterprise, Ross School of Business/SEAS, University of Michigan, USA

"The authors' holistic representation of sustainable globalization using a six-lens framework is an incredibly useful addition to the decision-making toolkit of business leaders and managers driving strategic initiatives in multinational firms. It is an especially valuable resource for managers seeking to design and execute global strategies that are aligned with sustainable objectives. This well-researched book not only draws readers' attention toward numerous environmental and social problems currently facing humanity, using up to date numbers and figures, but also provides insights and detailed examples of specific projects undertaken by multinational firms that have sought to address a few of these problems as part of their sustainability initiatives. This book urges leaders to place sustainability at the core of their business strategy. To this end, it provides conceptual tools and real-world examples to help business leaders find their way to sustainable profits."

Pallavi Shukla, PhD, Assistant Professor of Professional Practice, Rutgers Business School, USA

"*The Sustainable Enterprise Fieldbook: Building New Bridges* is an excellent resource for students just learning the ropes of organizational sustainability. It paints a clear picture of the current state of sustainable enterprise, where the gaps are, and what needs to be done by both individuals and organizations in order to cross the bridge to achieve true sustainability. In addition to theories and examples, this book provides the tools needed for people – at all levels of an organization – to take action to promote purposeful, sustainable enterprise, making it a valuable resource for both sustainability newcomers and seasoned experts alike."

Kinan Tadmori, Master of Business and Science student in Sustainability, Professional Science Master's Program, Rutgers University, USA

"The next time I teach my 'Sustainable Business' course, I will certainly be using *The Sustainable Enterprise Fieldbook* as the primary text. Having reviewed the advance copy of the fully revised and updated Second Edition, I am aware of no better resource for faculty and students than this text. The breadth of topics covered ensures an interdisciplinary approach to sustainable business practices with an emphasis on Human Capital, and the depth of each of the chapters, with numerous case studies, will facilitate engaged class discussion."

Ira Feldman, Founder & Managing Director, Sustainability Curriculum Consortium, USA

The Sustainable Enterprise Fieldbook

With deep thought and inspiring examples, this updated book engages readers by increasing their understanding and awareness of what sustainability means conceptually, practically, personally, and professionally. It provides readers with the tools and techniques to improve the social, environmental, and economic performance of their organizations in both the short and long term.

Since sustainability is not achieved in a siloed environment, everyone has a critical role to play on this journey. *The Sustainable Enterprise Fieldbook* engages today's managers and leaders of organizations, in both the private sector and civil society, who are being challenged as never before to find ways to play a proactive role in understanding and addressing the risks and opportunities of sustainability. It teaches them how to apply systems thinking to turn our most intractable problems into exciting business opportunities, and offers ground breaking frameworks in new chapters on globalization, strategy, metrics, and sustainability models for collaboration, technology, and community.

That is why this book is structured to be a fieldbook to provide practitioners the Activities, Cases, and Tools that they can use to help move their enterprise through progressively higher performing stages of sustainability. Readers will also gain access to the innovative *Living Fieldbook*: an online community forum filled with supporting materials.

Jeana Wirtenberg, Associate Professor of Professional Practice, Rutgers University, USA, and President and CEO, Transitioning to Green, USA.

Linda M. Kelley, Principal and Enterprise Ecologist, Transitioning to Green, USA.

David Lipsky, Head of Coaching, Assessment and Executive Onboarding at Samsung Electronics America.

William G. Russell, Principal with Transitioning to Green, USA.

The Sustainable Enterprise Fieldbook

Building New Bridges

Second Edition

Edited by Jeana Wirtenberg,
with Linda M. Kelley, David Lipsky,
and William G. Russell

Routledge
Taylor & Francis Group

LONDON AND NEW YORK

Second edition published 2019
by Routledge
2 Park Square, Milton Park, Abingdon, Oxon, OX14 4RN

and by Routledge
711 Third Avenue, New York, NY 10017

Routledge is an imprint of the Taylor & Francis Group, an informa business

First edition published by Greenleaf Publishing Ltd 2008

British Library Cataloguing-in-Publication Data
A catalogue record for this book is available from the British Library

Library of Congress Cataloging-in-Publication Data
A catalog record has been requested for this book

ISBN: 978-1-783-53527-9 (hbk)
ISBN: 978-1-783-53417-3 (pbk)
ISBN: 978-0-429-45347-2 (ebk)

Typeset in Garmond
by Out of House Publishing

First, we dedicate this book to honor the many heroes and heroines whose shoulders we stand on, and highlight here a few of the most notable ones who have passed since the first edition of our book was written.* Second, we dedicate our book to the millions of people around the world who work tirelessly every day to create a better world; and third, we dedicate it to the generations to come, who we hope will inherit a flourishing, sustainable world of endless possibilities for themselves, their children, and their children's children.

* **Jenny Ambrozek (contributing-author in our first edition)**
   Ray Anderson
   Mila Baker
   Warren Bennis
   Thomas Berry
   Fern Jones
   C.K. Prahalad

Contents

Figures

Tables

Boxes

About the contributors

Shakira Abdul-Ali, MSOD, CEO and Principal Managing Consultant, Alchemy Consulting, LLC, Trenton, NJ, USA
Abdul-Ali is an organization development specialist, trainer, and coach. Her principal areas of focus are diversity building and economic development initiatives, along with team building and performance improvement through training and coaching. Her clients have included New Jersey Transit; University of Minnesota; Head Start; Cornell University Management Development Program; Merck; Girl Scouts USA; various county colleges in New Jersey (Union, Middlesex, Essex, Camden, and Atlantic Cape); the Collaborative, Inc. (Boston, MA); and America Speaks. Before starting her own firm, Abdul-Ali held a number of public-sector roles, including Chief, New Jersey Office of Minority Business Enterprise; Administrator, New Jersey Small Business Division Office of Technical Assistance; and Assistant Director, New Jersey Governor's Study Commission on Discrimination in Public Sector Contracting.

Abdul-Ali received a BA in Economics and Urban Studies from Wellesley College, and an MS from the American University/NTL Organization Development program. She is an MBTI-qualified facilitator and a certified leader for the National Coalition Building Institute.

John D. Adams, PhD, Organizational Systems PhD Program, Saybrook Graduate School, San Francisco, CA, USA
Adams is Emeritus Professor of Organizational Systems, and was for many years the Chair of the Faculty and the Chair of the Organizational Systems PhD Program at the Saybrook Graduate School (San Francisco). He was also a guest faculty member at The Bainbridge Island Graduate Institute in the MBA in Sustainability program. These programs were each the first of their kind in teaching the principles and practices of sustainability to their learners.

His work in retirement continues to focus on the psychology of successful sustainability initiatives. He is author of *Thinking Today as if Tomorrow*

Mattered: The Rise of a Sustainable Consciousness (2000) and numerous articles and book chapters exploring the role of mental models for sustainability. Adams has been actively speaking, consulting, and writing on this topic since 1990, when he was the chair of the sustainable development task force at The World Business Academy.

Adams is the founder of Eartheart Enterprises, an international speaking, publishing, and consulting business. His clients have come primarily from the healthcare and high tech areas, including work with (HealthCare) the NIH, the NHS in the UK, Holy Cross system, Sisters of Mercy system; and (High Tech) Hewlett Packard, Digital Equipment Corporation (DEC), Sun Microsystems, Naval Air Systems Command. His work has focused on coaching and seminars in areas including sustainable development, health promotion and stress management, effective influence, and successful change implementation.

Adams has also previously served as Manager of executive development and of workplace effectiveness at Sun Microsystems; Director of Professional Development at the NTL Institute; and as Visiting Lecturer at The University of Leeds (UK). He has created 10 books and over 50 articles in the areas of health and stress management, sustainable development, personal effectiveness at work, mental models, and change.

Jenny Ambrozek, BA DipEd, SageNet LLC, Hastings-on-Hudson, NY, USA (1950–2016)

Ambrozek was Founder of SageNet (www.sageway.com), a consulting practice helping businesses create value by applying collaboration and participatory media tools connecting customers, partners, and employees. Ambrozek's online interaction work began in the mid-1980s with Edutel—an educational content service delivered on Prestel standard Videotex for the Australian Caption Centre. She was editor of *The Edutel Book: A Guide to Videotex in Education* (1985).

Coming to the United States in the 1980s, she joined Prodigy Services. In eight years at Prodigy, Ambrozek brought together a wide range of member-engagement components across a range of content areas. As Director, Community Development, she learned firsthand the importance of day-to-day operating practices in minimizing the cost of supporting interaction.

From 1996 Ambrozek helped clients implement successful online network and collaboration efforts to engage customers and promote internal knowledge sharing. With Joe Cothrel, she conducted the *Online Communities in Business 2004* study, contributing to the communities of practice organizational network survey instrument for the Network Roundtable, University of Virginia. Ambrozek was a co-founder and author of the 21st Century Organization blog, and provided her participatory media expertise to the University of Warwick Knowledge Innovation Network, Executive

Networks, and the start-up Acritas. She earned her BA DipEd at Macquarie University.

Gregory S. Andriate, EdD, Organization Innovation LLC, Palm Coast, FL, USA

Andriate is Executive Director of Organization Innovation, a consulting firm partnering with clients to develop sustainable enterprise capabilities for the 21st century. An expert in business innovation and transformational change, he helps organizations reframe, restructure, revitalize, and renew capabilities securing business value for customers and shareholders.

Since 1985, Andriate has led over 30 organizational transformation interventions in Europe and North and South America. His experience includes financial reporting/insurance savings plan conversions, agricultural/pharmaceutical product development cycle improvements, and workscape revitalization initiatives in 22 petrochemical manufacturing sites. His executive coaching experience includes reinventing corporate functions in engineering, communications, ecology/health/safety, finance, human resources, IT, logistics, and procurement.

Previously Andriate was Manager, Executive Development for BASF, responsible for executive competency and high-performance business capabilities development. Earlier, he was Assistant Dean, University of Bridgeport Metropolitan College, responsible for adult degree programs, and a faculty member at Bridgeport, Hartford, New Mexico, and West Virginia universities.

Andriate has published book chapters in *Information and Behavior* and *Communication Yearbook 6* and articles in such journals as *Communication, Communication Quarterly*, and *Communication Research Reports*, and has served on editorial boards of two academic journals. He earned his Bachelor's and Master's at Rutgers University and his Doctorate in Educational Psychology at West Virginia University.

Beth Applegate, MSOD, Applegate Consulting Group, Bloomington, IN, USA

Applegate Consulting Group (ACG) is an organization development (OD) practice with three decades of experience with national and international not-for-profit agencies, academic institutions, governmental agencies, and socially responsible for-profits. OD is a values-based system-wide process based on behavioral science knowledge. It is collaborative, and is concerned with the adaptive development, improvement, and reinforcement of strategies, structures, processes, people, culture, and other features of organizational life. OD is rooted in the constructs of human potential and development, empowerment equity, democratic processes and the importance of the use of self as a key to the leadership practices within organizations.

As Applied Behavioral Science practitioner Applegate is well positioned to bring to the fore the tradition of inquiry and dialogue in service of diversity and inclusion, social justice, and healthy individuals, groups, and organizations in the world. Working collaboratively with each client, ACG engages multi-sector organizational clients in a spectrum of change processes to strengthen leadership, team, and organizational effectiveness and sustainability. Applegate teaches a graduate course in the School of Public and Environmental Affairs (SPEA) for Indiana University on increasing understanding of one's own dimensions of difference, often a difficult and disorientating task as we rarely notice "the water in which we swim." Learners examine their own histories and how these inform the lenses through which they approach cultural differences. They are exposed to a variety of conceptual models and practical communication skills, which will allow them to make meaning of and engage effectively across differences.

Applegate has also served as adjunct faculty for American University and Trinity University and regularly speaks and presents at conferences and is an active contributor to the fields of Applied Behavioral Science and Organization Capacity-building. Applegate received the Cultural Competency Award in 2009 from the Alliance for Nonprofit Management for co-authoring *Embracing Cultural Competency: A Road Map for Nonprofit Capacity Builders* (2009). To learn more about Applegate Consulting Group please visit www.applegateonline.com.

Victoria G. Axelrod, MA, Axelrod Becker Consulting, New York, NY, USA

Axelrod is a management consultant and organization strategist. She has extensive experience developing, integrating, and executing company strategy. She is a Principal of Axelrod Becker Consulting (axelrodbecker.com), which develops sustainable growth by identifying new revenue opportunities based on the power of stakeholder networks. Clients are start-ups to *Fortune* 500 companies, nonprofits, and government agencies.

Axelrod is a former Senior Vice President and Head of Global Best Practices for the American Management Association where she doubled the revenue to $300 million in four years. She is also a Partner of Norman N. Axelrod Associates (a technology planning and solutions consulting firm). She co-founded the 21st Century Organization Group and blog to address issues in today's interconnected technology-driven global business environment (c21org.typepad.com).

Teaching at St. John's University, Tobin College of Business includes courses in Organization Systems for Sustainable Innovation, Business Plans and Entrepreneurship, and American Management and Leadership. She has published and made frequent presentations to groups such as US National Security Agency, Organization Development Network, Human Resource

Planning Society, and the US Chamber Institute. Axelrod has a BA from the University of Michigan and an MA from Columbia University.

James J. Colligan Jr., BSME, MBA, Manager—Operational Excellence Model & Continuous Improvement, PSE&G/PSEG Long Island, Newark, NJ, USA and Hicksville, NY, USA

James (Jim) Colligan is manager of the Operational Excellence Model & Continuous Improvement group for PSE&G and PSEG Long Island. PSE&G is the largest subsidiary of Public Service Enterprise Group (PSEG). PSEG is a publicly traded (NYSE:PEG) diversified energy company headquartered in New Jersey and is one of the 10 largest electric companies in the US. PSE&G currently serves nearly three-quarters of New Jersey's population in a service area consisting of a 2,600-square-mile diagonal corridor across the state. PSE&G serves 1.8 million gas customers and 2.2 million electric customers in more than 300 urban, suburban, and rural communities, including New Jersey's six largest cities. PSEG Long Island is also a subsidiary of PSEG and operates the Long Island Power Authority's transmission and distribution system under a contract which started in 2004.

Colligan is responsible for ongoing development and deployment of technical documentation and continuous improvement (CI) of processes to achieve operational excellence and balanced scorecard results. Through his staff in New Jersey and New York and an extended CI community of more than 300 Lean Six Sigma professionals, he manages progress and results for CI teams. He also supports and coaches senior leaders to develop CI capability in their respective areas to achieve business results.

Colligan joined PSEG in 1980 and has several decades of experience in a variety of line and staff roles in Fossil Production, Corporate Performance Management, Quality & Organization Effectiveness, Delivery Operations Support, Utility Operations Support, and currently Business Performance & Improvement. Colligan has a BSME from New Jersey Institute of Technology and an MBA from Fairleigh Dickinson University.

Colligan is Co-chair of the Conference Board Continuous Improvement Council. He also serves as Treasurer of Wayne Little League and has managed the Challenger League (a special needs baseball team for physically and mentally challenged children) for the past several years. Both in his personal and professional life, he finds his coaching experience to be his greatest asset. He maintains that whether your passion is baseball or business, there is no substitute for working hard, improving, and keeping score to ensure results.

Karen J. Davis, MA, New York, NY, USA

Davis has consulted with organizations globally for over 35 years. Her life's work is in the spirit of Earth wisdom, and her values and practices are grounded in multiple ways of knowing.

Davis is dedicated to building a global community and sustainability by working and learning with colleagues and groups worldwide. She is on the postgraduate faculty in Organizational Behavior and Development at the Universidad Diego Portales in Santiago, Chile. She is a board member of Open Space Institute, is active in the International Organization Development Association, and has been a Trustee of the Organization Development Network. Davis serves on the board of a large healthcare company and on boards of various community and cultural organizations.

Davis's educational background includes specializations in chemistry, counseling psychology, and social psychology. Her music training and experience are significant influences in her work and life. When not traveling or working around the world, she lives in New York City, returning regularly to her native Arizona. Summers, she is on her farm in rural Quebec, Canada, with her virtual office.

Davis describes herself as a "global citizen and gardener." The Earth is her playground and lifelong teacher.

Kent D. Fairfield, PhD, MBA, Silberman College of Business, Fairleigh Dickinson University, Madison, NJ, USA

Fairfield is Associate Professor of Management at the Silberman College of Business, Fairleigh Dickinson University. He spent his early career at Chase Manhattan Bank. Most of that time involved lending money and marketing services. After leading efforts there in training and development, he left Chase and set up Kent Fairfield Associates, consulting on organizational effectiveness.

He later added to his Harvard MBA by earning his PhD in Social and Organizational Psychology at Columbia. After four years at NYU's Wagner Graduate School of Public Service, he joined Fairleigh Dickinson 13 years ago. He soon became Principal in the Institute of Sustainable Enterprise, which does research, public outreach, and education on sustainability issues.

In addition, Fairfield has served a key role in experiential and applied learning for Silberman students. This entails arranging mentor experiences and requiring management students to do "learning management by doing management" through community service projects. He has been named New Jersey Teacher of the Year and FDU's Distinguished Professor for Education. In his off-hours, Fairfield indulges his passion for photography.

Alexis A. Fink, PhD, Intel Corp., Santa Clara, CA, USA

Fink is currently Director, Talent Intelligence Analytics at Intel. Her organization provides original organizational effectiveness research, HR analytics, talent marketplace analytics, and HR systems and tools. Prior to Intel, Fink spent seven years at Microsoft, where her roles included Director of Talent Management Infrastructure. Her career has been characterized by an integrative approach to HR, including developing and implementing competency systems and integrated talent management systems. Her background also includes work in large scale organizational transformation across multiple industries and contexts. Fink earned her PhD in Industrial/Organizational Psychology from Old Dominion University. In addition to practicing and leading in organizations, she continues to teach, is a frequent SIOP contributor, and an occasional author and journal editor.

Gil Friend, Chief Sustainability Officer, Palo Alto, CA, USA

Friend is Founder and CEO of Natural Logic, Inc., a strategy boutique creating and capturing value at the intersection of business and sustainability; Chairman of Gradient Capital, developing financial platforms to finance the future we seek; and Chief Sustainability Officer for Palo Alto, where he leads the city's "climate moonshot." A lifelong social entrepreneur and sustainability geek, Friend is widely considered one of the founders of the sustainable business movement and was named an inaugural member of the Sustainability Hall of Fame, with Ray Anderson, Amory Lovins, Karl-Henrik Robert, and Bob Willard, and "one of the 10 most influential sustainability voices in America" by *The Guardian*.

For more than 45 years, Friend has helped companies and communities design, implement, and measure profitable sustainability strategies. He served in the California Governor's Office developing early sustainability policies and programs. He was a founding board member of Internet pioneer Institute for Global Communications, founder and executive director of Foundation for the Arts of Peace, and co-founder and co-director of the Institute for Local Self-Reliance, a leading urban ecology and economic development "think-and-do tank," where he pioneered the current "green roof" trend 40 years ago.

Friend has served as MBA faculty at Presidio Graduate School, and California College of the Arts. He lectures widely on business strategy and sustainability issues. He holds an MS in Systems Ecology from Antioch University, has a black belt in Aikido, and is a seasoned practitioner of "The Natural Step" sustainability framework. He was a founding board member of the Sustainable Business Alliance, and currently serves on the board of directors of Inquiring Systems, Inc. and the advisory boards of CleanFish, the Green Chamber of Commerce, Green World Campaign, RePower Capital, Silicon Valley Net Positive Leadership Council, Sustainable Brands, and the Sustainability Accounting Standards Board, and was twice named one of the Bay Area's "top 25 movers and shakers in clean tech."

He is author of *The Truth About Green Business* and *Green Business Field Guide* (2009), hundreds of articles on business and sustainability, and is a contributor to other books.

Joel Harmon, PhD, Institute for Sustainable Enterprise, Fairleigh Dickinson University, Madison, NJ, USA

Harmon is Professor of Management in the Silberman College of Business at Fairleigh Dickinson University, a Distinguished Faculty Fellow of its Center for Human Resource Management, and Director of Research for its Institute for Sustainable Enterprise. During his 24-year academic career, he has served as Department Chair, President of the University Faculty Senate, President of the Eastern Academy of Management, co-leader of the Sustainable Practices Action Research Community workshop series (1997–2007) at the Academy of Management, and founding member of the Academy's Theory-to-Practice Executive Steering Committee. Before joining academia, he held several management positions in industry.

He specializes in organization strategy and transformation, focusing on linkages between people, learning, and sustainability practices and corporate performance. He has published widely in a variety of leading academic and practitioner journals including *Health Care Management*, *Case Research*, *Human Resource Planning*, *Cost Management*, *Group Decision & Negotiation*, and *Organization Behavior & Human Decision Processes*.

Harmon earned his PhD in Organization Communication and Change from the State University of New York at Albany and an MS in Environmental Policy and Planning from Rensselaer Polytechnic Institute.

Linda M. Kelley, Principal, Transitioning to Green, LLC, www. transitioningtogreen.com. Pittsfield, MA, USA

Kelley works at the nexus where big picture vision meets practical implementation to produce sustainable enterprise that is relevant and contributes to overall prosperity. She is a cultural creative who guides individuals and teams through the process of change to develop the mindset, presence, and capabilities they need to lead and collaborate in the building of a sustainable world.

Her focus is on cultivating professional and personal excellence that bridges the gap between knowing what to do and being able to do it. Kelley's whole systems approach to learning and change enables clients to navigate difficult issues in doable steps that produce rapid, genuine results. As happens with the turn of a kaleidoscope, our accumulated skills and experiences reorder and recombine to make new original patterns time after time; we're always a work-in-progress. It is the rich breadth and depth of our humanness, simultaneously simple and complex in its unfolding, that forms the foundation of Kelley's work as a consultant and coach.

She brings to her consulting, training, and coaching a pragmatic, hands-on perspective gained from 30 years of business experience coupled with her artist's sense of invention, play, and design, and an amateur naturalist's powers of observation. She works with both businesses and government agencies.

Kelley is a leader in forging new ground using virtual technologies for collaborative problem-solving, immersive learning, and advancing collective ingenuity. Delia Lake is Kelley's avatar representative in virtual platforms such as Second Life® where she has worked for over 10 years to raise awareness of and work collaboratively on real-world environmental and sustainability issues with people around the globe. She does this because she believes that virtual media will provide essential co-creative spaces and interfaces between local and global sustainability initiatives.

Kelley is a co-author of *The Sustainable Enterprise Fieldbook* (2008). She serves on the steering committee of the Downtown Pittsfield Farmers Market, is a member of the core team of the Pittsfield Working Cities Challenge, and formerly was on the board of the Sustainable Business Network of Greater Boston.

Richard N. Knowles, PhD, the Center for Self-Organizing Leadership, Niagara Falls, NY, USA

Knowles is Co-founder and Director of the Center for Self-Organizing Leadership. His work is focused on helping organizations become much more effective through the use of Self-Organizing Leadership.

He served in the DuPont Company for over 36 years beginning as a research chemist (40 patents), then in a variety of manufacturing assignments at Repauno, NJ, Chambers Works, NJ (as Assistant Plant Manager), Niagara Falls, NY (Plant Manager, 1983–1987), Belle, WV (Plant Manager, 1987–1995), and finally as Director of Community Awareness, Emergency Response and Industry Outreach. In 1995 he received the EPA Region III Chemical Emergency Planning and Preparedness Partnership Award.

His leadership work is featured in Tom Petzinger's *The New Pioneers* (1999) and Roger Lewin and Birute Regine's *The Soul at Work* (2000). He is author of *The Leadership Dance: Pathways to Extraordinary Organizational Effectiveness* (2002).

He has discovered and developed a unique approach to using the Process Enneagram, a highly effective tool for organizational transformation. It cuts to the heart of the key variables in dynamic situations enabling people to more successfully move forward through complex challenges. Knowles earned a PhD in Organic Chemistry at the University of Rochester and a BA in Chemistry at Oberlin College.

David Lipsky, PhD, Samsung Electronics America, Highland Mills, NY, USA

Lipsky is Head of Coaching, Executive Assessment and Onboarding at Samsung Electronics America. He has over 25 years of experience in building organizational and leadership capabilities that contribute to business success and personal growth. He has accomplished this by focusing on the potential and possibilities of the people and businesses he has worked with and using his extensive experience in strategic alignment, leadership development, and organizational transformation.

Lipsky has had the opportunity to work with many organizations in a variety of industries, including Sony, Unilever, United Technologies, Bank of America, Alpharma, KPMG Peat Marwick, and Merrill Lynch. Lipsky is also an Associate Professor at the Jack Welch Management Institute. He has lectured and authored articles and book chapters on internal consulting, organizational development, and sustainability. Lipsky received his undergraduate degree from Cornell University in Human Ecology and received a PhD in Applied Psychology from Hofstra University, focusing on leadership effectiveness and success.

Sangeeta Mahurkar-Rao, PhD, ProCelerité LLC, Clifton, NJ, USA

Mahurkar-Rao is Co-founder and CEO of ProCelerité (www.procelerite. com), an enterprise focusing on business process transformation for global businesses needing to align themselves with rapidly evolving market forces.

Mahurkar-Rao's business orientation and work in organization development has deep roots in systems thinking. She sees organizations consisting of numerous interrelated systems and believes that for a company to be sustainable it is imperative to understand both the whole and the interrelationship of the parts.

Formerly, Mahurkar-Rao was Global Head of HR and OD at Persistent Systems where she focused on aligning HR with business and led a strategic realignment to a role- and competency-based organization, while driving aggressive growth in the employee base. She has been retained by global companies to successfully lead strategic value-adding initiatives including organizational restructuring, visioning, and process alignment. She has been associated with NVIDIA, Winphoria Networks, Philips Software, and Tata Consultancy Services.

Mahurkar-Rao's research has been published, and she co-edited and co-authored *Roots of Reason: Science and Technology in the Ancient World* (2002). She received her PhD in Cognitive Science from the Bulgarian Academy of Sciences, Bulgaria.

Theresa McNichol, MA, Ren Associates, Princeton, NJ, USA

Theresa McNichol is President of Ren Associates, a consulting firm whose clients include government agencies, cultural institutions, and international foundations. A former museum executive director and curator, she is an independent scholar of Chinese art and culture affiliated with the Princeton Research Forum as well as an award-winning artist. McNichol has taught at Mercer County Community College for 25 years. As the developer of *imaginement*™, her research and arts-based science learning workshops for students and STEM faculty promote key 21st century learning skills: process oriented guided inquiry, attentional looking and exploratory writing in informal learning environments.

McNichol's publications and presentations at American, European, and Asian management conferences focus on stewardship and wise leadership. In 2012, she presented her paper "Networked Wise Management: How Self-Cultivation in the Classical Confucian Tradition Became the Way of a Global

Governance Model" at the conference Wise Management in Organizational Complexity at the China Europe International Business School, CEIBS, Shanghai, China PRC.

Her chapter, "The Art Museum as Laboratory for Re-Imagining a Sustainable Future," is included in Volume 3 of Advances in Appreciative Inquiry, *Introduction to Positive Design and Appreciative Construction: From Sustainable Development to Sustainable Value* (2010). McNichol holds a BA in Asian Area Studies and Chinese Language from Brooklyn College and an MA in Asian Art History from New York University.

Thomas K. Robinson, Waretown, NJ, USA

Robinson literally worked with PSE&G from the ground up. His 41-year career began as a summer employee while in college as a laborer in the company's Gas Department. After graduating with an Engineering degree from Duke University, he was hired into the company's Management Development program. His subsequent experiences included leadership positions in the company's Gas Distribution, Internal Auditing, HR-Management Development, Performance Excellence, Human Resource Planning, and Technical Training organizations. He championed the introduction and deployment of the company's Lean Six Sigma Performance Improvement effort; initiated the PSE&G Benchmarking and Performance Improvement Councils and led PSE&G's successful Health & Safety Culture Team. Prior to retiring, his final role as PSE&G's Manager of Health & Safety involved leading a team of 14 Health & Safety professionals in assuring the safety of PSE&G's 6,400 employees engaged in delivering safe and reliable electric and gas energy to customers across New Jersey.

Robinson served on the panel of judges for the New Jersey Governor's Award for Performance Excellence, earned an MBA from Rutgers Graduate School of Management, and was a member of the Conference Board's Business Performance Council. He is also an adjunct instructor at the Rutgers University Center for Management Development and Thomas Edison State University's School of Applied Science and Technology.

Since retiring, Robinson holds leadership roles in several community, non-profit, and volunteer organizations.

William G. Russell, Principal, Transitioning to Green, Leonia, NJ, USA

Russell is a Principal with Transitioning to Green, LLC, a sustainability consulting and training company and an adjunct professor at Columbia University where he teaches Green Accounting. He has over 30 years of diverse work experience in environmental engineering; information technology tool development and implementation; managerial and financial consulting; training, coaching, and teaching. His diverse experience has enabled him to attain a holistic global sustainability-aligned perspective and deep experience advancing each segment of the triple-bottom-line. He thrives on helping clients identify and actualize sustainability-aligned opportunities that interconnect with their core mission and objectives.

Areas of world class expertise include: sustainability metrics and performance management; sustainability accounting; financial analysis and intangible and natural capital value quantification. He is passionate about engaging with impactful enterprises and multi-stakeholder collaborations working to accelerate and scale experimental pilot project experiences, holistic sustainability-aligned corporate strategies and best practice programs, developing innovative tools, new system standards, and business and economic models. He formerly led the environmental practice of PricewaterhouseCoopers and was a founding member of initiatives such as the GHG Protocol, SRI and ESG investment tools and strategies, The Global Reporting Initiative, and The Business Alliance for the Future. He aspires to meaningfully contribute to evolving global systems and cultures that acknowledge science-based ecological conditions and promote personal and community values based on respect, equity, justice, being in service, and caring.

Daniel F. Twomey, DBA, Institute for Sustainable Enterprise, Fairleigh Dickinson University, Madison, NJ, USA

Twomey was Director, International Partnerships for the Institute for Sustainable Enterprise at Fairleigh Dickinson University (FDU), where he taught leadership and sustainability. He was previously Professor of Management at West Virginia University. He consulted for many large and small organizations and published more than 40 articles in national and international journals.

Twomey was a founder and director of four outreach organizations that link business with academia and teaching and research with practice, including co-establishing a two-day Academy of Management Workshop: The Practitioner Series. He has played a substantive role in forwarding FDU's mission of "global leader in education" by working with international universities and developing programs for both Executive MBA and undergraduate students. He codeveloped an innovative course that includes a stay in a small village in Costa Rica.

Prior to getting his doctorate, Twomey had a career in business, which he has continued as an academic, author, and consultant. Two of his recent publications include *Designed Emergence as a Path to Enterprise Sustainability*, *Emergence: Complexity and Organization* (2006), and *Democracy and Sustainable Enterprise* (2006). In 2012 he joined the anti-fracking movement with his wife, Rosemarie Twomey, organizing two community groups and publishing a weekly newsletter. In 2014, Twomey, now Professor Emeritus, with co-authors, submitted a paper to the International Conference of the American Society for Competitiveness. Their paper, "Fracking: Blasting the Bedrock of Business," one of 70 papers presented, was awarded "Best Paper" for the Conference.

Jeana Wirtenberg, PhD, President and CEO, Transitioning to Green; Associate Professor of Professional Practice, Rutgers University, Newark and New Brunswick, NJ, USA; Co-founder, Institute for Sustainable Enterprise, Fairleigh Dickinson University, Madison, NJ, USA

Wirtenberg helps companies and organizations make sustainability a mainstream, routine business practice. She is an expert on the leadership, organizational dynamics, and psychology required to make that happen. She is President and CEO of Transitioning to Green (www.transitioningtogreen. com). Her company develops individual and organizational capacity to make sustainability take root. She is Associate Professor of Professional Practice at Rutgers University, where she leads the Principles for Responsible Management Education (PRME) initiative, and was Co-founder of the Institute for Sustainable Enterprise at Fairleigh Dickinson University.

Her book *Building a Culture for Sustainability: People, Planet and Profits in a New Green Economy* (2014) shows how to holistically integrate sustainability throughout the culture of organizations. The book features nine case studies of companies leading the way, including Alcoa, BASF, Church & Dwight, Ingersoll Rand, Sanofi, and Wyndham Worldwide. Wirtenberg is lead editor for *The Sustainable Enterprise Fieldbook*, first and second editions (Greenleaf Publishing 2008; Routedge 2019).

Wirtenberg was HR Director for Development, Quality, and Organization Effectiveness at Public Service Enterprise Group (PSEG) where she led a variety of initiatives to transform the firm and build organizational capacity. Formerly, she held several leadership positions in AT&T Human Resources and Marketing. She started her career in the Federal government where she was a Social Science Analyst in the Office of Research at the US Commission on Civil Rights, and led the Women's Research/Social Processes team at the National Institute of Education.

She teaches Organizational Behavior in the Rutgers MBA program, Women Leading in Business, and Management Skills in the Rutgers Department of Management and Global Business. She received her Master's degree and PhD with honors in Psychology from UCLA.

Acknowledgments

We are grateful to the many people who contributed in direct and indirect ways to the completion of the second edition of *The Sustainable Enterprise Fieldbook*. In addition to each of our contributing chapter authors, we especially would like to acknowledge Jessica Bartenhagen, who helped compile the bios and worked on the *Living Fieldbook*; Elena Feliz as well as Jessica for their tireless commitment to our sister organization, the OD Collaborative for a Flourishing World (ODCFW); Nalini Kumaran, for her extensive contribution to the *Living Fieldbook*; and Sai Gayatri Ramanan for her help with the Sustainable Globalization chapter and references.

We are enormously grateful to all of our families for their support over the three years we worked on this book. They enabled us to do the work we needed to do, took care of our day-to-day needs, and made it possible for us to always keep making progress, despite untold obstacles, and health and life challenges along the way.

We are very grateful to our editors from Routledge, Rebecca Marsh and Judith Lorton, who exhibited great flexibility and continuous support throughout the process. We also want to acknowledge Penny Harper for her meticulous attention to detail and expert copy-editing to carry us all across the finish line.

Part I

Understanding reality: our context for *The Sustainable Enterprise Fieldbook*

Introduction and overview

Jeana Wirtenberg, Linda M. Kelley, David Lipsky, and William G. Russell

> Humanity is called to recognize the need for changes of lifestyle, production and consumption, in order to combat this warming or at least the human causes which produce or aggravate it.
>
> (Pope Francis, 2015)

Since the first edition of *The Sustainable Enterprise Fieldbook* was published in 2008, there have been many profound changes affecting people, the planet, and business, both positive and negative. Never has there been more attention globally on climate change, and the role of business in mitigating its impacts. While this is clearly insufficient for the problems we face, we continue to believe that it is the human side of sustainability that is the missing factor. So for the past 10 years we have focused intensively on building the leadership capacities, not just in the top echelon of leaders, but at all levels, to address our most intractable problems. We realized the need for an exponential increase in education, awareness, understanding, and, most important, action to address the problems that we face. As we updated our chapters on Leadership, Strategy, Change, Employee Engagement, et al., we were struck by the overall lack of progress and how relevant our advice and concepts still are today, and feel even more of a sense of urgency that more needs to be done. This urgency becomes even more pronounced as we observe the extreme divisiveness in the United States and around the world, with people lining up to take sides to either deny the realities of evidence-based science around climate change, or on the other side to try and ameliorate its impacts or attenuate its further degradation of our planet.

While we are making awesome advances in creating and applying highly complex technologies to improve our quality of life, we are also severely damaging the essential resources that make life on Earth possible. This is the greatest human irony of all time. We cannot develop much less sustain our lives and economies without the resources provided by Earth's natural environment. Though they may seem abundant, those resources are finite. Consuming them at the rate we are doing is unsustainable by all measures.

If we are to sustain ourselves, we must make different choices, changing our consumption habits and innovating so that we work well within the boundaries of our single, shared planet. We can invent businesses and lifestyles that align with planetary realities so that we will thrive. People, planet, profits are inexorably intertwined. It's up to each of us to pay attention, lead where we can, and be thoughtful, aware contributors when others are leading. We do our best when we work together.

It will take more than inventing new technologies, though. First, we must reconnect our values to what really matters, that deep, visceral understanding of our integral connection with the essence of Earth's bounty: water, air, food-nurturing soil, energy among those resources. Writing and rereading this last sentence, it seems too obvious to even state. Yet, our actions, individually and as societies, show we have been taking these absolutely essential resources for granted, giving them no more than minimal care on our part.

How have we gotten ourselves so disconnected in a world where we have so much, and what can we do about it?

Where are we, really?

> In spite of our total reliance on the natural world, we have become almost blind to it.
>
> (Stanislaw Trzebinski, sculptural artist,
> Woodstock, Cape Town, SA)

Nothing wipes away blindness to our unrelenting dependence on Nature faster than catastrophe does. Focus for a minute on the period of August–September, 2017. Two of the largest, strongest hurricanes ever recorded in the Atlantic basin hit the US mainland with little more than a week between them. Houston was deluged by Harvey that dropped almost 60 inches of rain in just the few days it was stalled over the area. Neighborhoods, oil refineries, chemical plants, all under water. Before a full assessment was made of that damage, all of coastal Florida was covered in Irma's storm surge, after that hurricane barreling through the Eastern Caribbean scouring Barbuda clean, then the knocking out of the Virgin Islands. Right behind came Maria blanketing Puerto Rico with winds that took out the island's electric power grid and water utilities. Each of these megahits left lingering devastation in its wake.

But that wasn't all. That same September, Mexico was hit by two earthquakes. The most damaging was to Mexico City where a 7.1 level earthquake turned busy city streets to rubble. And that was some of what happened in North America. In Europe, massive rainstorms flooded southern Norway, England, the Czech capital of Prague, Salzburg and Vienna in Austria, Bavaria and Saxony in Germany, the countryside surrounding the Black Sea, Croatia, Greece, Italy. Flash floods in Iran. Heavy monsoons raged floods through

India, Nepal, and Bangladesh forcing millions from their homes. Mudslides in China and the Philippines devastated communities.

Then there were the fires, some of the worst ever seen. Fifteen major wildfires raging in California alone. Over 120,000 acres burned at this writing with the fires still not under control and people praying for rain. Add to that, Oregon, Washington State, in the US. Wildfire events didn't stop at the US border though. During this same summer season of 2017, nearly 3 million acres of British Columbia burned. Brazil had its worst forest fire month ever. Hundreds of wildfires in Portugal. New South Wales and Queensland in Australia also suffered out-of-control fires. Fires in Siberia are said to be the worst in 10,000 years. Earlier in the year, wildfires rampaged through East, Central, and South Africa. Even icy Greenland is burning! Crackled from drought and burned to a crisp. Taken all together, it's overwhelming. It is not normal. It's not anyone's old normal.

Not surprisingly, the cost in lives and livelihoods from all this is gargantuan. People are not equipped to deal with multiple disasters on this scale. Each of these human disasters turns out to be a business disaster as well. Record clean up and rebuilding costs are looming over us with estimates for Hurricane Harvey as high as $200 billion. But the ultimate loss to business is even greater than close-in immediate costs to those in the affected areas. Do you do business in any of these devastated areas? Customers there? Suppliers? Do you know people who live in one or more of these areas? Do you have relatives there? Ask them what the real costs were—financial, environmental, and social.

We have not constructed our cities and towns, nor our businesses, nor our societies to handle 200-year events coming on the heels of 200-year events. Halfway through, 2017 was already the second hottest year on record, even without the effects of an El Nino event. If only 2017 were an anomaly. It's not. It follows recent record-breaking hottest years of 2014, 2015, and 2016. This is way off the norm for recorded history. So much environmental catastrophe happening simultaneously, and often with one event compounding another, that this is no longer theoretical. All of these disasters have hit us within a short, six-week period. The conditions favoring these formerly extreme environmental events are occurring more and more often.

Positive psychology enters the mainstream of sustainability thinking

Does how you think about a challenge like sustainability impact your success in addressing it? Positive psychology tells us it does. The approach of building on what works vs. focusing on fixing problems is more likely to result in the increased collaboration needed to solve many paradoxes of sustainability. In stark juxtaposition to this dark reality, we are transfixed by a profound paradox of almost infinite positive possibilities for a new age of humanity that is unfolding before our eyes. On the positive side, we are heartened and hopeful by the integration of principles of positive psychology into the mainstream of sustainability thinking, such as the focus on positive leadership and business practices (Cameron, 2013), the purpose economy (Hurst, 2014), the circular economy (Lacy & Rutqvist, 2015), the sharing economy (Mason, 2016), activating purpose in organizations, building meaningful work for people, the work of the Ellen MacArthur Foundation, and the movement to create a new narrative for business that encompasses a vision of a world that flourishes forever (Ehrenfeld, 2013; Laszlo & Brown, 2014). Throughout the second edition, we incorporate important advances on these principles of positive psychology and neuroscience, combined with our insights on the applicability of integrated and systems thinking to the sustainability discourse.

With cries from the Pope to CEOs of the largest corporations in the world to the UN all calling for fundamental rethinking of how we can and must create a sustainable and flourishing future for the next generation, and the next, we are convinced that it is not only possible, but that humanity is already moving inexorably towards a much needed and fundamental course correction. Yet sometimes it feels like one step forward and two steps back, in light of President Trump's dismantling of the Environmental Protection Agency (EPA), support for Arctic drilling, resurrection of the coal and fossil fuel industry, and departure from the Paris Agreement.

From a long-term change perspective, Kurt Lewin famously spoke about three stages of change—unfreezing, changing, and refreezing (Burnes, 2004). As we see it, we are somewhere between the unfreezing and change stage with regard to sustainability, with movements back and forth until we come to settle on the "new normal." Our hope is that the positive changes we are seeing around the new narrative for business in general, and business' support for the UN Sustainable Development Goals in particular, will proliferate from large multinational corporations into small and medium-sized enterprises, as well as NGOs. We believe that as the millennial generation moves further into the mainstream of corporate leadership, and our institutions of higher education embed sustainability into their teachings (especially in the business schools and MBA levels), that cultures for sustainability will become more and more embedded. The pattern is much like in the quality movement of the 80s and 90s, and eventually sustainable business practices will become the norm and the only way to do business. **We are writing this second edition to promote this vision, and make this prognostication not only possible, but doable!**

Global sustainability trends and solutions are still emerging, but becoming clearer. Systems and rules that caused current conditions to exist are changing. We may not know if the pace of change is quick enough or if the intended results of those changes will be attained, but their change is already ongoing and unstoppable. In the midst of this uncertainty, we must manage our lives and resources and corporations today for both short- and long-term needs. Our enterprise and capital market systems, rules, and strategies for investing and allocating financial capital are critical ones we rely upon to function. They are simultaneously experiencing innovative change and requiring sustainability-aligned strategic management.

Capitalism transformation

Capital market systems and rules establish value, facilitate global trade, and orchestrate the allocation of other interconnected natural, built, social, and human capitals. These systems directly or indirectly contributed to global risks such as asset bubbles; inflation and deflation; financial market technology infrastructure; unemployment and underemployment; and wealth and income gaps (World Economic Forum, 2017). New emergent financial system technologies are restructuring the industries' value chain and disrupting entrenched stakeholder roles.

While the trends and results appear positive, are they sufficient? People are already simultaneously anticipating more profound changes to the mental models, systems, and rules of capitalism itself. New economic models and corporate strategies such as the digital economy, the circular economy, and the sharing economy seek to decouple economic growth from material and human resource consumption constraints. The sharing economy is accelerating entirely new forms of ownership, lending, and legal contracts. As these innovations evolve they reduce the dependence on traditional capitalism to determine values, job skills, market prices, and resource allocations.

The great technological advance of the early 21st century consists not only of new objects and processes, but of old ones made intelligent. The knowledge content of products is becoming more valuable than the physical things that are used to produce them. But it is a value measured as usefulness, not exchange or asset value.

In his book, *The Big Pivot*, Andrew Winston (2014) provides a strategic framework for a resilient company. The framework anticipates resources becoming more scarce (and expensive) and external ecosystem-service values (i.e., climate change) being financially quantified and more internalized. Companies will need to radically collaborate with competitors and other stakeholders, and engage with and lobby for new government policies and rules. These next sustainability-aligned capital market transformation and value creation trends are already being successfully applied. Executives and investors must now reflect on the core purpose of their businesses, change their corporate visions, and implement new, emergent systems and rules to direct and accelerate their progress towards the sustainable future they are creating.

Rising investor demand for information on sustainability has spurred a flood of new research, both in the academic community and in the major brokerages that have formed dedicated teams assessing how companies are affected by everything from climate change and social pressures in emerging markets to governance records.

"Business case" for a sustainable enterprise

As much as businesses now recognize the "business case" for paying attention to sustainability, and even see it as a burning platform, we see on the horizon a tectonic shift taking place in corporations around the world. Today, many businesses are responding to the call to develop sustainability-aligned strategies because of their purpose, values, sense of corporate social responsibility, and their need to be and be seen as good corporate citizens. According to every executive survey from 2010 to 2017, sustainability is now "a key strategic priority" for most CEOs. Leading firms are seeing that an integrated "triple bottom line" (i.e., people, planet, profits) that balances attention to employees, society, and the environment with financial outcomes is critical not only to the world's sustainability, but also to their own long-term viability in the global marketplace.

Companies that want to succeed and thrive in the future are increasingly being encouraged to find ways to simultaneously meet both their own strategic needs and those of society (Porter & Kramer, 2011). More than ever before, companies are being asked to emphasize a broader and more balanced array of outcomes such as those characterized by the "triple bottom line" of people, planet, and profits (and to ensure sustainability is deeply embedded and not just bolted on) (Laszlo & Zhexembayeva, 2011; Wirtenberg, 2014). In the 21st century, rather than focusing singularly or even primarily on the "financial bottom line" and the financial assets they possess, the most sustainable companies are looking at themselves and their future through the lens of the "six capitals model" of natural, human, social, manufactured, intellectual, and financial capital. As discussed in Chapter 3, companies are fundamentally rethinking their strategies incorporating risks and opportunities emerging from the UN's Sustainable Development Goals, and new business models disrupting stagnant industries like energy and retail. Importantly, issues of climate change mitigation and adaptation, resource scarcity, rising consumer expectations, and radical transparency are all issues driving the new realities of business in the 21st century.

At the same time, evidence continues to mount demonstrating that corporate social-environmental performance is strongly associated with financial and marketplace success. For example, a study by Accenture/UN Global Compact (2013) showed that while the corporate sustainability movement has clearly been broadening and producing a deeper awareness and commitment all over the world, many business leaders are quite frustrated with the pace of change and the scale of their impact. There is clearly a "knowing-doing" gap at play which we address throughout this book.

On a positive note, a major potential advance which can help close this gap stems from the finding that sustainability can be seen as a key driver of innovation. In a recent Deloitte study, Aronson (2013) found that sustainability leaders are more than 400% more likely to be considered innovation leaders. Why? Because

> Sustainability can provide a different "lens" for thinking: it helps companies to approach situations differently … Thinking differently can unlock companies' innovative potential—they may see situations from a different point of view, they may re-examine their perspective of what's important, and they can tap into new ideas.
>
> (Aronson, 2013, p. 3)

And we see more and more evidence on almost a daily basis that the professional investment community, corporate executives, and directors appear to be increasingly focused on the degree to which firms are managed sustainably (Wirtenberg, 2014).

As an example, take Coca-Cola. What is the most important ingredient in Coca-Cola's success? Water. The syrup is what gives the product its competitive advantage, but without water Coca-Cola could not supply the world with its products. When the company became aware of the global challenge facing potable water, it co-founded the Global Water Challenge to address the problem. Sustainability makes business sense.

So why do we need *The Sustainable Enterprise Fieldbook*? And why now? Although the desired outcome of sustainability is becoming increasingly clear, the process by which one can best develop and implement sustainability is considerably less so. Our book is designed to help address both the what (what is a sustainability-aligned strategy for a company or organization?) and the how of sustainable enterprise (how do we go about building a sustainable enterprise?).

Although we use the term enterprise throughout this book (a term that is usually associated with the for-profit business sector), we firmly believe that the disciplines, case studies, tools, and references presented throughout our *Fieldbook* are applicable to organizations within the government, education, nonprofit, and nongovernmental organization (NGO) sectors as well. Furthermore, wherever possible we intentionally include examples of successful public–private partnerships, collaborative initiatives operating across multiple stakeholders and institutions, and organizations working in the "in-between space" to build sustainable enterprises. We believe these cross-sector, collaborative partnerships may offer the greatest hope for solving many of the globe's most intractable problems.

Humanity at a crossroads

We believe humanity is at the most profoundly critical crossroads in history, and the only acceptable solution is to move to a "human centric" world based on a caring and networked economy. We need to find a new balance between "me" and "we." We always need to remember the oxygen mask instructions the flight attendants give passengers when the plane is just starting. Put your own mask on first! You can't help anyone else if you don't take care of your own health and wellbeing.

We are especially drawn to the notion called "Ubuntu," a Nguni Bantu word, which roughly translates to: "we are because you are, and since you are, definitely I am." Loosely translated as "My humanity depends on your humanity; your humanity depends on my humanity." To be human is to affirm one's humanity by recognizing the humanity of others and, on that basis, establish respectful human relations with them. Desmond Tutu said: "You can't be human all by yourself, and when you have this quality Ubuntu you are known for your generosity."

As we realize the importance and potential of this interdependence of humanity, it can help us accelerate our progress towards thriving. We can move from the individual isolation of win-lose thinking to the possibilities of collaborating with the diversity required to innovate new solutions.

Humans are by nature social beings. Our obsession with "individual" would be an anathema to our ancestors. The primacy of individual over the public good is a very recent development in human history. We have yet to arrive at an optimal dynamic balance.

People are nothing if not inventive. From small band beginnings, people have spread around the globe inventing cultures and doing business along the way. This overwhelming success, though, has put humanity at a crossroads where sustainability now vies with unsustainability, and frankly the outcome is uncertain. In this *Fieldbook* we endeavor to lay out some essential areas where we must generate and grow sustainability's foundations.

Conscious capitalism

How should a person be if he or she has values aligned with sustainability? While making money is essential for the vitality and sustainability of a business, it is not the only or even the most important reason a business exists (Stout, 2012). Conscious businesses focus on their purpose beyond profit. We all need meaning and purpose in our lives. Purpose activates us and motivates us. It moves us to get up in the morning, sustains us when times get tough, and serves as a guiding star when we stray off course. Conscious businesses provide us with this sense of meaning and purpose. By focusing on its deeper purpose, a conscious business inspires, engages, and energizes its stakeholders, employees, customers, and others trust and even love companies that have an inspiring purpose.

Purpose of *The Sustainable Enterprise Fieldbook*

We like to think about life and sustainable development as a journey. For this moment and as a helpful metaphor to convey our messages, we imagine the journey to be traveling across a bridge. How we are currently being present for this passing moment in time is the cumulative collection of universal material, energy, intellectual and spiritual stocks and flows from all of our life experiences and actions so far. We live day to day and progress step by step. Each day we are alive our spirit, our living self-system, has sustained itself. We are fortunate, or lucky, or blessed with the opportunity to live another day. We get to decide again what we will do, how we choose to spend our time. Each new day we have journeyed another step along the bridge. The world has changed and we have changed. We are all interconnected and therefore are never traveling alone. We are individually powerful and weak at the same time. We are learning, having more experiences and impacts. Each day we reassess our context and decide how next to spend our precious and unknown remaining lifetime. How much more might we accomplish as we build another bridge increment? We are all some place along this bridge between the past and the future. The future has not yet happened and so for as long as we are alive we continue to control and influence some small aspect of some future outcomes. With greater collective wisdom, we can sufficiently transform our behavior and mental models, evolve and change for the better. With each renewed vision for a thriving future that we want to create, we set new sustainability-aligned goals and pivot to resiliently guide us onward.

The purpose of the *Fieldbook* is to help forge a path to a better world and a more sustainable, flourishing, and thriving future by supporting employees, managers, and leaders at every level and in every function, sector, and industry in three key ways:

- increasing their understanding and awareness of the meaning of sustainability on a conceptual, practical, and personal level;
- energizing and expanding their commitment to building sustainable enterprises that can contribute to enhancing the sustainability of the world and its ecosystems for generations to come;
- providing readers with the tools and techniques needed to individually and collectively take appropriate actions that will improve their personal and enterprise sustainability performance in the short and long term.

Missing ingredients and *The Sustainable Enterprise Fieldbook*

> The human environment and the natural environment deteriorate together: we cannot adequately combat environmental degradation unless we attend to causes related to human and social degradation.
>
> (Pope Francis, 2015)

The Sustainable Enterprise Fieldbook is designed to align with an emergent framework of best-practice enterprise qualities. In it, we pay particular attention to those areas with gaps between current and future practices as identified in a global sustainability survey of business leaders and managers (American Management Association [AMA], 2007), and that have been reinforced by many subsequent surveys.

This *Fieldbook* is unique in at least six respects:

1. We focus on the critical role that human capital (i.e., people) needs to play in the transformational journey to sustainable enterprise. We believe that this is the missing ingredient in transforming rhetoric into action, and we are committed to helping pave the way for people to take the actions needed to, quite literally, save the world.
2. It is based on a stream of original research, both qualitative and quantitative, focused on the qualities of a sustainable enterprise and state-of-the-art best practices. This research is summarized later in this chapter and interspersed throughout the book with specific illustrative examples from businesses and other organizations.
3. It offers concrete and practical ways to close the significant gaps that our and more recent worldwide studies revealed in the role that managers in every function need to play to build a sustainable enterprise. For example, we focus heavily on the "knowing-doing" gap, i.e., the significant gap between what managers know needs to be done, and what they and their organizations are actually doing about these sustainability challenges in their day-to-day practices.
4. We engage with you, our readers, by sharing the experiences some of our authors have had working with businesses, nonprofits, and educational institutions to design and implement elements of an organizational model founded on principles of sustainability, integrity, inclusivity, mutuality, and self-organizing leadership.
5. By offering a complementary online *Living Fieldbook* (see below) we strive to model sustainable principles and practices.
6. We see the entire journey as a form of action research and action learning, as we seek to continuously learn and improve on all elements of our current understanding and the future iterative learning we will all experience during the global journey to sustainability.

The Sustainable Enterprise Fieldbook and its innovative *Living Fieldbook* and online community support services offer a missing ingredient in the elements we think must come together to create a sustainable world.

Using *The Sustainable Enterprise Fieldbook*

The Sustainable Enterprise Fieldbook is designed so that the reader may quickly and easily reference any individual enterprise quality and find resources, case studies, tools, and related materials that can be used to help transform any enterprise from its current state to a more sustainable future state. Although all chapters cover distinctly different sustainable enterprise qualities, a consistent set of content categories are highlighted by icons throughout the *Fieldbook* to provide users with a quick visual guide and to enhance the *Fieldbook*'s utility.

Activities for awareness and understanding (A)

Throughout the chapters we introduce a number of activities, frameworks, thought questions, and the like. All of these are intended to increase awareness and understanding and are denoted by an **A**. Wherever an **A** appears, we suggest that professors and/or managers lead a simple activity, such as having their group read and discuss the associated text (essay, framework, and the like). In some cases, we supplement the **A** with an **L** for *Living Fieldbook* (see below). The **L** lets readers know they will find more detailed thought questions, discussion guides, and specific exercises aimed at further increasing awareness and understanding around that activity on the *Living Fieldbook*.

Case examples (C)

The Sustainable Enterprise Fieldbook uses case examples throughout the chapters as an effective way to make our messages more real to *Fieldbook* users. A **C** highlights case studies.

Tools (T)

The Sustainable Enterprise Fieldbook provides sample tools that lead to action. These were strategically selected by each chapter's authors as we discovered and used them during our work or learned about how others were using them by interviewing practitioners and identifying case examples. A **T** highlights tools.

Collectively we hope the Activities for awareness and understanding (**A**), Cases (**C**), and Tools (**T**) help inspire people to ACT.

Living Fieldbook collaborative workspace

Our collective community of authors recognize the constraints imposed by a physical book with hard page limits, deadlines, and production costs that make it impossible in one physical book to keep up with the rapid pace of learning and change related to sustainable enterprise practices. We hope to accommodate these limitations by supplementing the physical book content with an online Sustainable Enterprise Living Fieldbook workspace. The workspace is referred to throughout this book and can be freely accessed at https://TheSustainableEnterpriseFieldbook.com.

Since the beginning of our discussions, we determined that there was an abundance of highly valuable reference materials, tools, and case studies that individual team members were aware of and wanted to share. This shared knowledge became so expansive that we began to explore ways to introduce the best themes of these works within our book and offer readers an efficient way to identify and access our references and learn more deeply about any selected topic. We also recognized that, as standards and best practices rapidly evolve, our *Living Fieldbook* would provide a way to keep our insights current and even support open discussions and feedback forums where different opinions could be openly progressed, and completely unanticipated insights and solutions could naturally emerge.

We hope that the information and activities presented in the book, and the *Living Fieldbook*, will empower readers to effect positive change in their organizations, schools, and communities. Our aim is to build a socially, ecologically, and economically flourishing world, together. Toward this aim, the purpose of the *Living Fieldbook* is to provide a valuable and extensive supplemental online resource that expands the breadth and depth of material presented in *The Sustainable Enterprise Fieldbook*. The material you will find here has been carefully selected by the contributing authors of the book.

As mentioned above, throughout the book are icons for **A**ctivities, **C**ases, and **T**ools, with an "**L**" indicating that additional corresponding material may be found in this online space. As referenced in the book, here in the *Living Fieldbook* you will find that **A**ctivities, **C**ases, and **T**ools—as well as additional resources such as links to studies and videos—are listed by chapter.

Also featured in the *Living Fieldbook* are Learning Guide activities that enable professors, instructors, and managers to readily facilitate classroom exercises and lunch and learn activities. We invite you to explore and incorporate these materials and activities into your work, within your organizations, or in higher education. We welcome questions, comments, discussion, and encourage you to share your own ideas, experience, and research with the Organization Development Collaborative for a Flourishing World (ODCFW) on LinkedIn.

Context: Where are we now in the journey towards a sustainable world?

This section provides a window into how sustainable enterprise context and behaviors have changed from the first edition of the *Fieldbook* published in 2007 through the present time and including a vision of next behaviors through 2030, the timespan set by the United Nations to accomplish the Sustainable Development Goals.

2007 scenario predictions and 2017 result reflections

Writing this second edition of *The Sustainable Enterprise Fieldbook* presented a valuable opportunity to deeply reflect on what has happened over the past decade since our original publication. The first edition included three scenario predictions for the future. We shared at that time and repeat now that scenarios are fictional stories about possible futures. They are not intended to predict the future. Rather, they are intended to help readers challenge their own hidden assumptions about how the future may turn out. Some scenarios are based on ideas and trends that already exist. Newer scenario tools have expanded to include versions that set future goals and force people to imagine new paths and identify innovation needs and leverage points to accomplish those goals. Using today's mindsets and/or technology constraints some goals seem impossible. Scenarios that work back from a vision and goals for the future we want to create can serve to reveal new possibilities and previously unknown solution perspectives.

As predicted, this past decade's progress has been a combination of the proposed scenarios plus events and trends both positive and negative that were not foreseen at that time. The three 2007–2017 scenarios and a few reflections about each are:

1. **Things fall apart:** *Businesses see sustainability as a buzzword. Most businesses just want to survive in an increasingly anarchic world.*

   Reflections: Predictable, avoidable environmental trends including increasing greenhouse gas emissions and climate change; plastics waste pollution, coral reef bleaching, and overfishing of the oceans; and widening of the gap between the world's richest and poorest people continued to worsen. Current anti-globalization and escalating risks of military conflicts in Korea or the South China Sea could all be perceived as the fruition of things falling apart.

Box 0.1   If only ... sooner

How do we get people's attention who refuse to accept and act on critical areas of sustainability? One way is to start with a story:

Mother passed at 3pm on a cold, overcast wintery afternoon. Sitting bedside for 25 hours after taking her off life support, my sisters and brothers reminisced about our happiest and saddest memories mixed in with many "if only, sooner regrets." If only she had stopped smoking, checked for cancer, and saw that specialist sooner, we may have had her with us still. If the Mother in this story was our Mother Earth, how can we save her before going on life support? Sooner is now, we must change and move to action.

---

2. **Muddling toward sustainability:** *In 2017, sustainability is, at best, a mixed bag and, at worst, an utter mess. Countries keep trying to create global agreements on everything: fisheries, greenhouse gases, water conservation, pandemics, the reduction of global poverty, and so on. But the agreements are usually based on unchallenging consensus targets that, even when missed, are seldom punished by the larger community.*

    Reflections: Until recently, this path to sustainability was looking spot on. Now, however, the resiliency feedback levels identified to avoid various ecosystem and social crisis have narrowed. Future progress will have less room for muddling toward sustainability, and needs to rapidly accelerate.

3. **A global sustainability culture:** *The most hopeful scenario proposed for 2017 suggested a global sustainability culture might have taken root. Tipping point signals causing the cultural awakening would come from alarming scientific findings, changes in climate patterns, geopolitical conflicts, global media networks, and innovations in the marketplace including the success of "green" businesses.*

    Reflections: Feedback signals from each of the tipping point elements are amplifying attention that may still trigger a global mindset change and cultural shift. The rapid uptake by both countries and companies embracing the United Nations 2030 agenda and the Sustainable Development Goals gives us reasons to continue being hopeful for a thriving future.

Human and sustainability systems context: past, present, and future

Since we first published this book 10 years ago we have learned so much from our work in implementing the original concepts and tools. Reflecting on this learning helped us to adjust our vision, analytical models, and scenario stories, which we have included in this new edition. We see humans as the critical resource and ultimate purpose that sustainable enterprises both depend upon to operate and whose ultimate purposes they serve. We applied systems thinking (see Chapter 2) and input output modeling concepts to supplement the scenario stories and add richer context details to expand our openness to new ideas (mental models), guide our new behaviors (change management), shift our expectations (strategic goals) and feedback signals (metrics) as we simultaneously build and journey across our sustainability bridge into the future. In the table below we highlighted some of the key changes we have seen since publishing our first edition in 2007, second edition in 2019, and a look into the future in 2030 and beyond. In Table 0.1 below you will see "+" indicating positive contributors to sustainability progress and "−" for detractors.

The future looks bright, as we change our awareness, thinking, and collective action. We believe we will continue to make great strides in awareness and our thinking will continue to evolve using integrated thinking.

Table 0.1 Past, present, and future sustainability snapshot

	Past as of 2007[a]	Present as of 2018	Future (2030+)
Population	6.6 billion	7.6 billion	8.6 billion
Gross world production (GWP)	US$69.3 trillion	US$107.5 trillion as of 2014 US$78.28 trillion (nominal terms)	US$84.4 trillion
Financial Context	+ Economic systems were market-based and aligned with natural capital supplies and distribution efficiencies – 2007–2008 subprime mortgage crisis, feedback signals wrong, delayed, or missing – Americans lose quarter of their collective net worth[b] – Lehman Brothers' collapse	– Wider income gaps, continuing to increase + Enterprise income increasing – Employee wages decreasing	+ $6.6 trillion from productivity, businesses process automation, AI labor-force augmentation + $9.1 trillion from consumption side-effects, personalized and higher-quality goods (PWC estimate[c])
Human context	+ Sustainability enlightened thought leaders including: Buckminster Fuller, Donella Meadows, and Ray Anderson + Original Enterprise Sustainability Action Team who collaborated to produce the original edition of this Sustainable Enterprise Fieldbook	+ New leaders building upon and scaling past thought leaders' work with new goals, better technology, and mindfulness – Wider income and knowledge gaps, privileged control reduces trust	+ Historic generational shift in wealth and power from baby boomers to their younger children, influencing mindsets, goals, control of wealth, relationships to technology platforms, and sense of place or being in the universe +/– Urbanization and migration of talent +/– AI labor-force changing landscape of work
Triple-bottom-line systems context	+ Systems thinking and triple-bottom-line frameworks evolving + Social capital was evolving with the advent of the Internet, social media, and globalization	+ Growing understanding of systems thinking. A triple bottom line or three major aggregate systems of economic, social, and the environment are acknowledged and seen as integrated, but with acceptable tradeoffs between systems	+ Advanced understanding of fully integrated systems and feedback loop dynamics are evolving + Multi-capital inputs evolving to measure system stocks and flows across system scales

(continued)

Table 0.1 (Cont.)

	Past as of 2007	Present as of 2018	Future (2030+)
Population	**6.6 billion**[a]	**7.6 billion**	**8.6 billion**
	+ Machines and information technology continued to enhance Built Capital efficiencies, as well as extraction and distribution efficiencies	− Economic growth, defined as GDP or GNP, is the primary goal of development	+ The sustainable development goals are advancing a more aligned global vision
	− No broad awareness of or understanding of either systems thinking or triple bottom line within the general public	− Previously globalizing social systems enter a period of nationalistic pushback	+ Economic growth as our primary purpose is shifting towards a purpose of sustaining life on earth and human wellbeing
	− Systems thinking, environmental, social, and economic systems were evolving independently	− Short-term deterioration to environmental and social systems are seen as acceptable consequences for economic growth	+ Still three major aggregate systems of the environment or the planet, society, and the economy being managed, but with a greater appreciation of their interdependencies
	− Intellectual capital is closely held and difficult to transfer	− Long-term thresholds to natural capital and ecosystem services are starting to be questioned and monitored, but long-term consequences not consciously recognized by most	+ Social and economic systems pivoting to become more equitable and just
	− Natural capital is perceived to be plentiful/unlimited and the general public was not concerned	− Technology innovations are being relied upon to build resiliency and mitigate the risks of crisis caused by exceeding planetary ecosystem boundaries or thresholds	− Planetary boundaries and critical ecosystem services are exceeding sustainable thresholds and pose a risk to the long-term survival of humans
	− These advancements masked our perception of limits and perpetuated neo-classical economic models that depend upon perpetual, unlimited economic growth	− Technology and social media has unintended consequences of reinforcing peoples' biased perceptions of reality that fails to acknowledge long-term consequences	− Resiliency thresholds and rates and even the directions of change are uncertain
		− One outcome of these system breakdowns is focusing on the wrong system goals and feedback signals	

Notes:

a www.prb.org/Publications/Datasheets/2007/2007WorldPopulationDataSheet.aspx

b "Americans' wealth drops $13 trillion: Fed report shows a decline of home values and the stock market cut the nation's wealth to $50.4 trillion," Tami Luhby, CNN Money, June 11, 2009. http://money.cnn.com/2009/06/11/news/economy/Americans_wealth_drops/?postversion=2009061113 (accessed July 25, 2009). Luhby reports that in Q2 2007, collective American wealth totaled $64.4 trillion, and by Q1 2009 this value had fallen to $50.4 trillion.

c PWC (2017). Sizing the prize. What's the real value of AI for your business and how can you capitalize?, www.pwc.com/gx/en/issues/analytics/assets/pwc-ai-analysis-sizing-the-prize-report.pdf, p. 3.

Legend: "+" (contributors), "−" (detractors), "+/−" (both contributors or detractors) to sustainability progress.

This approach complements a societal purpose to preserve life today and focus our long-term economic and political systems' ultimate ends on maximizing the well-being of all people.

Hopefulness

Holistic and integrated systems thinking is an evolving skill that allows us as humans to do our best to understand our past and current realities. We are humbled as we reflect on the vastness of the universe, the expanses of time, and the interconnected and collective beauty that exists in the universe, our planet, and the world as we experience it. We will forever struggle to live in the paradox between our self-perception of what we think we know and believe to be true and all that is unknown and unknowable. Our lives and each moment's behaviors and actions are interconnected with everything past, present, and future. All lives matter for all time.

This book is our contribution to serve you and add value and quality to your personal wellbeing. We are inspired by the belief that you will become a better leader and positive contributor within broader movements to achieve positive and even transformational change. Our transcendent commitment is to contribute to transforming the business narrative, such that the purpose of business shifts from one of maximizing shareholder value to maximizing the wellbeing of all of its stakeholders and broader interconnected social and natural systems.

Social justice

As we review the current state of humanity, despite the best intentions of thousands of organizations and millions of people, we find alarming statistics. As of 2015, for well over 4 billion people—approximately 60% of all humanity including the majority of all people on the planet—are living in poverty with an annual income of less than $1,500 (Canaque & Hart, 2015). Poverty inevitably leads to malnutrition and children are the most vulnerable. According to Doctors Without Borders, malnutrition accounts for 45% of all deaths of children under five worldwide, and 3.1 million children die every year due to malnutrition (International Food Policy Research Institute, 2016).

Specifically, the most pressing issues going forward are summarized here and addressed throughout this book.

- **Persistent gender inequality:** Women face discrimination in obtaining work, economic assets, and participation in private and public decision-making. In 2015, almost 27% of women aged 20–24 were married before the age of 18. Women spent almost three times as many hours on unpaid domestic work as men (United Nations, 2017, p. 5).

- **Sustainably use our oceans and lands:** The proportion of marine fish stocks worldwide that have been overfished—that is, are at biologically unsustainable levels—increased from 10% in 1974 to 31% in 2013. Bleaching, driven by climate change and local impacts, has affected the health of coral reefs worldwide, which could disappear completely by 2050. Amphibians also face a high risk of extinction, with 41% already threatened (United Nations, 2017, p. 10).
- **Climate change and environmental degradation, with greatest suffering by the poor:** Sadly, global emissions of carbon dioxide have increased by more than 50% since 1990. Planetary warming continued in 2016, setting a record of about 1.1 degrees centigrade above the pre-industrial period. The extent of global sea ice fell to 4.14 million square kilometers in 2016, the second lowest on record (United Nations, 2017, p. 9).
- **Conflicts threaten human development:** Pervasive conflicts are forcing millions of people to abandon their homes (60 million in 2014 alone and increasing). "Every day, 42,000 people on average are forcibly displaced and compelled to seek protection due to conflicts." Sadly, children accounted for half of the global refugee population under the UN High Commissioner for Refugees in 2014 (United Nations, High Commissioner for Refugees, 2017).
- **Poverty and hunger persist:** Despite the progress reported above, about 770 million people still live in extreme poverty and are hungry. In 2016, an estimated 155 million children under the age of five were stunted (low height for their age), 52 million were suffering from wasting (low weight for their height), and 41 million were overweight (United Nations, 2017, pp. 2–3).

As we move forward, the Sustainable Development Goals, discussed further in Chapter 3 and Chapter 6, will take the lessons learned and build on these successes and work to remedy these continuing problems to create "a more prosperous, sustainable and equitable world."

On a positive note, over the last decade, the field of business and human rights has seen a dramatic evolution, from where companies and human rights activists were at odds, to one in which stakeholders have begun to approach a common understanding of the risks, challenges, and opportunities. While the 2011 UN Human Rights Council's endorsement of the Guiding Principles on Business and Human Rights, June 16, 2011 was a major watershed event, it was characterized by John Ruggie, former UN secretary-general, as only "the end of the beginning."

Yet we still see tragic failures of human rights protections, such as the Rana Plaza building collapse in which more than 1,134 garment workers needlessly perished in Bangladesh. From this horrific event, we learned that the suppliers of over a dozen well-known international brands were in the rubble, yet many of these companies did not even realize they had subcontractors working there.

This tragic situation casts a light on the fact that many companies don't really know where their clothes are made. And while we can do much more to protect garment workers' rights, momentum is finally starting to propel us in the right direction. The European Commission is looking to pass garment policies that help both member governments and companies manage their supply chains. And NGOs like LaborVoices are increasing transparency through crowdsourced worker data. On the positive side, many in the business community are more focused than ever on human rights and how to apply the 2011 Guiding Principles (United Nations, 2011).

We believe it is important to explore the moral case as well as the business case for respecting human rights. In the moral case, respecting human rights is an obligation, not voluntary. It stems from the recognition that **everyone participating in the system has shared responsibility** for any injustices, including the harm that results from **unintended consequences of our actions**. This is distinguished from a liability model which focuses on assigning blame and avoidance of complicity and liability. In the moral case, you share responsibility for the outcome; not just a responsibility to follow your duty not to infringe on human rights.

The good news is that a large majority of executives now believe that business is an important player in respecting human rights, and that what their companies do—or fail to do—affects those rights. However, the precise nature of these responsibilities has often been contentious. Where do we draw the line of what is the responsibility of business?

- 83% agreed that human rights are a matter for business as well as governments;
- 71% say their company's responsibility to respect those rights goes beyond simple obedience to local laws;
- most believe that their firms' operations have an impact on each of the 11 clusters of activities they identified.

Companies see human rights mainly as a stakeholder and ethical issue; a business case for respecting human rights focused on more immediate costs and benefits is less widely accepted. Only 21% say that a clear business case is driving their human rights policy (The Economist Intelligence Unit, 2015).

The Sustainability Pyramid model

Our previous study of nine of the world's most sustainable companies (Wirtenberg, Harmon, Russell, & Fairfield, 2007)[1] identified a "pyramid" of seven core qualities associated with successfully implementing sustainability

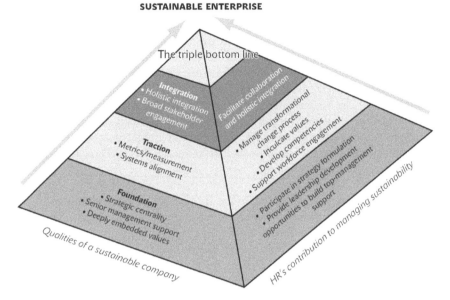

SUSTAINABLE ENTERPRISE

The triple bottom line

Integration
• Holistic integration
• Broad stakeholder engagement

• Facilitate collaboration and holistic integration

Traction
• Metrics/measurement
• Systems alignment

• Manage transformational change process
• Inculcate values
• Develop competencies
• Support workforce engagement

Foundation
• Strategic centrality
• Senior management support
• Deeply embedded values

• Participate in strategy formulation
• Provide leadership development
• Opportunities to build top-management support

Qualities of a sustainable company

HR's contribution to managing sustainability

Figure 0.1 The Sustainability Pyramid: qualities associated with highly successful sustainability strategies

Source: Copyright 2006, Institute for Sustainable Enterprise. Reproduced with permission.

strategies and achieving triple-bottom-line results. This model also illustrates the necessary contributions of human capital practices (see Figure 0.1).

The state-of-the-art sustainable enterprise

Global sustainability trends and solutions are still emerging, but becoming clearer. Systems and rules that caused current conditions to exist are changing. We may not know if the pace of change is quick enough or if the intended results of those changes will be attained, but their change is already ongoing and unstoppable. In the midst of this uncertainty, we must manage our lives and resources today for both short- and long-term needs. Our enterprise and capital market systems, rules, and strategies for investing and allocating financial capital are critical ones we rely upon to function. They are simultaneously experiencing innovative change and requiring sustainability-aligned strategic management.

For enterprises to operate in a way that actively fosters sustainability, we believe those organizations need to help restore—or at least not undermine—the capacity of the natural environment to provide resources and services. To earn the sustainability moniker, organizations must also actively contribute to the ability to thrive in the communities and economies in which they operate.

We define a "state-of-the art" sustainable enterprise as one that adopts a long-term, collaborative, "holistic" or systems-oriented mindset. It deeply embeds sustainable development into its core business strategy, and its activities result in the generation or regeneration of the planet's capital stocks: that is, natural, social, financial, human, intellectual, and manufactured capital. A state-of-the-art sustainable enterprise implements ethics-based business principles and sound corporate governance practices that consider the rights and interests of all relevant stakeholders, not only the immediate interests of company shareholders. Here we include advocates in areas of policy, economic systems, and consumerism.

A sustainable enterprise is likely to pursue a triple-bottom-line strategy that is tied to three broad domains of stakeholder needs: social, environmental, and economic. A sustainable enterprise is committed to transparency and accountability. Such an organization gives stakeholders opportunities to participate in all relevant decisions that affect them. A sustainable organization uses its influence to promote meaningful systemic change among its peers, within its neighboring communities, and throughout its supply chain. This is because it recognizes that, for sustainability to be achieved, it is not enough simply to change one's own organization; enterprises should also be a vehicle for encouraging the improved performance of others.

Most importantly, the AMA (2007) sustainability study found that the degree to which sustainability practices and strategies were being implemented—and the extent to which those strategies reportedly produce benefits—was significantly stronger among the higher-performing organizations. Arabesque Asset Management and The University of Oxford published a meta-study categorizing more than 200 different sources. Part One of the study reports that 88% of reviewed sources showed that companies with robust sustainability practices demonstrate better operational performance, which ultimately translates into cash flows. Part Two reports that 80% of the reviewed studies indicate that prudent sustainability practices have a positive influence on investment performance (Clark, Feiner, & Viehs, 2015).

The past decade's results are demonstrating positive reinforcing evidence that sustainability, responsibility, and profitability are not incompatible or tradeoffs, but in fact wholly complementary.

Overview of this book

The Sustainable Enterprise Fieldbook is organized into five parts and nine chapters. Each part and the subsequent chapters in this book follow the framework of our pyramid model and provide activities, case studies, tools, and techniques to forge a successful path toward creating a sustainable enterprise.

Our goal in this book is to forge a path to a better world and a more sustainable future by supporting employees, managers, and leaders at every level, function, sector, and industry by educating, energizing, and sharing best practices.

Part I. Understanding reality: our context for The Sustainable Enterprise Fieldbook

Introduction and overview

This Introduction attempts to provide you with an understanding of the current state of our environment, economic, and social systems, and the action research efforts we initiated in response to our ongoing question: What more is needed? We present our commitment to iterative learning and the research that focused our understanding and shaped the *Fieldbook*'s framework. The Introduction also provides the background and rationale for focusing on the people factor, the missing ingredient, in the field of sustainability and the importance of providing practical tools and approaches to drive positive sustainable action. We will use key principles and models to show how each of the book chapters contributes a key ingredient to the challenge of building a sustainable enterprise.

The Sustainable Enterprise Living Fieldbook is introduced as a means to capture and share best practices in collaboration technology, knowledge management, and social networks for sustainability.

Part II. Preparing the foundation for a sustainable enterprise

Part II presents the qualities of a sustainable enterprise that provide a foundation from which enterprise sustainability can be advanced:

- lead a sustainable enterprise (Chapter 1);
- think about a sustainable enterprise (Chapter 2);
- develop a sustainability-aligned enterprise strategy (Chapter 3).

Chapter 1. Leadership for a sustainable enterprise

Chapter 1 focuses on the way leaders see themselves and choose to be in relation to each other, employees, customers, communities, the larger society, the environment, and other stakeholders. Leaders in sustainable enterprise choose to purposefully engage with the people inside the organization as if it were a living system, while recognizing that they are simultaneously operating in the larger ecosystem of the world.

The processes of transformation and change begin with the leaders who then engage with the people in the organization; they all make it happen together. The aim of this chapter is to provide leaders with insights and examples of how this can be achieved in ways that produce superior results. To accomplish this, a **Leadership Diamond** model was developed, and essays that breathe life into the model are shared. The Leadership Diamond model integrates the roles of leaders in relating and influencing through the power of the enterprise intent and the embedded governing principles. It emphasizes the *way of being* that is so critical to sustainability. These essays focus on both theory and practical business examples. The essays significantly expand traditional ideas regarding leadership.

Chapter 2. Mental models for sustainability

Chapter 2 focuses on the all-pervasive nature of the prevailing patterns of thought and shows the importance of becoming aware of the currently dominant models that reinforce wasteful and unsustainable behavior. The chapter recognizes that, for sustainable initiative to succeed, the leaders, managers, and staff of organizations and enterprises must incorporate recognition and appreciation of the larger dynamic complex systems of which they are a part. In this way they can consciously co-create more versatile, inclusive patterns of thinking and acting. In this chapter, both theory and practices for making desired substantive changes in mental models are offered. John Adams' framework lays out six dimensions for assessing and working with mental models, and comes out of his many years of research and consulting. To illustrate the difference that mental models make regarding the challenges and opportunities corporations encounter along the journey toward sustainability, examples are presented from two companies—one in the energy industry and one chemical company—that have transformed their thoughts and actions in response to the communities in which they are situated. Three case studies follow that provide tools and exercises for effecting mental model changes, as well as cultivating personal and group operating systems that support a high-quality, sustainable future.

Chapter 3. Sustainability-aligned strategies

This chapter focuses on creating "smart" systems-based sustainability-aligned enterprise strategies by combining the best of current core strategy development practices with sustainability-aligned enhancements.

We review the current state of sustainable enterprise strategy with both a sobering assessment of our progress balanced with the enormous potential for a flourishing future. Government is not leading the movement and business is expected to do more. We also share a game-changing letter advocating every public company to have a clear strategy for Doing Well and Doing Good.

We introduce our Smart Strategy Bridge framework with four stages to accelerate our progress towards a flourishing future. Each stage contains system-based actions we can take to improve our sustainable strategies. The Bridge progressions move enterprises from: Being Stuck, to Doing Well, to Doing Well and Doing Good, and finally to Thriving. Tools introduced include: a sustainability-enhanced SWOT, an ROI Workbook, and The Big

Pivot. Case studies include: small farmers in Haiti leveraging trees for profits, GE's story of chasing the wrong purpose. Unilever and BASF are examples of integrating the SDGs within strategies for Doing Well and Doing Good. The Interface and Tesla cases are examples of disruptive strategies that embrace risks and unknowns, but are driven by a purpose to help their enterprises and society to Thrive.

Part III. Embracing and managing change sustainably

Part III includes specific sustainable enterprise qualities that infuse innovation and personal and group commitment. It also includes insights and tools to help you get started or adapt the performance measurement information and reporting systems that allow all enterprises and their stakeholders to appreciate their progress along the journey to enterprise sustainability:

- manage the change to a sustainable enterprise (Chapter 4);
- engage employees in the sustainability journey (Chapter 5);
- measure, manage, and report your progress (Chapter 6).

Chapter 4. Managing the change to a sustainable enterprise

Our path and pace to creating a more sustainable and thriving world depends on our ability to change. We need to change our beliefs, capabilities, and actions at an individual and enterprise level. This will require us to look, listen, and move differently. Looking differently at sustainability opportunities and challenges will open up new paths and possibilities. Seeing the larger, complex system we are operating in will lead to smarter actions like managing paradoxes vs. attempting to solve problems that are impossible to solve. Listening authentically and openly to a broader set of stakeholders will generate increased collaboration and shared ownership. Opening up dialogue and feedback vehicles to multiple stakeholders will improve our triple bottom line: social equity, ecological integrity, and financial profitability. Moving forward every day and testing out new paths and possibilities will generate the progress and innovative approaches needed for success. Utilizing organizational change methodologies like the FAIR model in this chapter that tap into the knowledge and energy of our employees and other stakeholders will result in our ability to change more quickly, with better results that can be sustained and built on over time.

Chapter 5. Employee engagement for a sustainable enterprise

Chapter 5 looks at the importance of engaging employees at all levels in co-creating the enterprise's future, a crucial accomplishment if even the most enlightened leaders are to get beyond their own best intentions. What approaches are recognized as necessary to involve employees in any major organizational change? What is unique about involving them in sustainability management?

This chapter suggests some of the psychological dynamics that contribute to achieving employees' sense of ownership and commitment to taking on sustainability. It describes the power resulting from people experiencing autonomy and interdependence, and belonging to a community of kindred spirits. It describes how authentic leadership can resonate with people at all levels of an organization, as positive energy and resolve become contagious.

Five in-depth case studies illustrate distinctive approaches to employee engagement. One describes how senior management set up conditions for self-organizing at a previously underperforming plant at DuPont. Another case study elaborates on a multiyear effort to bridge labor and management differences to radically improve safety; yet another infused safety concerns through the constant drumbeat of companywide activities. Eileen Fisher lives out the keen social consciousness of its founder. Employee engagement even spreads across company lines when Eileen Fisher enlists management at overseas suppliers to improve working conditions for low-paid employees. Similarly, a grassroots effort in India paid dividends with social and environmental benefits for a whole community. Each situation exemplifies sound management concepts for unleashing the power, creativity, and insights made possible only by engaging a broad swath of the workforce.

Chapter 6. Enterprise sustainability metrics and reporting

How do you measure sustainability? This chapter provides overviews of the enormous progress being made on sustainable development indicators, measurement frameworks, and systems at the global, national, and enterprise levels.

This chapter is about creating sustainability-aligned metrics and reporting systems that inform and monitor progress towards the "smart" sustainability-aligned Bridge strategy objectives presented in Chapter 3. Systems thinking is used to establish appropriate measurement boundaries and feedback signals. This requires establishing sustainability-aligned and stage-appropriate SMART goals. We introduce a multi-capitalism framework for measuring stock, flow, and threshold performance. Sustainability is integral to the core business and so there is only one strategy and one integrated measurement and reporting system that is enhanced and adapts as the enterprise strategy and performance progresses.

Measurement and reporting system design criteria, collaborations, tools, and case examples are presented for each of the four smart Bridge strategy stages. At the **Doing** stage companies realize how much they are already doing. **Doing Well** is the stage most sustainability-engaged companies are at today. Their performance management and reporting systems showcase competitor differentiation and optimize financial performance and value. At the **Doing Well and Doing Good** stage companies are implementing all prior stage performance objectives, but cannot become complacent. Their systems progress to be more holistic and interconnected with societal goals. At the **Thriving** stage companies are pioneering science-based measurement systems and collaborating to devise context-based allocation schemes that are ethical and fair.

Part IV. Connecting, integrating, and aligning toward the future

Part IV offers critical insights about how people relate to each other to create sustainable enterprises, and develop and envision their extended relationships, their communities, and the world. The two chapters in this section cover best and leading-edge practices regarding how to:

- operate in a global context (Chapter 7);
- create future sustainability by inventing the businesses and social networks to fuel our journey to prosperity (Chapter 8).

Chapter 7. Sustainable globalization: the challenge and the opportunity

Chapter 7 represents a breakthrough and a fundamental transformation in how we approach doing business in the increasingly globalized world in the 21st century. The authors use **six lenses of sustainable globalization** to provide fresh perspectives on global issues:

1. Economic/financial
2. Technology
3. Poverty and inequity
4. Limits to growth
5. Movement of talent
6. Geopolitical

With an emphasis on forward-thinking, technologically savvy, and multidisciplinary approaches, this chapter looks at the complex and globally interconnected nature of business today. Seeing the challenges and opportunities we face through each of these six lenses reveals new prospects for business and civil society. The chapter contains case studies to highlight innovative approaches that companies are inventing to address ecosystems under stress as well as rapidly growing urbanization while furthering long-term sustainability.

The six lenses sustainable globalization tool provides readers with guidelines for assessing opportunities and risks faced by their organizations from the perspective of each of these six lenses.

Chapter 8. Sustainability models for collaboration, technology, and community

Chapter 8 focuses on ways we can invent our sustainable future, with particular attention to the importance of collaboration, technology, and community. The chapter explores enterprises as complex systems operating in dynamic and increasingly unpredictable environments that include ecological disruption and social change. Drawing on lessons from the past and realistic assessments of where we are today, the chapter explores areas that are critical to inventing future sustainability for business and for society. Those are:

* integrated thinking;
* leadership and our complex networks of relationships including public-private collaborations;
* architecting participation;
* technology and ensuring the sustainability of essential resources.

The sections include tools, exercises and thought problems, and case studies about what it will take to reach baseline sustainability thresholds that can support prosperity and thriving within Earth's planetary boundaries.

Part V. Building new bridges to the future

Consistent with the major conclusions from previous research, our concept of sustainability has evolved from mostly separate streams of parallel conversations into a holistic notion that rejects the premise that social, environmental, and economic issues are competing interests. This integrative perspective contends that social, environmental, and economic performance can and must be optimized simultaneously for both short- and long-term success.

Chapter 9. A path forward: building new bridges to the future

Chapter 9 offers reflections on the journey we and our readers have traveled together. We have learned that the term conclusion may not be the best way to describe the ending of this physical book on sustainability. Each thing we collectively learn and share in our team makes us see even more clearly how much more information there is to learn and how many more insights and perspectives there are to explore if we are to have a lasting deep impact on the future of sustainability. In this chapter, we share what we have learned to this point and lay the foundation for a path forward that will provide for continued learning and sharing with the larger social network of sustainability we have chosen to contribute to. And, as members of this network, we hope to continue to contribute, engaging with others on the collective global journey to a sustainable world.

Note

1 The companies were Alcoa, Bank of America, BASF, The Coca-Cola Company, Eastman Kodak, Intel, Novartis AG, Royal Philips, and Unilever. All were listed in "The Global 100 Most Sustainable Corporations in the World," a project initiated by Corporate Knights. Details on its methodology and results can be found at www.global100.org (accessed January 17, 2008).

References

Accenture/UN Global Compact. (2013). *The UN Global Compact—Accenture CEO study on sustainability 2013.*

American Management Association (AMA). (2007). *Creating a sustainable future: A global study of current trends and possibilities 2007–2017.* New York: American Management Association.

Aronson, D. (2013). *Sustainability driven innovation.* New York: Deloitte.

Burnes, B. (2004). Kurt Lewin and the planned approach to change: A re-appraisal. *Journal of Management Studies, 41*(6), 977–1002.

Cameron, K. (2013). *Practicing positive leadership.* San Francisco, CA: Berrett-Koehler.

Canaque, F. C., & Hart, S. L. (2015). *Base of the pyramid 3.0.* Sheffield, UK: Greenleaf Publishing.

Clark, G. L., Feiner, A., & Viehs, M. (2015, March). *From stockholder to the stakeholder: How sustainability can drive financial outperformance.* Arabesque Partners, Oxford University. Retrieved May 5, 2018, from https://arabesque.com/research/From_the_stockholder_to_the_stakeholder_web.pdf.

Ehrenfeld, J. R. (2013). *Flourishing: A frank conversation about sustainability.* Stanford, CA: Stanford University Press.

Hurst, A. (2014). *The purpose economy.* USA: Elevate.

International Food Policy Research Institute. (2016). *Global Nutrition Report 2016: From promise to impact: Ending malnutrition by 2030.* Washington, DC.

Lacy, P., & Rutqvist, J. (2015). *Waste to wealth.* New York: Accenture Strategy, Palgrave Macmillan.

Laszlo, C., & Brown, J. S. (2014). *Flourishing: The new spirit of business enterprise.* Stanford, CA: Stanford University Press.

Laszlo, C., & Zhexembayeva, N. (2011). *Embedded sustainability: The next big competitive advantage.* Stanford, CA: Stanford Business Books.

Mason, P. (2016). *Postcapitalism: A guide to our future.* New York: Farrar, Straus & Giroux.

Porter, M. E., & Kramer, M. R. (2011, January–February). Creating shared value: How to reinvent capitalism—and unleash a wave of innovation and growth. *Harvard Business Review,* 63–77.

Stout, L. (2012). *The shareholder value myth: How putting shareholders first harms investors, corporations, and the public.* San Francisco, CA: Berrett-Koehler.

The Economist Intelligence Unit. (2015). *The road from principles to practice: Today's challenges for business in respecting human rights.* The Economist Intelligence Unit.

United Nations. (2011). *Guiding principles on business and human rights: Implementing the United Nations' "Protect, Respect and Remedy" framework.* HR/PUB/11/04. New York: United Nations.

United Nations. (2017). *The Sustainable Development Goals report 2017.* New York: United Nations.

United Nations, High Commissioner for Refugees. (2017). *Figures at a glance*. Retrieved January 15, 2018, from www.unhcr.org/en-us/figures-at-a-glance.html.

Winston, A. S. (2014). *The big pivot*. Boston, MA: HBS Press.

Wirtenberg, J. (2014). *Building a culture for sustainability: People, planet, and profits in a new green economy*. Santa Barbara, CA: Praeger/ABC-CLIO.

Wirtenberg, J., Harmon, J., Russell, W. G., & Fairfield, K. D. (2007). HR's role in building a sustainable enterprise: Insights from some of the world's best companies. *Human Resource Planning, 30*(1), 10–20.

World Economic Forum. (2017). *Global risks 2015* (10th ed.). World Economic Forum.

Part II

Preparing the foundation for a sustainable enterprise

Leadership for a sustainable enterprise

Richard N. Knowles, Daniel F. Twomey, Karen J. Davis, and Shakira Abdul-Ali

Introduction

Richard N. Knowles

This chapter on leadership raises awareness about a new state of being and explores the personal development and transformation necessary for the leader if she or he is to help bring about the change to sustainability. Authenticity, strategies, mental models, ways of engagement, collaboration, and construction of social networks are all ideas that depend on the leader seeing the organization in a new way. This requires a shift in paradigm, from seeing organizations as if they were machines to seeing them as if they were living systems, and this new perspective opens up vast possibilities for organizations, society, and the world.

Since the first edition of this book important, new insights from complexity science are having a profound impact on our understanding of how organizations actually work. Self-organizing criticality (Bak, 1996; Bak, Tang, & Wiesenfeld, 1988) provides insights about how change occurs, and the Process Enneagram© map (Knowles, 2002, 2013b), co-created by the people in the system, appears to be the strange attractor that helps to move the organization towards the edge of chaos and sustain it there where the energy and creativity are highest.

This chapter provides insights into the importance of developing and implementing a successful sustainability strategy and offers proven tools to help leaders create an environment that encourages the successful implementation of such a strategy. For a detailed discussion of the process of crafting and carrying out a sustainability strategy, see Chapter 3.

Companies that are carrying out sustainability strategies are often the best financial performers, as the *2007 AMA Sustainability Survey* in *Creating a Sustainable Future* (American Management Association [AMA], 2007) clearly reveals. The survey shows that, in companies that have successfully implemented sustainability strategies, top management strongly and visibly supports these practices and has deeply embedded the core values on which sustainability is based.

The most commonly used sustainability-related practices, according to the survey (AMA, 2007), focus on such issues as employee health & safety, eliminating workplace violence, accountability for ethical behavior, and a better balance between employee work and life issues. The data suggest that the most difficult to accomplish is advancing sustainability by reaching out to form collaborations not only inside the firm but outside, with stakeholders, other organizations, and the community at large.

Top management must become more visible inviting the people in the organization into conversations about how to make their companies safer, more sustainable, and cost-effective.

Many employees and managers, according to the AMA sustainability survey (AMA, 2007), are already concerned about sustainability issues and believe their interest is stronger than that of company leadership. Thus, there is a clear opportunity for senior management to align its sustainability strategies with the values of middle- and lower-level employees.

Several characteristics mark sustainability. One is the **zero footprint**, which entails preserving the environment through the use, for example, of renewable rather than nonrenewable resources. Another is employing methods that restore both the environment and the spirit of the people in organizations and communities.

The command-and-control approach of the machine paradigm requires a constant flow of power and energy from the top which shuts down the energy of the people deeper in the organization. People are seen as interchangeable parts; many do as little as possible, and their creative contributions are relatively low. This way of leading has its usefulness. However, if employed over the longer run, it is wasteful, ineffective, and inefficient; the organization becomes less sustainable. It is also responsible for driving a lot of counterproductive work behaviors.

A sustainable enterprise behaves as if it were a healthy, living whole. The organization's values and mission are connected with those of its people who in turn are fulfilling a greater purpose in service to the organization and the larger society. People find meaning and come alive; energy and creativity flow. Together, people co-create their collective future. As a result of this, resistance to change almost disappears, and healthy, more sustainable organizations are created.

Leaders for sustainable enterprise purposefully engage the natural tendency of self-organization. Leaders help create the conditions that inspire people to seek a higher purpose—openness, honesty, and transparency—and then invite people to come together to co-create their shared future. They co-create the organization's "BOWL,"[1] which consists of their values, vision, goals, standards of performance, and expectations. This way of leading requires the total commitment and active support of the people at the top of the organization as well as those in middle-management positions if it is to become fully internalized in the making of decisions and central to the business strategy. Knowles calls this way of leading Partner-Centered Leadership. The organization becomes **leaderful**: people from anywhere in the organization who see a need, may step forward, take the lead, and make things happen as long as they are working within the BOWL.

In this leadership mode, everyone can work at the high end of his or her skills moving purposefully toward the future together. The effectiveness of the organization rises by 30–40% when compared with the more common command-and-control organizations (Knowles, 2002).

This chapter consists of a series of holographic essays reflecting the contributors' own insights; no attempt has been made to blend them or force them into a uniform voice or set of ideas. Each will speak to different readers in different ways, providing a variety of insights about this way of leading. All are connected, however, at a deep level.

Richard N. Knowles's essay brings focus to a fundamental pattern of self-organization as an omnipresent, subtle, and powerful force that can be purposefully engaged by anyone who is willing to work in the ways described in this chapter. This idea runs through all the essays here, which recognize this force as a basic feature of the human way of being. Purposeful engagement results in a sense of urgency, clarity, resoluteness, and hope, and opens everyone to growth and new potential. Possibilities emerge that people can consider, develop, and embrace.

Knowles' essay introduces the concepts of Per Bak (1996) on self-organizing criticality which are fundamental to understanding the importance of focused, purposeful, disciplined conversations, how change occurs, and the way energy and creativity are opened up and sustained.

This essay also introduces ways to help leaders engage and experience this force presenting a novel, powerful, validated model of how to hold and preserve the difficult conversations that help people co-create their future and at the same time—using a model called the **Process Enneagram**©[2]—develop a strategic map for their journey ahead. The co-created Process Enneagram© map appears to be the strange attractor that enables the organization to work and live at the edge of chaos.

In the second essay, Daniel F. Twomey explores integrity, mutuality, and sustainability. The **Leadership Diamond**, a figure developed by Twomey, provides a visual picture of aspects of leadership that are critical for a sustainable enterprise revealing a new **way of being** that focuses on **integrity**, **mutuality**, and **sustainability**.

Twomey discusses domains of leadership that are critical for leaders to understand, to operate in, and to use. He identifies many of the processes, practices, and principles that will enable leaders to be more conscious of what they are doing and how they engage the world around them.

Karen Davis's essay holds up a vision of a "global wisdom society." Global wisdom embodies a system perspective and has a deep respect for natural systems, human needs, and future generations. It requires that people trust the dynamics of self-organization, learn from the new sciences, and serve society ethically. In this essay, Davis calls for a new *way of being* and invites the reader to listen deeply to rediscover the ancient lessons of indigenous traditions and Earth wisdom.

Shakira Abdul-Ali's essay emphasizes that leaders must listen to the voice of the community if they are to lead in a more sustainable way. The problems faced in the movement toward sustainability are too big and broad for any one individual or organization to go it alone. Leaders for sustainable enterprise must recognize the need to consent—rather than concede—to share power; this comes from an environment of authentic, trusting relationships. Abdul-Ali calls for co-creating and self-organizing shared values and processes.

The source of innovation and influence must emanate from all levels. Foundational theories of conventional management systems, accepted as valid, must be challenged. Ghoshal (2005) shows how the pretense of knowledge, unfounded negative assumptions about people, and other "bad theories" have made a substantial contribution to failed conventional practices, such as those employed by Enron.

The essays in this holographic ensemble bring together many of the key features of leadership for sustainable enterprise. One of these essays may make more sense to you than the others. If so, concentrate on the approach it offers; study it to develop your own thinking and leadership skills. There are many approaches, but no final answers. This offers all of us the opportunity to create our own approaches to building more sustainability and value into our own enterprises. Let's build a better world together.

Engaging the natural tendency of self-organization

Richard N. Knowles

Self-organizing criticality and the Process Enneagram©

When a typical manager walks around the facility, he or she often spots people talking together in small, informal groups. They are talking about something that is important and interests them. Perhaps it is a sports event or a political situation or family problem; maybe they are just getting caught up with each other; often they are talking about their work. Managers often interpret this as a waste of time, so they push the people to get back to work. Push, push, push takes a lot of energy, creates friction, and demoralizes everyone; it wears them out. It is a huge waste of time and energy, and thus an unsustainable way to lead.

What is happening when people gather to talk? What is going on here? Why? What can managers learn from this? Is it just a waste, or is there something deeper here that could be a key to opening up the energy and creativity of the organization? What would an organization be like if everyone was working to his or her best, applying herself to doing what it takes for the business to succeed? What would it be like if each person was working on an opportunity such as improving workplace safety while lowering costs and simultaneously improving productivity, quality, and customer service?

When leaders choose to purposefully engage with this way in which people come together, it can open up the effectiveness, efficiency, and productivity of the organization by 30–40% (Knowles, 2002).

This phenomenon is called self-organization, which sounds like chaos, anarchy, and potential failure. When I first heard of this, about 25 years ago, I almost fell out of my chair. After all, I was the plant manager and was supposed to keep things organized and tight. But over the years, in learning how to engage with this natural tendency of self-organization, I found that persistently talking with and listening to all the employees about important issues such as safety, quality, costs, sustainability, the enterprise's impact on the community, and the quality of work life, significantly improves the organization's performance. Injuries dropped by 98%, productivity rose 45%, emissions dropped 88%, and earnings rose 300%. Together we confronted and struggled with the issues and developed clarity about what we were trying to do and why this was important to all of us. This was done with openness, honesty, and hard work.

Engaging the natural tendency of self-organization

All living systems naturally "self-organize." This tendency can be seen throughout nature at all levels, from tiny bacteria to large ecosystems. In this essay, a system is loosely defined as a collection of similar things, a group or an organization. There is a shared identity that defines a sort of boundary around this collection of things.

This self-organization is so pervasive and subtle it's usually not even noticed. Yet it is occurring all the time. This natural tendency is powerful, yet subtle; it is like the current in a flowing river. Often people join the flow and engage purposefully in their conversations, in informal gatherings such as family reunions, or in high-performance work teams. Many of us who have been managers have, however, worked against this by trying to impose our wills on people, using a command-and-control approach, when we have had a specific task to do or a goal to reach. This is nonpurposeful engagement with the natural tendency of self-organization. Using the command-and-control approach is like trying to take the twists and turns out of a river and make it flow the way we want. But, in purposeful engagement, leaders join the river and draw great energy and focus from it.

Much of the vast literature on management and leadership is directed at ways that one's will can be imposed on the people in the organization to accomplish the tasks at hand. Most managers crave stability, reliability, pre-dictability, and control in their organizations. While imposing conditions such as these is necessary for a machine such as an airplane, this approach suppresses the vitality, energy, and creativity of people. When this command-and-control mode of managing and leading is used in an enterprise, people self-organize in ways that are seen by the organization as nonpurposeful, becoming lethargic, unresponsive, and resistant to change. Such organizations behave as if they are mechanical things that must be pushed and shoved by their leaders. They are like unhealthy living systems: torpid and passive. There is a growing frustration with this way of leading because of the less-than-hoped-for results, the effort required to keep things moving, the lack of sustainability, and the negative self-organizing behavior that it generates in people.

OUR LEADERSHIP CHOICE

As leaders and managers, we always have a *choice* to make about the way we engage the natural tendency for people to self-organize. There are times when the situation is such that one of these choices may be more appropriate than the other. However, if we can purposefully engage, we will be in the most sustainable position where energy and creativity build. This is about choosing the most effective way to lead in a particular situation, at a particular time. Leadership is a temporal process in which the leader must be conscious of what is happening and must choose the most appropriate leadership engagement process for the situation; this is the "leadership dance."

Most managers have learned how to use command-and-control management processes, but only a few have learned how to use management and leadership processes that purposefully engage the natural tendency to self-organize. Often, these few are the intuitive leaders who know that the command-and-control processes aren't very effective over the long term.

Increasingly, a language and models that are useful in working in this area are surfacing (see Chapters 2, 3, 4, and 5; and Knowles, 2002). Combining powerful models and explicit terminology with intuitive insights provides an effective way to purposefully engage the tendency to self-organize. I call leadership processes that purposefully engage this natural tendency "self-organizing leadership" or "Partner-Centered Leadership." With purposeful engagement, vitality, energy, and creativity increase, and the organization behaves as if it were a healthy, living system. The fundamental idea speaks to the nature of relationships as they are developed and expressed in conversations. Stacey (2001) is leading explorations into the importance of conversations and the exchange of gestures in organizations in his work on complex responsive processes (CRP).

The theoretical foundations of self-organization are critical to building a solid groundwork for this important work for leaders. CRP looks at the conversations among the people in the organization as temporal events. Leaders have direct engagement with people and are not separated from what is currently taking place in the organization. On the other hand, the theory of complex adaptive systems (CAS) looks at systems and organizations as things to be acted on. With the CAS approach, the engagement is with the people in the organization as if they were different from the leader, as if they were objects. Both CRP and CAS approaches are useful in helping develop deeper insights into what is happening in organizations, providing that the distinction between the two methods is understood and made explicit.

All leaders need to do to purposefully engage the natural tendency of self-organization is to begin to have the important, often intense, sometimes difficult conversations about the critical issues facing the organization and invite others to join in the exploration. Three areas provide important conversational pathways. These are the fundamental pathways for self-organizing leadership:

1. Abundantly sharing important, relevant information, such as aspects of how the organization is performing—the competitive situation, their safety and environmental performance, the cost of what the people in the organization are doing, earnings, and the potential impact of all this on the organization's future.
2. Building interdependent relationships and trust by spending time with people on their turf, being respectful, listening and sharing ideas, keeping one's word, taking public responsibility for mistakes, and talking together about how to correct the situation without blame or shame.
3. Helping people discover how they and their work fit into the whole picture, helping them to see the positive impact of their work—discovering meaning in the work.

Authentic conversations, one person at a time, begin to open up the connections that are the medium of successful self-organization.

These authentic conversations must be about the questions and issues that are truly important and critical to the success of the organization's work and its goals. The conversations may be difficult, so it requires courage, concern, commitment, and care to stay in the "heat" and find new ground on which to build. Leaders and employees have to be open, honest, and transparent. *If transformation is to occur, everyone in the organization needs to be engaged in the processes of the organization* and *must not act on the organization as if it were an external thing.*

There are a number of ways to open up these conversations. Leaders and employees together build trust and meaning as they talk and work together. They can ask questions about what they see or sense and ask why. Storytelling is a way for people to find meaning in what is happening. Margaret J. Wheatley (1992) was one of the early thinkers to reveal and publicize this way of leading. Leaders can use the "open space technology" of Harrison Owen (1991) to explore people's interests in a particular subject. The "future search" approach of Marvin R. Weisbord and Sandra Janoff (1995) helps find out what is important to people and identify those in the organization who care enough to carry it forward. David Cooperrider's "Appreciative Inquiry" approach (Cooperrider, Whitney, & Stavros, 2005) is also an effective way to open up the conversation. Sometimes it is necessary to have the hard conversations that Susan Scott talks about in *Fierce Conversations* (2004). Sometimes using Glenda Eoyang's approach (Eoyang, Olsen, Beckhand, & Vail, 2001) to explore the difference makes the difference. The challenge is to keep the conversations open, flowing, and authentic over time.

As new ideas are shared, exciting possibilities are discovered, and opportunities may open up for significant improvement. It's important to document the conversation, to keep the conversational space open, to keep the conversation alive, and to carry it forward to engage others.

Control shifts from management edicts and pronouncements to the co-creation during the Process Enneagram© workshops of what I term the "BOWL" (**A**) (Knowles, 2002, p. 99), which consists of the organization's mission, vision, expectations, principles, and standards of performance. All who are involved, at all levels, in the question being addressed by the Process Enneagram© workshops co-create this BOWL when developing the Process Enneagram© map. Once established, the BOWL provides order and focus for the organization, and within the BOWL people work with a high level of freedom to accomplish the tasks before them.

When people engage in this way, energy and creativity flow and the effectiveness of the organization improves significantly. Resistance to change almost disappears.

Self-organizing criticality and the role of conversations

Self-organizing criticality (SOC) is a natural phenomenon that occurs in the physical world. The SOC concept was introduced in 1988 by Per Bak, Chao Tang and Kurt Wiesenfeld. SOC is a property of self-organizing systems that, at their critical points, can suddenly shift to a new order. Examples of these phenomena are sand piles, earthquakes, mass extinctions, stock market fluctuations, and traffic jams. While these systems have attractors they are typically beyond discovery using traditional Newtonian scientific methods.

Bak's (1996) first examples were sand piles like at the bottom of an hourglass. As each grain of sand falls onto the pile, the pile gradually gets higher increasing its potential energy. **At some point, one that is not predictable, the next grain of sand causes the pile to experience a shift like a landslide releasing some of the potential energy.** As more sand is slowly added to the pile, it builds up again until the next slippage occurs. The shifts can be small ones that happen frequently, or intermediate in size occurring less frequently, or large ones that occur even less frequently.

SOC is typically observed in self-organizing, non-equilibrium systems where extended degrees of freedom and high levels of nonlinearity exist, like near the edge of chaos. The value in understanding SOC is its tendency to be a paramount guiding principle that reveals order from disorder, making visible the invisible and providing stability to the system.

Bak showed that the sizes of these landslides followed a power law. The graphical plots of the logarithms of the frequencies of events versus the logarithms of their sizes results in a straight line. He showed that earthquakes, volcanoes, and traffic jams also followed a power law. **He believed that his ideas accounted for how order emerges from disorder and how, in turn, the most enduring structures can unexpectedly collapse.**

SOC also applies to the buildup of energy in organizations. Knowles defines organizations as "complex, adapting, self-organizing networks of people." Since organizations are self-organizing the SOC process can take place within them. The more complex that human interactions become the greater the influence the SOC process has on systems and networks and the greater the importance of understanding the emergent properties of the attractor to hold the organization at the edge of chaos.

Instead of grains of sand building up on each other, one can visualize a myriad of purposeful, focused, and disciplined conversations in the organization building up energy over time.

No one knows when the next conversation will be really significant and shift things.

The challenge for organizations is the optimization of SOC for collective output and organizational gain. Understanding how to reveal attractors that influence SOC is important in solving complex problems and living at the edge of chaos. The organization's attractors provide order for the organization, a boundary and space within which the organization can hold firm yet allow freedom for the people within the organization to make the best decisions possible about doing their own work at the individual level.

Using Per Bak's ideas and extending them to organizations is a very useful way to see invisible patterns and attractors.

In pursuit of excellence

Most organizations are trying to grow and improve their safety performance and earnings. Many people in traditional management positions want to maintain a high degree of control so that their people do what they are supposed to do to make the organization more successful. These managers seek reliability, predictability, stability, and control. They see organizational challenges as systematic and machine-like with complicated issues that need reductionist thinking and linear tools like project planning, cost–benefit analysis, and training to fulfill the expectation that the people will work safely and do what the rules require.

These command-and-control cultures are often plagued with the unintended consequence of the people feeling cynical, frustrated, confused, fearful of and resisting change, and often angry (Knowles, 2002). Improvements in performance, safety, and production are difficult and slow. When the decisions are made at too high a level in the organization and the people are expected to unquestioningly follow these decisions, unintended as it may be, unproductive behavior often results. Information flows are constrained and restricted, trust is low, and managers lack the capacity to help the people to develop the collective purpose and identity of who they are and what they are trying to accomplish. The gulf between the work-as-imagined by those at the top and the work-as-done by those doing the work is unrecognized and huge.

For many managers this complicated, machine-like approach is seen as the proper and responsible way to lead. The roots of this go all the way back to Frederick Taylor and his 1911 book, *The Principles of Scientific Management* and are further influenced by Max Weber, A. M. Henderson, and Talcott Parsons in *The Theory of Social and Economic Organization* who refer in their 1947 book to layers of hierarchy, rigid status and structure, rules, and the role of experts. This way of leading is conservative, efficient, low-risk, and repeatable across many levels of the organization. It is what most managers have always done. They see the organization as if it is a machine, but, people and organizations are not machines; they are much more like living systems such as flocks of birds or schools of fish.

When managers shift their thinking and approach to their organizations to seeing them as complex, full of nonlinearity, feedback loops, and iterative processes, new opportunities open up for the organization and the people to become much more safe, effective, productive, profitable, robust, resilient, and better places to work. The cultures in these organizations become more vibrant and alive with the people feeling hopeful, having a sense of urgency with clarity of purpose, and openness to change and new possibilities (Knowles, 2002). Energy and creativity flow abundantly.

While this is a new and different place for most managers, they can develop the confidence to become significant change management leaders learning to live with the certainty that previously unseen properties will emerge enabling them to reach higher, more sustainable levels of safety performance with their teams.

To do this, though, requires an awareness and receptivity to the notion that human experience has evolved with SOC as a basic property behind the actions and thoughts of people. This is one reason the author understands organizations to be complex, adapting, self-organizing, networks of people. They are dynamical systems with changes occurring in both time and space. These networks are resilient and robust with information flowing freely throughout the networks in myriads of conversations. They can operate near the edge of chaos.

In addition to many conversations building up over time, a key for organizations to thrive and grow is the identification of the SOC strange attractor that holds the people and the organization in this dynamical space.

The hidden patterns behind the visible patterns of behavior are difficult to discover. However, once revealed they provide a region of order among the chaos as well as a space for freedom in which the people make the best decisions they can for their own work.

Knowles discovered a methodology to reveal the strange attractor that enables SOC to be a positive force in the organization. He realized that the strange attractor enables the organization to have sufficient stability to live in the ambiguity at the edge of chaos. He called the tool for discovering and creating the attractor the Process Enneagram© (Knowles, 2002). This tool helps people discover and reveal hidden patterns that allow creativity and energy to emerge, while at the same time maintaining order and focus for the organization, as well as the freedom for the people to make the best decisions for the work to be done.

Knowles calls the strange attractor the BOWL. It is a basin of attraction made up of the vision, mission, principles, and standards (of behavior and performance) and the ideas that emerge from the people co-creating their own Process Enneagram© map. The BOWL reveals how SOC can work collectively for the people and the organization by providing order and a boundary in which the people can coordinate and cooperate, yet also enabling the people within the BOWL to have the freedom to make the decisions that are appropriate and best for their particular work. As people see the need to do something they have the freedom and support to step forth to address this need and in doing so the organization becomes "leaderful" (Knowles, 2013a).

The Process Enneagram©

The Process Enneagram© is a tool for dealing with complexity. An enneagram is a Greek word for a nine-term figure. The Process Enneagram© builds on this figure and is focused on the patterns and processes taking place in organizations. Knowles identified the unique nature of each point, the way they interact, and the nature of the inner lines. Patterns for three leadership processes as well as for personal and organizational transformation were discovered. The use of this tool in a guided dialogue enables people to see who and what they are as well as discovering how and why things happen as they do (Knowles, 2013b). The business and people sides of the organization are reconciled and brought together resulting in the release of creative energy and commitment. In the course of the dialogue the people develop practical solutions to solve complex problems, make the connections with other people that they need to help them to do the work, and, in the course of the dialogue, energy and commitment emerge (Knowles, 2002). They co-create their living strategic plan. Beverly G. McCarter and Brian E. White (2013) suggest that the Process Enneagram© provides the missing link between complexity theory and practical application.

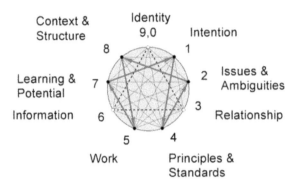

Figure 1.1 The Process Enneagram©
Source: Copyright 2002, Richard N. Knowles, Ph.D. Reproduced with permission.

The Process Enneagram©, Figure 1.1, guides and informs the conversations that are needed to move towards excellence in all aspects of performance. A breakthrough in developing the Process Enneagram© was Knowles' discovery that Bennett's (1996) systems could be placed around the circumference of the figure.

Point 1. The Monad renamed as "Intention"
Point 2. The Dyad renamed as "Issues and Ambiguities"
Point 4. The Triad renamed as "Principles and Standards"
Point 5. The Tetrad renamed as "Work" (the actual, physical things going on)
Point 7. The Pentad renamed as "Learning and Potential"
Point 8. The Hexad renamed for "Structure" (the internal structure of the organization) and "Context" (the external environment in which the organization exists).

Points 0, 3, and 6 were renamed from Function, Being, and Will to "Identity," "Relationship," and "Information," the three elements required for self-organization. These are the visible manifestations of Function, Being, and Will.

In the course of the dialogue with the Process Enneagram©, a map is co-created by the people in the organization. David Byrne and Gill Callaghan in their 2014 book, *Complexity Theory and Social Sciences: The State of the Art*, point out that everyone, including the managers, needs to be involved and engaged in the dialogue for it to be effective in the complex system of the organization. The dialogue process begins with a question that is important and compelling to the people like "How do we improve our safety performance?" This is followed by dialogue at each of the nine points writing onto the map the people's ideas and comments as they emerge. This is an enlightening process of self-discovery for the people; they realize that collectively they have a lot of knowledge they share together, and together they come to understand how SOC can work collectively for them.

The Process Enneagram© map that the people co-create is then posted on the walls of their meeting rooms and constantly discussed each time they meet, asking each other about their experiences since the last meeting as they are related to the Process Enneagram© map they created. As the people work together in this dialogue at each of the nine points, the organization becomes conversationful around their core work. These ongoing conversations keep the Process Enneagram© map alive allowing the people to make constant adjustments as the world changes and to sustain their work processes.

An important role for the leaders in the organization is to constantly maintain the ongoing conversations about their Process Enneagram© map, fully sharing information by going into their organization, listening to and talking with the people, learning together and helping them to see the importance of their contributions for the success of the whole organization. The Process Enneagram© map reveals the strange attractor (the BOWL) and is refreshed continuously ensuring the cohesiveness of the work and sustainability of performance.

In the hundreds of workshops that Knowles has led, the people shift from their old, traditionally led, low-energy organizational basin of attraction to their higher energy, more effective and efficient, self-organizing basin of attraction called their BOWL. This shift often happens in just a day or less. Then the leaders sustain the process through the ongoing conversations and dialogue each time the people meet. This is illustrated in Figure 1.2.

The Process Enneagram© is fractal and can be used at any level of scale. It begins with the starting question of importance. The opening question

Figure 1.2 Moving to the new state

Source: Copyright 2016, Richard N. Knowles, Ph.D. Reproduced with permission.

can be narrowly or broadly focused. The ideas, developed as the Process Enneagram© map are co-created by the people, are guided by the nature of the question. A narrowly focused question develops a Process Enneagram© map with a narrow focus and a broadly focused question develops a more broadly focused Process Enneagram© map.

The completed Process Enneagram© map co-created by the people becomes their living, strategic plan and is updated constantly as conditions evolve and change. This is their strange attractor, their BOWL enabling them to live and thrive at the edge of chaos, adapting, thriving, and growing by providing the stability and order to hold everything together and the freedom for the people to learn, grow, make the best decisions possible, and create new opportunities. Many of the changes they make are small, some of the changes are bigger but less frequent, and occasionally the organization reinvents itself. The organization is much more resilient as the people constantly make adjustments to improve things.

There are two transformation processes embedded within the Process Enneagram©. Personal transformation takes place as people work, on the right-hand side, on themselves and develop their co-created Principles and Standards. The organizational transformation occurs on the left-hand side as the people learn how to work together, learn, and develop new, potential possibilities. This brings the humanistic side of the organization together with the mechanical, Taylor side of the organization in a seamless way resulting in the release of energy and creativity. This is illustrated in Figure 1.3.

In using this approach when Knowles was the plant manager of a large, DuPont chemical plant in Belle, WV, as mentioned earlier in this chapter, the results were remarkable (e.g., earnings rose about 300%, injury rates dropped by about 98%, emissions dropped by about 88%, and productivity rose by about 45%).

Figure 1.3 Total business excellence

Source: Copyright 2014, Richard N. Knowles, Ph.D. Reproduced with permission.

SOC—purposeful use of a natural phenomenon

Many of you reading this chapter have experienced a major crisis in your organization like a fire or the loss of a very big customer. You have probably noticed how quickly the people self-organized, became a high-performing team, and successfully worked through the crisis. This was SOC in action. There is so much happening and so little real-time information for the managers that they are forced by the circumstances to open up and the people move through the upper path indicated in Figure 1.3. Great energy and creativity emerge as the people engage with the crisis. Morale and excitement build. But then when the crisis passes, the organization reverts to its former self with all the dysfunctional behavior resurfacing. Usually neither the people nor the managers know how to hold themselves at the edge of chaos and sustain the excellent performance so they slip back to the old ways.

Figure 1.4 shows the pathways for the two choices that a leader or manager can make each time he/she is faced with a complex decision. The lower, command-and-control pathway is followed when the manager decides that she/he has the answers and imposes them upon the organization. This

Figure 1.4 How organizations function

Note: The pattern used in this chart is built off the work of Bill McKelvey, April 24, 2008.

Source: Copyright 2014, Richard N. Knowles, Ph.D. Reproduced with permission.

pathway choice usually feels quicker for the manager and if the people just follow the instructions, things will be just fine. But many times things are not just fine because when the manager imposes his/her will onto the natural tendency for self-organization, the people in the system begin to pull back and shut down. Information flows become weak and blocked up. The energy dissipates. The levels of trust between the people in the organization and the leaders get broken, all sorts of dysfunctional behavior spreads, like the way people form cliques and resist change. The hidden elephants grow. People self-organize around the kinds of behaviors that drag the organization down and suck the energy out. Nothing basically changes; the culture is quite dysfunctional, the network breaks down, and the organization gradually dies.

However, when the leader follows the upper pathway, engaging the natural tendency of self-organization, he/she is now using the natural phenomenon of SOC, the path typically experienced as the people plunge into solving a crisis. As the conversations open up and the energy builds, the organization moves up along this path. New ideas and possibilities emerge; the elephants get rooted out, information flows freely enabling the network to better know itself. The excitement and interest in the work build. People become more creative, energized, and leaderful. The organization moves towards the edge of chaos where it is most dynamic, creative, and healthy. The people co-create their shared future using the Process Enneagram© thus enabling them and their organization to hold themselves successfully at the edge of chaos becoming a highly functioning organization with a positive, sustainable, strong culture.

The BOWL they create enables the people in the organization to live effectively at the edge of chaos. The leaders and others maintain the BOWL which provides order and focus. They broaden the people's understanding, continuing to learn together. Walking around among the people, learning, listening, talking with each other is one of the processes to sustain the BOWL. The BOWL is the strange attractor that enables the organization to live and work successfully at the edge of chaos and for the people to do their work most effectively and safely. A number of case studies showing completed Process Enneagram© map BOWLS are in Knowles (2002).

Here are some real examples of new things happening in organizations near the edge of chaos.

- In Niagara Falls, NY many small changes occurred like when one member of the City of Niagara Falls, NY Leadership Team shared a truck with another group, and another Team member provided temporary clerical help to another group. These kinds of behaviors are rare in Governmental organizations. The changes built upon each other resulting in the Leadership Team cutting $16,000,000 out of a $62,000,000 budget in the four years they worked together.

- Some intermediate-sized changes occurred like eliminating $600,000 a year in wasteful truck handling procedures in just two months. This was done by the operators at the Belle Plant. They decided that there were too many empty trucks just sitting around and began to return them to the vendors.
- Occasionally a large change occurred like when a new leader at the DuPont Niagara Falls Plant came into a dysfunctional, failing production organization that was not able to run. He declared that "failure was no longer acceptable" and opened up the conversations to smoke out the elephants. Change happened quickly and the operation is still productive and profitable 25 years later.
- Another example of a major shift occurred in the CSR Invicta Sugar Mill in Ayr, Australia when the people cut their number of injuries from about 35 per year to zero in just three weeks and sustained that performance for the next nine months.
- Another example of a large change occurred at the DuPont Belle, WV plant when 16 different conversions of chemical process control systems were made without building control processes in parallel to be sure that the new processes would work before the old ones were shut down. Every one of the conversions worked enabling the organization to cut the time and costs of these conversions by about 50%, saving millions of dollars of investment and months of time.

At the DuPont Belle, WV plant, where Knowles was plant manager, leading and using principles of the Process Enneagram© from 1987 to 1995, the people learned to sustain this high level of work for 17 years even though subsequent managers failed to follow through, retreating into their offices and themselves. Things gradually fell apart when the BOWL was not sustained and the SOC process broke down, in this case, to the point where a man was killed in 2010 in a preventable accident 15 years after Knowles had been reassigned and had left the plant.

Continuous dialogue and conversations along with the use of the co-created Process Enneagram© map keep the BOWL alive. They are the keys for the organization to move through SOC and thrive in highly energetic, creative, effective, productive, profitable, and safe ways of working at the edge of chaos. **The future is built one conversation at a time! Organizations ultimately ignore this at their peril.**

Some thoughts on emergence

I describe behaviors emerging from three different leading processes in *The Leadership Dance: Pathways to Extraordinary Organizational Effectiveness* (2002, pp. 169–176). These leading processes—each of which consists of three interdependent ideas—are embedded in the Process Enneagram© (Knowles,

2002, p. 30). In actual practice, all of these are running all the time, but it is useful for this analysis to look at them as if they were separate.

The most basic and important leadership process is the self-organizing leadership process of **identity**, **relationship**, and **information**. There are two other leadership processes embedded in the Process Enneagram©: **operational leadership** is focused on the issues (problems), structure, and assigning the work; **strategic leadership** is focused on the intention (the new thing that needs to be done), principles and standards (the new behaviors that the new thing that needs to be done requires), and learning (how to do and sustain this new thing).

Self-organizing leadership connects the Process Enneagram© points 0, 3, and 6. Operational leadership connects points 2, 8, and 5, and strategic leadership connects points 1, 4, and 7. All three of these leadership processes are embedded within the Process Enneagram©. Moving among these forms of leadership as the immediate situation requires is called the **leadership dance**.

Emergence in the self-organizing leadership process

Identity, relationship, and information emerge as everyone in the organization engages in dialogue about questions and issues that are very important to them. Through this dialogue, leaders are engaging the natural tendency of self-organization in purposeful ways. Reflecting on the importance of these conditions for self-organization, people can look at them from the perspective of their threefold relationship. They are forces that are interacting all the time. Through the interaction of the parts of this triad, new behaviors emerge releasing energy and creativity (Figure 1.5):

- When everyone has an interdependent relationship and an abundance of information, as people become clearer about their identity **meaning** emerges.
- When everyone has a clear sense of identity and an abundance of information, as people's relationships become more interdependent **trust** emerges.
- When everyone in the organization together has a clear sense of identity and an interdependent relationship, as new information becomes available people can move into **action**.

These new behaviors emerge depending on the ways leaders choose to engage the people in the organization. These choices can lead to vastly different outcomes. Purposeful engagement leads to a sense of urgency, clarity of purpose, resoluteness, hope, new potential, and new possibilities. Nonpurposeful engagement leads to fear, anxiety, confusion, struggle, cynicism, frustration, and resistance to change. These ideas are developed further in Knowles (2002).

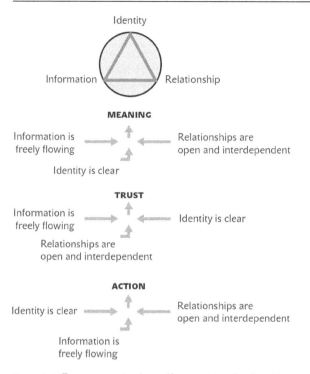

Figure 1.5 Emergence in the self-organizing leadership process

Source: R. N. Knowles (2002). *The leadership dance: Pathways to extraordinary organizational effectiveness* (p. 130). Niagara Falls, NY: Center for Self-organizing Leadership. Reproduced with permission.

The choice of the mode of engagement is simple, but the execution can be difficult.

Some examples

An example from when I was plant manager at the DuPont plant in Belle, WV, will help illustrate these ideas further. When we began a construction project to convert from pneumatic to electronic process control systems at Belle, we involved the engineers, operators, mechanics, and all supervision deeply in the communications and planning processes. Our goal was to convert to the new chemical process control systems without maintaining parallel systems for transition and backup. This was a high-risk approach, so we knew that everyone needed to be involved in the weekly project status reviews, planning sessions, design meetings, and the like; many of the operators, mechanics, and engineers were sent to the Honeywell School for computer training. All the information was shared on a continuous basis, and interdependent relationships were developed. There was a lot of give-and-take in these meetings as everyone tried his or her best to make the project a success. At the end of the project, the unit was started up without incident, making quality product in record time. This approach cut the costs and time in half, from the original estimate of US$6 million in investment and two years to implement. Then 15 more projects were successfully put into place in record time and at lower-than-forecast investment without running any parallel processes, clearly showing the success of self-organizing leadership processes.

In another example using engagement processes such as these, the City of Niagara Falls, NY Leadership Team worked together with the mayor in a way that resulted in cutting out US$15 million from a US$62 million budget over a four-year period. This was the first time in the city's history that the Leadership Team worked together this way, and saved so much money. Sharing information, building interdependent relationships, and getting very clear about the mission to make the city as strong as possible were keys to this success. A lot of the savings resulted from people talking about what was going on, so, for example, we knew to put the new sewers into place before paving the streets.

Surely, most of you reading this book can think of examples in which well-intended projects with high expectations were started from the top of the organization with little employee involvement. The people resisted the changes, slowing things down to the point that the organization lost energy and interest, finally giving up altogether. Many of the quality improvement efforts over the last 20 or more years have ended like this. However, this is not because of the poor quality of the technology, but rather the lack of deep involvement of all the people.

Application across cultures

The self-organizing leadership processes described in this essay have been used across many cultures for more than 25 years. For example, I have used them extensively in Australia, New Zealand, Malaysia, United States, Canada, and the United Kingdom in organizations ranging from heavy industry—such as steel, coal, and chemicals—to Leadership Institutes, school districts, accounting firms, the United Way of Niagara Falls, city government, and various community projects such as the Niagara County Study on Services for the Aging. Claire Knowles uses this approach very effectively in her work with women in transition (www.lightsonworkshop.com).

Tim Dalmau has used these processes in companies and communities in Australia, New Zealand, South Africa, Namibia, Thailand, United States, Mexico, Malaysia, Germany, Indonesia, China, and Singapore (www.dalmau.com). Steve Zuieback has used them extensively in the state of California school system (www.stevezuieback.com).

This approach is not limited to any particular sort of work, culture, or organization. It applies to situations ranging from individuals to very large groups; it is fractal in nature in that it works at multiple levels of scale.

There seems to be an archetypal nature to this work that makes it useful and transferable. Although the specific situations differ in each instance and are not transferable, the deeper patterns and processes of SOC and the Process Enneagram© are highly consistent and transferable.

Conclusion

As leaders, we have a choice to make about how we engage the natural tendency to self-organize. Historically leaders and managers have tried to impose their wills—there will still be occasions when leaders need to do this—but we are finding that purposefully engaging the natural tendency to self-organize produces vital, coherent, energetic, creative, highly effective, and more sustainable organizations. Self-organizing leadership provides pathways for leaders to effectively and purposefully engage the natural tendency of self-organization.

This work requires a high level of openness, integrity, courage, and commitment. For an organization to arrive at a point where people are listening deeply, asking the tough, deeper questions, and respecting and truly valuing each other requires the leader to be working from a deep sense of self, purpose, and integrity. This sustainable way of leading is more about *being* than about having a set of skills, as important as they are.

The Leadership Diamond: zero footprint and a life-giving workplace

Daniel F. Twomey

The **Leadership Diamond** (see Figure 1.6), created by Daniel F. Twomey, illustrates key ideas about a more sustainable way of leading.

The most important role of top management is enabling the self-organizing creativity and energy of the enterprise. This is largely accomplished by articulating a clear, compelling, and sustainable enterprise intent and embedding the principles that will govern behavioral relationships and routines. The enterprise intent and governing principles inform strategy formulation. Within this framework, everyone becomes a leader: she or he establishes positive and productive relationships and influences others within the unit as well as in the greater relevant network.

The leadership process starts with not-knowing and proceeds with an inquiry, learning–action cycle as individuals and units co-create innovative approaches to a sustainable enterprise. **Way of being** takes on much of the aligning, controlling, and disciplining functions of the traditional organization. It includes

Figure 1.6 The Leadership Diamond. Sustainable enterprise: zero footprint and a life-giving workplace
Source: Copyright 2007, Daniel F. Twomey. Used with permission.

the following: **integrity**—claims and behaviors are consistent; **mutuality**—genuinely connecting with others; and **sustainability**—development toward higher levels of awareness and commitment to society.

Our current situation is:

- Faulty (nonsustainable) assumptions
- Faulty (nonsustainable) processes and structures
- Lack of integrity, mutuality, and sustainability (way of being).

The elements of the diamond are:

- We need to acknowledge, "We don't know how to be sustainable"
- We need to address this by inquiry, learning, and entrepreneurship
- And, together, establish co-creating and self-organizing values and processes
- Which are guided and enabled by embedded governing principles
- This is directed and energized by enterprise intent
- And leads to sustainable enterprise: zero footprint and a life-giving workplace
- With an absolute and compelling vision (shared by all)

- The core of this is a shift in way of being: integrity, mutuality, and sustainability (self-awareness).

Nature and domains of leadership for sustainable enterprise

Daniel F. Twomey

Leadership is a complex part of the larger dynamic of human behavior that varies based on contextual factors. The 21st century presents special challenges, with its context of high connectivity and interdependency and its increasingly overstressed resources and unstable political and economic relationships. The question addressed here is: "What kind of leadership is needed to create thriving sustainable enterprises that will reverse the negative trends and help restore the environment and society?"

Leadership

As a society, we are facing a new and enormous challenge in a rapidly changing world. We need to release the creativity, initiative, and goodwill of all people inside and outside the enterprise. Within the enterprise, top management can no longer be the sole source of innovation and influence; these must emanate from all levels. Foundational theories of conventional management systems, accepted as valid, must be challenged. Ghoshal (2005) shows how the pretense of knowledge, unfounded negative assumptions about people, and other "bad theories" have made a substantial contribution to failed conventional practices, such as those employed by Enron.

The sustainable enterprise is focused, but not by top-down plans and controls or "aggrandized" leaders. Rather, a shared, noble, and compelling purpose; the principles that govern behaviors and routines provide the energy and integrity of the enterprise, self-organizing and self-disciplining at all levels. As enterprise moves to distributed leadership and self-organizing processes, the way of being of all employees becomes increasingly important, especially integrity, mutuality, and sustainability (Torbert & Associates, 2004).

These leadership qualities are the cornerstone of the leadership of a sustainable enterprise:

- **Integrity.** What we say or claim is consistent with our behaviors.
- **Mutuality.** Genuinely connecting with others to collaboratively create intent and actions.
- **Sustainability.** Capable of continuous learning and development toward higher levels of societal benefit for future as well as present generations.

The Leadership Diamond provides the context for leadership that both builds relationships and influences and is influenced by others, a radical change from conventional leadership. To appreciate this radical change, this essay examines the underlying dynamics, asking, "Is a fundamental change necessary?" Ways of being are used as lenses to explore this question.

We need to examine and change the language of leadership including the strongly entrenched words and concepts that assume a top-down articulated hierarchy of influence. Here I use **domain** to replace the top-down paradigm with one that enables self-organizing behaviors. The *American Heritage Dictionary* (1992) defines *domain* as "a sphere of activity, concern, or function." Domains are not defined by size, importance, title, or pay, which are associated with top-down hierarchy. Rather, domains are primarily determined by the spheres of activity within an organization. Someone in "top management" may have a small, not very important domain, and someone lower in the hierarchy may have a large and important domain. Furthermore, persons may operate in more than one domain.

Like the conventional organization, a sustainable enterprise needs to differentiate roles and responsibilities. Rather than distinguishing leadership roles by levels of unilateral power based on a top-down hierarchy, a sustainable enterprise determines them by the needs of the sphere of activity (domain) in which the individual operates. When people see the organization as a blended set of domains in which everyone exercises leadership within his or her sphere, it can become a life-giving workplace characterized by integrity, mutuality, and sustainability. Yet this aspect of sustainability is often neglected; leadership is viewed as a top-management or HR responsibility.

Leadership approaches and characteristics

The leadership model for sustainable enterprise is founded on the assumption that the best vehicle for providing goods and services to society is a free-market economy based on the innovation and productivity of profit-making businesses. Although leadership and the role and practices of business are different issues, they are linked. Mental models and values of fairness, equity, and mutuality underpin both leadership behaviors and business practices. For example, when top executives exploit employees by establishing disproportional salaries—such as CEOs who make 500–1,000 times the average employee's salary—one might expect the firm to also exploit its suppliers from small, emerging-market countries.

A radical approach: integrity

The underlying issue of whether one should advocate for radical leadership change is one of integrity—being truthful about the situation as one sees it. Do the vision and strategies that drive the actions needed for sustainability represent a paradigm shift from conventional practices? Is there a need for transformation, a fundamental change at the root level? It seems clear if we look at the theories-in-practice, rather than the espoused theories, of a few thought leaders, that Western leadership still operates within the top-down, charismatic decision-maker model in which the focus is on maximizing winning for the leader. This appears to be the case especially at the top of large corporations in which salary and privilege exemplify the belief that most of the intelligence and creativity belongs to the CEO, CFO, and other C-level executives and that the role of leaders is to drive their values and decisions down through the organization. A common "truth" throughout these organizations is that any initiative must have top management's approval and support. This belief seals a self-reinforcing dynamic that disenables bottom-up creativity and initiative.

A co-creative approach: mutuality

A fundamental difference in a new leadership model is the recognition of mutuality and interdependence. We are all part of the contemporary leadership model, and only by working together will we achieve the transformational change many of us seek. We who are writing this book and advocating change don't have the answers. Many of the answers must come from those, such as corporate executives, who have responsibility for action. We need to find ways to learn together to create the transformation. The people who populate the lower levels of organizations are as important to the change in leadership as those at the top, and they have as much right and responsibility to initiate and support change. Also, customers and others served by the enterprise, as well as those in the next generation who will populate these enterprises, are voices that need to be heard; they also can share in the leadership of sustainable enterprise.

A learning approach: sustainability

There is no particular leadership model that will carry us successfully into the future; rather, leadership will change as people and organizations learn and evolve. The ideas and distinctions made here about leadership provide signposts for inquiry, action, and learning, but they are not the immutable truth. As the values, beliefs, and salaries of top-down leadership topple, and as more people participate in the continuous process of leadership transformation, emerging forces will define a true sustainable leadership model. Argyris and Schön (1996) and Senge, Kleiner, Roberts, Ross, and Smith (1994) have contributed greatly to an understanding of the learning organization, yet those ideas still have only spotty application.

The question about radical change versus incremental change is, "Will a gradual modification of the existing leadership model meet the needs of sustainability?" I believe it will not for the following reasons: the world has a relatively short time to make fundamental corrections; the contemporary model, in its most fundamental values, beliefs, and behaviors, is diametrically opposed to what seems to be needed; and, despite growing public awareness and calls for change, the leadership structure and systems of major corporations seem unable to change significantly. Therefore, the best hope for sustainable enterprise is a new paradigm for a transformed leadership model.

Domains of leadership

Leadership belongs to everyone in the sustainable enterprise. Leadership is the enabling of others to be powerful and innovative in support of the organization's governing principles and enterprise intent. Although all leadership for sustainable enterprise has the common characteristics of awareness, not-knowing, inquiry, and learning from actions, different domains require specific perspectives and skills. Typically the organization designates each employee's role, activities, and responsibilities, which in turn determines his or her domain (sphere of activity) and, in part, the leadership capabilities needed in that position. I specify three possible domains to illustrate different spheres of activity. The activities in these domains call for particular leadership capabilities as well as the core leadership qualities: integrity, mutuality, and sustainability. Hence, domain C—macro-systems leadership—is different from, but not necessarily more important than, domain A—action-learning level. Not all domain C leaders are at the top of the organization, and not all domain A leaders are at the bottom of the organization.

In domain A, leaders create positive relationships and influence actions by fostering a culture of collaboration at the individual and group levels, thereby increasing value to the unit and to its output. In domain B—a systems-aligning sphere—the leader has an awareness of the larger system and the patterns and factors that affect the unit and its output, as well as the ability to collaboratively influence leverage points in ways that create systemic benefits. In domain C the leader has both an awareness of enterprise-level dynamics and the ability to co-design the enterprise intent and governing principles that will enable positive emergent dynamics and self-organizing leadership throughout the enterprise. Richard Knowles (2006), and in the essay "Engaging the natural tendency of self-organization" in this chapter (pages 38–55), asserts that self-organizing is a natural human behavior that is an omnipresent, subtle, and powerful force that can be purposely engaged.

A leader can shape and expand his or her domain, and leaders may operate in more than one domain. For example, an entry-level employee in a domain A role may be especially good at seeing patterns (domain B) before they become part of the internal system. A good self-organizing system would embrace this new perspective, which typically is ignored in conventional organizations. The idea is to create a more fluid and integrated structure, one that encourages the emergence of leadership within every domain.

Jim Collins (2001) describes qualities in sustainable leadership that would apply to any of the domains. He identifies five types of leaders in successful firms. Of these, level 5 leaders are best at creating sustainable enterprises. The level 5 leader is modest, relies principally on inspired standards, demonstrates unwavering resolve, apportions credit to others, and is a catalyst for transition from good to great. She or he frequently uses advocacy to challenge assumptions and the status quo, or changes the context of inquiry. The integrity, mutuality, and sustainability evident in level 5 CEOs are also needed for the individual, group, unit, systems, and each of the domains in the enterprise.

Domain A: relationships and local action

In the self-organizing enterprise, everyone has both the opportunity and the responsibility to create productive relationships and positively influence decisions and actions within his or her network. Each person and every conversation has the potential to have an impact on the nature and outcome of interactions with other people. Much of the culture and many routines of the enterprise are created and/or modified in individual-to-individual and informal group interactions. When these relationships and the culture are positive and aligned with the vision of the enterprise, opportunities for improvement are present, whether they are to better serve the customers, to make the workplace safer, or to create a new product. Leadership in domain A creates the mutuality and intent that supports high performance of the unit and the co-creation of improvement within that job, task, or unit. Integrity, mutuality, and sustainability may be centered at the group-peer level, but they extend to the entire enterprise, so that self-initiating and self-organizing behaviors are aligned across the enterprise. Without fully enabled leadership in this domain, the greatest resource of talent, energy, and potential in the enterprise is wasted. Yet contemporary enterprises do little to enable this leadership domain, and they do much to discourage it.

Domain A leadership is not only found in enterprises, but is frequently seen in communities where individuals create the relationships and provide the influence that enable the community to become a force for positive change.

Domain B: patterns and leverage

The domain B leader, in addition to being aware of and influencing events, sees, understands, and influences trends. This leader identifies routines, patterns of behaviors, and sequences of events in ways that reveal leverage points. Such an appreciation of historical and systemic patterns and forces enables the leader to shift the unit's relationships and expand the synergistic influences that are occurring at the local or event level.

Domain B leadership is strategic as well as synergistic at the unit level as well as across units. It involves bringing together the right people, creating the conditions, and sometimes reframing the conversation for self-organizing at the unit level and across unit levels. Integrity at this level is evident in the unit strategies. Mutuality and sustainability are seen in and across units, as well as aligned with the enterprise. As leaders take on more complex domains of leadership, there is an increased need for knowledge creation. Knowledge creation becomes a more deliberate and intensive process that uses experience and tacit knowledge from diverse sources to conceptualize understanding and actions (Nonaka, Toyama, & Noboru, 2000).

Domain C: purpose, design, and emergence

In domain C, the leader, while appreciating events and patterns, is closely attuned to the purpose of the firm and its role in society. She or he recognizes the global dynamics and trends presently threatening the survival of our civilization and understands that releasing the creativity and energies of the organization in service of a noble purpose is the best way to rise to this world challenge and ensure that the enterprise will thrive. To achieve this goal, the leader infuses the enterprise with a clear and compelling intent, as well as with values and principles about how people within the enterprise self-organize. This may include embracing paradoxes and shifting the paradigm. Domain C leaders design the factors that enable the emergent organization's structure, processes, and behaviors (Twomey, 2006). Design is a co-creation process that brings together diverse views in a context of knowledge creation that enables the experience and tacit knowledge of the group to synergistically emerge as actionable knowledge. Through this process, the leader demonstrates and embeds integrity, mutuality, and sustainability in the fabric of the enterprise in ways that encourage and support other enterprises to do the same for the benefit of the entire world.

Life-giving workplace

Many of the leadership practices that enable enterprises to make substantial gains in their quest toward a zero footprint—preserving the physical environment—also serve the enterprise intent of a life-giving workplace. While there is a synergistic relationship between achieving zero footprint and achieving a life-giving workplace, the life-giving workplace calls for some unique, and often overlooked, leadership traits. The trend line for many of the requirements is down.

A truly life-giving workplace would attract, develop, and retain the best, brightest, and most committed talent for all leadership domains and levels within the enterprise. It would provide a safe and secure environment in which all of a person's creative and productive capabilities are welcomed and nurtured, even when the individual has major life disruptions. It would be a place in which:

- Equity and diversity are a part of all relationships.
- Organizations, departments, and individuals with particular responsibility for people, such as human resources and organizational development, are empowered to be advocates and problem-solvers.
- Leadership encourages an environment that enables people to balance all aspects of their lives, family, community, work, and more.
- These life-giving values and practices are promulgated in all people in the enterprise and its network and supply chain.

Processes and practices for sustainable enterprise

Table 1.1 shows some distinctions that leaders and their teams may use for reflection and inquiry into the enterprise's leadership and its journey to sustainability. These dichotomies, principles, and practices are to be used to trigger deeper inquiry into current behaviors or future possibilities, and not as benchmarks to judge progress. Users are encouraged to add to these lists or create their own using personal experiences and the diverse perspectives in this leadership chapter.

Table 1.1 The enterprise's journey to sustainability

Issue	From	To
Goals	Fixed	Multiple, evolving
Paradoxes	Simplify/deny	Embrace
Focus	On self	On benefit to others
Decisions	Advocate/enforce	Shared inquiry, action
Solutions	Knowing, inflexible	Informed, committed
Design base	Past experiences	Emerging future
Value	Tangible/countable	Social/intangibles
Differences	Difficulties, barriers	Opportunities, enrichment
Perspective	Narrow, single	Wide, multiple
Business	Combative job	Noble profession
Status quo	Supports	Challenges
Facing threats	Fearful, reactive	Confident, proactive
Communications	Demanding/positioning	Inquiry to enable action
Competition	Dominating/exploiting	Level playing field
Competitors	Diminish	Collaborate with
Sharing	Never enough	Plenty

Sustainable principles and practices at all levels

- Reflections (e.g., at beginning and end of meetings).
- Nonauthoritarian action language: requests, offers, and the like.
- Nonjudgmental questions and inquiry.
- Structuring and welcoming diversity of ideas.

- Self-awareness: noticing one's own behavior.
- In all relationships, first establish mutuality.
- Systems thinking: ask why, assume interdependence.

Principles and practices for fostering a self-initiating culture

- Don't blame (Southwest Airlines avoids blaming to create high-performance, aircraft-turnaround-team effectiveness).
- Reduce win–lose dynamic of all reward systems.
- Create equity.
- Expect and enable self-resourcing: most individuals or groups can start initiatives without getting funding from the enterprise, if the enterprise doesn't discourage or prevent them from doing so.
- Fully share information.
- Create clear, compelling, and actionable vision (Fairleigh Dickinson University has a vision of being "The Leader in Global Education." It provides a clear and compelling direction, and almost every employee may take action at one or more of the leadership levels).
- Management "walks the talk" (integrity): top management truly and fully behaves in ways that are consistent with the vision.
- Map self-initiated and self-organized activities and projects. This shows the kind of initiation and organizing that is possible at each level of the enterprise. The ratio of top-down compared with bottom-up initiatives, as well as the degree of self-organizing, informs the continuous redesign.

Reflections on leadership from ancient traditions and Earth wisdom

Karen J. Davis

> The distorted dream of an industrial technological paradise is being replaced by the more viable dream of a mutually enhancing human presence within an ever-renewing organic-based Earth community.
>
> (Thomas Berry)

> Whatever befalls the earth befalls the sons and daughters of the earth. Mankind did not weave the web of life; we are but one strand in it. Whatever we do to the web, we do to ourselves … All things are bound together.
>
> (Chief Seattle)

Learning other cultures' stories and exploring their ways of knowing, being, and acting may compel us toward a sustainable society in which everyone is a leader. So where do we begin?

- What questions do we need to ask ourselves, each other, our organizations, and our world?
- What new stories are necessary to replace the currently engrained ones that only reinforce the dominant culture's ways of being and doing?
- What types of leadership are essential for people to co-create stories of sustainability?
- What and how can we learn from Mother Earth and all her creatures— and from Father Sky?
- How can multiple ways of knowing enhance the journey toward sustainability?
- How is what we are doing now affecting the lives of people seven generations in the future?

These are only a few of the questions that we might hold as we rediscover the values-based ways of being and knowing, individually and collectively, that are rooted in ancient and indigenous cultures and traditions, and in the wisdom of Earth.

Global wisdom organizations and leadership

From the information knowledge era (with its focus on the human mind and intellectual capital), we are approaching an era of spirit (with focus on consciousness and wisdom) in which community is the model.

A global wisdom society with global wisdom organizations values all cultures and traditions and skillfully utilizes multiple ways of knowing for the greater benefit of all life.[3] Institute of Noetic Sciences research suggests that a global wisdom society will be marked by the following:

- a profound recognition of universal interconnectedness among all peoples and all life;
- a commitment to right action for the benefit of all, guided by the mysterious intelligence of the whole;
- valuing learning and openness above certainty and closure, and embracing multiple ways of knowing;
- living in ecological balance;
- perhaps most important, acknowledging that humans exist in a universe alive with consciousness and spirit.

A global wisdom organization (Davis, 2003) embraces the following:

- holding a systemic perspective and always looking at the wholeness, interrelatedness, and harmony and balance of living systems and the universe;
- operating from a deep understanding of and respect for natural systems and cycles, human needs, and future generations (WindEagle & RainbowHawk, 2003);

- trusting the dynamics of self-organizing and collective consciousness (Owen, 2004) as well as co-intelligence; that is, having the capacity to evoke creative responses and initiatives that integrate each person's diverse gifts for the benefit of all (Atlee, 2003);
- learning from the new sciences;
- ethically serving society and Earth in life-affirming, sustainable ways, including those that are in harmony with natural ecological and global environmental systems; being in stewardship of the whole.

In a global wisdom culture, everyone is both leader and follower. The essence of leadership is co-creating and holding the space for people to talk and act with each other about what is important to them, their organization, their community, and the world. Rather than physical space, this is *energy* space for reflection and deep inquiry whereby a deeper source of meaning can arise. One function of a leader is to help people discover the expertise and wisdom in themselves and in others.

Other elements, which are not usually a focus of leadership, are important and worthy of consideration:

- **Asking and holding the right questions.** Native American wisdom is that the First People had questions, and they were free; the Second People had answers, and they became enslaved (WindEagle & RainbowHawk, 2003). Questioning taps wisdom. Knowing the answer limits possibilities.
- **Storytelling.** For indigenous peoples who have an oral tradition, story-telling is a way of life (Anguita, Baker, Davis, & McLean, 2005, p. 487):

   Through stories we can remember who we are and share experiences using past histories and accumulated wisdom, beliefs, and values … Stories tie us to our humanness, and they link the past, present and future by teaching us to anticipate the possible consequences of our actions.

- **Trusting oneself.** Trusting oneself precedes trusting someone else. Healthy trust implies the presence of honesty, integrity, and transparency.
- **Learning and relearning together.** Deep learning is seeing other world perspectives and leaving aside one's own judgments and stereo-types. Understanding one's own mental models strengthens economic, social, and environmental competencies. (For more on mental models, see Chapter 2.) Systemic thinking is fundamental to awareness of inter-dependence and the impact of one's actions (Anguita et al., 2005).
- Being comfortable with ambiguity, uncertainty, and paradoxes.
- Being one (in harmony and balance) with the universe.
- **Trusting multiple ways of knowing.** Being open to modes of con-sciousness that are beyond rationality. Insight into ways of knowing is gained by exploring intuition, the subconscious, and dreams. The con-tinuum of knowing ranges from a feeling, sense, or "the little voice inside" to technology.

In their profile of the fourth-wave biopolitical leader, Maynard and Mehrtens (1993) highlighted the importance of being aware of one's own unconscious programming and inner character, integrating feminine and masculine aspects of self, avoiding domination and passivity, having a positive frame of mind, living intentionally and intuitively, addressing moral, cultural, and economic questions, perceiving realities of global conditions, and dealing effectively with issues of ecology and technology.

Leaders in global wisdom organizations may attain these aspects of leadership, and more, through high levels of consciousness, intention, and responsibility.

Stories from nature

Through the years, I have found lessons and stories from nature to be powerful teachings and constant reminders of ways of knowing and being.

The stories and ways of being of some creatures in nature are lessons of leadership. How can individuals and groups reflect some of these leadership qualities?

- As hummingbirds, which fly right, left, up, down, backwards, even upside down.
- As geese, which fly in V formation, rotating and sharing leadership, encouraging one another through honking, and taking care of each other.
- As eagles, which soar the heights, thus having a broad perspective of the world. The eagle is sacred to some indigenous cultures and represents divine power and enlightenment. The eagle teaches us the importance of seeing the whole pattern or big picture. The eagle gently reminds us of connecting with our higher power.
- As monarch butterflies, whose lifecycle includes metamorphosis, and which migrate each year thousands of miles from Canada to Mexico and back involving three or more generations.

These are but a few of Earth's creatures and collectives from which leaders might learn. Over millennia of human life, people have continuously engaged in rediscovering and learning from the natural world and its complex living systems. There is little that is new; rather, knowledge is being rediscovered time and time again. By listening deeply to the universe and the collective consciousness, all people can receive this wisdom.

Lessons from indigenous cultures

There are endless possibilities for leaders in sustainable enterprise to learn from indigenous cultures whose people live as one with nature and Earth. Indigenous peoples do not see the environment as something apart from them; they see themselves as co-stewards of the land with other creatures (and, in some cases, with spirits).

It can be useful for a leader to reflect on some of the indigenous ways of partnering with complexity from the work of anthropologist Hugh Brody (Pollard, 2006):

- Generosity (both with knowledge and material possessions) and egalitarianism are essential elements of these cultures, and produce an environment of reciprocity and trust.
- Much of the activity enables the building of self-confidence and high self-esteem, freedom from anxiety (fear of the unknown), freedom from depression, the acquired respect and trust of others, and a culture of collaboration and consultation.
- Telling stories is the way of giving advice and instruction and of answering questions. The process is consultative rather than hierarchical. Elders, chiefs, and shamans are respected, but do not have or seek power or authority over others. Children learn about leadership from stories and example.
- People in these cultures not only depend on the conscious mind to process information, they appreciate how the subconscious, dreams, and instincts enrich their understanding and decision-making process.
- There is a profound respect for individual decisions; after sharing of knowledge, if there is no consensus on action, each individual is trusted to do what he or she thinks is right and responsible, and there are no recriminations for not conforming to what others think is appropriate.
- Authority is more horizontal than vertical—a result of the necessity of reaching unanimity on a decision before any action is taken (Harris, Moran, & Moran, 2004).
- Children are not asked what they want to be when they grow up (as in the dominant culture that lives mostly for the future). Children already *are*; they are children and they do not have to wait *to be* (Harris et al., 2004).

And finally a note on *time*, for which there is no word in many indigenous cultures (Pritchard, 1997). In the mainstream culture, time is to be used, saved, and spent; people are paid for their time. Indigenous cultures generally view time as a continuum that is related to the rising and setting of the sun and to the changes of the seasons.

Ancient wisdom council

Bringing Earth wisdom and indigenous traditions into the workplace and individual lives is a focus of the Ehama Institute (WindEagle & RainbowHawk, 2003). One powerful and holistic way is through the ancient wisdom council. This is an integral part of many tribal cultures for clarity and decision-making; it accesses wisdom for addressing an issue or solving deep conflict, allowing the community to put their agreement and energy behind new solutions.

The ancient wisdom council is based on universal intelligences that are held and expressed through the lens of a sequence of perspectives (Kinney-Linton, WindEagle, & RainbowHawk, 2007, p. 197):

> Creation Intelligence: freedom and creativity
> Perceptual Intelligence: present condition and appreciation
> Emotional Intelligence: power and danger
> Pathfinding Intelligence: purpose and direction
> Sustaining Intelligence: maintenance and balance
> Predictive Intelligence: interrelatedness and timing
> Decisive Intelligence: clarity and action
> Energia Intelligence: integrity and vitality

A leader embraces all perspectives while holding a safe space for people to bring forth universal intelligences.

The possibility of everyone's "leading" through a blending of Earth wisdom and high technology is a powerful way of being and making a difference in organizations and the world.

Knowing that every beginning is an ending and that every ending is a beginning, I invite us to again ask the "right" questions of ourselves and each other, including, "What do we need to be asking at this time for future generations?"

New frameworks for leading sustainable enterprise

Shakira Abdul-Ali

Leading an enterprise that follows the path of natural production—the path that leaves no footprint and facilitates life-giving workplaces—cannot possibly rely on the genius of the individual imagination. It is implausible, even unfair, to expect that individual insight and vision, regardless of the depth of inspiration, will be up to the task of gauging critical process factors that ensure waste-free production, while valuing people and maximizing profits—the process recognized as the triple bottom line. Leaders must acknowledge that an authentic birth of this kind of workplace comes from the tension that radiates from the merging of multiple sources of intelligence. Some believe that this will require new values and new paradigms. In fact, it may only require expanding the reign of knowledge and intelligence that is currently perceived as being "of value."

Lessons from nature

Elisabet Sahtouris, a noted evolutionary biologist, has often referred senior business leaders to lessons the natural world offers. Sahtouris is widely known for describing ways in which human communities can imitate and learn from the mature societies that live in the plant and animal worlds. Consider how she applies the lessons from the caterpillar to our economy (Sahtouris, 2003):

> The best metaphor I've found ... comes from the biological world ... It's the metamorphosis of a caterpillar into a butterfly [that is] bloating itself until it just can't function anymore, and then going to sleep with its skin hardening into a chrysalis.
>
> What happens in its body is that little imaginal disks (as they're called by biologists) begin to appear in the body of the caterpillar and its immune system attacks them. But they keep coming up stronger and they start to link with each other ... until the immune system of the caterpillar just can't function any more. At that point the body of the caterpillar melts into a nutritive soup that can feed the butterfly.
>
> I love this metaphor because it shows us [that] ... the caterpillar is unsustainable so it's going to die. What we have to focus on is, "can we build a viable butterfly?" ... because that's not guaranteed.

Consider those imaginal disks as being representative of the outlying sources of intelligence that are focusing on questions whose exploration will promote sustainable practices, eliminating waste and maximizing energy.[4]

Organization culture

How can leaders infuse those imaginal cells to which Sahtouris (2003) refers into the cultural milieu of their organizations? What might it look like when they transform their culture in order to achieve accountability within a framework of a triple bottom line? In fact, two prominent corporate leaders may demonstrate what it looks like when those imaginal cells are cut loose in an organization and empowered to thrive. One is Microsoft and the other is Toyota.

Note the informal online commentary of one Microsoft employee:[5]

> Everyone at Microsoft "gets" software—the managers, the administrative assistants, the vice presidents ... Even many of the "blue collar" workers (cooks, janitors, bus drivers) know something about software— it's not normal! ... Elevating the common denominator in this way makes Microsoft a wonderful workplace for people who love making software

... Microsoft gives software developers a lot of personal freedom over both the work and the work environment ...

For the most part, I determine what I work on and when I will get it done. There are exceptions—tasks others ask you to do for them, external deadlines or dependencies—but these goals are set cooperatively with your management and coworkers, taking into account your interests and abilities ... Very few projects at Microsoft have "small" impact ... You have the opportunity to earn, save, or cost the company millions of dollars through your work. It's an awesome responsibility, but an awesome chance to create widely influential software.

While it might seem like a risky venture to allow these imaginal cells of employees to go off on their own, who can argue with the genius of Bill Gates's leadership, his empowering of employees in this way? Yet perhaps a more widely practiced and better-known model for the creative use of teams may be found in an ostensibly more "regimented" organization than Microsoft. Toyota follows ISO 9000 procedures and in 2007 emerged as the world's leading automaker. Do Toyota employees—dedicated practitioners of "the Toyota Way"—operate as imaginal cells? Maybe, since any single employee:

can pull a cord to stop the production line at any time ... The plant is decorated with photos of company sports teams. Upbeat slogans (written by employees) hang from the ceiling. Each production team has its own cheery melody that rings out when a member needs to catch management's attention. Combined with perky beeps and electronic signals that mark important events, the plant sounds like a gigantic pinball machine.

(Christian & Hideko, 2006)

Clearly, there is something uniquely generative about the cultures that prevail in these companies—something that spurs their employees to behave independently for the greater good of the corporation, while pursuing their own personal objectives.

Two organizations that emerge from the African American experience may offer a methodology and models for achieving the kind of employee empowerment found in Toyota and Microsoft. These two organizations were created to transform the reality of the African American community and experience by way of supporting African Americans in their self-image and way of being. The method and models implemented in these organizations may offer a pathway for all institutions—private, public, and government, among others—to achieve sustainability through a way of communicating that enables a reassessment of what is really important.

Listening into transformation and being-ness

The International Black Summit and the Black African Heritage Leadership Development Caucus present a unique notion: "Listening" people and communities into transformation and being-ness.

The International Black Summit (IBS) was organized in 1991. It grew out of a conversation between two women who each had completed a course in personal empowerment run by the Landmark Education Corporation (LEC). The LEC is itself an offspring of Werner Erhardt's iteration of the "human potential movement" of the 1960s: "est" (Erhardt Seminar Training).

IBS's mission, known as the Declaration, was crafted during the first summit weekend in October 1991. This Declaration has been the driving force behind all subsequent IBS summits and initiatives since its founding.[6] The Declaration is a brief series of assertions that includes the following statement:

> WE STAND for the expression of our spirituality; ending the murders of our men, women and children; building economies responsible for funding our community; maintaining wellness of being in our bodies; providing human services; establishing nurturing relationships; altering the conversation of who we are in the media; empowering our youth.

Curiously, the Black African Heritage Leadership Development Caucus (BAH) was also born in October 1991. The BAH was established by people of black African heritage who were trainers and members of the National Coalition Building Institute (NCBI). NCBI is a diversity-training organization founded by Cheri Brown for the purpose of building relationships between black and Jewish students on US college campuses. According to BAH director Joyce B. Johnson Shabazz,[7] The Black African Heritage Leadership Development Caucus emerged as a leadership development resource team of the NCBI. The participating trainers of black African descent needed to explore a methodology to interrupt the limited perspectives on racism held by many well-meaning allies. To that end, during the course of an annual three-day intensive, BAH participants pursue a conversation that reconstructs the mindset of victimization based on the historical application of racial oppression.

What distinguishes each of these organizations from nearly all others in the African American community is that both organizations were created solely for the purpose of *transforming the behavior* of their members. To that end, they may offer a pathway toward organizational transformation, toward sustainability and the attainment of the triple bottom line.

Since their formation, both the IBS and the BAH have ushered thousands of individuals of African descent from around the globe (East, West, and southern Africa, Canada, the Caribbean, and Brazil, as well as the United States) through a conversation that has enabled participants to experience fundamental shifts in their attitudes about themselves and the lives that they lead. Many BAH participants say they have experienced, often for the first time, total liberation from the constrictions of internalized oppression. The conversations generated by each group support the participants in arriving at a common understanding; yet, remarkably, each participant is informed by the conversation in a manner that suits his or her own unique life framework and way of being.[8] In other words, while the participants move together, in the same direction—rafting in the same stream—each person in the communally oriented conversation is given the opportunity to hear and receive a message that is crafted through that conversation for her or his own personal transformation and guidance. This offers compelling lessons for leaders who seek to transform the behavior of employees toward sustainable, triple-bottom-line-oriented behavior that is self-generated and self-correcting.

Echoing the way Sahtouris describes nature's richly diverse ecosystem, one of the primary elements of the leadership model practiced within IBS and BAH is a near-reverence for diversity. Both organizations welcome, embrace, and appreciate individuals from all socioeconomic, political, and religious backgrounds and strive for total class integration. Further, within both organizations, leadership is not always vested in the people who have "the right" credentials—that is, the right education, work experience, or social pedigree. Instead, leadership is vested in the person who most effectively and convincingly "shows up" inside the task at hand. The IBS community describes this as:[9]

> looking for who the person [leader] is Being, in relationship to the task, and how well that person communicates intentionality and integrity in pursuit of that task. A leader is someone who can stay with the Conversation [and], the Alignment process until the last person in the room can see the Alignment, all the while staying detached enough to recognize when Alignment is not present.

The challenge that this type of deep diversity brings along with it is an ongoing presence of tension and confrontation—sometimes experienced as conflict. The quality of this conflict is rarely angry or mean-spirited. It is not the kind of conflict based on competition, where one idea *beats* another. Rather, it has the quality of birth—a high-energy struggle to deliver authentic, precious, and meaningful data.

Table 1.2 describes the qualities and characteristics of the "listening-into-being" leadership model practiced within these groups.

Table 1.2 "Listening-into-being" leadership qualities and characteristics

Leadership model: qualities and characteristics	International Black Summit	Black African Heritage Leadership Development Caucus
Organizing principles	• Commitment to the Summit Declaration • Authentic listening • Acknowledgment of *distinctions* as means of processing information within the context of life's conversation • Everyone's voice counts ("No insignificant person has ever been born" [N.D. Simmons]) • There's no "out there"; everything is a projection from that which lies within • There is already an answer to every question, at the moment it is asked • Trigger—the "rub" or charge that results in a new or deeper assessment of an issue or situation, relative to its impact (on an individual) • Ongoing self-actualization • We're all in it together • Operates simultaneously in the linear and nonlinear domains • Trust the process; it is as valuable/vital as the outcome	• Spiritual attunement • Authentic listening • A transformational continuum of an ongoing conversation given by life • Every voice is necessary; every voice must be heard • Open and full disclosure of issues/concerns (abuse occurs in secrecy and seclusion) • Complete significance in the black race social identity • Reclamation of personal power • Political and economic consciousness • Self-love and valuation of the black community • Acknowledgment and respect for ancestors • Being in relationship with our history • Cooperative economics
Decision-making process	• Alignment—a sacrosanct process through which the entire Summit Body (down to the last voice) acknowledges "the answer" (what's "so"; what "already is") • Alignment is *not*: majority rule; voting; cajoling; manipulating; not even consensus	• Contributory process; reliance on synergy • There is an expectation and a requirement for accountability to an outcome
Response to conflict/ resistance	• Embracing it/welcoming it/"going for the gold" in it • Acknowledging that any conflict is generally within an individual; usually points to something in the person that is unresolved • When conflict shows up, it offers direction; there is completion in conflict; it helps to move obstacles out of the way	• Seen as a necessary part of evolution; it is welcomed • Inviting it/exploring it/finding the direction in it • Anticipate it with open arms, acknowledging it as "a part of everything" • Living under a racist system requires that we make peace with conflict in order to sustain a quality of life

Sources: Personal communication with IBS leaders: P. Parks, Jr. (California), J. K. Young (Delaware), K. Copper (Georgia), S. Shelton (California), telephone interview, January 4, 2007; and IBS leaders R. Blake (New York), N. D. Simmons (New York), O. Sanders (North Carolina), telephone interview, January 6, 2007. Personal communication with BAH ... R ... telephone interview, January 8, 2007

Essay conclusion

Many of the characteristics of the IBS/BAH leadership practices are reflected in elements that are presented in the works of Sahtouris (1998, 2003). Such elements include self-creation, in which each participant must confront his or her own barriers to transformation within the context of the relevant inquiry; complexity (diversity of parts), whereby each participant is enriched by the views of people who are different from him or her; empowerment/employment of all component parts; and communications among all parts.

These models offer an atypical framework for exploring the challenge of achieving sustainable production. Natural lifecycles and organization culture are just two viable reference points for guidance in leading the sustainable enterprise. Other reference points will likely include perspectives from which the focus is on *integration* as opposed to *domination*. The message here is for leaders to be willing to acknowledge the value of information, practices, and leverage points that emanate from sources to which they are unaccustomed.

The IBS and BAH models have tapped into a conversation technology that empowers each participant to achieve alignment on his or her respective agendas. Participants arrive at a common ground, regardless of differences in status, professional achievement, public acclaim, national origin, or religious affiliation. Leaders of sustainable enterprise might wisely choose to explore the power of this process. It is hoped that, through this text, leaders throughout the organization will, together, create the tools, ideas, and strategies to help them on the journey toward this crucial goal.

Conclusion

The essays in this holographic ensemble bring together many of the key features of leadership for sustainable enterprise. One of these essays may make more sense to you than the others. If so, concentrate on the approach it offers; study it to develop your own thinking and leadership skills. There are many approaches, but no final answers. This offers all of us the opportunity to create our own approaches to building more sustainability and value into our own enterprises. Let's build a better world together.

Notes

1 The idea of the "Bowl" is developed in the essay "Engaging the natural tendency of self-organization," by Richard N. Knowles, later in this chapter (page 45).
2 An introduction to this model is developed in this chapter, in the essay "Engaging the natural tendency of self-organization," by Richard N. Knowles (pages 38–55).
3 Institute of Noetic Sciences, www.noetic.org (accessed July 9, 2002).

4 Sahtouris's reference to imaginal disks might be likened to the emergence within organizations of "green teams" that are tasked with alerting stakeholders at all levels of the organization to look for opportunities to conserve energy, minimize waste, and maximize quality-of-life practices for employees.

5 Michael Brundage's home page, "Working at Microsoft," www.qbrundage.com/ michaelb/pubs/ essays/working_at_microsoft.html (accessed January 7, 2007).

6 IBS home page, www.blacksummit.org/x_declaration.asp (accessed April 28, 2007).

7 Personal communication with J. B. Johnson Shabazz, telephone conversation, January 8, 2007.

8 Way of being, in this context, generally refers to an unconscious set of patterns and habits that an individual implements in order to conduct both the ordinary and the extraordinary day-to-day business of life.

9 Personal communication with R. Blake, telephone interview, January 6, 2007.

References

American Heritage Dictionary of the English Language. (1992). *The American Heritage Dictionary of the English Language* (3rd ed.). Boston, MA: Houghton Mifflin.

American Management Association (AMA). (2007). *Creating a sustainable future: A global study of current trends and possibilities 2007–2017*. New York: American Management Association.

Anguita, J., Baker, M. N., Davis, K. J., & McLean, G. N. (2005). Global organization development. In W. J. Rothwell and R. Sullivan (Eds.), *Practicing organization development* (2nd ed.) (pp. 467–492). San Francisco, CA: John Wiley.

Argyris, C., & Schön, D. A. (1996). *Organization learning II: Theory, method, and practice*. Reading, MA: Addison-Wesley.

Atlee, T. (2003). Co-intelligence: A vision for social activism. *IONS Noetic Sciences Review, 62*, 22.

Bak, P. (1996). *How nature works: The science of self-organized criticality*. New York: Springer-Verlag.

Bak, P., Tang, C., & Wiesenfeld, K. (1988). Self-organized criticality. *Phys. Rev. A, 38*(1), 364–374.

Bennett, J. G. (1996). *The dramatic universe: Vol. 3, Man and his nature*. Charles Town, WV: Coombe Springs and Claymont Communications.

Byrne, D., & Callaghan, G. (2014). *Complexity theory and social sciences: The state of the art*. New York: Routledge.

Christian, C., & Hideko, T. (2006, May 9) Corporate culture: The J factor. *Newsweek Magazine*. Retrieved February 16, 2007, from findarticles.com/p/articles/mi_hb3335/is_200505/ai_18039410.

Collins, J. (2001). *Good to great: Why some companies make the leap and others don't*. New York: HarperCollins.

Cooperrider, D. L., Whitney, D., & Stavros, J. M. (2005). *Appreciative inquiry handbook*. San Francisco, CA: Berrett-Koehler.

Davis, K. J. (2003). Global practice of OD. In M. Wheatley, R. Tannenbaum, P. Griffin, K. Quade, & National Organization Development Network (Eds.), *Organization development at work: Conversations on the values, applications, and future of OD* (pp. 103–105). San Francisco, CA: John Wiley.

Eoyang, G. H., Olsen, E. E., Beckhand, R., & Vail, P. (2001). *Facilitating organizational change: Lessons from complexity science.* New York: Jossey-Bass/Pfeiffer.

Ghoshal, S. (2005). Bad management theories are destroying good management practices. *Academy of Management Learning & Education, 4*(1), 75–91.

Harris, P., Moran, R., & Moran, S. (2004). *Managing cultural differences: Global leadership strategies for the 21st century.* Amsterdam: Elsevier.

Kinney-Linton, WindEagle, & RainbowHawk. (2007). Ancient wisdom council. In P. Holman, T. Devane, & S. Cady (Eds.), *The change handbook* (2nd ed.) (pp. 195–200). San Francisco, CA: Berrett-Koehler.

Knowles, R. N. (2002). *The leadership dance: Pathways to extraordinary organizational effectiveness.* Niagara Falls, NY: Center for Self-Organizing Leadership.

Knowles, R. N. (2006). Engaging the natural tendency of self-organization: Transformation. Retrieved April 29, 2007, from www.worldbusiness.org.

Knowles, R. N. (2013a). Guest Editor. *Emergence: Complexity & Organization, 15*(1). A Special Issue of Complexity and Organization.

Knowles, R. N. (2013b). *The Process Enneagram: Essays on theory and practice.* Litchfield Park, AZ: Emergent Publications.

Maynard, H. B., & Mehrtens, S. E. (1993). *The fourth wave: Business in the 21st century.* San Francisco, CA: Berrett-Koehler.

McCarter, B. G., & White, B. E. (2013). *Leadership in chaordic organizations.* Boca Raton, FL: CRC Press.

Nonaka, I., Toyama, R., & Noboru, K. (2000). SECI, Ba and leadership: A unified model of dynamic knowledge creation. *Long Range Planning, 33,* 5–34.

Owen, H. (1991). *Open space technology: A user's guide.* San Francisco, CA: Berrett-Koehler.

Owen, H. (2004). *The practice of peace* (2nd ed.). Circle Pines, MN: Human Systems Dynamics Institute and Open Space Institutes.

Pollard, D. (2006). Let-self-change: Learning about approaches to complexity from gatherer-hunter. Retrieved August 21, 2006, from blogs.salon.com/0002007/2006/08/06.html#a1606.

Pritchard, E. (1997). *No word for time: The way of the Algonquin people.* Tulsa, OK: Council Oak Books.

Sahtouris, E. (1998). The biology of globalization. Retrieved March 13, 2007, from www.ratical.org/ LifeWeb/Articles/globalize.html#p8.

Sahtouris, E. (2003). After Darwin. Lecture delivered at Wasan Island, Canada, August 30, 2003. Retrieved March 17, 2007, from www.ratical.org/LifeWeb/Articles/AfterDarwin.pdf.

Scott, S. (2004). *Fierce conversations: Achieving success at work and in life, one conversation at a time.* New York: The Berkeley Publishing Group.

Senge, P. M., Kleiner, A., Roberts, C., Ross, R., & Smith, B. (1994). *The fifth discipline fieldbook: Strategies and tools for building a learning organization.* New York: Doubleday.

Stacey, R. D. (2001). *Complex responsive processes in organizations.* London/New York: Routledge.

Taylor, F. W. (1911). *The principles of scientific management.* New York: Harper and Brothers.

Torbert, B., & Associates. (2004). *Action inquiry: The secret of timely and transforming leadership.* San Francisco, CA: Berrett-Koehler.

Twomey, D. (2006). Designed emergence as a path to enterprise sustainability. *E:CO Emergence: Complexity & Organization, 8*(3), 12–23.

Weber, M., Henderson, A. M., & Parsons, T. (1947). *The theory of social and economic organization.* New York: Oxford University Press.

Weisbord, M. R., & Janoff, S. (1995). *Future search.* San Francisco, CA: Berrett-Koehler.

Wheatley, M. J. (1992). *Leadership and the new science: Learning about organization from an orderly universe.* San Francisco, CA: Berrett-Koehler.

WindEagle, & RainbowHawk. (2003). *Heart seeds: A message from the ancestors.* Edina, MN: EHAMA Press/Beaver Pond Press.

Mental models for sustainability[1]

*John D. Adams, Linda M. Kelley, Beth Applegate,
Theresa McNichol, and William G. Russell*

> Mental models are the constructs that determine our behavior in any situation we are attempting to impact. They include what we know—what we value—what we believe—what we assume—out of which emerges a context for action or inaction. More often than not, we remain unaware of the mental models we are operating within.
>
> (John D. Adams)

Introduction

Linda M. Kelley

Mental models for sustainability are operating systems or paradigms that frame and hold values, and generate the qualities of respect that people exhibit for ourselves, for other people, for peoples and cultures, and for our Earth. Respect is a keystone for leaderfulness throughout any organization. As we saw in Chapter 1, an organization is leaderful when the information flow is open, relationships are healthy, employees are involved in decision-making, and initiative is encouraged. If an employee in the organization, regardless of level, sees something that needs to be done, she or he steps forward to meet the need and is supported in that effort by upper management. Intrinsic to mental models is that they operate both personally and socially. The social forms of mental models show in culture and traditions, and if persistent over time, they can become archetypes. People and our organizations are systems, living systems comprised of other systems that interact internally and externally, both individually and collectively.

Box 2.1 Values: a compass that guides

The *2007 AMA Sustainability Survey* (American Management Association [AMA], 2007) shows how important values are to the creation of sustainable enterprises. The survey's 1,365 respondents, from global, multinational, and national organizations, rated values second only to the support of top management in qualities necessary to build a sustainable enterprise. These two factors are closely related as leadership tends to set the tone in terms of corporate value systems.

Values related to sustainability are deeply ingrained in the "DNA" of companies well on their way toward sustainability, found Wirtenberg and her colleagues (Wirtenberg, Harmon, Russell, & Fairfield, 2007) in a study of nine companies across the globe. These values are typically embedded by organizational founders and are especially evident among the European-based companies in their sample. One executive said, "You can't talk to anyone [in our company] without them speaking about doing things that make a difference for people. So there is this interaction between the vision, the mission, and the culture, that is all wrapped up in a history of paying attention to this kind of stuff" (Wirtenberg et al., 2007, p. 14).

Another said, "People here don't get promoted if they don't have the values … a sustainable mindset. If someone is immune, they don't make it; they don't have the followership" (Wirtenberg et al., 2007, p. 17).

Although several of the companies in this study (Wirtenberg et al., 2007) had been through major changes, including downsizings, the unwavering commitment to their sustainability values was seen as the compass that guided them through those changes.

In this chapter, we offer both theory and practices designed to help people learn how to make substantive changes in their mental models, particularly in support of sustainability. Defining mental models as he does above, John Adams draws on his many years of research and consulting in the chapter's pivotal essay, "Six dimensions of mental models," in which he lays out a structure comprising six dimensions of consciousness: time orientation, focus of response, scope of attention, prevailing logic, problem consideration, and life orientation.

The three case studies that follow use these dimensions as a framework to show practices and exercises for making desired changes in how the people in the profiled organizations view and operate in the world.

In the first case study, "Cultivating mental models that support sustainability in a technically oriented organization," Linda M. Kelley demonstrates how people can make lasting fundamental changes. The objective of this program is to cultivate a broad base of leaders who understand both the details of the individual projects and the way in which these projects fit into the organization's overall purpose and goals. The exercises and practices Kelley presents integrate current scientific research and world-wisdom traditions, and expand systems thinking to include the whole thinking-feeling-acting person.

In "Mental models in civil society," Beth Applegate shows the importance of mental models to the development of a culturally competent[2] strategic plan. The organization featured is a progressive nonprofit agency whose staff and members had to change their mental models to bring their actions in line with what they said they valued. The clients are led through exercises designed to make important changes in one or more of Adams' six dimensions of mental models.

Finally, in "Appreciative Inquiry case study: executive MBA candidates," Theresa McNichol introduces readers to the framework of Appreciative Inquiry (AI) and shows how it can provide tools for transforming one's concepts and mental models from either/or to those that recognize inter-dependence and are inclusive, both–and systems. McNichol points out that it takes more than goodwill and a person's best thinking to effect this conversion. In addition, she emphasizes the importance of leveling the playing field so that the process is both collective and collaborative.

Each of the case studies presents work that brings about changes in ways that are respectful of people, their organizations, and the world in which they operate. The processes they highlight are complementary, and the exercises reinforce each other.

Mental models, systems, and systems thinking

Mental models are systems that play crucial roles in defining our thinking. They systemically comprise our beliefs and values, and consequent operating system instructions for how we live our lives and participate in our world. From within our mental models, we weigh what is good against what is bad, what is right against what is wrong, what is true against what is false. Our mental models are so ubiquitous it feels as though they are a natural part of each of us, but in fact the mainstays of each of our mental models are learned. These learned tenets embed themselves because we exercise them repeatedly, day in and day out. We can and do modify our mental models over time. Our success in making intentional changes to these pervasive systems is dependent on how well we understand them. The five key points below can help you to comprehend your own mental models, how they operate, and how they drive you, both personally and socially.

Five key points regarding people, mental models, and systems are:

1. People are natural systems thinkers. We're all born that way. Open and close your hand. Did you plan out all the steps needed to do that? Of course not. You thought it and automatically did it. Instructions to do that are already encoded in our systems. Now reach out and pick up an object. The same function as you did to open and close your hand activated, but so did your vision system, and your sense of touch and balance. Every person is a living system comprised of many subsystems all cooperating.
2. We are taught reason, logic, cause, and effect. We learn it at home. Don't touch that or else ... Do this because ... Our schooling builds on cause and effect reasoning to make sense of the world and get stuff done.

People have made great strides and accomplished amazing innovations by being able to drill down and expertly examine and experiment with parts of a system as though they were suspended in isolation. The final step should always be to reconnect and integrate the outcomes into functioning larger systems of which it is a part. This step helps to avoid many long-term negative consequences.

3. We are as oblivious of our complete dependence on our surrounding ecosystem as fish are to the fact that they swim in water. Even when we consciously ignore this, we interact with the world around us according to systems function. We breathe air, eat food, rest, develop social bonds, conduct business as the interconnected systems we are. Biomimicry may be a recent concept but it's an age-old evolutionary process.

4. People are people because of diversity. We depend on colonies of microbes to symbiotically perform our basic functions like digestion. Without this diversity and cooperation, we wouldn't function.

5. Mental models are operating systems that inform and instruct our voluntary actions and enable us to influence many of the involuntary ones our bodies perform. Since safety is imperative to survival, mental models and the habits they install contain many instructions that conserve and replace resources. If we ignored those, we'd die of exhaustion. This holds true for all living systems, and all constructs comprised of living systems, including our enterprises and Planet Earth.

Understanding people and enterprises from a systems perspective is crucial to guiding an enterprise toward sustainability.

Enterprise, systems thinking, and sustainability context

> System: A set of elements or parts that is coherently organized and interconnected in a pattern or structure that produces a characteristic set of behaviors, often classified as its "function" or "purpose."
>
> (Meadows, 2015, p. 188)

Throughout, our book introduces concepts, provides tools, and presents examples to further sustainable "enterprise systems." Most enterprise systems today force a siloed approach to operations, even those that purport to align around a common purpose. Systems and integrated thinking, which we advocate, break down the silos and align behaviors towards more holistic operations where enterprise components interact dynamically on purpose. In other words, from a systems perspective the right hand does know what the left hand is doing.

Systems thinking is an essential process for handling complex problems such as transforming sustainable development from a compelling idea into a reality. It has its foundation in system dynamics, advanced in 1956 by MIT professor Jay Forrester (Aronson, 1998). Donella Meadows who worked with Jay Forrester and the MIT Systems Dynamics group distilled her 30 years of wisdom learning and practicing systems thinking in the book *Thinking in Systems*. That work and others of her writings have greatly influenced sustainability thought leaders including many of the authors of this book. Meadows' fellow MIT colleague, Peter Senge, within his classic book, *The Fifth Discipline* more fully presents systems thinking concepts and includes numerous practical examples that pertain to analyzing sustainability problems and identifying possible solutions. Here and throughout this book, we share key insights from these works and explore deeper internal and larger external sustainable enterprise system interconnections.

The relevance of systems thinking as a tool for analyzing sustainability-aligned frameworks and discovering innovative changes, and also the wisdom of early practitioners, is appreciated more now than ever. Traditional problem analysis typically starts with acknowledgment of a problem and using traditional diagnosis tools to search for causes and symptom interventions by reducing the problem down to individual subsystems and pieces or parts being analyzed. Systems thinking, in contrast, looks at the thing being studied and how it interacts with other constituents of the system—a set of elements that produce a behavior—of which it is a part.

Current linear thinking has enabled systems to focus on smaller and smaller parts of greater world systems. They tend to implement interventions that seldom identify more complex root causes and by muting the symptom's signals, they encourage "bounded reality" destructive behaviors. That means that a number of important, influential elements that should be seen as system components are relegated to externalities. Systems thinking expands its analytical view to take into account larger and larger numbers of interactions as the problem or issue is being studied. This approach is particularly effective when attempting to analyze dynamically complex problems and/or problems with complex internal and external feedback loops. When viewing such complex issues holistically, analytical results often offer insights and conclusions drastically different than anticipated, or reveal solutions that were previously unknown and perceived as impossible (Aronson, 1998).

Systems thinking basics and key principles

Systems thinking in practice allows us to accept uncertainty, complexity, and our ability to learn. When we can work effectively in conditions of uncertainty, that is to accept uncertainty as one of life's givens, we learn to be wary and vigilant in a good and very important way. A person whose awareness is heightened catches onto, and can handle unexpected occurrences earlier in the process where they may still be able to do something about them.

The following are a few basics and key principles to support your understanding.

Box 2.2 Key system terms and principles

Adaptations & excerpts from Donella Meadows' *Thinking in Systems* (Meadows, 2015).

> I have yet to see any problem, however complicated, which, when looked at in the right way, did not become still more complicated.
>
> (Poul Anderson)

Systems:

- A system is more than the sum of its parts. It may exhibit adaptive, dynamic, goal-seeking, self-preserving, and sometimes evolutionary behavior.
- The least obvious part of the system, its function or purpose, is often the most crucial determinant of the system's behavior.

Stocks, flows, and equilibrium:

- **Stock:** An accumulation of material or information that has built up in a system over time.
- **Dynamic equilibrium** is when the sum of outflows equals the sum of inflows and the level of the stock will not change (though it's possible for this process to change the composition and quality of the stock).
- **Nonrenewable resources are stock-limited.** The entire stock is defined at once, and can be extracted at any rate (limited mainly by extraction capital). But since the stock is not renewed, the faster the extraction rate, the shorter the lifetime of the resource.
- **Renewable resources are flow-limited.** They can support extraction or harvest indefinitely, but only at a finite flow rate equal to their regeneration rate. If they are extracted faster than they regenerate, they may eventually be driven below a critical threshold and become, for all practical purposes, nonrenewable.

Feedback loops:

- **Feedback loop:** The mechanism (rule or information flow or signal) that allows a change in a stock to effect a flow into or out of that same stock. A closed chain of causal connections from a stock, through a set of decisions and actions dependent on the level of the stock, and back again through a flow to change the stock. *Author note: In other words, the output of an operation is fed back to inform an earlier condition, iteratively changing the quality of the original condition.*

- **Balancing or negative feedback loops** are stabilizing and goal-seeking. They oppose or reverse whatever direction of change is imposed on the system (e.g., Thermostat settings).
- **Reinforcing or positive feedback loops** reinforce the direction of change. These are vicious cycles and virtuous circles (climate change and atmospheric carbon mitigation).
- **Translating from systems operations:** If a reinforcing feedback loop rewards the winner of a competition with the means to win future competitions, the result will be the elimination of all but a few competitors. **Conventional wisdom:** The rich get richer and the poor get poorer.
- **Translating from systems operations:** Because of feedback delays within complex systems, by the time a problem becomes apparent it may be unnecessarily difficult to solve. **Conventional wisdom:** A stitch in time saves nine.
- *Author note: Feedback directly connected to one element of a system may also disrupt the flow of other elements by changing or resetting the operating conditions which can then ripple through not only the primary system but affect any system that is indirectly or weakly connected as well and in complex ways. This is one of the aspects that make systems unpredictable. This is certainly what is happening with climate change. It happens in economic markets too.*

Resilience, self-organization, and mindsets:

- Systems need to be managed not only for productivity or stability, they also need to be managed for resiliency.
- Systems often have the property of self-organization—the ability to structure themselves, to create new structure, to learn, diversify, and complexify.
- Many relationships in systems are nonlinear.
- There are no separate systems. The world is a continuum.
- The bounded rationality of each actor in a system may not lead to decisions that further the welfare of the system as a whole.
- Everything we think we know about the world is a model. *Author note: All these models have been conceived and created by humans.*
- Our models fall far short of representing the real world fully. *Author note: When systems are diverse, endlessly multivariate with semi-independent components, and dynamically complex, it is impossible for any model to represent them. The most advanced models will at best only be able to approximate primary system outcomes.*
- **Translating from systems operations:** A diverse system with multiple pathways and redundancies is more stable and less vulnerable to external shock than a uniform system with little diversity. **Conventional wisdom:** Don't put all your eggs in one basket.

Sustainable enterprise system boundaries and elements

Applying systems thinking within a triple-bottom-line framework ultimately interconnects enterprise and industry systems with economic, social, and environmental systems and feedback signals. How we pay attention, whether our mental models allow us to attend to certain categories of signals or not, directs both personal and organizational behaviors and purposes regarding enterprise sustainability or triple-bottom-line performance. With a lot of hard work and wisdom, we can humble ourselves, learn, self-organize inclusively, and restructure our enterprises and their interconnected component systems to align towards a shared vision and goals for a thriving future.

It's the interconnected relationships and shared purposes within the enterprise's functional subsystems (i.e., the interconnected corporate functions including sales, manufacturing, human resources, and finance) that determine sustainable enterprise performance. Successful ultimate outcomes enable the enterprise to continue to exist. Systems thinking encourages us to see the inputs, stocks, flows and feedback loops, and outcome interconnections within larger, more complex systems and networks of systems including the industry, locations, and markets an enterprise chooses to operate within. Sustainable performance depends in good part on system signals; how they follow familiar patterns, or not, and how these communications flow iteratively through the system via real and perceived positive (reinforcing) and negative (controlling goals) feedbacks.

If it sounds complex, it's because it really is. Because it is complex, people try to substitute more simple, linear models to represent important business conditions and hope for the best. But simple models often yield oversimplified results. They work well where you can anticipate likely outcomes. If conditions are hard to determine, more and more uncertain, information is ambiguous, and/or influences surge and wane with curious volatility, you are going to gain a much more valid, substantial understanding by taking a systems approach.

Not all the influences on a system are equal in their effects. Some enterprise systems are more affected by what happens locally. Other enterprises rock and are rocked by globe-spanning events. Both the actual effects and the perceived effects are important in that these combine in weighted, dynamic ways to determine the power and sustainability of an enterprise. Because people comprise enterprises, mental models that frame perceptions and behavior drive the people and consequently drive their enterprises.

System archetypes, functions, and purpose

On a practical level we each perceive reality through our own personal beliefs and life experiences, and the mental models that contain them. No one is capable of knowing and understanding true reality. Systems models have evolved to be consistent with the "real world" even though they cannot be complete in all aspects. People have constructed and modified best models, ones with the most valid outcomes, by interconnecting inputs from key worldviews, for example, along with economic and market data, include a worldview grounded by science (what is possible to do) with a worldview grounded by ethics (what we should do). Realistically, for a system model to be relevant to sustainability, it must be a viable system model. Economic and social systems are manmade; they are based on paradigms founded in sets of beliefs that have changed over time, and are subject to being shown to be no longer valid, as has happened many times in history. When people become invested in their comfort with how things are currently working for them, it becomes easier for them to deny our best available understandings of true reality. This is exacerbated by a guarded unease regarding the unknown future and our natural propensity to resist change.

The Daly Triangle, which we introduce in the next section, is one useful system framework for looking at sustainable development. By understanding common patterns of thinking and acting, and applying systems thinking, we can more clearly identify and pivot away from knowable "traps." Common pervasive traps are recognizable behaviors and outcomes that result when subsystem goals dominate at the expense of optimal outcomes for the overall system's goals, purpose(s), and ultimate sustainability-aligned, thriving outcomes. Attachment to personal benefits gained by continuing the status quo as mentioned above is one trap that can hinder achieving enterprise goals aligned with broader societal goals such as the 17 United Nations Sustainable Development Goals (SDGs). Achieving SDGs will be a transformational pivot towards a common purpose of achieving optimal human wellbeing within a thriving world.

Limits to growth or the Tragedy of the Commons archetype

When we treat complex systems as though they are isolated, over short periods they can operate as though their input stocks were unconstrained or limitless and wastes can be tossed out and will disappear. Over time, self-organization and the influence of other interconnected systems force system adaptations and modifications. As a result, continuing to treat the system, particularly if it's an enterprise, as though it is isolated, produces an unrealistic view of what's actually happening. For example, if someone said "The capital stocks of the Industrial Economy Model didn't require raw materials to produce product and service outputs," you'd be pretty sure the person was not perceiving the whole picture. Assessments of a growing population that didn't include a requirement for increased food supplies you'd clearly mark as incomplete and inaccurate, knowing it couldn't possibly happen that way. Yet people do produce studies and reports that are similarly incomplete and use those as the basis for important personal and business decisions. This kind of Trap and suggested Way Out were described by Donella Meadows as follows:

- **The Trap: Limits-to-growth also referred to as the Tragedy of the Commons:** In physical, exponentially growing systems, there must be at least one reinforcing loop driving the growth *and* at least one balancing loop constraining the growth, because no physical system can grow forever in a finite environment. When resources are plentiful and commonly shared every user benefits directly from its use, but also shares the costs of its abuse. If people are paying attention, there are weak feedback signals constantly relaying the condition of the resource to inform the decisions of the resource users. When people don't heed that feedback, the consequence is overuse of the resource, eroding it until it becomes unavailable to anyone. (Examples: inadequate planning and management of recyclables overburdens landfill space available for garbage disposal; overfishing of "desired" fish species in the oceans.)
- **The Way Out:** Educate and engage the users, so they understand the consequences of abusing the resource. Restore and strengthen the ignored or missing feedback link. Privatizing such scarce resources is a favored enhancement possibility for many who put their faith in the wisdom of markets. Another is public-private partnerships managed to care for resources held as commonwealths. Regulating access to scarce resources to all of its users is another possibility for those who sufficiently trust the regulators (e.g., pay as you throw options for municipal garbage collections) (Meadows, 2015, p. 59 and p. 191).

Eroding goals archetype

When setting goals without clear expectations, responsibilities, and relationship to vision and purpose, the results may be drastically different from desired behaviors and intended outcomes. The Trap and suggested Way Out were described by Donella Meadows as follows:

- **The Trap: Drift to Low Performance:** Allowing performance standards to be influenced by past performance, especially if there is negative bias in perceiving past performance, sets up a reinforcing feedback loop of eroding goals that sets a system drifting toward low performance (e.g., accepting "Fake News" as the new normal for journalism).
- **The Way Out:** Keep performance standards clear, well-understood, and supported by mutual commitments, then guided by standards that are enhanced by the best actual performances instead of being discouraged by the worst. When measuring, be especially careful not to confuse effort with result as system activity will produce effort, but not always desired

outcomes. Use this same archetype structure to set up a drift toward high performance (e.g., the SDGs) (Meadows, 2015, p. 123).

Other familiar system "traps" include Rule Beating (think taxes), Success to the Successful (the rich getting even more rich), Policy Resistance (some people are happy with the status quo when it favors their self-interests and others are simply afraid of change so resist as long as possible) among others. All of these traps represent knowable, expected behaviors and preventable consequences. Individuals and organizations are both susceptible to these traps.

The Daly Triangle

There are absolute, intractable limits to the planet's carrying capacity, as evidenced through planetary changes connected to global warming, climate change, and biodiversity loss. It is within this fixed planetary context that currently proposed tradeoffs between economic, manufactured or financial capital and natural resources or natural capital is deemed insufficient and ultimately unsustainable (United Nations, 2015).

The Daly Triangle (Figure 2.1) is one archetype for defining sustainability-aligned systems and supportive mental models. The framework accommodates complex interconnections and feedback signals, and thereby supports a strong sustainability approach for restructuring current systems. It provides a holistic perspective for analyzing aggregate global natural capital as being limited inputs or ultimate means for all subsystem elements, archetypes, and purposes. Each form of capital contributes to corporate purposes and human well-being in unique ways. Many people believe that the decline in natural assets can and should be managed. Weak and long-disregarded feedback signals have effectively impeded awareness about the needs of future generations. Short-term-oriented archetypes and mindsets have people believing that everything is good so long as there is economic growth.

Letting go of what is not needed to become hopeful for the future

As we get caught up in the pressures of day-to-day living, we get trapped by entrenched habits and beliefs that the way things are is how the world works. Our consciousness becomes myopic, focusing mainly on our own self-interests and short-term urgencies. We have trained our minds to give preference to an artificial, self-fulfilling perception of reality. The gap between "true" reality and "perceived" reality may never be greater than it is today. As we evolve to co-create a thriving future that we want for ourselves and society, we must undertake transformational change affecting each of us, and align our enterprises with core triple-bottom-line, environmental,

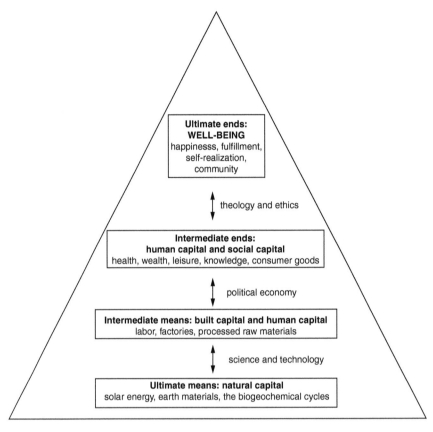

Figure 2.1 The Daly Triangle
Source: Copyright 1998, Donella Meadows. Used with permission.

social, and economic systems. This alignment with the Earth's resources and limits is the only sustainable way. If you ever need to reinforce the fact of our essential connection with Nature, step outside someplace where your feet touch the earth. Don't talk on a cellphone. Don't listen to music. Look up at the sky. Feel the air. Listen to the sounds of the wind, the birds, and even the bugs. Remember how wondrous and amazing life and our world truly is.

Donella Meadows suggested a new way of being unattached to all man-made paradigms. She advises us to stay flexible, to realize that no paradigm can be "true," and every paradigm is tremendously limited. She humbly reminds us that a true understanding of an immense and amazing universe is far beyond human comprehension. To become unconsciously competent, is to let go into Not Knowing, into what Buddhists call enlightenment (Meadows, 1999, p. 19).

Keeping with you a sense of the vastness of the universal that gives us life and yet in so many details is unknowable, return your attention to people and enterprises with a systems consciousness of how we operate in and on the world around us. While the fact that we are systems of systems may not always be front and center in our awareness, knowing that it is changes our perceptions and actions. From this space, delve into discovery about your own mental models, those of people close to you, and the collective mental models that drive your business enterprise.

Six dimensions of mental models

John D. Adams

Perhaps the best way to understand the relationship between mental models and sustainable initiatives is to start with a few quotes about the all-pervasive influence mental models have on all of our efforts and, consequently, how they determine our successes or failures.

> The range of what we think and do is limited by what we fail to notice. And because we fail to notice that we fail to notice, there is little we can do to change, until we notice how failing to notice shapes our thoughts and deeds.
> (Ronald D. Laing, quoted in Zweig & Abrams, 1991, p. xix)

> If we continue to believe as we have always believed, we will continue to act as we have always acted. If we continue to act as we have always acted, we will continue to get what we have always gotten.
> (Marilyn Ferguson)[3]

> It ain't what you don't know that gets you into trouble. It's what you know for sure that just ain't so.
> (Mark Twain, quoted in Gore, 2006, pp. 20–21)

> So do you not feel that, buried deep within each and every one of us, there is an instinctive, heartfelt awareness that provides—if we will allow it to—the most reliable guide as to whether or not our actions are really in the long-term interests of our planet and all the life it supports? This awareness, this wisdom of the heart, may be no more than a faint memory of a distant harmony rustling like a breeze through the leaves, yet sufficient to remind us that the earth is unique and that we have a duty to care for it.
> (HRH Prince of Wales, 2000)

> Once upon a time, there were four people. Their names were: Everybody, Somebody, Nobody, and Anybody. Whenever there was an important job to be done, Everybody was sure that Somebody would do it. Anybody

could have done it; but in the end Nobody did it. When Nobody did it, Everybody got angry because it was Somebody's job. Everybody thought that Somebody would do it; but Nobody realized that Nobody would do it. So consequently, Everybody blamed Somebody when Nobody did what Anybody could have done in the first place.

(Anon., quoted in Adams, 2000b, p. 101)

These comments remind us that our thought patterns determine our behaviors, and strongly influence the success or failure of our efforts to change. As Laing (Zweig & Abrams, 1991) points out, most of the time most people operate from a default mode of thinking that operates out of their conscious awareness; that is, the assumption that one holds an accurate and relevant view of reality is most of the time unquestioned and taken for granted. Those who disagree, by default, are considered to be wrong or misguided.

The mental models that prevail at the beginning of the 21st century are so far working to preserve the status quo and hindering the sustainable initiatives that most people now *know* are necessary to preserve a choice-rich human presence on the planet. For example, one of the most compelling mass mental models that has been instilled in the US public is that of consumerism—the concept that it is important for us to continually buy "things" in order to keep the economy healthy. We are told constantly that we will be happier if we buy the latest version of product X. It is so widespread that we generally don't think about it. For at least the last 50 years we have been inundated with "Buy now, before it's too late!" "Never again at this price!" and similar messages. Vance Packard (1957) wrote about this in the late 1950s, with extensive explorations into how marketing experts influence our inner minds (i.e., mental models). In the late 1960s, Toffler (1970) made consumerism one of the primary dimensions of "future shock," calling it *overchoice*. But modern marketing has prevailed, and these voices from the past are largely ignored.

As a result, today 10% of Americans have rented personal storage space because, even though house size has doubled in the last 30 years, people can't afford houses big enough to store all their acquisitions (Torpy, 2007; Vanderbilt, 2005). In addition, the average household credit card indebtedness, for households that have credit cards, is approximately US$10,000 (CNNMoney.com, 2007). Furthermore, in the aftermath of 9/11, the president of the United States encouraged us to go shopping—not to have compassion, not to care about the world, not to understand the underlying reasons for the attacks, not to get closer to our families, but to go out and buy things.

Lester Brown (2006) builds a compelling case that, with business as usual, the trends we see unfolding now may ultimately lead to the failure of our civilization itself. He argues that, if we continue on the course we are now on, more and more nation states will fail until civilization itself begins to unravel.

Table 2.1 Self-centered choices of modern organizations

	Sure, here and now	Unsure, far and later
Gains	Favored	Disfavored
Losses	Disfavored	Favored

Source: L. Zsolnai. (2002). Green business or community economy? *International Journal of Social Economics,* 29(8), p. 656. Copyright 2002, *International Journal of Social Economics.* Reproduced with permission.

The take–make–waste linear consumption model that prevails today is very nicely portrayed in an animated video called *The Story of Stuff*. The video develops an alternative circular consumption model that will be necessary for a high-quality sustainable future.

To illustrate how prevailing default mental models most often reinforce the status quo, making successful change difficult or impossible, I present a framework (Adams, 2000a, 2000b, 2004, 2006) consisting of six dimensions of thinking: time orientation, focus of response, scope of attention, prevailing logic, problem consideration, and life orientation. Preliminary surveys I've conducted of perceived mental models in five countries in North America, Europe, and South Asia suggest there is some degree of global universality of these ways of thinking.

Table 2.1 describes the primary drivers behind contemporary institutional strategy. Maximize profits now; defer losses and big costs to the future. However, the future is always "in the future," so the "big costs" of environmental degradation, depletion of nonrenewable resources, and overconsumption of renewables are deferred as long as possible. Equally irresponsibly, in order to maintain present-day economic "growth," governments are running up huge deficits that will have to be rectified by future generations.

Many years ago, I began asking groups of managers to use adjectives to describe "how people think around here." As time went on and the number of adjectives grew, it became clear that there were consistent themes: time orientation (urgency and short-term focus predominated); response focus (quick reaction to external stimuli); scope of attention (local or parochial—us versus them); prevailing logic (reductionistic and either/or thinking predominated); how problems get considered (finding fault and placing blame); and life orientation (life in the workplace most often focused on activity, workload, and materialism).

As categories emerged, I decided to set up each theme as one pole on a continuum, and then collect frequency data related to where along the continuum most people "did their thinking" most of the time. The following six dimensions were taken forward:

Time orientation: short term to long term
Focus of response: reactive to creative
Scope of attention: local to global

Prevailing logic: either/or to both/and
Problem consideration: accountability-and-blame to learning
Life orientation: doing-and-having to being

The results were quite revealing, as can be seen in Table 2.2, which contains a summary of how 158 managers and consultants from the United States, Canada, the United Kingdom, the Netherlands, and India experienced the predominant modes of thinking in their organizations and primary client systems. A high percentage of the responses cluster near the left-hand side of each category—short term, reactive, parochial, either/or, blame placing, and doing-and-having. Tables 2.3 and 2.4 provide more details on the left- and right-side focuses of the six dimensions.

Table 2.2 Mental models and sustainability: summary of responses (n = 158). Assessments by executives, managers, and organizational development (OD) professionals of prevailing mental models in their organizational environments

	Left ⅓	Middle ⅓	Right ⅓	
Short term: Focus on deadlines, immediate priorities, sense of urgency	93	48 *Time orientation*	17	**Long term:** Vision and strategies, potentials, opportunities
Reactive: External drives, prevailing rules and procedures	98	36 *Focus of responsiveness*	24	**Creative:** Taking initiative, new approaches, internal drives
Local: Focus on self or immediate group, competition	87	32 *Focus of attention*	39	**Global:** Whole organization, inclusive, ecumenical, larger community
Separation: Either/or, specialization	78	45 *Prevailing logic*	35	**Systems:** Both–and, holistic, interrelationships
Accountability/ blame: Clear assignments, self-protection, it's not my fault (don't get caught)	71	50 *Problem consideration*	37	**Learning:** Understanding, building on all types of experience
Doing/having: Materialism, greed, cost-effectiveness, financial performance, quantitative growth	81	40 *Life orientation*	37	**Being:** Having enough, self-realization, "greater good," intangibles valued, qualitative growth

Source: Copyright 2006, John D. Adams. Used with permission.

Table 2.3 Working with the left-side focuses

Focus	Messages that reinforce this focus	Questions to bring focus here	Positive value of focusing here	Result of overuse of this focus
Short term	• Don't fix it if it ain't broke • Just do it	• What needs attention now? • What are your immediate priorities?	• Establishing priorities • Acting with efficiency	• Lose the big picture • Overlook long-term consequences • Put bandages on symptoms
Reactive	• Do as you're told • If it feels good, do it • Life's a bitch and then you die	• What is the established policy, procedure, or practice? • What has been done before in this kind of situation?	• Consistency • Responsiveness • Loyalty	• Stuck in a rut • Unable to flow with change
Local	• Look out for "number one" • You've got to expect that from a ___!	• What makes you different or unique? • What is special about this situation?	• Survival • Protection • Maintaining position	• Loss of perspective • Ethnocentrism • Loss of diversity
Separation	• The best way to understand it is to take it apart • A place for everything, and everything in its place	• What are the relevant facts in this situation? • What do you get when you "crunch the numbers"?	• Convergence • Specialization • Rationality	• Fragmentation • Low synergy • Get lost in minutiae
Blaming	• It's not my fault! • All right, who's to blame here?	• What are your reasons for your actions? • What's wrong with this picture?	• Judgment, law, and rule enforcement	• Win–lose polarization • Risk aversion
Doing-and-having	• What's in it for me? • Faster, cheaper, better!	• What is the most cost-effective thing to do? • What's the bottom line?	• Financial performance and material comforts	• Attachment to possessions • Loss of human sensitivity • Burnout

Source: J. D. Adams. (2004). Mental models @ work: Implications for teaching sustainability. In: C. Galea (Ed.), *Teaching business sustainability: From theory to practice* (pp. 18–30). Sheffield, UK: Greenleaf Publishing, pp. 25–26.

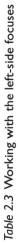

Table 2.4 Working with the right-side focuses

Focus	Messages that reinforce this focus	Questions to bring focus here	The positive value of focusing here	The result of overuse of this focus
Long term	• Create a vision • Plan ahead	• What do you anticipate? • Where are we headed? • Where do we want to go?	• Anticipation • Prediction • Possibilities • Contingencies	• Lose timely responsiveness • Ignore pressing realities
Creative	• Take responsibility for yourself • You can be anything you want to be	• Is there a different or better approach? • What would you do about this situation if you had a magic wand?	• Innovation • New ideas • New directions	• Overlook proven processes • Reinvent the wheel
Global	• Look at the big picture • Let's think about the consequences of this decision	• What's best for the organization as a whole? • How can you make a difference in the world?	• Comprehensive view • Inclusiveness • Value of diversity	• Idealism • Loss of initiative or drive • Inattention to detail
Systems	• Solving one problem almost always creates others • "The whole is more than the sum of its parts"	• Who are the key stakeholders? • If we take this action, what consequences can we predict?	• Divergent • Holistic • Finding key interrelationships	• Equate models to reality • Get lost in the clouds of complexity or theory
Learning	• "Let one who is without sin cast the first stone" • Here's another learning and growth opportunity	• What can you learn from this experience? • How might you benefit from letting go of that grudge?	• Ease of exploration • Seeking growth and learning	• May be taken advantage of • Self-sacrificing • Loss of discipline
Being	• You'll never walk alone • Trust the process • As ye sow, so shall ye reap	• What really matters in your life? • What does your "higher self" say about this?	• Self-realization • "Greater good" point of view	• Become ungrounded • Lose touch with "mainstream"

Source: J. D. Adams. (2004). Mental models @ work: Implications for teaching sustainability. In: C. Galea (Ed.), *Teaching business sustainability: From theory to practice* (pp. 18–30). Sheffield, UK: Greenleaf Publishing, pp. 27–28.

If these are the predominant styles of thinking (collective mental models) in contemporary "successful" organizations, then what sort of long-term sustainability can we expect to achieve? Because a person's mental models drive his or her focus and actions, if these mental models are maintained, Lester Brown's (2006) projection about China's rapid economic development and the attendant growth in its citizens' standard of living will not be able to be realized. Instead, organizations will continue to operate with a high degree of urgency and activity, short deadlines, and priority on immediate results and routing the competition at all costs, while blaming someone for the inevitable shortfalls and living the insupportable myth that working hard and earning ever more money will lead to fulfillment and happiness in life.

Building versatility to ensure a sustainable future

A key concept is **degree of versatility**: What is the normal range of collective thinking across each of the dimensions? What is the comfort zone within the company? Subjectively at least, each of the groups that contributed to the data in Table 2.2 *agreed that the versatility or comfort zones are narrow most of the time in most places.*

We will see versatility in action later in this essay when we look at the sustainability efforts of two large corporations in the chemical and energy industries. The remaining material here was provided by Thomas Stewart,[4] a consultant to these two companies.

Corporate mental models: chances and challenges

John D. Adams

Corporations provide simultaneously both the hope for and the challenge of developing a sustainable future. Corporations, by their nature, tend to be conservative in their actions, reacting slowly or even negatively to change, and avoiding new endeavors except within predefined parameters for growth and development. At the same time, they have highly effective channels for production and distribution, keen marketing and communication vehicles for promotion and sales, and powerful lobbying capabilities to protect their interests and ensure their continuation. Unfortunately, endeavors that fit within the current corporate context of growth and development probably don't often contribute to or support sustainable endeavors.

For example, changing the perspectives of business executives regarding planned obsolescence, what constitutes an acceptable rate of return on investment, or incorporating externalities into the price of goods or services may not fit within a corporate strategic model. Nonetheless, these actions, conscious or unconscious, intended or unintended, may affect the quality of people's lives or the environment in a negative way. Creating awareness within corporations is a continuing and uphill struggle. Yet significant opportunity exists for corporations to create sustainable endeavors—in no small measure because of their pervasive influence and control of capital, resources, and people. In the modern context of proliferating multinational corporations, and the resultant global enterprises, this multiplies and expands to include the very real potential to impact the planet for good or ill, for benefit or degradation, perhaps even for life itself as we know it. The opportunities and consequences are staggering.

One reason why mission and vision statements, and their related goals and objectives (or strategies and tactics), are so important within a corporate context is that these constructs define what an organization believes it is in business to do, what success looks like, and the steps that are necessary to get there.

As with any model for any system, there are inputs and outputs that define what that system or model can accomplish, as well as its limitations. Relating these mental models to major corporations and sustainable endeavors, we find that each organization has its own unique character, or "culture," that defines what the organization is ultimately capable of doing and the extent to which it is capable of acting or reacting as conditions change. If sustainability is a high priority, then moving toward practices that ensure that what we have today will exist, for ourselves and for future generations, is critical.

Within a "green" enterprise, such as a recycling operation or a buyback center, underlying assumptions might look like "the more we return to productive use, the better our bottom line in terms of sales of recycled materials." However, this presumes that return on investment is a priority. If that's not the case, then the volume of recyclables recovered and reintroduced into productive use might be the guiding priority and the yardstick against which our performance should be evaluated. Change the criterion for success and the target changes as well.

Alternatively, if a major corporation, say an industrial operation, incorporates into its mental models "valuing a clean environment," and, at the same time, doesn't wish to create negative impacts associated with the manufacturing processes, then it might opt to decrease the use of hazardous or toxic chemicals in those processes, or choose to invest in solar panels to offset the cost of electricity and reduce its carbon footprint. At the same time, to maintain competitiveness and still do what is environmentally responsible, citizens might cooperate with lawmakers to mandate the application of "green" regulations across an industrial sector, say oil extraction and refining. That action could have the effect of both creating a more sustainable environment and, at the same time, restricting competition to those corporations able to afford the cost of those regulations. Doing good can also mean doing well.

Yet the current pressure to expand without limits, which many have seen as a driving force behind globalization and the proliferation of multinational corporations, can be both a blessing and a curse. As a blessing, it exists within a corporation as the potential to apply best business practices to assure diversity and reduce discrimination, or it may be the use of best available control technology to reduce the magnitude and frequency of industrial incidents. However, it may also lead to one country's exploiting another's resources—including human resources—to fill its own needs because regulations are less rigorously enforced in one area and labor is cheaper and less organized.

The emerging global economy is also a global community in which globalization exists for the benefit of people who, in the past, might have been cut off from one another and exploited.

Chemical companies case overview: a community awakens

A chemical manufacturing plant and a petrochemical refinery, both San Francisco Bay Area facilities of multinational corporations, change in response to communities, both local and national.

Background

No one knows who the first person was to utter the phrase "knowledge is power." Few would dispute that what we are able to conceive can open up or, alternatively, limit what we are able to do subsequently. In the years since the first Earth Day (April, 1970), as people have witnessed such notable industrial incidents as Union Carbide's killing thousands and injuring many more in a chemical release (1984) in Bhopal, India, the *Exxon Valdez* despoiling the waters of Prince William Sound off the coast of Alaska (1989), and BP's Deep Water Horizon oil spill in the gulf of Mexico (2010), people have come to view industrial operations with suspicion and distrust, at a minimum, and often with outright fear.

Changing conditions: new conditions erode old mental models

Two companies operating chemical and refinery facilities in the San Francisco Bay Area initially opposed but subsequently embraced the realities of such conditions as global warming, species extinction, and climate change and recognized them as factors to be addressed now in their operations. These changes have not been easy to launch, and their magnitude and pervasiveness evolved over time, as new mental models emerged. Before the first Earth Day, industrial operations and related activities in these two companies existed as a sort of preemptive right to operate, without consideration for the communities or the environment in which these industrial facilities existed. In those days, the companies allowed their facility managers to operate essentially without oversight at the corporate level. "Profits at any cost" may not have been explicitly espoused, but it was certainly the norm.

This mental model began to erode as incidents multiplied, both globally and locally, impacting communities and resulting in damage claims against these corporations to the tune of hundreds of millions of dollars. The "hands-off" approach clearly was having unwanted effects. These claims eventually got the attention of shareholders and of management at the highest levels. They recognized that something needed to change. At the national and international levels, major incidents drew the attention of the media and both the courts of public opinion and of jurisprudence began to swing decidedly away from corporations and in favor of people and the environment.

Industrial corporations in the Bay Area began to be viewed as an evil: blighting their communities, they were seen as villains and interlopers. A post-Bhopal survey conducted by the then Chemical Manufacturing Association (CMA) showed that people did not distinguish between chemicals: sodium chloride (table salt) was judged to be just as harmful as sulfuric acid. Juries, regulators, and elected officials throughout the area became increasingly unsympathetic to the frequency and impact of industrial incidents. Grassroots organizations proliferated in the region in which these companies were operating and were able to litigate on behalf of communities, further contributing to a change in mental models that had existed since the industrial revolution. More significant still, the acceptance of the implied right of these facilities to continue to operate in these communities began to erode. People called for them to shut down.

Industry responds

Industry responded nationally and locally. At the national level, CMA instituted its Responsible Care initiative which included best practices review, risk assessment, the use of best available technology, emergency preparedness and response, and community interaction, among other initiatives. At the local level, county government introduced the first of its kind Industrial Safety Ordinance (ISO) which tied land use, a power vested at the local level, to enhanced safety reviews prior to any change in processing or facility expansion.

All these factors contributed to transforming the previous mental models from an unassailable, and ultimately unsustainable, prescriptive right to operate into a new and revolutionary concept first articulated by management in the county where the two companies operated. The facility managers and staff began to accept the fact that their companies only operate within the ongoing authority and approval granted by the communities in which they existed, an authority that, unlike a right, could be taken away depending on performance and, more recently, on the communities' perception of their value.

New mental models arise

These changes were fed up the corporate ladder and became manifest as changes in the corporate mental models of what constitutes a safe and sustainable relationship between a community and the industry that operates within it, with frequency and magnitude of incidents being the determining factors.

While not fully recognized at the time, other changes were occurring in the mental models. Specifically, because of the public's unwillingness or inability to distinguish a "good" (incident-free) facility from a "bad" (incident-ridden) facility, all were presumed guilty until proven innocent. The demonstration of innocence emerged as industries became more visible within their host communities, contrasted with the previous priority on invisibility and lack of interaction.

Expectations regarding the roles of the plant managers began to shift as well; no longer would they simply be responsible for the operations of the facility, they would also serve as the primary focus and representative of the corporation within that community. A new skill set was demanded of managers, most of whom were chemical engineers. These expectations became codified in the mission and vision statements, both locally and at the corporate level, and individual and collective bonuses became tied to safe and incident-free operation.

Change persists, in the community and in the corporations

This level of engagement has expanded over the years to the extent that a host community is regularly informed of its host industry's safety performance through public reports and ongoing engagement by means of community advisory panels (CAPs) or councils. Corporations and industrial facilities throughout the Bay Area regularly and routinely communicate with, and seek input from, their host communities regarding how that industry can contribute to that community's sustainability.

Key learnings

What has caused this "sea change" in perspective and in the mental models that support it, which one also sees emerging in corporations?

Corporations are comprised of people. Industry is not unaware or unconcerned about the growing inability of the planet to sustain life as we know it. Corporations, like individuals, wish to survive and, if possible, prosper. Those same perspectives appear within corporations in areas such as supporting diversity, respect for others, sensitivity to the environment, increasing emphasis on renewable sources of energy and products, and so on.

When communities self-empower, miracles can happen. The San Francisco Bay Area communities that are host to the two chemical corporations discussed here took ownership of their neighborhoods, with lasting, far-reaching results. Within communities, because of the Internet and the pervasive accessibility of knowledge, a violation in one community can be challenged in another to prevent the same thing from occurring in that community.

Authentic dialogue leads to accepted solutions. The overarching objective must be to establish effective, meaningful, and ongoing vehicles for authentic dialogue that leads to mutually beneficial and generally supported solutions. In the aftermath of 9/11, the county community warning system, paid for by industry to communicate with residents in the event of an industrial incident, has been evaluated as an "all hazard" system capable of notifying large numbers of people following a fire, earthquake, abduction, or other perceived threat. Through ongoing dialogue and interaction, the needs and priorities of communities can be addressed; and the mental models of what constitutes sustainability within those communities constructed and implemented.

Effective resolutions involve all. Solutions that incorporate *everyone* who has a stake in the issue and its resolution, to the extent that such is feasible, make everyone an *owner* of the success of the undertaking.

Lasting outcomes

One of the outcomes observed at the local level is community members standing up and opposing those they see as merely self-serving or as self-aggrandizing interlopers. Another outcome is the growth of trust through communication, which has resulted in a more connected and informed industry, better able to direct its community philanthropy. Believed to be a necessary cost of doing business, directing funds within a community where it will do the most good—after input from community members—leads to more sustainable communities.

Industries have become major advocates for an increased focus on vocational careers, recognizing that not everyone is going to go to a university and that existing highly paid employees in industry need to be replaced with local residents as the workforce ages. These local residents will, in turn, advocate for what they believe to be in the best interest of their communities and, this too, directly impacts the sustainability of these communities.

Conclusion

If one looks for problems, problems seem to abound. Likewise, if one looks for enemies, they will appear at every turn. Alternatively, if one looks for friends and solutions to the challenges faced by communities, in areas such as education, the environment, even in industry, these will likewise be found. Be it global or local, sustainability benefits from models that incorporate rather than isolate and that promote involvement, not exclusion. We are a social species, and are most content when we act in concert with others, most satisfied when we are helping others, and any model of a sustainable endeavor must incorporate these components.

Cultivating mental models that support sustainability in a technically oriented organization

Linda M. Kelley

This case study is about a program that prepares systems engineers to be leaders. To be the versatile leaders this organization requires, these engineers need to have mental models that are inclusive, global, creative, and promote learning. Technically oriented individuals who were assessed to have considerable potential were invited to participate in a special mentoring program. The sponsoring government agency recognized that it needed future leaders whose vision transcended the boundary of any specific project. My partners and I crafted a program to develop leaders who would understand the details—technical and nontechnical—of a variety of projects, see how those fit into the overall picture, and communicate effectively. The goal was to make these changes rapidly with lasting results.

This agency's mission is to pioneer the future and expand knowledge about the Earth, its solar system, and the universe. Its scientists and engineers pursue basic research and innovative technological development, much of which is transferred to the public domain. Work done by this agency has made possible significant advances in the fields of health and medicine, transportation, computer technology, and environmental management, and has greatly increased scientists' understanding of greenhouse effects on the Earth.

Background

Mental models constitute a personal operating system, complete with boundaries of perceptions, that structures the way a person thinks, feels, and acts. Mental models persist because a person exercises supporting neural pathways and muscular tensions again and again. These habit patterns confine people to predictable ways of thinking and acting. In order to shift a mental model, it is necessary to change the related habit patterns.

Might the difficulties people encounter while trying to change be due primarily to the approaches they are using to make those changes?

For the most part, people approach major changes by talking about the problems and possible fixes. As important as they are, words are seldom enough to effect major changes in how a person operates.

Words symbolically represent mental images from past experiences. According to the neuroscientist Antonio Damasio (1999, p. 318), these images are mental patterns constructed using our sensory modalities: "visual, auditory, olfactory, gustatory and somatosensory." These mental images revive associated neural networks from dormant states. When the desired change has similarities to a person's previous experiences, he or she may draw on these correspondences. When the changes are outside the realm of past experiences, there are no associated ways of thinking, feeling, and moving to revive. The person has to develop new networks of supporting neural pathways. No wonder substantive change seems so hard to achieve.

What could a person do differently to make intentional change both achievable and enduring? Richard Feynman, talking with Freeman Dyson about Einstein's process of genius, provides some insights (Gleick, 1992, p. 244):

> Feynman said to Dyson ... that Einstein's great work had sprung from physical intuition and when Einstein stopped creating it was because "he stopped thinking in concrete physical images and became a manipulator of equations." Intuition was not just visual but also auditory and kinesthetic. Those who watched Feynman in moments of intense concentration came away with a strong, even disturbing sense of the physicality of the process, as though his brain did not stop at the gray matter but extended through every muscle in his body.

When asked to describe his thinking processes, Einstein said they included elements that were visual and muscular, without words (Gleick, 1992). He described his thoughts as image entities that could be voluntarily reproduced and combined so he could play with them. For Einstein, according to Gleick, these thoughts-before-thoughts were visual and muscular in nature. Conventional words or signs weren't present until he arrived at a second stage of thinking, and even then he found it difficult to create logical constructs in conventional words to communicate his thoughts.

The process of communication appears to be consistent with what Einstein reported about his mode of thinking. According to research, less than 10% of what we convey comes from the words we say; 90% comes through our vocal and nonverbal presentation (Mehrabian, 1971). It is not surprising then that attempting change by verbal approaches alone leaves a gap between knowing *what* to do and actually being able to do it. Including the nonverbal dimensions dramatically increases the likelihood that a person will *be* the change he or she wants.

This leadership mentoring program integrates thinking, feeling, and moving—both verbal and nonverbal aspects—to produce change.

> Rather than something packed inside a solitary skull, [the mind] is a dynamic entity defined by its transactions with the rest of the world ... Just as gold's value derives not from its composition but from public agreement, the essence of thought is not its isolated neural basis, but its social use.
>
> (Brothers, 1997, p. 146)

Leadership mentoring program case study

Linda M. Kelley

> You are the first organization you must master.
>
> (Stuart Heller)[5]

A core part of this program was to help to change the meaning and the mental model of "systems engineer" from "someone who is an expert at everything" to someone who gains the respect of the project teams and adds value by asking good and sometimes difficult questions that further the agency's overall purpose. Through effective communication including voicing the needs and concerns of many projects, the engineer-leaders are able to clarify agency-wide issues, develop a common understanding, and work out meaningful solutions to critical problems. A key to the success of this program was that the engineer-leaders develop the confidence to take leadership roles without having project authority. Many projects in this government agency span years, so engineers typically stay teamed for a long time. During this program, the participants were removed from their regular project groups and assigned to other groups for six months at a time. At the end of each rotation, the participants presented the program advisory board with what they learned and shared their ideas about how projects could work differently and more effectively.

The cases shared here are examples of work with individual engineers in cross-functional, mid-level leadership positions. We held an initial three-day intensive workshop to lay out the basic principles and provide the program participants with strategies, models, and core practices they can use to produce rapid and real self-retooling. During the following six months, monthly group sessions were held in which participants learned to use their new tools effectively in real-time simulations. Additionally, each participant had private workouts addressing personal goals.

The technology we used, illustrated in *Retooling on the Run: Real Change for Leaders with No Time* (Heller & Surrenda, 1994), is designed to produce rapid and real acquisition of essential leadership qualities and competencies by facilitating *extraordinary learning* in ordinary states.

Leadership mentoring program: cases

Case 1. Scope of attention: local vs. global—a long shot comes in first

ASSESSMENT

This lead mechanical engineer had already proven she had the technical skills to be a top-rated systems engineer, but she was not perceived as decisive. Being relationship-oriented, it was easy for her to see expanding fields of overlapping details. Her challenge was to pull details together into a single, contained focus.

GOAL

She wanted to be seen as calm, solid, decisive, and authoritative, and be able to hold a vision of the big picture.

PRESCRIPTIVE PRACTICES

We coached this engineer helping her to better balance the details and the greater whole, to strengthen her ability to make decisions, and to make these changes an integral part of who she is. Her combination of exercises dramatically changed how she felt and was perceived by others. Since she was a doodler, this woman was shown that she could focus by intentionally drawing a square, then a second, then a third, placing each over the previous one. At the same time, she was to consciously keep her feet on the ground—legs uncrossed—and sit slightly forward in her chair.

RESULTS

Although less qualified on paper, this engineer applied for a senior systems engineering position with high visibility. The way she presented herself and handled the difficult "human systems" questions during her interview was a key factor in the decision to hire her. She impressed all the interviewers with her poise, knowledge, and leadership qualities. The panelists who knew her before she entered the mentorship program said they were impressed by how dramatically she had matured in such a short time.

Case 2. Focus of response: reactive vs. creative—from intimidation to effective communication

ASSESSMENT

This tall, male systems engineer and technical administrator is passionate about his work. He is also a hockey player, competitive and willing to go to the edge to accomplish his goals. Typically, he stood with his feet firmly planted on the floor, leaning slightly forward and looked intimidating. Colleagues found him threatening and felt he invaded their space, physically and intellectually.

GOAL

He wanted to be able to recognize when he was scaring someone. Once aware that his manner was not working, he wanted to be able to shift his attitude, style, and stance so he would be more effective and successful.

PRESCRIPTIVE PRACTICES

The coaching exercises helped him recognize when he was entering a high-intensity state. He practiced shifting his position and personal center of gravity, moderating his presence without burying his passion.

RESULTS

Now each time he finds people are no longer listening to what he is saying, he can shift, and then shift again, demonstrating versatility and inviting other people to be included, yet doing it in such a way that he isn't letting go of his intention to achieve his goals. He became a project manager. An ongoing exercise for him is "winning without fighting," in which he lets people's reactions move him, and then drops into an appropriate stance, as he does in hockey, but does not hold any position beyond its time.

Case 3. Prevailing logic: either/or vs. both–and—more effective power and real control

ASSESSMENT

This experienced systems engineer joined the program both to become more effective and to better control himself when confronting conflict. He had a habit of holding himself back, especially in situations of impending conflict. He maintained a wall between "being nice" and "being powerful," and he had no stops between "in control" and "going berserk."

GOAL

He wanted to be well considered, perceived as gentle yet powerful and in control during conflict.

PRESCRIPTIVE PRACTICES

This man was coached through conflict simulations using Filipino martial arts Escrima practice sticks. At first he shredded the padded covers with his forceful attack and the strength of his hits. But with practice, he found states between "being nice" and "going berserk" in which versatility of response can emerge.

RESULTS

He learned to express himself calmly and clearly with power and control. To accomplish his goal, he learned to reframe his negative characterization of "slow." Drawing on an analogy from fluid mechanics—when a tube is wide, the liquid moves slower, and when the tube narrows, that same liquid moves faster—he was able to use the familiar language of physics to help him make changes in his personal operating system. He no longer judges fast responses to be "better" or slow responses to be "worse." Now, he can employ the response that best fits any situation. He is now a mentor for the next group of participants.

More than two years into this coaching program, the careers of all participants have advanced more quickly than had been expected, and faster than they had done in the past.

Cultivating versatility and the capacity for change: key points for mental models of sustainability

- There is no real separation between the technical and the human. The unifier is the indivisible body–mind whole.
- The way a person moves through life can be seen in the way he or she moves through space. By working with how he or she moves through space, a person can change how he or she moves through life.

What a person is able to do depends on *where* the person is, *who* the person is at the time, and *where* he or she wants to go. Through the use of the language of movement, achieving lasting change is wholly consistent with the strategies of nature. Nature is inherently versatile. By paying attention to how nature works, and working with habits rather than fighting against them, people can make changes that endure.

> Human nature is not a machine to be built after a model, and set to do exactly the work prescribed for it, but a tree, which requires to grow and develop itself on all sides, according to the tendency of the inward forces which make it a living thing.
> (John Stuart Mill, 1859/1997, Chapter III, Section 4)

The heart of the technical leadership mentoring challenge

> … for the first time ever, our enemies are no longer outside us. We're quite well suited to battles with foreign powers, evil corporations or heartless states. But now we face many challenges where the enemy is us—our desires and our myopias may be what stand in the way of survival.
> (Mulgan, 2006, p. 34)

Sustainability requires the ability to harmonize situational leadership with principled leadership. Leadership is learned in action. New mental models are built in action. Fostering respect and trust among people, and engaging them to work toward a common goal, happens in action. These kinds of actions build supportive foundations for sustainable enterprise.

A mental model includes both internal focus and external vision. Well before acting, a person focuses attention either outward toward the external situation—people and events—or inward toward feelings, principles, and values.

Additionally, people rarely have access to their best thinking when they need it. The way of thinking required to build a spacecraft recognizes that change is a process that involves coordinated interactions among many different functions and organizations. However, when it comes to making personal changes, this process is often ignored. Albert Einstein (Gleick, 1992) said that one's job is to make things as simple as possible—but no simpler. In shifting one's mental models, there are important differences between the simple and the simplistic approaches.

Typical model for change

Figure 2.2 Intention drives Results
Source: Copyright 2007, Stuart Heller and Linda M. Kelley. Used with permission.

The simplistic equation, **I**ntention drives **R**esults, is the way most people try to effect change. Because it tries to drive results by force, and leaves out the process of change and accomplishment, this approach lends itself to swings between excitement and the depression that dashed expectations generate.

Including the change factors

Figure 2.3 Responsiveness shapes Results
Source: Copyright 2007, Stuart Heller and Linda M. Kelley. Used with permission.

The successful application of situational leadership depends on the leader's ability to see, listen, and adapt to what is actually going on. Therefore, it is necessary to add **R**esponsiveness shapes **R**esults.

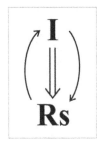

Figure 2.4 Intention and
              Responsiveness
Source: Copyright 2007,
Stuart Heller and Linda
M. Kelley. Used with
permission.

When designing a spacecraft or technical instrument system, engineers build in feedback mechanisms to connect the control systems with the sensor systems. The next factor to add is: **Intention**. **Intention** and **Responsiveness** influence each other.

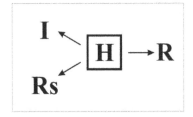

Figure 2.5 Habits bias everything
Source: Copyright 2007, Stuart Heller and Linda M. Kelley. Used with permission.

The final factor, and the one that makes the greatest difference, is: **Habits** bias everything. Habits link together thoughts and actions so one can accomplish often-repeated tasks without thinking. Unrecognized habits, however, are the enemy of change because by nature they maintain the status quo. "All of the learning that led to one kind of success becomes implicitly coded and works against your ability to unlearn. The challenge then becomes how to uncover those deeply ingrained assumptions" (Seely Brown, 1999, p. 85).

To change is to go through a process of keeping what is important, letting go of what is no longer needed, and adding what is now required. Although this may seem obvious, people often skip the step of letting go of what is no longer needed.

Holding on to habits beyond their time sabotages change initiatives and pulls people back into old behaviors—even when they have the best of intentions. Results suffer without alignment between intention and habit.

1. Intention drives results.
2. Responsiveness shapes results.
3. Intention and responsiveness influence each other.
4. Habits bias everything.
5. The interactions between these factors—intention, responsiveness, and habits—generate results.

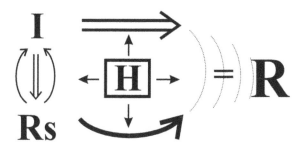

Figure 2.6 Change process: results model
Source: Copyright 2007, Stuart Heller and Linda M. Kelley. Used with permission.

From a systems view, the optimal solution for any particular situation must also be optimal for the system as a whole. "Think globally, act locally"[6] is more than a slogan. It must be the operational framework for acting as well as thinking. This attitude encourages breadth along with the depth essential for sustainability.

Models of sustainability are inclusive, holistic systems in which each aspect influences and is influenced by every other aspect (Figure 2.7). As Bruce Mau (2004, p. 129) said when defining integrated systems, "When everything is connected to everything else, for better or for worse, everything matters."

Versatility, essential to long-term success and sustainability, is a both–and mindset that includes being able to hold a vision of the big picture that transcends specific projects or circumstances *and* the detailed view required to drill down through the particulars by asking pointed questions. These abilities, required of systems engineers, are also essential to leadership for sustainable enterprises.

Human beings are integrated, complex, living systems. At their best, people are incredible learning systems who have the ability to purposefully shift styles, modes, and methods as appropriate to cultivate the versatility, strength, resilience, perception, and inspiration required for sustainability even when situations are unknown and unknowable in advance. People who grasp this can adjust their own mental models and help others to adapt, invent, and succeed under changed and changing circumstances.

These stories give a small taste of what is possible when people shift their mental models, by letting go of what is no longer important and including new possibilities for thinking, feeling, and moving. Sustainability is a process of release, grow, and nurture. With much at stake for individuals, enterprises, and the viability of the planet, people need inclusive, bold, generative mental models that support sustainability.

Figure 2.7 Versatility within a sustainable whole
Source: Copyright 2007, Stuart Heller and Linda M. Kelley. Used with permission.

Mental models in civil society

Beth Applegate

On the path to sustainability, enterprise leaders and staff will encounter situations in which formerly successful ways just don't work. If the leaders take a good look they will usually find that employees on all levels have numerous transferable skills and competencies that the organization may have missed. Often, important qualities are dismissed—discouraging talented people from taking on tasks outside their job descriptions—because the dominant mental models in the organization precluded them. When mental models of inclusion and respect predominate, however, people are seen as skilled and versatile, and they offer to help. They step up to challenges because they believe that who they are, what they know, and what they can do matters—and that their help will be appreciated. The journey to sustainability accelerates when people at all levels of an organization participate.

This is a case study about changing fundamental mental models in order to develop and implement a "culturally competent" strategic plan—that is, a strategic plan for building relationships, without dominance, that lead to just outcomes and accountability. The leadership of a progressive, advocacy-model-based civil rights organization proposed a new mental model to bring the organization into alignment with its mission.

The transformation in thinking that propelled this change was based on a framework for assessing and working with mental models presented by John Adams earlier in this chapter. Adams identifies six dimensions that reinforce the status quo, forestalling the journey toward cultural respect, inclusive community, and sustainability.

The board and staff leadership explicitly chose to engage in a culturally competent strategic planning process that required them to:

- reexamine their core values, vision, and mission, and develop new five-year goals viewed through a systemic lens of power, privilege, and oppression by the full board and staff;
- own, analyze, and share openly, knowledgeably, and compassionately both thoughts and feelings about the intersection of systemic privilege, power, and oppression in the organization as well as the different and overlapping individual cultural biases;
- strive to build a community of inclusion.

Mental models: the personal is political

Worldviews and personal belief systems are shaped by mental models that filter information and limit a person's capacity to understand the workings of the world. Like values, these models have many sources, including religion, race, age, gender expression, sexual orientation, class, and culture. All people subconsciously carry a repertoire of mental models that determine what they see, the interpretations they make, and the conclusions they draw about everything (Senge et al., 1994). These mental models shape and give meaning to reality. Most of them function outside people's awareness, and researchers and practitioners have only begun to realize the importance of learning how to bring mental models to consciousness and then to make intentional choices about whether to believe their meanings (Klein, 2001).

Just as mental models frame an individual's personal worldview, organizational mental models frame the way an institution values its core competencies. Even within an organization, people can use the same words to describe their objectives, but, if they hold conflicting mental models, it is difficult to reach common understanding. For the organization to succeed with a culturally competent strategic planning process, each board and staff member needed to reflect on and perhaps change her or his mental model of what an organization that advocates for equality and justice is. Each had to take a new look at the organization's policies, practices, and programs, and future strategic goals.

To help the board and staff bring to the surface their mental models of privilege and oppression, exposing hierarchical relationships as well as hidden advantages and penalties embedded in the system, tools based in systems theory and action research were introduced. Participants were also coached to reveal and shift mental models of white domination visited on people of color and indigenous peoples.

One goal throughout the process was to raise consciousness about operative mental models that impede the movement to sustainability. Another goal was to help participants reflect on and discuss mental models that shaped their current worldview regarding equality and justice. Together we helped them test whether those mental models were congruent with the programs, policies, actions, and behavior of the organization as a whole.

Revealing and changing mental models

The group used a variety of exercises to reveal prevailing mental models. Adams' six dimensions model presented earlier in this chapter helped us explore the versatility of the mental models of the organization and its stakeholders, better understand the organization's comfort zone, and identify which mental models needed to be reframed. This process resulted in demonstrable changes in the participants' personal and organizational mental models.

Aligning mental models with organizational mission: cases

Case 1. Timeframe: short-term vs. long-term

ASSESSMENT

The organization's day-to-day activities had increased significantly over the past few years and staffing levels had increased, but infrastructure planning lagged behind. The organization was operating without approved strategic or operational plans. Because longer-term strategic aspirations had not been established, nor had medium-term plans been developed or the required resources identified, staff were constantly struggling to meet existing fundraising, program, and policy commitments—and were not able to engage in the long-term thinking and acting necessary to create a sustainable organization.

CHANGE GOAL

From the beginning of the process, the goal we developed with the leaders was to close the gap between the organization's focus on the implementation of its short-term mandate and the need to engage in a strategic planning process for the long term.

TOOLS AND EXERCISES

"Fixes that backfire" is an exercise from *The Fifth Discipline Fieldbook* (Senge et al., 1994, pp. 125–129). We shared the story below (Senge et al., 1994, pp. 125–129) and then adopted a series of questions to raise awareness of and to reveal the prevailing mental models about time.

> How many times have you heard the saying, "The squeaky wheel gets the oil?" Whoever or whatever makes the most "noise" will often grab our attention. Now imagine someone who knows nothing at all about mechanics—and who, told hastily to grab oil, mistakenly picks up a can of water and splashes it on the wheel. With great relief, she'll hear the squeaking stop. But after a brief time, it will return more loudly as the air and water join forces to rust the joint. Once again, before doing anything else, she rushes to "fix" the problem—reaching for the can of water again, because it worked the last time.

Often, although people are aware of the longer-term negative consequences of applying a quick fix, the desire to immediately alleviate pain is more powerful than consideration of delayed negative effects. But the relief is temporary, and the symptom returns, often worse than before; unintended consequences snowball over a period of time, continuing to accumulate as the expedient solution is repeatedly applied.

Reflection questions:

- How does the "fixes" story help you understand the unintended consequences of focusing only on what begs for immediate attention?
- How does the story help you identify the real problems that the organization faces regarding the focus on time?
- How can you minimize the undesirable or unintended consequences created by attending primarily to short-term priorities or problems?

OUTCOME

Together, the board, staff, and constituent planning committee that led the 22-month internal process increased awareness of the unintended consequences of short-term fixes and made the commitment to address the real problem. According to the theory, every fix that backfires is driven by an implicit goal. By working through the questions, the group identified the root time-orientation problem the organization needed to address to move on to a strategic plan.

Case 2. Focus and response: reactive vs. creative

ASSESSMENT

This organization was hierarchical in structure, and did not allow for constructive questioning; nor did it create an environment that fostered responsibility, learning, or innovation.

CHANGE GOAL

We coached the leadership team members to help them understand their individual cultural biases in the context of the larger system of power, privilege, and oppression so that they could establish organizational norms that would support them in the journey toward establishing a more inclusive, respectful learning organization.

TOOLS AND EXERCISES

We developed an exercise, "creating common agreements," to reexamine the mental models underlying both a hierarchical structure based on positional power—the "do as you're told" culture—and the lack of individual and collective responsibility within the organization. We built on previous exercises to help the leadership team better understand their individual cultural biases within the larger societal and organizational system of power, privilege, and oppression.

OUTCOME

The common agreement exercise helped bring to the surface the organization's operative mental models and created a space for the leadership team members to express their values and desires. The common agreements that resulted reflected a set of culturally competent norms for the leadership team and the organization and established a foundation for creating innovative norms for the organization's future work.

Case study conclusion

Using Adam's six dimension framework to examine their mental models, the leadership team, staff, and board members became aware of the individual and collective mental models by which they were filtering information and inhibiting their understanding of how the world works, especially in relation to power, privilege, and oppression. Through the strategic planning process, the stakeholders in this nonprofit, progressive, advocacy-model-based organization acquired the awareness, confidence, and skills necessary to raise questions about decisions faced by the organization. Moreover, they became more conscious of their process of making choices, and of the importance of choosing whether to continue to believe their operative mental models or develop new ones, thus bringing their own mental models more into alignment with the values espoused by the organization.

Appreciative Inquiry case study: executive MBA candidates

Theresa McNichol

Mental models, as John Adams points out earlier in this chapter, have not kept up with the increasing focus on worldwide sustainability. Nor have science, applied research, and other disciplines come close to creating the global tipping point needed for building sustainability practices into the social and business terrain of our flattened world. However, there are signs that alternatives to the deficit approach to organizational design and development are pushing their way into the mainstream.

Consider this scenario: In a strategic planning session, two facilitators take radically different approaches with their respective groups. One facilitator asks the proverbial question, "What burning problem keeps you awake at night?" The other facilitator comes at the process from a completely different direction asking, "What has been a high point for you in the life of this company, a time when you were a member of the team that not only achieved maximum results but also had a positive impact on the community in which it operated?"

In Jim Lord's recent book, *What Kind of World Do You Want? Here's How We Can Get It* (2007), from which the above questions are adapted, the author reports on the profound impact of the second question. Often people become overwhelmed in response to the first question: there are so many problems, missed opportunities, and the like. What happens in the process, however, if the focus is taken off what is defective, and instead placed on what works—and, even more important, on what makes the entire enterprise soar?

Think back to a time when an idea generated excitement and energy, a time when no one minded pulling an all-nighter and everyone was energized by the process and the camaraderie. A way to engage this sense of excitement is through **Appreciative Inquiry**, a dynamic approach being used with positive and, more often than not, transformative results. Developed in the early 1980s, Appreciative Inquiry (AI) has provided an alternative to the deficit model by focusing on assets, resulting in the uncovering of a wealth of latent talent and creativity that was just waiting to be tapped. Using AI, individuals in systems start to work beyond mere function and co-create an entity that excels.

The Appreciative Inquiry process, framework, and tools

In 1980, while a graduate student at Case Western University, David Cooperrider co-authored a paper on Appreciative Inquiry (AI) with Professor Suresh Srivasta. They proposed that the art and practice of asking questions be employed as an intervention to strengthen (rather than diagnose) a system's capacity through the AI process of Discovery, Dream, and Design, thus surfacing its own untapped potential. Appreciative Inquiry, as well as being a practical philosophy for aligning a person's inner and outer worlds on a day-to-day basis, is a highly adaptable process for engaging people in building the kinds of organization and world they want to live in. AI involves a collaborative process of uncovering what gives a system life when it is at its peak on the human, economic, and ecological levels. It creates new knowledge that ultimately contributes to the fluidity and expansiveness of organizational lifecycles.

The tools

The 4D cycle of AI comprises the tools used in this case study:

- Discovery: appreciating and valuing the best of "what is"
- Dream: envisioning "what might be"
- Design: dialoguing "what should be"
- Destiny (deliver): creating "what will be."

The framework

The framework of Appreciative Inquiry provides tools to move our concepts to the far right of the continuum in Table 2.2, in John Adams' essay "Six dimensions of mental models" presented earlier in this chapter (page 94). As Adams explains, this is the optimum zone, but a person's best thinking does not get him or her there. Instead, people get stuck in their default zone, repeating the same action over and over but expecting different outcomes. To effect change in an organization, two things need to take place:

- The field must be leveled so that information does not move only hierarchically from the top down but rather throughout the organization in all directions—circular, horizontally, vertically, and diagonally. Unlike in the "expert" model, everyone participates, so the process is both collective and collaborative.
- Knowing the facts is seldom enough to move people to the right side of the continuum, so AI is used to tap the uncultivated part of thinking where insight, imagination, and innovation reside.

Executive MBA candidates: case

In this case, we work with executive MBA candidates, a "cohort" of ten students and three coaches who are preparing for their third integrated course as a unit. They have been focusing on stretch goal breakthroughs in their organizations and assessing their own personal effectiveness. Here, using Appreciative Inquiry, we coach them through a long-term look at their leadership capabilities, identifying past core strengths as a way of illuminating possibilities for the future.

Discovery process

Interview is one process of discovery. Participants work together in pairs for about 30 minutes—15 minutes to interview and 15 minutes to be interviewed. Rather than being analytical during the process, participants are to focus on emotion—what animates the speaker—and note that aspect of the story.

Participants begin by surfacing glimpses from personal experience that may inform future possibilities. To help articulate what's possible, they consciously focus on those situations that have enlivened and animated them, as it is from one's best experiences that the inspiration and confidence to aspire and act with boldness and conviction arise.

- Participants are asked to think back to a time in their careers when they experienced a peak moment, a glimpse into themselves as a level 5 leader (Collins, 2001),[7] which energized them and made them feel sure this was exactly what they wanted to be doing now and forever. What about that situation made them feel that way? Who was involved and what was going on?
- In considering what each participant values most deeply, he or she is asked, "What is the most important thing your company has contributed to your life? To the lives of others? Without being humble, what do you value as your most important contribution to your work?"

Each interviewer prompts: "Tell me more . . .," "How did that affect you?" "Why was that important to you?"

After this, the interviewers debrief, one-on-one.

Dream

Thirty minutes is allowed for participants to work on the dream section. In this part of the exercise, the original pairs come together and self-organize into two groups, still remaining in pairs. They imagine it is five years later and company XYZ or ABC (depending on the group) has been featured in

Harvard Business Review because it had just received the Geraldine R. Dodge Foundation's prestigious "Most Livable World Award."

Box 2.3   Handouts given to MBA executive group #1 and MBA executive group #2

ABC Corporation's mission is to focus leadership's and staff's unique energy, technology, manufacturing, and infrastructure capabilities to develop tomorrow's solutions, such as solar energy, hybrid locomotives, fuel cells, lower-emission aircraft engines, lighter and stronger materials, efficient lighting, and water purification technology.

XYZ Corporation, an architectural firm, specializes in four categories: residential, community design, commercial, and institutional. With its staff of architects, planners, and leaders in sustainable design, the firm helps clients worldwide craft designs for buildings and communities that embody new and enduring standards of economic, ecological, and social effectiveness.

A facilitator asks each participant questions that had been crafted prior to the event by the facilitators in conjunction with the sponsoring organization, such as, "What is all the excitement about?" "What type of guidance and advice are other company leaders looking to you to give them?"

Design

Each group is instructed to give form to the dream so they can articulate it to the other group. Props are provided, so the groups can describe their version of "a most livable world" in 2D, as a chart, drawing, or map; in 3D as a small-scale model; or on stage, as a collaboratively conceived performance or skit.

Destiny (deliver)

It is not enough to have a dream or a vision if it is not paired with a plan for delivery. The fourth stage of the Appreciative Inquiry framework stimulates action so that participants leave firmly intending to take the first step toward making the dream become a reality. One approach is "constructing the provocative proposition" (see Figures 2.8 and 2.9), coined and described by David Cooperrider (2002) in "Tips for Crafting Provocative Propositions."

Provocative proposition

The participants crafted a provocative proposition designed to encapsulate themes that each group identified from their interviews. Group #1 (ABC Corporation) identified a pattern of words that began with the letter C: *Communities, Connectiveness, Contagious courage,* and *Continuous learning.* Group #2 (XYZ Corporation) recognized three themes that surfaced in their interviews: the vision to see beyond the task at hand; the passion that an individual of integrity brings to his or her work; and the empowering engendered by a safe creative workspace imbued with vision and passion.

The provocative proposition reads:

> ABC and XYZ corporations will collaborate so that together they can create the kind of world they want to see in the future. By combining human capital locally and globally, they will enhance the intellectual and economic vitality of their enterprises. In addition, they will contribute to a new economic framework based on the vision of a more equitable distribution of goods worldwide.

Case conclusion

The participants reflected on the right-side focuses of Adams' six dimensions of mental models (see Table 2.4 on page 96), particularly those in column 4, "The positive value of focusing here." They agreed that the AI component had imbued them with a sense of anticipation rich with possibilities, but that to bring these possibilities into reality they had to adhere to their conscious commitment to collaboration—and to Adams' "right-side focuses," long term instead of short term, global rather than local, systems over separation, and the like. Information sharing, a keystone to their vision of the future, presents a risk, but they determined it is worth taking given the likelihood it will lead to innovation and new ideas.

With a blueprint for the future, the members of the cohort determined that, when they returned to their organizations, in addition to following time-honored leadership traditions, they would strive to realize their vision of a more livable world of the future.

Conclusion

For all the people in these case studies, power issues surfaced: inequalities of power, overbearing power, and, especially, the fear of having less power. Transforming our ideal of leadership from that of powerful, solitary hero to that of leader who engages people to work with one another to create the values, vision, and practical innovations necessary for sustainability is one of the biggest challenges enterprises face today.

→ Is it <u>provocative</u> . . . does it stretch, challenge, or interrupt?

→ Is it <u>grounded</u> . . . are there examples that illustrate the ideal as real possibility?

→ Is it <u>desired</u> . . . if it could be fully actualized would the organization want it? Do you want it as a preferred future?

→ Is it stated in <u>affirmative</u> and bold terms?

→ Does it follow a social architecture approach (e.g., 7-S model, etc.)?

→ Does it expand the zone of "proximal development?"
  • Use of third party (outside appreciative eye)
  • Complemented with benchmarking data

→ Is it a high involvement process?

→ Is it used to stimulate intergenerational organizational learning?

→ Is there balanced management of: continuity, novelty, and transition?

Figure 2.8 Criteria for good propositions

Source: D. Cooperrider. (2002, February). *Tips for crafting provocative propositions.* Cleveland Heights, OH: Weatherhead School of Management, Case Western Reserve University. Retrieved July 18, 2007, from connection.cwru.edu/ai/uploads/Crafting%20prov%20propos2-02.doc. Copyright 2002, David Cooperrider. Reproduced with permission.

A provocative proposition is a statement that bridges the best of "what is" with your own speculation or intuition of "what might be." It is provocative to the extent to which it stretches the realm of the status quo, challenges common assumptions or routines, and helps suggest real possibilities that represent desired possibilities for the organization and its people.

In many ways, constructing provocative propositions is like architecture. Your task is to create a set of propositions about the ideal organization: what would our organization look like if it were designed in every way, to maximize and preserve the topics we've chosen to study. Organizational elements or factors you may wish to include:

strategy	structures	systems
style	shared values	skills
stakeholder relations	societal purposes	staff

Figure 2.9 Constructing provocative propositions

Source: D. Cooperrider. (2002, February). *Tips for crafting provocative propositions.* Cleveland Heights, OH: Weatherhead School of Management, Case Western Reserve University. Retrieved July 18, 2007, from connection.cwru.edu/ai/uploads/Crafting%20prov%20propos2-02.doc. Copyright 2002, David Cooperrider. Reproduced with permission.

Enterprises in the developed world operate primarily from mental models where prevailing logic = either/or and time orientation = short term. In combination, these position sustainability incorrectly and in opposition to competition and profitability. What changes would come about if the overarching mental model became both–and?

Switching from the individual level to the global or societal level, in his book, *Capitalism at the Crossroads*, Stuart Hart (2007, pp. xxxix–xl) says:

> Global capitalism now stands at a crossroads: Without a significant change of course, the future … appears increasingly bleak … Failure to address the challenges we face—from global-scale environmental change, to mass poverty, to international terrorism—could produce catastrophe on an even grander scale than that experienced in the first half of the twentieth century: Constructively engaging these challenges thus holds the key to ensuring that capitalism continues to thrive in the coming century—to everyone's benefit … By creating a new more inclusive brand of capitalism, one that incorporates previously excluded voices, concerns, and interests, the corporate sector could become the catalyst for a truly sustainable form of global development—and prosper in the process. To succeed, however, corporations must learn how to open up to the world: Strategies need to take into account the entire human community of 6.5 billion, as well as the host of other species with which we share the planet.

Do your mental models, and your organization's, keep you blind to the opportunities sustainability presents? Do they maintain illusions of security while buttressing obsolete technologies, reinforcing dysfunctional attitudes, increasing risk, and inhibiting innovation? Or, do they enable the values, understanding, creativity, and strategies essential to adapt, invent, and lead for a sustainable future? Real sustainability requires supportive mental models.

The late American fiction writer Philip K. Dick (1978) gave us a useful touchstone for determining what is real and what is not. He said, "Reality is that which, when you stop believing in it, doesn't go away."

Human beings are truly wondrous. As a species, humans have engaged with life in ways that have changed the world, some for better and some for worse. We have learned many skills, made our own technologies, and gone through many transformations in the process. We have not yet, however, become sustainable—nor have we established sustainable communities or businesses. This is our new frontier and a true opportunity for advancement.

Sustainability of our world will only come about if each of us does his or her part, individually and collectively with others, aware of our thinking patterns and making the conscious choice to be sustainable. Getting to sustainability is an iterative process in which every present step is a new beginning, informed by the past and anticipating the future. As we move ourselves and our enterprises toward sustainability, our concepts of success, rewards, satisfaction, and even what is true and real will change with us.

Notes

1 The authors gratefully acknowledge contributions from Thomas Stewart to this chapter.
2 **Cultural competency** is the ongoing and ever-deepening practice of building genuine relationships that lead to just outcomes and accountability without dominance.
3 Personal communication with M. Ferguson, Rhinebeck, New York, March 1983.
4 Personal communication with T. Stewart, San Francisco, December 18, 2007.
5 Personal communication with S. Heller, Boston, January 1990.
6 This phrase was coined by David Brower when he founded Friends of the Earth in 1969.
7 For more on Collins's level 5 leader, see page 61 in "Nature and domains of leadership for sustainable enterprise" by Daniel F. Twomey in Chapter 1 (pages 57–63).

References

Adams, J. D. (2000a). Six dimensions of a sustainable consciousness. *Perspectives on Business and Global Change, 14*(2), 41–51.
Adams, J. D. (2000b). *Thinking today as if tomorrow mattered: The rise of a sustainable consciousness.* San Francisco, CA: Eartheart Enterprises.
Adams, J. D. (2004). Mental models @ work: Implications for teaching sustainability. In C. Galea (Ed.), *Teaching business sustainability: From theory to practice* (pp. 18–30). Sheffield, UK: Greenleaf Publishing.
Adams, J. D. (2006). Building a sustainable world: A challenging OD opportunity. In B. Jones & M. Brazzel (Eds.), *Understanding organization development: Foundations and practices* (pp. 335–352). San Francisco, CA: Pfeiffer/John Wiley.
American Management Association (AMA). (2007). *Creating a sustainable future: A global study of current trends and possibilities 2007–2017.* New York: American Management Association.
Aronson, D. (1998). Overview of systems thinking. Retrieved December 25, 2017, from www.thinking.net/Systems_Thinking/OverviewSTarticle.pdf.
Brothers, L. (1997). *Friday's footprints: How society shapes the human mind.* New York: Oxford University Press.
Brown, L. R. (2006). *Plan B 2.0: Rescuing a planet under stress and a civilization in trouble.* New York: W. W. Norton & Company.
CNNMoney.com. (2007). Money 101: Top things to know. Retrieved December 20, 2007, from money.cnn.com/magazines/moneymag/money101/lesson9.

Collins, J. (2001). *Good to great: Why some companies make the leap and others don't.* New York: HarperCollins.

Cooperrider, D. (2002). *Tips for crafting provocative propositions.* Cleveland Heights, OH: Weatherhead School of Management, Case Western Reserve University. Retrieved May 18, 2018, from https://appreciativeinquiry.champlain.edu/educational-material/tips-for-crafting-provocative-propositions/.

Damasio, A. (1999). *The feeling of what happens: Body and emotion in the making of consciousness.* New York: Harcourt.

Dick, P. K. (1978). How to build a universe that doesn't fall apart two days later. Retrieved November 29, 2007, from deoxy.org/pkd_how2build.htm.

Gleick, J. (1992). *Genius: The life and science of Richard Feynman.* New York: Pantheon.

Gore, A. (2006). *An inconvenient truth.* Emmaus, PA: Rodale.

Hart, S. L. (2007). *Capitalism at the crossroads: Aligning business, Earth, and humanity* (2nd ed.). Upper Saddle River, NJ: Wharton School Publishing.

Heller, S., & Surrenda, D. S. (1994). *Retooling on the run: Real change for leaders with no time.* Berkeley, CA: Frog.

HRH Prince of Wales. (2000, May). Sacredness and sustainability: A reflection on the 2000 Reith Lectures. Retrieved May 18, 2018, from https://www.princeofwales.gov.uk/speech/speech-hrh-prince-wales-titled-reflection-2000-reith-lectures-bbc-radio-4.

Klein, D. (with Morrow, K.). (2001). *New vision, new reality: A guide to unleashing energy, joy, and creativity in your life.* Center City, MN: Hazelden.

Lord, J. (with McAllister, P.). (2007). *What kind of world do you want? Here's how we can get it* (Pre-publication honorary gift edition). Retrieved May 18, 2018, from http://wkw-download.s3.amazonaws.com/what_kind_of_world_do_you_want.pdf.

Mau, B. (2004). *Massive change.* London: Phaidon Press.

Meadows, D. H. (1998). *Indicators and information systems for sustainable development: A report to the Balaton group.* Hartland Four Corners, VT: Sustainability Institute.

Meadows, D. H. (1999). *Leverage points: Places to intervene in a system.* Hartland Four Corners, VT: Sustainability Institute.

Meadows, D. H. (2015). *Thinking in systems: A primer.* Edited by D. Wright. White River Junction, VT: Chelsea Green Publishing.

Mehrabian, A. (1971). *Silent messages.* Belmont, CA: Wadsworth.

Mill, J. S. (1997). *On liberty* (original work published 1859). Retrieved June 21, 2007, from www.serendipity.li/jsmill/on_liberty_chapter_3.htm.

Mulgan, G. (2006, September/October). The enemy within. *Resurgence, 238,* 34.

Packard, V. O. (1957). *The hidden persuaders.* New York: The David McKay Company.

Seely Brown, J. (1999). The art of smart. *Fast Company, 26,* 85. Retrieved July 23, 2007, from www.fastcompany.com/magazine/26/one.htm.

Senge, P. M., Kleiner, A., Roberts, C., Ross, R. B., & Smith, B. J. (1994). *The fifth discipline fieldbook: Strategies and tools for building a learning organization.* New York: Doubleday.

Toffler, A. (1970). *Future shock.* New York: Random House.

Torpy, B. (2007, December 5). Lots of stories in storage, and business is booming. *Dallas Fort Worth Star-Telegram.* Retrieved December 20, 2007, from www.star-telegram.com/business/story/ 337563.html.

United Nations. (2015). *Integrating the three dimensions of sustainable development: A frame-work and tools*. Retrieved May 17, 2018, from www.unescap.org/sites/default/files/Integrating%20the%20three%20dimensions%20of%20sustainable%20development%20A%20framework.pdf.

Vanderbilt, T. (2005). Self-storage nation. *Slate Magazine*. Retrieved December 20, 2007, from www.slate.com/id/2122832.

Wirtenberg, J., Harmon, J., Russell, W. G., & Fairfield, K. D. (2007). HR's role in building a sustainable enterprise: Insights from some of the world's best companies. *Human Resource Planning, 30*(1), 10–20.

Zweig, C., & Abrams, J. (1991). *Meeting the shadow*. Los Angeles: Jeremy P. Tarcher.

Sustainability-aligned strategies

Smart enterprise strategies to progress
along a bridge to thriving

William G. Russell and Joel Harmon

> We live in a fundamentally changed world. It's time for your approach to
> strategy to change, too.
>
> (Andrew Winston)

How can we create "smart" enterprise strategies that will collectively guide
us over the complex bridge of sustainability to a thriving future? Earlier
chapters have helped develop an increased and shared awareness of many
of the factors that impact our journey. These include defining sustainability,
highlighting global and enterprise systems and the forces driving them,
mindsets that help us and hinder our progress, and the unique leadership
approach needed to achieve success. These are all key aspects we build upon
as we share our bridge strategy framework to help you formulate and execute
a sustainability-aligned strategy.

This chapter is about how to create adjustable or "smart"[1] strategies
that can guide enterprises along a progressive sustainable enterprise
journey. Stated in simple terms strategies guide you from where you are,
or your current state, to where you hope to move, or your desired state.
We use a sustainability lens to describe four discrete and progressively holistic stages to orient an enterprise's purpose and progress. Here and again
within Chapter 6, we suggest progressive, but interconnected smart goals to
assess and iteratively evolve the founding mental models and performance
expectations of the enterprise itself and the strategy guiding it. A sustainability-aligned strategy is not a fixed one, but adjusts and adapts as the enterprise progresses. Executing a sustainability-aligned strategy will be more
integrated and interdependent than traditional strategies. It requires wise
change management practices, diligent employee and stakeholder engagement, and a strong appreciation of global conditions and trends discussed in
the chapters to follow.

The basic notion of sustainability is evolving toward a more aspirational
vision of creating a "flourishing" or "thriving" desired state for the planet
and society (Ehrenfeld & Hoffman, 2013; Laszlo & Brown, 2014). It is aspirational and we believe with the right blend of humility, precaution, and

enlightenment, it is truly possible. We understand that we don't actually know how we will get there. Our strategies will reveal multiple paths where we must assess the near- and long-term risks and opportunities.

An effective strategy requires reviewing the state of global environmental and social systems. Our understanding about planetary boundaries, natural resource thresholds, and ecosystem services that support life is limited and evolving. The implications of what we are learning are alarming. Previously unknown or misunderstood risks are manifesting. Our strategies must manage the paradox between the near-term urgent risks and long-term, less certain, but important and life-sustaining, environmental risks. Our understanding of current social and economic system conditions is also evolving. These systems have knowable macro-system weaknesses and alarming feedback signal conditions that beg for mindset and performance reviews and system adaptation. Conversations and change-oriented collaborations are questioning the basic purpose of business and the economic and regulatory systems that drive its beliefs and behaviors.

It gives us renewed hope to see that sustainability is now "a key strategic priority" for many leading CEOs, according to several executive surveys from 2010 to 2017. Leading firms are seeing that an integrated "triple bottom line" (i.e., people, planet, profits) requires vigilant engagement and collaboration with employees, their external stakeholders, and society. Responsible stewardship of the environment, people, and financial resources must build resiliency and enhance wellbeing, our ultimate outcomes. Successfully navigating enterprises into the future is critical not only to each enterprise's own long-term viability in the global marketplace, but to sustaining and hopefully enhancing the wellbeing of all humans.

The goal of this chapter is to help leaders re-imagine their company from a more holistic and interconnected systems perspective. From this open mindset they can apply a mix of pragmatic strategy-informing tools to create a progressive, agile, and even adjustable or "smart" strategy. The progressive or smart sustainability-aligned strategy bridge framework, introduced later in the chapter, provides enterprises with a clear purpose, vision, goals, and values. The bridge strategy process reveals uniquely appropriate paths for action and achieving progress. It adjusts for each enterprise's current state, and provides an approach to obtaining a more diverse foundation by engaging employees and stakeholders into the strategy process and understanding each other's mindsets, biases, and capacities as we communicate together.

The chapter reviews some core strategy development concepts and best practices. We then review sustainability-aligning concepts and how processes that align strategies with sustainability have evolved to work with today's new understandings and goals. We then introduce the idea of strategies that are more iterative, progressive, and adjustable or smart. We build upon the systems thinking messages presented in the Mental Models chapter by presenting brief stage-setting perspectives for the co-evolution of interconnected human and enterprise systems. Throughout the chapter we include contextual observations, statistics, and trends that inform and remind us of the current progress and challenges ahead for the sustainability movement. Sustainability-aligned enterprise strategies and the outcomes they produce will transform the businesses that apply them and the lives of every employee, customer, and broader communities they serve.

We introduce an epoch story with quests to build bridges and cross chasms as a way to creatively help guide you through four progressive sustainable enterprise stages. The stages of our journey are inclusive and depict diverse enterprise types with diverse stakeholders all traveling together. We must be respectful of each other and formulate inclusive strategies that meet people and enterprises where they are today. For most, this is a difficult mindset shift to grasp as they re-imagine their enterprise's beginning state. Each of our four chasm-crossing missions starts with having enterprises choose that stage's mission and formulate their strategy to progress towards their new re-imagined strategic purpose and goals. Even these smaller segments of the more complete journey seem daunting at first and have risks that can cause the company to fail. Case studies are provided that assure you and others you work with that you are not traveling alone. Heroes have been working hard to understand what lies ahead, and innovate new tools to help you travel. Pioneering enterprises are attempting new paths that you can follow.

Achieving sustainability will require everyone's engagement and hard work. That said, it is important to be present as we travel, take time to reflect, have fun, and make this journey an enjoyable ride.

Enhanced strategic management process

> The industrial system takes too much, extracting and frittering away Earth's natural capital on wants, not needs. It wastes too much. It abuses too much. It takes stuff and makes stuff that very quickly ends up in landfills or incinerators—more waste, more abuse, more pollution.
>
> (Ray Anderson)

In our first edition of the *Fieldbook*, we presented the Sustainability Pyramid (also featured in the Introduction to this second edition). That framework insightfully emphasized that making sustainability central to an organization's overall strategy was a foundational quality for cre- ating a sustainable enterprise (American Management Association [AMA], 2007; Wirtenberg, Harmon, Russell, & Fairfield, 2007). The journey's vision at that time was more internally oriented focusing on building traction by engaging employees and aligning internal systems and performance metrics. Broader stakeholder engagement and the need for holistic integration was identified, but not urgently required. Most people were not (and still are not) yet aware of or have accepted the scenario modeling signals of Limits to Growth (Meadows, Meadows, Meadows, & Behrens, 1972) and other insightful, but undervalued or dismissed work released in more innocent times. Even through today, very few enterprises have sustainability groups— and those that do are still operating as silos—and are generally not well integrated with other core business functions. Leadership from large investor groups including Blackstone and BlackRock (Sorkin, 2018) are shaking things up, but for the moment, growth and single-bottom-line performance are still the primary drivers for governments and the formulators of risky, even bad, corporate strategies.

The basic strategic management process

This section reviews the general strategic management process and the SWOT framework for strategy formulation and execution. Enhancements for sustainability-alignment and insights learned over the past decade are included to help deepen understanding and promote further learning and adaptation in the future.

Viewed through a strategic management lens, a good strategy for sustainability must first and foremost be a fundamentally sound strategy. A good strategy promotes positive, system-reinforcing competition within industries, markets, and communities. Diversity builds resiliency and stakeholder-valued advantages that help assure the better performing enterprises also are the most viable and survive (Porter & Kramer, 2006). This applies to any type of enterprise, whether a large corporation that strives for market share and profitability, a small family-owned business serving local markets or an NGO (nongovernmental organization) that competes for clients and funding support. Thus, from this perspective, creating a good sustainability-aligned strategy essentially represents a critical enhancement of a solid basic strategic management process.

Figure 3.1 visualizes the essential elements of the strategic management process. In essence, a successful strategy is one that positions the organization so as to create an alignment or "fit" between its inside and outside worlds at any point in time. One aspect involves taking an "outside-in" perspective, analyzing the general and industry-specific forces in the organization's external environment to discern opportunities and threats.[2]

Another aspect involves taking an "inside-out" perspective, analyzing the organization's value chain, resources, and capabilities to discern its own "core competencies": What can it do to create value that is relatively rare among its rivals and hard for them to easily imitate?[3] A good strategy adopts a mission and goals that continually position the organization favorably in the outside world and that guide the creation and re-creation of the competencies necessary to succeed there in a resilient and sustainable manner.

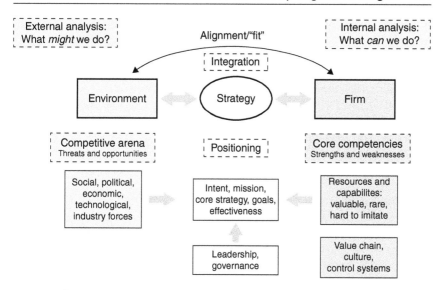

Figure 3.1 Strategic management: alignment of organization–strategy–environment
Source: Copyright 2008, J. Harmon. Used with permission.

Traditional strategic process enhancements

When reflecting on this process after a decade of application, two enhancements are noted. First, the system boundary between the firm and the environment on the left should be viewed as porous and adjustable depending upon the issues being considered and expansive to include the holistic triple-bottom-line economic, social, and environmental system interconnections of threats and opportunities at both the industry value chain and broader macro-level national and global boundaries. Second, when examining internal firm core competencies, more attention must be paid to the human capital (employees) mindsets and capacities and stakeholder engagement processes than what previous nonsustainable strategic processes required.

Understand the mission

Strategy is best formulated by a diverse team with diverse perspectives. A small group within senior leadership may have unconscious biases which risk missing vital insights that fresh broader stakeholders can infuse. A more inclusive and diverse team of enterprise leaders and stakeholders will require more time for collaboration. A diverse team, supported by leadership that is open to new ideas and an arsenal of tools to stimulate dynamic probing of key challenges, opportunities, and mindsets will produce better strategies. The outcomes will be better and more transparently reflect on the enterprise's current state and mission being confronted. Thinking strategically is to understand the problem you are trying to solve and seeing the problem from different views. Sometimes, the problem you need to address is not the one you originally set out to tackle. When a leader attempts to formulate a strategy in isolation or only with internal staff too similar in shared views and experiences, they may falsely believe that they completely understand the situation. All sorts of biases including groupthink may result, as the actual problem is frequently broader, more nuanced, or different than the leader or team originally may assume.

Formulating and executing activities

It is useful at this point to distinguish two interrelated sets of strategic management activities. The first set involves *formulating* (or developing) the direction and content of a strategy: its purpose, mission, and goals. The second set involves *executing* a strategy: the numerous activities that an organization needs to engage in to sustainably-align and apply the guidance of its strategy. It is also vitally important to recognize the back-and-forth iterative and emergent nature of the strategy formulation–execution process (Mintzberg, 1978). An organization tries to adopt approaches to the world that it believes will create success but adjusts its intentions according to realities encountered along the way. Senior enterprise executives are not the only ones who have a critical leadership role to play in developing strategies fit for the more complex, rapidly changing, 21st-century global economy. People at all levels, especially those who work at the organization's boundaries with customers, suppliers, regulators, and community groups, often can make powerful contributions to shaping and modifying their organization's strategy.

Performing a sustainability-aligned SWOT

Finally, for *strategic action-planning* purposes, it is useful to introduce the notion of a "SWOT" analysis as shown in Table 3.1. Strategic management is often pragmatically defined as the pattern of management actions to accomplish mission and goals by leveraging **S**trengths and addressing **W**eaknesses to capitalize on **O**pportunities and counter **T**hreats (see, for example, any good basic strategic management text, such as Hill & Jones, 2008).

Note that when done well a SWOT analysis requires an organization to:

- scan and make sense of both the broad and the industry-specific dynamics that to some extent drive its behaviors and results;
- assess the organization both for valuable resources and capabilities and for areas of relative weakness.

Distilling this analysis (which would go into the gray cells of Table 3.1) provides the strategic framework for formulating actions (the white cells of

Table 3.1 A SWOT framework for strategic analysis

	Opportunities *What conditions in the* *outside world could we* *really take advantage of?*	*Threats/risks* *What conditions in the* *outside world might really* *hurt us?*
Strengths *What things do we do* *really well or possess that* *have great value?*	How can we leverage our strengths to exploit these opportunities?	How can we leverage these strengths to neutralize or minimize these threats/risks?
Weaknesses *What things do we lack or* *do very poorly?*	How can we address these weaknesses to exploit these opportunities?	How can we address these weaknesses to neutralize or minimize these threats/risks?

Table 3.1). See the *Living Fieldbook* for a sustainability-specific SWOT tool for analysis and planning activities.

Strategy versus plans: Why versus how you do something

There are important distinctions between a strategy and a plan. A plan is usually a list of steps taken to accomplish a goal. A plan tackles questions like how, when, where, who, and what? A plan is a good thing to have, but a strategy is bigger than a plan. Strategy tackles the question of why? It has a large scope and looks at the end result as well as the many paths to the desired outcome. A strategy looks at every possible influencing factor, both seen and unforeseen and comes to terms with the whole situation, not just one end result.

Good versus bad strategy

A good strategy does more than urge us forward. "Let's get going," is not a strategy. A good strategy is one that reaffirms the enterprise purpose and refocuses its vision for the future. It reflects an awareness and honest assessment of current reality. It incorporates a SWOT analysis to capture current conditions, and also adapts the strategy as execution progresses. This implies checking and monitoring progress towards goals. It means incorporating qualitative and quantitative feedback, and having that feedback iteratively adjust the initial assessments of how things are.

A good strategy can look simple and obvious in retrospect. Conversely, bad ones can kill momentum, cause great delays, and even backslide an enterprise's progress. Any perceived improvements are likely achieved through dumb luck. Bad strategy ignores the power of choice and focus, trying instead to accommodate a multitude of conflicting demands and interests.

Sustainability-aligned enterprise strategies

This section offers a few distinctions between traditional strategies and ones that are sustainability-aligned. Sustainability strategies as initially depicted in our original book have evolved substantially and are poised for scaled progressive application.

Sustainability-aligned strategy, purpose, and goals

The journey to corporate sustainability can be viewed as a progression of stages and steps toward meeting societal expectations (Hitchcock & Willard, 2006; Willard, 2005, pp. 26–27). The earliest stages have tended to be compliance-driven, with a focus on reputable business practices (e.g., laws, regulations, contracts). In midpoint stages, organizations move beyond mere compliance to concerns for customer expectations (e.g., quality) and employee needs (e.g., health, safety, quality of work life). Advanced stages are characterized by a more integrated strategic approach infused with purpose and passion and marked by environmental stewardship and deep concerns for community needs. Some early adopters of advanced-stage sustainability qualities were founded on social-environmental ethical principles and have it in their "DNA." It is simply how they operate: what they do and have always done. More recently, with a particular emphasis on climate change risks, corporations have started to integrate science-based goals into their long-term strategies and plans. We have reorganized this continuum of strategic logic, purposes, and goals into a sustainability-aligned bridge framework presented later in this chapter.

Systems thinking advancements

Systems thinking in theory and practice was introduced in Chapter 2, and is a core enhancement for formulating sustainability-aligned strategies. Some will argue that systems theory has been applied for sustainability framing for decades. Sustainability thought leaders including Donella Meadows (Meadows, 1999; Meadows, 2015), Peter Senge (Senge, 1994), Hunter Lovins (Lovins & Lovins, 1989), and Daniel Aronson (Aronson, 1996) and others, have been applying and promoting this for over 30 years. That work however, like other thought leaders who were ahead of their time, has not been given enough attention. It has yet to become mainstream and scale as we desire. We hope that through this book and the work of other fellow sustainability leaders who also are aware of it and applying it now (Baue, 2017), its wisdom will finally be appreciated and its application vastly scaled. The aggregate state of the enterprise movement, as reviewed later in this chapter, is still nascent. Broad, inclusive, adoption of systems-based sustainability-aligned strategies can be transformative to any enterprise and the broader systems with which they interconnect.

The following are systems thinking advancements applied to sustainability-aligned strategies:

- articulating a systems view of an enterprise with interconnected and interdependent purposes, functions, mental models and elements;
- use of the Daly Triangle to establish ultimate means, intermediate means, intermediate ends, and ultimate ends;
- multi-capital ecological accounting including the acknowledgment of limited nonrenewable (technical) and renewable (organic) natural capital;
- blind spots, disruptive technologies, system weaknesses, and critical assumptions positive or negative are probed;
- agile quick pivots and velocity adjustments are made as new feedback signals are monitored and adjusted.

Adjustable or smart strategy for clear purposeful vision

We tell our story as if it takes place linearly in time. One arc from start to finish. Or in our case four arcs creating a bridge crossing four potentially journey-ending perilous chasms. Implementing a systems-oriented holistic, sustainability-aligned strategy in reality will be more complex. The sustainable enterprise strategic journey integrates or blends the view ahead through multiple time periods and is adaptive, agile, and multidimensional.

The linear version of our bridge story is viewed like looking through progressive lens glasses. Progressive glasses allow you to see clearly across distances from close to far away. Our progressive bridges allow enterprises to see clearly through time from near term to times further and further out into the future. A progressive sustainability-aligned strategy must allow you to see anything ahead, close and far. As you react to these multi-distant sights, you process risks and opportunities. With the help of feedback signals (i.e., good metrics), you adjust the strategy and continue progressing ahead with a clear purposeful vision.

While progressive glasses are wonderful advancements for seeing clearly, technology has advanced to the next level with the innovation of adjustable or "smart" lenses. Smart glasses come with liquid lenses that can automatically adjust their focus, which means that you don't have to take reading glasses on and off (Chang, 2017). This technology can also replace bifocals, or progressive glasses as we propose. Bifocals, which itself would be an improvement in strategy development, help you see through one prescription at a distance, and another for nearby objects. Now imagine the future of sustainability-aligned smart strategies. "The major advantage of these smart eyeglasses is that once a person puts them on, the objects in front of the person always show clear, no matter at what distance the object is," (Carlos Mastrangelo quoted in Chang, 2017).

Ultimately the aggregate smart strategy reveals a jagged, but precautionary path with the highest probability of progressing in a positive direction for the longest foreseeable time periods. This path is inclusively iterated between the enterprise and its stakeholders throughout the process. Each progressive insight helps avoid both impasses caused by human paradox priority differences (tradeoffs) and delayed or inaccurate environmental and or economic feedback signals. Illustrative priority performance risks include:

- current economy value propositions and finances during startups;
- competitor and customer reactions and feedback signals in the medium term;
- expanded more complex market and supply chain perspectives;
- geopolitical and environmental risks and opportunities.

If strategic conditions change, the strategy needs to be updated and a new strategic direction or velocity developed.

Sustainability-aligned human/enterprise systems perspective

> I believe that a sustainable society depends totally and absolutely on a new mind-set to deeply embrace ethical values. Values that, along with an enlightened self-interest, drive us to make new and better decisions.
>
> I also believe that it doesn't happen quickly … it happens one mind at a time, one organization at a time, one building, one company, one community, one region, one new, clean technology, one industry, one supply chain at a time … until the entire industrial system has been transformed into a sustainable system, existing ethically in balance with Earth's natural systems, upon which every living thing is utterly dependent.
>
> (Ray Anderson)

As discussed in earlier chapters, we are constraining our ability to influence effective progress towards a more sustainable thriving future in part because of our failure to think holistically. Systems thinking helps us do that. It tells us that, like all systems, humans and enterprises lean toward self-organizing. Nature and the people who came before us evolved the environmental, social, and economic systems that define our reality and influence mindsets and our way of being.

Human and enterprise evolution

According to the International Geological Congress, humanity's impact on the Earth is now so profound that a new geological epoch—the Anthropocene—was declared (Carrington, 2017). From a human systems perspective, this new "epochal" story is about humans finally recognizing weak or delayed planetary feedback signals. The signals took scientists about

60 years to appreciate. That clearer vision caused them to declare that a new story had begun. Those signals included the radioactive elements dispersed across the planet by nuclear bomb tests, plastic pollution, soot from power stations, concrete, and even the bones left by the global proliferation of the domestic chicken (Carrington, 2017).

According to the Smithsonian Institute, our ancestors have been around for about six million years. Our more evolved or "modern" form of humans only evolved about 200,000 years ago. Humans adapted and learned how to self-organize. They formed early social enterprises in the form of families and tribes. They innovated and used tools. The societal system that we consider to be "civilization" has only existed for about 6,000 years with the industrial age starting in the 1800s (Howell, 2015).

While we've accomplished much in a geologically short time, our shared responsibility to serve as caretakers for the planet is becoming more clear and urgent. We are reaching and even surpassing certain safe resilient threshold limits of both the supplies of natural resources and the ability of the planet to accept and absorb our wastes. The effects of humans on Earth cannot be understated. There are now 7.5 billion people on Earth who need food, shelter, and energy. This represents growth opportunities that can be incorporated into the strategies of businesses, but they also require sustainability-alignment to avoid blind spots, unintended consequences, and causing externality impacts and economic costs beyond whatever revenues and profits they might earn today.

Enterprise system construct for sustainability-aligned strategies

If any individual enterprise within the broader economic, social, and environmental systems goes away, if the good or service is still adding value to the system, a new enterprise will self-organize to replace it. As described in Chapter 2, a sustainable enterprise system is also interconnected with internal subsystem functions like sales, manufacturing and procurement, and broader external systems like cities or industrial sectors within which it operates and serves as a part.

The following are the key system constructs that enterprises explore when re-imagining their enterprise as a sustainable enterprise system. The Daly Triangle perspectives were previously introduced in Chapter 2 and sustainability goals and multi-capital accounting are presented in more detail in Chapter 6.

Sustainability-aligned strategies examine the assumptions, priorities, relevance, and performance expectations regarding the following enterprise system constructs:

- **Functions or its purpose**: Why is it in business? What role do its products and services contribute to its customer's wellbeing? (Ultimate ends)

- **Resources, multi-capital system elements:** Stocks, flows and thresholds for:
  - Natural capital: Raw materials and ecosystem services (Ultimate means)
  - Human capital: Enterprise and supplier employees and gig contractors (Intermediate means and intermediate ends)
  - Built capital: Facilities, inventory and equipment (Intermediate means)
  - Social capital: Supplier and other stakeholder relationships (Intermediate means and intermediate ends)
  - Financial and economic capitals (Intermediate means)
  - Intellectual capital: Experiences, innovations, and technology (Intermediate means and intermediate ends).
- **Time horizons:** Critical, resilient, thresholds for capital flows with particular focus on constraining resources that might cause the enterprise to fail. Constraining resources included financial capital, but also might be some other capital such as labor or a critical supplier relationship.
- **Strategic goals and resiliency:** Goals define how much the enterprise wants to progress along some set of key system conditions. Resiliency conditions are precautionary reserves related to system feedback expectations and/or critical capital stocks and flows. Reserves or buffers bring security and confidence to business leaders as they make sustainability-aligned, purposeful, strategic choices about risks and opportunities among diverse paths ahead.
- **Boundaries, interconnections:** What internal **(SW)** systems (e.g., procurement, manufacturing) and progressively broader external **(OT)** system developments (e.g., technology innovations, political risks, climate change, economic growth), feedback loops, and other relevant nexuses that the enterprise's operations, products, and/or services impact broader systems and/or the broader systems may impact the enterprise.
- **Mental models:** Enterprise system behavior expectations and rules, organizing frameworks, and business models. Mental models and archetypes of connected and broader global systems should also be examined as appropriate for the strategic purpose.
- **Networks and collaborations:** How might the enterprise system and its strategy be different if it were able to acquire, merge, or develop strategic partnerships and collaborate with other stakeholders? What might be gained through sharing perspectives, resources, information, and insights to collectively travel farther, more successfully and resiliently to pursue common purposes together?

With hope and a clear strategic purpose, complex systems become comfortable (we can never actually manage a complex system). We next present a brief overview of the state of the sustainability movement and the collective challenges enterprises face as they formulate their sustainability-aligned strategy to resiliently progress them towards their thriving future.

The current state of the sustainability movement

As Andrew Winston pointed out in the quote which opened this chapter, we live in a fundamentally changed (or in our view changing and evolving) world. We need new and better strategies to guide us and the systems that we depend upon. It is helpful, but sobering, to reflect briefly on the broader context of our global governance, economic, and enterprise systems. What are the system levers driving the movement? What is the current state of wellbeing of people? The wellbeing of all people everywhere matters and is the ultimate ends of the movement and for the businesses enabling it. Business systems convert limited natural capital ultimate means to higher states creating unlimited shared value at both the intermediary and ultimate end states. From these honest holistic systems perspectives, we get a better understanding of the magnitude of challenges and leverage points for the amount of change truly needed to accelerate sustainability movement, accomplish goals, and enhance wellbeing for all.

The movement from a macro-level perspective is stuck. No clear collective purpose, no strategy, no chance of getting unstuck and safely resiliently functioning without collaborative engagement by people everywhere to do what they can to effect change. We believe that sustainability or its alternative, more inviting visions of flourishing or thriving, is our best compass to guide the purpose and direction of the changes ahead. It is the best lens through which to view our current state of reality and guide us to better future states of progress. Sustainability-aligned strategies to guide us are needed at all system levels, but especially so for businesses. Business has been identified as the most effective system lever through which progress towards our environmental, personal, and societal goals can be attained.

We set the journey's stage with a few brief statistics and observations about the current reality of the sustainability movement generally. We add some perspectives on the human and enterprise "travelers" whose systems interconnect and interdependently are progressing along the journey together.

Context: negative global outlook, business needs to do good

We provide insights on the sustainability movement's current state from the lenses of business and government. We first use the World Economic Forum's *2018 Global Risks Report* to provide business perspectives. We use the World Bank's *Global Economic Prospects Report* for 2017 to depict a government perspective and we close with comments from a more focused green business and environmental impacts perspective from the GreenBiz *2018 State of Green Business* report.

The World Economic Forum: business sees fractures and failures in global systems

The *2018 Global Risks Report* presents a perception survey of nearly 1,000 experts and decision-makers about the likelihood and impact of 30 global risks over a 10-year horizon. Over this medium-term period, environmental and cyber risks predominate. While acknowledging recent encouraging global growth, they express caution noting: "Any breathing space this offers to leaders should not be squandered: the urgency of facing up to systemic challenges has intensified over the past year amid proliferating signs of uncertainty, instability and fragility" (World Economic Forum, 2018, p. 5).

Klaus Schwab, Executive Chairman of the World Economic Forum, summed up the *2018 Global Risks Report*[4] by saying:

> The World Economic Forum presents the latest Global Risks Report at a transformational time for the world … Globally, people are enjoying the highest standards of living in human history. And yet acceleration and interconnectedness in every field of human activity are pushing the absorptive capacities of institutions, communities and individuals to their limits. This is putting future human development at risk. In addition to dealing with a multitude of discrete local problems, at a global level humanity faces a growing number of systemic challenges, including fractures and failures affecting the environmental, economic, technological and institutional systems on which our future rests.

The World Bank: the economy and government overreliant on fragile growth

A few statements from the World Bank's *Outlook Report* for 2017 present a slight, but fragile upturn in economic growth prospects. That said, governments of diverse forms, locations, and means are collectively struggling to achieve their purposes for their citizens. Acknowledging many alternative government systems, we offer the US constitution's language as one helpful example expressing the purpose of a government system. The purpose of the Federal Government of the United States of America, as found in the Preamble of the Constitution, is to "establish Justice, insure domestic Tranquility, provide for the common defense, promote the general Welfare, and secure the Blessings of Liberty to ourselves and our posterity." Let those words sink in as we consider our reality today. It appears that government leaders and politicians responsible for leading their diverse governing enterprises are not able or willing to effect real policy reforms and invest the resources needed to slow and redirect negative sustainability movement trends.

Economic growth is viewed as the solution to world problems. It is the mental model governments rely upon to produce the financial capital they need (taxes) to invest for sustainable progress. Through this mindset, financial capital is governments' limiting resource for moving sustainability ahead. Not only the World Bank, but the World Economic Forum, the United Nations, and most governments share this growth-dependent mindset. From that perspective the feedback signals anticipate weak global trade growth. Cascading systems risks occur as financial conditions become volatile. The World Bank also added that rapid reassessment of risk could also be triggered by a spike in geopolitical tensions, bouts of volatility in commodity markets, or financial stress in major emerging market economies (World Bank, 2017). Paradoxically, if the economy grows without disconnecting limited natural capital stocks and flows, successful economic growth accelerates planetary ecosystem deterioration!

Business progress is mixed but hopeful

With government stalled, our hopes shift to the business community to lead the movement. A report by Globescan/SustainAbility (2012, p. 5) pointed to a deep systemic role for business, stating,

> the private sector has both the capability and reason to play a catalytic leadership role where collective action and change to underlying system conditions are required. This will demand that businesses improve and evolve their own strategies and practices, as well as stimulate and support the shifts in policy, capital markets and consumption that will be required to achieve sustainable development.

The GreenBiz Group[5] has been tracking the sustainability movement and reporting on "how" and "what" the private sector is doing for over a decade now. It collaborated with TruCost[6] to produce the *2018 State of Green Business* report. Joel Makower, GreenBiz, Group Chairman summarized its assessment, noting:

> To be sure, this is no rose-colored view of planetary problems. When it comes to transforming products, value chains and entire economies to align with the environmental and social goals of sustainability, the dynamics are significant. They include a lack of US political leadership but the rise of subnational actors, such as cities and companies; the short-termism of investors but the rising awareness of the relationship between climate and risk; the many difficulties of transforming supply chains but the growing number of companies investing in their suppliers'

well-being. Simply put: This is hard work, and progress at times can be elusive. But we are seeing such obstacles being overcome in company after company, across sectors and borders.

(Makower, 2018)

Human perspectives: heroes; unemployed; displaced

Be the change you want to see in the world.

(Mahatma Gandhi)

When viewing society from a global systems perspective, people are the human capital that drives the economic and enterprise systems. They also are residents and citizens within nations, states, cities, and communities. People evolved government, economic, and enterprise systems to serve their needs. If enough people's needs are not being met by those systems, the systems will change. Today's question is not, "Are people's needs being met?" but "When will these failing systems be changed and evolve?"

The quest for the sustainability movement is to move ALL people to have thriving lives. We take a moment to acknowledge both people who are leading others in this journey and others who are insufficient and deserve help to progress and thrive.

Heroes

Positive Mavericks, a term coined by Preventable Surprises Founding CEO Raj Thamotheram (Baue, 2017 p. 18), along with Ray Anderson's radical industrialists are heroes in this story. They provide us with hope, inspiration, and much appreciated leadership as we get engaged through our own life's work. We dedicated this book to a few of these heroes who have left us, but whose shoulders we stand upon now.

Heroes tend to be heroes because of their deeds rather than what they say. Countless ordinary people are already quietly setting the example of sustainable living. They work hard and lead within their enterprises and communities. Sustainable Jersey, a nonprofit that works with communities and schools throughout New Jersey showcases just such people. Heroes who are humbly serving their communities.[7]

Unemployed and impoverished

Unemployed and underemployed people inhibit human capital productivity and wellbeing. The International Labor Office shared these statistics and trends in their 2016 outlook report (ILO, 2016). They also noted that the global economy was weakening and as a consequence, global unemployment increased to over 197.1 million, 1 million more than in the previous year and over 27 million higher than pre-crisis levels. They also noted that the increase in jobseekers in 2015 occurred mainly in emerging and developing countries.

Some of our travelers are living in extreme or moderate poverty and have insufficient financial means to enjoy sufficient or secure lives. Thinking about the previous employment statistics, an estimated 327 million who are counted as employed are still living in extreme poverty (those living on less than US$1.90 a day in Purchasing Power Parity terms) and 967 million live in moderate or near poverty (between US$1.90 and US$5 a day in PPP terms) (ILO, 2016).

Refugees, displaced, and incarcerated

According to the United Nations High Commissioner for Refugees, an unprecedented 65.6 million people around the world have been forced from their homes. Among them are nearly 22.5 million refugees, over half of whom are under the age of 18. There are also 10 million stateless people who have been denied a nationality and access to basic rights such as education or healthcare (United Nations High Commissioner for Refugees, 2017).

By the end of 2016 there were 40.3 million people living in internal displacement as a result of conflict and violence in the world. This number has nearly doubled since 2000 and has increased sharply over the last five years (IDMC, 2017).

There were 31.1 million new internal displacements by conflict, violence, and disasters in 2016. Of these, 6.9 million were displacements by conflict and violence, and 24.2 million were caused by weather-related disasters (IDMC, 2017).

According to the World Prison Population List (WPPL), more than 10.35 million people are held in penal institutions throughout the world. Including the numbers reported to be held in detention centers in China and in prison camps in North Korea, the total may well be in excess of 11 million (Walmsley, 2016).

There are more than 2.2 million prisoners in the United States of America, more than 1.65 million in China (plus an unknown number in pre-trial detention or "administrative detention"), and 640,000 in the Russian Federation (Walmsley, 2016).

Enterprise perspectives: the big; the small; the emergent

> To grow a business, you need to spot a gap within a given market, fill it and establish ownership of the space.
>
> (Allie Webb)

The quest for the sustainability movement is to move ALL enterprises to re-imagining their purposes and produce ultimate ends of human wellbeing and thriving.

The big

The GreenBiz report showcased several leading corporations and mixed progress within the top 1,500 publicly traded companies in the world. That said, there are approximately 630,000 companies traded publicly throughout the world.

The total number of employees among all Fortune 500 companies is estimated to be 26,405,144 and the average number of employees per firm is 52,810.[8]

The small and independent

Small businesses in the US (enterprises with 500 employees or fewer) are representative of the relative contribution these enterprises have in regional economies around the world. In the US, they make up 99.7% of US employer firms, 64% of net new private-sector jobs, and 49.2% of private-sector employment.[9]

There are about 28 million small businesses in the US. Of these over 22 million are self-employed with no additional payroll or employees (these are called non-employers) (United States Census Bureau, 2011).

Over 50% of the US working population (120 million individuals) works in a small business (US Census Bureau, 2011).

Small businesses have generated over 65% of the net new jobs since 1995.

The number of non-employer firms are rapidly increasing in the emerging gig economy. The 22 million self-employed in the US in 2011 was a 2% rise from the prior year. Of those 19.4 million non-employer businesses were sole proprietorships, 1.6 million were partnerships, and 1.4 million were corporations (Small Business Administration Office of Advocacy, 2012).

The majority of employees globally work for small and medium-sized businesses, and 91% of employees believe it's important to work in a mentally healthy workplace. Some 75% of employees believe employers need to provide the support to achieve this (Marcos, 2015).

The emergent

The US averaged between 500,000 and 600,000 new companies every year from the late 1970s to the mid-2000s. That trend has adjusted due to the impacts of big box stores on mom and pop ones, more regulation, and more adaptation by large companies to support entrepreneurial projects and cultures internally. Startup companies around the world are important contributors to local economies and will benefit from aligning with sustainability and applying smart strategies from their inception.

Sustainability-aligned strategy chasms and bridges

> I can't change the direction of the wind, but I can adjust my sails to always reach my destination.
>
> (Jimmy Dean)

Chapter 9 presents a force field diagram that includes our suggested top 10 forces driving change (tailwinds) and top 10 restraining forces impeding change (headwinds). All of these topics represent knowable opportunities to proactively formulate or adapt enterprise strategies and systems. Depending upon the current direction of an enterprise, a tailwind for one enterprise may be a headwind for another. Following the strategic formulation process in Figure 3.1, each force could manifest within an internal system Strength or Weakness or through an external system Opportunity or Threat. Strategies are the navigation tool that position these and reveals choices of when to change course and tack. Large, less maneuverable sailboats, like large companies may move slower and ignore small gusts. Their momentum tends to require longer-term thinking and less volatile speed and/or rudder adjustments. They are resilient and can travel far, withstand high seas, and heavy winds. Small boats are more agile and changing speeds and/or direction can be done quickly. That said, even minor waves or wind gusts represent risks of capsizing. There are overwhelming numbers of people and enterprises whose sails are luffing and are stuck in irons. With this reality, we saw the need to build an inclusive progressive strategy bridge framework and use hope to fill their sails with wind.

A bridge framework and systemically formulating chasm crossing stories

Borrowing from gamification best practices, we introduce our sustainability-aligned strategy bridge framework as an "epochal" story of the time of man on Earth. Some storytellers, like Ray Anderson, used climbing a mountain or "mount sustainability" as their metaphor for sharing their vision and strategy for the journey (Anderson & White, 2011). We use chasms and building bridges as our metaphor. Figure 3.2 depicts four progressive bridges and four treacherous chasms that characterize generic, but customizable and scalable segment quests and a holistic story arc for the sustainability movement's journey.

The sustainability-aligned strategy bridge framework helps enterprises re-imagine themselves from a systems perspective. Good sustainability-aligned strategies include clearer vision, appropriate goals, and reveal resilient purposeful execution paths. The framework inclusively meets every unique enterprise where they are now (their "as is" state) and guides them toward

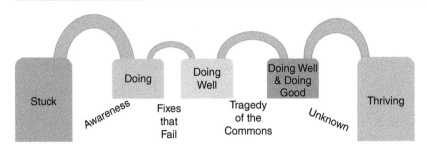

Figure 3.2 Sustainability-aligned strategy chasms and bridges
Source: William G. Russell, with permission.

their desired destination (their "to be" state). Using this framework, a company creates one integrated strategy that every enterprise function and all of its employees and stakeholders can use as their compass. The selected paths are resilient and informed by sustainability insights and opportunities. The framework also helps identify blind spots and avoid knowable risks in both the short and long term. The bridges in our story are being built as they are being crossed.

Each segment has heroes leading self-organizing communities of travelers who opt in and engage. Each treacherous chasm-crossing mission seems daunting at first, but there are tools that reveal insights and generate innovative ideas on how to proceed. Case studies are provided that assure you that you are not traveling alone and that others have already been where you are going. Prepare yourself to be moved into action creating progressive systems-based sustainability-aligned segments or holistic smart strategies. Set your goals and chart a path to cross chasms and reach new levels of human and enterprise wellbeing.

Learning maps and systematic bridge story development

Transitioning to Green,[10] the sustainability strategy and training consultancy that formed to advance and scale insights from the original *Fieldbook*, developed learning map tools for building sustainability awareness and systematically creating innovative bridge-crossing stories. These bridge stories get generated in a three-stage process. The general process is fueled by using open-ended questions throughout to promote broader discussion. Participants are also reminded to be mindful of their own listening behaviors and biases. Other good process behavior practices include soliciting input from all the voices in the room and encouragement to be open to new and different ideas and inputs from any and all participants. There is no one single fix to complex problems or processes. Allow solutions to emerge rather than endorsing ideas from the most powerful or vocal stances presented.

- The first stage is to use a structured conversation to get as complete an understanding of a problem including what caused it and what the consequences really are. We review the current "as is" state by reviewing three Elements:
  - Drivers: i.e., mental model flaws that created problems or traps. Lack of awareness/consciousness; thinking win-lose vs. both/and; and too focused on the single bottom line;
  - Systems and measurements: i.e., GDP/GNP as signals for a good economy; revenue and sales growth of low margin or even loss leading products (see Chapter 6); and
  - Outcomes: Waste of any and all capital resources (see Bridge 2, Doing Well for more about this); military conflicts; poverty and inequity; over-consumption; water pollution; unemployment.
- The second stage is to create a vision for what is possible in a future "greener" state for the specific stage of progress towards some longer-term future-fit and thriving state of performance. The vision is informed by reviews of best practices and purpose-specific goals of competitors within your industry as well as best in class performers across industries.
- The third stage is to utilize story-aiding prompts and create a bridge story of how you propose to "build a bridge" to move from your current "Gray" state to your envisioned "Greener" state. Specific attention is given to exploring how the enterprise might benefit through adopting some known "green" best practices. It also explores opportunities for collaboration that reduce risks and scale impacts of each path identified.

As we move through these stages, a strategy team can acknowledge what is gray (Threats) about our world and honor green efforts that our society and companies are doing, as a work-in-progress. They share several bridge story scenarios while systematically re-imagining their enterprise as it moves from wherever it is to the next progressive state of sustainable performance.

Watch out for chasms

At this time we wish to briefly alert you to a few persistent and tricky chasms that if not seen early enough can slow and even reverse expected progress or in some cases cause the enterprise to go over its resilient guardrails and fall into the chasm and go out of business completely. These are pitfalls, traps, or blind spots that every enterprise runs into when they are busy and don't take the time to reflect fully while re-imagining the company. Chasms can be identified and resiliently navigated around as part of a good strategy. Chasm risks can arise at any moment in time. When a disruptive chasm is identified, agile adjustments or new or next strategies must be adapted. Blindly following an existing strategy knowing the "bridge is out" just ahead is foolish.

The sustainability-aligned strategy bridges are introduced in the next section and elaborated on to include more specifics about the system constructs, tools, and case examples for each strategy segment (Bridge) proposed.

CHASM 1: AWARENESS

The first chasm that keeps enterprises stuck is that they don't know what they don't know. Warning signs include being stuck using old mindsets, complacency, arrogance, insularity, and a general lack of curiosity. They fail to see a truth as a result of groupthink, blind spots, and related biases.

CHASM 2: UNINTENDED CONSEQUENCES (ALSO KNOWN AS FIXES THAT FAIL)

Ignoring the balancing forces of a paradox and looking for "silver bullets" and overly simplistic solutions to intractable problems, rather than a willingness to deal with complexity and whole systems. For example, when ethanol was first introduced many people failed to take into account the fact that it would lead to reduced land and crops for food production.

CHASM 3: TRAGEDY OF THE COMMONS

When Garrett Hardin first proposed this concept in 1968, he demonstrated the idea that a small increase in use of a shared resource (e.g., one extra cow grazing on the grass) provides a great benefit to an individual, while the cost of that additional use (decreased grass supply) is shared by all. Therefore, each user has an incentive to use (and exploit) the resource to the greatest of his or her ability. Ultimately there is a decrease in yield for both the group and the individual.

This has many applications today as we experience shared and finite resources in oil, water, and other natural resources. This chasm also has many social and economic applications that emerge through our mental models and feedback signals about what a just, fair, and caring society chooses to provide. Relevant topics from today include: healthcare, minimum wage, immigration practices, access to education and the arts, and freedoms of many forms.

The situation is made worse by what is known as the Lauderdale Paradox, first enunciated by the seventh Earl of Lauderdale in 1804. He observed that rising private riches were associated with declining public wealth, including a shrinking commons. In modern terms, as the riches of a minority elite grow, their ability to deprive the majority of the commons is strengthened (Standing, n.d.).

CHASM 4: THE UNKNOWN

Nothing keeps us stuck more than our deep-seated collective fear of the unknown. As we move from Doing Well and Doing Good today to Thriving, we don't know how we are going to do it. No company is Thriving now. Also complex systems behaviors with long-delayed feedback signals will not be known until the unknown chasm is too close to be avoided. Two hopeful comments are offered now to preemptively sensitize you and avoid common barriers of getting overwhelmed, depressed, or fearful of an unknown future. First, know there are hundreds of heroes and leading enterprises already hard at work exploring the unknown paths ahead. Second, we actually don't need to know and can't even know everything anyway. Current trends are not inevitable indicators of our future outcomes. We have the ability to create the future we choose.

Sustainability-aligned bridges

As we built out the progressive bridge strategy, it evolved to a more highly iterative and integrated, smart strategy concept blending sustainability-aligned and traditional core strategy segments within evolving enterprises and across diverse client groups. The smart bridge is an adaptable framework that can scale to be as simple or complex as it needs to be. An enterprise just starting its first steps is free, so long as it incorporates a few core behavior principles, to focus its strategy on a near-term purpose. As externalities are assessed and common resiliency boundaries or threshold risk bands become known, corporations which are already resilient will need to begin responsibly adapting their behaviors and as needed help smaller suppliers, customers, and communities. Those less resilient stakeholders are also expected to do their parts and get their own resiliency levels up in order to progress themselves. The final bridge to Thriving will need pioneer companies like Interface Carpet has been already. Those companies large or small that understand the consequences of operating beyond safe thresholds will choose to take risks that lead the way and test unknown approaches to arrive at our ultimate destination of Thriving.

The four bridge segments are briefly introduced here and then elaborated on in the progressive chapter sections that follow. Those sections include the key system construct elements, frameworks and tools, and case examples for each progressive bridge segment.

Doing

Doing is our phrase for enterprises that are just starting up or have been operating insufficiently. We present tools to help them get unstuck. Some are stuck due to external threats and poor, difficult circumstances which they had little control over. Others are stuck or even in motion, but don't have a sense of direction. Sustainability awareness and best practices for these enterprises serve to offer hope and a direction that allows them to confidently take their first steps on this first progressive bridge and get started on their sustainability journey.

Doing Well

Doing Well is our phrase for companies that are already profitable, but do not yet have sufficient financial or some other strategically vital stock inventory to safely take risks and invest money and other resources towards worthy, but long-term sustainability-aligned risk mitigation or growth opportunities. Using tools like Bob Willard's ROI Workbook, introduced in more detail in the Doing Well section ahead, enterprises can identify sustainability-aligned efficiencies to reduce material and energy wastes, increase employee productivity, and innovate. Most companies can improve profits substantially while also reducing risks to cashflow without needing to make big investments or take on debt. Such obvious self-serving strategies also have synergistic positive benefits to society in the form of reduced environmental and social footprints. These opportunities abound and are not being pursued.

It is also important to note that companies traveling on this bridge are only doing what they should have been doing all along, or catching up to work they have ignored. These enterprises should only be granted a limited time before other stakeholders would force them to progress further or fold.

Doing Well and Doing Good

Doing Well and Doing Good is an enhanced version of the former strategy of Doing Well by Doing Good. That original strategy was grounded in a purpose of gaining a competitive advantage. Using that mode to guide the strategy was therefore no different than the companies that use sustainability-alignment to do well. It just so happens that their best opportunity to do well was aligned with a need in a market that served the customer and a broader community.

Doing Well and Doing Good is more evolved. Doing Well and Doing Good are not separate or separable efforts over the long term. Enterprises choosing this strategic purpose must still compete in the global economy. At the center of their efforts is the premise of service. Service to a truth larger than self, a demand more pressing even than its financial performance. While its leaders are still accountable to owners and shareholders, they also recognize and accept a responsibility to use their wealth and strength to work, in the context of a for-profit business, for the common good. Business cannot survive in a society or environment that fails.

Thriving

Thriving is the phrase we chose to depict those companies that are accomplishing their purpose for their customers while having no net decline in natural capital, improving the wellbeing of their employees and the communities within which they operate and their products are used. This bridge completes the holistic arc of our journey. Enterprises achieving this level of performance are Thriving within their system's context responsibility. For more on context sustainability goals see Chapter 6.

A TOOLBOX FOR SUSTAINABILITY-ALIGNED BRIDGE STRATEGY FORMULATION

Every bridge strategy and their holistic interconnected progressive or smart versions all begin by applying sustainability-aligned SWOT assessments. These are done for various perspectives and system boundaries. Similarly the tools presented within any specific bridge category are also helpful to creating the strategies within the other bridge sections. We have placed a few highly effective tool introductions within the bridge section that seemed to most fit its innovations and strategic insights. Collectively these are a powerful toolbox for sustainability-aligned strategy formulation.

Doing: starting the journey, stepping onto the bridge

The purpose of a business is to create a customer.

(Peter Drucker)

We are at a unique moment in history, where we can and must create a new future for enterprises—indeed for all humanity—to thrive into the future and for perpetuity. It starts with a commitment to work together to accelerate the journey from awareness to understanding and, most important, to action. We use the enterprise system constructs presented earlier to outline key perspectives for each of the four sustainability-aligned strategy bridge segments. Each segment can be implemented independently, if appropriate. This is particularly true for the millions of startup, small and independent enterprises with little or no resiliency guardrails to buffer them from falling into one of many chasms these enterprises face every day. They can be fueled by hope that comes from increased sustainability awareness (Bridge 1's primary chasm impeding force) and confidence gleaned from the cases and tools ahead to get started on their journeys.

Sustainability-aligned strategic system perspectives to get started

The following are selected enterprise system construct items most relevant for enterprises formulating sustainability-aligned strategies for **Bridge 1, Doing**:

- **The purpose for Doing:** Enterprises in this stage likely don't have a defined purpose or a good strategy for pursuing it. Now is the time to reflect and ask: Why are we doing this business? How might our products and services contribute to the wellbeing of our customers? Another reality-grounding question vitally relevant to enterprises on this bridge is: Which strategic path most safely progresses the enterprise to break even financially?
- **Take inventory of multi-capital stocks and most vital threshold flows:** For most businesses on the Doing strategy bridge, financial capital including personal assets and friends and family investments is the most limited stock. Do also inventory other multi-capital assets relevant to your business and its strategy.
- **Time horizons:** Resilient thresholds for independent non-employment and startup companies are expected to have time horizons of two years or less.
- **Strategic goals and resiliency:** The goal for companies either just starting up or operating independently on the margin of being insufficient is to get to break even from a cash flow perspective. It must do so using a sustainability-aligned respect for how it treats its employees, suppliers, and community. Fair compensation and policies that support gender equality, religious freedoms, and health and wellness are normal cultural expectations. Once profitable, these enterprises can move to the second bridge and begin building up financial and other stocks. Just like a rainy day buffer in a personal bank account, this class of traveler must operate frugally and build capital stocks.
- **Boundaries, interconnections:** The primary boundary of interest for Bridge 1 travelers is between the enterprise and the customers it is serving. Assuring its product or service enhances value to the customer's wellbeing in a differentiated way. Transparent, respectful, and collaborative relationships with employees, investors, and suppliers are all important and can buy some flexibility during this volatile period.
- **Mental models:** Startups and independents must be sensitive to the full costs and impacts of the business model. Strategies that are dependent upon government subsidies or not paying equal and fair wages to employees are not sustainably-aligned. When considering partnerships, beware of exploitative schemes that fail to account for the full boundary and capital elements that the business must operate within to be viable.

- **Networks and collaborations:** Partnering with other individuals and enterprises within the industry or local community may serve to more efficiently add capital stocks to the enterprise's resources and help reduce personal risk and stress.

Strategic tools for Doing

The two tools picked for enterprises developing sustainability-aligned strategies for Doing are Crossing the Chasm, and the Lean Business Model Canvas. These are both highly successful traditional strategy formulation tools that emphasize the importance of understanding the customer's needs, examining business models, and focusing on critical resources (stocks) that create the enterprise's value proposition. These tools help enterprises that are stuck to review and re-imagine their enterprise.

Crossing the chasm

Geoffrey Moore used *Crossing the Chasm* with an urgent D-Day battle strategic analogy (Moore, 1999). Early-stage technology companies are alerted to a chasm of failing to anticipate the change in customer expectations as the company attempts to navigate from a sufficient state working with early adopter customers to a mainstream state working with pragmatic and conservative customers. Figure 3.3 provides a typical chasm-crossing journey within

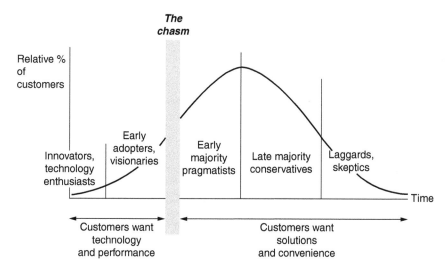

Figure 3.3 Crossing the Chasm Strategy Framework

Source: Geoffrey A. Moore, *Crossing the Chasm*, 3rd edition. New York: Harper Business. Copyright © 1991, 1999, 2002, 2014, Geoffrey A. Moore. Used with permission.

the technology industry. His insights and strategic recommendations are highly appropriate for any Bridge 1 company. The approach suggests that the enterprise proactively think further ahead into the future and from a broader more holistic system perspective of competitors, partners, and customers. This strategic process works for all of our chasm-crossing challenges as well. Sustainability-alignment application simply includes more diverse, but mostly knowable chasms. The right blend of capital(s) investing and collaboration with strategic partners and stakeholders will reveal the best path ahead.

Lean Business Model Canvas

Lean Canvas also prioritizes getting your customer-problem-solution foundation in order first. It is ideal for guiding strategy formulation discussions of early stage innovation projects and startups. Figure 3.4 depicts the Lean Business Model Canvas Framework (LBMC). It helps strategy developers answer critical questions. Who are your target customers? What problem are you solving? How does this solution create value? The solution box becomes critical to aligning the strategy with the enterprise stated purpose and value(s). At this stage the discussions are not fixed, but a tool for guiding inclusive participation from other employees to comment and provide their inputs.

Lean Business Model Canvas   **Model Name:**

Problem	Solution	Unique Value Proposition	Unfair Advantage	Customer Segments
Top 3 problems	Top 3 features	Single, clear, compelling message that states why are you are different and worth buying	Can't be easily copied or bought	Target customers
	Key Metrics Key activities you measure		**Channels** Paths to customers	

Cost Structure	Revenue Streams
Customer acquisition costs Distribution costs Hosting People, etc	Revenue model Lifetime value Revenue Gross margin

Figure 3.4 The Lean Business Model Canvas Framework
Source: www.heflo.com, Creative Commons license.

Startup and stuck enterprises find their purpose and begin doing

The following two case stories represent the transformative opportunity and impact that hope ignites. Each case included education and training to raise awareness and enhance employee skills. Both had supportive sponsors and investors to get them started. Both developed their own tools for scaling their progress and impacts. Lastly, both are being performed as collaborations and building up networks to further scale their learning and successes. Neither are subsidized models, but are frugal ones that work within reasonable startup capital thresholds while moving the enterprise from subsisting or startup to Doing Well and Doing Good. These enterprises have all discovered their purpose and with hope are working hard converting strategy into actions and deeds.

Timberland and Small Farmers in Haiti

Hugh Locke, President and Co-Founder of the Smallholder Farmers Alliance in Haiti and President and Founder of Impact Farming, is a hero to Bridge 1 travelers. He has helped thousands of smallholder farmers in Haiti to finance their way out of extreme poverty. The innovation is scalable and has the potential to be applied with and transform millions more of the world's 500 million subsistence farmers (impacting nearly a third of all people on the planet) into impact farmers. This social business used income from carbon credits or "tree currency" as a business model breakthrough which led to over 6.5 million trees being planted to date. Timberland was initially a strategic investor and corporate sponsor of the initiative (a classic Bridge 3 strategy). Now Timberland is becoming a customer and purchasing its organic cotton raw material inputs from these farmers. That relationship uses an innovative supply chain business model based on tree currency. It also connects smallholders to the global economy and has potential for application throughout the developing world.[11]

Smallholder farmers are enrolled into the Smallholder Farmers Alliance (social capital), trained in farming best practices (human capital), provided with a few critical tools (built capital), and seeds (natural capital) to get started. In just a few years they are profitable. The alliance is scaling a self-financed global force to combat climate change, improve food security, and empower women. Hugh's work is the subject of a documentary "Kombit: The Cooperative." View his TED talk and hear him tell his story.[12]

AIM2Flourish: Doing Well and good deeds

AIM2Flourish accelerates the shift to a Business for Good mindset by recognizing the positive impact of today's business leaders, and changing the way tomorrow's leaders are taught. It is showcased within our Doing Bridge because of its Flourish Prize case companies and its impact nurturing of next-generation business leaders and startup enterprises that, like the small farmers in Haiti, move from Doing to Doing Well and Doing Good. This initiative is a collaboration between the Fowler Center for Business as an Agent of World Benefit at Case Western Reserve University, a network of higher education partners, the United Nations Sustainable Development Goals (see Doing Well and Doing Good and Chapter 6), and a global community of Business for Good companies.

Using the SDGs as their lens, students identify an innovation, conduct an "appreciative inquiry" in-person interview with a business leader working to apply the innovation, and then write about what they learned. The AIM2Flourish innovations page contains 1,000+ student-written stories about business innovations that are both profitable for their businesses and making a positive contribution to one or more of the UN SDGs.

The creation of Flourish Prizes is especially noteworthy. These award-winning case companies are each inspirational examples of using sustainability-aligned purpose and frugal strategies that expect profitability while responsibly serving customers and society. Throughout 2016, business students around the world submitted 422 AIM2Flourish Innovation Stories to the AIM2Flourish.com platform. A distinguished jury evaluated 48 semi-finalists and selected the 17 best-of-the-best—one for each SDG.[13]

Doing Well: risk management and business case for building resiliency

> Do what you can, with what you have, where you are.
>
> (Theodore Roosevelt)

Every enterprise operating profitably can focus on advancing to the next phase, using their sustainability-awareness to improve resource efficiencies, engage employees, explore product and business model innovations that reduce their footprints and improve their profits. Smaller footprints and some financial reserves are important or critical to improving the company's resiliency.

Sustainability-aligned strategic system perspectives to Do Well

The following are selected enterprise system construct items most relevant for enterprises formulating sustainability-aligned strategies for **Bridge 2, Doing Well**:

- **The purpose for Doing Well:** Efficiency improvements have interconnected financial and footprint benefits. Also, synergistic opportunities to Do Good, that do not require taking on high risks, should be pursued.

- **Increase efficiency and productivity of vital stocks with most vulnerable threshold flows and/or greatest flow volatility.** Material, water, energy efficiencies reduce footprints and save money. Engage with employees to solicit diverse ideas for efficiencies, risk management, and innovations. These actions in turn will increase margins reinforcing the objectives and extending capital threshold runways.
- **Time horizons:** Profitable enterprises cannot rest or become complacent. The ROI Workbook tools below suggest a 3–5 year time horizon.
- **Strategic goals and resiliency:** At this stage of operations, best practice benchmark efficiencies and practices of both competitors and best in class non-competitors should be reviewed. Drawing from Green to Gold presented in more detail below and related works (see also, Hitchcock & Willard, 2006; Lazlo & Zhexembayeva, 2011), the potential immediate benefits of sustainability-aligned strategies with a purpose to Do Well include:
  - reduced operating expenses;
  - increased employee engagement and productivity;
  - increased revenue/market share (in existing and particularly in new markets);
  - reduced risk (especially to cash flow)/easier financing;
  - increased innovation (in both processes and new products);
  - better recruitment and retention of talent;
  - increased social/reputational capital.
- **Boundaries, interconnections:** Engaging with industry associations, community groups, and sustainability initiatives are helpful while also enhancing core relationships.
- **Mental models:** Companies crossing the chasm of unintended consequences need to be sure they have defined their purpose and problems properly. One unintended consequence of early low hanging fruit successes is complacency. The efficiencies highlighted within this purpose change constantly and can be repeated over and over again for continued benefits. See the Blackstone case below for more on this.
- **Networks and collaborations:** Focus on strategic partnerships that have direct benefits to the core business performance and add to capital stocks and enterprise capacities.

Strategic tools for Doing Well

It appears that many businesses are responding to the call for them to develop sustainability strategies as much because of the "business case" as because of their sense of citizenship. The two tools showcased here are both particularly effective at guiding enterprises to identify their best paths to enhanced profitability and resilience. More tools are included within the Blackstone case details below and additional *Living Fieldbook* supplemental materials.

Green to Gold

Green to Gold is a classic book for sustainability advocates written by two long-time heroes within the sustainability movement, Dan Esty and Andrew Winston (Esty & Winston, 2006). The book's tagline, *How Smart Companies Use Environmental Strategy to Innovate, Create Value, and Build Competitive Advantage*, is also the primary purpose of enterprises traveling on the path from Doing to Doing Well. The book, like our own, has a supplemental website with additional materials and a blog where the authors bring more depth to this class of business strategic opportunities.[14]

Sustainability ROI Workbook[15]

The Sustainability ROI Workbook is a proven simulator tool, informed by real company results, to estimate 3–5 year bottom-line benefits for an enterprise (Willard, 2012). This Excel workbook monetizes all direct and indirect benefits arising from sustainability-related projects and automatically does return on investment (ROI) calculations, based on user input. The model was initially developed by Bob Willard, one of the original leaders for articulating the business case benefits to companies. He is a hero to all companies seeking to cross the chasm of unintended consequences and Do Well. In the true spirit of service and Bob's sense of urgency to enroll as many users of this tool as possible, he selflessly offers the tool as a free, open-source resource. Figure 3.5 provides an overview of the ROI Workbook including key decision-making criteria, and related, quantified business case elements. The tool improves the success rate of sustainability initiatives so that enterprises can increase their resiliency and take risks on next projects that also need to be done.

Sustainability-aligned enterprises Doing Well

The two case examples chosen to guide companies on this seemingly uneventful section of the sustainability movement demonstrate that even this stage is far from business as usual. Done poorly, the unintended consequences and blind spot risks are treacherous and have serious business consequences. We begin by updating our perspective on GE. It had been a poster child for Doing Well, but failed to be alert to more holistic system conditions. That case is followed by the insights shared by Don Anderson, Chief Sustainability Officer of the Blackstone Group. The two companies demonstrate that sustainability-aligned strategies can be complex or simple, but not too simple.

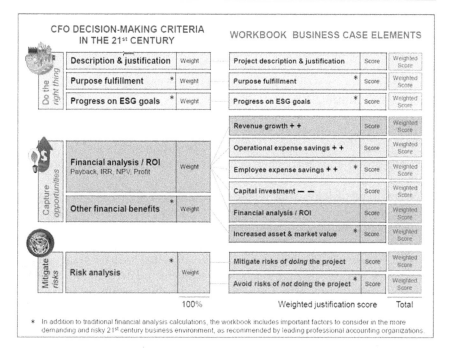

CFO DECISION-MAKING CRITERIA IN THE 21ˢᵗ CENTURY			WORKBOOK BUSINESS CASE ELEMENTS		
Description & justification	Weight		Project description & justification	Score	Weighted Score
Purpose fulfillment *	Weight		Purpose fulfillment *	Score	Weighted Score
Progress on ESG goals *	Weight		Progress on ESG goals *	Score	Weighted Score
			Revenue growth + +	Score	Weighted Score
			Operational expense savings + +	Score	Weighted Score
Financial analysis / ROI	Weight		Employee expense savings + + *	Score	Weighted Score
Payback, IRR, NPV, Profit			Capital investment — —	Score	Weighted Score
Other financial benefits *	Weight		Financial analysis / ROI	Score	Weighted Score
			Increased asset & market value *	Score	Weighted Score
Risk analysis *	Weight		Mitigate risks of *doing* the project	Score	Weighted Score
			Avoid risks of *not doing* the project *	Score	Weighted Score
	100%		Weighted justification score		Total

* In addition to traditional financial analysis calculations, the workbook includes important factors to consider in the more demanding and risky 21ˢᵗ century business environment, as recommended by leading professional accounting organizations.

Figure 3.5 ROI Workbook overview
Source: Bob Willard through free, open-source, unrestricted permission.

GE: complex enterprise missed knowable strategic signals

Our original book contained a case on GE's Ecomagination initiative. While that was a poster child for Doing Well at that time, recent events discussed next are a precaution that Doing Well performance must be achieved from a sustainability-aligned holistic perspective. Environmental efficiencies and certain risks to cash flows were knowable, but missed. GE's structure was complex and investors could not understand how the whole and the sum of the parts added up. Simultaneously, its purpose was not sufficiently clear as its core "industrials" perspective was clouded by its substantial purposes of financial services (GE Capital and Insurance businesses) and most recently Internet of Things data and knowledge-based business models. How do these diverse feedback signals get prioritized and synergized within its strategy? How is that clearly communicated to investors in order that they sufficiently match their risk, impact, and return criteria?

Throughout the past three CEOs one gets the impression that the purpose of GE was to say good things while doing whatever it took to satisfy investors. Under Jack Welch, the company had a "take no prisoners" attitude toward the Environmental Protection Agency. During his tenure, the company was criticized and dubbed an environmental bad actor. It avoided responsibility to clean up pollutants its factories had dumped into the Hudson and Housatonic Rivers.

The baton was passed to Jeff Immelt. GE became a world leader on corporate environmental matters. Executives saw environmental issues as opportunities for competitive advantage and marketplace success. So from a smaller Ecomagination perspective, GE was best in class. The company, however, was more than just Ecomagination. The company was and is complex. Growing profits and satisfying shareholder demands still were the company's main drivers.

With the exit of Jeff Immelt it quickly became clear that the emperor wasn't wearing any clothing. How did the market (and analysts) get it so wrong for so long? What we do know is—in business and investments—complacency kills. Knowable sustainability-related risks were festering.

John Flannery, GE's new CEO, initially appeared to have things under control. He was able to go through every segment and detailed the strengths and weaknesses of each business line and what he thought the immediate future held. It was classic "competitive strategy" type analysis. So how is it possible that only a few months later investors described a recent call with shareholders as looking "Enron" or "Tyco-like" or, "a pleasant fiction" (Gilmartin, 2018)?

The reality of GE was that it was a large complex company. It has an opaque financial structure and traditional financial reporting makes it difficult to analyze and understand for even the most astute investor. As a reliable dividend paying stock, GE did not treat its financial capital responsibly. Instead, it spent $22 billion in open market purchases of its own stock. It paid shareholders over $8 billion. A total cash outflow of over $30 billion. Cash declined by approximately $22 billion year over year. With $6–7 billion in free cash flow from operations, something had to give. That something was a 50% dividend cut (Miller, 2017).

Next came underfunded long-term liabilities from both its insurance and financial businesses. Reinsurance reserves associated with North American Life & Health were failing to adjust, knowing the general population is living longer and consuming more nursing, assisted living, and home health services. That knowable system misread required a minimum of $6.2 billion of additional reserves. Another $15 billion in statutory contribution needs to be funded by GE Capital through 2024. There are still more issues including latent subprime mortgage business liabilities, underfunded employee pensions ($31 billion), and last but not least, billions more tax-related obligations (Gilmartin, 2018). It appears this was the case of "let's make money now, and let someone else clean up the mess later." Well, it's later now and shareholders are left to clean up the mess (Dergunov, 2018). Rather than a sustainability-aligned strategy for the future, this company is strategizing a capital raise or breakup. There is no clearer signal that an enterprise system has failed than when the sum of its parts (SOTP) are worth more than its whole.

Blackstone: complex signals pragmatically focused for Doing Well

To preemptively clarify, the Blackstone Group and BlackRock who you will hear more about in the next section are both financial firms that Do Very Well. The two respective CEOs, Steve Schwarzman of Blackstone and Larry Fink of BlackRock, were partners back in the 1980s who had a breakup. That said, it appears both are playing powerful leadership roles transforming business expectations and behaviors with respect to sustainability. Both companies are demonstrating how sustainability is a transformational lens to guide any company. Blackstone is leading by pushing enterprise travelers across the bridge to Doing Well and BlackRock is pulling enterprise travelers onto the bridge to Doing Well and Doing Good.

Don Anderson is Chief Sustainability Officer of the Blackstone Group. His 12-page report, "Sustainability: Myth, Madness and Magic," is a foundational reference for everyone on Bridge 2, Doing Well (Anderson, 2017). Blackstone invests mostly in private equities and alternative investments. Its private equity business alone has 81 portfolio companies with more than 500,000 employees across a diverse set of industries and geographies. Its real estate business has one of the most expansive residential and commercial footprints in the world. Blackstone's approach to sustainability is, in short, to pursue measurable, action-oriented operational interventions that improve a company's bottom line and its impact on the environment. It first seeks to embed measurable, high return-on-investment (ROI) strategies that drive earnings and improve environmental performance.

Anderson shared three examples of "the magic" that allows it to scale, act nimbly, and start fast out of the gate. And this approach is replicated again and again across its portfolio companies:

- Playbooks—Playbooks codify good practice, including dashboards, scorecards, Portfolio Managers (utilizing Toolkits), and guidance on finding and fixing low- and no-cost operational and maintenance issues.
- Summits—Where employees are brought together to learn how to launch and run a performance improvement program.
- Legislation—Rapid responses to legislation such as the EU Energy Efficiency Directive (EED) give the ability to aggressively comply with this dynamic legislation.

The company consistently sticks to this simple formula. It believes these efforts are not tangential, but mission critical.

Doing Well and Doing Good: resilient enterprises seize opportunities and are called to be in service

Sustainability-alignment of doing well and doing good strategies is not new. Porter and Kramer argued in their award-winning 2006 *Harvard Business Review* article that a strategy of "corporate social integration" (Porter & Kramer, 2006, p. 92), takes two forms: "inside-out linkages" in which company operations impact society, and "outside-in linkages" in which external societal forces impact companies (Porter & Kramer, 2006, p. 84). Looking outside-in requires a company to understand the social-environmental influences in its competitive context that affect its ability to improve productivity and execute strategy. Looking inside-out requires a firm to map the social-environmental impact of its value chain.

In their 2011 *Harvard Business Review* article "Creating Shared Value" Porter and Kramer argue that no business can solve all of society's problems. In short, they assert that the strongest mutual business–societal impact comes from applying corporate strategic thinking to both leverage positive social and environmental benefits and mitigate negative social and environmental impacts in ways that enhance competitive advantage (Porter & Kramer, 2011). This was the standard playbook of many of the world's largest and most resilient companies. That said, it was all being done at their own pace and not necessarily the pace that larger social and environmental systems require.

On Tuesday, January 16, 2018, a game-changing shift took place. The chief executives of the world's largest public companies received a letter from one of the most influential investors in the world. What it said is likely to have caused a firestorm in the corner offices of companies everywhere and a debate over social responsibility that stretches from Wall Street to Washington.

Box 3.1 presents key excerpts from the letter Larry Fink, Chairman and CEO of BlackRock sent out. BlackRock manages more than $6 trillion in investments through 401(k) plans, exchange-traded funds, and mutual funds, making it the largest investor in the world. He opens by acknowledging the economic system's long-manifesting paradox between the wealthy and the poor. He describes it as a paradox of "high returns and high anxiety." He follows with a second observation that the government system is failing to acknowledge known long-term deteriorating conditions and that society is now looking to the business community to help fix them. He has accepted this as a challenge (and opportunity) that he and BlackRock have accepted with the understated promise that their systems will "adapt." His ultimate comments, which are game changing, is that BlackRock now is expecting every one of the companies that it is an owner of (actual or fiduciary) to have a clear strategy. That strategy must include, not only how does the company intend to earn a profit (being profitable is still a requirement), but ALSO, how will the company be serving society? This is a much needed pull to jolt all business leaders into a new reality. This new reality will have enterprises representing trillions of dollars in financial capital, developing their strategies to cross the chasm of the tragedy of the commons and guide them through the paradox of high returns and high anxiety to Do Well and Do Good.

Box 3.1   A sense of purpose: Larry Fink letter to shareholders

Dear CEO,

… We are seeing a paradox of high returns and high anxiety. Since the financial crisis, those with capital have reaped enormous benefits. At the same time, many individuals … don't have the financial capacity, the resources, or the tools to save effectively …

… We also see many governments failing to prepare for the future … As a result, society increasingly is turning to the private sector … Society is demanding that companies, both public and private, serve a social purpose … Without a sense of purpose, no company, either public or private, can achieve its full potential. It will ultimately lose the license to operate from key stakeholders. It will succumb to short-term pressures to distribute earnings …

… BlackRock recognizes and embraces our responsibility to help drive this change. … We have undertaken a concentrated effort to evolve our approach …

Your strategy, your board, and your purpose … companies must be able to describe their strategy for long-term growth.

… The statement of long-term strategy is essential to understanding a company's actions and policies, its preparation for potential challenges, and the context of its shorter-term decisions. Your company's strategy must articulate a path to achieve financial performance. To sustain that performance, however, you must also understand the societal impact of your business as well as the ways that broad structural trends from slow wage growth to rising automation to climate change affect your potential for growth.

These strategy statements are not meant to be set in stone—rather, they should continue to evolve along with the business environment …

… We also will continue to emphasize the importance of a diverse board. Boards with a diverse mix of genders, ethnicities, career experiences, and ways of thinking have, as a result a more diverse and aware mindset. They are less likely to succumb to groupthink or miss new threats to a company's business model. And they are better able to identify opportunities that promote long-term growth …

... a company's ability to manage environmental, social, and governance matters demonstrates the leadership and good governance that is so essential to sustainable growth ...

Today, our clients—who are your company's owners—are asking you to demonstrate the leadership and clarity that will drive not only their own investment returns, but also the prosperity and security of their fellow citizens. We look forward to engaging with you on these issues. Sincerely,
Larry Fink
Chairman and Chief Executive Officer

Source: www.blackrock.com/corporate/en-us/investor-relations/larry-fink-ceo-letter.

Sustainability-aligned strategic system perspectives to Do Well and Do Good

The following are selected enterprise system constructs most relevant for enterprises formulating sustainability-aligned strategies for **Bridge 3, Doing Well and Doing Good**:

- **The purpose for Doing Well and Doing Good:** Companies on this bridge may be smaller companies that had sustainability-aligned strategies from their beginning or larger successful companies that are now expected to demonstrate their social responsibilities. While the startups and small nimble businesses are likely to have clear innovative solutions for their customers as the strategic driver for Doing Good, the role of the larger companies is not as clear-cut. Some good can be accomplished by assisting suppliers to improve their practices. They also may be asked to support communities to advance broader social goals that are further removed from their core business and capacity strengths.
- This is a good time to re-imagine how the enterprise's strengths might be applied more expansively. Ask again from a secure foundation: Why are we doing this business? How might our products and services contribute to the wellbeing of our customers, stakeholders, and society? What investments can I make with my, not unlimited, capital (as Porter says, no company can fix society alone) to continue building resiliency while accelerating progress towards responsible goals?
- **Increase efficiency and productivity of vital stocks with most vulnerable threshold flows and/or greatest flow volatility.** Both the business world and the investment world must be vigilant about the chasm of complacency. They have enjoyed a long period of excess capitals which were not being used with sufficient responsibility. As

Blackstone (Anderson, 2017) suggests, material, water, energy efficiencies will continue to be expected normal business practices for reducing footprints and saving money. Employee and stakeholder engagement are also critical during this all hands on deck strategic shift.

- **Time horizons:** The new rally cry for business, "2 degrees and the SDGs," emerged from the convergence of the United Nations releasing of the Sustainable Development Goals (see following section and throughout this book) and the commitments that emerged out of the Paris climate accord to limit global temperature rise to under 2 degrees Celsius. The SDGs are using 2030 or about 10 years as their horizon for Doing Well and Doing Good. Some thresholds, especially those interdependent with cash flow or the capital markets, may still be shorter. Environmental thresholds may have more time.
- **Strategic goals and resiliency:** Business goals may still look similar to those for Doing Well. Societal goals can now align with the UN SDGs. See Chapter 6 for more on how enterprises are aligning their metrics and goals with the SDGs.
- **Boundaries, interconnections:** The boundaries of Bridge 3 travelers are expanding. Longer-term environmental and societal feedback signals might be knowable. That said, if those signals are too delayed, some different system boundaries may be helpful to determining safe resilient paths ahead.
- **Mental models:** Companies crossing the chasm of the tragedy of the commons must spend sufficient time determining their own historic exploitation of the commons and accept responsibility to end unjust, unequal, and overly privatized solutions.
- **Networks and collaborations:** For Doing Well and Doing Good travelers, collaborative solutions are essential. No company and no government can thrive alone. Large or more resilient enterprises (and governments) can do more good and do more to support other enterprises and communities with fewer means.

Strategic frameworks for Doing Well and Doing Good

The Sustainable Development Goals (SDGs) are proving to be a unifying framework for aligning the efforts of all stakeholders and especially those of government, investors, and the business community. We provide a brief introduction here and more on how to measure progress towards them in Chapter 6. We also include an introduction of the Big Pivot strategy framework. That framework, devised by Andrew Winston, might arguably have been grouped as a tool for Thriving. No matter where you first learn about it, the thought-provoking insights and guidance it reveals are extremely helpful to formulating a sustainability-aligned (resilient) strategy for Doing Well and Doing Good.

The sustainable development goals (SDGs)[16]

Corporate social integration has exploded with the release of the UN Sustainable Development Goals or SDGs. We review them in more detail in Chapter 6, but need to assure all who are formulating strategy about their existence and the enthusiastic reception and integration they are getting within both governments and businesses around the world. The goals and other societally desirable system improvements may represent business risks in some industries, but many governments, corporations, and investors see these interconnected desirable solutions as opportunities for growth.

The SDGs define global sustainable development priorities and aspirations for 2030 and seek to mobilize global efforts around a common set of 17 goals and 169 targets. The SDGs call for worldwide action among governments, business, and civil society to end poverty and create a life of dignity and opportunity for all, within the boundaries of the planet. Figure 3.6 depicts the 17 SDGs.

The SDGs expand the challenges that must be addressed to eliminate poverty and embrace a wide range of interconnected topics across the global economic, social, and environmental systems. The SDGs were developed using an inclusive process with substantive input from all sectors of society and all parts of the world. Through the UN Global Compact alone, more than 1,500 companies provided input and guidance. The goals are universally applicable in developing and developed countries alike. Governments are expected to

Figure 3.6 The Sustainable Development Goals (SDGs)
Source: https://sustainabledevelopment.un.org/sdgs.

translate them into national action plans, policies, and initiatives, reflecting the different realities and capacities their countries possess.

While they primarily target governments, the SDGs are designed to rally a wide range of organizations and sectors to help shape priorities and aspirations for sustainable development efforts around a common framework. Most importantly, the SDGs recognize the key role that business can and must play in achieving them.

The Big Pivot: a strategic tool for resilient enterprises

New economic models and corporate strategies such as the circular economy and the sharing economy (see Chapters 7 and 8) and the Daly Triangle (see Chapter 2) seek to decouple economic growth from material and human resource consumption constraints. Andrew Winston in his book, *The Big Pivot*, provides a strategic framework for a resilient company (Winston, 2014). See Figure 3.7 below. The framework anticipates a hotter (climate change), more resource-constrained or "scarcer" (and more expensive) and better-connected world. He also seeks to build a better economy that properly quantifies investment returns and if appropriate can incorporate externalities or more specifically, the costs and benefits of our common and mostly external ecosystem services. Chapter 6 includes more details on the value of ecosystem services.

Companies will also need to radically collaborate with competitors and other stakeholders, and engage with and lobby for new government policies

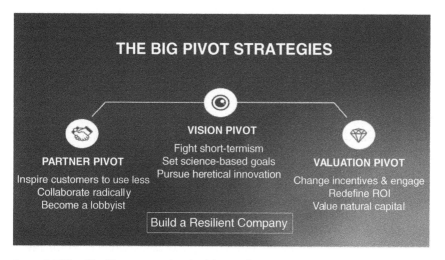

Figure 3.7 The Big Pivot strategies: build a resilient company

Source: Andrew Winston, based on his framework from *The Big Pivot* (Harvard Business Press, 2014). Used with permission.

and rules. These next sustainability-aligned capital market transformation and value creation trends are already being successfully applied. Executives and investors must now reflect on the core purpose of their investments and businesses, change their corporate visions, and implement new, emergent systems and mental models to guide, direct, and accelerate their progress towards the sustainable future they are creating.

Leading companies Doing Well and Doing Good

In September of 2017, *Fortune* Magazine put out an issue with a listing of 56 companies that would "Change the World." The list included Accenture, which is using data to reduce Emergency Room visits; IBM, for helping urban high schools close the STEM skills gap; and Levi Strauss's effort to make life better for some of the 300,000 garment workers who make its jeans. The list also included Unilever which we discuss in the next section. There are many more companies in this segment of the journey and as we recognize a few, it is important that all resilient companies begin to re-imagine themselves in service of both their customers and society.

Unilever: visionary leadership and Doing Well and Doing Good deeds

One of our foundational principles of a sustainable enterprise which was covered in depth in Chapter 1 was the importance of leadership. We follow with sustainably aligned values and then the good strategy. When we look at Unilever from a holistic sustainable enterprise perspective, it is the complete package. Its founder, Lord William Lever, built a business around the sale and distribution of soap that not only proved to be profitable and sustainable, but which also played a pivotal role in transforming the health of Victorian Britain's poor (Mars, 2017). That baton has been handed on many times since then and today it is held by another of our sustainability heroes, Paul Polman.

Mr. Polman's sustainability-aligned strategy for Unilever is known as the Unilever Sustainable Living Plan (USLP). It includes pursuing paths that decouple its growth from environmental footprint and increase its overall social impact. It takes this responsibility across the total value chain, and for all of its brands around the world. The USLP has helped the company grow its revenues and profits as well. When Unilever announced its first-half results for 2017 the news was good. Revenue of about $30 billion was up 5.5%, and earnings per share were up 24% over the previous year (Fry & Chew, 2017). The company is Doing Well. The USLP also has guided it to address external issues such as food security, deforestation, and sanitation. The company is Doing Good.

So what does Paul Polman think are the biggest challenges to companies progressing their sustainability journeys?

Unilever saw the challenge of corporate sustainability as more clearly defining the "tactical" and "systemic" issues. And defining the terminology. On tactics: labeling claims need to be clear about what standards to develop, and disclosure and materiality. Systemic: system change, moving from short-term focus in politics and finance, and changing consumer preferences & habits. These need to change at the systems level; the first step is identifying the problem.

(G&A Institute, 2017)

We could not have said it any better!

Samsung: STEAM Challenge Doing Good through the SDGs

Samsung Electronics America, Inc. sponsored the Global Classroom STEAM Challenge, bringing teachers and students from five countries together to find solutions for sustainable development issues around the globe. The students were challenged to work collaboratively to use STEAM (science, technology, engineering, arts, and math) skills to build out possible solutions that align with the United Nations Sustainable Development Goals (SDGs). Samsung also demonstrated technology aligned with its core business as the teams used a virtual classroom platform developed by IVECA, a nonprofit organization that supports international collaborative learning. Schools and projects included:

- Ross High School's Butler Tech in Hamilton, Ohio and Science Academy of KAIST in Busan, Korea, which are addressing the "No Poverty" and "Zero Hunger" SDGs by developing a website and an NGO to collect and distribute food.
- Downtown College Prep in San Jose, California and Zhenjiang Vocational Technical College in Jiangsu, China, which are addressing the "Clean Energy," "Climate Action," and "Life on Land" SDGs thanks to co-developed devices to reuse recyclables and plastic to cool and filter the air and conserve water.
- Northwest Pennsylvania Collegiate Academy in Erie, Pennsylvania and International School of Tunis from Tunis, Tunisia, which are addressing the "Decent Work and Economic Growth" and "Industry, Innovation and Infrastructure" SDGs through educational programs to create jobs and improve their economy through tourism and workplace equality.
- The Lawrence County High School in Moulton, Alabama and Luiza Formozinho Ribeiro Public School in Sao Paulo, Brazil, which are addressing the "Good Health and Well-Being" SDG through co-developed websites and a mobile app to reduce and better manage waste and litter in their communities.[17,18]

The company continues to develop programs that inspire the next generation of innovators through STEAM skills that prepare students for their future.[19]

BASF: creating chemistry for a sustainable future[20]

With natural capital being our limited, ultimate means, it is comforting to know that one of the leaders advancing their sustainability-aligned strategy is also in the natural capital, chemicals, business. BASF has prominently stated that its purpose is: "We create chemistry for a sustainable future." It is harnessing 114,000 employees to contribute to the success of its customers in nearly all sectors and almost every country in the world. With sales of over $70 billion and a healthy profit, BASF is Doing Well and Doing Good! It has a fully integrated sustainability-aligned strategy. It is purposefully guiding itself on a path that combines economic success with environmental protection and social responsibility. We will share more in Chapter 6 about its work to not only talk about doing this, but to actually rigorously quantify it through its Value-to-Society methodology. "This approach has the potential to transform the way corporations assess their impacts on society and will influence the way they are running their businesses in the future," states Christian Heller, head of BASF's Value-to-Society program. By measuring the impact on the health and well-being of people, the results reflect the "real" value contribution of BASF's business activities: the benefits and costs created for society.

The Value-to-Society approach creates a more comprehensive picture of BASF's impacts along the value chain and demonstrates how chemistry is enabling sustainable growth. Managing and improving its impact is key to keeping and strengthening BASF's license to operate and to fostering its license to grow. BASF provides its approach and learnings to current debates on the monetary value of the economic, environmental, and social impact of business decisions. The company also shares its experience in networks and conferences like Sustainable Brands, GreenBiz, and more, to support transparency, and to contribute to the continued standardization and operationalization of impact valuation.

The Global Opportunity Explorer for SDG innovations[21]

The Global Opportunity Explorer is a joint project of Sustainia, DNV GL, and the UN Global Compact. The tool was created on the conviction that the SDGs offer a myriad of business opportunities with great value to companies, society, and the environment. The tool maps cutting-edge innovations and new markets. Over 300 innovative urban climate solutions from four years of Cities100 reports are showcased. It also helps business leaders, entrepreneurs, and investors connect with new partners, projects, and markets to foster more partnerships for the SDGs and a greener and fairer world by 2030.

Thriving: enlightened leaders accepting risks and embarking to create the new world

The final span along our sustainability-aligned strategy is Bridge 4, Thriving. In this span the company is actually accomplishing its purpose for its customers while having no net decline in natural capital, and simultaneously improving the wellbeing of its employees and the communities within which it operates and its products are used.

The sustainability movement requires collective bold and focused efforts like those performed to transport humans to the moon. In fact, Elon Musk, one of our heroes working to create enterprises that Thrive, is the founder of SpaceX among many other businesses. Companies choosing to compete in this sector of innovation may or may not be earning a sufficient profit to maintain their financial stock wealth. They are doing whatever it takes, failure is not an option for these individuals. The sobering truth is that there are no thriving companies today. That said, there are companies, business leaders, and sustainability professionals already hard at work on the journey.

Sustainability-aligned strategic system perspectives for Thriving

The following are selected enterprise system construct items most relevant for enterprises ready to take bold risks in order to explore the unknown frontiers of the final segment of our story, **Bridge 4, Thriving**:

- **The purpose for Thriving:** Progressing the enterprises' natural capital impact to 0 or positive regenerative performance while sustaining or enhancing the wellbeing of its employees, customers, and community stakeholders today without compromising the ability of future generations to thrive.
- **Increase efficiency and productivity of vital stocks with most vulnerable threshold flows and/or greatest flow volatility.** Material, water, energy efficiencies reduce footprints and save money. Engage with employees to assure diverse ideas for both efficiencies and innovation. These actions in turn will increase margins reinforcing the objectives of building up a financial reserve and extending other capital threshold runways longer out into the future.
- **Time horizons:** 2050 or longer for this mission. But as cases show, financial thresholds are a barrier to long-term strategies and business models with substantial volatility and unknown risks.

- **Strategic goals and resiliency:** Companies seeking to advance to Thriving are assuming large risks, but likely necessary ones as business as usual will not sustain society or their organization in the long term.
- **Boundaries, interconnections:** The boundaries of Bridge 4 travelers are highly fluid. Diverse enterprises can see their visions from vastly different perspectives and it is not knowable if one or another is more or less valid.
- **Mental models:** Companies crossing the chasm of unknowns must get comfortable with failures. It won't be the failures we remember, but how we learn from them and adapt and keep moving.
- **Networks and collaborations:** Sharing unknown risks to advance the needs of society and avoid tragedies of the commons seems like a logical path to pursue. Both science-based goals and future-fit business frameworks presented next are striving to do so.

Frameworks and collaborations advance Thriving strategies

The following are a few initiatives making initial probes across the unknown chasm. These pioneers like the astronauts before them accept the risks with the belief that their service will make a difference.

Enterprises collaborate to integrate science-based goals

The Science Based Targets[22] initiative champions science-based target setting as a powerful way of boosting companies' competitive advantage in the transition to the low-carbon economy. It is a collaboration between the Carbon Disclosure Project (CDP), World Resources Institute (WRI), the World Wide Fund for Nature (WWF), and the United Nations Global Compact (UNGC) and is one of the We Mean Business Coalition commitments. So far over 337 companies have signed on and are pioneering these goals that align with mitigating climate change threshold risks.

Lila Karbassi, Chief, Programmes, United Nations Global Compact, while expressing her enthusiasm for this initiative, noted, "We cannot thrive in a world of poverty, inequality, unrest and environmental stress—all exacerbated by climate change," (Karbassi, n.d.). See Chapter 6 for more on the Science Based Targets goal setting methodologies.

Enterprises commit to thriving and Future-Fit Business Benchmark[23]

Since the 1990s an international group of scientists, led by the founders of The Natural Step, co-created and refined an academically rigorous, systems-based framework designed to guide progress toward a flourishing future. They

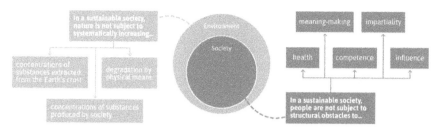

Figure 3.8 Future-Fit Business Benchmark Framework: eight social and environmental system conditions

Source: Future-Fit Business Benchmark, with permission.

collaborate to mobilize business in pursuit of "future-fitness," empowering any enterprise and eventually all market actors to recognize and reward the right kinds of action. This starts with understanding that companies don't exist in a vacuum: business can only thrive if society prospers, which in turn demands that we safeguard Earth's life-support systems. Future-fit companies add value to the holistic system ensuring that business in no way hinders, and ideally contributes to, society's progress toward future-fitness. Figure 3.8 presents the Future-Fit Business Benchmark Framework including eight social and environmental system conditions. More information is available on its website and in the *Living Fieldbook*.

Disruptive companies take risks to Thrive

Some leaders have studied the science and believe humans are plundering the Earth's resources. Other leaders look at possibilities and want to be the first to achieve success and go beyond what is currently possible today. Interface Carpet and Tesla are working hard to have their companies be the ones out in front and demonstrating the behaviors and practices they believe will make the world a better place. They know the risks, but also see that our practices today must change.

Interface Carpet: Mission zero to Thriving

In 1994, Ray Anderson had an epiphany that started his journey to transform Interface Carpet into a sustainable enterprise that thrived. At that time the supportive tools and communities of science-based goals and future-fit business benchmarks did not exist. He chose to be a sustainability movement pioneering astronaut and Interface Carpet was his rocket. He set a seemingly radical strategic goal for the firm: "Mission Zero," a commitment to eliminate any environmental impacts by the year 2020. Shortly before his death, he estimated that the company was more than halfway towards this vision. At that time in 2011, Interface had been on the journey for 17 years.

It had reduced greenhouse gas emissions by 24%, fossil fuel consumption by 60%, waste to landfill by 82%, and water use by 82%, while avoiding over $450 million in costs, increasing sales by 63%, and more than doubling earnings.

The good news is that Interface persevered after Ray retired. He passed the baton to Daniel Hendrix, who served as CEO for nearly 16 years. During that time, Interface adapted its sustainability-aligned strategy as it secured its position as the leading global manufacturer of modular carpet, while continuing its Mission Zero™ quest. Hendrix successfully drove the company's business by focusing on Interface's core carpet tile business and diversifying its market segmentation through expansion into the education, hospitality, healthcare, retail, and institutional spaces. Hendrix will continue to bring his industry expertise and counsel to bear as Chairman of the Board, but has passed the CEO baton to Jay Gould as of March 2017. Gould is primed to lead the organization into its next phase of growth.

Interface is demonstrating what a thriving enterprise aspires to be. It has battled hard to make sustainability-aligned progress every day. It has done so while honoring its ambitious Vision and Mission statements.[24] Its journey, as expected, includes failures which it does not hide, but shares so others might learn. The company accepts that it doesn't know now how it is going to accomplish its ambitious goals, but remains hopeful. While some claimed it will take a miracle, Jim Harzfeld, a former Interface executive who was the head of the first Environmental Task Force in 1994, claimed that it is business as usual: "People don't realize that it took five or six miracles to get this far; Interface has always been in the miracle business" (quoted in Davis, 2014).

We are grateful to Ray and everyone at Interface for being leaders. We wish you long-term success as you continue to work to be the first company that, by its deeds, shows the entire industrial world what sustainability is in all its dimensions: people, process, product, place and profits—by 2020—and in doing so we will become restorative through the power of influence.

Tesla: a thriving vision disrupting the status quo, but chasm warning signs loom

Brave risk-taking pioneer Elon Musk has made it his life's purpose to carry multiple industries simultaneously toward his vision of a thriving future. As we think about the chasm of the unknowns that will need to be tamed, disruptive innovations such as the ones he is pursuing will be needed. We are now at Bridge 4 for Thriving, but the company doing the disrupting is strategically behaving like a bad Bridge 1 Startup. Let's briefly review what we can see that is knowable.

Elon Musk thinks and acts on a larger, more cosmic scale than we're accustomed to from entrepreneurs. He has become a household name synonymous with the future and is not shy about promoting his work. Whether he's working on electric vehicles (Tesla) or sending rockets into space (SpaceX), he has obtained hero worship. He also has accomplished some deeds that keep him in the game while working hard to do industry-disrupting innovations within eight industries simultaneously (CBInsights, 2018).

Tesla by the numbers feels like another GE in the making. The company has a lot of work to do to improve its image of being able to produce positive results. Tesla is now on its fourth vehicle model and still cannot seem to get the manufacturing angle figured out. The result is that institutional investors are leaving. Because Tesla did not follow the Bridge 1 strategy playbook of getting to profitability before taking on the next risk bridge and the next, its ultimate viability will be subject to traditional investor behaviors.

If institutional investors don't continue to buy into the vision, it is game over and Chapter 11 here we come. Learning from GE's history, Tesla also does not seem to have the cash flow yet to stop raising funds. Since the Model 3 was unveiled, the cash reservations for new products have jumped from $1,000 to $5,000, $20,000, $50,000, and even $250,000 for the Roadster Founder's Series. It is pretty obvious we are degrading into a quasi-Ponziesque situation where today's reservation monies are building the previously promised vehicles or paying the bills to keep the lights on. That cannot continue (Bailey, 2018).

There are other chasm warnings that might keep a normal human up at night. Let's look at two. From an inside systems perspective, the history at SolarCity which is now owned by Tesla did not demonstrate sustainability-aligned values. By 2013, it was the leading installer of solar systems in residential buildings in the United States. Its key innovation, though, was less on the technology side and more on the accounting side. SolarCity pioneered the "solar lease" strategy, which allows homeowners to get their roofs installed for free and pay back the installation costs over time. To grow sales, SolarCity used aggressive sales tactics and savings promises that critics say "bent the truth" of the numbers. Customers, once they realized they wouldn't be saving as much as they'd been promised, canceled their installations in droves. That enterprise system hit a cash flow challenge, investors sold, and in February 2016, the stock price dropped by a third. Tesla subsequently bought SolarCity giving that startup a cash flow lifeline. And now Tesla's business purpose shifts to absorb SolarCity. In some ways, it can make sense if, as Geoffrey Moore suggests, Tesla is going to attempt to cross the chasm with a more holistic product that makes it easier for mainstream customers to buy.

From a broader systems perspective, two different visions are colliding. Elon Musk's vision is to disrupt the existing automobile industry. Tesla is a car company working to make the "car company" a thing of the past. Without going further, the alternative reality is that several more established automobile companies are reacting to the same opportunity of electric and autonomous vehicles. Tesla is not the only investment option. Using our sustainability lens, we believe that betting on electric vehicles becoming mass market makes sense. Great Britain and France voted to ban diesel and gasoline auto sales starting in the year 2040. China has made it a point that one in five cars sold in the country should run on some alternative source of fuel by 2025. GM plans to have 20 electric vehicle models on the road by 2023. Volvo has decided to get rid of traditional fuel-powered cars entirely by 2019.

Our sustainability-aligned bridge strategy story ends on an unknown. Elon Musk is hard at work creating the future he wants. He is leading at this moment and like Ray Anderson before him, radical industrialists are needed.

Conclusion: *Be hopeful, Do your best, Thrive*

Welcome to the next phase of the sustainability movement. We thank you for being a leader dedicated to helping your enterprise align its strategy with sustainable, safe, and resilient paths. Relentlessly make progress towards your goals and know all progress advances us closer to achieving the SDGs. You know you are not traveling alone. Students have started through programs like Aim2Flourish. Small farmers in Haiti have joined in. Be hopeful as you take the first steps of your journey.

We have explored together the basics of both systems thinking and how to develop a good strategy. Now is the best time to form a diverse team of enterprise leaders, employees, and trusted stakeholders and begin to re-imagine your vision for the future you want. Use all of the tools in your toolbox, from SWOTs; to the Lean Business Model Canvas and ROI Workbooks; to the Big Pivot and Future-Fit Business Benchmarks. Follow the learning map process and create your enterprise's epochal story. This will take time, hard work, and there will be many learnings (failures) along the way. Don't get down and lose confidence, learn, adjust, and keep striving to do your best.

The sustainability movement is stuck, but there is a clear path forward. Government is failing its citizens and so business is expected to do more. We'll give you a few years to build up your stocks, but not much more. Complacency is a blind spot chasm that pulled down many great companies such as GE. Larry Fink and investors will be watching. Accept and embrace your responsibility to serve others and make a profit while doing so. Use precaution as you navigate across the chasm of the tragedy of the commons as limited stocks are stressed. Get comfortable with the unknown and formulate the smart bridge strategy that puts you on a path to Thrive.

Notes

1 We derive our use of "smart" from its use in the eyewear industry as explained later in the chapter. We also support its use to describe SMART goals which are defined as ones that are specific, measurable, attainable, relevant, and timebound.

2 Students of strategy will recognize this perspective as grounded in neo-Darwinian theories of population, ecology, and industrial ecosystems; see, for example, Aldrich (1979).

3 Students of strategy will recognize this perspective as grounded in classic resource-based theories of the firm; see, for example, Barney (1991) and Prahalad and Hamel (1990).

4 www3.weforum.org/docs/WEF_GRR18_Report.pdf

5 www.greenbiz.com

6 www.trucost.com

7 www.sustainablejersey.com/media-communications/sustainable-jersey-heroes/

8 www.quora.com/How-many-employees-does-each-Fortune-500-company-have

9 www.sba.gov/sites/default/files/FAQ_Sept_2012.pdf

10 www.TransitioningtoGreen.com

11 www.SmallholderFarmersAlliance

12 www.youtube.com/watch?v=Z0dvYFxVkUQ

13 https://weatherhead.case.edu/centers/fowler/aim2flourish/flourish-prizes/

14 www.eco-advantage.com/

15 http://sustainabilityadvantage.com/

16 https://sustainabledevelopment.un.org/sdgs

17 www.csrwire.com/press_releases/40750-Samsung-Challenges-Students-Around-the-World-to-Tackle-Sustainable-Development-Issues-Through-STEAM-Skills

18 A live webcast of the program on the United Nation's YouTube channel is at www.youtube.comunitednations

19 https://news.samsung.com/us/tag/steam/

20 www.basf.com/en/company/sustainability.html

21 http://explorer.sustainia.me/about

22 http://sciencebasedtargets.org/about-the-science-based-targets-initiative/

23 http://futurefitbusiness.org/

24 www.interfaceglobal.com/Company/Mission-Vision.aspx

References

Aldrich, H. (1979). *Organizations and environments*. Englewood Cliffs, NJ: Prentice Hall.

American Management Association (AMA). (2007). *Creating a sustainable future: A global study of current trends and possibilities 2007–2017*. New York: American Management Association.

Anderson, D. (2017, August). Sustainability: Myth, madness, and magic. *Blackstone*. Retrieved January 20, 2018, from www.blackstone.com/docs/default-source/black-papers/sustainability-myth-madness-and-magic.pdf.

Anderson, R. C., & White, R. A. (2011). *Business lessons from a radical industrialist*. New York: St. Martin's Press.

Aronson, D. (1996). Overview of systems thinking. *Thinking.net*. Retrieved December 25, 2017, from www.thinking.net/Systems_Thinking/OverviewSTarticle.pdf.

Bailey, D. (2018, January 16). Fidelity continues to dump Tesla shares. *Seeking Alpha*. Retrieved January 16, 2018, from https://seekingalpha.com/article/4137829-fidelity-continues-dump-tesla-shares?li_source=LI&li_medium=liftigniter-widget#comments.

Barney, J. B. (1991). Company resources and sustained competitive advantage. *Journal of Management, 17*, 99–120.

Baue, B. (2017). *Blueprint 3. Data integration, contextualization & activation for multicapital accounting.* Reporting 3.0.

Carrington, D. (2017, November 28). The Anthropocene epoch: Scientists declare dawn of human-influenced age. *The Guardian.* Retrieved January 10, 2018, from www.theguardian.com/environment/2016/aug/29/declare-anthropocene-epoch-experts-urge-geological-congress-human-impact-earth.

CBInsights. (2018). From energy to transport to healthcare, here are 8 industries being disrupted by Elon Musk and his companies. *CB Insights.* Retrieved January 21, 2018, from www.cbinsights.com/reports/CB-Insights_Elon-Musk-Disruption.pdf.

Chang, L. (2017, February 13). Bye-bye bifocals: These smart specs use liquid lenses to focus at any distance. *Digital Trends.* Retrieved January 14, 2018, from www.digitaltrends.com/cool-tech/smart-glasses-liquid-lenses/.

Davis, M. (2014). 20 years later, Interface looks back on Ray Anderson's legacy. *GreenBiz.* Retrieved May 18, 2018, from www.greenbiz.com/blog/2014/09/03/20-years-later-interface-looks-back-ray-andersons-legacy.

Dergunov, V. (2018, January 22). GE's $21 billion stumble: I was wrong, the bottom is not in, and it could get worse. *Seeking Alpha.* Retrieved January 22, 2018, from https://seekingalpha.com/article/4139004-ges-21-billion-stumble-wrong-bottom-get-worse?auth_param=1ekhcg%3A1d6b930%3A4ce6b2fd993625f3d57e7b16979c8c63& uprof=14&dr=1.

Ehrenfeld, J. R., & Hoffman, A. J. (2013). *Flourishing: A frank conversation about sustainability.* Stanford, CA: Stanford University Press.

Esty, D. C., & Winston, A. S. (2006). *Green to gold: How smart companies use environmental strategy to innovate, create value, and build competitive advantage.* New Haven, CT: Yale University Press.

Fry, E., & Chew, J. (2017, September 7). How *Fortune*'s "change the world" companies turn doing good into good business. *Fortune.* Retrieved January 22, 2018, from http://fortune.com/2017/09/07/change-the-world-money/.

G&A Institute. (2017, December 18). *Harvard Business Review:* Increased focus on corporate sustainability convening CEOs for critical conversations on the theme. Retrieved January 3, 2018, from www.ga-institute.com/newsletter/press-release/article/harvard-business-review-increased-focus-on-corporate-sustainability-convening-ceos-for-critical.html.

Gilmartin, B. (2018, January 21). Requiem for a GE bull. Retrieved January 21, 2018, from https://seekingalpha.com/article/4138895-requiem-ge-bull?auth_param=1ekhcg%3A1d68sf3%3Ace2e1461d293173e36be83d6e3b7efa1&uprof=14&dr=1.

Globescan/SustainAbility. (2012). *Extending corporate leadership on sustainable development. Final report of the regeneration roadmap: Changing tack.* Globescan/SustainAbility.

Hill, C.W., & Jones, G.P. (2008). *Strategic management: An integrated approach* (8th ed.). Boston, MA: Houghton Mifflin Co.

Hitchcock, D., & Willard, M. (2006). *The business guide to sustainability: Practical strategies and tools for organizations.* London: Earthscan.

Howell, E. (2015, December 23). How long have humans been on Earth? Retrieved January 3, 2018, from www.universetoday.com/38125/how-long-have-humans-been-on-earth/.

IDMC. (2017). *Global report on internal displacement.* Retrieved January 15, 2018, from www.internal-displacement.org/global-report/grid2017/.

ILO. (2016). *World employment and social outlook: Trends 2016.* Geneva: ILO.

Karbassi, L. (n.d.). Further, faster, together with corporate science-based targets. Retrieved January 18, 2018, from http://sciencebasedtargets.org/2017/11/14/further-faster-together-with-corporate-science-based-targets/.

Larry Fink's letter to CEOs. (2018, January 16). Retrieved January 17, 2018, from www.blackrock.com/corporate/en-us/investor-relations/larry-fink-ceo-letter.

Laszlo, C., & Brown, J. S. (2014). *Flourishing: The new spirit of business enterprise.* Stanford, CA: Stanford University Press.

Laszlo, C., & Zhexembayeva, N. (2011). *Embedded sustainability: The next big competitive advantage.* Stanford, CA: Stanford Business Books.

Lovins, L. H., & Lovins, A. B. (1989). *How not to parachute more cats: The hidden links between energy and security.* Old Snowmass, CO: Rocky Mountain Institute.

Makower, J. (2018, January 16). *2018 state of green business.* GreenBiz.com. Retrieved May 3, 2018, from www.greenbiz.com/article/state-green-business-2018.

Marcos, O. V. (2015, September 16). 200 global facts about the state of small businesses in 2015. *SlideShare.* Retrieved January 9, 2018, from www.slideshare.net/marcosluis2186/200-global-facts-about-the-state-of-small-businesses-in-2015.

Mars, A. (2017, December 6). Doing well by doing good: An interview with Paul Polman, CEO of Unilever. *Huffington Post.* Retrieved January 22, 2018, from www.huffingtonpost.com/alexandre-mars/doing-well-by-doing-good-_1_b_9860128.html.

Meadows, D. H. (1999). *Leverage points: Places to intervene in a system.* Hartland Four Corners, VT: Sustainability Institute.

Meadows, D. H. (2015). *Thinking in systems: A primer.* Edited by D. Wright. White River Junction, VT: Chelsea Green Publishing.

Meadows, D. H., Meadows, D. L., Meadows, J. R., & Behrens, W. W. (1972). *The limits to growth.* New York: Universe Books.

Miller, S. L. (2017, December 12). GE by the numbers. *Seeking Alpha.* Retrieved January 22, 2018, from https://seekingalpha.com/article/4131264-ge-numbers?auth_param=1ekhcg%3A1d2vkbl%3A6c76a692451abf568584fc5e73543a9d&uprof=14&dr=1#comments.

Mintzberg, H. (1978). Patterns in strategy formulation. *Management Science, 24*(9), 934–948. doi: 10.1287/mnsc.24.9.934

Moore, G. A. (1999). *Crossing the chasm: Marketing and selling high-tech products to mainstream customers.* New York: Harper Business.

Porter, M., & Kramer, M. (2006, December). Strategy and society: The link between competitive advantage and corporate social responsibility. *Harvard Business Review,* 78–92.

Porter, M. E, & Kramer, M. R. (2011). Creating shared value. *Harvard Business Review,* 3–17.

Prahalad, C. K., & Hamel, G. (1990). The core competencies of the corporation. *Harvard Business Review, 68*(3), 79–93.

Senge, P. M. (1994). *The fifth discipline: The art and practice of the learning organization; with a new introduction and tips for first-time readers.* New York: Doubleday/Currency.

Small Business Administration Office of Advocacy. (2012). Frequently asked questions. www.sba.gov/sites/default/files/FAQ_Sept_2012.pdf.

Sorkin, A. R. (2018, January 15). BlackRock's message: Contribute to society, or risk losing our support. *New York Times*. Retrieved January 17, 2018, from www.nytimes.com/2018/01/15/business/dealbook/blackrock-laurence-fink-letter.html#story-continues-1.

Standing, G. (n.d.). We have plundered the commons. Retrieved January 18, 2018, from www.weforum.org/agenda/2018/01/we-have-plundered-the-commons/.

United Nations High Commissioner for Refugees. (2017). *Figures at a glance*. Retrieved January 15, 2018, from www.unhcr.org/en-us/figures-at-a-glance.html.

United States Census Bureau. (2011). *2011 Nonemployer Statistics*. US Department of Commerce. Retrieved May 5, 2018, from http://censtats.census.gov/cgi-bin/nonemployer/nonsect.pl.

Walmsley, R. (2016, February 2). *The World Prison Population List (WPPL)*. London: The Institute for Criminal Policy Research, at Birkbeck, University of London.

Willard, B. (2005). *The next sustainability wave: Building boardroom buy-in*. Gabriola Island, BC, Canada: New Society Publishers.

Willard, B. (2012). *The new sustainability advantage: Seven business case benefits of a triple bottom line*. Gabriola Island, BC, Canada: New Society Publishers.

Winston, A. S. (2014). *The big pivot: Radically practical strategies for a hotter, scarcer, and more open world*. Boston, MA: Harvard Business Review Press.

Wirtenberg, J., Harmon, J., Russell, W. G., & Fairfield, K. D. (2007). HR's role in building a sustainable enterprise: Insights from some of the world's best companies. *Human Resource Planning, 30*(1), 10–20.

World Bank. (2017). *Global economic prospects: Weak investment in uncertain times*. World Bank Group, January.

World Economic Forum. (2018). *World Economic Forum 2018 global risks report*. Geneva: World Economic Forum.

Part III

Embracing and managing change sustainably

Managing the change to a sustainable enterprise

David Lipsky, Linda M. Kelley, Gregory S. Andriate, and Alexis A. Fink

Achieving sustainable enterprise in the 21st century

Look, listen, move! I can imagine the guides shouting out to the Discovery Corps team as they traveled west. Look out for potential danger, new animals, bugs, and plants. Listen and follow your Indian guides and officer's lead. Move, always keep moving, keep your blood flowing, and make progress every day. In 1803 President Thomas Jefferson challenged Lewis and Clark to find a passage west before the Europeans. Their objectives included learning about the area's plants, animal life, and geography as well as building relationships with the native populations and establishing trade with them. They were energized and empowered by a clear vision and challenge from President Jefferson and they learned and adjusted their path by partnering with many of the Native American Indian populations.

Box 4.1   Lewis and Clark and the Corps of Discovery Expedition

In 1803 President Thomas Jefferson acquired the Louisiana Purchase for the United States from France. He tasked Meriwether Lewis and William Clark with leading this journey of exploration. Although both were army men, these two brought to the task very different skills and knowledge sets. Lewis was President Thomas Jefferson's private secretary, and like Jefferson, Lewis was fascinated by the quite new discipline of science.

Lewis read everything he could get his hands on and conducted his own experiments when possible. From imagining wide ranges of situations they might encounter, he prepared a traveling store of tools, ordinances, provisions, medicines, and goods for trade that he hoped would keep the group safe.

Clark's experiences as a commanding officer had taught him the value of building interpersonal relationships. He knew that simply commanding was inadequate, that inspiring his people to also develop supporting relationships was essential to the group's wellbeing. Without the skillfulness and preparation of each of these men it is likely the expedition would have ended in failure.

Together they were able to traverse and map very challenging territories, handle the many surprises, engage the assistance of the native peoples whom they encountered, and reach the mouth of the Columbia River in what is now Washington State. Because of the care they took on all fronts, they lost but one man and that to appendicitis.

Their Expedition of the Corps of Discovery took the good part of two years—starting out from St. Louis in the summer of 1804 and arriving at the Pacific Ocean, in what is now Oregon, during the winter of 1805–1806, and made a successful return to St. Louis with journals and maps in September, 1806.

Sustainability can be seen as our modern-day version of the Discovery Corps' challenging passage into the unknown west. While their vision of the desired future was clear, ours is still hazy. The challenge is clearer; we must take care of our planet and people so our following generations can thrive. This will require us to improve our capability to accommodate change, to innovate on many fronts, to look, listen, and move differently. Looking differently at sustainability opportunities and challenges will open up new paths and possibilities for us as individuals and for our organizations. Changing into a sustainable enterprise is systemic by nature; each individual and each team contributes in some form or manner. How you contribute makes a difference. Listening authentically and openly with a broad set of stakeholders will generate increased collaboration and shared ownership, shared vision and shared commitment.

Enterprise sustainability requires inclusive change at the systems level, it involves all stakeholders. Systems change, like all change, is challenging, it disrupts our lives. Whether they are small or big, disruptions force people to make changes. As soon as possible, existing habits that frame what has become "normal" activate to attempt to regain the former normal state. It doesn't matter if change is intentional, or forced upon us, old habits of thinking and doing surface. They creep back in like subtle sabotage so dealing with habits, as mentioned in Chapter 2, "Mental models for sustainability," is important. Add to that, external conditions are moving along too, and not necessarily at a steady pace. While each of us is working out our own changes, other people in the organization are making their own changes. As

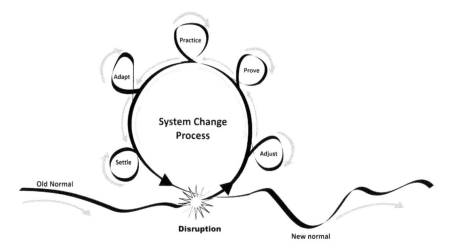

Figure 4.1 Systems change process
Source: Linda M. Kelley, 2010. This work is licensed under a Creative Commons Attribution Non-Commercial 4.0 International License.

each change large or small takes hold, it also changes the greater organization in ways that are difficult to predict. The change process starts to feel a lot like wandering through a bowl of spaghetti. One strand moves and it shifts everything around it. Even changes that sound simple may not be easy. It's no wonder that people find it hard to manage to linear diagrams of change that depict change as a straight line with distinct, orderly steps. If the model of systems change is not a straight line cause and effect one, what does systemic change look like? Systems change is roughly circular and it is iterative.

Sometimes people disrupt the normal flow intentionally. Often, though, disruption happens and people have to respond. The first action is to get one's bearings. Where am I?

We can view the process of systems change (see Figure 4.1) cycling through seven basic stages: 1. Disrupt, 2. Adjust, 3. Prove, 4. Practice, 5. Adapt, 6. Settle, and 7. Return to the flow and the New Normal.
If we flesh it out a little, it would look something like this:

1. Disrupt—What happened and where am I?
2. Adjust—Find my feet and get my bearings where I am now. Can I move?
3. Prove—What are my options? I'll try this first. No, that's not it ... and another, and another, experimenting until something seems to work.
4. Practice—Take what worked to the next level. Practice it over and over, change the circumstances a little, and practice some more.
5. Adapt—The new practiced ways seem almost right. What if anything needs further tweaking? Smooth the edges, adjust the fit, modulate the connections ... seems pretty good.

6.   Settle—get comfortable with the new ways, new balance. It's OK now.
7.   Return to the flow at the level of the New Normal.

For complex systems, this is the simplified process of change. At any stage in this process, another disruption can happen, and the stages cycle through at whatever that level is. For instance, say a new disruption happens during the Adapt stage. Attached to that state, a change cycles through the seven stages with the Adapt functioning as the Old Normal and at the completion of that cycle, the flow of New Normal returns into that Adapt stage. The process looks almost fractal. This is why when immersed in any significant, complex change it feels like you are wading through the spaghetti bowl.

Issues related to sustainability are forcing individuals, organizations, and industries to make significant changes at fundamental levels of operation. While these kinds of changes are not easy, there are some things we can do to prepare ourselves. First is to assess readiness to change. Forcing change on people or organizations that are not ready, that do not have the knowledge, skills or capacity, is a recipe for failure.

You might use the framework shown in Table 4.1 as a starting point in preparing for change. Filling out the boxes will give you a good idea of where you are prepared and where you will have to do more work to get ready. A word about stress level. On an individual level, remember that while people may want to leave personal problems at the door, functionally that's just about impossible to do. If something is wrong at home or with the family, that person will not be functioning at prime competence no matter how much they might try. In addition, a person who is already loaded down with critically important work and deadlines won't be able to handle more. Don't expect that person to engage in fundamental change in addition. We only have so much capacity for stress and change. If you want and need overloaded people to participate, lighten their load to make it possible. The same goes for organizations. If a team is overloaded or stressed out, none of the people will be able to contribute their best efforts to the change initiative.

For industries, and companies that comprise them, stress shows up in a somewhat different way. The level and intensity of competitiveness in an industry is one way stress shows up. It's not to say that this kind of stress is bad, or good, just that it's important to acknowledge it is present. Another stressor is emerging disruptions. Are there technologies on the close horizon that have the potential of broadsiding the whole industry? That's another stressor, even if it isn't fully formed yet. There are others, but the point is to take these into account when assessing change readiness for a business or industry.

One more piece that's important to address regarding change readiness is the strengths and weaknesses of an individual and organization, and threats and opportunities that may shift how strong or weak those qualities are under

Table 4.1 Organization readiness to undertake system-level change

The issue: _____

	Individual	Organization	Industry
Urgency of change			
	☐ Knowledgeable about the issue ☐ Believe the issue is important ☐ Expect positive outcome	☐ Knowledgeable about the issue ☐ Believe the issue is important ☐ Expect positive outcome	☐ Knowledgeable about the issue ☐ Believe the issue is important ☐ Expect positive outcome
Capacity for change	Attitude: Beliefs: Stress level: Bandwidth:	Structure: Culture: Stress level: Bandwidth:	State of maturity: Degree of regulation: Level of Competitiveness: Likelihood of disruption:
Capabilities			
<u>Relevant competencies></u>	Skills: Talents: Knowledge base:	Skills: Expertise: Intellectual capital:	Skills: Expertise: Currency of Data:
Reliable support			
Resources>	Human: Financial: Material and technological:	Human: Financial: Material and technological:	Human: Financial: Material and technological:
Networks>	Personal: Professional:	Internal: External:	Intra-industry: Cross-industry:

Source: Copyright 2017, Linda M. Kelley and Transitioning to Green, LLC. Used with permission.

different conditions. This is critically important for preparing for systems change because it's always iterative. It is these interactions that make SWOT assessments (see Figure 4.2) for systems a little different than what you might do for simple changes. In systems change, changes made on an individual level iteratively shift the basic conditions of the whole system to greater or lesser degrees. Because of this, systems change can also present paradoxes. It's as the old African proverb says, "You can never step into the same river twice."

Taken together, these tools will give you a decent sense of where you and your organization stand regarding change. You can also use these tools as a lens through which to look at other systems changes.

> When you change the way you look at things the things you look at change.
> (Wayne Dyer)

A Systems View of SWOT

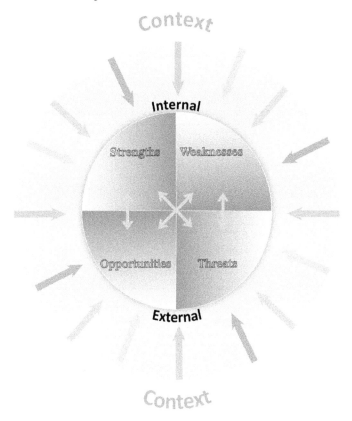

Figure 4.2 A systems view of SWOT
Source: Copyright 2013, Linda M. Kelley and Transitioning to Green, LLC.

Look

Many of our sustainability challenges are not problems to be solved, they are paradoxes to be managed.

> There is paradox at the heart of things. Life will never be easy, or perfectible, or completely predictable. It will be best understood backwards, but we have to live it forward. To make it liveable at all levels we have to learn to use the paradoxes—to balance contradictions and inconsistencies—as an invitation to find a better way.
>
> (Charles Handy)

Human beings can often be very stubborn, especially when they narrowly focus on a small number of factors and think they can solve these. Fifteen years ago, one of the authors offered his brother-in-law an extra used computer he had so he could learn his craft of typesetting in the new world of technology, which was evolving rapidly. His brother-in-law politely declined the offer, thanked him, and explained that typesetting jobs will never go away. He thought the newly increased union fees would be used to lobby the government to prevent typesetting jobs from getting offshored. In terms of what we reviewed in the previous section, his habits of thinking and doing kept him from seeing the emerging disruption of the typesetting industry by computer technology. He currently repairs elevators, a noble job but very challenging with his advancing age. A computer would not have solved his problem, neither would the lobbying efforts. Looking at this as a paradox, union dues could have been used for training in new technologies over time, which could have sustained him in his industry.

This narrow thinking can be exaggerated when we go from the individual to the group level. We believe singular actions can solve our most pressing problems. Looking through a pinhole limits our field of view and allows us to focus on individual issues, sometimes this blinds us to the competing forces of paradoxes.

> I will bring back the coal jobs!
> (Donald Trump, *Washington Post*, March 29, 2017)

The promise that then-US Presidential candidate Donald Trump made to struggling coal miners was similar to the brother-in-law's belief that his union could protect his job. By treating coal narrowly as a problem, reacting and pursuing what we see as an easy path forward—often solving a perceived problem from a singular perspective (e.g., country or stakeholder group)—has resulted in many dead ends and failed initiatives, bringing about untold unintended consequences, and wasting efforts and time that we cannot afford. Recognize that many of our problems result from addressing only a small number of variables while disregarding more complex multi-variable and multi-stakeholder issues. It is just about impossible to bring back "the old normal" when the conditions that constituted them have changed. Today, even in West Virginia's heart of coal country, there are more jobs in solar energy than there are in mining coal. The world is moving on. The markets moved on. Where would former coal miners be now if at all levels we had invested in developing a new, comprehensive economy in coal country based on renewables and used the money spent on marketing coal to retrain our coal miners for new roles?

Identifying paradoxes vs. problems

On the surface, many issues appear to be problems we need to solve. Globally, getting children into school earlier and keeping them in school longer will raise their ability to provide for themselves and their families over a lifetime. But many poor families rely on their children to help out around the house and take care of siblings so parents can earn enough money to sustain the family in the short term. The wrong question is how can we solve this problem— the right question is, how might we balance the paradox of both providing an education while allowing enough time for children to contribute to their families?

NASA scientists commissioned a way to 3D print a pizza in space

"Think globally, act locally" may need to be adjusted to "think galactically, act inclusively." While we know that local sourcing and production reduces our carbon footprint, ubiquitous technology expansion plus marketing and advertising campaigns drive consumer behavior and create a paradox where people are pushed to desire products that disregard both needs for the sustainability of resources and also for vibrant local economies.

In Economics, a "Jevons Paradox" has two parts. First, improvements in a technology (say, an engine) cause that technology to use resources (say, fuel) more efficiently. This seems all well and good, until you meet the second part. In the second part of a classic Jevons Paradox, people consume more of the resource as a result of the new, more efficient technology—because, hey, why not, right? Now we can afford it! Therein lies the paradox: in attempting to conserve resources, sometimes our technological advances end up making them less costly, and thereby increasing their consumption by the general public—the exact opposite of the intended effect. Nineteenth-century economist William Stanley Jevons first described this phenomenon in his observations of coal consumption in England following the introduction of the steam engine (Correll, 2015).

While working at UNICEF, one of our authors in his first month offered many uneducated, uninformed, and not always welcome suggestions for improvement. Speaking to a leader he suggested, hypothetically, that we should break the organization up into two separate organizations. The first organization would be an emergency-based logistics organization, ready at a moment's notice to assist in a crisis. The second would be an evidence-based advocacy group that could lobby governments to change policies to better support women and children in countries around the globe. Since they did such different things, it made sense to break up the organization. What he did not understand was that the credibility and relationships built by UNICEF Country Leaders and their staffs allowed them to influence government policies in the countries they served. Our author learned that the paradox of emergency focus and advocacy focus needed to be managed rather than trying to solve the problem by breaking the organization apart.

Listen

Getting the right stakeholders into the conversation can lead to powerful and long-lasting solutions. These efforts create the space and energy for committed action that can become viral and flourish. Effective paradox identification and management require that all stakeholders be heard. This contributes to identifying the key competing forces and provides the creativity and ownership needed to set up a sustainable management system.

When you have multiple stakeholders recognize something as a paradox, the potential for agreement is much greater than if they're individually trying to solve problems from their own individual stakeholder perspectives. An example of this is when a single stakeholder group argues against closing down a nuclear power plant because of short-term pricing impacts, or job losses, seeing no room for compromise until they achieve their objective. While other stakeholders might point to recent nuclear failures and are adamant that there are real risks to the safety of surrounding communities. While it's tempting to dig in, pitting one side against the other with each going for the win, in this example the arguments live on different planes. With a paradox, this approach doesn't work. First, we must listen without judgment to these different stakeholders with different views, then both parties can work together to achieve a solution that balances the paradox. For example, phasing out a reliance on nuclear power over a 10-year period while investing in renewable energy might make the most sense.

Generating the right conversations

In the leadership chapter in this book Dick Knowles discussed the importance of leading through partner-centered approaches that are at once *dynamic, non-linear, conversational, and leaderful.* This approach with the right set of ingredients will leverage the potential of people and the power of self-organizing to help change and sustain an organization.

Listen for the conversation seed

Listen to the organization, its people, their stakeholders—what do you hear? What's important, what topics have generated informal self-organizing teams? What you might hear are inclusive, organic conversations where every individual feels valued and understood for where they are and what they bring to the discussion. These change conversations organically grow and lay the required groundwork for highly organized change processes needed to drive sustainable change. It is the potential of people to drive change at both individual and collective levels, leveraging both organic and organized approaches.

Move

> If you can't fly then run, if you can't run then walk, if you can't walk then crawl, but whatever you do you have to keep moving forward.
>
> (Martin Luther King Jr., 1963)

Moving as a group was one of the keys to the Corps of Discovery Expedition's success. Daily progress goals created the discipline to stay focused, documenting learnings like new plants and paths but not staying in one place. In our sustainability journey, we must be careful not to get stuck in fighting current reality where so much of our energy can be exhausted in unfreezing the current state (Lewin, 1951).

Sharing best practices and leveraging the potential of many voices can help us choose the better paths and support each other on our ascent. It is by leveraging the potential of individual strengths that we collectively make progress. Each day we must set realistic goals, measuring our success by advancing the triple bottom line (TBL) of social equity, ecological integrity, and financial profitability. To do this we must collectively change mental models, including our beliefs, language, and behavior, managing the many paradoxes needed to increase long-term shareholder value by integrating social, environmental, and economic opportunities into our strategies (Saling & Kicherer, 2002; United Nations Industrial Development Organization, 2002).

The three-step conversational dance that leads to positive action

For enterprises to effectively change they must have a mix of conversations that supports the desired change, not forces that change but ones that allow concerns to be surfaced and appreciated as the foundation of negotiating mutually satisfactory agreements. We can have Why, What, and Who/When conversations. Check your own meetings and keep track of the mix of conversations you are having to drive change. Then adjust by building time into your agenda to cover all three conversations.

- Why or Heart conversations stimulate people's beliefs and passions for what they care most about.
- What or Head conversations inform and educate individuals and groups and can lead to either action or the parking lot. With increased knowledge people begin to see the possibility of a problem solved, opportunity leveraged, or a paradox managed.
- Who/When or Hands conversations lead to coordinated, connected, and collective action, unleashing the potential of people to drive the change forward.

Is the "#MeToo" movement a new form of organizational change?

The problem of sexual harassment in the workplace has existed for many years. Why are we now finally taking action? #MeToo has been used by social activist Tarana Burke over the last decade and has been reignited and popularized by actress Alyssa Milano, encouraging women to tweet about their own experiences of being harassed. This has resulted in millions of individuals sharing their own stories, sparking numerous investigations and action. High-profile and powerful individuals like Harvey Weinstein, Matt Lauer, and Bill O'Reilly have been quickly fired although accusations of misconduct had existed for years. Past practices of organizations have been to protect their executives and talent, often by quietly settling these cases away from the view of news and social media. With movements from the bottom up like #MeToo, these issues will not be re-hidden any more than the genie could be shoved back into Aladdin's lamp. This grassroots-driven issue took a lot of people by surprise. Some were surprised that it surfaced at all. Many were shocked at the size, scale, and reach. Millions and millions of women from around the world, women on every one of the continents of the globe posted #MeToo! This has now provoked systems change in many corners. As with all fundamental, complex systems change, this one will have bursts of progress and times of falling back. We don't know how long it will go on or what the outcomes will be. What we do know is that resultant changes are already rolling through many public and private organizations of all kinds. With the power of social media cutting across many boundaries, we must ask ourselves what will the next social media movement be and how will enterprises be prepared to change?

Starting with a change in mental models, and then the consequent languaging and approach we use, we must continue to evolve the threshold where we can sustain our world as the foundation for the more positively charged goal of thriving (Ehrenfeld & Hoffman, 2013; Laszlo & Brown, 2014). Our efforts must focus on both the enterprise level and on engaging individuals to drive these positive sustainability changes. "Never depend upon institutions or government to solve any problem. All social movements are founded by, guided by, motivated and seen through by the passion of individuals" (Mead, 1928).

Enterprises must have both the right culture and design to foster these new ideas, often bubbling up from the sea of organic conversations both inside and outside of the organization's network of relationships, often from members closest to the customers, and sometimes from the customers themselves. These ideas can bud from the beautiful organic flowers of possibility and blossom into the deep, disciplined, and complex structures and processes needed to take root and change the organization.

The soil of organizations must be fertile to support the growth of inclusive, organic conversations. These conversations can germinate and spread when technology can facilitate connections among people with fruitful ideas and resources. Through a series of filters focusing on viability and ROI some ideas grow into strategic bets and sometimes require significant investment and sophisticated change management. One example of this is a program that IBM has deployed, the "Technology Adoption Program." An internal website is provided where innovators can test their applications with early adopters and prove business value through adoption. This accelerates the process of conversation, to prototyping to testing and launching. Value is determined by usage rather than politics, which results in better market success. These types of solutions can be used so that the individual feels valued and understood for where they are and what they bring to the discussion. These change conversations organically grow and lay the groundwork for accelerated change. It is the potential of people to drive change individually and collectively, leveraging both organic and organized approaches.

Managing the change to sustainable enterprise

A little more on the behavior of complex systems undergoing change. It's important to make a distinction between management and guidance. While management is important for some aspects of systems change, management only works when situations and people are functioning with a large degree of predictability. These are usually cases where not only are the surrounding conditions relatively stable, but also the people are well prepared, the particular change is not overwhelming, and it's likely that the shifts can be made within a short period of time.

In times when stress abounds and where disruptions force change, management is less effective and sometimes even detrimental. When the changes to the system come about by forceful disruptions, guidance, and leading by example is much, much more important than management. Think of it like a complex situation of driving on ice, or shooting pool. If you are driving on an icy road and you apply direct pressure, try to control the situation, i.e., hit the brakes, you are almost guaranteed to slip and perhaps slide completely out of control. Counterintuitively, not touching the brakes and turning into the slide and using the existing momentum of the car, in other words, guiding what is already happening but gently, usually yields much better results and the possibility of regaining some influence over the direction the vehicle goes. Now think about playing the game of pool. If you hit the ball squarely and directly toward the pocket, most often the ball doesn't go in. If it did, there wouldn't be much of a game. Instead players need to carefully assess not only the positions of the other balls on the table but also the surface of the table. Then, mentally playing through possible outcomes, choose a less direct hit to the ball, often bringing other balls into play as well as the sides of the table, to guide your ball through a more complex trajectory that will result in your ball finding the pocket via a path of least resistance. A skillful player can often guide a ball to go where he or she wants it to go, but not always.

Regarding complex systems of people, the process of guiding requires the guides to let go of attachments to what worked last time and reassess the situations anew. The process of management though is often to apply best practices from the past to the current situation where one can reasonably expect the results to be similar to what happened in the past. The rule is to be sure you know which field you're playing on so you can manage or guide accordingly.

While we do believe that we have made sustainability progress in the last 10 years since the first edition of *The Sustainable Enterprise Fieldbook*, many of the most important challenges remain that we identified in a worldwide sustainability study conducted by a number of authors of this book (American Management Association [AMA], 2007, pp. 24–25). Many high-performing enterprises have already embraced the challenge of creating and nurturing sustainable enterprise business practices. Not surprisingly, most organizations recognized by leading sustainability indices (such as Dow Jones Sustainability Index, Domini 400 Social Index, and FTSE4Good Index Series) have a well-established business culture that values and balances elements of economic viability, environmental responsibility, and social equity (Assis & Elstrodt, 2007; Benson, 2007; McGraw-Hill, 2007; Wirtenberg, 2014). These enterprises have learned to deliberately and consistently pursue environmentally and socially responsible goals, balancing immediate needs of investors and consumers without sacrificing the long-term viability of our planet or its inhabitants (Spivey, 2006). Individual investors can have a significant impact on influencing organizations they choose to invest in with an expectation of increased enterprise sustainability efforts. Other innovative financial organizations are providing alternative more sustainable investment options for consumers and businesses like flowmoneysystem.com. We believe that thriving in the future will depend on innovations in the sustainability space. Lux Capital is one example of a venture capital firm focused on investing and bringing these solutions to market. It seeks out innovators who not only want to make money, they also want to make a difference.

> If you are a scientist, inventor, or entrepreneur with an idea that can lead the world into a brighter future, we hope you will reach out to us. We make long-term bets on contrarians and outsiders. We believe the next generation of industrialist titans will be scientists, technologists and inventors who are doing more than challenging the status quo—they're literally challenging the laws of physics.[1]

For such organizations, the future challenge involves emphasizing, extending, and reinforcing core organization values to perpetuate sustainable enterprise practices. For other organizations, the future challenge will be far greater, potentially requiring the creation and installation of new values throughout the enterprise. In the words of one senior executive, creating a business culture that embraces sustainable development values may well require "fundamental changes in organizational DNA" on a global basis. Taken together, accountability for social equity, ecological integrity, and financial profitability form a triple bottom line measuring sustainable development practices. Our approach to managing the change to sustainable enterprise in the 21st century is based on six assumptions:

1. Achieving sustainable enterprise requires a fundamental shift in managing and measuring enterprise success via TBL metrics.
2. Achieving successful performance on TBL metrics requires fundamental changes in traditional approaches to markets, customers, stakeholders, and stockholders.
3. Changing traditional approaches to markets, customers, stakeholders, and stockholders requires driving TBL concepts into key enterprise processes and daily business practices and decisions.
4. Driving TBL concepts into daily business decisions requires new sustainable enterprise values that are readily understood and embraced by decision makers at multiple levels of the organization.
5. Installing sustainable enterprise values (people, planet, and profit) often requires cultural transformation at all levels of the organization.
6. Creating sustainable enterprise business cultures may require behavior change from every person at every level of the organization.

Sustainability-related factors driving key business decisions

A global survey (AMA, 2007) reported several findings relevant to managing the change to sustainable enterprise. First, respondents (N = 1,365) believed that sustainable enterprise values are more important to them personally than they are to the company for which they work. This suggests that increasing alignment between individual and company values would capture the minds and hearts of those working to add value to all TBL constituencies. This will, in turn, help harness the discretionary effort essential for installing a sustainable enterprise culture and successfully propelling the entire organization into the future.

A second, and perhaps more important, finding revealed that respondents expected a shift in the top three sustainability-related factors driving key business decisions over the 10 years following 2007. This shift in the importance of "sustainability-related key business drivers" suggests that enterprises nurturing capabilities to "improve image, enhance innovation, and secure diverse top talent" are more likely to reap the benefits of sustainable enterprise than those simply installing and practicing basic TBL policies. Consequently, cultivating an enterprise culture that embraces and promotes sustainable development values is likely to create positive advantages essential for achieving and sustaining success in the 21st century. These findings are more recently corroborated in nine case studies featured in *Building a Culture for Sustainability* (Wirtenberg, 2014).

Creating cultures that embrace sustainable business practices, and are based on seeing the organization as if it were a living system, grows progressively more important to long-term success in all types of organizations (Wirtenberg, 2016). Increasing economic globalization necessitates ever more frequent reviews and adjustments to enterprise portfolios, creating significant turnover and fluidity in workforce members. New workforce entrants from diverse backgrounds are likely to increase as we continue to move toward flattened workscapes and virtual employee populations (Aydinliyim & Wirtenberg, 2017). These new entrants must all learn ways of doing business that ensure perpetuation of sustainable enterprise values, even in those organizations presently demonstrating best-in-class sustainable development practices. Thus, cultivating enterprise cultures that embrace sustainable development values will remain a core capability essential to achieving and sustaining success in the 21st century (Wirtenberg, 2014).

Challenges in changing enterprise culture

Creating significant cultural change at every level of the organization is far easier said than done. Even a casual review of contemporary management literature suggests that most companies dramatically underestimate the challenge faced in creating and implementing change.

Box 4.2   Success vs. failure in enterprise-wide change

It is no secret that most change initiatives fall short. Findings across multiple studies suggest that 50–80% of corporate change efforts fail to achieve desired results. Even worse, this is especially true for attempts to change corporate culture. In his 1996 book *Leading Change*, John P. Kotter reports that 85% of companies fail to achieve their change objectives. Paul Strebel (2000), in his *Harvard Business Review OnPoint* article, reports that 50–80% of change efforts in *Fortune* 1000 companies fail. A *Wall Street Journal* (Lancaster, 1995) review of 1,005 reengineered companies reports that only 50% met cost targets; only 22% achieved projected productivity increases; about 80% ended up rehiring some laid-off employees; less than 33% achieved profit expectations; and only 21% achieved satisfactory return on investment.

Capra (2007) provides insights as to why so many change efforts fail:

> Although we hear about many successful attempts to transform organizations, the overall track record is very poor. In recent surveys, CEOs reported again and again that their organizational change efforts did not yield the promised results. Instead of managing new organizations, they ended up managing the unwanted side effects of their efforts. When observing our natural environment, we see continuous change, adaptation, and creativity; yet our business organizations seem to be incapable of dealing with change.
>
> Indeed, the same business culture can provide both an advantage and liability, depending on prevalent business conditions. Studies of DEC (Digital Equipment Corporation) reveal that the same culture contributing to the once-mighty company's success also prevented it from adapting to a changing context—even though the need for change was recognized (Schein & Kampas, 2003). This cultural rigidity ultimately cost DEC its existence as an independent company. Choices made by entire societies about their cultural values, and the ultimate outcomes that those choices have on sustainability, have been similarly investigated (Diamond, 2005).

Change is difficult in organizations with experts reporting that (see Box 4.2 "Success vs. failure in enterprise-wide change"):

- only 20–50% of strategic change initiatives fully realize expected benefits;
- less than 50% of planned change efforts successfully overcome employee inertia;
- failure to fully implement strategic change undermines realization of business results and jeopardizes achievement of competitive advantage.

Most cultural change initiatives fail because they are driven by the need to cut costs in the short term. All too often, this involves reductions in force that decimate organizational expertise and severely reduce capability to reach enterprise goals. As such, cost-driven transformation efforts are nonsustainable.

Factors essential for successful change

The good news is that we know what differentiates success from failure in creating sustainable change. Successful enterprise-wide change efforts are visibly championed by senior management, and include:

- committed leadership willing to engage, make, and support essential investments (information technology [IT], capital, training, and the like);
- shared mindset and co-created values: agreement on what's needed and how to get there; shared priorities; willingness to take risks; aligned incentives; and reward systems;
- adaptive change management using integrated project structures, clear roles and responsibilities, recognition and management of resistance, and willingness to provide resources (time and budget) required to implement changes;
- effective communication and stakeholder management generating critical mass of stakeholder support by providing access to information, focusing on desired outcomes, and frequently reporting progress;
- organization culture characterized by high degrees of trust between management and workforce, embracing collaboration, teamwork, empowerment of individuals to act without permission within the scope of their own role, and commitment to staff development.

Decisions to initiate major change in a company provoke side effects in its highly complex and dynamic systems. To encourage successful outcomes leaders must engage the people who are likely to be affected by upcoming changes, preparing them to expect the unexpected and giving them support for coping with significant upheavals. Change leaders recognize that everything is connected. As changes ripple through the system, consequences are uncertain and therefore unpredictable. Even decisions to make absolutely critical alterations meet with resistance when they upset projects on which the people involved are measured according to the results they've produced (Sterman, 2001). Mindfulness at all levels increases awareness of situations, emerging problems, and their possible solutions (Harvard Business Review Staff, 2014).

When undertaking a major change initiative, how might your company's leadership provide the policies, structure, resources, and slack—in time and space—so that many people can become invested in its success?

Indeed, successful transformational change may involve looking at the organization in a new way, which embraces the messy complexities of the natural world. Capra (2007) argues: "Once we have that understanding, we can design processes of organizational change accordingly, and create human organizations that mirror life's adaptability, diversity, and creativity." Thus, an understanding of natural change processes is a prerequisite to establishing lasting change in the organization.

Transforming enterprise culture

Enterprise transformation approaches provide valuable insights for generating successful change. Seeing the whole organization as a system allows us to be more thoughtful, balanced, and accurate in the change areas we target. Proven approaches typically rely on creating organizations that accept and embrace deliberate renewal of workforce talent; responsible use of environmental resources; and alleviation of major societal ailments (Aydinliyim & Wirtenberg, 2017). In particular, we advocate the orchestrated redesign of organizational "DNA" using four transformational elements: **Framing**, **Aligning**, **Igniting**, and **Refreshing** (FAIR):[2]

Framing. Shifting corporate mindsets to develop fresh mental models[3] of *what we are* and *what we can become*; expanding corporate identity to infuse new visions, aspirations, and new resolve.

Aligning. Adjusting economic models, aligning physical infrastructure, and redesigning workplace processes and procedures to achieve a competitive level of performance. This is more than simply restructuring organization charts to cut heads and reap fast financial payoffs; reinvention requires comprehension and apprehension of fresh capabilities needed to sustain enterprise advantage.

Igniting. Kindling growth by achieving market focus, inventing new businesses, and using technology to change the industry rules of competition; promoting organic growth and stimulating new competitive capability most clearly differentiate organization transformation from mere downsizing.

Refreshing. Adjusting enterprise information metabolism to foster creativity, generate energy, and restore *esprit de corps*; investing individuals with new skills and purposes, thus permitting the organization to regenerate itself; revitalizing enterprise *sense of community* is the most challenging, yet potentially most potent, transformation tool available to organization leaders.

The FAIR model represents the fundamental life skills that any organization needs to survive and thrive in the sustainable development world of the 21st century.

Participative change and sustainable enterprise cultures

Organizations can change only as quickly as the people in them change. Successful organization transformations require expansion of conversational space, thus enabling all employees to think and act differently. William Ury (2014 TEDx San Diego) emphasizes the importance of listening, which can unleash the potential of people's minds, transform relationships, and lead to better solutions. We know that people learn in many different ways, and good organizational change will leverage several of them, including social and individual learning experiences, as well as active versus passive (or observational) learning.

We have found an *immersion approach* to be most effective in helping people make these transformations. Change immersion relies heavily on the principle of modeling; with modeling, people learn not only through their own experience, but also by observing the experiences of others. Creating visible examples of the consequences of embracing or rejecting new behaviors fosters organization-wide learning, which can have a profound effect on employee decisions to embrace new behaviors.

Adult learning theory holds that people need time and reinforcement to adjust to the idea of new behaviors and learn associated skills. Employee understanding is itself only a first step in driving successful enterprise transformations. Beyond ensuring that workforce members have the time to help co-create, understand, and embrace the purpose of the changes (at least enough to give it a try), we must also address three additional factors. First, we must revamp reward and recognition systems to ensure new behaviors are adequately maintained over time; this typically involves significant adjustment to core human resources and management systems, and is seldom undertaken lightly. Second, we must deliberately recruit or create active, visible role models who practice the new enterprise behaviors; people are far more likely to try out (and continue engaging in) new behaviors if they see them modeled by others (especially those they respect and admire). Third, we must ensure that everyone is provided with the time and resources to learn new skills to do what is required of them in the future. For adults, this typically involves five steps: listening, co-creating, absorbing, using experimentally, and integrating into existing knowledge. Many organizations set themselves up for failure by "scrimping" on this vital component of successful transformations.

Thus, creating an environment of participative learning is essential to the success of any cultural transformation, and the chances of achieving sustainable change are far greater when all four of the above factors (co-creating a new understanding with the employees, revising reward systems, ensuring the presence of visible role models, and providing the means for employees to acquire new skills) are present.

Many change initiatives fail because they focus only on the tangible components of the business enterprise: its basic structures, technologies, systems, and work processes. The reality is that transformational change is fundamentally about changing the intangible components of the business enterprise: the way people perceive their roles, approach their jobs, and make choices on a daily basis. In our work, four elements have proved essential for successfully changing the way people work together: co-creating a compelling future state to which people can aspire; co-developing shared values and behaviors aligned with achieving the future vision; ensuring that everyone receives the knowledge and skills required to succeed in the future environment; and creating an environment in which people at all levels see visible, functional examples of the behaviors they've been asked to embrace.

Seasoned managers recognize that alterations in basic work routines often pose a daunting challenge. They have learned that any attempt to alter habitual work behaviors requires a *deliberate effort*, necessitating conscious examination of assumptions about *why and how* someone works. These questions inevitably lead to reexamination of personal and professional priorities, and can often entail fundamental reassessment of *employment value propositions*. Such excursions can be perilous, and are seldom lightly undertaken.

Box 4.3   Value propositions for internal vs. external stakeholders

The challenge of optimizing value propositions for internal versus external stakeholders increases as organizations grow in size and complexity. This is primarily because those directly accountable for delivering value to external stakeholders (such as shareholders, local community, government) are seldom directly responsible for delivering products or services to clients or customers on a daily basis. See Chapter 1 for insights addressing the alignment challenges senior executives face when they become further removed from those they rely on to deliver target results on a daily basis.

Iterative transformational change methodology

An integrated approach for managing the change to sustainable development cultures can be created by merging the FAIR model, participative change management, and traditional project management methodologies. This method combines an understanding of how organizations change (FAIR), how people learn (participative learning theory), and four conditions essential for changing the way people behave at work. The intentional, tenacious application of integrated concepts, driven by action-learning teams advocating sustainable development principles, produces organization-wide changes in how people think about their work: how work is structured, how success is measured, and how materials and information move through the organization. In our experience, this total approach consistently creates, develops, and installs sustainable enterprise cultures that balance people, planet, and profit goals in the development of sustainable value propositions essential for achieving triple-bottom-line success in the 21st century. A common misconception about transformational change interventions is the notion that they follow traditional "beginning–middle–end" sequences so ingrained in Western thinking. Perhaps, paradoxically, transformational change actually starts with an *ending*. Lewin (1951) conceived a three-stage change model ("unfreezing–changing–refreezing") suggesting that individuals must first "let go of"—literally stop—old behaviors before they can begin engaging in new behaviors. That is, rather than beginning with what the new will be, effective change actually requires letting go of the old before addressing the new directly. Although starting at the end is counterintuitive for many, it is absolutely essential for changing the way people think about their work.

Overlaying the FAIR model onto traditional change management stages provides a neat solution to this dilemma. This approach permits us to think about managing transformational change interventions in discrete stages, with each of the FAIR elements operating iteratively within sequential stages of the change process.

This **iterative transformational change methodology** (see Figure 4.3) has proven particularly effective for creating and implementing sustainable enterprise values, while simultaneously providing powerful developmental experiences for emerging leaders; creating internal advocates for reinvented work processes and practices; and building the foundation for an adaptive culture that continually strives to tackle future challenges in the struggle to achieve sustainable enterprise practices.

The recommended methodology ensures all elements essential for successful enterprise change are assessed, addressed, and monitored throughout the transformational change engagement. This systematic, systems-level approach to creating and managing change employs principles of modeling at multiple stages and multiple levels of an organization to systematically transform the way everyone thinks about and performs their work on a daily basis.

The key to transformational success involves creating cross-functional collaboration across a set of interdependent interventions managed as a single, integrated organizational intervention. (See Chapter 8 for more on collaboration,

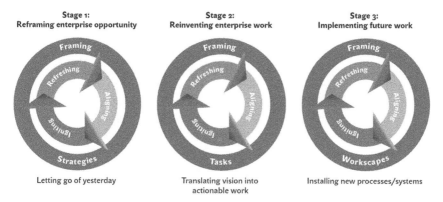

Figure 4.3 Iterative transformational change methodology
Source: Copyright 2008, Organization Innovation. Used with permission.

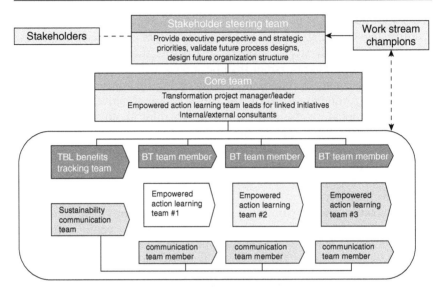

Figure 4.4 Empowered team intervention structure

Note: Typical project structure for empowered action learning team interventions employed in iterative transformational change methodology stage 2: "Reinventing enterprise work."

Source: Copyright 2007, Organization Innovation. Used with permission.

including models and frameworks, tools, exercises, and best practices.) The primary driving mechanism is an empowered action learning team (the **core team**, Figure 4.4) charged with managing stakeholder interests and coordinating intervention activities across multiple project stages or phases. As owners of the transformational change methodology, the core team must ensure application of the FAIR model with each new constituency encountered as the intervention iterates through multiple levels and functions within the larger enterprise. Our empowered action learning team approach ultimately involves chartering and launching multiple teams over sequential 100-day periods. The principle "7–70–700" refers to the number of workforce members engaged in three successive 100-day periods. In a typical transformational change project, each core team member in stage 1, "Reframing enterprise opportunity," becomes the leader of a natural work redesign team in stage 2, "Reinventing enterprise work." Similarly, one or more members of each redesign team in stage 2 will lead implementations teams in stage 3, "Implementing future work."

The empowered action learning team approach is equally appropriate for use in business enterprises, civic organizations, and social networks. Major elements include co-creating and identifying organizational performance opportunities, reinventing core work processes, aligning employee engagement and commitment, and mobilizing workforce resources to implement new ways of delivering value to all stakeholders (customers, employees, shareholders, local community, and the like). This approach has been successfully applied in a variety of industries, countries, and cultures, including Argentina, Brazil, Canada, the United Kingdom, Germany, Mexico, Spain, and the United States. This approach, having proven equally effective with workforce members in Europe, North America, and South America, is offered without hesitation to anyone seeking a robust methodology for creating and implementing new values within existing enterprise cultures.

Box 4.4   Assess your organizational readiness to move to sustainable enterprise: change readiness diagnostic tool

This tool measures organizational readiness to meet major challenges encountered in the journey to sustainable enterprise: meeting today's needs without compromising the ability of future generations to meet their own needs. Best-practice enterprises define success in terms of an integrated triple bottom line: accountability for social equity, ecological integrity, and financial profitability. To assess your organization's readiness to move to sustainable enterprise, simply rate the following 12 statements on a scale from 1 to 5, where:

1 = not characteristic; this never happens here
2 = somewhat characteristic; this seldom happens here
3 = characteristic; this sometimes happens here
4 = very characteristic; this frequently happens here
5 = extremely characteristic; this always happens here without exception

1. Senior leaders visibly support and communicate benefits of sustainable enterprise business practices
2. People here appreciate how embracing sustainable enterprise values will impact our company, businesses, and jobs
3. People here agree about what does and does not need to change as we move toward sustainable enterprise
4. People here understand the scope and time requirements for becoming a sustainable enterprise
5. Managers typically recognize and address individual resistance to adopting sustainable enterprise business practices
6. Management recognizes and rewards those leading and supporting the change to sustainable enterprise
7. People here respect and value those working to create a sustainable enterprise culture
8. Employees get time and support for learning new skills essential for future success
9. Managers rebalance job responsibilities of people assigned to change projects

10. Goals of sustainable enterprise efforts are aligned across company departments
11. People here are willing to share information and ideas to achieve the best results
12. We have high levels of trust and cooperation between management and employees

Calculate your score: total the 12 numbers assigned to each statement. If your score equals:

55–60: Change master—primed and ready to handle major challenges
46–54: Change leader—likely to cope with challenges, with some bumps in the road
36–45: Change dilettante—proceed with caution; high risk of unrealized benefits
<36:   Change novice—seek guidance from organizational change masters

Note: This assessment provides a high-level overview of several more robust diagnostic tools, supplying a preliminary diagnosis of five major change dimensions impacting successful transformation to sustainable enterprise for the 21st century.

Source: Copyright 2005–2007, Organization Innovation LLC. Adapted with permission.

Iterative guide to sustainable development workscapes

Stage I. Reframing enterprise opportunity

Reenvisioning enterprise opportunity is the first step in the enterprise evolution. It's about moving beyond the confines of *who we are* and *what we do* to address *what we must become.* Changing enterprise identity strikes at the root of fundamental organizational DNA, involving adjustments to:

- dominant approach to conducting business;
- standards for measuring performance;
- workforce motivation and engagement;
- freedom to innovate, experiment, and push the boundaries of acceptable practices for achieving the long-term mission.

Thus, reframing the enterprise invariably requires mobilizing workforce engagement, re-creating a shared vision of the future, and building new metrics for determining individual and organization success in achieving enterprise goals. (See Chapters 5, 6, and 8 for additional insights into addressing these challenges.)

The core team functions as a primary engine and integrative force, and is specifically chartered to deliver results for all key activities addressed in stage 1.

Typically, the team must be equipped to diagnose and address the following critical success factors: thorough understanding of current state; assessing gaps between current and best practice capabilities; and building a business case for enhancing organizational performance on TBL metrics (social equity, ecological integrity, and financial profitability). The ultimate goals of the "Reframing enterprise opportunity" stage are improving the value proposition for all stakeholders (employees, customers, local community, government, and shareholders), while simultaneously engaging the minds and hearts of the people working to deliver increased shareholder value.

Box 4.5   Employee engagement and organizational renewal

There's a chicken-and-egg aspect to the relationship between employee engagement and organizational renewal. Organizational renewal offers employees the opportunity to more fully leverage their potential. As seen in Chapter 5, engaged employees are proud of their organizations and offer discretionary effort.

Both of these topics are deep and rich—too much to cover here with any justice. Instead, we offer a thought: A key component of employee engagement is pride in the organization. To encourage engagement, especially in times of change, organizations can be "pride-worthy." Taking a TBL perspective is a great start to being pride-worthy. Doing right by your employees, doing right by the community, and doing right financially all contribute to an organizational image that employees feel good about. (See Chapter 5 for a detailed discussion of this robust concept.)

A typical core team includes members representing multiple levels and a cross-section of key functions within the current organization. In our experience, a fulltime team leader (100% time allocation), with team members assigned at 50% workload, has the greatest probability for meeting or exceeding targets defined in the team charter. Although there is no absolute core team member profile, those selected typically bring deep expertise in the following disciplines: project management (team leader), finance/accounting, manufacturing/engineering, logistics, maintenance, communication/change management, and organization structure and design. All members will be expected to function as change agents in their own areas, and must therefore be credible, respected, and viewed by colleagues as capable of representing the greater interests of the entire group. In keeping with principles regarding social equity, core teams should also reflect multiple aspects of diversity (e.g., gender, ethnicity/nationality, profession, age/seniority).

Box 4.6   Quick wins: "earnest money" on the change

Often, as you begin to explore a problem space in earnest, you'll come across a golden opportunity to start the change. Something so easy, so obvious, so visible! Grab those low-hanging fruits with both hands and make a big show of it. These *quick wins* should be carefully positioned as little baby steps and not the end game, but there is tremendous power in demonstrating your commitment to change. Doing a small thing well—executing well and communicating well—increases others' trust in you. They begin to believe that maybe you'll be able to do a big thing well. It also puts a chink in the armor of denial; right out of the gate, with this project, things are different. Busting old beliefs is a powerful approach accelerating change. In addition to early wins try making a list of all the reasons why a particular change can't happen and then one by one change the assumptions to possibilities that have the power to change people's beliefs.

Once assembled, the core team will introduce and manage a portfolio of tools designed to mobilize and engage the entire workforce in identifying and quantifying potential opportunities for improving organizational efficiency and effectiveness; for creating a more positive workplace; and for implementing a *quick hit/quick win* process, or workplace enhancement improvements on an accelerated schedule. Typical opportunity identification activities include:

- **Creating transparency in value creation dynamics, metrics, and current performance.** This normally requires reviews of financial statements, strategic initiatives, capital investment plans, and the like. This work often forms the skeleton around which the rest of the opportunity identification activities are built.
- **Assessing workforce readiness for transformational change** (see Box 4.4 "Assess your organizational readiness to move to sustainable enterprise" on pages 205–206 and also Table 4.1 on page 187. Formally assessing change readiness of the organization informs change management.
- **Extensive interviews.** Although ostensibly for information gathering, these function more as a step in the change management effort. They are an opportunity to set expectations, allow people at multiple levels and in multiple functions of the organization to feel heard, and they begin to get people engaged. These interviews can also be a time to begin identifying potential team members for the next phase of the project.

- **Process opportunity mapping.** Application of high-touch–low-tech methodology engaging key stakeholders in capturing optimization opportunities for key work processes and work flows.
- **"Day in the life of" (DILO) assessments of people, process, equipment** (see Box 4.7 "Understand the problem you are solving").

Throughout all these activities, the team demonstrates new sustainable enterprise values, modeling a new approach to conducting business and introducing

---

Box 4.7   Understand the problem you are solving

Good, thorough research can yield surprising answers to mundane questions. The opportunity identification tools are designed to help understand not just the "obvious" solutions, but the root causes.

One important such identification tool is the day in the life of (DILO) exercise. Here, team members meticulously follow a person, object, form, sample, order, or other unit of analysis all the way through the system.

A favorite example of a DILO is the "great forklift shortage." Operators in a particularly sprawling facility spent inordinate amounts of time—several hours of every shift—hunting around for available forklifts. The shortage of forklifts was a real problem. Just buying more posed a problem, because of the requirements for safe operation in this particular facility. The ones they needed were very, very expensive.

Enter the DILO, conducted by operators from the very same plant, people with a clear agenda to prove they needed more of the expensive forklifts. What did they find? It wasn't the *availability* of the forklifts that was the problem; it was the *location*. By following several forklifts around over the course of several days, they learned that each one was used for only a very small percentage of any given shift. The wasted time was all in hunting around, for 30 minutes or more at a time, to find one. Each person just left it parked wherever it had last been used.

The solution? A set of designated parking spots. In the end, rather than purchasing more forklifts, the plant was actually able to retire some, another step in its efforts to reduce its environmental footprint.

The magic of a DILO is its irrefutability. In the forklift example, how would such a solution have been received if it had been dictated from on high? Instead, a group of peers set out to solve their own problem— and they did, though not in the way that they intended. When lunchroom grumbling about needing to put things away started up, the DILO researchers were there to set the record straight. Management was happy with the cost avoidance. Employees were happy with the reduced frustration that never being able to find the equipment they needed had engendered. Win–win was achieved!

TBL standards for measuring performance. At the same time, they actively engage employees at all levels in actions demonstrating freedom to innovate, experiment, and push the boundaries of acceptable practice.

Leadership alignment and support are essential components of any transformational change effort. Typically conducted in workshop format, this work ensures senior managers understand how to use the empowered team process to simultaneously deliver improved organizational performance and develop essential business and team skills throughout the organization. In the ideal situation, leadership workshops take place before teams are formally commissioned. In cases in which pre-positioning is unrealistic, workshops may be run in parallel with work redesign teams described above, or, if absolutely necessary, even scheduled as a direct lead-in to organization redesign work. Leadership alignment workshops are essential to the smooth, sustainable operation of the empowered action learning team model, for both practical and political reasons. Empowered action learning team methodology is fundamentally bottom-up in nature, and requires that leaders await team recommendations before taking action. This runs counter to the normal management practices (and perhaps even instincts) of most leadership teams. Therefore, it's essential to help senior leaders resist the urge to impose order, accelerate actions, or otherwise disrupt the empowered team process.

Experience demonstrates patience is far easier when leaders are confident that empowered teams will return solutions aligned with company priorities and management time schedules. Consequently, it becomes incumbent on core team members to make sure that senior managers receive solutions they can live with, and successful projects most frequently require core team members to bridge any potential gaps between company priorities and team member/employee self-interests. Fortunately, this alignment is often a natural outcome of the frequent, candid discussions between the core team and the enterprise or organization's leaders or leadership team; in a typical project, the leader of the core team not only has a standing one-to-one briefing with the enterprise leader each week, he or she also typically becomes a full member of the enterprise's leadership team for the duration of the project.

The culmination of stage 1: "**Reframing** enterprise opportunity" is a recommended case for change. Although a case for change may take many forms, at minimum it should include a reinvention plan supported by a sustainable enterprise business case. (Note: a case for change is also the typical culmination of any change management intervention. This can contribute to confusion regarding our approach, in which some expect neat, linear steps in the change process.) A good business case for change will invariably include *three buckets* supporting recommended changes: quantitative/financial analyses ("real money") projections demonstrating benefits to shareholders; nonquantified/financial analyses (real money impacts expected from changes, with no specific or reliable data available for accurately estimating benefits); and nonquantifiable benefits (intangible but "real" benefits; these may be necessary enablers or preconditions for benefits in the first two categories) that may be expected to result from changes. It is important to note that nonquantified financial benefits are included intentionally. First, they hold the promise of an additional financial upside beyond those quantified in the first category (i.e., quantified financial). Further, identifying but not calculating benefits providing low return on investment of time and effort supports the credibility of the team and its work. Although some change efforts advertise suspicious numbers, based on several layers of assumptions, our methodology explicitly separates the "hard, take-it-to-the-bank" benefits of a project from the "expected, aggregated, increased value" sorts of return.

The *three-bucket* approach permits integration of TBL metrics (*Living Fieldbook*) into the business case, and ensures change decisions are based on more than simple short-term profit motives. This balances the needs of external and internal stakeholders and recognizes that increases in shareholder value are inextricably tied to improving the employee value proposition. Therefore, the case for change reframes business priorities, optimizes returns for all constituencies, and clarifies the path for achieving environmentally and socially responsible goals balancing immediate needs of investors and consumers without sacrificing long-term viability of our planet or its inhabitants.

Stage 2. Reinventing enterprise work

The **reinventing** component of enterprise transformation entails redesigning key activities embedded in the processes, systems, and tools supporting achievement of organizational goals. This work focuses on creating new economic models for pursuing and measuring sustainable success, redesigning work architectures to achieve a competitive level of performance, and aligning physical infrastructure to ensure resource focus on areas providing optimal results for all constituencies.

Primary goals of the reinventing stage include: designing future work processes and systems; clarifying key organizational roles and responsibilities; defining future organization structures; improving morale and motivation by promoting trust, encouraging teamwork, and alleviating *fairness* concerns; and creating employee ownership and commitment to sustainable enterprise values.

During reinvention, the active engagement of workforce members is formally expanded beyond the original core team, which now assumes a project management coordination function. This allows the knowledge and experience of those core team members to scale more broadly, as each core team member takes leadership of a specific work stream in the reinventing phase. As depicted in Figure 4.4 on page 204, people are assigned to multiple empowered action learning teams formally chartered to design the future processes essential to achieving sustainable enterprise. The number of teams generally depends on the key changes identified in the sustainable enterprise business case; 5–12 is a typical range. These generally take the form of natural work teams (redesigning future work processes), coordination teams (core, benefits/metrics), governance teams (leadership alignment, organization design, steering), and enabling teams (communication, workforce competence enhancement); the organic formation of these teams is congruous with the perception of the organization as a living system (Wirtenberg, 2016).

Box 4.8   How to leverage internal resources with little or no added expense

The content or process expertise that a good consultant brings can be an essential component of effective change. However, the credibility brought by your current workforce—their expertise in your work processes, your culture, all the details that make your workplace unique—is beyond value. The sincere advocacy of one skeptical, informal leader in your organization may be the single greatest change tool you have. That sincere advocacy can't be bought, but it can be earned through the approaches outlined in this chapter.

Using our "7–70–700" rule, we now increase the total number of immersed employees by a factor of 10. This necessarily involves revisiting many of the same issues originally addressed by members of the core team during stage 1. Although this may seem like the process is slowing down, this is a critical step in achieving successful transformation; in this case, slowing down will help us go faster in the long run as it provides an opportunity for team members to be fully immersed and engaged. Permitting new participants to ask the same questions, address the same concerns, and discover the same answers is an absolutely essential element for increasing the critical mass of employees actively embracing the core elements of the new sustainable development culture.

Though this may seem inefficient, there is no substitute for permitting each team member to learn the *new company truths* at his or her own pace and in his or her own way. This issue may be particularly problematic for members of the senior management team, who are understandably anxious to capture benefits of new opportunities as quickly as possible. Successful change consultants have learned to leverage this leadership impatience by creating champion roles that give leaders an active role in shaping empowered team thinking. This satisfies the leaders' need to move forward while providing empowered teams with the space to explore and address the new sustainable development concepts at their own pace.

Frequently, an essential component of the reinvention stage is **igniting** the enterprise, or reinventing primary components of the business model. This may take the form of igniting growth by achieving market focus in existing markets, migrating to new geographic regions, inventing new businesses, or utilizing technology to change the industry rules of competition. Igniting provides an opportunity to breathe new life into an organization. In situations in which igniting opportunities have been identified in the business case for change, empowered action learning teams are tasked with designing and implementing work processes, systems, and tools required to bring each opportunity to fruition. It is interesting to note that the same workplace reinvention processes used to streamline operations and cut costs may also be applied to designing and implementing enterprise growth opportunities. We have run interventions in which some natural work teams focus on improving operational efficiency and effectiveness while others focus on creating the growth engines that will sustain the enterprise during changing business conditions. This combination is particularly effective, as it offers the opportunity to align the organization to capture both relatively immediate, or short-term (efficiency), and longer-term (growth) benefits, rather than setting up a conflict between the two.

Igniting and aligning the fundamental value propositions underpinning basic business models is often an essential component of moving to a sustainable enterprise. The people, planet, profit perspective inherent in a TBL approach frequently necessitates reexamination of fundamental operational assumptions, many of which were developed and conceived during periods when organizations were designed primarily around a single bottom line.

Igniting is the single greatest factor distinguishing organization transformation interventions from mere downsizing. (See Box 4.9 "Do you need to downsize?" below.) In our experience, the most successful and sustainable enterprise transformations are conducted in organizations on the verge of significant (or even exponential) growth. The willingness to optimize and transform organization cultures as they approach periods of significant capital investment often distinguishes sustainable enterprises from those companies merely struggling to remain afloat. Even in cases in which downsizing may be essential, it still makes sense to engage the line employees in redesigning their future. It is discouraging to read accounts of companies that involved workers as simply a ploy to pacify workforce members, and it is important to note that true transformation requires more than mere lip-service to employee participation in the change process.

It is impossible to overstate the importance of pilot testing during this phase. Smart pilot testing is an iterative process, which takes advantage of opportunities to refine improvements on a small scale. This approach has the advantage of fostering broader engagement with the ultimate solutions as well as allowing additional people to contribute to refinements. Hallmarks of smart pilot testing:

- **Position it specifically as a pilot test.** Pilot tests nearly all have hiccups, glitches, and things you just didn't think about. Set the stage by declaring that this is a "beta" version!

- **Start in fertile ground.** Maximize your odds for success in the first pilot test. Ideally, the first pilot test will provide you with lots of feedback, including feedback to make corrections and improvements if needed.
- **Integrate learnings.** All your work to build credibility may come down to this moment: your ability to accept that some things could be better and you might not have been completely right on a thing or two. Some find analyzing pilot tests invigorating; others are crushed by small failures. A smart leader, firmly in the "invigorating" camp, recently said, "We had a successful pilot. We learned that our model doesn't work. Thank goodness we didn't go straight for the global launch!"
- **Pilot again.** This time, pilot in the most hostile conditions that your process will face. You've demonstrated that it *can* work at this point; now you are demonstrating that it *will* work, even under adverse circumstances.

Box 4.9   Do you need to downsize?

Despite substantial evidence that downsizing, especially "knee-jerk" downsizing, rarely leads to business success, it still seems to be a popular technique. Beyond the instant gratification of a reduced payroll, there's a quiet mythology that dramatic downsizing will exert a sort of Darwinian force on the work to be done. Only the most critical work will be completed. Products will ship, services will be rendered, invoices will be sent, bills will be paid. Presto, we eliminated all the unnecessary tasks with none of that pesky analysis or understanding work. We're heroes!

The above unkind characterization is not to suggest that downsizing is never necessary, or that, when necessary, it cannot be done with intelligence and integrity (Cascio, 2002). Armed with a thorough understanding of the work to be done and the staffing required to do it, one can make intelligent staffing-level decisions. In the ideal case, changes can be absorbed in the natural ebb and flow of the organization over the change period. In other instances, wise use of vendors and contractors is indicated. When staffing legitimately needs to be reduced, it is still possible to approach the situation with a TBL perspective. These people that you let go—they go somewhere. They accept positions with your suppliers, with your customers, with your competition, as your competition, on your city council, and on your kids' school board. In this world of mergers and acquisitions, they frequently end up back on your payroll. When planning a downsizing, be sure to consider not only the financial bottom line of the process, but also the human and community outcomes as well. Below are the best practices for downsizing well:

- Transparency and high integrity. Be clear and honest about why the steps you are taking are necessary, perhaps including alternative scenarios, or multiple options. Don't ask any questions or offer any options unless you are willing to live with the answers. Make clear the criteria for who is staying and who is going, and state any exceptions upfront. Occasionally, employees can be retrained or dedicated to new tasks, or groups of employees can move to reduced work schedules; if these are options, the same guidance regarding transparency and high integrity applies.
- Allow sufficient, appropriate, and clearly defined timelines. Depending on the circumstances, this may vary dramatically. We've shared examples here of planned transitions lasting over a year. Others will be much shorter.
- Provide some exit support. Many organizations have severance policies that include pay and/or benefits continuation. Not all organizations can afford such exit support. Depending on circumstances, organizations can offer exit support in the form of a guest office for a limited time for job hunting purposes, and to offer a sense of normalcy to the former employees. Human resources or recruiting can offer guidance on résumé writing, can make connections with other recruiters, or take other steps to help former employees with their job searches such as offering outplacement assistance.

Essentially, through pilot testing, you are creating a *bulletproof* process, as well as creating a growing group of advocates. Throughout the change, but especially in this phase, the role of leadership is to set direction and communicate priorities. Leadership alignment workshops focus management energy on clarifying enterprise mission, vision, values, and guiding principles that everyone will follow on the journey to sustainable enterprise. Many interventions include clarification of business drivers and/or anticipated obstacles the organization must overcome during its multiyear transformation process. Our interventions all include a **transformation map**, providing a powerful communication tool illustrating specific milestone goals, metrics, critical success factors, and high-level action plans to be achieved on a multiyear journey to sustainable enterprise. (See Box 4.10 "The case for mission statements," below; see Richard Knowles's essay "Engaging the natural tendency of self-organization," in Chapter 1 for additional insights into co-creating organizational or project "bowls" capturing employee imagination.)

Stage 3. Implementing future work

Implementing sustainable development work routines involves three distinct components:

- co-creating integrated implementation plans;
- refreshing workforce capabilities;
- mobilizing workforce resources.

Refreshing the enterprise entails refreshing the *esprit de corps* of the people investing their lives in the success of the organization. Refreshing is all about investing individuals with new skills and purposes, thus permitting the organization to regenerate itself. Renewal is an integral component of the empowered action learning team approach, and every aspect of creating, developing, and sustaining positive team dynamics must be modeled and practiced at every stage of the transformational intervention.

The nature of this work results in changes that truly are *better*: not simply more profitable, but solutions and approaches that eliminate persistent frustrations. The use of iterative pilot studies offers the opportunity to tangibly engage a growing portion of the organization. Combined with effective communications, and an intentionally inclusive project approach, tools such as pilot studies help these projects take advantage of natural tipping points to convert skepticism and resistance into enthusiasm.

Throughout this process, there is a gradual transfer of ownership for the change. In its initial phases, the change is driven very much by a small set of experts. However, as a project progresses, that small set of experts programmatically fades into the background. The job of this elite group is more to stretch the others with whom they work than it is to deliver results single-handedly. Though they may initially take a very directive role, by the end of a project they are entirely in the background. The crucible of an intense change project often hones capability in a dramatic way. The gradual transfer of ownership through the three phases—**reframing**, **reinventing**, and **implementing**—of this work and the intentional scaling by an order of magnitude at each step means that progress is less likely to halt when or if the core group is transitioned to new work. Rather, ownership and engagement are sufficiently diffused that the change will continue even after the original architects of the change have moved on.

Box 4.10   The case for mission statements

Most mission statements are useless, forgotten documents, full of meaningless clichés. Energy is poured into endless wordsmithing, and the final product is unveiled with much fanfare, only to be forgotten by the end of the quarter. Take a look at your organization's mission statement: Is there anything in that paragraph that is unique to your organization? Mission statements are commonly mundane and indistinct. And that's a pity.

Useful mission statements function in two ways. First, crafting a meaningful, common understanding of the purpose of an organization is an important exercise. Here, leadership teams can come to agreement on fundamental points of their business model—points that might otherwise have created discord, and suboptimal results. In one dramatic, and painful, example, a struggling leadership team battled over whether their job was to maximize profits for their division, or maximize profits for the business as a whole, through driving the value chain of the larger organizational *big bet*. This situation of dual, unarticulated priorities had existed for years and drained money and energy from the business. Only by confronting it head-on, as a leadership team, were they able to come to a unified strategy. As a result of the mission conversation, behavior changed. Thinking changed. And the business turned around.

The second way a good mission statement is useful is as a decision aid for the organization as a whole. A good mission is specific enough to help employees decide, should I do A or B? It will add transparency and accountability to the priorities set by leadership.

Even the best mission statement, however, is only as good as the leadership team backing it up. Actions do speak louder than words. A mission cannot drive sustainability in a system where all the reward systems are calculated on quarterly results.

Conclusion

Look, listen, move. Simple guidelines for the challenging sustainability road ahead to change and transform our enterprises. The Discovery expedition showed us that the ingredients of a clear challenge, excellent preparation, collaborative approach, and disciplined commitment to hard work could generate success. This is what is needed for organizations to drive internal and external change that will contribute to increased TBL success.

Achieving sustainable enterprise in the 21st century requires fundamental changes in the ways organizations manage enterprise processes and approach markets, customers, stakeholders, and shareholders. This chapter has discussed approaches to making that transition. The concepts and ideas discussed in this chapter are really just the next step in a natural evolution.

Both the development of an organization with a supportive culture and a skillful workforce, and the process of change to become a sustainable enterprise employ a systems approach advocating a multidimensional perspective of a complex whole. The evolution to embracing triple-bottom-line perspectives simply applies this same sophistication to sustainable development outcomes that we already recognize as inputs and throughputs in any organizational system.

Transformational change typically requires everyone to adopt new ways of thinking and behaving. The bottom line is that any enterprise will only perform differently when its people adopt new habits and work behaviors supported by realigned systems, tools, and talent management processes. Simply stated, this means co-creating and embracing new priorities and assuming new work routines in the daily course of adding value to the overall enterprise.

The secret to successful transformation to sustainable enterprise lies in the application of TBL perspectives on an organization-wide basis. This requires the willingness to expand traditional definitions of external stakeholder interests, while simultaneously engaging the minds and hearts of employees working to deliver increased value to all stakeholders. Sustainable enterprises embrace win–win–win strategies optimizing the needs of customers, employees, shareholders, communities, and governments, while avoiding attempts to maximize returns for any one group (such as shareholders) at the expense of others. They recognize that increases in shareholder value are inextricably connected to improved value propositions for all constituencies, and deliberately balance the needs of external and internal stakeholders. This multidimensional balance must be sustained through co-created conversations, at all levels, addressing issues critical to all enterprise stakeholders.

We can look at sustainable enterprise change most effectively by differentiating paradoxes from problems and considering the landscape of the whole system. Listening to be more inclusive, leaderful and authentic can provide the fertile ground for organic conversations to help us focus on the most impactful and lasting change. Moving together will generate both the shared ownership and disciplined testing of new approaches that will build new bridges of possibilities that will help us thrive.

Notes

1 www.luxcapital.com/about/
2 The FAIR model and its description are copyright 2008, Organization Innovation LLC. Used with permission.
3 For more on transforming mental models to bring them in sync with sustainable enterprise, see Chapter 2.

References

American Management Association (AMA). (2007). *Creating a sustainable future: A global study of current trends and possibilities 2007–2017*. New York: American Management Association.

Assis, V., & Elstrodt, H.-P. (2007). Positioning Brazil for bio-fuels success. *The McKinsey Quarterly, Special Edition: Shaping a New Agenda for Latin America, 2*, 1–6.

Aydinliyim, L., & Wirtenberg, J. (2017). Reimagining the twenty-first-century employment relationship: Aligning human resources and corporate social responsibility through employment policies and practices. In L. A. Berger & D. Berger (Eds.), *The talent management handbook* (3rd ed., pp. 456–470). New York: McGraw Hill.

Benson, J. (2007). DEP—Use sustainability as a standard: Commissioner delivers keynote speech at UConn Natural Resources Forum. *The Day*. Retrieved March 10, 2007, from www.theday.com.

Capra, F. (2007). Life and leadership: A systems approach (Executive summary). Retrieved December 21, 2007, from www.fritjofcapra.net/management.html.

Cascio, W. F. (2002). *Responsible restructuring: Creative and profitable alternatives to layoffs*. San Francisco, CA: Berrett-Koehler.

Correll, D. (2015, February 23). Three Jevons Paradoxes for the future of sustainable supply chain management—and one way to resolve them all. *CSR Wire*.

Diamond, J. (2005). *Collapse: How societies choose to fail or survive*. New York: Viking-Penguin.

Ehrenfeld, J., & Hoffman, A. J. (2013). *Flourishing: A frank conversation about sustainability*. Stanford, CA: Stanford University Press.

Harvard Business Review Staff. (2014, March). Mindfulness in the Age of Complexity. *Harvard Business Review*. Retrieved August 28, 2015, from https://hbr.org/2014/03/mindfulness-in-the-age-of-complexity.

King, M. L. (1963). I Have a Dream Speech, August 28. Retrieved May 5, 2018, from www.archives.gov/files/press/exhibits/dream-speech.pdf.

Kotter, J. P. (1996). *Leading change*. Boston, MA: Harvard Business School Press.

Lancaster, H. (1995, January 17). Reengineering authors reconsider reengineering. *Wall Street Journal*, 81.

Laszlo, C., & Brown, J. S. (2014). *Flourishing: The new spirit of business*. Stanford, CA: Stanford University Press.

Lewin, K. D. (1951). *Field theory in social science: Selected theoretical papers*. New York: Harper & Row.

McGraw-Hill. (2007). *Greening of corporate America* (McGraw-Hill SmartMarket Report: Design & Construction Intelligence Series). New York: McGraw-Hill Construction.

Mead, M. (1928). Author quote. Retrieved August 26, 2015, from www.goodreads.com/author/quotes/61107.Margaret_Mead.

Saling, P., & Kicherer, A. (2002). Eco-efficiency analysis by BASF: The method. *International Journal of Life Cycle Assessment, 7*(4), 203–218.

Schein, E. H., & Kampas, P. J. (2003). *DEC is dead, long live DEC*. San Francisco, CA: Berrett-Koehler.

Spivey, A. (2006, Fall). A golden rule for business: How sustainable enterprise serves the triple bottom line. *UNC Business*, pp. 7–11.

Sterman, J. D. (2001). System dynamics modeling: Tools for leading in a complex world. *California Management Review, 43*(4), 8–25.

Strebel, P. (2000). Why do employees resist change? In *Harvard Business Review* OnPoint Collection, *Creating followers: Framing change initiatives to maximize employee participation* (pp. 23–36). Boston, MA: Harvard Business School Publishing.

United Nations Industrial Development Organization (UNIDO). (2002). *Eco-efficiency for SMEs in the Moroccan dyeing industry. Phase I: A sustainable approach to industrial development* (UNIDO Project Report). Vienna: United Nations Industrial Development Organization.

Wirtenberg, J. (2014). *Building a culture for sustainability: People, planet, and profits in a new green economy.* Santa Barbara, CA: Praeger.

Wirtenberg, J. (2016). The living organization: Designing a new landscape for OD. In W. J. Rothwell, J. M. Stavros, R. L. Sullivan, & J. D. Vogelsang (Eds.), *Organization development in practice* (pp. 150–167). San Francisco, CA: Organization Development Network.

Employee engagement for a sustainable enterprise

Jeana Wirtenberg, Kent D. Fairfield, Richard N. Knowles, William G. Russell, and Sangeeta Mahurkar-Rao

> What is the point of hiring all these brilliant people and then telling them what to do?
>
> (Steve Jobs)

Over the past decade, employee engagement has risen to the top of the business agenda—HR professionals have been alarmed about the ubiquitous low levels of employee engagement for decades—but for senior business leaders as well (Deloitte University Press, 2015). Gallup's 142-country study on the State of the Global Workplace found that only 1 in 8 workers—roughly 180 million employees in the countries studied—were psychologically committed to their jobs and likely to be making positive contributions (Gallup, 2013). Recent research reported by WeSpire (2015) corroborated this statistic, finding that only 13% of global employees are engaged in their work.

Business leaders have come to realize that having an engaged, purpose-driven workforce is not only essential for them to become a high performance workplace, but is a necessity for their business to survive. Why? Because an engaged workforce gives them a competitive edge in the hypercompetitive marketplace for top talent and in turn leads to increased productivity, creativity, innovation, and bottom-line results. Moreover, an engaged workforce drastically reduces HR costs related to attraction, recruitment, and retention.

Research shows that highly engaged employees can improve business performance by up to 30%, and that fully engaged employees are 2.5 times more likely to exceed performance expectations than their "disengaged" colleagues (Willard, 2012). The Corporate Leadership Council (2007) found that companies with engaged employees grew profits three times faster than their competitors, had 87% less staff turnover, and achieved 20% better performance than average. A global study by Towers Perrin-ISR (2014) found that operating income of companies with engaged employees improved by 19% in one year versus a decline of 33% for companies with low levels of employee engagement.

Enhancing employee engagement through sustainability

So how do we define employee engagement, how does it relate to sustainability, and what do we do about it? This chapter lays out some fundamental principles of employee engagement in the context of sustainability management, provides illustrative case studies of five exemplary organizations, and offers some conclusions about how today's managers can use this knowledge in their own organizations.

> Real engagement unleashes our potential, and leverages our innate need to experience ourselves as creative beings.
>
> (Renee Lertzman)

Employee engagement is a combination of commitment to the organization and its values, plus a willingness to help out colleagues. It is closely related to the notion of organizational citizenship. It goes beyond job satisfaction and is not simply motivation. Engagement is something the employee has to offer. It cannot be "required" as part of the employment contract.

Engagement subsumes a myriad of employees' perceptions, including their satisfaction, commitment, pride, loyalty, personal responsibility, and advocacy for the organization. When employees are engaged, they are able to withstand limited periods of lower work satisfaction and still remain highly committed. When employees are fully engaged, they are more conscientious, productive, and committed to their work. The essence of engagement can be described as "psychological ownership."

The key to employee engagement is unlocking what already resides in people, including their natural creativity and inventiveness. According to the World Business Council on Sustainable Development (WBCSD, 2010), 59% of engaged employees say their job brings out their most creative ideas versus 3% for disengaged employees. To increase employee engagement we need to open the doorway for employees to "give it their all" at work, using their unique gifts and powers as they apply their valuable discretionary energy.

Research has shown that employee engagement manifests in four essential domains: employees' (1) feelings of urgency; (2) feelings of being focused; (3) feelings of intensity; and (4) feelings of enthusiasm (Macey, Schneider, Barbera, & Young, 2009, p. 20). Unleashing these feelings on behalf of sustainable business practices will benefit the employees, the organizations they work for, and the world.

How to do this is rapidly becoming the Holy Grail and organizations are experimenting with many different approaches. Underlying all these approaches are two fundamentally different views about the psychology of sustainability and what makes people do what they do. On the one hand, we have rewards and incentives, games (discussed in detail below), competitions, pledges, and even mandates.

Renee Lertzman (2015) proposes another view, arguing persuasively that we need to go beyond "nudging, gaming and competing" and find a new

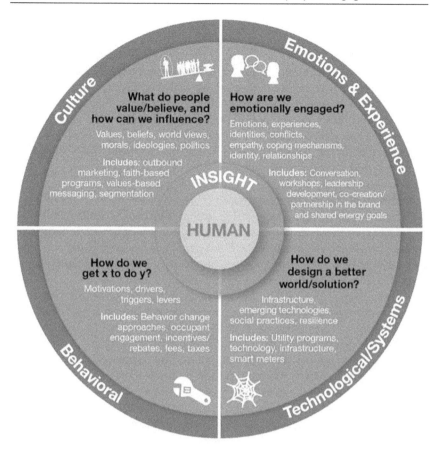

Figure 5.1 Designing real engagement
Source: Copyright 2015, Renee Lertzman. Reproduced with permission.

psychology of sustainability that is in its own unique category. According to Lertzman (Figure 5.1), we need to attend to all four ways that people think, behave, and practice engagement. From a *cultural* perspective, we need to understand what people value and believe, and figure out if and how we can influence their *values*. From a *behavioral* perspective, we need to figure out if and how we can get people to *act* sustainably. From a *technological systems* perspective, we need to figure out how we can design a better world *solution* to the problems we are addressing so behavior change isn't even required but just emerges organically. Most importantly, and least understood, we need to get at people's deep *emotions, experiences, and identities*, and how they can find ways to gratify these through their work.

The greatest threat to our planet is the belief that someone will save it.
(Robert Swan)

By its very nature, sustainability conversations call up deep-seated fears, anxieties, and ambivalence in people. These conversations threaten everything people think they know and need to survive. At the same time, it has the potential to elicit people's highest callings, life purpose, aspirations, hopes, and dreams. It paves the way for people to make a difference with their lives and build mastery over new challenges. It can lead them to develop new competencies and discover new pathways for exploration on the never-ending search for a sense of oneness and connectedness.

A great many employees today are craving this sense of shared purpose; they want to know how what they do will contribute to not only their organizations, but to themselves and society. But our approaches to employee engagement are all too often one-sided.

According to Bill Jensen's (2014) recent Future of Work study, our approaches are fundamentally lopsided; they use too much of a corporate-centric lens, focus too much on how the employee can benefit the company, and are missing at least half of what the future of the work relationship is about. Employees of the future

> see companies as vehicles to achieve their goals and dreams—vehicles that can amplify their passions, achievements and community relationships beyond what they could have done on their own or elsewhere. A company's and leader's vision is absolutely crucial to this—employees [will stay] only if that vision matches what's already in the worker's soul, and only if the company creates an exciting space for the worker to explore his/her passions and push them further. *Vision excites people* … But the way many companies run their business destroys the excitement.
>
> Add in other trends—continued growth in freelance workers, GenY/GenZ views about work, tenure with any one company continues to decrease—and the workforce's view of seeing companies as vehicles to fulfill their own needs will only get stronger.
>
> (Jensen, 2014, p. 13)

Furthermore, Jensen's Future of Work study provides a very different perspective on all the reports of chronic disengagement at work. In this view, the lack of engagement does not mean that the workforce is disengaged from working on what matters to them. In fact, they are extremely engaged in their quest to achieve their hopes and dreams. What it does mean is that the workforce is extremely frustrated with business' lack of desire or ability to be a vehicle for achieving their dreams and goals. Only 29% agreed with the statement, "I can achieve my dreams and goals where I currently work." Significantly, nearly three-quarters of the people who work do not believe they can meet their personal goals in today's work environments (Jensen, 2014, p. 15).

Recent research sheds light on how we can address these employee concerns through sustainability. Studies have shown that employees want to be involved with sustainability initiatives. The participants in one survey reported overwhelmingly that they would rather be employed by a company that practices sustainability; 96% said they would like to work at a successful company that also aspires to be good (Willard, 2012). Furthermore, considerable evidence exists that employees welcome the chance to exercise autonomy and creativity when given the opportunity (Goleman, Boyatzis, & McKee, 2013; Pink, 2011). By this thinking, managers need to lay out the direction, provide resources and guidance, and then move to a supportive role.

A key aspect of sustainability is how seriously the company takes its corporate social responsibility (CSR) (Wirtenberg, 2014). Employees who say they have the opportunity to make a direct social and environmental impact through their job report higher satisfaction levels than those who don't by a 2:1 ratio (Net Impact, 2012). CSR and employee engagement are highly correlated and often go hand in hand, since both bring about increases in pride, satisfaction, advocacy, and retention.

CSR drives good business results through such human resource outcomes as attraction, retention, and even compensation. According to the WBCSD People Matter study (2010):

- 70% of employees with a favorable perception of their company's community engagement plan to stay for the next two years, versus 50% of those with a less favorable perception.
- 75% would recommend their company if they feel it is environmentally responsible versus fewer than 50% if it is not.
- 47% of job seekers are more likely to join/stay with a company that addresses social issues.
- 75% of employees who consider their employers to pay enough attention to environmental protection and sustainable development exhibit higher levels of commitment.

All other things being equal, a significant percentage of employees would even be willing to take a 15% pay cut to work for a company that is committed to corporate social responsibility, according to Net Impact's (2012) "Talent Report: What workers want":

- 35% would be willing to take a 15% pay cut to work for a company committed to CSR;
- 45% would for a job that makes a social or environmental impact;
- 58% would to work for an organization with values like their own.

Furthermore, PwC's 2011 study of millennials at work found that:

- 88% of graduate students and young professionals factor an employer's CSR position into their job decision; and

- 86% would consider leaving a job if their employer's CSR performance no longer held up.

Factor into the equation that it costs two to three times an employee's salary to replace him or her, and we have a strong business case for CSR from a strictly financial perspective as well as a human one!

Gamification-enhanced employee engagement

Gamification has emerged as an innovative tool for elevating awareness, enhancing learning experiences and changing behaviors. American Express (2012) defined gamification as "using game technology in a Website, service, community or application in order to drive participation. It's a perfect way to create customer engagement or employee participation."

Employee engagement has been an obvious context for developers to produce gamification platforms and "gamified" applications. Corporations are integrating "gameful" design elements into a diverse set of existing employee engagement activities such as training, performance management, and sustainability program implementation systems.

The Marriot Group was an early adopter of gamification for engaging employees and customers. The My Marriott Hotel game is a brand awareness and educational tool that gives people a behind the scenes look at what it takes to run a hotel. WeSpire is an example employee engagement platform used by companies including MGM Resorts International, McDonald's, and Unilever. Its platform includes proven gamified programs for sustainability, corporate citizenship, volunteering, and wellbeing.

GlobStrat, another illustrative tool, is a triple-bottom-line business simulation platform. GlobStrat is used by numerous universities to better integrate sustainability concepts into the teaching of topics such as strategy, leadership, and finance. Companies including Apple, L'Oreal, and Renault see GlobStrat as a safe place to obtain critical sustainability-aligned experiential learning for current and potential new business leaders and to improve the effectiveness of cross-functional employee resource groups and green teams. GlobStrat is the centerpiece of Transitioning to Green's Leadership for Sustainability program and Rutgers Executive Education Mini-MBA on Sustainability-Aligned Leadership and Strategy, providing hands-on experiential learning for managers and executives in all functions of the corporation.

While effective design and implementation are critical for achieving successful outcomes, the initial user feedback and superior outcomes of gamified programs indicate even broader adoption and expansion of gamification tools in the future. See the *Living Fieldbook* for more details about gamification genres and tools, gamefulness design attributes and related company case studies.

What employee engagement looks like

If you want to go fast, go alone. If you want to go far, go together.
(African proverb)

In their well-known book *The Leadership Challenge*, Kouzes and Posner (2007) say that employee engagement has to build on a foundation of creating a climate of trust, listening in depth, and sharing information and resources. They urge leaders to build a sense of interdependence, which, they say, stems from cooperative goals and roles, norms of reciprocity, and face-to-face interactions. They stress the importance of employees feeling powerful and in control of their lives. Skillful leaders engender this sense of self-determination, which breeds ownership and motivation. One young manager was thrilled when his boss asked his opinion and gave him the leeway to make an important decision about how to carry out a demanding task. "He backed me up completely ... and I subsequently did everything I could to ensure our success. There was no way I was going to let us not be successful" (Kouzes & Posner, 2007, p. 254).

This manager exemplifies the natural dynamic in which more power and authority lead to a greater sense of accountability. As people doing collaborative projects begin to trust that their colleagues will perform their tasks, everyone feels responsible for carrying out his or her own job. Thus, more power and autonomy interact with more accountability and more ownership, which increases the chance for success. Kouzes and Posner (2007) also hold that developing competence and confidence are foundational to employee involvement. As people develop their competence and confidence, they feel effective in what they do. Research shows that such self-efficacy contributes greatly to taking initiative, persisting under duress, and even enjoying better heath (Bandura, 1997; Saks, 1995).

Another approach engages employees by building on what is seen as the natural tendency to self-organize. Practitioner and consultant Richard Knowles argues that people will organize themselves around anything that is important to them, whether management intends it or not (Knowles, 2002, 2006; see also pages 39–43). If unprompted, they may work out problems together, gossip together, or work counter to corporate intentions: self-organizing will continue no matter what, and, depending on whether leadership encourages it, the self-organization will be productive or non- or counterproductive. The challenge of management, he says, is to set up conditions for employees to enthusiastically address the key issues for success—productively self-organizing. He recommends a series of conversations in which leadership shares important information with workers. These conversations build interdependent relationships and trust and help people discover how they and their work fit into the work at large—thereby encouraging employees to find meaning in their work.

People's natural energy fuels such an approach, as opposed to a command-and-control mode, which "is like trying to remove the twists and turns from a river and forcing it to flow the way we want" (Knowles, 2006, p. 2). Instead, management's real role is to help clarify the foundation principles co-created by leadership and employees, such as vision, mission, and standards of performance—a "Bowl" in which everyone operates—and then step back allowing the workers to self-organize into teams for the work ahead. At the DuPont plant in Belle, West Virginia, according to Knowles (see the DuPont case in this chapter, pages 231–234) workers self-organized into scores of teams and management moved out of the way, thus encouraging the productive self-organizing tendencies of the workers to come to the fore.

A third perspective that focuses on mobilizing energy comes from Linda Gratton (2007), who asserts that the most outstanding performance arises from "hot spots," work units characterized by cooperation, energy, innovation, productivity, and excitement. Organizations that create such hot spots elicit people's potential around what they find most meaningful. Gratton argues that hot spots arise from a cooperative mindset, spanning of boundaries, and an igniting purpose, in concert with productive capacity.

More recently, Gratton (2011) describes five forces that are already causing a profound and fundamental shift in how employees engage at work: technology, globalization, demography and longevity, society, and energy resources. Each of these forces is explored further throughout this chapter and book.

Employee engagement in sustainability management

The value generally derived from employee engagement can be further amplified in organizations that aspire to sustainability management. Most executives in such organizations will articulate the vision of an enterprise that is prospering economically, contributing to social values in-house and in the world, and encouraging environmental stewardship, or, taken together, the triple bottom line. Employees tend to relate these goals to their own values. One HR executive at a multinational firm commented (Wirtenberg, Harmon, Russell, & Fairfield, 2007, p. 16) on how employee engagement and sustainability work together for corporate success:

> A big advantage to sustainability is getting employees engaged because they want to make a difference in the world. I work with a lot of committed people whose lives are about making a difference and choose to do it here at [our company] … Everyone agrees that's what is going to help make us one of the greatest companies in the world.

The AMA sustainability survey (AMA, 2007) asked how important 18 different sustainability-related issues—such as a safe work environment, clean water, fighting corruption, affordable clean energy, and global climate change—are to the respondents. They rated 80% of them as highly important, averaging 4.3 on a scale of 1.0–5.0, ranging from 3.8 to 4.8. Interestingly, the respondents also said they believed their organizations viewed every one of these issues as being appreciably less important than they did. Presumably they would find it more satisfying if their organizations pursued such sustainability factors more vigorously. If their leaders issued the invitation, the people would follow.

In fact, organizations engaged in sustainability management are at an advantage in hiring top talent. In a study (Wirtenberg et al., 2007, p. 16) of the most highly regarded sustainability management companies, one HR executive said,

> The better [our firm] is branded as a company that's sustainable and doing the right thing, the better I'm going to be able to attract talent, because the talent wants to work with the best companies, and the best companies are those that not only get results, but do it in a way that creates a sustainable environment.

Recent psychological research helps explain how people working for what they regard as a good cause feel better physically and are galvanized to exert exceptional effort toward related goals. Martin Seligman (Seligman, 2011; Seligman & Csikszentmihalyi, 2000) has done seminal research in this area and founded a school of thought called "positive psychology." His research shows how people engaging in acts of altruism, generosity, and the like exhibit beneficial physical symptoms and higher levels of happiness. Over the past decade, organizational researchers have established a new field—"positive organizational scholarship"—that embraces the impact of positive actions in the context of an enterprise or community (Cameron, Dutton, & Quinn, 2003). To the extent that employees feel deeply about the aims of sustainability—and they can see the connection between their job and those aims—they can regard their work as holding special meaning. Studies have shown that people perform at a higher level when their work is not "just a job" but is more of a calling (Wrzesniewski, 2003), and "those with callings often feel that their work makes the world a better place" (Hurst, 2014; Wrzesniewski, 2002, p. 232). Some have described this dynamic, in which employees feel part of something greater than themselves and realize personal aspirations and potential, as achieving "transcendence" (Ashforth & Pratt, 2002). More recently, Clayton Christensen, a leading thinker on innovation, invited his readers to deeply explore this for themselves in his *New York Times* bestseller *How Will You Measure Your Life?* (2012).

Goleman and his colleagues (Goleman et al., 2013) explain how neuroscience helps to elucidate the biochemical reasons for these reactions. They argue that excellent leaders exhibit high levels of emotional intelligence, founded on keen self-awareness of their own emotions, the ability to regulate their emotions, and a high degree of empathy for the emotions of others. As a result, such leaders are skilled at managing relationships with others, including building rapport, leading teams, solving conflicts gracefully, and inspiring others to action. Such *resonant leaders* are transparent in what they do. They are genuinely authentic in that their actions and language are fully congruent with their values, which is essential to the move toward sustainability management.

Boyatzis and McKee (2007) reported their research that resonant leaders are mindful, or fully conscious, of themselves, others, nature, and the larger world. They deal with the world with hope and an optimistic, confident vision of achieving their dreams. In addition, resonant leaders exhibit compassion toward their co-workers and those whom they serve. Neuropsychological research has provided evidence for why such emotions are literally contagious insofar as others react positively at a subconscious level. This dynamic can produce powerful collective action.

Some companies have taken concrete steps to engage their employees in highly personal ways in the cause of sustainability. For example, the multinational mining and metals company Alcoa has invited employees' children to do drawings of what a sustainable world would be like. This naturally prompts family discussions that can help employees see the subject through youthful eyes—and through a lens of their legacy for future generations.

While many people associate Wal-Mart with its well-known efforts to provide low prices through rigorous cost controls, outsourcing, and low wages, the company has taken major strides to place environmental sustainability at the center of its strategic focus (Scott, 2005). One far-reaching program of employee engagement arranges for thousands of Wal-Mart employees at all levels to attend workshops about sustainability. They return to their stores and offices and invite their co-workers to design a "personal sustainability project." These projects may be as simple as replacing light bulbs with low-energy alternatives at home or riding a bike more. Discussions about the projects take place at work, and headquarters tracks their progress (Sacks, 2007). Such a program clearly attempts to encourage employees to feel a new affinity for the environment and to begin to align their own values with those of the company—deriving meaning from being a part of something bigger. While each project may be small, the potential impact on the thinking of some portion of the company's 1.9 million employees and the cumulative effect on the world could be considerable.

Case studies

Five case studies illustrate some of the above approaches to employee engagement and provide a basis for developing other strategies and tactics for outstanding management.

1. **A story from the DuPont Plant in Belle, West Virginia.** The author describes his own experience helping the people to enhance their safety, operating results, and morale in a large chemical plant handling hazardous materials by enabling self-organizing practices and a holistic approach that resulted in opening up the opportunities for people to step forward and take the lead when they saw a need for improvement. In engaging *with* the people, rather than trying to do things *to* the people, many began to give their gift of discretionary energy; this is the energy over and beyond that needed to do the minimum job requirements. This enabled the plant to move to sustainable levels of safety and performance excellence lasting for 16 years at which time management had drifted back into the old, command-and-control ways and performance fell apart; they then had a fatality.

2. **Energizing people to create a safer, healthier workforce at PSE&G.** A multi-stage effort brings union members and management together with new initiatives reducing accidents and stimulating creative solutions.

3. **Engaging employees in social consciousness at Eileen Fisher.** An apparel manufacturer founded on principles of simplicity, joy, and human connection achieves consistent profitability while remaining devoted to improving the lot of women and the environment.

4. **Environmental, health, and safety issues at Alcoa Howmet.** One man conducts a long-standing campaign to ensure that safety concerns are infused into every activity and person in a high-precision metals fabricator.

5. **Employee engagement at T-Systems: sustaining the organization and beyond.** A grassroots employee effort to deal with intolerable traffic conditions becomes an organization-wide change project that spreads over the whole community, with clear human and environmental benefits.

This section starts with a first-person account of a broad-based management effort in a DuPont manufacturing plant.

Case 1. A story from the DuPont Plant in Belle, West Virginia

Richard N. Knowles

When I was appointed plant manager at the Belle, West Virginia, plant, I found its overall performance was dreadful, especially in safety. Although people were trying to do a good job, they had been performing so poorly for so long that it seemed acceptable. The main task of the 1,300 workers was to safely handle highly hazardous materials to make chemical intermediates and products. The plant dealt with large quantities of these materials. For example, from time to time, there would be 10–15 tank cars of hydrogen cyanide and up to 10,000 tons of anhydrous ammonia awaiting use as raw materials.

Actions

At the corporate level, DuPont had long singled out safety as a critical value, and the Belle Plant was nearly the poorest performer in the company. As I met everyone over the first three weeks, I was very clear that we had to get safety under control. My core belief was, "I don't have a right to make my living at a place where it is okay for you to get hurt." Most of the operators, mechanics, truck drivers, and railroad operators were intrigued by this, since they were the ones who were sustaining the injuries.

My safety focus began with the plant staff; this was serious, and the staff needed to establish new standards. I used a tough, top-down approach and had to terminate a few people because of safety performance problems. I walked the plant four to five hours a day, talking about this. There were many heated arguments about sticking to necessary procedures. Twice a week, I had one-hour business meetings in an operating area, shop, office, or the lab. After reviewing our safety and environmental situation, I invited questions and answered every one. I promptly distributed meeting minutes to everyone. After many acrimonious sessions in which people vented their frustrations, the meetings became more purposeful. Together we talked about the plant's challenges and how we should go forward. I placed responsibility for safety clearly on the shoulders of line supervisors rather than on staff safety specialists, who were to function in a support role. During these times, people told me they began to see me as focused, honest, determined, and fair.

Within about 18 months, the plant's safety performance improved to about average for DuPont. However, people were still getting hurt, so this was not good enough. The top-down process was moving us in the right direction, but the results were only mediocre. Furthermore, the arguments over safety had become tiresome and insufficient. The top-down approach was clearly unsustainable.

As new leadership staff came on board, we decided to use a plant-wide team approach that we thought could be much more effective if we did it right. The staff began with the development of the "Belle Treatment of People Principles."

These were simple statements about how we on the management staff wanted to work with everyone. They included such principles as the importance of interesting, challenging work with the potential for learning and growth, personal accountability, involvement in decision-making, and the need for fair and consistent management. The management staff posted these principles around the plant, asking for people to hold staff accountable for living up to them. The workers' first reaction was to laugh at us. "You SOBs won't do this." But when they saw the managers were trying, they held us to it and really castigated us if we messed up. In fact, after about nine months of this rough-and-tumble approach, most of the people were adopting these as *their own* values—a fundamental shift.

Having established a clear mission and values and clarified the issues facing us, we introduced a team approach. The management staff spent about six months talking with everyone about teams and training people to be team leaders and facilitators. Everyone in the entire plant then moved, over one weekend, to form about 125 self-organizing teams, markedly transforming how we worked together. The transition was a bit ragged as everyone gradually became accustomed to the new system, but our total performance, including safety, did not drop during this time. Nearly all the self-organizing teams were coming up with better ways to improve performance and lower costs; valuable new bottom-up change initiatives went from a trickle to three or four a month. The work that started on safety issues had spread to all aspects of the plant. In safety, our plant became the third best in all of DuPont, even though the plant had to make reductions in the workforce.

All through this work, the leadership approach had to be flexible and responsive to the business- and people-related situations that came up. Our preferred approach was centered on engaging purposefully with the force of people's self-organization tendencies by actively sharing information, increasing trust, and building interdependence. In our conversations together, I helped everyone see how they fit into the larger picture and were helping to make a difference. Still, there were times when the standards dropped, and I had to take decisive action to reestablish them. Shortly before I moved on to another assignment, a supervisor committed what everyone acknowledged was a gross safety violation, and I had to fire him.

I regard this way of leading as a "dance" that requires leaders to pay attention to patterns and processes and constantly adjust to the demands of the present moment. I am proud to say that during these seven and a half years, the patterns and processes of sustainability became so deeply embedded within the people at the Belle plant that even a decade later their safety performance has continued to improve. For several years, the Belle plant actually posted the best safety record in DuPont.

Critical results

Over a period of less than eight years, the injury rate dropped 98%, plant emissions dropped 87%, productivity rose 45%, and earnings rose 300%. This persuasively exemplifies the triple-bottom-line benefit of sustainability management. It could not have happened unless everyone was pulling together. No one person could have brought this about. This employee-involvement effort was one in which I invited everyone to come together to help make the plant the best it could be. My role evolved from slave-driver to cheerleader, which was a lot more fun and satisfying.

Key learnings

Achieving this kind of transformation with vigorous employee engagement and high levels of performance requires leaders who:

- can see the patterns and processes of behavior involved in how work really gets done;
- understand that different situations require different leadership approaches;
- are willing to share information freely with employees and be as transparent as possible, maintaining conversations across all levels;
- can build trust and interdependence between workers and managers;
- help people create a vision and mission that is credible and important for everyone, allowing them to see how they fit into the larger picture;
- have the courage, caring, and commitment to stay in the process and help make it happen;
- have the courage and willingness to talk with the people, listen to them, discover new ideas with them and build a shared future together. Looking together for both/and solutions rather than getting stuck with either/or solutions leads to performance excellence. Doing things with the people rather than to them is a powerful shift in the culture.

The cornerstone of this employee engagement rested on management's genuine desire to enlist the best ideas and effort from employees while standing firm for standards that were nonnegotiable. Leadership had to be authentic, open, and honest. When we made mistakes, we apologized and moved on. Eventually employees sensed a calling to take responsibility for success and could see every day how their behavior contributed to it.

Key ideas and tools illustrated here

- Taking a stand for high standards and humane practices.
- Seeing the limitations of top-down management and transitioning to more employee-driven methods.
- Inviting all levels of an organization into dialogue and acting on resulting ideas.
- Building engagement around self-organizing teams.
- The gift of discretionary energy is available only when we are working *with* each other with integrity, trust, and authenticity. Trying to force this from people does not work.

In the years since this work I have come to see, with many organizations, how fundamentally important this way of leading is to building sustainability. Organizations are Complex Adaptive Systems; this is how to engage with the people, as partners, in co-creating a sustainable future. I call this way of leading Partner-Centered Leadership.

The next case study concerns another industrial challenge, but here the challenge is faced by PSE&G, a company with hundreds of different sites.

Case 2. Energizing people to create a safer, healthier workforce at PSE&G

James J. Colligan Jr., Thomas K. Robinson, and Jeana Wirtenberg

Public Service Electric & Gas, New Jersey's largest energy company, reacted to several workforce fatalities by commissioning a team in 1997 to benchmark other companies to determine the critical elements of their success in health & safety. This led to a multifaceted safety system, a Commitment Statement endorsed by management and union leaders, and a grassroots-led council structure.

Although consistently improving over the five years after the team was commissioned, the safety record seemed to plateau by 2003 at around the 2.5 OSHA (Occupational Safety & Health Administration) Incident Rate, meaning that approximately 150 people were injured annually. While this represented a significant improvement over previous years, the new president of PSE&G challenged a small team of safety and organizational effectiveness people to devise an approach that would enable the company to reduce the rate even more. This effort took place during a period of uncertainty caused by a highly publicized pending merger and resulting staff reductions. While initial efforts in the early 2000s were successful in improving the company's safety culture and results, it still wasn't reaching its Top Decile performance goal for the OSHA Incident Rate.

After winning a contract to manage LIPA's (Long Island Power Authority) Transmission & Distribution operations in 2011, the President of PSE&G renewed the challenge for both PSE&G and PSEG Long Island (PSEG LI) to achieve Top Decile safety performance. He rallied the management and unions of both companies to renew their efforts to achieve this level of performance to ensure the company's employees returned home in the same condition they arrived at work.

Actions

In formulating its plan, PSE&G could build on strong working relationships between company and union leadership that were forged during earlier total quality management initiatives. Together they built a new effort on this foundation, using well-established change management principles, including a

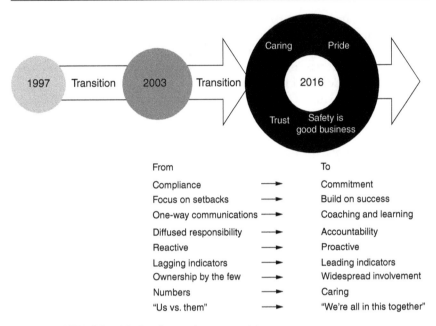

From		To
Compliance	→	Commitment
Focus on setbacks	→	Build on success
One-way communications	→	Coaching and learning
Diffused responsibility	→	Accountability
Reactive	→	Proactive
Lagging indicators	→	Leading indicators
Ownership by the few	→	Widespread involvement
Numbers	→	Caring
"Us vs. them"	→	"We're all in this together"

Figure 5.2 PSE&G health & safety culture transition
Source: Copyright 2017, PSE&G. Reproduced with permission.

clear, compelling vision, leadership support, employee engagement, regular reporting, recognition and celebration of short-term wins, and reinvigoration with new projects and people.

Creation of vision

Leaders conducted a series of facilitated visioning sessions in mid-2003 with approximately 150 grassroots employees representing many locations. Participants identified four major components of the desired culture of the future: pride, caring, trust, and "health & safety is good business." They also envisioned a variety of desired values and practices that represented a significant departure from the early days' sometimes distant labor management relations (see Figure 5.2).

Leadership commitment and employee participation

Armed with the new vision, the consulting team formed the Health & Safety Culture Transition Team, comprising about 70 people. The team's initial objectives were to:

- develop alternative measures for safety and benchmarking where applicable;

- create a strategy where union and management trust each other and work well together;
- design and develop a robust, interactive approach to safety communications;
- originate a method to build a learning organization;
- construct a plan to develop and nurture an expanded cadre of safety leaders.

All participants volunteered for a particular subteam, each of which was championed by a member of the PSE&G senior leadership team and supported by a subject matter expert, such as internal communications or health and wellness. The leadership also appointed a core team, consisting of the subteam leaders and champions, union safety leaders, and subject matter experts. The core team was to monitor progress and approve initiatives as they were developed by the subteams. Approved initiatives became part of the agenda for the full team at subsequent quarterly update meetings.

Reinvigoration with new projects

Based on the successful outcomes of the first two years and input obtained by the benchmarking subteam, project leadership created in 2006 two additional subteams, driving safety and ergonomics. Patterned after the original subteams, both of these groups have made significant contributions to ongoing results. In fact, the driving safety team's efforts led to the creation of a new safety system component. Such evolving contributions reinforce the important principle of emergence to continually reinvigorate an initiative and remain open to new learnings.

To build on the company's prior safety team accomplishments, the President of PSE&G commissioned a Lean Six Sigma Team in 2013 to develop a common Incident Investigation and Analysis process for both PSE&G and PSEG LI. The goal was to determine and share root causes and action plans for safety incidents in order to improve organizational learning and results. The initial process and associated data were shared in an MS SharePoint system which has now transitioned to a web-based Safety Information Management System (SIMS). Documenting and sharing safety incident root causes and action plans has supported the improvement of the company's OSHA Incident Rate for both companies. In 2016, PSE&G achieved Top Decile OSHA Incident Rate performance and PSEG LI is dramatically improving. Leveraging the success of the Incident Investigation and Analysis Team, the President of PSE&G further commissioned best practice studies in 2016 for general safety (OSHA, First Aids) and motor vehicle incidents to determine if its processes and procedures were in line with Top Decile performing utilities. These teams provided new areas for the company to improve in 2017 in order to reach and sustain Top Decile safety performance. These areas include: (1) the establishment of an Executive Safety Forum comprised of top union and management leaders; (2) improving the company's safety training for general safety and motor vehicle incidents; (3) consistent development and use of job hazard analyses/field observations; (4) identification and training of high-risk drivers; and (5) review and appropriate utilization of motor vehicle technology.

Critical results

The health & safety culture transition and subsequent safety team accomplishments include:

* a safety and wellness intranet site providing access to resources;
* A common Safety Information Management System to improve learning;
* annual health & safety plans for each location;
* the safety leading-indicator measurement system;
* knowledge-sharing sessions with external best-practice organizations;
* ongoing ergonomic efforts to decrease the incidence and severity of musculoskeletal injuries.

PSE&G's OSHA Incident Rate has steadily declined; the 2006 results were almost half those of the previous five years. Also the injuries that have occurred have been less serious. Employees at many locations have worked for extended periods without a personal injury. These results were especially noteworthy considering the reduced staffing levels in anticipation of a pending merger and related uncertainty about employees' future. Our continued team efforts have led to PSE&G achieving Top Decile OSHA Incident Rate performance in 2016 and PSEG LI dramatically improving over the past several years (Figures 5.3 and 5.4).

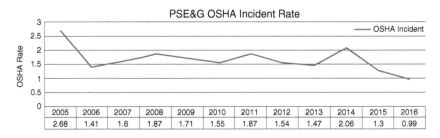

Figure 5.3 PSE&G OSHA Incident Rate
Source: Copyright 2017, PSE&G. Reproduced with permission.

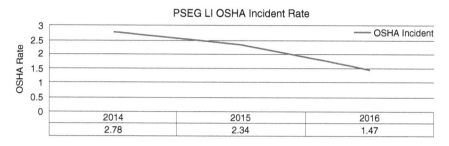

	PSEG LI OSHA Incident Rate	
2014	2015	2016
2.78	2.34	1.47

Figure 5.4 **PSEG LI OSHA Incident Rate**
Source: Copyright 2017, PSE&G. Reproduced with permission.

Learnings

This case illustrates that sustainability is a journey that must start from a solid foundation of focus, commitment, and participation. It also highlights how application of solid change management principles can enable the creation of a safer and healthier work environment, ultimately contributing to improved performance. It clearly shows that creative, focused efforts by a group of dedicated people can achieve extraordinary results, even during periods of exceptional change, uncertainty, and distraction. These efforts have laid the foundation for continued improvement into the future.

Key ideas and tools illustrated here

*   Building on strong working relationships between management and union leadership.
*   Visible senior leadership support as a critical lever.
*   Use of total quality management tools in supporting health & safety initiatives.
*   Importance of having a clear and compelling vision that everyone creates and supports.

Other companies approach sustainability with a focus on social justice and human welfare. Eileen Fisher founded her company around such principles, as described in this case study.

Case 3. Engaging employees in social consciousness at Eileen Fisher

William G. Russell

Eileen Fisher invested her US$350 in savings in 1984 to purchase materials and have a seamstress make up four pieces of clothing that she herself wanted to wear, products that would simplify life and delight the spirit. She promptly caught the eye of retailers at an industry show, and an enterprise was born. By 2007, this still privately held company boasted US$225 million in sales, 39 of its own retail stores, and 1,000 department store outlets. Some 700 employees, 80% female, work for the firm, augmented by an extended labor force in suppliers' factories located in the United States, China, India, Western Europe, and South America.

Actions

Fisher built her company on a foundation that stressed social consciousness, particularly for enriching the lives of women. These principles are evident in the company's leadership, employee policies, and relationships with suppliers.

Leadership

Employee engagement for Eileen Fisher begins with its leadership and the enterprise's values, vision, and performance standards. The enterprise is highly decentralized and promotes the development of cross-company teams, but operations are relatively simple and encourage connection among people and groups. The Social Consciousness Team bears direct responsibility for shepherding the firm's employee engagement.

The corporate mission statement demonstrates how central employee engagement is to the company's foundation principles. The mission is "to inspire simplicity, creativity, and delight through connection and great design" and specifies four core practices: individual growth and wellbeing, collaboration and teamwork, joyful atmosphere, and social consciousness (Hall, 2006).

Employee policies

Eileen Fisher infuses its values and social consciousness messages across all stages of an employee's experience, beginning even before hiring (Hall, 2006). A potential employee finds the company's vision, values, and commitment to social consciousness throughout its website. During the interview process, recruits experience the office's scenic views, eco-friendly products, and energy-efficient lighting. They hear about the firm's concern for global standards for workplace conditions and employment practices and are asked about their own interests regarding social issues.

New hires receive more than standard training programs. Each is paired with a peer partner who personally reinforces the company's values and social consciousness programs, which appear in strikingly handsome print and electronic materials. The company's values and social programs are the focus of periodic brown-bag lunch sessions and further reinforced in newsletters, which also highlight charity events the company gets involved in. Employees can take advantage of on-site wellness programs and savor organic and locally produced catered food. Everyone receives an annual US$1,000 allowance to spend on her choice of outside wellness activities. All communications encourage employees to express company values in both their work and personal lives. In addition, the company affords employees numerous opportunities to grow professionally by joining one or more socially conscious committees, participating in in-store and community service events, and obtaining additional learning and leadership development training.

Supplier workforce practices

More than a decade ago, Eileen Fisher executives came to realize that their concern for their own employees needed to be expanded to embrace those people working for their suppliers. Like the company itself, these contractor partners hire predominantly women. They came to view suppliers as not just sources for clothes but also extensions of their own values and workforce. This realization drove the company to engage with suppliers to improve local working conditions. The UN SA8000 standards, governing the treatment of employees, child labor, and health & safety, became the working benchmark.

Eileen Fisher successfully persuaded many suppliers that certain humane practices produce short- and long-term financial benefits. Most of these companies were run by tough businessmen who reflected their national cultures, which were often characterized by rote learning and discouraged creativity. The company sometimes ran into resistance and distrust, with such responses as, "We have always done it this way."

Eileen Fisher has conducted its own training programs for suppliers' workers in some parts of the world. In China, for instance, where the typical wage earner has only a middle-school education, and may not have learned about feminine hygiene, sexual topics, or workplace rights, Eileen Fisher has instituted programs that address these subjects. Likewise, the company may teach workers techniques for, say, gracefully speaking up to a manager. The company has convinced some contractors to consider less punitive approaches toward employees and to move to more positive reinforcement and rewards. Many contractors have been delighted that these can really motivate employees, and they often report new levels of employee morale and loyalty. These suppliers are themselves becoming more creative, and some neighboring companies are starting to emulate them. Similarly, deeper partnerships between Eileen Fisher and suppliers are focusing more on environmental considerations, including lighting, air quality, and water quality.

In 2014, Eileen Fisher began a project to map its supplier network. What started as a fairly simple mapping has expanded to include not only its direct suppliers but also the suppliers of its suppliers. A goal of this project is to increase transparency and encourage responsible manufacturing aligned with human rights and principles of sustainability. The company began sharing its progress from 2018.[1]

Critical results

Eileen Fisher's 18-member leadership team is committed to balancing "Business, Product, and People and Culture," considering all of them equally. For example, it encouraged the company to integrate social consciousness and sustainability into product design decisions, which led to a line of garments made from organic cotton. Over the years, the vice president of people and culture and the social consciousness head have attempted to align their compensation practices with their values, by introducing, for instance, flat rate increases in salary. People are rewarded with growth opportunities, making it more of a place for growth and discovery, although not everyone has accepted this.

The company has been profitable since its founding. Refraining from becoming a broadly held public company, it set up an employee stock ownership plan (ESOP) in 2006. By 2012 employees owned 33% of the shares. Although the company does not, at the time of this writing, quantitatively measure the benefit of its social consciousness program, in the past it was primarily guided by what feels right. It is striving to better quantify the payoff from these investments and it is experiencing visible change in workforce practices. For instance, turnover has averaged just 15%, compared with an industry norm of 30–40%. The company's reputation attracted a dazzling 6,000 résumés in one year to fill 75 positions, one-quarter of which were filled internally (Hall, 2006). Eileen Fisher is highly rated by the Great Places to Work Institute, ranking no. 7 out of the top 25 companies identified. Management aspires to be no. 1.

Eileen Fisher clearly exemplifies the positive outlook of its founder. As Amy Hall, the director of social consciousness, reported, "We celebrate successes—individuals and teams, anniversaries, anything!"[2] The company listens to all the voices. In the spirit of collaboration, it doesn't dwell on mistakes; instead, it aims to make them a learning experience. Such openness can present a challenge (Hall, 2006, p. 51):

> Our staff has so much energy and so many ideas that it is often difficult to rein in people's well-intentioned enthusiasm … Helping staff see the big picture, and not focus just on their own sphere of influence, is time-consuming.

Heightening the challenge is the company's insistence on extending most initiatives to its far-flung supplier network, which requires such special efforts as translating key materials into Chinese and Spanish.

Unlike companies that have slowly come to incorporate social conscious-ness and sustainability management into long-standing practices, Eileen Fisher has built these into its corporate "DNA" from the beginning. While this offers the advantage of not having to retrofit new ideas onto old habits, it presents new challenges of how to find one's way. Through the continuing influence of its founder, the company has boldly broken much new ground and achieved remarkable results.

Key ideas and tools illustrated here

- Creating a culture that is aligned with the enterprise's distinctive values, vision, and performance standards, including consistent messages through peer partners, lunch-time discussions, newsletters, and commu-nity service events.
- Engaging employees by emphasizing social consciousness, which incorporates individual growth and wellbeing, collaboration and team-work, and a joyful atmosphere.
- Integrating sustainability concerns into fundamental human resource practices, product design, and corporate facilities.
- Extending the company's social consciousness agenda by working actively with its network of suppliers.

Another industrial case study illustrates how Alcoa Howmet deals with crit-ical safety management through comprehensive employee engagement.

Case 4. Environmental, health, & safety issues at Alcoa Howmet

Kent D. Fairfield

> The key differentiator for success is not how we use Six Sigma, lean manufacturing and that sort of thing; it's *engaging people* into observing, identifying, and solving problems.
>
> (Jim Johnson)

Alcoa Howmet, a major business of Alcoa Inc., is a global leader in airfoil and structural castings, serving the aerospace and industrial markets. Such products result from a dirty and potentially dangerous production process. The division's 28 plants constitute what was formerly Howmet Corp., whose management has traditionally devoted considerable attention to safety and environmental concerns.

When Alcoa purchased the company in 2001, however, Alcoa manage-ment introduced extensive new strategies and more demanding standards for environment, health, & safety (EHS). Jim Johnson had seen the protocols for handling EHS evolve over more than 30 years. Starting on the shop floor at Howmet in 1978, Johnson became a firstline supervisor, later the plant manager, and eventually vice president of manufacturing for the whole division. He reports that, when he was plant manager, safety was just one of many issues he concerned himself with until its importance came home to him in brutal terms. "I thought hitting my numbers was the most important thing," he told one interviewer, until one day a mold broke "and I had a guy pour molten metal down his boot. It was a life-changing experience for me" (Kowalski, 2005).

Since this accident, Johnson has championed safety as the most important goal in all his plants. The assistance he gets from the Alcoa corporate office has reinforced his shift in priorities, including formalizing a robust EHS management system. For one thing, Alcoa ties incentive compensation to EHS results. When operations people meet, Johnson says, they ask each other, "Have you gotten anybody hurt? What did you do about it?" Naturally, industrial facilities have had basic safety measures in place for decades—the Occupational Safety & Health Administration (OSHA) requires detailed reporting—and Johnson says[3] it is possible to achieve basic safety benchmarks, "the low-hanging fruit," by simply demanding it of employees. He had done that in one of his earlier management jobs, but he discovered people slipped back into more unsafe behavior after he left that location for a new assignment.

Johnson says that driving down accident rates further for more enduring results depends on engaging employees in more direct ways. One way Alcoa Howmet does this is by training all managers not only to execute safety procedures themselves but to train all their people in EHS. Although the company sometimes relies on outside consultants to design its training, it insists that all plant managers and others deliver the training themselves.

One exercise teaches participants to observe an operation with an eye toward potential breaches of safe practices. In the "Red Flag" program, all employees visit another department and place a red flag by any piece of equipment or action that appears to be a risk. Johnson reported that this program helps raise employees' consciousness of safety, not only in other people's work areas but also in their own.

Management pushes hard to get people to scrutinize working conditions from the EHS perspective and continually urges employees to feel free to speak up about any unsafe situation. Johnson quotes his boss challenging people: "Would you bring your kids in here and let them work where you work?" In an environment of molten metal and high-speed grinding and cutting machines, this sets a high bar for acceptable work practices. One way the company ensures that managers focus on their training obligations is to require a detailed work plan. Managers have to draw up their own **leader standard work**—patterned after the standard work associated with line workers—in which EHS training activities may constitute as much as 40% of their time.

A smart investment in training people about safety and sound environmental practices translates into less time dealing with emergencies and quick fixes. In fact, the company's most promising future plant managers devote most of their time to learning how to do the necessary EHS teaching and coaching. Even an invitation to a senior manufacturing manager to help in a sales presentation for customers does not preempt a planned safety activity. In addition, the company dispatches its best managers to other Alcoa Howmet facilities to conduct peer audits. Seeing outside executives scrutinize their facility helps employees recognize the importance of the right kinds of behavior.

Critical results

The various safety initiatives put in place since the Alcoa acquisition have paid off. The lost work day rate of 1.00 in 2001 was cut to only 0.034 in 2006. Average total OSHA recordable injury rate dropped over the same time from 7.06 to 1.90. The company could not maintain such a low rate in 2007, though, and the lost work day rate increased to 0.13, still a sizable improvement on the past. The company determined that 48% of recent accidents involve employees who have worked there less than one year, suggesting the need for better training and coaching of newer employees. Senior management also wants to instill in these workers the ability and confidence to speak up without fear of reprisal whenever uncertain or concerned about a safety issue.

Key learnings

Alcoa Howmet's record of improvement in safety exemplifies the progress that can occur when a company places high priority on the issue. Its executives clearly model the importance of safety; they do not just mouth vapid clichés about its desirability. Employees seem to get the message. This also illustrates the notion that setting goals and executing strategies in the name of sustainability coincides with improved business results. Fewer accidents represent the humane outcome and avoid the expense, regulatory entanglements, and bad publicity of an unsafe work history. Johnson's devotion to employee engagement is obvious when he insists, "Everybody has to understand the role that they play in assuring that all of our workers go home safe every night." And how does he justify all the attention to safety? If not, "I couldn't live with myself," he says (Kowalski, 2005).

Key ideas and tools illustrated here

- Going beyond demanding safe work practices and engendering employee-driven improvements.
- Training the managers to train others in safe and proper practices.

- Conducting peer safety audits between departments and across facilities to identify potentially dangerous conditions and practices and raise awareness for all.
- Living out a passion for safety to achieve humane goals as well as pragmatic corporate objectives.

The final case study here concerns employee engagement that originated at the grass roots and had repercussions for an entire community. It all started at the Indian offices of a major German information technology firm, T-Systems.

Case 5. Employee engagement at T-Systems: sustaining the organization and beyond

Sangeeta Mahurkar-Rao

The employees in the Pune, India, office of T-Systems were having tremendous difficulty reaching their office on time in June 2006. The traffic signal intersection at the corner by the office caused intense congestion, and irate commuters took to aggressive, undisciplined driving. The resulting gridlock meant that crossing the junction sometimes took as long as 40 minutes, affecting all T-Systems employees. Employee productivity was down and stress was up. In addition, the long wait exposed many employees on motorbikes and scooters to high pollution levels from the idling vehicles. This bottleneck was a consequence of enormous growth in the city. Many new office buildings and shopping areas had recently mushroomed along this road, straining an already stretched law enforcement capability and civic infrastructure.

Employees voiced their distress at a staff open-house meeting, along with their concern about the larger social issue it posed: the congestion affected countless people beyond their company. Employees decided to step forward and try to resolve the problem. They formed a task force including senior management, functional heads, and team members in June 2006 and took on the task of developing a suitable plan.

Actions

The task force brainstormed various possibilities and finally decided to try to facilitate the traffic flow themselves during peak hours. The initiative had the full support of senior management, which was vital, as it involved considerable investment of the employees' normal work time. The management believed it was part of their commitment to social responsibility.

The task force contacted the local traffic police and discussed its proposed initiative. The traffic police officers welcomed their suggestions, as their force was stretched too thin to tackle such localized problems. They also promised to support the effort however they could.

After gaining approvals and support from the management and local agencies, the task force developed the following plan:

1. Each morning from 8:30 to 10:30, employee volunteers would assume the role of traffic wardens and be physically present on the road to direct traffic.
2. To enforce more disciplined movement, the wardens would use physical barriers to prevent vehicles from jumping signals.
3. Other employee volunteers would hold placards that held messages for saving fuel and controlling pollution.
4. Another group would hold placards that would reinforce the importance of following traffic rules, augmenting similar messages to be posted on nearby billboards.
5. The employees would arrange to have tree branches cut to avoid obscuring important traffic signs.
6. The task force would inform the local traffic police of its specific plan and seek any support required.

This initiative had the active participation of the entire senior management team, which greatly encouraged broad employee involvement, and more than 100 of a staff of 500 employees volunteered their time.

Critical results

A key accomplishment is that having participated in achieving a sustainable social benefit, employees felt deeply satisfied. The initiative had a positive effect on all commuters at the signal. After a couple of unpleasant instances when commuters questioned the authority of the volunteers, people soon accepted the new arrangements. T-Systems employees were delighted to be able to reach the office on time. The previous waiting period of 35–40 minutes to cross the junction dropped to just 3–5 minutes, a vast improvement. The traffic police have taken note and helped ensure that during peak hours traffic wardens are posted for signal monitoring. Many residents expressed their appreciation, including parents of schoolchildren in the area. There was a visible improvement in the disciplined driving of local commuters as they began observing the traffic signals, contributing to the smoother flow.

The unique initiative received considerable coverage in local media, which helped inform the community of the project's underlying spirit and the reasons for the effort. The obvious improvements and the media attention motivated many other organizations located on the same road to offer their own volunteers. A rally was organized on Independence Day, August 15, during which responsibility was handed over to a larger contingent made up of volunteers from companies, social service organizations, government retirees, and youth, along with some traffic police. T-Systems employees took pride in having initiated and served as catalysts for this triumph of civic improvement.

Key learnings

This case is a powerful illustration that improving the sustainability of a single organization can have a positive impact that extends beyond the organization's boundaries. It reinforces the systems thinking view that what affects the organization necessarily affects the rest of the system of which it is a part, including other organizations and the community at large. The outcome benefited T-Systems employees, the company's productivity, neighboring commuters and organizations, pollution levels, and overall civic welfare.

Engagement of employees can result in powerful outcomes if the employees are suitably empowered and supported by management. It can also engender a strong sense of accomplishment, itself a critical factor for nurturing a sustainable organization.

Key ideas and tools illustrated here

- Listening to the serious concerns of employees about their welfare.
- Endorsing grassroots efforts by providing management participation and support.
- Sparking increased self-reliance and self-efficacy through projects outside people's job description.
- Aiding employees with the practical concerns of getting to work and contributing to broader community welfare as well.

Conclusion

The five case studies illustrate how certain well-established psychological dynamics form a foundation for vigorous engagement by employees. The cases share a number of strategies and tactics that managers can use to bring about sustainability management with highly desirable outcomes.

Psychological dynamics

The work of Kouzes and Posner (2007) and Gratton (2007) stresses the psychological sense of ownership of a company's mission, particularly when employees experience their work as pertaining to the meaning in their life. Employees at Eileen Fisher and DuPont experience autonomy and self-determination, thanks to management values and practices that give them considerable leeway. Employees feel very much a part of a community of kindred spirits. In addition, they all tend to work in a system founded on interdependence, which Kouzes and Posner identified as critical to collective performance. Their positive attitudes are contagious, as Boyatzis and McKee (2007) would have predicted.

Strategy and tactics

While the cases describe a range of settings, from the industrial to white collar to manufacturing, considerable similarity exists in their strategy and tactics. Executives in all cases lay out certain understandings, standards, and guidelines for employee behavior. They also grant considerable freedom for employees to execute their plans and actions. As Knowles (2002, 2006) recommends, they often conduct conversations in the form of town hall meetings, or training sessions. Interestingly, leaders at both DuPont and Alcoa concede that a command-and-control approach achieved middling improvements for safety and employee cooperation, and both found they had to genuinely involve their employees to achieve higher-level, long-lasting results.

One common strategy is to break down traditional barriers imposed by people's positions in an organization. PSE&G built its safety initiative on cross-level task forces. Alcoa placed frontline workers in the role of safety detectives. Another successful organization we came across promoted egalitarian communication through informal, outdoor dialogues and a simple "rule": when you are within six feet of someone, whether a porter or top executive, say "hello." In a further attempt to dissolve the obstructions that organizational hierarchy can generate, the CEO of this same organization made a simple, authentic gesture; she moved her office from the top floor executive suite to a small office on the first floor near the cafeteria. Now when she leaves her office, she is in immediate contact with both clients and people from all levels of the organization, and spontaneous conversations arise daily.

A related strategy is to allow employees a clear line of sight to the outcomes stemming from their efforts. T-Systems' management nurtured a grassroots initiative so that staff experienced firsthand the improvement in traffic flow. The self-organizing initiative at DuPont allowed employees to see how their behavior improved the plant's safety record, increased its productivity, and contributed to a 300% escalation in earnings.

Outcomes

Employee engagement in each case study contributed to exceptional outcomes. Operating results improved markedly in all cases. The improvements were, for the people, both a cause and a consequence of this improvement. Employees felt called to new levels of self-reliance and autonomy, and they responded with energy, drive, and creativity. They exhibited new levels of ownership and accountability for unprecedented results. The all-too-typical resistance to change was minimal. A computer programmer acquires a new sense of self-efficacy when discovering his or her own ideas for solving a traffic problem are executed for communitywide benefit. Participants inside a "hot spot" feel the resonance of being a part of a winning team and experience a whole new sense of being in a community of kindred spirits.

In sum, we have seen in previous chapters that leaders need to craft inspiring visions, adopt constructive mental models, and manage complex change for sustainability management, but their efforts come into full flower only when they skillfully engage their employees. The concepts discussed in this chapter in the context of these exemplars of exceptional practice demonstrate how employee engagement can produce extraordinary results for the individual, the team, the organization, and the larger world.

Notes

1 Vision 2020. Retrieved February 5, 2018, from www.eileenfisher.com/vision-2020/.
2 Personal communication with A. Hall, telephone interview, September 20, 2007.
3 Personal communication with J. Johnson, Dover, New Jersey, October 5, 2007. All information and quotes in this case study are from this interview unless otherwise indicated. Sadly, Jim Johnson has since passed away. He was a true inspiration to us all. For more on Alcoa Howmet's journey and how Jim's legacy carried on, see Wirtenberg, 2014, Chapter 3.

References

American Express. (2012, July 19). Using games can help drive employee engagement. Retrieved September 1, 2015 from www.americanexpress.com/us/small-business/openforum/articles/using-games-can-help-drive-employee-engagement/.

American Management Association (AMA). (2007). *Creating a sustainable future: A global study of current trends and possibilities 2007–2017*. New York: American Management Association.

Ashforth, B. E., & Pratt, M. G. (2002). Institutionalized spirituality: An oxymoron? In R. A. Giacalone & C. L. Jurkiewicz (Eds.), *The handbook of workplace spirituality and organizational performance* (pp. 93–107). Armonk, NY: M. E. Sharpe.

Bandura, A. (1997). *Self-efficacy: The exercise of control*. New York: Freeman.

Boyatzis, R., & McKee, A. (2007). *Resonant leadership: Renewing yourself and connecting with others through mindfulness, hope, and compassion*. Boston, MA: Harvard Business School.

Cameron, K. S., Dutton, J. E., & Quinn, R. E. (2003). *Positive organizational scholarship: Foundations of a new discipline*. San Francisco, CA: Berrett-Koehler.

Christensen, C. (2012). *How will you measure your life?* New York: Harper Collins.

Corporate Leadership Council. (2007). *Upgrading the organization's employee engagement strategy*. Retrieved May 18, 2018, from http://ir.cebglobal.com/phoenix.zhtml?c=113226&p=irol-newsarticle_pf&id=983769.

Deloitte University Press. (2015). *Global human capital trends 2015*. Retrieved May 17, 2018, from www2.deloitte.com/content/dam/insights/us/articles/cognitive-technology-in-hr-human-capital-trends-2015/DUP_GlobalHuman CapitalTrends2015.pdf.

Gallup. (2013). *State of the American workplace*. Retrieved May 17, 2018, from https://collaboration.worldbank.org/docs/DOC-18331.

Goleman, D., Boyatzis, R., & McKee, A. (2013). *Primal leadership: Unleashing the power of emotional intelligence*. Boston, MA: Harvard Business School.

Gratton, L. (2007). *Hot spots: Why some teams, workplaces, and organizations buzz with energy—and others don't*. San Francisco, CA: Berrett-Koehler.

Gratton, L. (2011). *The shift: The future of work is already here*. London: Harper Collins.

Hall, A. (2006). Engaging employees in social consciousness at Eileen Fisher. *Journal of Organizational Excellence, 25*(4), 45–52.

Hurst, A. (2014). *The purpose economy*. Boise, ID: Elevate.

Jensen, B. (2014). *Search for a simpler way: Future of work study*. Retrieved May 17, 2018, from https://peoplexpert.ch/website/wp-content/uploads/FutureOf WorkReport.pdf.

Knowles, R. N. (2002). *The leadership dance: Pathways to extraordinary organizational effectiveness*. Niagara Falls, NY: Center for Self-Organizing Leadership.

Knowles, R. N. (2006). Engaging the natural tendency of self-organization. *World Business Academy Transformation, 20*(15), 1–10.

Kouzes, J. M., & Posner, B. Z. (2007). *The leadership challenge* (4th ed.). San Francisco, CA: Jossey-Bass.

Kowalski, R. (2005). Interview with James Johnson. Unpublished manuscript, Case Western University, Cleveland, OH.

Lertzman, R. (2015). *Going beyond nudging, gaming, and competing: An open discussion about designing real engagement*. San Diego, CA: Sustainable Brands 15 Conference, June 3, 2015.

Macey, W. H., Schneider, B., Barbera, K.M., & Young, S.A. (2009). *Employee engagement: Tools for analysis, practice, and competitive advantage*. West Sussex, UK: Wiley-Blackwell.

Net Impact. (2012, June). *Talent report: What workers want in 2012*. Retrieved May 17, 2018, from www.netimpact.org/research-and-publications/talent-report-what-workers-want-in-2012.

Pink, D. (2011). *Drive: The surprising truth about what motivates us*. New York: Riverhead Books.

PwC. (2011). *Millennials at work: Reshaping the workplace*. Retrieved May 17, 2018, from https://scholar.google.com/scholar?q=PwC%E2%80%99.+(2011).+Millennials+at+work:+Reshaping+the+workplace.&hl=en&as_sdt=0&as_vis=1&oi=scholart.

Sacks, D. (2007, September). Working with the enemy. *Fast Company, 118*, 74–81.

Saks, A. M. (1995). Longitudinal field investigation of the moderating and mediating effects of self-efficacy on the relationship between training and newcomer adjustment. *Journal of Applied Psychology, 80*, 211–225.

Scott, L. (2005, October 24). Wal-Mart: Twenty-first century leadership (Speech). Retrieved December 21, 2007, from walmartstores.com/Files/21st%20Century%20 Leadership.pdf.

Seligman, M. (2011). *Flourish: A visionary new understanding of happiness and well-being.* New York: Free Press.

Seligman, M. E .P., & Csikszentmihalyi, M. (2000). Positive psychology: An introduction. *American Psychologist, 55,* 5–14.

Towers Perrin-ISR. (2014). *The ISR employee engagement report.*

WeSpire. (2015, May). *The evolution of employee engagement: An annual report and research.* Retrieved May 17, 2018, from www.wespire.com/resource/evolution-of-employee-engagement-research-2015/.

Willard, B. (2012). *The new sustainability advantage.* New York: New Society.

Wirtenberg, J. (2014). *Building a culture for sustainability: People, planet, and profits in a new green economy.* Santa Barbara, CA: Praeger.

Wirtenberg, J., Harmon, J., Russell, W. G., & Fairfield, K. D. (2007). HR's role in building a sustainable enterprise: Insights from some of the world's best companies. *Human Resource Planning, 30*(1), 10–20.

World Business Council on Sustainable Development. (2010, August). *People matter—engage: Inspiring employees about sustainability.* Retrieved May 17, 2018, from http://docplayer.net/19382068-People-matter-engage-inspiring-employees-about-sustainability-world-business-council-for-sustainable-development.html.

Wrzesniewski, A. (2002). "It's not just a job": Shifting meaning of work in the wake of 9/11. *Journal of Management Inquiry, 11,* 230–234.

Wrzesniewski, A. (2003). Finding positive meaning in work. In K. S. Cameron, J. E. Dutton, & R. E. Quinn (Eds.), *Positive organizational scholarship: Foundations of a new discipline* (pp. 296–308). San Francisco, CA: Berrett-Koehler.

Enterprise sustainability metrics and reporting

Performance measurements for resilient strategic progress

William G. Russell and Gil Friend

> Counting sounds easy until we actually attempt it, and then we quickly dis-
> cover that often we cannot recognize what we ought to count. Numbers
> are no substitute for clear definitions, and not everything that can be
> counted counts.
>
> (William Bruce Cameron)

This chapter is about creating sustainability-aligned metrics and reporting systems that inform and monitor progress towards the "smart" sustainability-aligned Bridge strategy objectives presented in Chapter 3. A sustainability-aligned measurement and reporting system will include: Creating stage appropriate SMART[1] goals, identifying and implementing multi-capital stock, flow, and threshold performance indicators,[2] and implementing continuously improving sustainability-aligned business management and reporting systems.

Our approach uses systems thinking to establish appropriate measurement boundaries and feedback signals. Systems thinking is a holistic approach to analysis that focuses on the way that a system's constituent parts interrelate, and how systems work over time and within the context of larger systems. The systems thinking approach contrasts with traditional analysis, which studies systems by breaking them down into their separate elements.[3] Strategic choices for the future need to adapt to the enterprise's current context and future-facing performance goals. Every enterprise's performance management system operates with its own uniquely appropriate feedback loop signals, based on those contexts and goals, and the multiple relationships and interrelationships that make up any business system. Those signals if well designed help the system learn and adapt to change. If poorly designed they can cause unintended consequences to itself or to other interconnected systems. There is no single tool or right way to measure performance; the challenge is to learn the options available and select the most appropriate tools for your particular enterprise's context and purpose.

This chapter reviews some essential practices for defining and measuring sustainable enterprise system performance. We introduce multi-capital frameworks as a tool for more helpful measuring and analysis. Multi-capital accounting—valuing natural, human, and social capital, as well as financial capital—has been rapidly gaining acceptance as a more robust and nuanced lens through which to assess, measure, and report sustainability-aligned performance (Gleeson-White, 2015; McElroy, 2011). Multi-capital stocks, flows, and thresholds integrated with purposes and outcomes framed through the Daly Triangle (Meadows, 1998), (featured in Chapter 2, pages 89–90) bring complex global, local, and sustainable enterprise systems into more holistic alignment and clear focus.

We build upon the Smart Strategy Bridge framework presented in Chapter 3 by presenting system criteria, collaborative approaches, and best practices for sustainability metrics, as well as tools and case studies for each of the four sustainability-aligned strategy stages.

The first Bridge progression stage is **Doing** and includes companies that are just starting up and/or beginning to align with sustainability practices. Companies begin by assessing what they already measure and initiatives they are already doing. Initial sustainability measurement systems expand performance indicators and goals beyond single-bottom-line financial capitals and performance indicators to include nonfinancial capital stock and flow measurements and peer and best practice benchmark goals. Sustainability-aligned versions of traditional value chain mapping and Balanced Scorecard tools are presented to minimize resistance to change and develop confidence as resiliency improves.

The second stage are companies that are **Doing Well**. These companies are primarily interested in measuring financial performance and nonfinancial information as needed to drive efficiency, reduce risks to cashflow, and for preparing environmental, social, and governance (ESG)-aligned sustainability reports. Tools presented include the ROI Workbook from Chapter 3, the World Economic Forum's Global Risks Report, and the Sustainability Accounting Standards Board (SASB) materiality maps. Four interconnected sustainability reporting initiatives are introduced: The Global Reporting Initiative (GRI), SASB, The International Integrated Reporting Council (IIRC), and the Reporting 3.0 Initiative. Each are advancing important standards or guidance including how to assess materiality within this currently unstructured but rapidly evolving discipline. Efforts to monetize natural and social capitals are provided as critical interconnected perspectives that supplement the basic Doing Well insights.

The third Bridge stage are companies that are **Doing Well and Doing Good**. In addition to measuring prior stage performance objectives these companies must also add measurements pertaining to their contributions towards the UN Sustainable Development Goals (SDGs) and other socially beneficial outcomes. We review the World Business Council for Sustainable Development (WBCSD) SDG Compass tool and showcase BASF's efforts to measure social impacts. We share key questions increasingly being asked by long-term institutional investors. These questions backed by hundreds of influential investors (representing more than $15 trillion of Assets under Management (Tett, 2018)) and CEOs of major international companies could trigger or accelerate a shift from companies focused only on Doing Well, pulling them into the Doing Well and Doing Good strategic realm and beyond.

The fourth Bridge stage are companies that wish to **Thrive**. These companies seek to measure and apply context-based allocations of global planetary boundary risks, in order to operate within natural capital and ecosystem services carrying capacities. They also measure social impacts and contributions to societal wellbeing. The Thriving section introduces a mix of global scientific research collaborations, methods for assessing global environmental and social resiliency conditions, and methods to allocate limited resources and social obligations to individual enterprises. The Stockholm Resilience Centre and Future Earth are centers leading the scientific research needed to support carrying capacity performance measurements and allocation schemes. Many scientists are concerned that our ecosystems and planetary boundary thresholds have already been exceeded.

Some business leaders have heard this message and are collaborating to set science-based environmental goals. Initial applications are primarily emphasizing the more easily measured GHG emissions and climate change. Eventually they will need to integrate all of the planetary boundary risks. Simultaneously, other groups are collaborating to develop context-based allocation methods that allow individual industries and companies to evaluate their enterprise's value chain impacts and resource requirements. The Future-Fit Business Benchmarks and other tools are already available to help enterprises measure strong sustainability performance while not crashing into vital capital constraints or strategic Bridge performance guardrails.

The four stages collectively measure all of the elements and interconnections included within the Daly Triangle and related science-based frameworks. Enterprise leaders and scientists don't know how strong sustainability goals will be met. Pioneering companies are already piloting innovations to transform efficiency and effectiveness expectations. These efforts coupled with developments with institutional investors indicate shifting norms to longer term (still only 3–5 years) strategic visions that stress both financial AND socially positive performance. CEOs have been put on notice. Complacent companies and industries will get disrupted. Leading companies delivering enhanced wellbeing for their stakeholders will be rewarded.

Sustainability performance measurement context

> In the 21st century, I think the heroes will be the people who will improve the quality of life, fight poverty and introduce more sustainability.
>
> (Bertrand Piccard)

We've come a long way since the first edition of this *Fieldbook* was published. We refer readers to the original metrics chapter as it contains a wealth of useful tools appropriate for how sustainability had been framed at that time. This sustainability metrics chapter is substantially re-aligned and updated.

Today the world is more interconnected. No person, company, or country can become sustainable alone. Some technological breakthroughs will help, but ultimate solutions will require compounding beneficial effects from a multitude of seemingly small, isolated actions. An enterprise's vision of sustainability is the holistic aggregation of the life experiences of its leaders, employees, and stakeholders. It is shaped by their mental models for how they believe the world works. Their smart strategy vision is formed by: the lenses—purpose(s) they choose to pursue; the quality and quantity of the light (technical and qualitative data); unbiased, mindful, awareness of current conditions; and the degree of alignment along common goals. From this perspective, sustainability metrics provide the lens that sees through the fog and presents a clear view of reality today and a clear vision of prospects for a thriving future.

Sustainability measurement leaders and foundational work

We want to acknowledge the foundational work of a few mentors who came before us, and highly recommend that all readers become familiar with it. First, Donella (Dana) Meadows, who passed away in 2001 at the age of 59, is acknowledged as one of the most influential thinkers of the 20th century. She was principal author of *The Limits to Growth* (1972), which sold more than 9 million copies. Her work is preserved by the Academy for Systems Change which she founded in 1996.[4] We specifically acknowledge her for her role as lead author of the 1998 report to the Balaton Group, "Indicators and Information Systems for Sustainable Development" and its influence on the authors of this chapter (Meadows, 1998). That report has fondly been referred to as the "Bible" of sustainability indicators (Baue & Thurm, 2017). Another highly relevant core document that linked systems thinking and sustainability for transformational change was her provocative paper, "Leverage Points: Places to Intervene in a System" (Meadows, 1999).

The United Nations and the World Bank sponsored many early reports and continue to contribute today through their leadership of the Sustainable Development Goals, Responsible Investing, Sustainability Education and more. Herman Daly has influenced our thinking and is acknowledged for creating the Daly Laws and the Daly Triangle introduced earlier in this book (Chapter 2, pages 89–90). Our learning from their work and the many others contained in the chapter and more give us hope and a sense of optimism that we are headed in the right direction. We are not traveling alone. There are people who we know and some unknown who we are yet to meet as we connect and collaborate to build a bridge to the future we are in the process of creating.

Acknowledging The Limits to Growth

As sustainable development awareness was still emerging in the early 1970s, one group of researchers, commissioned by the Club of Rome, developed World3, an interactive computer model designed to simulate the consequences of interactions between the Earth and human systems. *The Limits to Growth* (Meadows, Meadows, Meadows, & Behrens, 1972) provided an initial preview of the consequences of a rapidly growing world population and finite natural resources. The model simulated the holistic interdependencies of technology innovation, economic markets, and five risk factors: world population, industrialization, pollution, food production, and resource depletion. Three simulation scenarios were presented: a standard "business as usual" scenario; a second "aggressive technology innovation" scenario assumed the expansion of available resources, but no significant culture changes in human behaviors would occur; and a third "resource-stabilizing policies" scenario assumed we could alter human behaviors and manage to stabilize the consumption of limited resources. Both the "business as usual" and "aggressive technology innovation" simulations resulted in resource overshoots and significant catastrophic impacts to our quality of life.

At the time of its release, many prominent economists, scientists, and political figures criticized *The Limits to Growth*. They attacked the methodology, the computer, the conclusions, the rhetoric, and the people behind the project. In 2010, Professors Peet, Nørgård, and Ragnarsdóttir reflected again on this work and called the book a "pioneering report," but said "unfortunately the report has been largely dismissed by critics as a doomsday prophecy" (Nørgård, Peet, & Ragnarsdóttir, 2010).

The model continued to be updated and its results validated. The paper entitled "A Comparison of *The Limits to Growth* with Thirty Years of Reality" (Turner, 2008) examined the actual data in place of the simulated model predictions made in 1972 and found that, over the three decades, the changes in industrial production, food production, and pollution were all in line with the "business as usual" predictions of economic and societal collapse in the 21st century as presented in *The Limits to Growth*.

While the business community was in the early stages of embracing eco-efficiency with the intention of Doing Well and improving profits, a parallel message of dire threats to human survival advanced and began driving an urgent intention for more transformational change. A small, but rapidly growing community of sustainability heroes and positive mavericks started to openly discuss limits to growth (planetary boundaries, carrying capacities, thresholds, and context allocations discussed later in the chapter). Today, many more sustainability practitioners are reflecting on the state of the planet and how to resiliently guide sustainable progress in our ultimate outcome(s) of human wellbeing. New business models including the circular economy and the doughnut economy introduced in this chapter and others discussed in Chapter 7 are examples of scientists and businesspeople truly beginning to confront these limits.

Current focus for sustainability measurement systems

A decade ago, much of our measurements focus was on physical "stuff." We focused systems to measure resource efficiency and the physical "metabolism" of our organizations. Today, measuring stuff is still important and expected, but new lenses of materiality and value have evolved. Other perspectives changed as well:

- Initially, we were very concerned with reporting. Today, we're increasingly concerned with how reporting contributes to strategic insight.
- We focused on the metrics of the tangible, the physical resources and financial resources being reported separately within traditional financial reports. Today, we recognize the large and still rising value of the intangibles. Intangibles including reputational value of brands and risks from climate change or supply chain disruptions account for over 80% of the value of a typical publicly listed company today.
- We were working to think about natural capital alongside financial capital; now, we're working to bring six capitals into the management equation.
- We were focused on the numbers themselves; now, we're beginning to understand the critical importance of context and the power of science-based goals.
- Our conversation was on the fringes of the business world; now, it's moved closer to the core strategies of enterprises (Friend, 2017).

The biggest competitive advantage in this century will belong to those enterprises able to see through the fog and progress themselves resiliently across perilous chasms that the fog obscures for the unaware or unsuspecting competitor (Friend, 2017).

Ecological Footprint

The Ecological Footprint has emerged as one of the world's leading measures of human demand on nature, and the ability of nature to ongoingly meet that demand. It allows us to calculate human pressure on the planet and come up with facts such as: If everyone lived the lifestyle of the average American, we would need five planets to support us. Conceived in 1990 by Mathis Wackernagel and William Rees at the University of British Columbia, the Ecological Footprint launched broader Footprint (Environmental impacts) and Handprint (Social impacts) measurement initiatives. The Ecological Footprint is an eloquent metric capable of communicating both a science-aligned measure of strong sustainability performance of the planet and society as a whole while also serving as a context-allocated measure of strong sustainability performance for smaller community, company system boundaries, and individual lifestyle impacts.

The Global Footprint Network[5]

The Global Footprint Network (GFN), founded in 2003, is an international think tank that develops Ecological Footprint accounting tools and leverages its research to influence policy decisions in a resource-constrained world. It works collaboratively with local and national governments, investors, and opinion leaders to ensure all people live well, within the means of one planet. The *Working Guidebook* to the National Footprint Accounts (NFA) describes the methodology along with detailed descriptions of calculations and data sources. The *Ecological Footprint Atlas* explains the purpose behind Ecological Footprint accounting, addressing research questions and basic concepts, as well as the underlying science of the calculations. The *ERISC: A New Angle on Sovereign Credit Risk* report describes the rationale and methodology used to substantiate the business case for financial institutions and ratings agencies to include ecological criteria as a key component of country risk analysis.

The Ecological Footprint quiz[6]

The Global Footprint Network has developed a remarkably effective "quiz" tool used by individuals, schools, and enterprises throughout the world to measure their own unique context-allocated Ecological Footprint. How much land area does it take to support your lifestyle? In just a few minutes you can take this quiz to find out your Ecological Footprint, discover your biggest areas of resource consumption, and learn what you can do to tread more lightly on the earth. Figure 6.1 provides an example quiz result. This person's lifestyle requires 3.7 Earths to support it. Overshoot Day for this person, the day they surpass their allocated share of biocapacity resources for the year, was April 10th.

Figure 6.2 shows the Land Type, Consumption Categories, and relative contributions to the overall Ecological Footprint for this person's lifestyle. Visit the endnote link to take the quiz and see the stories of others who have also taken this quiz and learned what actions they can take to reduce their footprints and responsibly journey across their bridge into the future.

We wanted you to have these different sustainability performance perspectives in your consciousness as you now proceed to review the remainder of the chapter and book. No matter how well we think we are performing, we must appreciate that our resources are limited and that our personal lifestyles have a biocapacity requirement to sustain it. If we believe the environment is a common resource and all people have equal rights to its use, then all lifestyles

Figure 6.1 Footprint quiz results: overshoot and earths
Source: Ecological Footprint Calculator, Global Footprint Network, date performed: February 5, 2018. Published with permission.

that require more than 1 Earth to sustain them are exceeding a fair context share of the planet's biological assets. We must collectively create transformational resource efficiency innovations and adapt our consumption habits and lifestyles before we surpass some currently unknown resiliency threshold and trigger a "Tragedy of the Commons" collapse.

Enterprise sustainability and systems measurement essentials

> Systems thinking is a discipline for seeing wholes. It is a framework for seeing interrelationships rather than things, for seeing "patterns of change" rather than static "snapshots."
>
> (Peter Senge)

This section introduces a few essential sustainability performance measurement concepts, frameworks, system qualities, and technology trends.

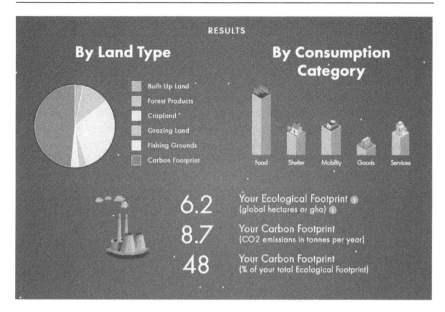

Figure 6.2 Footprint quiz results by land type and consumption category

Source: Ecological Footprint Calculator, Global Footprint Network, date performed: February 5, 2018. Published with permission.

Whether you are a world-leading expert or an enthusiastic beginner, this section establishes a common foundation of understanding before more contextualized topics, tools, and initiatives are presented. Potential pitfalls of sustainability measurement are also presented for consideration as you establish or re-align and adapt your own system.

Business management systems with sustainability metrics are powerful tools to inform leaders, employees, and stakeholders throughout the company value chain and product and service lifecycles. These measurement systems, along with a common vision of the desired future state, are the critical ingredients for sustainable, even regenerative performance in a thriving world.

Enterprise system boundaries, mental models, and feedback loops

This section introduces a business management framework for designing and evaluating a sustainability-aligned enterprise performance management system. We also describe a few best practice system qualities and advancements in information technology. While sharing similar system model and framework components, each enterprise's measurement and reporting system is uniquely designed to serve and align with the enterprise's purpose, organizational structure, stakeholders, and the intermediary and ultimate ends it produces.

Sustainability-aligned business management system lenses and boundaries

Sustainability-aligned business management systems use value chain or life cycle boundaries. Figure 6.3 provides a business management framework with multi-dimensional lenses and strategic risk and opportunity perspectives. The x-axis shows the value chain or product lifecycle boundaries including upstream supply chains, operations, downstream customer use, and its ultimate community and global environmental, social, and economic outcomes. The y-axis shows the multi-capital resources and related triple-bottom-line risk and opportunity perspectives. The z-axis incorporates the aspects of a continuously improving system, including formulating the smart strategy, identifying policies and related rules the enterprise operates within, the goals and indicators identified to build resiliency and manage progress towards the goals, information needed to guide ongoing operations of the company, information used by management to monitor performance from an internal perspective, and reporting information used by management and external stakeholders.

Each of the multi-dimensional perspectives in the sustainability business management system can reveal a range of relevant data points for enabling the enterprise to measure its efforts and outcomes. Once specified, these data points can help the organization uncover trends along both temporal (past, present, and future) and material (quantitative and qualitative) scales.

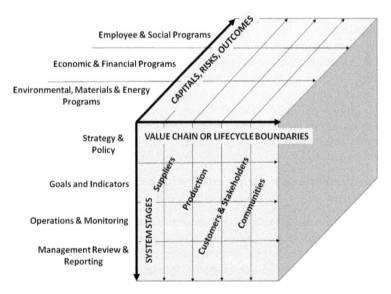

Figure 6.3 Enterprise sustainability-aligned business management framework
Source: William G. Russell, with permission.

Integrated thinking and enterprise risk management interconnections

Integrated thinking is an emerging skill set to help enterprises think more holistically about how the enterprise operates and how trans-functional coordination and trans-organizational collaborations can be improved. (For more on Integrated Thinking, see Chapter 8, pages 394–395.) The Committee of Sponsoring Organizations of the Treadway Commission (COSO) and the World Business Council for Sustainable Development (WBCSD) are developing draft application guidance for using an enterprise risk management framework that includes environmental, social, and governance-related (ESG) risks. That guidance is designed to supplement COSO's updated enterprise risk management (ERM) framework as presented in *Enterprise Risk Management—Integrating with Strategy and Performance* (COSO, 2017).

COSO's ERM framework supports companies establishing ERM governance and processes to manage increasing volatility, complexity, and ambiguity of the business environment—internally and externally. The business management framework in Figure 6.3 is compatible with this objective. An ESG-inclusive management framework preserves value and reduces downside exposure. It also better interconnects risk management with strategy and operations decision-making while enhancing corporate performance (COSO & WBCSD, 2018).

Mental models and feedback loops

Each enterprise, industry, and locality has certain norms that formulate the mental models and system archetypes it uses to guide strategic decisions. Here are some practices to keep in mind as the enterprise system is being reviewed and continuously improved (Friend, 2017):

- Open everything. Resist the automatic temptation to play your cards, whether Intellectual Property (IP) or performance data, close to the vest. The world is becoming more transparent and there is likely more value from shared learning than incremental value of control.
- Be inclusive and diverse. None of us is as smart as all of us.
- Find patterns without resorting to the easy escape of mechanistic reductionism.
- Don't obsess about the wrong things. Stay focused on what is relevant to the enterprise's stage strategy and outcome goals.
- Embrace and navigate uncertainty and nurture emergence.
- Ground uncertainty with science that underlies all we value and do. See the Thriving stage section for helpful resources and examples for aligning the enterprise around consensus science, shared commitments, big goals, and systematic action.

Every system operates with feedback loop signals. Those signals if well designed help the system learn and adapt to change. If poorly designed they can cause unintended consequences to the system itself or to other interconnected systems. When considering appropriate indicators for monitoring a system, the following perspectives are important:

- Are the signals or indicators lagging or leading the performance aspects they are measuring? What might be the lag or lead time delays of those signals? What delay periods exist between the indicator signals and expected impacts?
- Many systems collect historic, backwards-looking results metrics. Is historic performance a relevant perspective for future performance? What assumptions are made that might be wrong when the time view is shifted towards the future?
- What insights are helpful for guiding us ahead with strategic decisions that must be made today? Data modeling and scenario analysis are the tools emerging to help assess indicators of future performance (United Nations, ESCAP, 2015).

Choosing the right measures

> When indicators are poorly chosen they can cause serious malfunctions ... The choice of indicators is a critical determinant of the behavior of a system.
>
> (Donella Meadows)

Choosing the right performance measures is a critical aspect of designing a great sustainability-aligned performance management and reporting system. There are specific indicators that provide timely, reliable, and cost-efficient information on the current state of social, economic, and environmental elements of sustainability. These may include input, output, and outcome indicators. Those indicators may be aggregated into a compressed set of composite indicators (lifecycle assessment, Ecological Footprint, and the like). Composite indicators are useful in simplifying a long list of indicators to provide a visible indication of key trends.

There is no one set of agreed-upon "rules" for what makes a good measure. Best practice shows that good measures typically are:

- **Useful**: The measure provides information that is valuable to the system being assessed, enterprise department, or to decision-makers.
- **Self-evident/understandable**: The measure does not need a lot of explanation.
- **Evaluative**: The measure helps the reader evaluate something, not just describe something.

- **Instructive or important**: The measure tells the reader something significant or something that would not be known from other sources.
- **Valid, reliable, and economical**: The measure captures the intended information in an accurate and cost-effective manner (Meadows, 1998).

Performance measurement of a viable system has three measures of capacity producing three measures of achievement. The capacity components are:

- **Actuality**: "What we are managing to do now, with existing resources, under existing constraints."
- **Capability**: "This is what we could be doing (still right now) with existing resources, under existing constraints, if we really worked at it."
- **Potentiality**: "This is what we ought to be doing by developing our resources and removing constraints, although still operating within the bounds of what is already known to be feasible" (Beer & Lane, 1972).

The achievement components are:

- **Productivity**: is the ratio of actuality and capability;
- **Latency**: is the ratio of capability and potentiality;
- **Performance**: is the ratio of actuality and potentiality, and also the product of latency and productivity (Beer & Lane, 1972).

Selecting indicators that accurately reflect the system attributes we need to understand while avoiding data collection and indicators that distract us from what is important and relevant to measuring performance and purposeful outcomes is a key skill for designing a quality management system. Like the smart strategy they inform, the metric system should be regularly reviewed and enhanced.

Multi-capitalism

The Daly Triangle presented in Chapter 2 and our systems-aligned Bridge strategies presented in Chapter 3 use a multi-capitals framework to categorize the Ultimate Means (natural capital) and other intermediate capital stocks. The triple bottom lines continue to be an effective view of aggregate sets of nonfinancial and financial topics and indicators. As the fields of ecological economics and integrated reporting progress, a multi-capital orientation of sustainability issues and indicators is gaining support (Eccles & Krzus, 2015; IIRC, 2008).

Multi-capital frameworks provide a basis for understanding sustainable development in terms of the economic concept of wealth creation or "capital." Forum for the Future developed a Five Capitals approach in the 1990s

(Forum for the Future, 2011). The model presented at that time described five capitals as:

- **Natural capital:** The natural resources (energy, environment, and matter) and processes needed by organizations to produce their products and deliver their services. (Our ultimate means in the Daly Triangle.)
- **Human capital:** Incorporates the health, knowledge, skills, intellectual outputs, motivation, and capacity for relationships of the individual. (Intermediary means [labor] and intermediary ends [education, health, entertainment] in the Daly Triangle.)
- **Social capital:** Any value added to the activities and economic outputs of an organization by human relationships, partnerships, and co-operation.
- **Manufactured capital:** Refers to material goods and infrastructure owned, leased, or controlled by an organization such as tools, technology, machines, buildings, and all forms of infrastructure. (Intermediary means [tools, equipment] and intermediary ends [consumer products] in the Daly Triangle.)
- **Financial capital:** Reflects the productive power and value of the other four types of capital and includes those assets of an organization that exist in a form of currency that can be owned or traded.

These definitions have continued to evolve. Intellectual capital is now a sixth capital that many organizations have adopted (IIRC, 2008; Reporting 3.0, n.d.; United Nations, ESCAP, 2015). This capital's specific interpretation is still being debated. IIRC defines intellectual capital as organizational, knowledge-based intangibles, including:

- intellectual property, such as patents, copyrights, software, rights, and licenses;
- "organizational capital" such as tacit knowledge, systems, procedures, and protocols.

Jane Gleeson-White noted that a revolution in accounting was taking place and urged enterprises to go beyond merely accounting for traditional financial and industrial capital and take account of the benefits and detriments to the natural world and society. Accounting should include four new categories of wealth: intellectual (such as intellectual property), human (skills, productivity, and health), social and relationship (shared norms and values), and natural (environment). She states that making them part of our financial statements and GDP figures may be the only way to address the many calamities we face (Gleeson-White, 2015).

The IIRC humbly notes that all organizations depend on various forms of capital for their success and that enterprises are not required to adopt this exact categorization. The capitals are stocks of value that are increased, decreased, or transformed through the activities and outputs of the organization. The overall stock of capitals is not fixed over time. There is a constant flow between and within the capitals as they are increased, decreased, or transformed. For example, when an organization improves its human capital through employee training, the related training costs reduce its financial capital. The effect is that financial capital has been transformed into human capital. The critical aspect of multi-capital accounting acknowledged within the Daly Triangle is that natural capital is a limited (and really the only limited) capital and described as our "ultimate means" (Meadows, 1998). All other capitals are intermediate means or intermediate ends of enterprise activities. Mark McElroy shows that there are no limits to social capital growth (McElroy, Jorna, & Engelen, 2007), but also cautions that attempts to use traditional economics to value nonfinancial capitals can result in unintended consequences (McElroy, 2014). This reality will come up again when we discuss efforts to monetize natural and social capitals in an effort to correct current economic system value measurement flaws.

A multi-capital scorecard tool is presented later in the chapter (page 308–309) as a tool for assessing context-based enterprise sustainability performance. The *Living Fieldbook* also contains more information on the background and applications of multi-capital accounting.

When selecting measurement topics and indicators for your enterprise performance management system, it is important to note that no theme and topic taxonomy is perfect and that to a certain extent, every theme and every topic has interdependencies with every other. Given the advancements in data collection technologies and tagging, multi-capital data tags appear to be useful to conducting insightful data analytics in support of a company's corporate strategy, sustainability vision, and performance management and reporting system.

Setting goals and targets

We need to set, pursue, and monitor progress towards individual, local, national, and global goals that facilitate interconnected, equitable, and thriving quality of life for all human beings. This section introduces a framework, a tool, and a case study for setting sustainability-aligned goals and targets.

SMART goals for "smart" sustainability-aligned strategies

We previously established our four progressive Bridges and adjustable or smart sustainability-aligned strategies. It seems appropriate to guide those strategies with SMART goals. SMART goals are:

- Specific: Objectives should specify what they need to achieve. (Be clear if objectives are aggregates of multiple diverse system aspects.)
- Measurable: You should be able to measure if you're meeting the objectives or not. (But remember, not all measures are numerical or linear.)

- Attainable: Are the objectives you set achievable or attainable? (See Interface case in strategy, and NASA case Box 6.1 below, for when impossible goals must be attained.)
- Relevant: It must support outcomes important to you and the organization's success. (Note that many metrics are needed and relevant to support outcomes that are not direct outcome or results measures.)
- Time-bound: The objective must have a date identifying when the result is to be accomplished as well as milestones along the way. (Be careful when attempting to align time-bound goals with both leading and lagging data and feedback loops.)

Smart does not necessarily mean simple. Sustainability-aligned goals, carrying capacities, flows, targets, performance impacts, and benchmarks are hard to establish and even harder to measure and monitor progress towards. Sustainability performance analysis must accommodate complex realities such as unknown interconnections and long lag times between causes and effects and significant uncertainty in the measures themselves and/or their threshold limits. This reality runs contrary to decision-makers' tendency to look for easy, clear methods to delineate progress and success.

We present a case study on goal setting by NASA as sustainability goals require Apollo mission-like focus and commitments. We also present the PivotGoals tool as it enables stakeholders to easily see the publicly shared goals and targets of most major companies. The SDGs, Science-based Goals, and Future-Fit Business Benchmarks were all previously introduced in Chapter 3 and will be discussed again from a measurements perspective in the sections to follow in this chapter. See the *Living Fieldbook* for more case studies and details on setting goals and targets.

Box 6.1   NASA and Apollo goals: starting with the end state

Only the more courageous among us match the stretch goals standards of the Apollo mission. NASA realized that challenging technical achievements required for the moon mission would have to be supported by powerful social innovations. The first act of the Apollo project was to throw a victory party—at which the NASA organization celebrated the successful moon launch and return. After the party, they sat down and asked themselves, "How did we do it? What did we do at the end of the process that enabled us to fulfill this mission? What were the actions in the last year, and the year before that and the year before that?"

When the gap is big, and the pathway not clear, this reverse mental engineering can make it possible to see a path—from the goal to the start—that may be obscured by the dizzying permutations that exponentially multiply when looking from the start toward the goal, when the branching possibilities are too numerous to see clearly. (To deal with the challenge of apparent technical impossibility—or at least of large gaps between "need to" and "know how"—NASA created the department of "It Can't Be Done," which dispassionately turned impossible demands into design specifications that could be systematically invented and engineered into possibility.)

Most companies prefer to set reasonable goals that they are confident they will achieve. Others select aggressive and public goals that demand both technical innovation and organizational breakthroughs. A stretch sustainability goal—such as 100% renewable energy portfolio within 10 years—may seem equally outlandish. "Can we do it?" some will ask. "Is it even possible?" On the other hand, the more useful question to ask, given that people will need to trend in that direction at some rate in any case, may be "what would it take to achieve that goal (and not at the expense of business goals)?" Radical efficiency gains? A new kind of deal with an energy provider? Something we haven't thought of yet? It's in the stretch beyond the goals already within reach that "invention" comes into play. Not "can we?" but "how can we?"

Source: Adapted from Friend (2004), with permission.

Pivot Goals[7]

PivotGoals, a tool developed by Jeff Gowdy and Andrew Winston, is an attempt to bring together two ideas: companies are critical to our collective future, and the goals companies set matter enormously. Most companies prefer to set reasonable goals that they are confident they will achieve. PivotGoals is founded on the belief that there is a correlation between setting aggressive targets, reporting on them transparently, and ultimately improving performance. In an effort to accelerate the speed of adoption, the PivotGoals tool developers collected the goals of the Global Fortune 500 companies across 58 macro and micro-industries, categorized them, and made them easily searchable. In addition to searching by company name or industry, additional search categories include:

*   Goal Type: Five descriptor categories such as Specific & Dated for goals with clear end dates, "We will cut our energy use across our operations

20% by 2015," and Intentional for goals that are stated vaguely without numbers or dates, such as "we will reduce air emissions."

- Value Chain: Categories such as Supply Chain, Product Use, End of life.
- Absolute or Intensity: An absolute goal is one set for a numeric reduction, regardless of the growth of the business, such as "We will be zero waste by 2015" or "We will cut emissions 20% by 2020." A relative/intensity goal is one with a denominator (per sales, employee, ton of product, etc.), such as "We will cut emissions 20% per car we produce."
- The PivotGoals developers envisioned users and uses such as the following:

  - Benchmarking: Corporate managers and executives can compare their goals to others in their sectors and from a wider comparison pool.
  - Driving performance: Closely correlated to benchmarking, employees and managers can use the goals they've set, along with others their peers have posted, to create a sense of urgency for the organization to drive change in the organization.
  - Research: Students and academics studying how companies manage our mega-challenges can utilize the data as input to new research projects/publications on corporate sustainability.
  - Accountability: NGOs and other stakeholders can use this data to hold companies accountable to what they've publicly stated now or in the recent past.

Management system qualities and technology

Our world is experiencing significant transformational change. Amazing technological tools are streaming continuous information, multi-media stories, pictures, and video clips. We are easily overwhelmed and numbed as events unfold before our eyes: natural disasters including earthquakes, hurricanes, and tsunamis, regime changes, terrorist attacks, and random, senseless shootings. Our irrational behavior, fear, and ignorance is constantly exposed. We have the ability to ignore knowable feedback signals. Complacency and denial about government processes, healthcare, credit card debt, or the mortgage markets have all been exposed as imperfect and ready for re-imagination and system change.

While there are obvious challenges in the world today, advancements in science and information technology combined with proven history of the human ability to adapt and innovate, provides a source for optimism. The opportunities and impacts of augmented reality and artificial intelligence are still emerging. We must reflect more deeply on what it means to be human as we are humbled when IBM's Watson defeated our best humans on Jeopardy.

Management system qualities

A smart strategy supported by SMART goals with appropriate metrics and a technology-enabled performance management and reporting system will:

- provide a clear line of sight that connects smart strategy's purpose, goals, actions, and impacts for the enterprise value chain and your communities of interest, so everyone can see the impacts of their actions;
- enable the risk management controls, responsibilities, and accountabilities;
- enable diverse teams to balance between autonomy and working as a coherent whole;
- include the metrics that could reveal blind spots and disclose transformational opportunities and disruptions including those that could disrupt your metrics system itself (e.g., Big Data, Blockchain, Cyber security).

Management systems and technology

With advancement of business management systems and systems thinking, managing a business has become inextricably linked to data management and information technology. Today's business managers depend on real-time data and automated metrics management systems to inform their day-to-day operating decisions and long-term strategic plans.

Companies are deploying a variety of technology solutions such as PC-based spreadsheets and risk analysis software to collect data, calculate metrics, and generate reports. Enterprise resource planning (ERP) systems automate and improve manufacturing processes and resource management, and support input–output evaluations and material-flow cost accounting.

Enterprise databases, intranets, and web-based portals are supporting metrics management systems such as balanced scorecards, a variety of environmental and social indicators, and financial and sustainability reporting. As these systems become more interconnected with the suppliers and customers, a more holistic system with an enterprise's value chain as its boundary is emerging.

Other even more holistic measurement systems interconnect large-scale government and other public data sets with enterprise data in order to analyze regional and social impacts. Traditional management systems were not designed for a balanced view of financial, environmental, and social metrics. They were developed to measure performance data for quality, risk, and cost control. Next-generation systems integrating sustainability aspects with data analytics, graphics, and augmented reality technologies promise clearer views of complex issues with more holistically aligned functionality.

With the advancements in technology, big data analytics, and process automation, we are also seeing the possibilities of, and progress toward, a future when more intelligent metrics systems will facilitate unconsciously competent behavior. People will prosper, flourish, and thrive simply because it is how things work.

Sustainability metrics pitfalls

> It ain't what you don't know that gets you in trouble. It's what you know for sure that just ain't so.
>
> (Mark Twain)

Proactively contemplating potential metric pitfalls and unintended consequences is important when designing and implementing sustainability metrics and reporting systems. All measurement systems include estimates, inaccuracies, ambiguities, and are susceptible to cyber-attacks and fraud. At the enterprise level, people manage what they measure, but often measure what they have data for while not measuring what truly matters.

Examples of pitfalls for measuring sustainability performance include:

- Poorly presenting and managing uncertainty.
- Presuming balance and relevancy between measures or competing story arguments.
- Ignorance bias or believing that what you know for certain is right. The mortgage industry failure is one catastrophic example of this pitfall. The Gapminder Foundation's Ignorance Project[8] (Box 6.2) provides more examples of this pitfall.
- Ignoring insights from behavioral economics and the effects that scarcity can have on a person's ability to rationally interpret data and apply its signals to make decisions (Feinberg, 2015).

Box 6.2   Gapminder Ignorance Project

The Gapminder Foundation started the Ignorance Project to investigate what the public knows and doesn't know about basic global patterns and macro-trends. The project introduction draws upon observations that:

> Statistical facts don't come to people naturally. Quite the opposite. Most people understand the world by generalizing personal experiences which are very biased. In the media the "news-worthy" events exaggerate the unusual and put the focus on swift changes. Slow and steady changes in major trends don't get much attention.

Source: Gapminder Ignorance Project.

See the *Living Fieldbook* (**L**) for more information on Pitfalls.[9]

Doing: get started measuring sustainability performance

> Efficiency is doing things right; effectiveness is doing the right things.
>
> (Peter Drucker)

"Doing stage" enterprises include companies that are just starting up and/ or beginning to align with sustainability practices. Over 500,000 companies are started in the US alone each month. There is a huge opportunity and need to catch them early and get them engaged. They need to be players on the field and in the game. They need to be taking steps on this first Bridge. They need to set up sustainability-aligned strategies and metrics systems that help them know the score from the start. The guidance and resources presented in this section can also be used by any enterprise that is re-imagining itself and is now integrating sustainability with its existing strategy and performance management and reporting systems. Companies farther along on their sustainability journey can also review the steps and tools presented here to avoid the pitfall of complacency and boost their confidence and resolve as they reflect on where they are and where they started from.

This section builds upon the purpose and system construct presented in Chapter 3 and the performance management essentials from the previous section. We first outline measurement and reporting system design criteria appropriate for supporting Bridge 1 Doing stage strategies and programs. We then review a six-step sustainability measurement program implementation process. Sustainability-aligned versions of traditional value chain mapping and Balanced Scorecard tools are also presented. Tools that align traditional methods with sustainability help minimize resistance to change and develop confidence as resiliency improves. Note that the original metrics chapter tools available on the *Living Fieldbook* include the Natural Logic Business Metabolics methodology; the IMU Flow cost accounting methodology; US Green Building Council LEED criteria for measuring building performance, and other helpful sustainability metric resources to help you get started.

Doing stage measurement and reporting system design criteria

The following are selected enterprise performance management and reporting system construct items most relevant for enterprises just getting started formulating sustainability-aligned strategies and metrics management systems for **Bridge 1, Doing**.

- **Get started, performance measurement purpose for Doing:** Enterprises in the Doing stage will range from startups with no prior measurement systems to smallholder farmers and family-owned private businesses up through medium-sized businesses that have operated for some time. They all share a purpose to define their sustainability-aligned purpose to serve customers and get to sufficiency or profitability. A smart sustainability-aligned strategy and enterprise will use metrics to guide them. A beginning system need not be overly complex. The tools that follow can help you quickly leapfrog to a highly effective system.
- **Take inventory:** Getting started is mostly about the business management system's framing (Figure 6.3) and sustainability-alignment. Enterprises are already measuring many important items. They have bank accounts and keep track of expenses. You have time sheets and expense reports. Before advancing to any specific aspect of profitability modeling or reviewing sustainability reporting standards, take an inventory of what you already are doing and already measuring. That is the best place to start when identifying relevant activities to measure and improve. This step also provides confidence. You realize how much you already are **Doing**.
- **Time horizons:** Resilient thresholds and time periods for Bridge 1 enterprises are typically two years or less. Annual reporting will still be needed for tax purposes and provide a good moment for performance, strategy, and systems reviews. Beginning measurement systems also need to balance data entry requirements and operating decision analytics. Vital operating equipment or product quality systems are likely to have existing and rigorous metrics associated with them. New data entry and metrics for sustainability objectives such as energy efficiency, waste minimization, and most employee-related performance can start with monthly data entry and indicator analytics.
- **Strategic goals and resiliency:** The urgent goal for companies starting up is to get to break even from a cash flow perspective while respecting environmental, social, and employee relationships. An initial performance management system need not be expensive to implement. Excel or equivalent technology can work for many companies. Traditional measures pertaining to the cost of goods sold, product pricing, and margins are the key performance indicators. Costs of selling, average sale amounts, and sales cycle times are additional key performance indicators for this stage.
- **Boundaries, interconnections:** The primary boundary of interest for Bridge 1 travelers is between the enterprise and the customers it is serving. Assuring its product or service enhances value to the customer's wellbeing in a differentiated way. Transparent, respectful, and collaborative relationships with employees, investors, and suppliers are also important. A formal sustainability report is not anticipated for companies at this stage of progression. That said, we believe a transparent strategy supported by relevant metrics and reporting systems enables

good management and efficient and effective communications and engagement with these stakeholders.

- **Key performance indicators and priority capital stocks and flows:** Building upon the inventory of what you are already doing and already measuring, beginning stage enterprises can follow a six-step process for implementing a great initial sustainability-aligned performance management system. This process interconnects with the ROI Workbook tool previously introduced in Chapter 3. It allows you to get sufficient insights for each major lever that drives efficient and productive use of capitals, risks to cash flow, the intangible value of brands, and profitability.

- **Mental models:** Initial performance management systems begin with innocent and vital intentions to measure "what counts" for the enterprise's purpose in order that it can be managed. One unintended consequence of this practice that requires sensitive employee engagement is the negative reaction of employees as they emotionally believe that the system is intended to "control" their activities, and even find justifications to eliminate their roles altogether. Advanced proactive engagement and training are important supplements to any actual metrics system being implemented.

- **Networks and collaborations:** To keep up with sustainability trends and practices regardless of the industry, we recommend becoming active with Sustainable Brands[10] and GreenBiz.[11] Industry and sustainability professional associations are also helpful resources to learn other relevant trends and best practices.

Beginner's guide to implementing sustainability metrics

Fairleigh Dickinson University's Institute for Sustainable Enterprise (ISE) hosted a series of five roundtable meetings over a two-year period sharing developments and insights on implementing sustainability metrics programs. The roundtable participants were leaders in measuring sustainability performance and reporting their progress to diverse stakeholders. These leaders realized that more companies and especially their suppliers and small and medium businesses within their communities needed to be engaged and supported to start collecting data and reporting on their current performance and future progress. Ultimately sufficient data collection and reporting would enable analytics and performance management of entire value chains and communities.

Create a guide and share tools

It was determined that creating basic tools and an implementation guide could help unaware or stressed companies to shift from blind unconsciousness to purposeful actions. They are taking the first steps in a journey towards enhanced financial prosperity; efficient, responsible, and regenerative environmental stewardship; engaged, productive, and thriving employees; healthy and fulfilled customers; and flourishing virtual and physical communities. Sustainability-aligned metrics contribute to their business intelligence and inform day-to-day decision-making and long-term strategic planning and performance reporting. Box 6.3 provides a six-step process that beginning companies can follow to implement an initial sustainability-aligned metrics program. Measurement system boundaries can include company-controlled assets, employees, and owned or leased facilities, and extend across the entire value chain of suppliers, customers, and stakeholders.

Box 6.3   Beginner's steps for implementing a sustainability metrics program

Step 1. Metrics program planning
   a. Define system purpose
   b. Schedule, budget, and skills
   c. System structure and components
   d. Program approach (e.g. Phased, Instant-on)
Step 2. Inventory current metrics practices and tools
   a. Review sustainability metrics and reporting standards
   b. Establish strategy-aligned metrics and reporting system vision and priorities
      i. Improving financial performance and profitability modeling
      ii. Stakeholder business risk and materiality assessment
      iii. Competitor, industry, customer goals
   c. Analyze the business case and establish budgets
Step 3. Profitability modeling
   a. Balance sheet inputs: revenue, cost of goods, cost of labor, profits
   b. Material and waste data and costs
   c. Labor data and costs
   d. Cash flow risk assumptions
   e. Model efficiency benchmarks and reduction goals
Step 4. Implement basic program
   a. Establish goals
   b. Select metrics and targets
      i. Existing operational and reporting metrics in use
      ii. Profitability model parameters
      iii. SDG compass tool list

  c. Create data collection and tracking systems
    i. Natural capitals and environmental data collection
      • Materials, water, water, waste, and recycling
      • GHG and air emissions
    ii. Manufactured capital and operations data collection
      • Facilities, capital equipment, supplies and parts
    iii. Human capital data collection
    iv. Social capital data collection
    v. Intellectual capital data collection
    vi. Financial capital data collection
Step 5. Program training
  a. Basic sustainability employee training
  b. Performance management system training
Step 6. Sustainability performance reporting and communications
  a. Internal metrics performance graphics and dashboards
  b. Metrics and employee accountability/employee engagement
  c. External sustainability performance reporting

Source: William G. Russell, with permission.

Value stream mapping

Value stream mapping is a lean manufacturing technique used to analyze and design the flow of materials and information required to bring a product or service to a consumer. At Toyota, where the technique originated, it is known as "material and information flow mapping." It can be applied to nearly any value chain. It is a powerful tool for measurement systems design for sustainability which can uncover the massive potential economic value.

A typical value stream map shows the current steps, delays, data and information flows required to deliver the target product or service. A sustainability focused Value Stream Map also shows the energy and materials that flow into and out of each process along the way. It looks at which processes add value, and which don't. Maps identify the value leakage at each stage—the loss of physical materials and energy quality, as well as economic value. These could include, for example, excess energy use and spend, insufficient product yield and excess non-product output, hazardous products or non-products, lost sales, unrecovered resources, and more—anything that doesn't add value to customers, shareholders, stakeholders and/or the earth's living systems.

Next you quantify, prioritize and look for synergies—the strategies and tactics, spanning everything from product design and manufacture to sales offerings and contract terms that can reduce or eliminate value leakage and generate substantial new value.

(Friend, 2012)

The value stream exercise also supports the selection of relevant performance metrics, and the development of a comprehensive strategic roadmap to guide your organization to capture all that potential value. Box 6.4 provides a series of questions you can review as you map and assess your enterprise value stream. Of course this is easier said than done. It takes inspired leadership, an engaged multi-stakeholder team, and the experienced, integrative, and even provocative approach (Friend, 2012).

Box 6.4   10 things you need to know about your value stream

Be sure you understand these questions about your value stream:

1. Where is the money being made in your value stream?
2. Who's harvesting it?
3. Where's the sustainability impact—and opportunity?
4. Where are you leaking—instead of adding—value?
5. Where could someone else take value from you?
6. Where could you take value from them?
7. Where could you create more value together?
8. Where could you deliver more value to customers?
9. What would you need to know—and do—in order to do that?
10. With whom?

Source: Friend, 2012, with permission.

Sustainability balanced scorecard

The balanced scorecard process is an example of an enterprise-wide measurement system that has been successfully adapted to support sustainability-aligned metrics and business management systems (Möller & Schaltegger, 2005). The purpose of the balanced scorecard is to help organizations manage results more effectively with a balance of measures in four categories: financial, customer, internal processes, and learning/growth. Once developed, a balanced scorecard becomes an instrument for aligning organizational performance with strategy.

Broadening balanced scorecard measures to include environmental and social issues creates an effective tool for measuring enterprise sustainability. In their paper "The Sustainability Balanced Scorecard," Figge and colleagues provide a systematic approach for organizations to use when creating their own sustainability balanced scorecard (SBSC) (Figge, Hahn, Schaltegger, & Wagner, 2002).

The authors suggest three methods for creating an SBSC to fit an organization's needs:

- integrating environmental and social into the four pillars of the balanced scorecard;
- addition of a nonmarket perspective into the balanced scorecard; and
- deduction of a derived environmental and social standard (Figge et al., 2002, p. 8).

Case 1. Sustainability balanced scorecard: Rent a Plant

Rent a Plant was a participant in a research initiative conducted by Shanon Boerrigter at the University of Twente on the use of the Sustainability Balanced Scorecard Framework to measure the performance of the sustainability strategies for Dutch SMEs (Boerrigter, 2015). Rent a Plant provides and maintains interior landscaping throughout the Netherlands. Its emphasis is on the quality of the plants provided to the customer. The entire organization is designed towards maintaining the highest level of customer service. Figure 6.4 shows the core part of the applied sustainability balanced scorecard for the organization, across all five balanced scorecard perspectives.

The sustainability strategy of Rent a Plant is currently implemented by two executives. They stressed that integrating the strategy and scorecard outcome measures with all employees and all stakeholders is very important to the company, but that the company still has a lot to do. They see their customers as direct stakeholders and encourage them to implement better practices such as using emails to correspond instead of correspondence by post. The government is viewed as an indirect stakeholder with whom they had to work on initiatives such as the separation of waste.

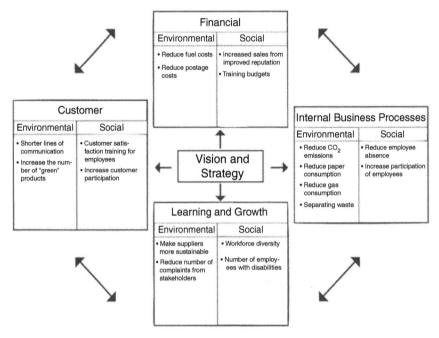

Figure 6.4 Example sustainability balanced scorecard for Rent a Plant
Source: Adapted from Boerrigter (2015).

Doing Well: financial and sustainability performance reporting

> Money is not the thing ultimately or even actually aimed at. Money is not what really counts, though it must be counted.
>
> (Rhinelander)

Doing Well companies are already profitable, but do not yet have sufficient wealth to resiliently take potentially beneficial actions unless they have obvious and high probability positive financial returns. Many companies are stuck in this stage. They are not able to change their mental models of greed, self-interest, growth, or complacency in the capital market systems, and pursue short-term profits. The sustainability mindset at this stage is often still not fully committed. This is the stage to exercise mindfulness and learn to harness sustainability practices for enhanced profits and value. Learn to play the competitive game of sustainability-aligned business better. The good news is that sustainability-aligned strategies and performance have positive financial returns and correlate with better investor returns in the capital markets. Playing this stage of the progressive differentiated competition well prepares you for being a long-term winner.

This section builds upon the Doing Well purpose and system construct presented in Chapter 3, the performance management essentials and earlier stage strategy and performance management tools and insights. From that foundation, we outline measurement and reporting system design criteria and enhancements appropriate for supporting Bridge 2, Doing Well stage strategies. We provide helpful research sharing indicators and targets for Doing Well and demonstrate that sustainability-aligned investments have positive ROIs, improve profitability, and reduce cash flow risks. We also review research that demonstrates sustainability-aligned enterprises outperform their peers in the capital markets. We share global risk insights and align those perspectives with environmental, social, and governance (ESG) risk ratings, sustainability-aligned reporting, and materiality assessments. We close the chapter reviewing the perplexing paradox of monetizing natural and social capitals. The *Living Fieldbook* contains supplemental information pertaining to each of these headwind and tailwind forces influencing our desire to **Do Well**.

Doing Well stage measurement and reporting system design criteria

The following are selected enterprise performance management and reporting system construct items most relevant for enterprises formulating sustainability-aligned strategies for **Bridge 2, Doing Well**.

- **Performance management purpose for Doing Well:** Performance management systems for Doing Well are similar, but progressively more complex than those of Stage 1 enterprises. Additional supplier information for their needs and transparently sharing additional performance information needed by their investors are major adjustments. As resiliency and confidence are growing, more attention to nonlinear disruptive risks, e.g., supply chains and intangible risks associated with brands and reputation, become important.
- **System and data inventory review:** Doing Well stage enterprises are expected to already be doing core data collection and performance management activities from Stage 1. Doing Well stage companies continue to be primarily focused on measuring financial performance and nonfinancial information as needed to drive efficiency, reduce risks to cash flow, and optimize profit. That said, many of the companies within this stage are larger, relatively successful, and if already publicly traded, have more developed regulatory and financial reporting systems in place. Internal project performance tracking becomes necessary as more and more projects are being implemented simultaneously. Adding key performance indicators in anticipation of environmental, social, and governance (ESG) ratings and sustainability reporting will also be needed.

Several system cycles and reviews will happen as the business management system settles in and becomes a powerful tool for guiding operations and strategic discussions and decisions for the future.

- **Time horizons:** Profitable enterprises cannot rest or become complacent. The ROI Workbook tools below suggest a 3–5 year time horizon for an enterprise to operate within this stage. Performance systems must support annual sustainability-aligned ratings and reporting data requirements. The frequency of data collection and reporting remains similar to Stage 1 systems.

- **Strategic goals and resiliency:** At this stage of operations, best practice benchmark efficiencies and practices of both competitors and best in class noncompetitors should be integrated into the performance metrics and data collection systems. For publicly traded companies picking priority GRI indicators and aligning data with selected ESG ratings questionnaires and analytics will be an exciting advancement. Preparing for and then issuing initial external reports are also progressive goals for this stage.

- **Boundaries, interconnections:** Reviewing Figure 6.3 will become a routine practice. Doing Well stage companies are not quite measuring and monitoring their complete value chains and product lifecycles. Tier 1 suppliers and investors are the next value chain stakeholders engaged in the strategy and included in systems measurements and performance monitoring. The risk axis will have all of the environmental, economic, and social elements engaged, but there will be more complexity regarding the number of projects and initiatives.

- **Key performance indicators and priority capital stocks and flows:** Natural capital accounting is still early and focused on material, water, and energy efficiencies. This process interconnects with the ROI Workbook tool and additional project management software tools helpful as a portfolio of actions are simultaneously implemented. Monitoring requires flexibility to continue collecting discrete data at the smallest scale while also enhancing the ability to efficiently analyze and aggregate the data through multiple strategic lenses. ESG risk topics and performance indicators are also added to initial key performance indicators.

- **Mental models:** This stage of strategy is a period for mental model transitioning. We accept that the financial and stock market performance enhancements are achieved by leaning into leadership and investor greed impulses and short-term thinking. The key is not to believe that is how the world works, but to be mindful and as you complete initial low hanging fruit wins, gain confidence and resiliency, start shifting perspectives toward stakeholder service and longer-term risks and opportunities.

- **Networks and collaborations:** Peer best practice sharing networks can be added to the sustainability awareness and practices networks. Industry and accounting associations are also active in advancing the practices introduced within this stage of progression.

Measuring performance for profits, risk, and value

Performance management systems support both the internal and external communication of an enterprise's sustainability performance. Operations equipment has its pressure and temperature gauges, smart meters measure energy consumption, and metrics software delivers its analytics through spreadsheet files, customized dashboards, websites, and more.

The following tools and research provide helpful benchmarks and calculators for measuring performance and demonstrating that sustainability-aligned investments have positive ROIs, improve profitability, and reduce cash flow risks.

SHIFT platform: best practice tools and collaborating community[12]

SHIFT is an online platform that allows you to search an extensive collection of sustainability tools greatly accelerating your strategic path and progress. SHIFT was developed by a cross-sector collaboration led by the Sustainability Initiative at MIT Sloan and Valutus. SHIFT is also a community of practitioners working together to review tools based on their own experiences. The SHIFT community includes corporate sustainability practitioners, sustainability-oriented entrepreneurs, impact investors, and more. Over 400 companies have contributed tools to the platform. Tools are searchable and can also be viewed using Sector, ESG Issues, Job Function, and Free or Pay filters. We support this collaboration with respect to tools for assessing profitability; there were 20 tools (including our favorite ROI Workbook from Bob Willard) included on the platform.

Sustainability advantage and the ROI Workbook

Bob Willard, a long-time leader in expressing the business case for sustainability, developed a Sustainability Opportunity Model in his book *The New Sustainability Advantage* that blends actual corporate data and industry results benchmarks to quantify eight areas of sustainability-aligned enterprise investment opportunities. Chapter 3 introduced his open source ROI Workbook tool for quantifying sustainability-aligned ROIs. For companies in the Doing and Doing Well strategic stages, the original spreadsheet tool is a great place to begin. On average the model conservatively indicates that companies can increase profits over a 3–5 year period between 50% and 80%, while reducing risks to future cash flows to between 16% and 32% (Willard, 2012).

Project ROI: competitive and financial advantages of sustainability

Research sponsored by Verizon and Campbell's quantified potential financial returns on investment from corporate responsibility (CR) actions for large, publicly traded companies. The report, *Project ROI: Defining the Competitive and Financial Advantages of Corporate Responsibility and Sustainability*, showed positive financial results across several different financial performance categories (Rochlin, Bliss, Jordan, & Yaffe Kiser, 2015). Box 6.5 shows a summary of the Project ROI positive research findings.

Box 6.5   Project ROI research findings summary

CR's potential value for marketing, sales, and brand/reputation:

- increase revenue by up to 20%
- increase price premium by up to 20%
- increase customer commitment in:
  - a core segment of 1–20%
  - the total segment of 60%
- establish CR brand and reputation value as 11% of the total value of the company
- avoid revenue losses of up to 7% of the firm's market value

CR's potential value for Human Resources:

- reduce the company's staff turnover rate by up to 50%
- save per additional retained employee 90–200% of the employee's annual salary
- improvements in CR performance has the same effect on retention as an increase in annual salary of $3,700/year
- workers' willingness to accept variability in pay including 5% pay cut
- increase productivity by up to 13%
- increase employee engagement up to 7.5%

CR's potential value for market value, share price, and risk reduction:

- increase market value by up to 4–6%
- over a 15-year period, increase shareholder value by US$1.28 billion
- increase valuation for companies with strong stakeholder relationships 40–80%
- reduce the cost of equity by 1%
- reduce share price volatility 2–10%
- avoid market losses from crises estimated at US$378 million
- reduce systematic risk by 4%
- reduce the cost of debt by 40% or more

Source: Adapted from Project ROI.

Evidence continues to mount demonstrating that corporate social-environmental performance is strongly associated with financial and marketplace success. There is still a "knowing-doing" gap at play which this book helps address. In addition to direct profit and shareholder value benefits, another major potential advance which can help close this gap is that sustainability can be seen as a key driver of innovation. A study done by Deloitte found that sustainability provides a different "'lens' for thinking and unlocking innovative potential and tapping into new ideas" (Aronson, 2013, p. 3).

Sustainability investing and capital markets

Capitalism does not permit an even flow of economic resources. With this system, a small privileged few are rich beyond conscience, and almost all others are doomed to be poor at some level. That's the way the system works. And since we know that the system will not change the rules, we are going to have to change the system.

(Martin Luther King, Jr.)

Sustainability can drive outperformance

Arabesque Asset Management and The University of Oxford published a meta-study *From the Stockholder to the Stakeholder: How Sustainability Can Drive Outperformance* categorizing more than 200 different sources (Clark, Feiner, & Viehs, 2015). They report positive correlations between diligent sustainability business practices and economic performance. Part one reports that 88% of reviewed sources showed that companies with robust sustainability practices demonstrate better operational performance, which ultimately translates into cash flows. Part two reports that 80% of the reviewed studies indicate that prudent sustainability practices have a positive influence on investment performance.

The Arabesque reports along with many others ultimately demonstrate that sustainability, responsibility, and profitability are not incompatible or tradeoffs, but in fact wholly complementary. Every company large or small, manufacturing or services can create financial value by strategically implementing a portfolio of sustainability-aligned actions. Strategies are adapted to the current financial resources available and the enterprise's unique competitive and market context.

Capitalism transformation

Capital market systems and rules establish value, facilitate global trade, and orchestrate the allocation of other interconnected natural, built, social, and human capitals. These systems directly or indirectly contributed to global risks such as asset bubbles; inflation and deflation; financial market

Table 6.1 Capitalism 2.0

Characteristic	Capitalism 1.0	Capitalism 2.0
Purpose of the firm	Maximize **shareholder** value; short term	Maximizing **stakeholder** value; short and long term
Legitimate capitals	Financial	Financial, natural, social, human, manufactured, and intellectual
Bottom lines	Profit	Profit, planet, people
Strategic focus	Growth; consumption	Stakeholder wellbeing
Source of financial capital	Stock market and big financial institutions	Co-ops; communities; credit unions; crowd-sourcing
Market focus	Global	More local
Powered by ...	Fossil fuels	Renewable energy
Negative impacts	Externalized	Internalized
Accountability	The firm	The firm's value chain
Transparency	As little as possible	Naked; fair taxes
Business model	Sell products; linear; take-make-waste	Sell services; circular; borrow-use-return

Source: Adapted from Bob Willard, Creative Commons, no permission required.

technology infrastructure; unemployment and underemployment; and wealth and income gaps (World Economic Forum, 2018). New emergent financial system technologies are restructuring the industries' value chain and disrupting entrenched stakeholder roles. While the trends and results appear positive, are they sufficient? Many people are anticipating more profound changes to the mental models, systems, and rules of capitalism itself. For example, Table 6.1 provides a summary of features for what Bob Willard calls Capitalism 2.0.

Monitoring ESG risks and ratings

Businesses are facing an evolving landscape of emerging environmental, social, and governance (ESG)-related risks that can impact a publicly traded company's profitability, credit rating, capital market performance, and even long-term survival. Investors have also expressed increased interest in ESG performance and a desire to understand how companies are managing a selection of long-term risks such as climate change and water scarcity. A survey of 320 institutional investors conducted in 2017 revealed that more than 80% agreed: that CEOs should lay out long-term board-reviewed strategies each year; that companies have not considered environmental and social issues as core to their business for far too long; that generating sustainable returns over time requires a sharper focus on ESG factors; and that ESG issues have real and quantifiable impacts over the long term (Nelson, 2017).

Serious money is lining up behind sustainability-aligned investing. Advancements in data collection, analytics, and emerging innovative insights are influencing investment strategies and shifts in capital allocations, markets, and the financing of urgently needed sustainable goods and services. The ESG and ratings companies have evolved and consolidated since the original *Fieldbook* was published. Previously, we had showcased Innovest, KLD, and TruCost. Innovest and KLD along with RiskMetrics and GMI were all acquired by MSCI. TruCost—another ratings and valuation company—was acquired by Dow Jones Indexes. Today MSCI, Dow Jones Sustainability Index, and still many others are advancing and developing new sets of metrics to quantify the quality, diversity, governance, carbon, social practices, and most any other risk factor you can think of, to analyze ESG risks. They share a common objective to use these metrics to identify and select leading companies for investment purposes.

The reinforcing performance results of sustainability-aligned investment strategies, and greater production and insightful analytics from enhanced financial and nonfinancial performance metrics, are helping sustainability-aligned investing to grow rapidly (over 60% between 2012 and 2014). These strategies are outperforming traditional investment strategies, increasingly capturing market share of investor dollars, and rapidly approaching mainstream tipping points (Esty & Cort, 2017). The *Living Fieldbook* provides additional elaboration on this segment of the capital markets industry, and the diversification of investing strategies it has spawned.

Although positive results such as those noted above are beginning to convince CEOs and boards that profitability and sustainability can go hand in hand, some words of caution are warranted. Quantifying sustainability performance is a tricky business and the indices of MSCI, Dow Jones, Goldman Sachs and others are still works in progress. In addition, sustainability-aligned investment research/analysis by its nature is not proactive. They are specifically designed to assist investors to "pick" the few stocks with the best sustainability-driven return on investment. They make no attempt at raising capital markets overall to a level where all companies are efficient and sustainable.

It is also worth noting that the statistics linking sustainability to performance were achieved even though the current market does not explicitly recognize value chain-wide risks, or external costs and benefits related to an enterprise's more holistic sustainable performance. As resources become more scarce (and expensive), and external ecosystem service values (e.g., climate change) become more internalized or at least appreciated by shareholders, the stock performance gaps between good and bad sustainability performers may well widen.

Sustainability-aligned reporting, materiality, and assurance

How do you use your sustainability metrics and reports—as a rearview mirror displaying past performance, or as a radar system illuminating the path ahead? As a box you need to check, or as a tool to help your people and partners be smarter?

(Gil Friend)

Figure 6.5 provides an overview of the capital markets sustainability reporting ecosystem. It depicts how companies must understand and manage financial and regulatory reporting requirements, and voluntary reporting requirements. Both of those report types have different assurance requirements. There are initiatives to develop standards for ESG reporting across various global stock exchanges including the Sustainable Stock Exchange Initiative and Global Initiative for Sustainable Ratings (GISR).

Three interconnected sustainability reporting initiatives are introduced and presented in more detail below: the Global Reporting Initiative (GRI), the Sustainability Accounting Standards Board (SASB), and the International Integrated Reporting Council (IIRC). A fourth initiative, Reporting 3.0, is another reporting initiative. That initiative is presented in the final Thriving section as its approach more explicitly requires using a science-based and context-allocated approach to strong sustainability performance. All of these

Capital Markets – Sustainability Reporting System

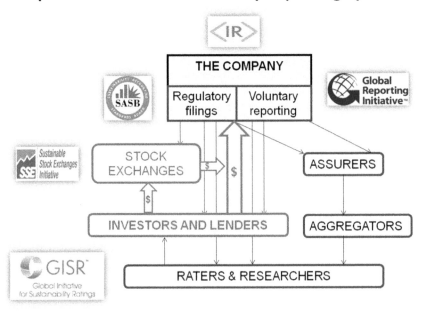

Figure 6.5 Capital markets—sustainability reporting system
Source: Bob Willard, Creative Commons, no permission required.

initiatives are advancing important standards or guidance to this currently unstructured but rapidly evolving discipline.

Raising the bar

The United Nations Environment Programme (UNEP) developed an excellent summary of the state of environmental disclosures in sustainability reporting. It analyzes what the key and most common environmental disclosure items are, and provides practical recommendations for companies and other reporting organizations on how these items should be measured and reported. That document also made recommendations on how sustainability reporting could be improved in the future (UNEP, 2015). Some aspects of the field—including ESG ratings and rankings—continued to fragment, while other aspects, such as how to determine materiality and stakeholder engagement processes, were maturing and standardizing. The World Business Council for Sustainable Development (WBCSD) has created a tool that organized these standards (WBCSD, CDSB, Ecodesk, 2018). The Sustainable Stock Exchange Initiative and the Global Initiative for Sustainability Ratings (GISR) are additional examples of efforts to bring more standards and structure to this emerging discipline.

The Global Reporting Initiative (GRI)[13]

The Global Reporting Initiative (GRI) is the most widely used standard for reporting sustainability performance to stakeholders. The initiative was launched by former CERES Executive Director, Dr. Robert Massie and Dr. Allen White of the Tellus Institute in 1997. In 2013, GRI released the fourth generation of its Guidelines, G4. The standards include Reporting Principles, Standard Disclosures, and an Implementation Manual for the preparation of sustainability reports by organizations of any size or sector. The standards provide guidance on the format and content of the reports as well as providing assistance on how to normalize and verify data. They contain a comprehensive set of organizational, management system, and performance parameters relating to a company's economic, social, and environmental performance. The guidelines encourage companies to set targets and commitments, and then to report on the extent to which these are being met, and provide reasons for any gaps or failures. The GRI strongly encourages the adoption of a stakeholder engagement process, with the aim of reporting on those issues of greatest relevance to stakeholders. GRI maintains a sustainability report disclosure database of over 9,000 organizations.

Tim Mohin, the current CEO of GRI, acknowledges that the reporting landscape is increasingly crowded, and that there is an alphabet soup of different standards. He lists along with GRI, IIRC, and CDP, SASB, and newest on the block, the TCFD (Task Force on Climate-Related Financial

Disclosure), which applies to financial, rather than sustainability reporting. He believes that confusion among standards is overblown, but is also a leader in reaching out to all of these and fostering greater collaboration (Slavin, 2018).

The Sustainability Accounting Standards Board (SASB)[14]

The Sustainability Accounting Standards Board (SASB) was founded in 2011 to develop and disseminate sustainability accounting standards that help public corporations disclose material, decision-useful sustainability information to investors in mandatory SEC filings, such as the Form 10-K and 20-F. SASB uses a legal definition for materiality. It feels that when certain risks have been determined to be material ones, then companies are legally required to include disclosures about those risks in their regulatory filings. They could also include disclosures within a sustainability or integrated report, but the first disclosure would have been a required one. Through 2016 SASB has developed sustainability accounting standards, materiality maps, and metrics for more than 80 industries in 10 sectors.

The International Integrated Reporting Council (IIRC)[15]

The International Integrated Reporting Council (IIRC), founded in 2011, is a global coalition of regulators, investors, companies, standard setters, the accounting profession, and NGOs. The coalition is promoting communication about value creation as the next step in the evolution of corporate reporting. The IIRC's vision is to align capital allocation and corporate behavior to wider goals of financial stability and sustainable development through the cycle of integrated reporting and thinking. The IIRC has been a major advocate for a multi-capital accounting approach which has brought that concept to the attention of the mainstream accounting associations, institutes, and societies.

Global Initiative for Sustainability Ratings (GISR)[16]

As an impartial, multi-stakeholder initiative, GISR will advance excellence in ESG ratings, rankings, and indices for measuring corporate sustainability performance. By advancing standards of excellence for financial market ratings, GISR aims to accelerate the integration of environmental, social, and governance factors in corporate and investment decision-making. Elevating usage of ESG factors in company and investment decision-making will contribute to long-term positive change on social and environmental issues. GISR maintains a research hub of ratings methods and best practices. It also has developed 12 principles that guide the process and content of sustainability report aspects. They inform the selection of issues and indicators, and signal to financial markets, companies, consumers, and the public at-large that ratings practices are credible (GISR, n.d.).

Reporting Exchange Tool[17]

In 2017, the WBCSD, in partnership with the Climate Disclosure Standards Board (CDSB) and Ecodesk, launched the Reporting Exchange. This is a free, online platform for navigating the complex provisions and requirements of sustainability reporting. Key research findings for just the United States and Canada revealed 290 reporting provisions and 156 reporting requirements. It was also telling that even among the WBCSD member companies—who are the global leaders in reporting and disclosures—that 24% of those companies in the US and Canada show no alignment between the issues highlighted as "material" in their sustainability report, and the risks in the financial filing (WBCSD, CDSB, Ecodesk, 2018).

Materiality

Each of the reporting initiatives above has differing definitions and interpretations of what is material and how to assess materiality. The following are the different definitions:

AMERICAN INSTITUTE OF CERTIFIED PUBLIC ACCOUNTANTS, AICPA SAB 99

Information is material if its omission or misstatement could influence the economic decisions of users taken on the basis of the financial statements. Materiality depends on the size of the item or error judged in the particular circumstances of its omission or misstatement. Thus, materiality provides a threshold or cut-off point rather than being a primary qualitative characteristic that information must have if it is to be useful (SEC, 1999).

GRI: MATERIALITY PRINCIPLE

The GRI didn't provide an explicit definition for materiality, but developed a very helpful principle with more detailed guidance about how to apply and test materiality.[18] Its principle is: "The report should cover Aspects that: Reflect the organization's significant economic, environmental and social impacts; or substantively influence the assessments and decisions of stakeholders" (GRI-G4, 2013) Figure 6.6 depicts a materiality matrix that aligns with the GRI-G4 principle. The dots represent environmental, social, or governance materiality aspects objectively identified and positioned on the x-axis by the enterprise. The y-axis positioning of the aspects is not well defined and must deal with the issue of how to reconcile different assessments from different stakeholder groups.

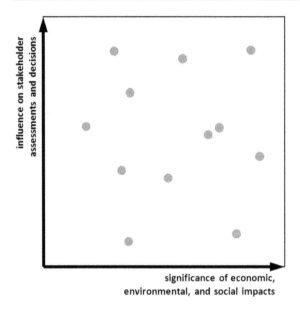

Figure 6.6 GRI-G4 materiality matrix
Source: Bellantuono et al. (2016), Creative Commons, no permission required.

GRI in partnership with RobecoSAM reviewed materiality from multiple stakeholder perspectives in *Defining Materiality: What Matters to Reporters and Investors* (GRI, RobecoSAM, 2015).

Bellantuono and colleagues conducted further research regarding both the qualitative and quantitative methods being used to assess materiality. They successfully piloted a multi-attribute group decision-making approach that was relatively simple. This approach is helpful as it makes the process available to small and medium enterprises who otherwise didn't have the resources to conduct these reviews (Bellantuono, Pontrandolfo, & Scozzi, 2016).

Accounting and assurance

Both US and international accounting standards boards and their respective CPA authorities are all waking up to the realization that their current principles, standards, and rules are in need of adaptation in order to deal with weaknesses and integrate new tools and technology relevant to identifying, assessing, and integrating sustainability risks and opportunities within traditional accounting and assurance practices. Collaborations and efforts to bring alignment among the diverse and somewhat competitive professional associations and standards initiatives will be a welcome element toward improving sustainability performance management systems and reporting for the future.

Jane Gleeson-White thinks that accountants will become the leaders of a new sustainability revolution. She saw 2012 as the sea-change year with the forming of IIRC and an international movement to transform how corporate accounting is calculated and the rise of incorporating the effects on the environment to the accounting of national and global economies. She sees multi-capital accounting as only the second revolution in accounting since double-entry bookkeeping began. She sees the shift as being of seismic proportions and that it was driven by the 2008 financial crash and our ongoing environmental crisis. These changes are profound and far-reaching, transforming the way the world does business, and the nature of capitalism (Gleeson-White, 2015).

Natural and social capital accounting

Expanding our boundaries for financial measures will be an important advancement for making better sustainability-aligned economic choices. This broader mindset is becoming possible through recent methodology and indicator advancements for financially quantifying intangible value, the value of natural capital, and ecosystem services. Monetization efforts are one helpful step towards progressing "Doing Well and Doing Good" strategies.

We appreciate that there are potential pitfalls from monetizing selected capital stocks and flows. They are subject to assumptions that are still relatively immature and difficult to calibrate. They have large confidence ranges. (See ecosystem services valuation example.) Natural and social capital systems also may not lend themselves to economic supply and demand responses. That said, they can help provide a compelling sustainability frame for current accounting systems.

The Natural Capital Protocol Toolkit[19]

The WBCSD and the Natural Capital Coalition launched the *Natural Capital Protocol Toolkit*. The protocol is a standardized framework for measuring business impacts and dependencies on nature. The Protocol and Toolkit help businesses address natural capital depletion by improving understanding, measurement, and decision-making. The Toolkit is a free and interactive database with over 50 tools for businesses to use in exploring, experimenting with, and carrying out natural capital assessments across their operations. The toolkit will help any enterprise to better measure and assess broader financial risks and opportunities associated with natural capital and ecosystem services. Over time, the toolkit will evolve and provide important data about which tools are the most commonly used by business.

TEEB report: Natural Capital at Risk

The Economics of Ecosystems and Biodiversity (TEEB) commissioned TruCost to apply its Guide to Corporate Ecosystem Valuation to estimate in monetary terms the financial risk from unpriced natural capital inputs to production, across business sectors at a regional level. TruCost used an environmentally extended input-output model (EEIO), to develop those estimates and at a high level, how these may flow through global supply chains to producers of consumer goods. It showed that some business activities do not generate sufficient profit to cover their natural resource use and pollution costs (TruCost, 2013).

The primary production and processing sectors analyzed in this study were estimated to have unpriced natural capital costs totaling US$7.3 trillion, which equated to 13% of global economic output in 2009. The majority of unpriced natural capital costs are from greenhouse gas emissions (38%) followed by water use (25%), land use (24%), air pollution (7%), land and water pollution (5%), and waste (1%) (TruCost, 2013).

Environmental Profit and Loss[20]

The Environmental Profit and Loss analysis was conceived by PUMA Chairman, Jochen Zeitz and first conducted in 2010. The associated methodology was developed with the support of PricewaterhouseCoopers LLP and TruCost (Confino, 2011). Kering, the parent company for Puma, has released its Environmental Profit and Loss Accounting methodology in an open source mode (Kering, n.d.). Kering has also made the methodology part of the Natural Capital Coalition's Toolbox resources. Because the methodology has continued to evolve since its launch, the results between Puma's original assessment and today's holistic assessment of the Kering value chain from extraction all the way through disposal are not comparable. Kering publishes its Group EP&L on an annual basis. The EP&L is used as a day-to-day decision-making tool and is fully embedded into the business. The EP&L revealed that 93% of Kering's impacts lie in the supply chain and, in particular, from the production and processing of raw materials which represent 72% of the total. Its operations represent only 7% of the impacts. Kering focuses on solutions and leveraging change along the supply chain while avoiding high impact sources. Kering is currently expanding its natural capital accounting work to assess biodiversity and also linking natural capital accounting to Planetary Boundaries (WBCSD, n.d.). More information on the EP&L is available on the *Living Fieldbook*.

Revised global ecosystem services value measurement: US$125 trillion per year

The first edition of the *Fieldbook* reviewed a 1997 study by world-leading ecological economist Robert Costanza and his colleagues (Costanza et al.,

1997). That study said services of ecological systems and the natural capital stocks that produce them are critical to the functioning of the Earth's life-support system. They contribute to human welfare, both directly and indirectly, and represent part of the total economic value of the planet. Costanza and colleagues revised their study in 2014 (Costanza et al., 2014). They adjusted the two values for inflation and used 2007 US$ to compare the revised estimate to the original. The 1997 estimate becomes $46 trillion when adjusted for inflation. The 1997 economy was also valued at about $46 trillion. The 2011 revised value of ecosystem services was $125 trillion and the entire global economy in 2011 was only $75 trillion. In the updated analysis, the value of ecosystem services (on which the entire global economy depends) was estimated to be two-thirds larger than the global economy itself. They also noted that between 1997 and 2007, there was between $4.3 trillion and $20.2 trillion loss of ecosystem services per year due to development and declines in productive lands. We'd suggest that's material. Very material ...

The *Living Fieldbook* contains additional references, case studies, and tools.

Doing Well and Doing Good: measuring financial and social performance

> Even if we can never quantify [satisfaction or happiness] ... as precisely as we currently quantify GNP ... perhaps it is better to be vaguely right than precisely wrong.
>
> (Herman Daly)

Doing Well and Doing Good companies are ready to break through in their performance. They are wealthy enough to resiliently take on more risk and responsibility. They have the freedom to move beyond the inhibiting beliefs of greed and welcome new opportunities to serve their stakeholders. Stage 3 companies have played the game well, but now see the need to change the rules of the game, or possibly play a different game altogether that better aligns innovative business models with sustainability-aligned outcomes and values. Performance success indicators expand their boundaries, and include measuring actions and performance towards mitigating global risks, and pursuing new opportunities aligned with societal goals.

This section again builds upon the strategic purpose and system construct presented in Chapter 3, the performance management essentials, and each earlier stage strategy and performance management tools and insights. We build on these and outline measurement and reporting system design criteria and enhancements appropriate for supporting Bridge 3, Doing Well and Doing Good stage strategies. Stage 3 strategies are more holistic and interconnect with global risk insights. We introduce the World Economic Forum global risks report series as a tool for monitoring enterprise risks and assessing materiality. We share key questions now being asked by long-term institutional investors.

These questions backed by hundreds of influential investors and CEOs could trigger an accelerated shift from companies focused only on Doing Well pulling them into the Doing Well and Doing Good strategic realm. We also introduce the WBCSD's SDG Compass tool, and BASF's efforts to measure social impacts as best practices measuring business and social performance together. We close this section by calling out a few potential pitfalls of our current economic system whose feedback signals are known, but continue to cause headwinds with unintended consequences as we scale efforts to achieve the SDGs. See the *Living Fieldbook* for supplemental information.

Doing Well and Doing Good measurement and reporting design criteria

The following are selected enterprise performance management and reporting system criteria construct items most relevant for enterprises formulating sustainability-aligned strategies for **Bridge 3, Doing Well and Doing Good**.

- **Performance management for Doing Well and Doing Good:** Their performance management systems interconnect and track external performance across their value chain and with the communities with whom they interact. In addition to measuring and reporting on all prior stage performance objectives, they are guided from a long-term triple-bottom-line global system context. Enterprises progressing at this level see their purpose as responsibly and synergistically contributing to the needs and wellbeing of customers and society.
- **System and data inventory review:** Stage 3 enterprises are already doing core data collection and performance management activities from all prior stages. The metrics and reporting systems appropriate for this stage of performance will likely interconnect with external "big data" sources, and include more complex product and service lifecycle impact assessments and full cost financial modeling.
- **Time horizons:** The SDGs are using 2030 or about 10 years as their horizon for Doing Well and Doing Good. Some thresholds, especially those interdependent with cash flow or the capital markets, may still be shorter. Environmental thresholds and climate change may have longer time horizons. The performance management systems however are now likely going to integrate with more real-time artificial intelligence and automated decision tools—large big data collection technologies—that have the potential to disrupt current practices and enable transformational efficiencies and monitoring capabilities.

- **Strategic goals and resiliency:** Business goals and societal goals will converge. Climate change is a dominant common environmental risk with the goal of keeping temperature rise to less than 2 degrees. Closing the income and wealth gap is another commonly held goal. The entire set of 17 SDGs will be aggressively advanced over the next decade. They represent both risks and opportunities for resilient, synergistic, performance breakthroughs.

- **Boundaries, interconnections:** The boundaries of Bridge 3 travelers are expanding their focus to include their holistic value chains and lifecycle impacts. The risk dimension of Figure 6.3 is also holistically covered such that the entire business management system interconnects with global environmental, economic, and social systems.

- **Key performance indicators and priority capital stocks and flows:** Multi-capital accounting will be an evolving practice for all enterprises already following Bridge 3 strategies or which are going to be pulled onto this Bridge by institutional investors. Social performance criteria will be developed and monitored. More natural capital flows will be tracked across entire value chains.

- **Mental models:** Companies crossing the chasm of the tragedy of the commons must spend sufficient time determining their own historic exploitation of the commons and accept responsibility to end unjust, unequal, and overly privatized solutions. When they suspect system flaws they proactively engage, and take actions to improve and fix them. They take their perspectives to broader and longer-term visions that reveal synergistic and transformational opportunities.

- **Networks and collaborations:** For Doing Well and Doing Good travelers, collaborative solutions are essential. No company and no government can thrive alone. As such, innovative and large-scale public, private partnerships will emerge. Avoiding the tragedy of the commons pitfalls that accompany most current privatization solutions—that exacerbate wealth divides and restrict access to the commons to the poor and middle-class people—will be critical.

The World Economic Forum and enterprise risk assessment[21]

Each year the World Economic Forum (WEF) conducts an assessment of the most significant global risks to business as determined by the business community itself. These reports are released in conjunction with the annual WEF gatherings in Davos, Switzerland. Reports include extremely insightful observations and trends gleaned from tracking global risks for over a decade. Over the past decade, the prevalence of ESG-related risks has steadily increased while the more traditional economic, geopolitical, or technological risks are less dominant. The 2008 Global Risk Report only included one societal risk—pandemics—in the top five risks in terms of impact. Ten years later, in the Global Risks Report 2018, four of the top five risks were societal or environmental, including extreme weather events, water crises, natural disasters, and failure of climate change mitigation and adaptation. These reports also highlight the interconnectedness that exists between the risks themselves—such as water crises and involuntary migration, and their interconnections to more aggregate global topics and trends.

The Global Risks Report 2018 is published at a time of global growth. The WEF members are business CEOs that view economic growth as being a good thing, but many also appreciate that there are many other potentially known and unknown consequences of growth that will need monitoring as well. (See the next section for more on macroeconomic indicators.) They say that any breathing space provided because of the current growth should not be squandered. They acknowledge an urgent need to face up to systemic challenges that have intensified over the past year amid proliferating signs of uncertainty, instability, and fragility.

These WEF Global Risk reports should be used by enterprises that are thinking more strategically and holistically about global risks and opportunities as a frame and context within which their own strategies and performance can be formulated and gauged. It is not necessary that an enterprise measures all risks. Rather companies should use the list of potential risks for discussions, and to assert that all the WEF risks were qualitatively reviewed. Then they can cite that only selected risks were determined to be of sufficient importance to include with their strategies and report disclosures.

The 2018 report covers more risks than ever, but focuses in particular on four key areas: environmental degradation, cybersecurity breaches, economic strains, and geopolitical tensions. A new series was also released, called "Future Shocks," cautioning against complacency, and emphasizing the need to prepare for sudden and dramatic disruptions (World Economic Forum, 2018). All of these perspectives will help shape resilient strategic plans and risk monitoring processes of enterprises with the purpose to Do Well and Do Good.

The Sustainable Development Goals (SDGs) and opportunity

The scale and ambition of the United Nations Agenda 2030 was expressed through the Sustainable Development Goals (SDGs) previously introduced in Chapter 3, and discussed throughout this book. The SDGs define global sustainable development priorities and aspirations for 2030 and seek to mobilize global efforts around a common set of 17 goals and 169 targets. The SDGs call for worldwide action among governments, business, and civil society to end poverty and create a life of dignity and opportunity for all, *within the boundaries of the planet.*[22]

Like the WEF Global Risk Reports, the SDGs expand the challenges that must be addressed to eliminate poverty, and embrace a wide range of interconnected topics across the economic, social, and environmental dimensions of sustainable development. While they primarily target governments, the SDGs are designed to rally a wide range of organizations, and shape priorities and aspirations for sustainable development efforts around this common framework with shared goals.

As with all sustainability-aligned measurement systems, some precautionary thinking and acknowledgments of potential pitfalls is prudent. The United Nations has made economic growth a vital element of achieving several of the interconnected goals. The rates required for the goals are likely unrealistically high. We also note in the next section how economic growth measures are imperfect—and if used without proper context—can result in unintended, but knowable negative long-term consequences. We also note in the next section that growth does not necessarily lead to the desired outcome of reduced poverty.

The SDG Compass[23]

One extremely helpful resource, the SDG Compass, was developed by GRI, the Global Compact, and the WBCSD. It is a knowledge-base to explain how the SDGs affect a business and provides tools to integrate the SDGs into a corporate strategy. The SDG Compass includes a pragmatic guidance document on how companies can align their strategies and implement the SDGs as well as measure and manage their contribution to the realization of the SDGs. The web resource features information for each SDG, including the role of business, and illustrative examples of business solutions, indicators, and tools.

The SDG Compass guide presents five steps that assist companies in maximizing their contribution to the SDGs. The five steps rest on recognition of the responsibility of all companies to comply with all relevant legislation, respect international minimum standards, and address all negative human rights impacts. The SDG Compass is developed with a focus on large multinational enterprises. Small and medium enterprises and other organizations are also encouraged to use it as a source of inspiration, and adapt as necessary. The SDG Compass is designed for use at the entity level, but may be applied at product, site, divisional, or regional level as appropriate.

The five steps of the SDG Compass guide are:

1. Understanding the SDGs.
2. Defining priorities to seize the most important business opportunities.
3. Setting goals to help foster shared priorities and better performance across the organization.

4. Integrating sustainability into the core business and governance, and embedding sustainable development targets across all functions.
5. Reporting and communicating sustainable development performance to stakeholders using common indicators and a shared set of priorities.

Measuring and motivating Doing Well and Doing Good

> Rank does not confer privilege or give power. It imposes responsibility.
>
> (Peter Drucker)

We have introduced tools and perspectives about what the most critical global risks and global goals are for business. These can feel overwhelming or too removed from the day-to-day operations of a struggling small or medium-sized company. As such, guidance developed by future thinking organizations and case examples of what leading companies are doing can help reduce this reaction and help any company continue to progress with its sustainability journey.

BASF: integrating SDGs and measuring social impacts[24]

BASF has developed a core corporate strategy that integrates sustainability risks and opportunities and is aligned with the UN SDGs. It has developed a "Value-to-Society" approach that provides a more comprehensive picture of BASF's impacts along its value chain and demonstrates how chemistry is enabling sustainable growth. It sees reducing its impact as being key to keeping and strengthening its license to operate (Wirtenberg, 2014).

The CEO Force for Good (CECP):[25] encouraging companies to Do Well and Do Good

CECP is a CEO-led coalition that believes that a company's social strategy—how it engages with key stakeholders including employees, communities, investors, and customers—determines company success. Founded in 1999 by actor and philanthropist Paul Newman and other business leaders to create a better world through business, CECP has grown to a movement of more than 200 of the world's largest companies that represent $7 trillion in revenues, $18.6 billion in societal investment, 13 million employees, and $15 trillion in assets under management. CECP helps companies transform their social strategy by providing customized connections and networking, counsel and support, benchmarking and trends, and awareness building and recognition.

The explicit endorsement of Doing Good and Doing Well that this network makes is a much needed pull to jolt all business leaders into a new reality. This new reality will have enterprises take more necessary risks and develop strategies to cross the chasm of the tragedy of the commons and guide them through the paradox of high returns and high anxiety to Do Well and Do Good.

Doing Good and Doing Well precautions and pitfalls

The tailwinds accelerating a transition from merely Doing Well and working within the constraints of our current economy and Doing Well and Doing Good are strong. However, the chasm of the tragedy of the commons and other headwinds associated with our current economy are also strong. The transition may get turbulent. We must remind ourselves of a few of these headwind measures that warrant continuous feedback signal monitoring as we simultaneously adapt our global economy, capital markets, employment, and lifestyle/consumption mindsets to support a new way of being.

The first edition of the *Fieldbook* discussed GDP as a measure of economic performance, and introduced the Genuine Performance Indicator (GPI) as a more sustainability-aligned alternative. Additional macroeconomic indicators that enterprise must monitor include interest rates (Kosse, 2002), unemployment rates (Dixon, 2016), and income inequality (DeSilver, 2015) among others. We continue to raise awareness about the potential pitfalls behind the improper use and misunderstanding of the context behind each.

More information on each of these topics is provided on the *Living Fieldbook*.

Thriving: enlightened leaders establishing thresholds and context allocation methods

> The best way to predict the future is to create it.
>
> (Peter Drucker)

Thriving is where the company is at once: accomplishing its purpose for its customers; having no net decline in natural capital; creating value; all while improving the wellbeing of its employees, customers, and stakeholders. This Bridge completes the holistic arc of our journey. Enterprises achieving this level of performance are Thriving within their system's context responsibility.

Companies operating with the strategic goals of Thriving will first and foremost be committed to science-based, strong sustainability business model constraints. Unlike all of the prior stage strategies, these companies realize that sustainable, Thriving, performance is not a competitive game being played by businesses. It is a long-term requirement for humans to continue to live on the planet. The Daly Triangle reminds us that natural capital is our ultimate means for sustaining life and enhancing human wellbeing. It is integral to every enterprise's ability to preserve its license to operate in the long term. Some business and investment leaders are already working hard to design and pilot more enlightened economic and governance systems to support Thriving companies.

Hundreds of leading companies have heard this message and are collaborating to set science-based environmental goals. At this time most companies are embracing science-based goals for GHG emissions and climate change. Simultaneously, other groups are collaborating to develop context-based allocation methods that allow individual industries and companies to evaluate their enterprise's value chain impacts and resource requirements. The Future-Fit Business Benchmark initiative introduced in Chapter 3 and other tools are already available to help enterprises measure strong sustainability performance while avoiding crashing into vital capital constraints.

Thriving stage measurement and reporting system design criteria

The following are selected enterprise performance management and reporting system construct items most relevant for enterprises ready to take bold risks in order to explore the unknown frontiers of the fourth strategic Bridge stage of **Thriving**:

- **The purpose for Thriving:** Progressing the enterprise's natural capital impact to 0 or positive regenerative performance while sustaining or enhancing the wellbeing of its employees, customers, and community stakeholders today without compromising the ability of future generations to Thrive.
- **Inventory practices:** Assess performance management practices for each of the multi-capital stocks and flows and carrying capacity thresholds where available.
- **Multi-capital accounting of vital stocks with most vulnerable threshold flows and/or greatest flow volatility.** Thriving companies will have performance management systems holistically aligned with a multi-capital accounting framework that monitors the stocks, flows, and thresholds of all the capitals.
- **Time horizons:** 2050 or longer for this mission. But as the WEF recommends our systems must be resilient and expect to adapt to "future shocks" that are unknown.
- **Strategic goals and resiliency:** At this stage, the Thriving goal for a resilient enterprise is for that enterprise to operate within the context-allocated planetary boundary environmental conditions, and be safely above all of the context-allocated social floor conditions. See the doughnut economics section for more specific environmental and social risk items.
- **Boundaries, interconnections:** The boundaries of Bridge 4 travelers are highly fluid. For the purpose of business management, we see the

boundaries as being the entire enterprises value chain and lifecycle stages and all of the environmental, economic, and social issues or multi-capital risks at all cascading levels between the enterprise and the planetary systems.

- **Mental models:** Companies are still crossing the chasm of unknowns. They must learn to work productively in unstructured environments and make decisions with ambiguous criteria and incomplete information.
- **Networks and collaborations:** At this stage our networks are inclusive. Adding networks such as the Future-Fit Business Benchmark and Reporting 3.0 communities will be helpful for setting and monitoring threshold limits.

Science and strong sustainability

The Brundtland definition[26] is noble, but not testable; where's the target? Sustainability frameworks including the GRI, IIRC, and SASB Sustainability Reporting initiatives and the aspirational UN SDGs help define, measure, and monitor sustainability performance. That said, each perpetuates embedded mindset biases, or is beholden to a stubborn allegiance to a single bottom line, self-interest first, growth-dependent, economic system. These frameworks are all alarming people who are disconnected from science-based insights regarding global realities and risks.

Social, science, and capital market transformation initiatives are already in progress now to define and produce powerful science-aligned sustainability performance measures and market mechanisms. These efforts are fragmented and have competing governance, stakeholder, and scientific perspectives, and are in different stages of design and application. Each also must acknowledge and manage significant uncertainties associated with foundational science-based thresholds, ethical and economic allocation approaches, and leave open the question of how aggressively to pursue them.

Strong versus weak sustainability

The concept of strong sustainability is based on the scientific fact that all human life and activity occurs within the limitations of planet Earth, or the "biosphere" where human, plants, and other animals live. Without a functioning biosphere there can be no society, and without society there can be no societal functions, including an economy. The notion of the triple bottom line as normally presented using overlapping circles represents a weak sustainability-oriented system.

Weak sustainability systems assume that natural capital can be substituted by other capitals and that there are no differences between the kinds of well-being they create. The economy's goal is growth through capital accumulation, and that the total value of the aggregate stock of capital should be at least maintained or ideally increased for the sake of future generations (Pelenc, Ballet, & Dedeurwaerdere, 2015).

Strong sustainability systems believe that natural capital is more than a mere stock of resources. Rather, natural capital is a set of complex systems consisting of evolving biotic and abiotic elements that interact in ways that determine the ecosystem's capacity to provide human society directly and/or indirectly with a wide array of functions and services (Brand, 2009; De Groot, Van der Perk, Chiesura, & van Vliet, 2003; Ekins, Simon, Deutsch, Folke, & De Groot, 2003; Noël and O'Connor, 1998; Pelenc et al., 2015).

Table 6.2 summarizes the main differences between weak and strong sustainability.

In terms of scientific methodology, strong sustainability is greatly preferred as the perspective for establishing sustainability goals and performance metrics. Managing natural capital as the "critical" nonsubstitutable capital resource providing ecosystem services and sustaining human life itself should be embedded within societal beliefs and human behaviors.

Science and its role driving technological innovations will be an important element in achieving development goals and strong sustainability conditions. Eradicating poverty and hunger has been helped through new high-yielding varieties of rice that can withstand drought in Africa and flooding in Asia. Science is also helping African farmers, who lose as much as half of what they produce to pest infections, through

Table 6.2 Weak versus strong sustainability

	Weak sustainability	Strong sustainability
Capitals substitutability	Natural and other capitals are perfectly substitutable	Substitutability of natural capital is severely limited
Consequences	Technical innovation and monetary compensation for environmental degradation	Human actions can entail irreversible consequences
Sustainability issue	Total value of aggregate stock of capitals should be maintained or ideally increased for future generations	Conserving irreplaceable stocks of vital natural capital for the sake of future generations
Key concept	Optimal allocation of scarce resources	Critical natural capital
Thresholds and environmental norms	Instrumental rationality *(Technical and scientific approach for determining threshold)*	Procedural rationality *(Scientific knowledge as input for public deliberation)*

Source: Adapted from Pelenc et al. (2015).

new technologies for better biological pest control. Another area of scientific progress is in reducing childbirth mortality, thanks to the discovery of magnesium sulfate given to mothers immediately after birth, which is drastically reducing maternal deaths (Naicker, 2015). Technological innovation that solves one—or even synergistically improves several of the world's sustainability problems—also represents the biggest business opportunities of our time.

Planetary boundaries and the Stockholm Resilience Centre[27]

The Stockholm Resilience Centre is a leader in conducting transdisciplinary research. It advances the understanding of complex social-ecological systems to improve ecosystem management practices and long-term sustainability. Its research on planetary boundaries (PB) is the seminal work connecting strong sustainability ecosystem service risks and science-based goals with performance measures. The PB framework was first introduced in 2009, when a group of 28 internationally renowned scientists identified and quantified the first set of nine planetary boundaries.

Figure 6.7 depicts the most recent PB state. Four of nine planetary boundaries have already been crossed as a result of human activity (Steffen

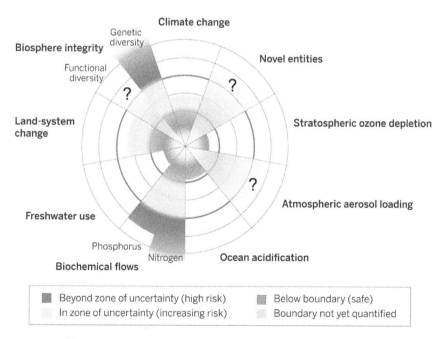

Figure 6.7 Planetary boundaries

Source: Will Steffen, Senior Fellow, Stockholm Resilience Centre, with permission.

et al., 2015). The four are: climate change, loss of biosphere integrity, land-system change, and altered biogeochemical cycles (phosphorus and nitrogen). Two of these, climate change and biosphere integrity, are what the scientists call "core boundaries." Significantly altering either of these "core boundaries" would "drive the Earth System into a new state". Transgressing a boundary increases the risk that human activities could inadvertently drive the Earth System into a much less hospitable state, damaging efforts to reduce poverty and leading to a deterioration of human wellbeing in many parts of the world, including wealthy countries (Steffen et al., 2015).

Social performance and Doughnut Economics

Kate Raworth, an economist and Senior Visiting Research Associate at the Environmental Change Institute of Oxford University, has developed a visualization of conditions that make a zone habitable for humanity. Raworth shows the zone where humanity thrives as a doughnut sandwiched between the environmental ceiling of planetary boundaries and the social foundation of governance and accessed ecosystem services. Figure 6.8 provides this Doughnut Economy visualization.

The inner circle contains the 11 dimensions of human deprivation, from Rio + 20 submissions. Social foundations of safety and justice are constructed on and with the availability of these 11.

The outer layer represents critical planetary boundaries. The safety zone for human prosperity is within the doughnut that lies between the environmental ceiling and the social foundation. It is within this doughnut that we make sustainable livelihoods and work "to eradicate poverty and inequity for all, within the means of the planet's limited resources" (Raworth, 2012).

Future Earth: scientists in service of sustainability[28]

Future Earth is a consortium based in five countries that came together between 2012 and 2015 to coordinate and steward several vital global scientific data collection and research initiatives necessary to assess the health of the planet. Future Earth builds on more than three decades of global environmental change research through the World Climate Research Program (WCRP), the International Geosphere-Biosphere Program (IGBP), DIVERSITAS, and the International Human Dimensions Program on Global Environmental Change (IHDP). This is just one example of the type of scientific community collaborations that will be needed as we advance our understanding of planetary boundaries, natural capital carrying capacities, and other interconnected global systems health monitoring.

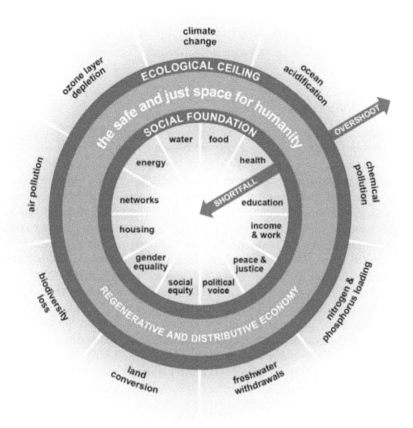

Figure 6.8 The Doughnut Economy

Source: Raworth, K. (2017). *Doughnut Economics: Seven ways to think like a 21st century economist.* London: Penguin Random House, with permission.

Context-based enterprise goals and indicators

Context-Based Sustainability (CBS)[29] is an approach to enterprise sustainability accounting (and target setting) that takes social, economic, and environmental thresholds and limits in the world (upper and lower ones pertaining to vital resources or capitals) explicitly into account. It then allocates fair, just, and proportionate shares of either the available capitals or the shared burden to maintain them to a specific enterprise (including its unique value chain system) in order to assess the sustainability (and at this point we are looking for Thriving) performance of enterprises. Mark McElroy and Bill Baue have been heroes leading both multicapitalism and CBS to better measure and assess strong sustainability performance (Baue, 2017; McElroy, 2011). Their efforts and a broader network of practitioners have been lobbying the GRI to more explicitly require context-based performance assessments by the users of that standard (McElroy, 2017). Like with materiality, GRI has developed a principle with guidance and a process for testing context when developing sustainability reports.[30]

MultiCapital Scorecard™ (MCS)[31]

The IIRC framework and the GISR Ratings Standard endorse Context-Based Sustainability (CBS) and multi-capital accounting, but are also only principles-based and nonprescriptive in this regard. Enterprises have been left to their own devices as to how to operationalize these principles. Operationalizing CBS principles and multi-capitalism metrics raises some basic questions. What does it mean, for example, to assess performance in terms of multiple capitals and how might one do so in a formal or structured way? What exactly is the capital theory of performance and what are its practice implications? The MultiCapital Scorecard™ was created as an open source methodology and tool to answer these questions (McElroy & Thomas, 2015).

In 2013, Thomas & McElroy LLC (T&M) was formed when Mark McElroy joined forces with Martin Thomas, a 30-year veteran of Unilever, with the express intent of developing a more complete, triple-bottom-line implementation of CBS. Ben & Jerry's had been an initial pilot company for applying CBS methods. It later became the first company in which the MultiCapital Scorecard™ was piloted. This tool is the first context- and multi-capital-based integrated measurement, management, and reporting system. In practice, the MultiCapital Scorecard™ follows a three-step process:

1. Scoping and materiality.
2. Areas of impact (AOI) development.
3. Scorecard implementation.

We have previously discussed scoping (the Business Management System [BMS] framework) and materiality assessments. Once a material set or portfolio of AOIs (a selected group of enterprise system aspects of the BMS) has been identified each of the associated AOIs must be further researched and developed in preparation for the role it will play in measurement and reporting. The MultiCapital Scorecard™ methodology does this in two parts. First is the specification of sustainability norms or goals and second is the development of an associated data collection protocol. Sustainability norms (SNs) are defined as standards of performance for what an organization's impacts on vital capitals must be in order to be sufficient, sustainable, and supportive of stakeholder wellbeing. Sometimes, the SNs identified by an organization for particular AOIs will not be achievable anytime soon, in which case the MultiCapital Scorecard™ allows for the specification of Trajectory

Targets (TTs) as interim goals. (See the science-based targets section next for examples of goal setting.) As with our smart bridge strategy from Chapter 3, this tool acknowledges that most organizations are not resilient enough to achieve Thriving performance all at once. It suggests that TTs be defined in a way that provides a transition pathway, or trajectory, from some current state of affairs to the target state represented by an SN.

Once SNs and TTs have been defined for individual AOIs, data collection protocols for each must be developed. A data collection protocol is a system for gathering the data required to describe an organization's impacts and populate a MultiCapital Scorecard™. The data collection protocol includes people, process, and technology dimensions. The people dimension will identify the parties responsible for gathering the data; the process dimension will determine when and how the data should be collected; and the technology dimension will specify the role of technology, if any, in capturing, computing, and reporting the data required (McElroy & Thomas, 2015).

Operationalizing the MultiCapital Scorecard™ required a refinement to the definition of economic capitals from that of the IIRC and others presented earlier. Using the refined capitals definitions, the tool used another innovation to enable a performance scoring. It developed a seven-point scoring schema in the MCS to assess performance towards achieving SNs and TTs (McElroy & Thomas, 2015). These are exactly the kinds of pioneering efforts that help our entire universe of companies and ultimately the economy itself evolve to the next greener iteration.

Finally, there is nothing in the design of the MultiCapital Scorecard™ that calls for the monetization of impacts on capitals other than for financial capital itself. Instead, it calls for the identification of capital limits and thresholds in their own terms (e.g., gallons of water, tons of greenhouse gas emissions, product safety levels, conformance to ethical standards, etc.). Whether or not the use of natural capital is occurring at a sustainable rate, for example, may not necessarily be reflected in the price we put on it and instead will have everything to do with biophysical limits. The same is true for the other capitals and their own stocks and flows (McElroy & Thomas, 2015). The *Living Fieldbook* also contains more information on the background and applications of the MultiCapital Scorecard™.

Frameworks and collaborations advance thriving metrics

Accepting the sustainability challenge is daunting to many. It requires embracing and simultaneously coping with multiple "wicked" problems with complex system boundary overlaps. Solving wicked problems requires system change and changing systems cannot be accomplished alone. Multi-disciplinary, multi-national, and multi-generational collaboration between diverse stakeholders arriving at the table with different ethical, economic, and political philosophies is required. Add to that significant amounts of distrust, ignorance, short-term thinking, and expectations of immediate and gratifying results, and we are challenged as never before.

Science-based targets (SBTs)

The science-based targets[32] initiative introduced in Chapter 3 is a helpful collaboration advancing both the importance of respecting scientific trends and their respective environmental and social impact risks, and developing fair and relevant allocation schemes so that enterprises can set meaningful targets. There are several science-based target setting methods that fall under three main approaches. The first two are related to the "carbon budget"—the remaining amount of carbon that can be emitted into the atmosphere to limit global temperature rises to well below 2 degrees Celsius.

- Sector-based approach: This divides the carbon budget by sector and then allocates it to companies in that sector.
- Absolute-based approach: This assigns to companies the same percentage of absolute emission reductions as is required globally—i.e., 49% by 2050 from 2010 levels.
- Economic-based approach: The carbon budget is equated to global GDP and a company's share is determined by its gross profit.

These approaches are similar to those being advanced by other initiatives developing context allocation schemes. We chose to showcase Mars as the case example here specifically because it saw science as being more than just carbon, and used the planetary boundaries as its framework for assessing risks and strategic actions.

Mars: making an impact with operations and value chain[33]

Mars is a family-owned business with diverse products and brands including Milky Way, M&Ms, and more. Mars wanted to help build a planet that is healthy and thriving and build a sustainable business. It is investing in renewable energy, improving conditions in its supply chains, and speaking out about climate change. Among other things, it makes sure that the people it relies on—from smallholder farmers to suppliers—benefit from the growth of its business.

Mars acknowledges that it needs to protect the earth so that there are fewer impacts for the people that live on it. To do so, it has chosen to focus its efforts using the "planetary boundaries" and set science-based targets to help it prioritize and decide what to do. With the planetary boundaries as its guide, the company used internal information and public, accepted data, and was able to identify three broad areas in which it could make the biggest difference. It identified greenhouse gas emissions, impacts of water use, and impacts of land use. Over time, Mars has progressed and improved sourcing processes for palm oil, paper and pulp, beef, soy, rice, mint, fish, tea, coffee, and other raw materials.

Enterprises commit to thriving and Future-Fit Business Benchmark[34]

The Future-Fit Business Benchmark (FFBM) framework, also introduced in Chapter 3, is one of the group's leading collaborations to establish enterprise goals and performance indicators that are science-based and also identify human wellbeing conditions. The FFBM framework was developed by scientists and used the Natural Step principles as its foundation. It is collaborating to co-create and refine an academically rigorous, systems-based framework to guide progress toward a flourishing and thriving future. Future-fit companies add value to the holistic system ensuring that business in no way hinders, and ideally contributes to, society's progress toward future-fitness. The Benchmarks help business measure—and manage—the gap between what they are doing today and what science tells us they will need to do tomorrow. The FFBM community is collaborating with the Reporting 3.0 community presented next and many others as well.

Reporting 3.0[35]

Reporting 3.0 is a global good initiative serving as a global platform to scout out and accelerate reporting innovations and help bring the global economy onto an inclusive, sustainable path. Like the other initiatives working to advance sustainability reporting, it sees a need for consolidation and convergence in the fragmented sustainability reporting market.

GLOBAL THRESHOLDS & ALLOCATIONS COUNCIL

Reporting 3.0 held a multi-stakeholder event in the first quarter of 2018 to initiate the Global Thresholds & Allocations Council (GTAC). The mission of this council is to establish an authoritative approach to reporting economic, environmental, and social performance in relation to generally accepted boundaries and limits. GTAC will operate as a partnership between leading organizations and individuals from science, business, investment, government, and civil society, focused on assessing and validating methodologies for allocating fair shares of responsibility to organizations for their impacts on the stocks and flows of capitals—natural, human, social, and other resources—within their carrying capacities. Building on related efforts to establish science-based targets, GTAC will be working to accelerate progress toward contextualizing company disclosures commensurate with the ecological, social, and economic urgencies facing societies and companies alike in the coming decades (Reporting 3.0, n.d.).

THE DALY HOURGLASS

As part of their work developing a series of blueprints that advance distinct aspects of sustainability management and reporting, the Reporting 3.0 community did a virtual dialogue review of the Daly Triangle which was introduced in Chapter 2 and has been a guiding tool for this metrics and reporting chapter. They did not feel a triangle shape effectively visualized the thresholds concept. Their reassessment of the Daly Triangle resulted in the following three tweaks:

- They equalized their representation of the Ultimate Means (natural capital) and Ultimate Ends (wellbeing) by placing two triangles side by side and fusing them together to form an hourglass shape.
- They flipped the progression, with natural capital atop as the "sands" of capital resources that flow through the hourglass (which introduced a missing element of "time").
- Finally, they introduced the sustainability thresholds using the ecological ceilings and social foundations established by Kate Raworth in Doughnut Economics.

They called the resulting graphic (Figure 6.9) the Daly Hourglass. Its highly significant meanings now underpin the advocacy for a design document (R3 Data Blueprint), a holistic integral information system which the Reporting 3.0 and collaborating community of partners is now hard at work creating (Baue, 2017).

Conclusion: *measure what matters and manage it*

Welcome to the still unstructured world of sustainability performance measurement and reporting. Numbers alone cannot capture the deepest meanings of sustainability. Yet we have little choice but to relentlessly pursue, and rely on, those quantitative and qualitative measures that will empower us to preserve that which is beyond measurement.

We have attempted to provide some context to impress upon you that measuring sustainability performance is good for your enterprise and vital to society. We know from experience with clients in every sector that the right metrics properly applied can help enterprises improve performance and align with the SDGs and strong sustainability goals. These topics, tools, and case stories present an initial system overview to get you started on your journey. Implementing and trusting technology-enabled, sustainability-aligned performance management systems, even knowing their limitations and weaknesses, present our best understanding of current reality and help identify and prioritize the most desirable pathways ahead.

Executives managing change have long acknowledged the importance of metrics to assess baseline conditions and progress toward goals.

DALY HOURGLASS

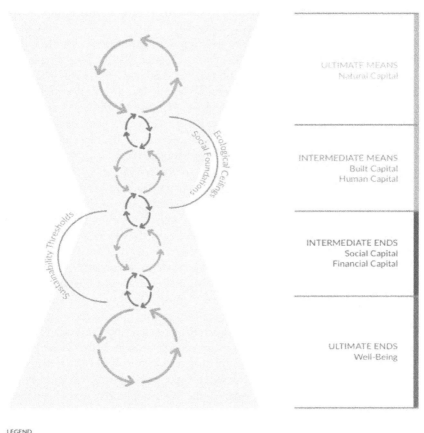

LEGEND

— Capital Flows
— Capital Stocks

Figure 6.9 The Daly Hourglass
Source: "Daly Hourglass," Bill Baue, Blueprint 3. Data Integration, Contextualization & Activation for Multicapital Accounting, Reporting 3.0, 2017, with permission.

Stage-appropriate measurement system criteria and implementation resources were presented for each of the four purposeful enterprise strategy Bridges. Beginners are comforted to see how much they were already doing and can fill in a few gaps to help see strengths and weaknesses and enhance material, energy, employee, customer, and financial performance.

For those already on this journey, this information helps you check your bearings. Do you feel better prepared to re-imagine your next destination and begin re-orienting your measurement and reporting systems? Tools such as the PivotGoals and SDG Compass are powerful and allow you to rapidly innovate, surpassing competitor performance, and delivering meaningful value to customers and society. We also have introduced networks of enterprises collaborating to advance the methods and standards for measuring and reporting sustainability progress.

We introduced the work of the Stockholm Resilience Centre, Future Earth, and the Global Thresholds & Allocations Council (GTAC) all working to measure and monitor planetary boundaries and carrying capacities. The Global Footprint Network's Ecological Footprint and its quiz showed us the gap between our current lifestyles and the capacity of the earth to regenerate the biocapacity resources required to support it. These science-based initiatives present alarming realities. The magnitude of the challenge and the ultimate performance gaps to be closed are substantial.

We also included comments alerting us to potential pitfalls associated with metrics systems generally and measuring sustainability performance specifically. We must acknowledge that metrics systems are subject to frauds and how much is simply unknowable. This is especially so when setting science-based goals, social service floors, and fair and equitable context allocations of resources and performance obligations.

Sustainability is an ever-changing end state in an unknowable future. The still limited monitoring of the resiliency of our planetary boundaries indicates that we are currently not responsibly caring for fragile life-supporting ecosystems. The ecological footprint reminds us that we only have one planet Earth and we must preserve and regenerate its biocapacity while adapting our lifestyles to live within one planet biocapacity constraints. We can build upon the experience of NASA's Apollo mission and establish next "departments of it can't be done." Let's throw a victory party and then get busy reverse-engineering the pathways to accomplish the SDGs and turn today's seemingly impossible environmental, social, and economic conditions into strategic opportunities and design specifications. Let's be optimistic, despite all the challenges we face, and be inspired by nature's resiliency and humanity's innovation as we systematically invent the future we want.

> People are fond of counting their troubles, but they do not count their joys. If they counted them up as they ought to, they would see that every lot has enough.
>
> (Fyodor Dostoevsky)

Notes

1 SMART = Specific, Measurable, Attainable, Relevant, and Time-Bound.
2 The concept of multi-capitals was introduced with the Daly Triangle and stocks, flows, and threshold performance were elements of systems. Both were previously introduced in Chapter 2, pages 89–90.
3 http://searchcio.techtarget.com/definition/systems-thinking

4 www.academyforchange.org/
5 www.footprintnetwork.org
6 www.footprintcalculator.org/
7 www.pivotgoals.com
8 www.gapminder.org/ignorance/
9 The *Living Fieldbook* includes 20 articles on the Pitfalls of Metrics by Matt Polsky et al.
10 www.sustainablebrands.com/
11 www.greenbiz.com/
12 https://shift.tools/
13 www.globalreporting.org
14 www.sasb.org
15 http://integratedreporting.org/
16 http://ratesustainability.org/
17 www.reportingexchange.com/
18 https://g4.globalreporting.org/how-you-should-report/reporting-principles/principles-for-defining-report-content/materiality/Pages/default.aspx
19 http://naturalcapitalcoalition.org/
20 www.kering.com/en/sustainability/epl
21 www.weforum.org/reports/the-global-risks-report-2018
22 http://17goals.org/
23 https://sdgcompass.org/
24 www.basf.com/en/company/sustainability.html
25 http://cecp.co/
26 The Brundtland Commission, in a report often considered the beginning of the global dialogue on sustainability, recognized sustainable development as "a process of change in which the exploitation of resources, the direction of investments, the orientation of technological development, and institutional change are made consistent with future as well as present needs" (World Commission on Environment and Development, 1987, p. 38).
27 www.stockholmresilience.org
28 www.futureearth.org/
29 www.sustainableorganizations.org/
30 https://g4.globalreporting.org/how-you-should-report/reporting-principles/principles-for-defining-report-content/sustainability-context/Pages/default.aspx
31 www.multicapitalscorecard.com/
32 http://sciencebasedtargets.org/about-the-science-based-targets-initiative/
33 www.mars.com/global/sustainable-in-a-generation/our-approach-to-sustainability/planning-and-measurement
34 http://futurefitbusiness.org/
35 https://reporting3.org/

References

Aronson, D. (2013). *Sustainability driven innovation: Harnessing sustainability's ability to spark innovation*. New York: Deloitte.

Baue, B. (2017). *Blueprint 3. Data integration, contextualization & activation for multicapital accounting.* Reporting 3.0.

Baue, B., & Thurm, R. (2017, August 11). How to transform today's "senseless" ESG data into tomorrow's actionable knowledge. *Sustainable Brands.*

Beer, S., & Lane, A. (1972). *Brain of the firm: The managerial cybernetics of organization.* London: The Penguin Press.

Bellantuono, N., Pontrandolfo, P., & Scozzi, B. (2016). Capturing the stakeholders' view in sustainability reporting: A novel approach. *Sustainability, 8*(12), 379. doi:10.3390/su8040379

Boerrigter, S. (2015). The use of the Sustainability Balanced Scorecard Framework for Dutch SMEs as a tool for measuring the performance of their sustainability strategy, 5th IBA Bachelor Thesis Conference, July 2, 2015, Enschede, The Netherlands. University of Twente.

Brand, F. (2009). Critical natural capital revisited: Ecological resilience and sustainable development. *Ecological Economics, 68,* 605–612.

Clark, G. L., Feiner, A., & Viehs, M. (2015, March). *From stockholder to the stakeholder: How sustainability can drive financial outperformance.* Arabesque Partners, Oxford University. Retrieved February 19, 2018, from: https://arabesque.com/research/From_the_stockholder_to_the_stakeholder_web.pdf.

Confino, J. (2011, May 16). Puma world's first major company to put a value on its environmental impact. *The Guardian.* Retrieved February 19, 2018, from www.theguardian.com/sustainable-business/puma-value-environmental-impact-biodiversity.

COSO. (2017, June). *Enterprise risk management—Integrating with strategy and performance.* COSO.

COSO, & WBCSD. (2018). *Forthcoming draft application guidance: Enterprise risk management framework: Applying enterprise risk management to environmental, social and governance-related risks.* COSO, WBCSD.

Costanza, R., d'Arge, R., de Groot, R., Farberk, S., Grasso, M., Hannon, B., et al. (1997, May 15). The value of the world's ecosystem services and natural capital. *Nature, 387,* 253–260.

Costanza, R., Erickson, J., Fligger, K., Adams, A., Adams, C., Altschuler, B., et al. (2004). Estimates of the Genuine Progress Indicator (GPI) for Vermont, Chittenden County and Burlington, from 1950 to 2000. *Ecological Economics, 51,* 139–155.

Costanza, R., de Groot, R., Sutton, P., van der Ploeg, S., Anderson, S. J., Kupiszewski, I., Farver, S., & Tyrner, K. (2014). Changes in the global value of ecosystem services. *Global Environmental Change, 26,* 152–158.

De Groot, R., Van der Perk, J., Chiesura, A., & van Vliet, A. (2003). Importance and threat as determining factors for criticality of natural capital. *Ecological Economics, 44,* 187–204.

DeSilver, D. (2015, September 22). The many ways to measure economic inequality. Retrieved February 19, 2018, from www.pewresearch.org/fact-tank/.../the-many-ways-to-measure-economic-inequality/.

Dixon, A. (2016, November 22). Top 5 problems with the unemployment rate. Retrieved February 14, 2018, from https://smartasset.com/career/problems-with-the-unemployment-rate.

Eccles, R., & Krzus, M. (2015). *The integrated reporting movement.* Hoboken, NJ: John Wiley and Sons, Inc.

Ekins, P., Simon, S., Deutsch, L., Folke, C., & De Groot, R. (2003). A framework for the practical application of the concepts of critical natural capital and strong sustainability. *Ecological Economics, 44*, 165–185.

Esty, D. C., & Cort, T. (2017). Corporate sustainability metrics: What investors need and don't get. *Journal of Environmental Investing, 8*(1), 13–59.

Feinberg, C. (2015, May–June). The science of scarcity. *Harvard Magazine*. Retrieved May 5, 2018, from http://harvardmagazine.com/2015/05/the-science-of-scarcity.

Figge, F., Hahn, T., Schaltegger, S., & Wagner, M. (2002). The sustainability balanced scorecard: Theory and application of a tool for value-based sustainability management. Presented at Greening of Industry Network Conference, Gothenburg, Germany.

Forum for the Future. (2011). *The Five Capitals Model—a framework for sustainability*. Brooklyn, NY: Forum for the Future.

Friend, G. (2004, June 30). How high the moon: The challenge of "sufficient" goals. *New Bottom Line, 13*(3). Retrieved January 29, 2008, from www.natlogic.com/new-bottom-line/v13/25-v13/ 194-new-bottom-line-volume-13–3.

Friend, G. (2012). Is your value stream leaking? *Natural Logic*. http://natlogic.com/is-your-value-stream-leaking/.

Friend, G. (2017, December 21). Counting what counts: The evolution of new metrics. *Sustainable Brands*. Retrieved May 5, 2018, from www.sustainablebrands.com/news_and_views/new_metrics/gil_friend/learning_count_what_counts_evolution_new_metrics.

GISR. (n.d.). *Principles*. Retrieved February 19, 2018, from http://ratesustainability.org/core/principles/.

Gleeson-White, J. (2015). *Six capitals, or can accountants save the planet?* New York: W. W. Norton & Company.

GRI-G4. (2013). *Sustainability reporting guidelines—reporting principles and standard disclosures*. Retrieved February 19, 2018, from www.globalreporting.org/resourcelibrary/GRIG4-Part2-Implementation-Manual.pdf.

GRI, RobecoSAM. (2015). *Defining materiality: What matters to reporters and investors*. GRI, RobecoSAM.

IIRC. (2008). *The international IR framework 2.1*, pp. 11, 12. IIRC.

Kering. (n.d.). *Kering environmental profit & loss (EP&L) methodology & 2013 results*. Retrieved on February 20, 2018, from www.kering.com/sites/default/files/document/kering_epl_methodology_and_2013_group_results_0.pdf#page=24.

Kosse, V. (2002). *Interest rates and their role in the economy during transition: The problem of high interest rates in the case of Ukraine*. The National University of Kyiv Mohyla Academy.

McElroy, M. (2011, March 10). Key issues in sustainability metrics and indicators, Presentation at Sustainability Leadership Forum, Chicago, IL, Center for Sustainable Business.

McElroy, M. W. (2014, October). *Context-based monetization curves: A sustainability model for assigning monetary values to organizational impacts on vital capitals*. V1.4, Center for Sustainable Organizations.

McElroy, M. (2017, November 7). Is it possible that GRI has never really been about sustainability reporting at all? *Sustainable Brands*.

McElroy, M., Jorna, R., & Engelen, J. (2007). Sustainability quotients and the social footprint. In R. Welford (Ed.), *Corporate social responsibility and environmental management*. New York: John Wiley and Sons Ltd.

McElroy, M. W., & Thomas, M. P. (2015). The MultiCapital Scorecard. *Sustainability Accounting, Management and Policy Journal, 6*(3), 425–438. doi:10.1108/sampj-04-2015-0025

Meadows, D. H. (1998). *Indicators and information systems for sustainable development*. Balaton Group report.

Meadows, D. H. (1999). *Leverage points: Places to intervene in a system*. Hartland Four Corners, VT: Sustainability Institute.

Meadows, D. H., Meadows, D. L., Meadows, J. R., & Behrens, W. W. (1972). *The limits to growth*. New York: Universe Books.

Möller, A., & Schaltegger, S. (2005). The sustainability balanced scorecard as a framework for eco-efficiency analysis. *Journal of Industrial Ecology, 9*(4), 73–83. doi:10.1162/108819805775247927

Naicker, I. (2015, May 24). The role of science in reaching development goals. *The Conversation*. Retrieved February 15, 2018, from http://theconversation.com/the-role-of-science-in-reaching-development-goals-42071.

Nelson, M. (2017, April 25). *The importance of nonfinancial performance to investors*. EY.

Noël, J-F., & O'Connor, M. (1998). Strong sustainability and critical natural capital. In S. Faucheux & M. O'Connor (Eds.), *Valuation for sustainable development: Methods and policy indicators* (pp. 75–99). Cheltenham, UK: Edward Elgar Publishers.

Nørgård, J., Peet, J., & Ragnarsdóttir, K. (2010, February 26). The history of the limits to growth. *The Solutions Journal*.

Pelenc, J., Ballet, J., & Dedeurwaerdere, T. (2015). Weak sustainability versus strong sustainability. *GSDR*. Retrieved from https://sustainabledevelopment.un.org/content/documents/6569122-Pelenc-Weak%20Sustainability%20versus%20Strong%20Sustainability.pdf.

Raworth, K. (2012, February 12). Can we live inside the doughnut? Why we need planetary and social boundaries. *Oxfam Policy & Practice*. Retrieved March 21, 2018, from https://policy-practice.oxfam.org.uk/blog/2012/02/can-we-live-inside-the-doughnut-planetary-and-social-boundaries.

Raworth, K. (2017). *Doughnut economics: Seven ways to think like a 21st-century economist*. London: Random House Business.

Reporting 3.0. (n.d.). Global Thresholds & Allocations Council [Press release]. Retrieved February 14, 2018, from https://reporting3.org/wp-content/uploads/2018/01/GTAC-ConceptNote-Final.pdf.

Rochlin, S., Bliss, R., Jordan, S., & Yaffe Kiser, C. (2015). *Project ROI: Defining the competitive and financial advantages of corporate responsibility and sustainability*. IO Sustainability.

SEC. (August 12, 1999). SEC staff accounting bulletin: No. 99—materiality. Retrieved February 19, 2018, from www.sec.gov/interps/account/sab99.htm.

Slavin, T. (2018, February 4). Tim Mohin: "The world doesn't need more CSR reports." *Ethical Corporation*. Retrieved May 4, 2018, from www.ethicalcorp.com/tim-mohin-world-doesnt-need-more-csr-reports.

Steffen, W., Richardson, K., Rockström, J., Cornell, S. E., Fetzer, I., Bennett, E. M., & Sörlin, S. (2015, February 13). Planetary boundaries: Guiding human development on a changing planet. *Science*. Retrieved February 15, 2018, from http://science.sciencemag.org/content/347/6223/1259855.

Tett, G. (2018, February 1). In the vanguard: Fund giants urge CEOs to be "Force for Good." Retrieved March 30, 2018, from www.ft.com/content/a28203d8-067d-11e8-9650-9c0ad2d7c5b5.

TruCost. (2013). *Natural capital at risk: The top 100 externalities of business.* TEEB, WBCSD.

Turner, G. (2008). *A comparison of* The Limits to Growth *with thirty years of reality.* Commonwealth Scientific and Industrial Research Organization (CSIRO).

UNEP. (2015). *Raising the bar: Advancing environmental disclosure in sustainability reporting.* UNEP.

United Nations, ESCAP. (2015). *Integrating the three dimensions of sustainable development: A framework and tools.* Greening of Economic Growth series. United Nations.

WBCSD. (n.d.). *Kering: Environmental profit and loss (EP&L) accounting.* Retrieved February 20, 2018, from www.wbcsd.org/Clusters/Natural-Capital-and-Ecosystems/Business-Examples/Kering-Environmental-Profit-and-Loss-EP-L-accounting.

WBCSD, CDSB, Ecodesk. (2018). *Corporate reporting in the United States and Canada.* WBCSD, CDSB, Ecodesk.

Willard, B. (2012). *The new sustainability advantage: Seven business case benefits of a triple bottom line.* Gabriola Island, BC, Canada: New Society Publishers.

Wirtenberg, J. (2014). *Building a culture for sustainability: People, planet & profits in a new green economy.* Santa Barbara, CA: Praeger.

World Commission on Environment and Development (WCED). (1987). *Our common future.* Oxford, UK: Oxford University Press.

World Economic Forum. (2018). *World Economic Forum 2018 global risks report.* Geneva: World Economic Forum.

Part IV

Connecting, integrating, and aligning toward the future

Sustainable globalization
The challenge and the opportunity

Linda M. Kelley, Victoria G. Axelrod, William G. Russell, and Jeana Wirtenberg

> The major challenge—and opportunity—of our time is to create a form of commerce that uplifts the entire human community of 6.5 billion[1] and does so in a way that respects both natural and cultural diversity. Indeed, that is the only realistic and viable pathway to a sustainable world. And business can—and must—lead the way.
>
> (Hart, 2007, p. 228)

Globalization in perspective

Technology has tied our world together more tightly than ever before in history. News cycles around the globe within minutes. Nonlocal entertainment, social movements, weather events appear on our screens, large and small. Apples grown in Washington State are enjoyed in Shanghai; strawberries from China (now the world's largest producer) are served for dessert in New York. Connect the OEMs for our cars, phones, appliances, medical equipment, and yes, buildings, and you'll have a network of lines that circle the globe. We truly are global through and through. Unless we make globalization sustainable at multiple levels, sustainability will elude us.

The good news is that we can employ many of the technologies that have accelerated this phase of globalization to spread sustainability as well. By taking a holistic perspective of the many challenges and opportunities of sustainable globalization, we can apply practical lenses and frames that help to reveal fertile interconnections where businesses and organizations can create increased economic value and societal wellbeing while benefiting the natural environment.

In this chapter we provide concepts, insights, and inspirational stories and examples, as well as activities, tools, and practices to help you and your organization find your own path toward greater sustainability. Humanity as a whole has realized enormous benefits from globalization: significantly improved health, accessible education, superior knowledge and technology, and advanced infrastructure among them. And this process continues. Not surprisingly, those gains have been accompanied by real costs—especially in the degradation of natural environments and upheavals in social realms. Moving forward, it is essential that we redress these very real problems, individually and cooperatively, with ingenuity, care, and respect across the globe. It's a tall order. We can do this. The driving question is, will we?

Globalization has had many stages spanning eons. Each of globalization's stages has had distinctive twists and turns. Each has environmental, economic, and social consequences. A pivotal thread underlying them all is the migration of perceived value and the quest for betterment that accompanies that, leaving the old behind to create and embrace the new. Over time the value we invest in ideas, technologies, political organization, culture, business practices, and mental models declines. When what we had prized becomes widely available, it's taken for granted and we perceive it to have less value. We seek out new objects of desire, engineered ones that we perceive to be of greater value. What often gets lost in this process is the inherent value of the services we get from water, air, food, and community support—services on which our lives depend. Without these services we do not survive, plain and simple. When we ignore, contaminate, and degrade the quality of any of these four essentials, we put ourselves at risk. This is not a new problem for humanity. Many before us have pointed to the folly of ignoring the basics. You need only to read the preface of Ben Franklin's *Poor Richard's Almanac*.

> All for the want of a nail
> A little neglect may breed mischief …
> for want of a nail, the shoe was lost;
> for want of a shoe the horse was lost;
> and for want of a horse the rider was lost.
>
> (Benjamin Franklin, *Poor Richard's Almanac*, preface, 1758)

Water, air, food, and community are more basic and essential than is a nail. It's not that we don't know this. But in our pursuit of betterment we have neglected to safeguard these irreplaceables. We've stopped perceiving the value of what is truly important.

Today's globalization stands in stark contrast to previous stages. This phase involves not only acquisition of resources and migrations of people, at all levels, but also privileges the flow of capital and technical know-how with unprecedented, accelerating speed. Too often the effect of this combination is to gin up facilities and communities then remove resources, from location after location, country after country, in pursuit of the next financial reward, more, better, faster, and leaving a wake of dashed expectations, shattered capacities, and depleted resources.

This form of globalization flurry has brought humanity to the cusp where sustainability teeters on a precipice. We, as residents of our various localities, citizens of the world, and leaders in business have a choice to make. Will we embrace principles of sustainability, and engage other people to generate a sustainable world with widespread prosperity? Or not?

Future sustainability demands that we alter some favored ways of making our way in the world. Reflecting on our past accomplishments, looking toward our hoped-for future, we ask again the question posed in 2007, by The Intergovernmental Panel on Climate Change (IPCC): What changes in lifestyles, behavior patterns, and management practices are needed, and by when? (Pachauri, 2007, slide 15).

Sustainable globalization, and the globalization of sustainability

Sustainable globalization presents at once the greatest challenge and the greatest opportunity of our lifetime. It's become clear that business models and practices that worked so well in the recent past are unsustainable financially, socially, and environmentally. Consumption as a way of life is hitting an overshoot wall. Overshoot is "the date when humanity's demand for ecological resources and services in a given year exceeds what Earth can regenerate in that year" (Earth Overshoot Day, n.d.). Currently, humanity uses a year's worth of nature's regenerative bounty well before the end of that year. In 2016, we consumed a whole year's stock before the middle of August; in 2017, we hit that consumption wall even earlier, on August 2. We're maintaining our consumption by devouring basic fecundity thereby reducing the level of ecosystem services regeneration. Living beyond our environmental means year after year is not sustainable by any measure.

Since business provides a large portion of the goods and services on which we depend, savvy business leaders will be at the forefront of making production globally sustainable. While visions that inspire may encircle the globe, each implementation takes form locally, in the here and now, person by person, business by business. If global is the field of dreams, local is home base.

Throughout this book, we attempt to address what will be required of us in order to be sustainable. We look from multiple perspectives. Each viewpoint provides vital considerations. Together they are intended to advance our readers' understanding and facilitate the creation of workable, practical solutions, using an overall lens we call *sustainable globalization*.

Because globalization has intertwined our functional economic systems everywhere, the effects of multi-directional flows of trade, investment, and capital (social, cultural, and technological) are felt worldwide. Events and disruptions that happen in one area of the world, for better or for worse, now hit us all. No longer are any regions being left out. World trade has been the engine of unprecedented economic growth during the last 60 years but its benefits are still unevenly distributed. That is changing swiftly as China, South Asia, East Africa, and West Africa blossom into technology-enabled, social, and business innovation and economic hubs.

Sustainable globalization is a fundamental transformation in how people approach doing business. It's a 21st-century shift from a zero-sum, win–lose approach to one that fully takes into account short- and long-term impacts of people's actions within Earth's ecosystems. Only by respecting the planetary boundaries is it possible to employ precious natural resources prudently and produce goods and services of real value. Sustainable production supports communities of people who are motivated to conserve, transform, and rejuvenate resources so that they build a good future for all. Sustainable globalization takes this community-minded purpose and translates it into principle-centered operations. An important touchstone for this is the 2030 Agenda for Sustainable Development: people, planet, prosperity, peace, partnership (Transforming our world, n.d.). This UN-produced document of principles lays out a global development founded in inclusion, responsibility, service, collaboration, and the triple-bottom-line integration of accountability for people, planet, and profit. The globalization of sustainability provides the impetus to create multi-layered real value that becomes the foundation of widespread prosperity.

Sustainability as a global organizing principle

Today the effects of globalization permeate the lives and work of people in all regions of the world. These effects do not spread evenly. Sometimes they roll through like a cue ball on a pool table, knocking out opponents and bystanders alike in the drive to capture rewards. Fortunes are made and lost. Boundaries renegotiated. Power reordered. The tide of globalization raises some boats more than others, and some boats not at all. Globalization is fraught with fits and starts, with expansion and contractions, and exuberance and anxiety. But onward it spreads. Wherever you live, no longer is it possible to retreat into an insulated cocoon. A decision not to participate is a decision to place the prospects of your future being sustainable in the hands of those who do choose to be active players.

The globalization of sustainability will happen. Whether intentional or not, it will come about through the collective reconfiguration of humanity's place in the world and of the real value of business. A question we all must answer is "How will we design and develop livelihoods so that economic prosperity is both widespread and decoupled from the consumption and waste of resources?"

Six lenses

To deepen our understanding and provide a strategic context by which to assess where we are and how we can best effect change, we introduce, and organize this chapter around, a "six lens" practical framework for thinking about sustainable globalization:

- economic/financial
- technology
- poverty and inequity
- limits to growth
- movement of talent
- geopolitical.

Using these six lenses, we take a systemic view of complex and interrelated issues and bring them together into an integrated whole. First, from a practical perspective, we look sequentially through each individual lens, highlighting contributions of each. Then we look at how they comprise a holistic presentation of sustainable globalization (see Figure 7.1). To do this we focus on articulating issues in combination with examples of how some trailblazing, globally diverse enterprises are addressing sustainability with their organizations.

As we have seen in other chapters, leaders, and managers in every function play key roles in shaping the sustainable future of their organizations and setting the conditions for success. How rapidly companies develop mental models, capabilities, strategic business innovations, with supporting management systems, organization structures, and processes that support sustainability depends on how effectively people champion necessary shifts. The ability to innovate and the skill of collaborating effectively are important; so are the resiliency to recover and the agility to adapt. How do you modernize the base of your business? How do you translate your assets?

We are heartened to see that a number of businesses are already beginning to address environmental issues in areas such as water pollution, renewable energy, and carbon emissions. Still, we have only scratched the surface. Clearly, much more remains to be done to contend with the immense challenges before us. Although reducing the effects of carbon emissions is urgent and critical, concerns for the availability of clean water isn't far behind on today's list of sustainability priorities. And water issues may turn out to be the most compelling driver for change.

An awakening to the degeneration of critical environmental conditions is pushing more and more businesses and industries to reevaluate their business models. Companies are exploring what they need to do to reconstitute themselves sustainably while creating real customer value in a complex, evolving global network of markets where they buy and sell.

Each of these six lenses gives us a useful perspective into the business opportunities of sustainable globalization. Front-runners and early adopters are already demonstrating what is possible. By the time you read this, the initiatives in some of these examples may have succeeded wildly while others may have slowed or ceased. No one has "nailed" sustainability yet but the businesses and organizations whose stories follow are out there on the line, working to make a difference every day. Be inspired. Join with them. Do better. Help them do better. It is your future. It is our future.

(1) Looking through the economic and financial lens

People believe environmental "bads" are the price we must pay for economic "goods." However, we cannot, and need not, continue to act as if this trade-off is inevitable.

(UN Under Secretary-General Achim Steiner,
UNEP's Executive Director, 2011)

Figure 7.1 Six lenses for sustainable globalization

Source: Copyright 2016, V. G. Axelrod, J. Harmon, L. M. Kelley, W. G. Russell, and J. Wirtenberg. Used with permission.

The UN Global Compact encourages businesses to take a comprehensive approach to instilling sustainability into their business. It lists five essential elements:

> (1) operate responsibly in alignment with universal principles and (2) take strategic actions that support the society around them. Then, to push sustainability deep into the corporate identity, companies must (3) commit at the highest level, (4) report annually on their efforts, and (5) engage locally where they have a presence.
>   The defining features of the Compact are: principle-based, public-private, multi-stakeholder, global-local, voluntary yet accountable.
>
> (United Nations Global Compact, n.d.)

Some of the world's leading enterprises have the economic power to exert enormous influence over their own sustainable future as well as that of others.

They have the power to convene NGOs (nongovernmental organizations), government leaders, policy think tanks, and professional and trade associations for collaboration to address global issues. Leveraging their influence, they have begun to make major strides in expanding participation in sustainability.

Two issues stand out against the background as we look at sustainable globalization through an economic and financial lens. First, we see the need to look at economies, and the companies and markets that comprise them, through an environmental, social, and governance (ESG) framework, and second, we see the need to fundamentally redefine how we measure business success.

Environmental, social, and governance (ESG) framework

The ESG framework lays out three areas for measurement and accounting: environmental concerns, social concerns, and corporate governance concerns. With increased focus on long-term value creation, ESG is rapidly becoming a new reference point for financial analysis and decision-making.

Many companies now produce Corporate Sustainability Reports that comply with the Principles for Responsible Investment (n.d.) to tell the world of their progress in addressing ESG concerns. In terms of sustainable globalization, governance must encompass more than just the internal corporate concerns. This chapter section is being written on the heels of Britain's vote to exit the European Union. Within hours of that vote tally, a huge cloud of uncertainty and instability rumbled through global financial markets. How this directive will ultimately affect investments, trade and tariffs, labor force, and movement of people, no one knows. Whatever the future outcome, it is a pointed reminder that enterprise sustainability requires us to weigh and question the foundational assumptions that enable our businesses to operate. It has become clear that business as usual is anything but. Global companies and markets are more tightly coupled than ever before. Debt burdens are intertwined. Sustainability of companies and even their industries requires that business strategies take into consideration the possibilities and consequences of substantial upheavals in social and environmental arenas. Vigorous sustainability requires a business to align with a purpose greater than profit alone, and that company governance lead the way.

Rethinking the fundamental model of business: placing sustainability at the core

The three following companies, DSM, Interface, and Eileen Fisher, have each rethought fundamentals of their business to include principles of sustainability. Because of this commitment, each has developed important new business initiatives.

CASE I. DSM: BRIGHT SCIENCE. BRIGHTER LIVING

Linda M. Kelley

Health • Nutrition • Materials   Why would a company choose to put sustainability at the heart of its business? If the company is purpose-driven to create better lives for people, embracing sustainability makes good business sense. Placing sustainability as a core value of the company positions Royal DSM to take the long view where governance is proactive and drives the innovation that will realize DSM's purpose. It also raises the question, what is to be sustained? And from what is to be sustained, what can be developed? For DSM what can and should be developed is science-based, scalable solutions in health, nutrition, and materials.

Feike Sijbesma, CEO since 2007, believes sustainability is a business imperative that allows DSM to position itself at the forefront of megatrends where the greatest business opportunities will be found. Sustainability is not only the right move for a company, it's also a smart business move. Businesses that wait around for government to develop regulations will forgo significant competitive advantages.

> Sustainability is not only about compliance or corporate social responsibility. It has become a business driver based on our core values. Throughout DSM, sustainability is integrated in how we do business. Our products and solutions positively contribute to the world's current and future challenges. "Nobody can be successful—or even dare to call themselves successful—in a world that fails," says Sijbesma.[2]

No stranger to change, the company began life in 1902, as the Dutch State Mines. Over the years the company diversified, privatized, then transformed itself into the forward-thinking company it is today. Restructured to be a fully integrated company, DSM sees very good growth, margins, and returns from its purpose and strategy. The company sees three platforms for sustainable growth: nutrition, climate change, and the circular economy.

One of the DSM's innovative materials products is EcoPaXX®, a high-performance, bio-based plastic made primarily from tropical castor beans. Versatile and carbon-neutral certified, EcoPaXX can be used for many products such as packaging, fuel vapor separators for cars, low-voltage power distribution connectors, and water faucet valves. With its flame retardant, chemical resistant, and lightweight, innovative plastics, DSM Engineering Plastics won the award for Best Plastics Design at PlasticsEurope in 2016.

On another front, as one of the largest producers of micronutrients, DSM has set issues of malnutrition as a priority to address. Partnering with the World Food Programme, UNICEF, and World Vision, and with Scaling Up

Nutrition Business Network, DSM works to provide nutritious, sustainable food to the hungry poor, particularly young children and pregnant and nursing women. Micronutrients are important, but so is sustainable protein. DSM innovation has developed Clean Cow feed additive that aims to reduce the amount of methane emitted in vivo by 30% (Ramsey, 2015). Again, from CEO Feike Sijbesma, "achieving good quality nutrition for the world is everybody's business" (SUN Business Network, n.d.).

DSM takes its global responsibilities seriously. The company is committed to making a lasting, positive difference socially and environmentally—throughout their own operations, and in their work with their suppliers, customers, and end-users. For DSM, bright science, brighter living means sustainable business that supports a compelling purpose.

CASE 2. INTERFACE, A PIONEER AND STALWART OF SUSTAINABLE BUSINESS

Linda M. Kelley

Twenty years into the sustainability journey, award-winning Interface Europe has achieved major milestones: 90% reduction in carbon, 100% renewable energy for operating their European plant, zero landfill waste, and almost no water in the manufacturing process. Well known for bold innovations and superior design in carpeting, with Net-Works™, Interface is applying its know-how to cleaning up the oceans by recycling discarded fishing net into carpet fiber. So far, it has collected 100 tons of net and in the process provided more secure financial opportunities to hundreds of families. Net-Works is business and community conserving and innovating together. "This is just the beginning. By 2020 we aim to improve the lives of *1 million people* and better protect *1 billion square meters of the ocean*."[3]

Interface is actively looking for opportunities to replace its product raw materials with retrieved, reprocessed materials. Looking at your company's business, where might it replace virgin resources with reclaimed, reprocessed materials? Make a list of possible areas. Talk with colleagues. Do some brainstorming. Do some research. What opportunities do you see? What challenges and barriers do you find? Thinking outside the box, what might you be able to do?

CASE 3. EILEEN FISHER ON EMBODIED PURPOSE[4]

Linda M. Kelley

> We don't want sustainability to be our edge, we want it to be universal.
>
> (Eileen Fisher)

Eileen Fisher is both a visionary leader, and a purpose-driven brand. Listening to her, it's clear she loves what she does—the clothes, the fabrics, the timeless fashion, and most of all the people. Not only has the company organization always relied on teams of people, in 2005 Fisher decided that the future of the company did not lie in going public, but in becoming employee owned. She sold one-third of the then $300,000,000 company to her 875 employees through an employee stock ownership plan.[5]

Inspired by a trip she took to Bhutan, Fisher and the company began doing some personal transformation work. She learned that to fully embody purpose, she had to fully "show up." As founder, president, and chief creative officer of a company with strongly held values about the responsibilities that businesses have for the condition of the environment and people, Fisher knew she had to do better. At the beginning of 2016, EILEEN FISHER became certified as a B Corporation, aligned with the company's triple-bottom-line approach to business success and embodied values.[6] The B Corp Declaration includes "envisioning an economy that uses business as a force for good." Fisher says, "A business can be a movement that can change the world." Although the company has been practicing sustainability for a long time, the fashion industry as a whole is one of the most polluting in the world. About one in eight people work in the fashion industry. We have to change it. (The global apparel is more than a $3 trillion market and accounts for 2% of the world's GDP.)

As Fisher says, for the most part CEOs don't want to be interviewed about sustainability because it's scary that what we're doing isn't good enough. She started asking herself every morning, what matters to me today? What will I do with this day? Our voices matter. Now Eileen Fisher, the person, is showing up and speaking out. EILEEN FISHER, the company, is continually reevaluating its overall operations through a sustainability lens. The technology is out there. So is its vision: Vision 2020.[7]

> Our vision is for an industry where human rights and sustainability are not the effect of a particular initiative but the cause of a business well run. Where social and environmental injustices are not unfortunate outcomes but reasons to do things differently.
>
> (Vision 2020, n.d.)

When we meet our company goals, and we will, it still won't be enough, Fisher says. We need to inspire and engage the rest of the industry to come with us. So, we are becoming sustainability ambassadors, speaking out, knowing that our voices matter. We're sharing what we know and learning from people we meet. It's about showing up, doing the best you can every day. Along with Eileen Fisher, we ask how can each of us, how can we all use our work, our business, our voices to make the world a better place?

(2) Looking through the technology lens

Technology as a driving force for global growth and democratization

CASE 4. WATSON GOES TO WORK

Linda M. Kelley

Watson was introduced to the wider world as a game contestant on *Jeopardy* in 2011. That was fun but IBM's Watson was destined for greater things. Fast forward to 2016 and Watson is hard at work. Rather than competing, Watson with cognitive computing and its Internet of Things (IoT) technology is partnering with physicians at the Cleveland Clinic to deliver faster diagnoses and improved healthcare. Watson is also working with Beijing Environmental Protection Bureau to cut smog pollution in that city. Focused on air quality and renewable energy, the Green Horizons program combines the Internet of Things with Big Data and Cognitive Computing to collect and analyze enormous amounts of environmental data. Understanding the impacts enables officials to make better decisions to manage courses of actions over the following 7–10 days. Warning people of air quality, reducing traffic, and restricting industrial pollution output are a few ways officials are using this information.

Speaking of traffic, there's more. Driverless cars have made the headlines, but look behind that to the real power of the technology to drastically improve traffic flow and reduce pollution regardless of whether the vehicle is driven by a person or computer. Powered by Watson, meet Olli, a sleek, 3D printed, electric minivan that holds up to 12 passengers. Schedule your pick-up with your smart phone app. The system uses lidar, camera, and GPS to navigate along a pre-set route (Counts, 2016). Watson Olli will remind you to bring your umbrella if rain is in the forecast, pick up your colleagues with whom you're meeting, and even drive away so you can hold your meeting right in this large-windowed minivan. Meeting complete? Ask Olli for recommendations for nearby restaurants. The van will drop you off and be there when you're finished your meal. Local Motors street tested 30 vehicles in Maryland with National Harbor Transportation during the summer of 2016. With summer tests successfully completed, Olli, now prepared to run in normal urban traffic, has expanded to Miami, FL, Las Vegas, NV, with plans for Buffalo, NY. In addition, Olli's artificial intelligence has been upgraded for increased accessibility, including a ramp for wheelchairs, the capability to read braille and give audio cues for visually impaired, text messages for hearing impaired, and verbal guidance for people with dementia. Regular production starts in 2018 (Harris, 2018).

From Olli's design through manufacture to first 10 sold and running = just 3 months. This first version of Olli is perfect for terminal to terminal shuttles at airports, or large university or corporate campuses. But think ahead. Imagine what could be. Local Motors Strati Roadster is 75% 3D printed on huge machines with ABS plastic and carbon fiber. It's road-ready and for sale to beta testers. LM is experimenting with new, lighter weight materials. Nine other companies have 3D printed cars in the prototyping state (Mensley, 2017). Some are crowdsourcing designs and funding. Interior comfort, mobility, functionality, and style are all on the design table given the capabilities of computer design.

Now for fun let's imagine the car skin embedded with solar cells that are thin enough to sit on a bubble, and drive along a solar powered road. A small section of the famed Route 66 in Missouri is taking up the asphalt to test a glass road. No ordinary glass, this tempered, rough-textured version is embedded with solar collectors and computer chips. So the road not only processes information but also powers itself. And no more worries about snowy, icy roads because the surface clears itself. Here you have the possibility of car or truck and road working together, transferring data between them and to big data collectors and processors such as Watson. These technologies are already in the testing stage. Big change is in the works.

Looking to the natural world provides some insights to truly effective management of traffic. Leafcutter ants are masters. With colonies of up to 100,000, they manage daily highway traffic of tens of thousands of individuals bringing resources in and removing waste. Transportation and traffic issues are one of the many areas where nature provides us with excellent examples of effective, efficient management practices. For instance, "rather than slowing down, ants speed up in response to a higher density of traffic on their trails, according to new research published in Springer's journal *The Science of Nature—Naturwissenschaften*. When the researchers increased the supply of food by leaving food next to the trail, ants accelerated their speed by 50 percent. This was despite more than double the density of traffic."[8] Managing human traffic with comparable adjustments and density of vehicles takes more dedicated, concentrated attention than most drivers pay, but perfect for big data processing.

Technology + design thinking

IBM isn't the only familiar office name working on traffic issues. When you hear the name Xerox, what do you think? Copiers? Document management? How about traffic systems? From electronic toll collection to intelligent transit and fleet management, Xerox is helping cities rethink the end-to-end, multi-modal customer transportation system.

What could carry 1,400 passengers, run on electricity above city streets—so cars can pass underneath, and cost much less than a subway? A straddling bus of course! Even the idea sounds fantastical, but the Chinese are building a scale model. This concept was first proposed by American architects Craig Hodgetts and Lester Walker in 1969, but wasn't developed. Now, it's being fast-tracked. Introduced as a computer simulation at a tech show in May,

2016, a working prototype went live on August 1, in the Beidaihe District of Qinhuangdao Hebei Provence, China.[9] Will some version ever actually be built? If this technology could live up to its promise, would straddling buses be a way to significantly reduce both fuel consumption and urban air pollution while also reducing traffic congestion in major cities? Gridlock of enormous numbers of transport vehicles is a huge and growing problem in the world's largest cities. Increased urbanization and aging inner-city transportation infrastructures make moving people and goods efficiently, without polluting, one of today's urgent challenges.

Technology will not resolve all the issues surrounding sustainability, but it can make an important contribution. These examples of how people are rethinking, redesigning, and right-sizing transportation are already under way. It will include implementation of smart, multi-modal transportation: motorcycles, performance and commuting bicycles, buses, and planes. Airbus is another company that sees its future in 3D printing of vehicles. The company introduced its first printed aircraft, THOR, at the International Aerospace Exhibition in Schoenefeld, Germany on June 1, 2016. This drone mini-plane is the beginning of an aircraft future where planes are faster and less expensive to produce as well as more efficient to operate. Airbus is taking to the ground with its design capability too. The company is now designing and 3D printing lightweight, performance motorcycles. You don't need the motor? Montague Bikes makes 3D printed performance bikes that fold so you can ride from home to public transportation, carry on and off, then ride to your destination and fold it away until you're ready to leave.

As the songwriter-philosopher, Bob Dylan, says, "The times they are a changin'" (released 1964).

You may be wondering what these initiatives have to do with sustainable globalization. There are some enormous problem areas where these initiatives can make a beneficial difference. In the US alone 26% of the greenhouse gases emitted come from the transportation sector. At the beginning of this section, we spoke about traffic management in Beijing. This is not a trivial matter. In summer of 2013, Beijing suffered a traffic jam that extended over 100 km and lasted more than nine days![10] People stuck in automobiles, goods stuck in transport trucks, and the pollution from idling engines added to Beijing's already high level of almost daily smog impacted the health of millions of people. Though air pollution in Beijing regularly makes the news, it is not the only densely populated urban area with severe air quality challenges or even the worst offender. On the World Economic Forum's 2016 list of the most polluted megacities, Beijing comes in at #5. Delhi and Cairo have the highest levels of air pollution (Shirley, 2016). There is ample opportunity for technological innovation and a ready global market. Looking for new ideas, innovations, and inspirations? Look for the intersections of art, craft, and technology. Keep an eye on hackathons, mashups, and crowdsourcings from around the world.

Inquiry is one good way to raise awareness. A question to ask yourself is what contributions do my business and lifestyle make to exacerbating and/ or resolving transportation and traffic issues? Seriously, what is the actual transportation impact—beneficial and detrimental, and especially in environmental and social terms, of the supplies and tools you use? Of the products you make and services you provide? Do you know? What might you do differently to have less negative impact or more positive impact? To apply your capabilities to helping other businesses and municipalities lessen their impact? Have you factored any of this in to your own sustainability?

Technologies applied to address basic needs

While transportation and traffic are an emerging global crisis, lack of access to clean water is already a crisis. Right now, one in ten people do not have access to safe drinking water (Water Cooperation 2013, n.d.). It's easy for those of us who live in Europe or North America to take access to clean water for granted. You're thirsty? You turn on the tap and fill your glass, or if you're on the run, grab a bottle of water and go. Want a shower? No problem. Wash your clothes, wash your car, water your yard, no problem. Well, it's no problem until "suddenly" it is and your access to water is cut. In reality, even regions that typically have adequate water supplies suffer floods, droughts, and contamination that turn safe water supplies unusable.

As important as leading-edge high-tech, complex innovations are to resolving many critical global problems, some can be addressed well by using tightly targeted technologies that can be implemented and maintained by communities to ensure access to essential services like local water for drinking and sanitation. One in ten people globally do not have access to safe water. Water-related diseases kill; a child succumbs to a water-related disease every 90 seconds (Water Cooperation 2013, n.d.).

CASE 5. CHARITY:WATER

Linda M. Kelley

> Our mission is to bring clean, safe drinking water to every person in the world.

What does it take to make this bold statement a reality? In 2004, Scott Harrison, founder, had a crisis of conscience and rediscovered faith. He gave up being a professional party boy and nightclub promoter to become a volunteer photographer on Mercy Ships. After two years in West Africa witnessing extreme poverty and disease, Harrison's life-changing perspective brought with it a new commitment. Over half of the diseases found in less developed countries are due to drinking unclean water. "No one needs to drink dirty water.

There's no cure we're waiting for to arrive from a lab. There's no mystery. We know how to provide this," says Harrison (Timalsina, 2016). He founded charity:water in 2006, committed to build wells in Uganda, and raised $15,000 from old nightclub friends to get started. Today, charity:water boasts 20,062 water projects funded, partnering with 25 organizations in 24 countries. These projects have reached 6,300,000 people around the globe: Africa, Central and South America, and Asia. At charity:water "we invest the money we raise into organizations with years of experience to build sustainable, community-owned water projects around the world."[11]

charity:water has partners who are involved on various levels: brand partners such as Google, Caterpillar, and Keurig Green Mountain, and corporate sponsors like Authentic Jobs and Do Amore. And then there are partners who actually work in the selected communities, such as Action Hunger, Clear Cambodia, Splash, and Water for People to name a few.

But the heart of this story isn't about Scott Harrison. It's about Tencia Desmata of Mozambique, single mother and bread entrepreneur, and all the people like Tencia who have a renewed lease on life because they now have access to clean water.

When Tencia's husband took ill and died, she became the sole provider for her three young sons. They got by, though barely, on the few crops she raised plus baking a little bread to sell near her sons' school. But much of her day was consumed fetching barely potable water from the river in a Jerry Can. Until 2010, that is. That year the village had a well drilled. Now clean water is available to all. As a consequence, the village children are healthier, and so are their parents. Girls can go to school full time instead of trying to fit schooling in between fetching water. And Tencia has plenty of clean water for making her delicious banana maize bread from a recipe handed down to her by her grandmother. This bread is so delicious that at the local market she sells out all she can make every day. Her bread is so in demand that Tencia is planning to expand her maize field and hire an employee to help her bake and sell. And all because she has available clean water.[12]

Tencia's story is one of collaboration on a global scale among people who have never met face to face. Each of these partners—the fundraisers, the technology providers, the NGOs, the local community—brings something essential, without which Tencia wouldn't be able to entrepreneurially lift herself and soon some neighbors out from under the weight of coping day to day with the scarcity of safe water.

(3) Looking through the lens of poverty and inequity

> More than eight million people around the world die each year because they are too poor to stay alive. Our generation can choose to end that extreme poverty by the year 2025.
>
> (Sachs, 2005, p. 1)

Today we face extreme contrasts between extraordinary levels of material wealth for a small minority on the one hand, and extreme poverty for hundreds of millions of people on the other. We believe that this condition inhibits global sustainability. At the turn of the 21st century, the wealthiest top percentile owned 48.9% of global household wealth. After a dip during the world financial crisis, those wealthy have regained what they lost and more. In 2015, those in the wealthiest percentile own 50% of all household wealth.[13] It is estimated that the top decile controls 87.7%. Proportionally, the poor spend more of their income on the basics of food and housing. They put more of their money back into the economy than do the wealthy.

> Income distribution itself matters for growth as well. Specifically, if the income share of the top 20 percent (the rich) increases, then GDP growth actually declines over the medium term, suggesting that the benefits do not trickle down. In contrast, an increase in the income share of the bottom 20 percent (the poor) is associated with higher GDP growth.
>
> (Dabla-Norris et al., 2015)

Fortune at the bottom of the pyramid

In their seminal article "The Fortune at the Bottom of the Pyramid," C. K. Prahalad and Stuart L. Hart (2002) made a strong case for the enormous opportunities to bring prosperity to the poorest people of the world—that demographic sector they refer to as "the bottom of the pyramid." The fortune opportunity is to be found by multinational corporations changing their view and seeing through a new, more inclusive lens:

> Low-income markets present a prodigious opportunity for the world's wealthiest companies—to seek their fortunes and bring prosperity to the aspiring poor. This is a time for multinational corporations (MNCs) to look at globalization strategies through a new lens of inclusive capitalism. For companies with the resources and persistence to compete at the bottom of the world economic pyramid, the prospective rewards include growth, profits, and incalculable contributions to humankind.
>
> (Prahalad & Hart, 2002, p. 1)

Furthermore, they describe the opportunities and the business case that lie ahead for companies that are willing to grapple with the enormity of the challenge and put their toes in the water:

> Collectively, we have only begun to scratch the surface of what is the biggest potential market opportunity in the history of commerce. Those in the private sector who commit their companies to a more inclusive capitalism have the opportunity to prosper and share their prosperity

with those who are less fortunate. In a very real sense, the fortune at the bottom of the pyramid represents the loftiest of our global goals.

(Prahalad & Hart, 2002, p. 15)

Looking back from a vantage point of 16 years after Prahalad and Hart wrote "The Fortune at the Bottom of the Pyramid," we see a picture that is more complex even in its incompleteness. Yes, businesses reaching out from a well-established foundation to serve those who don't have access to needed resources is important but it is only one aspect of the business of sustainable globalization. This chapter highlights some examples of innovation and entrepreneurship on the part of those who, though they are under-resourced from a Western perspective, demonstrate that "wastes" are not refuse but important resources. If we can all learn this lesson, we have a good chance of co-creating a sustainable future and constructing an inclusive foundation of global prosperity. Only if the developed and the currently less developed sectors can work together to bring the true sustainable development that Stuart Hart envisions can we make a "Green Leap." For this to come about, both multinational and local businesses must recognize that their financial success is inherently intertwined with social equity and the responsible use of the natural environment, globally locale by locale by locale.

Market creation at the base of the pyramid

As a preface to this section, we refer back to discussions about the leader's mindset in Karen Davis's essay in Chapter 1, and the application of a local business SWOT analysis in Chapter 3 (see Table 3.1).

INDIGENOUS BUSINESS DEVELOPMENT, SCALING SOCIAL INNOVATION: "SPECIALIZING IN HOME-GROWN SOCIO-ECONOMIC INNOVATION"

According to Dorette Steenkamp, executive director, Uthango Social Investments, South Africa,

> Sustainable development and related enterprise growth in communities will only be possible if we prioritize true engagement of communities. Listening in an active, responsive way to community members requires putting aside one's own agendas and often asks for organizational courage to innovate existing processes. The fears and aspirations of communities have a direct influence on the sustainable practices embedded in their enterprises and actions—especially at a micro-enterprise and local economic level. Globalization is not the greatest threat at grassroots, but lack of engagement on authentic indigenous solutions disrespects community building principles and perpetuates non-sustainable development

practices. Endorsement of any form of development starts with listening and engaging communities through appropriate technology and relationship economics.[14]

Alvarez and Barney (2006) distinguish two dimensions of business development in the new global sustainable paradigm: discovery-based versus creation-based. In the discovery-based paradigm, businesses "target" the unmet needs in the BoP, estimate the size of the market, "deploy" new technologies, extend their current business model via structural innovation, and then "scale up." In contrast, in creation-based business development, the process begins with humility and an open mind. Competitive imagination is sparked, and something new is co-developed. A new business model is built based on trust and social capital. Rather than "scaling up" it is "scaled out."

CASE 6. MARKET DEVELOPMENT FROM THE BOTTOM UP: THE ZABALEEN

Linda M. Kelley

Cairo generates over 15,000 tons of waste every day. With 18,000,000 people, that makes Cairo one of the dirtiest major cities in the world. The Zabaleen, the garbage people, make a living out of trash. Starting their day at 4 am, the men run two shifts of garbage collection, bringing the materials back to home base, mostly to the Moqqatam district, where the women sort it for reuse. Organic waste is separated out and used to feed livestock. Almost all the rest is turned into other useful products.[15]

> The output is eventually turned into quilts, rugs, pots, paper, livestock food, compost, recycled plastic products such as clothes hangers, and much more. Reusing and recycling about 85% of all waste that they collect, the Zabaleen have far surpassed the efficiencies of the best Western recycling schemes, which have so far only been able to reuse 70% of all material.
>
> (Kadduri, 2015)

How did this happen? The Zabaleen are a Coptic Christian community who live in the Moqqatam district of Cairo. Drought in southern Egypt during the mid-1940s forced some pig farmers to move north to the outskirts of Cairo. They began collecting garbage in order to get organic waste to feed their pigs. The drought continued and more of the pig farmers migrated north. For generations this community has made their meager living by picking garbage and recycling what they could. Working with garbage is a dangerous job. They became garbage experts who provided pickup service right at the customer's door. They had to. The income of the whole community comes from recycling trash. Cairo had no contracted solid waste removal services. In 2003, Egypt's former leader, Hosni Mubarak, contracted with three multinational waste management companies with the intent of modernizing the collection. Those contracts required only 20% of the garbage be recycled and the rest would be landfilled or dumped without treatment into local waterways (Aguirre, 2015). The Zabaleen had no contracts. Though they worked diligently, it was at best an informal arrangement. A stipulation in the contracts with the waste management companies stated that those companies owned the garbage, shutting out the Zabaleen.

Was there despair in the community? Of course. But the Zabaleen are a tight-knit community that has cultivated a sense of mutual responsibility so they decided to fight back. They dreamed of reclaiming their trade. For that fight, they didn't gather weapons but instead collected money, whatever people could give, and with the help of an NGO sent a few of the community's young men to Wales to learn modern methods of waste collection and recycling.

Determination and hard work paid off. Using what those men learned, the community started a Recycling School to teach and integrate modern techniques with their own practices further improving their trade. They learned that doing the work and planning for sustainability are not separate. They are nested within systems, in this case their community, within the city of Cairo, and now in the waste management and recycling larger industry.

The way forward for the Zabaleen is not without its difficulties and setbacks. In 2009, and despite the World Health Organization saying those pigs had no bearing on the epidemic, the Egyptian government, worried about a possible swine flu epidemic, killed 300,000 pigs and gave the Zabaleen no compensation. Was this necessary to prevent swine flu? Or possibly driven by the cultural differences where the Muslim majority hold the Coptic Christian minority as unseemly, as second class? Both of these motivations have been cited.

On the positive side, the Cairo residents preferred the convenience and efficiency provided by the Zabaleen over the large waste management companies. The Egyptian government has registered 44 Zabaleen collection companies and awarded them work to take over garbage collection in the south of Cairo as part of a pilot project to improve conditions. It's a story still unfolding. "We have always been treated as a backward people incapable of managing the refuse of such a large town. And yet we are the ones who invented an eco-city model," says Ezzat Naem. He has always worked in collecting trash. He and his community have been through bad times and they're still worried but also hopeful (Guenard, 2013).

This vignette raises some of the real tensions and thorny issues of globalization. What are ones that occur to you? Environmental? Economic? Social? Make a list. Discuss them with your colleagues. Are you as a leader considering these kinds of issues and consequences in the operation of your enterprises? What opportunities and risks are you not considering? How might you do better? What difference would that make?

Exit north-south divide, enter connectivity

Categorizing countries or peoples by coupling their economic status with their geographic location has become less and less relevant. Given today's technology that enables people everywhere to not only connect with one another but also do business together, looking at connectivity is a much more important window into global business developments. Whether it is electronics or food production, clothing or cars, we are all inextricably intertwined.

Electronic technology is pervasive. We have become interdependent in ways that would not have been imagined a mere 20 years ago. It's more than importing products from other countries or exporting them. There are many benefits in terms of employment and knowledge transfer. There are also some dirty secrets that need to be brought out into the light of day, because we can and must do better.

DISPLACED COSTS OF PROGRESS: RARE EARTH METALS MINING IN MONGOLIA

How many times a day do you use your mobile phone? For many people that phone is more than a convenience, it is their lifeline. There are 7.5 billion people on Earth and as of 2017 there were almost 5 billion mobile phone users. Of course not everyone has a mobile phone yet, but service spans the globe. Even in the less developed areas there are almost 90 phones per 100 people. People use mobile phones to keep in touch with family, and as a primary tool for conducting business. Phones are manufactured in over 30 countries. There's competition in design to make phones more and more capable, to make them "smarter." Rapid obsolescence. But, and here's the big but … the smart parts of mobile phones depend on rare earth metals (Rohrig, 2015). Color, florescence, display switching, smash resistance, and more, require one or more rare earth minerals. "Rare" is a bit of a misnomer. It's not that there is precious little of most of these metals, but that they are rarely found if at all in most areas of the world. These metals are considered rare because they are concentrated in only a few locations on Earth. Western U.S, South Africa, Brazil, India, Japan, Tanzania, Australia, and Greenland all have some rare earth metal deposits. But a large portion, and the major production, is found in Inner Mongolia, China. What is it like there?

Tim Maughan at the BBC describes it first-hand:

> From where I'm standing, the city-sized Baogang Steel and Rare Earth complex dominates the horizon, its endless cooling towers and chimneys

reaching up into grey, washed-out sky. Between it and me, stretching into the distance, lies an artificial lake filled with a black, barely-liquid, toxic sludge. Dozens of pipes line the shore, churning out a torrent of thick, black, chemical waste from the refineries that surround the lake. The smell of sulphur and the roar of the pipes invades my senses. It feels like hell on Earth.

(Payne, 2015)

Previously farmland, this tailings lake is a hell hole of enormous proportions. The environmental destruction makes the devastated tar sands of Alberta, Canada look tame by comparison. This dreadful site is one example of many ugly sides of our critical smart technologies (Dickerson, 2015). Clearly unsustainable, we can't keep this up. We need smart technology to green our cities and communities but the current process of manufacturing is anything but green!

If this isn't enough, let's take a brief look at the end-of-life of a cell phone. In particular, what happens to the rare earth metals locked inside? People throw away an enormous 40 million tons of e-waste a year, part of which are mobile devices. This comprises 70% of the total toxic waste in landfills. Less than 15% of e-waste is even designated for recycling. The vast majority are trashed, shipped to waste sites in developing countries. One of those sites is on the outskirts of Accra, Ghana. In this vast scrapyard the e-waste is set on fire so that adults and children both can pick through the smoldering debris to try to recover rare earth metals from scorched ground while breathing the poisoned air.[16] These metals are mined in large quantities in Mongolia, recovered in minuscule amounts in Ghana with huge amounts of toxic waste generated on both ends. It doesn't take complex thinking to grasp that there's something horribly wrong with this picture!

This is one of the ominous problems that will continue to eat into sustainability initiatives globally as we increase our production of and dependence on smart technology. It is solvable. It starts with reconceptualizing. You can help. Ask yourself, your colleagues, your friends, your competitors, how do we conceive and design products respectfully of the state of Earth's resources: bioresources that regenerate, and mineral resources that occur only in fixed amounts? How do we extract needed materials then manufacture high tech products without destroying our environment?

Corporate social responsibility (CSR), doing well by doing good

Business must be run at a profit, or else it will die. But when anyone tries to run a business solely for profit … then also the business must die, for it no longer has a reason for existence.

(Henry Ford)

At the beginning of the 21st century, many companies are concerned about being good corporate citizens. One way they address this is through corporate social responsibility initiatives. Usually these involve some aspect of triple-bottom-line sustainability such as improving the local environment, engaging with social services agencies, or teaching business-related skills to under-resourced populations, often partnering with NGOs.

Along with CSR, a number of companies are setting up Sustainability Advisory Councils (SAC) and encouraging employees to form Employee Resource Groups (ERGs). The more entry points, the more people working on specific issues, the more progress on sustainability, and the more insights about fruitful next steps—especially if they share information widely.

Yes, each of these kinds of initiatives helps to resolve important problems. But how the programs are orchestrated is almost as important as the project itself. Holistically conceived projects can spread their effects well beyond the specific issues addressed. The long-term, broad-reaching outcome is that people get to apply their values as well as their skills to do things that are really meaningful to them. It's not only that they gain satisfaction at having made a positive difference, but also the enthusiasm and insights from working outside the normal channels gets people in touch with what really matters.

(4) Looking through the lens of limits to growth

> Every natural system in the world today is in decline … We are drawing down resources that took millions of years to create in order to supplement current consumption … As a consequence, habitats are destroyed, species become extinct, and in the process, the productive health of the environment is compromised and decreased.
>
> (Hawken, 2005, p. 23)

This book focuses on sustainability for businesses and their leaders. We have rooted it in the recognition that businesses are conceived and managed by people within complex, dynamic contexts where differing perspectives and diverse cultures operate simultaneously on multiple levels. This is the reality where we all make our living. The challenge we face is to use the bounty of Earth within the constraints of renewability. People make decisions. Decisions involve actions. Actions have consequences. To achieve sustainable globalization in the 21st century, we the people must make our livings within the limits of boundaries of the planet on which we live. These constrain how, where, and when we can use available natural resources while we develop broad-based prosperous enterprise. Our current methods of doing business not only produce enormous waste but also throw many ecosystems into such stressed conditions that they are unable to recover or regenerate resources we've extracted up to levels that replace what we've taken. Nature will set "limits to growth" that caps our consumption of resources (Meadows,

Meadows, & Randers, 2004). In whatever endeavor we pursue, nature has the last say.

Ecosystems under stress

As Paul Hawken describes in his chapter "The Death of Birth" in *The Ecology of Commerce* (2005, pp. 19–36), every single ecosystem of our planet is under profound stress. Since Hawken wrote that book, we have not decreased but increased stresses on Earth's natural resources. Some critical areas about which we should be concerned:

- Numerous fish species are facing collapse. Among the causes are overfishing, eutrophication due to fertilizer and waste runoff, and higher water temperatures.
- Productive land for raising food is decreasing. Among the causes are soil depletion, water aquifer drawdown, urbanization, and prolonged armed conflict.
- Forest ecosystems worldwide are under attack. The effects of climate change are all too evident: drought, mega-storms, infestations of pests. But that's not all. Every year swaths of forests are clear cut for both mining and industrial monoculture crops. Rainforests—tropical and temperate— provide ecoservices of carbon storing and air filtering, thereby providing critical global ecosystem services beyond their harvesting value.

What makes these and other emerging crises intractable is that they are approached as being independent of one another, and they are not. Looking from a systems perspective, some of the interconnections are obvious while others take some parsing out. As an example, let's take a closer look at fisheries.

According to the World Wide Fund for Nature (WWF), the world's oceans are massively overfished. "53% of the world's fisheries are fully exploited, and 32% are overexploited, depleted, or recovering from depletion."[17] There have been fisheries collapses in the past. John Steinbeck's *Cannery Row* (1945) revolves around the collapse of the sardine fishery in Monterey, California. World War I drove a huge increase in demand for canned sardines to feed servicemen. Though there was a lull during the Great Depression, this fishery boomed again during World War II. Because of the favorable conditions of Monterey Canyon, this is one of the most productive forage fish (includes sardines, anchovies, herring) areas of the world. Brought on by a combination of overfishing and cyclical changes in the ocean, this profitable sardine fishery collapsed in the mid-1940s. Recovery took almost 40 years. But recovery was relatively short lived. Peaking in 1999, between 2007 and 2016, this sardine fishery stock plummeted, losing almost 90% of its population (Hill, Crone, Corval, & Macewicz, 2016). In the spring of 2015, the Federal government shut down the commercial sardine harvest; that ban was renewed in 2016; at this writing, there appears to be a slight uptick in that fishery population. This time the collapse deserves a closer and more comprehensive look though. Is it a localized event as it has been in the past? Or this time is the sardine collapse part of a larger picture of global overfishing and changes related to global warming? If so, a local ban may not produce long-term recovery.

One-third of the global fish harvest is forage fish. Some are eaten directly, many are processed into fertilizer and pet food. We aren't the only ones who depend on sardines and other forage fish. These are primary food sources for whales and dolphins, seals and sea lions, brown pelicans, and a host of other species. Continued growth in human population has increased fishing—from increasing the number of fishing families to increasing the number of factory fishing ships deployed—all of which leads to rampant overfishing. Changes in ocean conditions, particularly increased temperatures and coastal pollution, plus inadequate global fisheries management policies and policing have put many fisheries at great risk. As with many other environmental ecosystems, the comprehensive study of global fisheries and the impact of species loss is in early stages. Forage fish are showing to be ecosystem keystone species. Loss of any of these smaller species will have effects that ripple up and down the whole of the marine ecosystem food web, and negatively impact human food production as well.

There are many interacting dynamics of this marine ecosystem of which sardines are a part. And there are also influences that affect the coastal forage fish ecosystem but are not integral to it: overfishing by humans, influx of nitrogen, phosphorus, and heavy metals, and higher or lower sea surface temperature to name a few. Too much stress to the system and it will begin to break down. For sardines that is showing up as compromised immune systems in juveniles.

This vignette of a sardine fishery has important similarities to what is happening in other ecosystems—both natural and constructed. Take a serious look at any of a number of the ecosystems on which people depend for sustenance. What supports each system's integrity? What stresses a particular system? How much stress can that system take? What kinds of stress, and where can the system accommodate stress before it begins to break down, lose resilience, and plummet toward collapse? Then consider the natural ecosystems that are key to the operation of your businesses.

Additionally, what natural ecosystems are your business practices affecting or even disrupting? Do you know? Are these considerations reflected in your strategic plan? If so, how are you tracking these effects? If not, what do you have to do to include them? Beyond those, what other companies, industries, and sectors are dependent on these same ecosystems? Do you know? How are they affecting the resources you need? If there are multiple businesses using the services of the same ecosystems, are you coordinating the mitigation of your impacts? These are important questions to ask and address regarding the true health of your business. If you do not know and account for the conditions that maintain critical eco-system services, you are putting your business at considerable risk.

"Traditionally, business risks have been fires, floods, and dangers related to employee health & safety—risks to tangibles. There is a growing, daunting list of mega-issues that threaten both tangible assets and intangible assets like reputation" (Willard, 2005, p. 93). Today businesses must include and account for a host of risks that have previously been lumped and ignored as externalities. The nature of these new risks is variable and likely not solely under your control. But they are very real and may make the difference in the sustainability or unsustainability of your business. If you include these true costs and risks, what does it do to the assessment of the viability of your business? How much of your profitability depends on burden-shifting the true costs of the ecosystem services you use? If you are not paying these costs, who is paying them for you, and how? How likely is it that others will continue paying these ecosystem services costs for you in the future?

There will always be limits to growth in any semi-contained, materially finite system such as our Earth. In 2016, just about every major ecosystem on Earth is affected by humanity's acquisition of resources. Traditional business practices almost guarantee that these ecosystems will suffer and degrade. Key to sustainability is decoupling value creation across the board from exploit-ation and waste of Earth's natural resources. This shift in conceptual model and operations of business is doable. It will not happen on its own. It requires that forward-thinking leaders champion the process. Innovations in business models and practices that successfully achieve this decoupling will produce opportunities for greatly increased future rewards.

Ecological footprints

Currently, there are over 7.5 billion people on our planet Earth and that number increases by 200,000 more people each day. We are adding another 74 million people per year to the total population.[18] Increased population amplifies stress in many natural and social resources that enterprises depend on for their livelihood. This is further exacerbated by the fact that a number of the fastest growing populations are located in environments that are already over-stressed. If the current trajectory continues, this combination has potential to seriously disrupt our efforts toward sustainability.

The ecological footprint previously introduced and described in Chapter 6, shows impacts related to two critical questions:

- How much of the regenerative capacity of the biosphere is used by human activities?
- How much biocapacity is available for use within a given region?

Beyond those questions there is another very significant one that impacts future biocapacity, one that is exacerbated by globalized trade. It is:

> How much of ecological systems services—such as water, fertile soil, and biodiversity—are removed from one location as raw materials or as products then post use discarded to be deposited in another region?

The demand for ecosystem services, for use of the Earth's biocapacity, is outstripping the capacity of regeneration, not just this year but for a number of years now. Using the United States and 2012 numbers as an example, the ecological use demand in the US equates to use of the biocapacity of 8.2 global hectares (GHA) per person per year. The carrying biocapacity of the US is 3.8 GHA per person. Therefore, the US runs a deficit in biocapacity of 4.5 GHA per person. This can only happen in one of two ways: using the biocapacity of some other region of the world or eating into the replenishment capacities which will impact what will be available to people in the US in the future. The bioresources use in the US as well as in some other countries significantly exceeds the available regenerative capacity each year. By any measure this is unsustainable. The developed world is able to service consumption demands only by depleting its regenerative capacity thereby reducing the capacity to meet future needs.

Figure 7.2 provides a depiction of the world in terms of ecological creditors and debtors. This gives a view of the world that shows regional use in light of available resources. Today we tend to create a false separation between developing nations and developed nations or its close analogy of Northern and Southern Hemisphere national alliances. Because of globalized trade and flow of both information and capital, resources are moved around from one region of the globe to another.

The ecological footprint worldwide has been steadily increasing. In a nutshell, it would require approximately one and a quarter Earths to satisfy current global demand. It would take more than four Earths to satisfy people's use of the bioresources if all persons currently alive in underdeveloped regions were suddenly elevated to a middle-class lifestyle with those consumption patterns. That clearly is impossible to do when we share a single Earth. Use of bioresources is not spread evenly across the world's population. To support their current lifestyles, many developed countries are in ecological deficit, that is they are using more biocapacity than they have so they are importing biocapacity from other areas of the world. As you can see from the map, the United States and Germany are using 100–150% of their country's biocapacity. The United Kingdom, China, and Japan are all using over 150% of their biocapacity.

If ecological footprint trends continue toward depletion of critical ecological resources on a global scale, driven by a "get mine before it's gone," a tragedy of the commons mindset, humanity will find it seriously challenging to provide

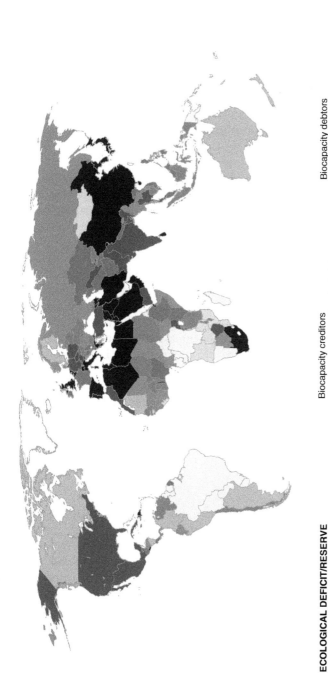

Biocapacity creditors
Biocapacity greater than footprint

>150%   100%–50%   50%–100%   50%–0%

Biocapacity debtors
Footprint greater than biocapacity

>150%   100%–50%   50%–100%   50%–0%

Figure 7.2 Ecological Footprint of consumption and biocapacity

Source: Ecological Footprint. Used with permission.

for the health and wellbeing of our world's still growing population. If this were to come to pass, it's likely that nations that are not yet using all of their biocapacity, ecological creditors, could become protectionist in regard to selling their resources. Countries that have credits because they use less than their available biocapacity are becoming aware of the rising demand for the ecosystem services they provide to debtor nations. Quite naturally they are exploring market mechanisms to more appropriately monetize and trade these currently undervalued ecological assets. Given the current business models in vogue this will put increased stress on multinational corporations that depend on use of disparate resources. It is also feasible that, acting in their societal self-interests, nations would resort to military aggression to meet their level of demand for food, clothing, technology, and many other desired products. Control of desired resources has been the impetus for war many times throughout history and could be again should weaker, but more ecologically viable, nations either refuse to "share" or attempt to politically and economically assert themselves.

At the time of this writing, no country is ranked as sustainable according to any organizations that produce rankings on assessments that include social, economic, and environmental measures. Frequently the Nordic countries are ranked highest, but none are deemed sustainable. Fortunately, many countries are now aware of sustainability issues and are developing programs to establish national practices in sustainable governance, human rights, and responsible use of resources. How aware are employees in your company of initiatives in your country, region, locale? How does this level of awareness show up in strategies, initiatives, and operations?

If this section on limits to growth implicit in ecological resources and stresses makes anything clear, it is that in an interconnected world, there are just about no firewalls left. These highlighted risks and many others not detailed here have associated consequences for enterprises. None of these will resolve to our benefit on their own.

What can we do?

Get creative! Rethink and redesign for the better. adidas is doing that: They're rethinking shoes to make them all around much better.

Lots of considerations go into constructing a great running shoe. Among those, it has to protect a foot, support posture while in motion, and cushion a foot from excessive impact shocks. So far as design goes, they've come quite a way since the early mentions of running shoes—in 1852. While styling has evolved, until recently running shoes have been constructed from new materials. In the early 1990s, Nike set up a reuse and recycling program for old running shoes. It helped move the industry toward reducing waste all around, and using recycled or post-consumer materials whenever possible. Closing the loop in manufacturing is critical. So is cleaning up the waste already generated. What if materials for running shoes were ... scavenged?

CASE 7. DESIGNED FOR SUSTAINABILITY AND RESTORATION: ADIDAS—TURNING OCEAN TRASH INTO SHOES

Linda M. Kelley

Recent studies estimate about 269,000 tons of plastic trash float on the surface of our oceans (Parker, 2015). Some has been tossed on the shore by beach goers, more has fallen off cargo ships, and even more is dumped as garbage generated by coastal cities. Four of 13 adolescent sperm whales stranded on the North Sea shore of Schleswig-Holstein had large amounts of plastic in their stomachs, including large chunks of a bucket and one 13-meter-long shrimp industry safety net.

adidas wants to change that. Eric Liedtke, adidas Group Executive Board member responsible for Global Brands, says,

> The industry can't afford to wait for directions any longer. Together with the network of Parley for the Oceans, we have started taking action and creating new sustainable materials and innovations for athletes ... We want to bring everyone from the industry to the table and create sustainable solutions for big global problems.[19]

The entire upper part of this new adidas shoe is made from reformed ocean-reclaimed plastic waste.

Where did the company start? It started with rethinking design, by reaching outside the normal operating zone, and seeking collaborations at the edges where one discipline rubs against another. It talked with a manufacturer whose machines are used for carbon fiber airplane parts and for car seats to find new ways to manufacture shoe components. Rather than going it alone, adidas floated its idea to musician/performer, creator of style Pharrell Williams—who was already collaborating with adidas—and to Parley for the Oceans. In addition to being a featured celebrity in adidas ads, Williams is a co-founder of Bionic Yarn. Bionic "turns things we discard into raw materials we can be proud to use in our everyday lives."[20] Already making yarn from recovered plastics, Bionic Yarn was eager to partner. But there was more. Ocean trash is laden with detritus such as dead, rotting marine life. One of the missions of Parley for the Oceans is to get the waste out of our waters. Founded by Cyrill Gutsch, Parley is concerned with major threats to our oceans, particularly waste pollution. The organization brings together people from many walks of life including artists, musicians, actors, journalists, inventors, architects, and scientists who are committed to develop ecologically responsible business models and products. With oceans as their focus and plastics as their rally point, and already working in the sportswear industry, Parley for the Oceans "committed to turning that concept into a consumer-ready product within a year" (George, 2016). On June 29, 2015, at a climate conference at the UN, adidas and Parley presented a prototype made with 3D printed midsole, recycled PET, and gillnet from the Arctic Sea reprocessed into nylon thread. adidas introduced its limited-edition shoe on World Oceans Day, June 8, 2016. Perfecting the process has a way to go still, so instead of selling, adidas set the first 50 pairs out for people to earn via Instagram. Born of a collaboration among many, here's what shoe designer Alexander Taylor has to say about the project. "A designer can be the agitator and the agent for change. He must be entrepreneurial in spirit, seeking out collaborators to reach amazing solutions which outperform and offer truly viable alternatives to current methods" (Howarth, 2016).

This adidas example as well as the other ones in this chapter originated because people cared, cared about what happened to our planet and to its people. Caring connects us to each other and to what we can do together. Caring connects us to what really matters. It's what another star performer, Charlie Chaplin, said years ago.

> We think too much and feel too little. More than machinery, we need humanity. More than cleverness, we need kindness and gentleness.
> (Charlie Chaplin, the final speech from *The Great Dictator*, n.d.)

Is there a place for caring in our capitalist model of business with its increasingly globalized reach? The road to date for caring capitalism has been a rocky one over the 20 some years since Ben and Jerry's brought it to the fore. Faced with so many issues and challenges regarding sustainability, a very real question now is can we afford capitalism without the caring? The companies highlighted in this chapter believe that caring and capitalism can exist together. When they are united purposefully by committed, forward-thinking leadership, the investments of capital are leveraged to improve quality of life for many, engage stakeholders in meaningful work, and better the performance and profitability for the company through responsible use of Earth's resources.

Caring shows up in values. What values are core to your company? How are they translated into strategy and operations? How do your company policies encourage or discourage collaborations for the greater good? What about innovations in repurposing and reuse of resources? Reviewing what some of the companies highlighted here are doing, what kinds of things might you now begin, expand, or stop?

Water—food—energy interconnection

While the interconnections between water, food, and energy are obvious on some levels, the extent of dependence among them is broad and deep. The vast majority of those interconnections fly below our radar. It is critical to sustainability that we explicitly address our dependence on widespread

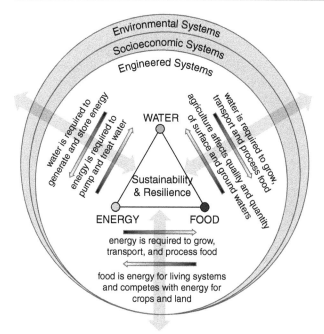

Figure 7.3 Food, energy, and water system (FEWS)

Source: Michael Chang (2016). Food-Energy-Water Systems: Opportunities at the Nexus. Retrieved from https://collections.elementascience.org/food-energy-water-systems/ (Forum at Elementa: Science of the Anthropocene www.elementascience.org). Used with permission.

availability of all three of these essentials. Though we often attempt to manage food, water, and energy as separate categories, it's more realistic to treat them as the interconnected systems they are—water system, food system, energy system—nested into critical services systems of Environmental Systems, Socioeconomic Systems, Engineered Systems.

Underlying all our social systems, underlying the day-to-day lives of each and every one of us are a few basic assumptions. Those include the ongoing availability of water, food, and energy.

There are many important considerations regarding water, food, and energy. One of those is how our use of materials in one area impacts each of the other two areas.

What if we ran out of phosphorus?

That will never happen. But phosphorus could become unavailable in the volumes we need. Why would that be so bad? We'd simply find a replacement. For many of its uses, not really. There are some troubling facts about phosphorus that business as usual has ignored.

Its transparency in its purist form is symbolic of how phosphorus seldom enters our conscious awareness. Its uses are practically invisible to us even though it is used for many, many functions in our lives. Where is phosphorus used? It's an anti-caking agent in baking powder, a brightener in paints, a preservative and flavor enhancer in processed foods. Phosphorus is also used in safety matches, in fireworks and explosives, and as a flame retardant as well. But that's not all. Phosphorous added to cleaning products softens water and removes grease, so it's also used in manufacturing to clean the metal surfaces and in toothpaste to remove tartar. It's used in fine china and in antacids. Phosphorus is also used in semi-conductors and because of its tenability, holds great promise in thin film technology and optics. If this were it, phosphorus would clearly be needed. First and foremost, though, phosphorus is important because it is essential to cell metabolism—for us and all of the rest of Earth's life forms. Phosphorus is one of the building blocks of life on Earth.

Where do we get phosphorus? If it's everywhere, it must be available everywhere. Yes and no. In order of abundance on earth, phosphorus is number 11. While phosphorus is ubiquitous, it's found in large enough quantities to be gathered for practical application in only a few places. Primary sources for phosphorus are phosphate-high rocks, the concentrated accumulations of ancient guano, and old bones. For centuries, farmers have known they needed to replenish soil minerals. Farmers have collected and ground old bones into meal and added that to the soil for hundreds of years. The supply of old bones is limited though. Deposits large enough to support today's large-scale agriculture and industries are found in only a few places in the world. Currently, much of the world depends on the vast deposits in the Western Sahara, principally in Morocco. While the majority of this mineral, essential for life and used by people around the globe, comes from a small area of northwest Africa, as of 2016, there is no comprehensive global political policy agreement that addresses the absolute need for continued availability of phosphorus.

A cautionary tale of excess and abuse is the mining and devastation of Nauru (Micronesia). A place you've probably never heard of, today only the thin rim of the island is habitable for humans, and that only barely. Barren of its former natural resource and the profits it brought, tiny Nauru has few options. All the accoutrements of modern life have to be imported, including food. That takes money and the money paid is gone. Nauru has now become a haven for shady, internet banks. Could they have managed their resources differently? Of course. But there as in so many other places, the lament is "But I just didn't know."

Will we learn the lessons of Nauru in time to save the Peace River watershed on Florida's Gulf Coast? The US has 19% of the world's phosphorus. Of that, 65% is in Florida, just north of the Peace River watershed known as Bone Valley. The mines cover about 58,000 acres and include holding pools of toxic clay sludge. On days of adequate flow, the Peace River supplies about 6 million gallons of drinking water to residents who live in Charlotte, Sarasota, and Desoto counties. Usually unseen, the phosphate mining operations inland have left a moonscape of slag hills and poisoned pools. While phosphorus is essential to life, too much can be harmful to human health, unbalancing the body's calcium–phosphorus balance. We know what phosphorus runoff does to the coastal areas. It enables algal blooms which foul the seawater prized by tourists for fishing and swimming, but even more important the algae explosions are temporary food for numbers of marine creatures on up the food chain. When the phosphorus supply slacks off, the algae die triggering a food chain die-off. The decomposition of large volumes of deceased animals sucks the oxygen out of the waters prompting further die-off, resulting in a coastal dead zone.

If this were all it would be bad enough, but it's not. Central Florida is prone to sinkholes. Phosphorus mining and the production of fertilizer byproduct, the weakly radioactive phosphogypsum, is stacked there as waste, lots, and lots of it. About 1 billion tons worth stacked in 25 stacks in Central Florida alone. When the underlying karst can't support that kind of weight, the ground underneath collapses, exposing the porous substrate and its aquifers to water laden with the toxic waste.

Postscript. A few weeks after the above section on phosphorus was written, a sinkhole 45 feet across developed in one of the Mosaic Company's stacks, sinking the slag and draining an enormous pool of toxic waste water. An estimated 215 million gallons of contaminated, radioactive water dumped into the Floridian Aquifer, a primary source of drinking water for the State.[21] First estimates are that it will cost up to $50 million to fix. But how widespread and long lasting this disaster will be is yet to be determined. It is not the first nor will it be the last crisis involving the phosphorus mining and fertilizer manufacture in West Central Florida. Sinkholes that form under these pools atop of huge waste stacks sitting on porous substrate are not accidents; they are constructed setups for disaster. These disasters are preventable. So far, we have not done what it takes.

Commercial agriculture is highly dependent on the application of additional phosphorus. Crops that are deficient in phosphorus have stunted growth and weakened immune systems. Take grain for example. To produce 130 tons of grain it takes about 1 ton of phosphate. By the late 20th century, we had developed a powerful agricultural sector that feeds billions of people. This phosphorus vignette is one part of the ugly underbelly of that industry. It doesn't have to be this way.

Our supplies of food, in fact our own lives, are dependent on adequate supply of available phosphorus yet we are wasting it away. Phosphorus is used in life processes then, after use, much of it is excreted. That's why we have ancient guano as a source today. We actually could recover much of the phosphorus we use now, but we don't. Instead we wash it away in fertilizer runoff, in manufacturing waste, and in vast amounts in sewage. We have recovered almost none of it.

Another option is to compost food waste regionally on a scale large enough to provide a great percent of the nutrient resupply for industrial agriculture so that some of the phosphorus is returned to the farmland soil so it will be available to the next season's plantings.

Taking a critical look at the issue of phosphorus through the lens of sustainability, we have either a global scale disaster in the making or a real business opportunity. We get to choose which it will be. Business as usual puts us on the path to catastrophe. "At current production levels, the world will exhaust these reserves in fewer than 80 years."[22]

In the same sense that sardines are a keystone species of marine ecosystems, phosphorus is a keystone mineral for human productivity, including survival. Yet the need for coordinating the acquisition and use of phosphorus isn't on political agendas. Managing this essential resource, fairly and responsibly, on a global scale will be one of the great, looming geopolitical challenges of the 21st century.

Does your business need phosphorus? If so, how are you managing those supplies? Have you thought about phosphorus recovery? Are you doing anything about it? Are you coordinating with other companies in your industry and sector? Across sectors? Once again, for many of its uses, there is no replacement for phosphorus.

What happens when conditions we count on change significantly?

FALSTAFF: I will not lend thee a penny.
PISTOL: Why then the world's mine oyster, Which I with sword will open.
(William Shakespeare, *The Merry Wives of Windsor*)

People have treated Earth's bounty as though it should be ours for the plucking, but is the world really our oyster? Can we consume resources with impunity?

As humanity has traversed the globe searching, taking, cultivating, exploiting, it's clear we have neglected to take into account factors that constitute essential supports for human life. Some consequences of this long-term disregard are now becoming apparent. Global warming is one of them. Although we have made some progress in reducing the amount of carbon we off-gas from fossil fuels, it is not enough. In that regard, human minimum habitability factors become critical because these are the real boundaries. As a practical matter, normal temperature range and duration makes a difference. Prolonged high, or low, temperatures negatively impact people and the bioresources on which we depend.

People are not well suited for surviving much less thriving in Earth's most extreme conditions without an enormous expenditure of supporting resources. This is why we construct buildings with heating and cooling systems, and are willing to pay for them. Although it isn't hard and fast, many people today seem to work and sleep better within an ambient temperate range with a minimum above 60 degrees Fahrenheit and maximum below 80 F. Prolonged exposure to too hot or too cold and we suffer hyperthermia or hypothermia. Under either of these conditions our body functions become impaired. In recent years there have been numerous record-setting, summer high temperatures that significantly exceeded 120 F. People die from extreme heatwaves and cold waves. Heat waves have claimed many lives across the globe in recent summers where temperatures exceeded 120 F in some populated areas. Through ongoing research, this temperature range assessment is being refined so weather services, for instance, can include temperature danger warnings. One such project is NOAA's Wet Bulb prototype which measures heat stress.

Even if we don't exceed the upper limits, pushing seasonal norms into our highest habitable range will take its toll on our health, or productivity, and our infrastructure.

Extended extreme heat, coupled with either drought or prolonged rain, stresses our food crops, so that even when they are not wiped out they yield less. Drought has gripped the wheat-producing US high plains in the summer of 2017. Farmers figure the crop output will be only half of what it usually is, and the outlook for peas, soybeans, barley, and corn isn't much better. Ranchers sold off cattle because the grazing grass is too poor to support them. Recent studies indicate that the world's dry zones are expanding (Chan & Wu, 2015). Prolonged drought in any of the world's breadbasket areas would reduce available food for a world population that is still growing. It's not just the farmlands that are already being affected though. Sea surface temperatures are rising, and the already reduced fish populations are shifting migration and zones, again reducing reliable food sources for large numbers of people.

Meanwhile, this same summer (2017), both the Mideast and the American southwest are suffering scorchingly high temperatures. Iran has seen some of the highest temperatures ever recorded in cities, over 129 F. Arizona's temperatures weren't much lower. The State has had a dozen large, destructive wildfires since Spring in dry, hot forests. And many flights were canceled out of Phoenix because smaller planes can't get enough lift to take off in the thinner air of such extreme heat. Climate change has real consequences in our everyday lives.

Why touch on this area in a book focused on the business of sustainability? Because impaired sustainability of societies presents inordinate risks to business as well, and these very real risks are seldom considered. More than that, when they are considered, most often the focus is on the symptoms rather than on the underlying issues and causes. If we are to address problems that have the potential to derail business, and even societies, we need to be able to identify what the real issues are so we can address their causes rather than getting bogged down in trying only to counter symptoms. A real issue is that people need sufficient habitable zones as our foundation for sustainability. We can only fulfill our goals of prosperity and thriving if we maintain this base platform.

Reframing the conversation about climate change

First, Earth's climate has changed many, many times over its few billion years and will continue to change over time. Sometimes the climate has been significantly warmer and sometimes very much colder than it is now. Whatever life was on Earth has either adapted to the changes or has died out. No one is going to stop Earth's climate from changing. Right now, all credible climate research shows that the average surface temperature of Earth is rising. Our Earth is warming. This global warming threatens to reduce the zones that can support the activities and ecosystems essential to human survival. For humanity, this should be a huge concern. In the past few years we have experienced sustained temperature highs that have not been seen in recent history. Four of the world's leading climate research organizations, NASA Goddard Institute for Space Studies, Met Office Hadley Center/ Climate Research, NOAA National Climactic Data Center, and the Japanese Meteorological Agency are in close agreement and show tracking temperature data that is rising rapidly since the 1980s.[23]

All indications point to the spike in temperature rise being caused by human activity. Global warming is not an underlying issue though. Our imprudent management of vital resources is exacerbated by burning of fossil fuels that increases atmospheric CO_2 and wasting irreplaceable resources. Global warming is one unintended yet dangerous symptom of our push to advance humanity's progress. Because of the inherent interconnections between climate and habitable zones, it is likely that continuing on our current course business will precipitate environmental crises and enormous human suffering. Forward-thinking business leaders can create new, real economic value by going beyond risk mitigation and open up opportunities through innovations that may even birth new industries.

Why do people live where they do? Habitable zones for human life

Although people circle the globe, populating diverse terrains, the most dense populations are concentrated in latitudes that are neither extremely hot nor extremely cold.

One way to look at the health of habitable zones is to overlay a population map with a global temperature range map, an environmental footprint map, an arable land under cultivation map, and a map of stressed water areas. Where are the convergences of stresses? Do conditions that pop out look like the setup for a perfect storm?

Access to potable water is one of the essential supports for human life. "Multiple climate studies project continued climate inaction will put some one-third of the currently-habited and arable landmass of the planet into a state of near permanent drought post-2050. This new study finds that we are well on our way" (Romm, 2015).

Sustainability is not just about global warming and its human and environmental costs, drastic though they are likely to be given that the effects from the greenhouse gasses we've already pushed into the atmosphere are projected to last many years into the future. If by some miracle the warming trend abated and the greenhouse gases magically disappeared from the atmosphere, we'd still be polluting our critical water supplies and draining aquifers that serve millions. We would still be doing business as though natural resources were in endless supply and therefore consumable and disposable. We would still be leaving environmental wastelands from resource extraction and processing. Our worldwide population would still be rising with all of us billions trying to satisfy our basic needs plus bettering our own standards of living. The predominant models by which we conduct business would still make us by all measures unsustainable.

Recognizing that there are issues of development that span borders, nations of the world have come together through the UN to address some of the most egregious problems. Common goals are laid out in *The Future We Want* (2012). First on the list in the common vision is eradication of poverty and freeing humanity from hunger. The vision is broad and inclusive.

> We therefore acknowledge the need to further mainstream sustainable development at all levels, integrating economic, social and environmental aspects and recognizing their interlinkages, so as to achieve sustainable development in all its dimensions.[24]

Within this framework sit the Millennium Development Goals (2013, Outcome document), the 17 Sustainable Development Goals (2015), and the Development Agenda 2030. Though countries have started on strategies and implementation processes, as of this writing, systems for monitoring and evaluation are still in early development phases. How countries coordinate their efforts, share their successes, and cooperate on addressing the larger challenges will determine whether these goals are realized globally or not.

Achieving the Sustainable Development Goals is important to our global future and excellent progress, but they don't go far enough in identifying and addressing critical underlying issues that inhibit sustainability from a business or planetary perspective.

Our Earth is almost a closed system with semi-permeable boundaries. What's in stays in; very little is added. Nested within the system of the whole Earth are many interdependent environmental and social systems that rely on the overall health of the whole planet. It's been said many times, but we should never forget that we have available to us the resources of only one planet, and they're shared.

In pursuing our desired lifestyles, what are we really willing to risk with the increase in global warming due in large part to human activity? Food supply and security? Availability of potable water? Weather extremes? Human suffering, individually and on a large social scale? What costs are we really willing to pay? How much can we actually borrow from our future without sending critical, life-supporting, present day systems into positive feedback loops that result in habitat loss and species extinction? When will we, our businesses and communities take the necessary steps to ensure that the habitable zones are sufficient to provide the resources for the business of taking care of Earth's human population?

"Borrow" is a key word in all of this. In effect, Nature lends us resources. From our perspective, we use and consume these resources. Eventually, Nature gets used resources recycled. Nature doesn't waste. The problem is that we have been irresponsible borrowers. We should be returning what we've used in good condition. Yet when we borrow from Nature we behave badly, taking what is lent and disregarding any obligation to return them in as good or better shape than they were when we took them. In many instances, we make those borrowed resources unavailable for reuse in the foreseeable future. We burn, poison, and dissipate resources as though there was an infinite store but there is not. Such flagrant misuse results in good part from poor conceptualization and design. As has been shown in a number of cases and examples in this chapter, taking a systems approach to conceptualization and design reveals new opportunities for creating value responsibly. Smart design connects the kinds of resources used, how they are obtained and processed, how they are used, and what happens to them when their usefulness is finished. Smart design can reduce waste and enable recycling for reuse. Designing products for recycling, reuse, repurposing is the way of our future, the best way to a sustainable future.

Climate change: impacts, mitigation, and migration

INTERGOVERNMENTAL PANEL ON CLIMATE CHANGE: MITIGATION

Among the key findings from the recent Intergovernmental Panel on Climate Change (IPCC) Fifth Assessment Report (November, 2014):

- It is extremely likely that more than half of the observed increase in global average surface temperature from 1951 to 2010 was caused by the anthropogenic increase in GHG concentrations and other anthropogenic forcings together.
- Anthropogenic influences have likely affected the global water cycle since 1960 and contributed to the retreat of glaciers since the 1960s and to the increased surface melting of the Greenland ice sheet since 1993. Anthropogenic influences have very likely contributed to Arctic sea-ice loss since 1979 and have very likely made a substantial contribution to increases in global upper ocean heat content (0–700 m) and to global mean sea level rise observed since the 1970s.
- Many aspects of climate change and associated impacts will continue for centuries, even if anthropogenic emissions of greenhouse gases are stopped. The risks of abrupt or irreversible changes increase as the magnitude of the warming increases.
- It is virtually certain that global mean sea level rise will continue for many centuries beyond 2100, with the amount of rise dependent on future emissions.
- Many adaptation and mitigation options can help address climate change, but no single option is sufficient by itself. Effective implementation depends on policies and cooperation at all scales and can be enhanced through integrated responses that link adaptation and mitigation with other societal objectives.
- Adaptation and mitigation responses are underpinned by common enabling factors. These include effective institutions and governance, innovation and investments in environmentally sound technologies and infrastructure, sustainable livelihoods and behavioral and lifestyle choices.

The sustainable development goals cannot be achieved if we don't tackle climate change … The World Bank has actually warned us that by 2050, around 1.3 billion people will be at risk from climate related disasters. And at least 100 million of these will be pushed back in poverty. There is no business case in enduring poverty and it would be wise for any business to decarbonize their total model.

(Paul Polman, CEO, Unilever, at COP22, November 12, 2016)

Climate change is a strategic security threat that sits alongside others like terrorism and state-on-state conflict, but it also interacts with these threats. It is complex and challenging; this is not a concern for tomorrow, the impacts are playing out today.

(Former Rear Admiral Neil Morisetti, UK Maritime Forces and the UK's Climate and Energy Security Envoy, 2016)

The 21st Conference of the Parties

The CoP21 invited the Intergovernmental Panel on Climate Change to provide a special report in 2018 on the impacts of climate warming of 1.5 °C above pre-industrial levels and related global greenhouse gas emissions pathways. If ever there were an area of concern that demanded widespread inclusion and expertly researched input to understand the impacts, it's changes occurring in Earth's climate.

Changes in Earth's climate, in the cycles of heat and cold, wet and dry, have the potential to be the most disruptive forces humanity has ever encountered. If the effects aren't touching you at this moment, it's easy to be lulled into believing that you are going to dodge this bullet, but none of us, anywhere around the globe, is or will be immune to the effects. Global climate change has no regard for political boundaries. Addressing this challenge will require efforts, contributions, and cooperation from all the different sectors including businesses, governments, and nongovernmental organizations. Weather extremes: water—floods and droughts, temperature—record highs and lows, high winds, that disrupt everyday life ripple through business and upend economies. These disasters come with a high price tag. For example, a year later the *Insurance Journal* estimated the economic costs of a single superstorm, Superstorm Sandy (East coast landfall, October 29, 2012), to have reached $70 billion. At this point in time, rather than treat these extremes as one-time events, it would be prudent for all of us to take stock globally as to such effects and what we need to do to mitigate them right now.

Assessing progress and updating mitigation workplans are critical if we are to understand and address the most pressing implications for sustainability. No one will be able to do this alone. The framework and inherent biases of each organization makes its perspective necessarily incomplete and transorganizational collaboration mandatory.

We all know that severe weather causes frustrating delays in transportation and travel. The more extreme the weather, the more it upends lives and seriously disrupts business. Obviously, too much water or too little, and temperatures that are overly hot or frigid play havoc with food and other agricultural crops. But, even businesses that aren't hit directly feel the effects when critical components of their supply chains are. Most manufacturing today runs lean. While there are many advantages to just-in-time manufacturing, it does increase vulnerability to supply chain disruptions especially those caused by natural events.

Today, business is highly dependent on complex electronics, whether they are essential components of their products or critical tools that enable the conduct of business. Climate change induced megastorms have the potential of creating disruptions on the level of the 2011 earthquake-generated tsunami that hit Japan. It decimated supply chains of numerous industries globally and shut down production. Because Hitachi, north of Tokyo, was shut down, both General Motors and Peugeot-Citroen productions were delayed because they didn't have their airflow sensors. Sony, Texas Instruments, and Toshiba all had their supply chains of computer chips and liquid crystal display screens disrupted. All this and more from a single natural event. Over $20 trillion of intermediate goods and services are acquired through global trade. As many corporations have already recognized, ignoring the potential consequences of climate change puts business at significant risk.

What are some climate change risks and mitigations that should be included in your business strategy? Are they currently being considered? Are your current practices for obtaining and assessing risks sufficient to protect your business? Who is included in your advice network, internally and externally? Are there others who should be included in order to reduce risk and increase resilience?

While climate change induced migration is only beginning, the International Organization for Migration, The UN Migration Agency, has started planning for significant, complex displacements of people.

> There are no reliable estimates of climate change induced migration. But it is evident that gradual and sudden environmental changes are already resulting in substantial population movements. The number of storms, droughts and floods has increased threefold over the last 30 years with devastating effects on vulnerable communities, particularly in the developing world. In 2008, 20 million persons have been displaced by extreme weather events, compared to 4.6 million internally displaced by conflict and violence over the same period. Gradual changes in the environment tend to have an even greater impact on the movement of people than extreme events. For instance, over the last thirty years, twice as many people have been affected by droughts as by storms (1.6 billion compared with approx. 718m).
>
> Future forecasts vary from 25 million to 1 billion environmental migrants by 2050, moving either within their countries or across borders, on a permanent or temporary basis, with 200 million being the most widely cited estimate.[25]

(5) Looking through the movement-of-talent lens

Movement of talent in perspective

Talent moves. When we think of talent on the move, typically we think about the capabilities and potential represented by key employees leaving one company or industry to join another, or to start a new venture, or even retire. Certainly, that is one important area but focusing solely on highly valued professionals tells only a small part of the story regarding the movement of talent.

In very real ways, the movement of talent shapes the sustainability of globalization. Talent in motion, geographically and intellectually, is fertile ground for innovation. When new people and new talent arrives on the scene, it's unsettling to individuals and to organizations, even when they invite the change. Ordinary assumptions about one's values, position, and how things should be done lose transparency. How people negotiate disruptions, how they resist or accommodate added capabilities, resets working climates. It's in the bumping and rubbing together of differing perspectives, experiences, and practices that cracks appear in the old "normal." These often-uncomfortable transition spaces are gateways to innovation. These "workout" spaces force new perspectives that reveal heretofore unrecognized opportunities. Challenges to the status quo push people to change what they think and do, and in the process, they develop talents. Such generative mashups move people to achieve what they had previously thought impossible.

Today, geographic migration is at an all-time high. Over 232 million people live for a year or more in a country that is not their country of birth.[26] That's close to three-quarters as many people as live in the United States. Worldwide, 65 million people have been displaced due to war or persecution, half of them children.[27] Not included in that displacement number are 19 million people who lost their homes due to environmental disasters such as earthquakes and floods. Where do all these people go? A few countries host the bulk of the migrants. The United States has the highest number by far with 46 million people, followed by Russia with over 11 million, and Germany with almost 10 million. Where are these people coming from? The largest number come from India where 14 million people have emigrated.

People on the move bringing talent affects business in many ways.

> Migrants by virtue of their inherited and acquired knowledge of the business and the institutional environment of their country of origin and their country of residence can be valuable sources of knowledge for firms.
>
> (Shukla & Cantwell, 2016)

Inevitable mashups that result generate platforms that then foster the development of new talents that spread and seed more creative mashups, and create new value in the process. One of the effects over the past 50 years has been a significant shift in market capitalization evaluation. Where profitability in the middle of the 20th century was still dependent on exploitation of natural resources, by the early 21st century services became the focus of profit generation. Further, it has become increasingly clear that profit alone is not sufficient to ensure sustainability. Without talent, there is no business. Without growing talent, there will be no broad base of prosperity to generate business sustainability.

Talent and skill

To better understand the significance of the movement of talent in regard to globalization, it's important to lay out what is meant by some of these terms. People have been migrating since humanity's beginnings. In fact, migration may be one of the primary characteristics that has defined humanity. People on the move are seeking to improve their conditions, their options to make their living, whether the initial motivation is moving away from something or moving toward something else. Sometimes people are moving away from situations they can no longer tolerate, other times they move toward conditions they perceive to be preferable.

Talent in the original sense of the word referred to inclination and disposition, balance and support. Recently talent has become more narrowly defined as natural abilities. More often than not, talent that is assessed to be natural abilities is taken out of context and those abilities are considered to be absolutes. Yet when we really consider this we realize there are very few abilities that actually manifest consistently over time and across contexts. Most of what we hold as talent is skillfulness developed over time, applied generatively to specific contexts, and translated to new contexts when possible.

An important question to ask is, when large numbers of people move, how do we seed the ground so that transferable talent surfaces and new talent develops to address critical issues of lifestyle standards such as increased population density, availability of essential natural resources, and the wherewithal to prosper sustainably?

Source: Linda M. Kelley, 2016. Creative Commons Attribution. Used with permission.

CASE 8. THE REINVENTING OF RWANDA

Linda M. Kelley

When crisis strikes with an enormity that shivers people to their core, are they able to remake themselves?

Devastation comes in many forms. Some are environmental in origin: massive earthquakes, relentless drought, or megastorms to name a few. Others are social in origin and effect: financial crises, collapse of an industry, or severe political conflict such as ethnic cleansing, revolution, or war. Whichever the cause, the worst of those rupture the transparency of everyday life in irreversible ways, forcing people to rebuild their lives. Resilience is important but it isn't enough. Returning to stability is only the first step. It's what people do to regenerate themselves following catastrophe that determines their future, and how sustainable they will be.

Twenty years ago, few if any would have considered that the Central African country of Rwanda could become a budding tech hub. Yet that is just what's happening. At a glance, Rwanda would seem to have many strikes against it. A small, landlocked country of great natural beauty but few tradable natural resources, Rwanda burst onto the global stage in 1994 ablaze with horrific genocide—800,000 killed in 100 days—that ripped apart Rwandan society.

Fast-forward, today, Rwanda is a country in the process of transforming itself. Without a doubt, Rwandan President Paul Kagame is a remarkable leader who has a reputation for being both impressive and repressive. He's shrewd, complicated, and controversial: part rebel military commander and strongman, part social engineer, part visionary who continues to push Rwanda to transform from a poor, agrarian economy into a middle-income, knowledge-based, technology-enabled society by 2020. Fortunately, though, success doesn't ride on the leadership of a single individual. Rwanda Vision 2020 has grown into a team effort.

Enacted in 2000, "Vision 2020 aspires for Rwanda to become a modern, strong and united nation, proud of its fundamental values, politically stable and without discrimination amongst its citizens" (Kaberuka, 2000). The Vision has six pillars:

- reconstruction of the nation and its social capital anchored on good governance, underpinned by a capable state;
- transformation of agriculture into a productive, high value, market-oriented sector, with forward linkages to other sectors;
- development of an efficient private sector spearheaded by competitiveness and entrepreneurship;
- comprehensive human resources development, encompassing education, health, and ICT skills aimed at public sector, private sector, and civil society. To be integrated with demographic, health, and gender issues;
- infrastructural development, entailing improved transport links, energy and water supplies and ICT networks;
- promotion of regional economic integration and cooperation.

There are a few aspects that make this Vision unusual. The very first pillar is "reconstruction of the nation and its social capital," in other words, the development of Rwanda's talent base. This is critical because it roots the development of infrastructure, technology, markets, and the economy in human resources, as emphasized again in the fifth pillar. In addition, Rwanda also subscribed to the UN Millennium Goals. By the close of 2015, it had made significant progress in all eight areas: (1) Eradicate extreme poverty and hunger; (2) Achieve universal primary education; (3) Promote gender equality and empower women; (4) Reduce child mortality; (5) Improve maternal health; (6) Combat HIV/AIDS, malaria, and other diseases; (7) Ensure environmental sustainability; (8) Develop global partnership for development.[28]

Essential infrastructure development in this new Rwanda includes not only roads, water, and electricity but also, education, healthcare, and information and communication technology (ICT). Because of public/private cooperation and investment in ICT, by 2015, over 3,000,000 Rwandans had mobile phones and internet access. With fiber-optic, high-speed 4G LTE broadband and connections internationally via both wireless and undersea cables, Minister for Youth and ICT, Jean Philbert Nsengimana says, "We are increasing accessibility and Internet speed, we are making it easier for people to do business and have impact on fellow citizens." As of January 2018, the 4G LTE network covered 95% of Rwanda (Tumwebaze, 2018). From Nsengimana again, "In just 15 years, what was once considered as an object of luxury and privilege for rich people has become a basic necessity for Rwandan urban and rural daily lives" (Ben-Ari, 2014).

With 95% of children going to school, Rwanda's primary school enrollment is the highest in Africa. Organizations such as Innovations for Learning, and One Laptop Per Child, which has provided thousands of laptops to students, are working in the country. There is still a long way to go. Despite the great progress made already, a 40% skills gap still exists and 42% of youths are either unemployed or underemployed. Among the universities that are on board with Rwanda's transformation are the Massachusetts Institute of Technology (MIT) and Carnegie Mellon. MIT International Science and Technology Initiatives has run Global Startup Labs at Kigali Institute of Science and Technology, particularly focused on technology entrepreneurship and agroeconomy.

In 2012, in partnership with the government, Carnegie Mellon opened the CMU Information and Communication Technology (ICT) Center of Excellence (CoE) in Kigali. It has already graduated its first cohort of students. The wide-ranging technical program extends into rural health delivery, solar energy, smart farms, and big data. Carnegie Mellon University Rwanda will be the anchor tenant of an "innovation city" within Kigali that will house technology companies and institutions. Both driving and enabled by their technology innovations, Rwanda and the US Energy company, Contour Global, have built a methane-fired power plant on Lake Kivu (with gas extracted from the lake). This plant adds 25 megawatts of generating capacity. It is expected that more companies will follow suit, not only providing needed energy but also avoiding poisonous lake turnover from excess submerged methane. Rwanda is becoming a magnet for tech investment with direct foreign investment rising every year, in 2016 reaching $1.5 billion (Hill & Butera, 2016).

As of the end of 2016, that outlook is promising. Through public/private partnerships, Rwanda is supporting entrepreneurial startups, particularly through business-friendly policies, infrastructure, and incubators. A 2016–2017 World Bank Doing Business Report puts Rwanda as the second-best country in Sub-Saharan Africa for starting a business. The likes of KLab

(Knowledge Lab), Think (Millicom), FabLab (government innovation hub) offer startup space and support for entrepreneurs. And it seems to be working. Companies such as HeheLabs and Go LTD, both mobile apps companies, have gained traction. Attracted by the tech skilled workforce, Positivo GBH, an Argentinean company, is assembling computers in Kigali.

Will Rwanda succeed over the long term? That will likely hinge on how well and how fast the country develops a sustainable, innovation-friendly entrepreneurial foundation. So, it will be for many of the world's population centers that must reinvent themselves to be relevant, sustainable contributors in a world that is increasingly tech-enabled. A key factor will be whether or not they develop the talent base they require. In a very real way it comes down to how do you understand and use the resources you have.

The urbanization of globalization

> I don't think this is an idle dream; the city has served as a focus for active social life, for the conflict and play of interests, for the experience of human possibility, during most of the history of civilized man.
>
> (Sennett, 1977, p. 80)

Urbanization is hardly a new phenomenon. Archaeologists have found vestiges of early cities, dating back nearly 10,000 years. It's estimated that by 100 CE, Rome had a population of 1 million people. Two thousand years later, that city is still going strong. Many cities are more stable and have lifespans longer than nation states. With the Industrial Revolution of the 18th century, urbanization accelerated greatly. For example, in the early 1800s, London had a population of just over 1,000,000; by 1914, London's population was over 7,000,000.[29] By 1950, 749 million people lived in urban areas. Jump to 2014 and more than half the world's 7.2 billion people live in urban areas. By 2045, it is anticipated that over 6 billion people will be city dwellers with India, China, and Nigeria experiencing the largest growth in urban populations. Urban growth brings with it huge opportunities and challenges—social, technological, economic, and environmental.

> Managing urban areas has become one of the most important development challenges of the 21st century. Our success or failure in building sustainable cities will be a major factor in the success of the post-2015 UN development agenda.
>
> (John Wilmoth, Director of UN DESA's Population Division, 2014)

THE RISE OF MEGACITIES

While Boston, New York, San Francisco, and London have persistently stood out as cities renowned for technology development and social evolution, they have been joined, non-exclusively and in no particular order, by Beijing, Helsinki, Cape Town, Stockholm, Christchurch, Medellin, Bangalore (Bengaluru), Shanghai, Tokyo, Vancouver, Paris, Chicago, Seoul, and Singapore.

Sustainable urbanization depends on supportive structures. Physical location still counts but location in relation to infrastructure is becoming the greatest differentiator between urban areas that are growing in dominance and those that are not. Superior infrastructure means superior access. If you look at global communications networks, not surprisingly those with the most activity networks track with both dense populations and high economic value. By mid-2016, there were over 3.5 billion internet users globally.[30] Combine a map of transport of goods and services with communications networks and one can begin to see hub areas around the globe where likely megacities are coalescing. This economic geography looks rather different than the current global arrangement of nation states. In addition to occupying a physical geography, each megacity is tightly knit together electronically in virtual networks in highly complex social, economic, and environmental systems. Because of their considerable power, how they develop and manage their considerable resources will shape the sustainability of those urban megaregions and ultimately of the planet.

According to world Internet Usage Stats in 2017, Hong Kong (87.3%), Taiwan (88%), South Korea (92.7%), and Japan (94.0%) have some of the highest percentages of internet-connected populations in the world. Over half the world's population and almost half of the world's internet users

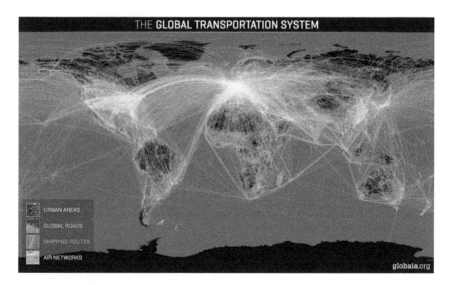

Figure 7.4 The global transportation system
Source: Félix Pharand-Deschênes/Globaïa. Used with permission.

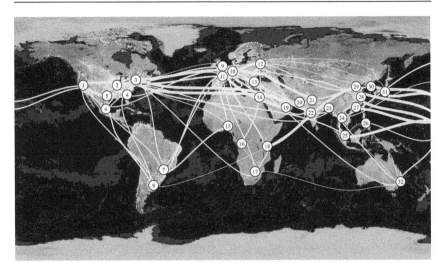

Figure 7.5 Global internet connects emerging megacities
Source: Linda M. Kelley, 2017. Creative Commons ShareAlike.

Table 7.1 Connected emerging megacities

Connected emerging megacities

1. San Francisco–Los Angeles– Vancouver–San Diego	17. Johannesburg
2. Chicago–Toronto	18. Nairobi–Dar es Salam
3. Boston–New York–Washington DC	19. Abu-Dhabi
4. Atlanta–Miami	20. Karachi
5. Dallas–Ft. Worth–Houston	21. Greater Delhi
6. Mexico City	22. Mumbai–Pune
7. Sao Paulo–Rio de Janeiro	23. Dhaka
8. Buenos Aires	24. Bangkok
9. London	25. Singapore–Jakarta
10 Rhine–Ruhr	26. Manila
11. Paris	27. Pearl River Delta
12. Moscow	28. Shanghai–Nanjing
13. Greater Istanbul	29. Beijing–Tianjin–Hebei
14. Cairo	30. Seoul
15. Lagos–Benin City	31. Tokyo–Osaka–Kobe
16. Kinshasa	32. Sydney

Source: Linda M. Kelley. No copyright.

are in Asia, and the numbers of people there with online access is growing rapidly. It's in Africa, though, where the percent of internet connection is growing the most rapidly, with an increase in connectivity of over 8,000% between 2000 and 2017.[31]

WHAT DO DYNAMIC MEGACITIES MEAN FOR BUSINESS?

I've been [in] Boston now six weeks and you just walk out the door. You're in the middle of an ecosystem that quite honestly for a big company, it makes you afraid. You're where the ideas are. You get more paranoid when you're doing that and that's a good thing … When you're a big company, it can get hidden but it's important that you're in touch with what the next idea is or what the next disruption is. And so I'm kind of a big believer that that's the wave of the future.

(Jeffrey Immelt, CEO, General Electric[32])

Of the 100 largest economic entities in the world, 42 are cities. That number is still rising. What does it mean for business and political power when some cities have a larger GDP than many countries do? Will cities reshape the world order? Cities attract and support the largest and most influential businesses in the world. There are also companies that are more powerful and influential than many nations. Of 25 at the top of that list, 14 are headquartered within emerging megacities. Resourceful cities are driving global economic growth. It has been projected that by 2025, current megacities with the highest GDP plus a handful more on a path of rapid emergence and their network of surrounding midweight cities—a total of 600 cities—will account for well over 60% of global GDP. Although urban regions are leading economic growth, rural areas still hold about half the world's population. Progress and sustainability requires that the urban dwellers work with their rural cousins, considering their needs, buying power, and knowledge, yes, their problem-solving abilities, ideas, and know-how if we all are to thrive. Urban–rural collaboration and mutual support is essential for global sustainability.

In a May 2016 speech, GE's CEO Jeffrey Immelt said that with 70% of the company's revenue outside the US, future "sustainable growth will require a local capability inside a global footprint." Immelt added, "In the face of a protectionist global environment, companies must navigate the world on their own" (McGregor, 2017).

Because they are as vulnerable as they are powerful, these burgeoning megacity centers of commerce and culture must take on the responsibility and the opportunity to initiate changes needed for sustainability. Many of these cities are already dealing with effects of climate change. Cleaning up our cities, reducing smog and pollution, developing clean, renewable energy to power our businesses via public-private partnerships would increase overall value and further sustainability. Many of the largest cities are along coasts where they will feel the brunt of rising seas from global warming. To date, neither governmental policies nor physical infrastructure are sufficiently robust to handle the challenges that will accompany significant climate change. Organizations such as 100 Resilient Cities, and The Global Covenant of Mayors for Climate & Energy are focused on developing the wherewithal of cities to not only withstand economic and environmental shocks, and social stresses, but also thrive sustainably in this highly urbanized emerging future.

Rapid population growth in megacities brings with it many challenges. Already suffering economic inequalities, if these cities are to be safely habitable the governing bodies of these urban centers must not only remedy these current gaps but also put in place institutional capacity to accommodate and integrate large numbers of immigrants with widely differing needs and abilities. While business will benefit from this influx of potential employees and customers, this sector will also need to partner with municipal authorities to make cities smarter and more capable. In doing this they will create a pathway for more and more people to become contributors to the overall wellbeing and create new value in meaningful ways.

(6) Looking through a geopolitical lens

> The problem with most of today's variants of capitalism is that they produce unintended consequences on a planetary scale. They ignore key externalities (particularly things like species loss and climate change), assuming that growth can continue almost indefinitely.
>
> (Elkington, 2012)

> International success depends on business leaders' having the foreign policy acumen to distinguish between what they can and can't do in a sanctions environment or tough diplomatic climate.
>
> (Chipman, 2016)

Does your organization consider geopolitical factors in your strategy? Are geopolitical factors even discussed?

For better or for worse, the combination of hyper-urbanization plus economic globalization plus peer-to-peer technologies is disrupting the authority of nation states. There are increasing discrepancies between the functional relevance of emerging networked megacity clusters and geographically bounded countries. Shifting affinities are reforming the complex networks that comprise urbanized regions. These interconnected webs are transforming how our societies are organized. Jockeying between megacities and nation states is already under way. Which of them has jurisdiction over people and their business activities is likely to be sorted and resorted a number of times during the near future. Navigating this new global geopolitical and economic landscape will require that businesses undertake some serious assessments to align sustainability strategies for creating value with a realistic view of the state of global affairs. This current business landscape is ripe with opportunities for innovation to increase sustainably created value. But there are many potential pitfalls along the way. With the social, economic, and environmental all intertwined, unintended consequences of our lifestyles are creating problems that bleed through into other areas. For example, when a widespread financial crisis happens, it provokes social unrest and migration that further disrupts business and adds stress to an already overburdened water supply. Put any of the three—social, ecological, or economic—in the trigger position and consequential events will ripple through the other areas. Today's geopolitical issues are tightly coupled and highly complex. While business must plan and manage with these considerations in mind, there are no easy answers.

Our only pathways to sustainability are ones we create with many other people. How and at what levels and touchpoints do we, as individuals and businesses, need to coordinate our approaches and actions? Together we must develop umbrella strategies for systems that enable us to address critical environmental, social, and economic problems fairly and effectively. Together we are co-creating a new global future. If we work cooperatively, we can make it a sustainable future.

Pressures are pushing leaders to grab for quick solutions, especially ones that give fast, visible results. While that kind of decisive action may have worked well in the past, the more uncertain the times are the less likely they are to yield desired results, especially if they inadvertently increase instability in any way. Focusing on good, challenging questions that require hard looks at reality offer the better paths forward into sustainability. Formulate questions that relate to real values and concerns. The best questions reveal inherent interconnections between geopolitical issues and actions material to your business. Addressing them well is a strategic imperative.

Using the lens framework, develop your questions around important, challenging, pivotal geopolitical issues to consider and address appropriately in your business strategy, including:

Governance—Who regulates what aspects of the organization and how? Nation states, powerful megacities, industry organizations, and professional networks all influence governance and therefore the opportunities and threats to a business. What are the parameters and areas of authority—both internal corporate and external political? Who sets policy and compliance? How do concerns of investors fit with demands of regulators? Are compensation and rewards aligned with or in conflict with long-term sustainability objectives?

Terrorism and security—Obvious when you think about it, terrorism (violence against civilians) and insurgency (violence against States or governments) affect business operations. But do you consider possible effects and consequences in developing company strategies? Have you accounted for possible stranded assets? Reduction in productivity? Decreased demand for products and services? Disruption or elimination of key parts of your supply chain? What about security of your facilities and employees, and your distribution network?

Globalism + localism—Think globally and act locally is a nice catch phrase but an insufficient guide for strategic planning. Local operations affect global conditions; global conditions have local consequences. How do your local operations account for possible global disruptions that could ripple through the economic, environmental, and/or social foundational assumptions on which your business is based? There are a number of relevant gradations between global and local, each pulling and pushing on the stability of the established order, in both cooperative and competitive ways: State to State, Alliance to Alliance, Nation State and megacity or region are some in play today. How does your business strategy account for disruptions in relationships that can cause shifts in power?

Capitalism and democracy—Capitalism benefits from a degree of autonomy and self-determination, yet businesses in nondemocratic states have embraced and excelled in capitalist markets. Where is your business dependent on certain freedoms to operate, and where can it tolerate greater constraints? How do you pick up on signals that significant changes are probable? Political climates shape expectations. Investment is one of the areas in flux. Activist investors of various stripes are pressuring companies to change how they operate. On one hand, some investors push for ever lower costs to reap higher profits. Other activist investors push companies to lessen exposure to environmental risks. Use of targeted media by investor groups to influence customers and regulators has an effect on corporate reputation and freedom to operate. How do your strategies address these kinds of investor pressures that if ignored can challenge the very integrity of the company?

Holistic integration

The world is truly at a crossroads in defining and determining the future of humanity. Viewing current local, regional, and global situations through a single lens is no longer an option. Each of our six lenses for sustainable globalization—**Economic/financial**, **Technology**, **Poverty and inequity**, **Limits to growth**, **Movement of talent**, and **Geopolitical**—is a necessary perspective from which to address some aspects of the complex, interconnected challenges confronting humanity. If we look only from a single perspective, seemingly intractable problems abound, including: resource depletion in energy, food, and water; global warming; widening economic gaps and entrenched poverty; healthcare crises and potential pandemics; high healthcare costs; drug abuse; leadership vacuums and lack of ethics in business; racial, religious, and ethnic siloing; terrorism and war. The "solutions" we have applied in the past have been primarily from only a single discipline (e.g., economics, politics, or the environment), sector (public/private/nonprofit), industry, or region, which are inadequate to cope with these complex challenges.

Systemic, multi-causal, entrenched problems require systemic, long-term solutions that engage all the key constituencies in a deep inquiry into both their sources and their solutions. Fortunately, a number of people and organizations worldwide are beginning to take an overall systems approach. One of those is the Belfer Center for Science and International Affairs at Harvard, whose mission is to "provide leadership in advancing policy-relevant knowledge about the most important challenges of international security and other critical issues where science, technology, environmental policy, and international affairs intersect."[33] This is just one of many resources using a multidisciplinary approach. An ongoing project of The Belfer Center is Science, Technology, and Globalization (STG) that focuses on the nexus of technological innovation, public policies, and social evolution.

As stewards of the planet, it is incumbent on individuals and businesses to develop new interdependent and interdisciplinary/cross-functional models of collaboration to address global issues including climate change, which is rapidly approaching a "point of no return." With a growing world population and increased demands for planetary resources, people must begin to think globally while acting locally in communities and businesses. Start wherever you are now. Take positive actions at an individual as well as an organizational level.

Conclusion

> Don't measure yourself by what you have accomplished, but by what you should have accomplished with your ability.
> (John Wooden, UCLA Basketball Coach, Retired)

Globalization always has been about access to resources and consequently it is also about power and control—who gets to use what resources, how, and where. With a population of 7.4 billion people and rising, globalization and access to resources today is also very much about equity. Doing business, making a living, by plucking resource after resource—whether materials or people, from one region and depositing it, depleted of usefulness, in another region is unsustainable. Sustainable globalization demands that people and their organizations prudently manage essential-to-life resources, and share them equitably. "Business as usual" has been highly dependent on exploitation, waste, and consumption. Any realistic assessment of conditions of our one and only Earth leads to the conclusion that if we want important resources to continue to be available, we must design our lifestyles to include renewing these resources. Privileging of single-bottom-line profits at the expense of people and planet has put humanity on a path hell-bent for disaster.

We conclude this chapter by repeating the question posed by Rajendra Pachuri at the 27th session of the IPCC (Pachauri, 2007, slide 15). If we are to become globally sustainable, "What changes in lifestyles, behavior patterns, and management practices are needed, and by when?"

As each of us asks this important, practical question of ourselves, our business partners, our politicians, scientists, technologists, academics, and educators, we are grounding the process of sustainability in our ordinary activities. It's not enough to ask only once. We must question ourselves relentlessly, vigorously, and openly, each time peeling back a layer, each time filling in new details about those changes and how we can make them real.

We can't puzzle through complex, global, wicked problems that we face today with the same level of thinking that produced them in the first place (hat tip to Albert Einstein). We must peer through our old perceptions as though they were haze rather than walls to see what else is out there. We must confound and break apart our normal thinking channels, open our minds so as to check and verify whether concepts that drive us are actually valid in the context of the globalized world where business must champion sustainability. If we do not, unsustainability-induced fragility will shatter business as we know it.

It's not so easy to unburden ourselves from the hold that standardized worldviews have on us. Our thoughts can be captured more easily than we'd like to believe. When someone says to you, "Don't think of an elephant." What do you do immediately? Think of an elephant! Our thoughts are seized and held in this way, day after day, again and again. We seldom even notice much less monitor this process, in good part because mental models we've adopted preference worldviews of exploitation for profit. Because it's what we've been taught as the road to success, it "rings true." As we explored in Chapter 2 of this book, "Mental models for sustainability," mental models shape what we believe and how we perceive the world. Mental models are the framework for how we make sense of the world. They're insidious because the role they play is to confirm or refute everything we think and do. This "common sense" about the world governs how we participate in globalization, and how we engage with sustainability.

It's important for each of us to know our own tendencies to hold certain concepts as priorities over others. These show themselves both subtly and forcefully in our decisions—personally and professionally. It might help to return to the Mental Models chapter and reread a few of the pieces there, and consider what your own mental models are. Or bump yourself out of ordinary perceptions by donning old 3D glasses, maybe ones accidentally brought home after watching the movie *Avatar* and forgotten. Don't have any of those? Try putting on someone else's prescription glasses upside down and looking in a mirror. It's not quite the same as the crazy mirror in a funhouse but it will do. Unable to see as you normally would, what do you notice? What are you thinking? If you can, try walking around a bit. Do you find yourself hesitating and quickly making an assessment of your position before taking a step? No glasses? On the computer a lot? Find some magic eye tricks online. Look at the dots. Find the patterns. Then try to ignore those patterns and return to seeing random dots. Not so easy? Once we see a solution, just as the thought of an elephant does, it captures and filters our perceptions. If you have a pet, try to imagine looking at the world as a dog might see it, or a cat. Let yourself be drawn in. Then, after you've confounded your perceptions, stay in that state and consider one of the wicked global problems we face and the trailblazing efforts of some of the projects highlighted in this chapter. What do you notice about them that you missed before?

The suggestions above may seem irrelevant or even silly at first glance. They are not. What these exercises are doing is slipping underneath your normal tendencies and thinking modes, and shifting your perceptions and assumptions off kilter just enough that aspects of reality you don't ordinarily notice reveal themselves to you. Disrupting the filters on our perceptions is an effective way of opening up new space for envisioning and rethinking. It allows us to access levels beneath our ordinary, habitual ways of seeing to a deeper awareness where wisdom traditions operate. At these more funda-mental levels of awareness, insights can translate readily from one area of perception to another.

However we do it, revealing our learned preferences for unsustainable "business as usual" practices is crucial to discovering how we can contribute to global sustainability. The leaders of companies highlighted in this chapter all had awareness-raising experiences that changed their perceptions of their business and propelled them to initiate sustainability supportive ventures.

When viewed through a holistic lens from a systems perspective, many of today's unsustainable business practices have surprisingly weak connections to how the natural world actually functions. Fully grasping the business opportunities sustainability presents for your organization requires leaders to see beyond the confines of their traditional mental frameworks and achievements. Only then can leaders recognize that sustainability is not at odds with business success, but instead is the essential foundation of future business prosperity. We have offered some examples in this chapter. The next first steps are up to you. If you want to be a leader who takes part in gener-ating global sustainability, question your assumptions, small and grand. The leaders of businesses featured in this chapter search, assess, question, listen, test, then assess and question again. No one can see these superb opportun-ities if they are looking for them from within the "more, more, faster, faster" business as usual mindset that predominates today. That model obscures sustainability-aligned opportunities from your view.

As good as the current sustainability initiatives of forward-thinking com-panies and their leaders may be, as Eileen Fisher says, they aren't enough. The world needs all of our best efforts. If we are to develop a sustainable world that's not only habitable but prosperous, we all need to "show up."

If we who see the rewards of sustainability and the pitfalls of current mainstream business practices do not show up and speak out, then the power to define and determine the courses of action will remain with the still large numbers of traditional businesses on unsustainable paths. Whether or not what they offer furthers or hinders sustainability, or is even validly founded, is irrelevant because as the only voices on the channels of information they will be the ones heard and followed.

We believe we have outlined major issues of globalization and some means by which organizations can begin to shift their orientation so that they generate solutions. Using the six lenses for sustainable globalization, and the perception shifting exercises by yourself and with your team can jumpstart your creative thinking. There is no magic bullet; the sustainability journey requires leaders to make bold choices, and engage others in real collaboration.

Given the increased awareness surrounding the need for more sustainable solutions, the initiatives presented and their growing momentum gives cause for optimism. There is still a lot more to do. Leaders must champion deep transformations, strategically nurtured, and implemented. Global sustainability depends on business, governments, civil society, and informed people engaging with each other to raise the bar and develop new models of real sustainability. Sharing our resources, we must monitor the condition of the world in the complementary context of these six highly interconnected global lenses so that we can make valid, informed decisions which lead to changes necessary to support sustainability on the local, regional, and global scale.

In our view, sustainability solutions must include all six of these lens realms. Each lens shines a light on some of the keys to achieving fundamental, profound transformations or paradigm shifts in what we think we know (i.e., "the way it is") and consequently what actions are possible where. Those fundamental transformations in our mindsets and values precipitate shifts in assumptions about the need for consumerism, the basis of economic systems, and the effectiveness of management systems.

Whether it's increased air pollution, disruptive cultural memes, or adaptations of disease-causing viruses, the unstoppable force of globalization has ensured that operating in isolation is no longer possible for any of us, no matter where we are. The tentacles of globalization have infiltrated into so much of life today that the choice we are left with is whether we will do what it takes to ensure that the globalization process takes place sustainably, or decline and leave our fate to someone else. We the authors of this book choose to work for sustainability.

While global sustainability has no quick fixes, globalization that furthers sustainability offers great return on investment for enterprise, for society, and for the environment. Global sustainability will only come about if we leverage natural resources, technology, innovation, responsibly and equitably so that we unleash human potential around the world. To do this, we need to make it normal practice to perceive our world inclusively, with all its problems and in all its glory, while envisioning how we can bring about sustainable prosperity across the globe, for all. This is the heart of sustainable globalization.

Notes

1 World population in 2017 is estimated to be just over 7.5 billion and climbing. Current World Population. Retrieved July 18, 2017, from www.worldometers. info/world-population/.

2 How can companies integrate sustainable development goals? (October 12, 2015). Retrieved June 29, 2016, from www.theguardian.com/sustainable-business/2015/ oct/12/united-nations-sdg-un-global-compact-sustainability-world-business-council.

3 Empowering communities by turning waste into opportunity. Retrieved June 29, 2016, from http://net-works.com/.

4 A Conversation with Eileen Fisher, Sustainable Brands. (May 26, 2016). Retrieved May 26, 2016, from www.sustainablebrands.com/digital_learning/event_video/ brand_innovation/conversation_eileen_fisher.

5 How I Did It: Eileen Fisher. As told to Liz Welch. (November 1, 2010). Retrieved, June 30, 2016, from www.inc.com/magazine/20101101/how-i-did-it-eileen-fisher. html.

6 Private conversation between author and Amy Hall, Director of Social Consciousness, EILEEN FISHER (July 19, 2016).

7 Private correspondence with Amy Hall, Director of Social Consciousness, EILEEN FISHER (July 18, 2016).

8 Traffic control: What we can learn from ants. (April 22, 2015). Retrieved July 12, 2016, from www.sciencedaily.com/releases/2015/04/150422084350.htm.

9 China's elevated bus: Futuristic "straddling bus" hits the road. (August 3, 2016). Retrieved August 3, 2016, from www.bbc.com/news/world-asia-china-36961433.

10 Highway jam enters its 9th day, spans 100 km. Retrieved July 5, 2016, from http:// news.xinhuanet.com/english2010/china/2010-08/23/c_13457295.htm.

11 charity:water projects. Retrieved July 24, 2016, from www.charitywater.org/ projects/#stat-info-3.

12 More bread for the baking. (January 23, 2015). Retrieved July 24, 2016, from https://medium.com/charity-water/more-bread-for-the-baking-cff67702f525# .i6i2wyu9a.

13 Global Wealth Report 2015. Credit Suisse. (2015, October). Retrieved August 1, 2016, from https://publications.credit-suisse.com/tasks/render/ file/?fileID=F2425415-DCA7-80B8-EAD989AF9341D47E.

14 Personal communications with Kelley, L.M. (aka Delia Lake in Second Life[R]). (January 9, 2008).

15 The Zabaleen of Garbage City. Retrieved July 25, 2016, from www.peterdench. com/the-zabaleen-of-garbage-city.

16 Electronic waste in Ghana. Retrieved August 9, 2016, from www.theworldcounts. com/counters/waste_pollution_facts/electronic_waste_facts.

17 Overfishing. Retrieved July 1, 2017, from www.worldwildlife.org/threats/ overfishing.

18 Current world population. Retrieved July 1, 2017, from www.worldometers.info/ world-population/.

19 adidas and Parley for the Oceans stop the industry's waiting game. (December 8, 2015). Retrieved August 21, 2016, from http://news.adidas.com/US/Latest-News/ALL/adidas-and-Parley-for-the-Oceans-Stop-the-Industry-s-Waiting-Game/s/770e492e-544f-4eda-9b8b-f9e2596569b1.

20 Bionic[R] transforms recovered plastic into durable materials. Retrieved August 25, 2015, from www.bionicyarn.com/about.html.

21 Massive sinkhole leaks more than 200 million gallons of radioactive water from fertilizer plant into Florida's main source of drinking water (but plant owners insist there's no risk!). (September 17, 2016). Retrieved September 21, 2016, from www.dailymail.co.uk/news/article-3794074/Sinkhole-Florida-fertilizer-plant-leaks-200-million-gallons-radioactive-water.html.

22 Phosphorus supply and demand. (2016). Retrieved September 7, 2016, from http://web.mit.edu/12.000/www/m2016/finalwebsite/problems/phosphorus.html.

23 Earth's temperature record (graphic). Retrieved September 18, 2016, from http://climate.nasa.gov/climate_resources/9/.

24 The Future We Want – Outcome document. Retrieved September 21, 2016, from https://sustainabledevelopment.un.org/futurewewant.html.

25 A complex nexus. Retrieved March 7, 2017, from www.iom.int/complex-nexus.

26 How many expats are there worldwide? Retrieved October 1, 2016, from www.theexpatblog.com/how-many-expats-are-there-worldwide/.

27 Unprecedented 65 million people displaced by war and persecution in 2015— UN. (June 26, 2016). Retrieved September 29, 2016, from www.un.org/apps/news/story.asp?NewsID=54269#.WXD8S7LqKUk.

28 Fact sheet on current MDG progress of Rwanda (Africa) (December 5, 2015). Retrieved November 26, 2016, from www.mdgmonitor.org/mdg-progress-rwanda-africa/.

29 List of largest cities throughout history. Retrieved February 3, 2017, from https://en.wikipedia.org/wiki/List_of_largest_cities_throughout_history.

30 Internet World Stats. Retrieved September 30, 2017, from www.internetworldstats.com/stats.htm.

31 Internet World Stats. Retrieved September 30, 2017, from www.internetworldstats.com/stats.htm.

32 Interview with Walter Issacson, Aspen Institute for *The Atlantic*'s Washington Ideas Forum, Wednesday, September 28, 2016.

33 Harvard Kennedy School, Belfer Center for Science and International Affairs. Retrieved May 18, 2018, from www.belfercenter.org/about.

References

17 UN Sustainable Development Goals. (n.d.). Retrieved May 16, 2016, from www.undp.org/content/undp/en/home/sdgoverview/post-2015-development-agenda.html.

Aguirre, I. (2015, June 12). Cairo's "Zabaleen" garbage collectors: Egypt's diamond in the rough. Retrieved July 30, 2016, from http://globalriskinsights.com/2015/06/cairos-zabaleen-garbage-collectors-egypts-diamond-in-the-rough/.

Alvarez, S., & Barney, J. B. (2006). *Toward a creation theory of entrepreneurial opportunity formation*. Retrieved January 30, 2008, from www.cefe.net/forum/Creation_Theory.pdf.

Ben-Ari, N. (2014, April). Big dreams for Rwanda's ICT sector. Retrieved November 20, 2016, from www.un.org/africarenewal/magazine/april-2014/big-dreams-rwanda%E2%80%99s-ict-sector.

Chan, D., & Wu, Q. (2015, August 28). Significant anthropogenic-induced changes of climate classes since 1950. Scientific Reports 5, Article number: 13487. Retrieved July 3, 2017, from www.nature.com/articles/srep13487#f2.

Chaplin, C. (n.d.). The Final Speech from *The Great Dictator*. Retrieved July 17, 2017, from www.charliechaplin.com/en/articles/29-The-Final-Speech-from-The-Great-Dictator-.

Chipman, J. (2016, September). Why your company needs a foreign policy. Retrieved September 18, 2016, from https://hbr.org/2016/09/why-your-company-needs-a-foreign-policy.

Counts, R. (2016, June 16). The Local Motors Olli is a driverless EV minibus with IBM Watson inside. Retrieved July 1, 2016, from www.autoblog.com/2016/06/16/local-motors-olli-autonomous-shuttle/.

Dabla-Norris, E., Kochlar, K., Suphaphiphat, N., Ricka, F., & Tsounta, E. (2015, June). Causes and consequences of income inequality: A global perspective. Retrieved August 15, 2017, from www.imf.org/external/pubs/ft/sdn/2015/sdn1513.pdf, p. 4.

Dickerson, K. (2015, May 12). The world's lust for new technology is creating "hell on Earth" in Inner Mongolia. Retrieved August 9, 2016, from www.businessinsider.com/the-worlds-tech-waste-lake-in-mongolia-2015-5.

Earth Overshoot Day. (n.d.). Retrieved June 20, 2017, from www.overshootday.org/.

Elkington, J. (2012, February 29). Your grandchildren have no value. Retrieved June 30, 2017, from www.theguardian.com/sustainable-business/sustainability-with-john-elkington/investors-longterm-sustainable-finance.

Franklin, B. (n.d.). *Poor Richard's Almanac, preface (1758)*. Retrieved July 10, 2016, from https://founders.archives.gov/documents/Franklin/01-07-02-0146.

George, K. (2016, June 7). adidas x Parley: From fishnets to footwear in just a year. Retrieved August 25, 2016, from www.gameplan-a.com/2016/06/adidas-x-parley-from-fishnets-to-footwear-in-just-a-year/?section=main.

Guenard, M. (2013, November 13). Cairo puts its faith in ragpickers to manage the city's waste problem. Retrieved August 1, 2016, from www.theguardian.com/world/2013/nov/19/cairo-ragpickers-zabaleen-egypt-recycling.

Harris, J. (2018, January 25). Accessible Olli: The driverless shuttle that adapts to your age and ability. Retrieved May 18, 2018, from https://sanvada.com/2018/01/25/accessible-olli-driverless-shuttle-adapts-age-ability/.

Hart, S. L. (2007, March 12). *Capitalism at the crossroads: Aligning business, earth & humanity* (2nd ed.). Upper Saddle River, NJ: Wharton School Publishing.

Hawken, P. (2005). *The ecology of commerce*. New York: Collins Business.

Hill, K. T., Crone, P. R., Corval, E., & Macewicz, B. (2016, March 16). Assessment of the Pacific Sardine Resource in 2016 for USA Management in 2016–17. Retrieved August 10, 2016, from www.pcouncil.org/wp-content/uploads/2016/03/H1a_2016_Sardine_Update_Assmt_FullElectricOnly_APR2016BB.pdf.

Hill, L., & Butera, S. (2016, May 19). Exploding lake, blood-laden drones spur Rwanda's tech boom. Retrieved November 23, 2016, from www.bloomberg.com/news/articles/2016-05-19/exploding-lake-volcano-skirting-drones-spur-rwanda-tech-boom.

Howarth, D. (2016, June 8). adidas launches trainers made from ocean plastic with Parley for the Oceans. Retrieved August 26, 2016, from www.dezeen.com/2016/06/08/adidas-trainers-parley-for-the-ocean-plastic-design-recycling/.

Intergovernmental Panel on Climate Change (IPCC). (2007). Retrieved June 5, 2016, from www.ipcc.ch/pdf/presentations/valencia-2007–11/pachauri-17-november-2007.pdf.

Intergovernmental Panel on Climate Change (IPCC). (2014). Climate Change 2014, synthesis report. Retrieved July 23, 2017, from www.ipcc.ch/pdf/assessment-report/ar5/syr/SYR_AR5_FINAL_full_wcover.pdf.

Kaberuka, D. (2000, July). Vision 2020 Rwanda. Retrieved November 20, 2016, from www.sida.se/globalassets/global/countries-and-regions/africa/rwanda/d402331a.pdf.

Kadduri, A. (2015, May 26). Turning waste into wealth with Cairo's garbage people. Retrieved July 24, 2016, from www.yourmiddleeast.com/culture/turning-waste-into-wealth-with-cairos-garbage-people-photos_31874.

McGregor, J. (2017, February 2). The art of a China deal. Reciprocity and the Trump Pacific Partnership. Retrieved February 3, 2017, from www.chinafile.com/view-point/art-of-china-deal#sthash.HZkSsYem.dpuf.

Meadows, D. H., Meadows, D. L., & Randers, J. (2004). *Limits to growth: The 30-year update* (paperback ed.). White River Junction, VT: Chelsea Green.

Mensley, M. (2017, May 17). 10 coolest 3D printed cars. Retrieved July 1, 2016, from https://all3dp.com/3d-printed-car/.

Pachauri, R. K. (2007, November 17). *IPCC fourth assessment report, synthesis report.* PowerPoint presentation given at the 27th session of the Intergovernmental Panel on Climate Change. Retrieved January 6, 2008, from www.ipcc.ch/graphics/presentations.htm.

Parker, L. (2015, January 11). Ocean trash: 5.25 trillion pieces and counting, but big questions remain. Retrieved August 18, 2016, from http://news.nationalgeographic.com/news/2015/01/150109-oceans-plastic-sea-trash-science-marine-debris/.

Payne, C. (2015, April 3). China's massive toxic lake will make you question buying another electronic device. Retrieved August 9, 2016, from http://inhabitat.com/chinas-massive-toxic-lake-will-make-you-question-buying-another-electronic-device/.

Prahalad, C. K., & Hart, S. L. (2002, 1st quarter). The fortune at the bottom of the pyramid. *Strategy + Business, 26,* 54–67. Retrieved February 3, 2008, from www.cs.berkeley.edu/~brewer/ict4b/ Fortune-BoP.pdf.

Principles for Responsible Investment. (n.d.). Retrieved September 25, 2016, from www.unpri.org/.

Ramsey, L. (2015, August 3). Scientists found an ingenious way to cut down on a hidden source of one of the most harmful air pollutants. Retrieved June 29, 2016, from http://scalingupnutrition.org/the-sun-network/business-network.

Rohrig, B. (2015, April). Smartphones, smart chemistry. Retrieved August 9, 2016, from www.acs.org/content/dam/acsorg/education/resources/highschool/chemmatters/archive/chemmatters-april2015-smartphones.pdf.

Romm, J. (2015, September 3). New study shows how climate change is already reshaping the earth. Retrieved August 22, 2016, from https://thinkprogress.org/new-study-shows-how-climate-change-is-already-reshaping-the-earth-ef9c83c97799#.exfvd6z8x.

Sachs, J. D. (2005). *The end of poverty.* New York: Penguin Books.

Sennett, R. (1977). *The fall of public man.* New York: Alfred K. Knopf, Inc.

Shirley, A. (2016, May 12). Which are the world's most polluted cities? Retrieved July 13, 2016, from www.weforum.org/agenda/2016/05/which-are-the-world-s-most-polluted-cities/.

Shukla, P., & Cantwell, J. (2016). Migrants and the foreign expansion of firms. *Rutgers Business Review, 1*(1), 44–56. Retrieved July 10, 2017, from www.rbusinessreview.org/rbr010103.

Steinbeck, J. (1945). *Cannery row*. New York: Viking Press.

SUN Business Network. (n.d.). Retrieved June 29, 2016, from http://scalingupnutrition.org/the-sun-network/business-network.

Timalsina, N. (2016, June 27). From nightclub promoter to CEO: Scott Harrison, founder of charity:water. Retrieved July 24, 2016, from https://medium.com/startup-grind/from-drug-addict-to-ceo-the-incredible-journey-of-scott-harrison-founder-of-charity-water-a1e9e89d6422#.t69c01w8m.

Transforming our world. (n.d.). The 2030 Agenda for Sustainable Development. Sustainable Development Knowledge Platform. Retrieved June 25, 2016, from https://sustainabledevelopment.un.org/post2015/transformingourworld.

Tumwebaze, P. (2018, January 3). 4G internet network coverage reaches all districts—KT Rwanda. Retrieved May 20, 2018, from www.newtimes.co.rw/section/read/226815.

United Nations Global Compact. (n.d.). Our global strategy. Retrieved September 18, 2016, from www.unglobalcompact.org/what-is-gc/strategy.

Vision 2020. (n.d.). Retrieved June 30, 2017, from www.eileenfisher.com/vision-2020/.

Water Cooperation 2013. (n.d.). Retrieved July 14, 2016, from www.unwater.org/water-cooperation-2013/water-cooperation/facts-and-figures/en/.

Willard, B. (2005). *The next sustainability wave: Building boardroom buy-in*. Gabriola Island, BC, Canada: New Society Publishers.

Wooden, J. (n.d.). Quotes. Retrieved June 8, 2016, from www.goodreads.com/author/quotes/23041.John_Wooden?page=2.

Further reading

Airbus APWorks launches the "Light Rider": the world's first 3D-printed motorcycle. (2016, May 19). Retrieved July 10, 2016, from www.airbusgroup.com/int/en/news-media/press-releases/Airbus-Group/Financial_Communication/2016/05/en_APWorks-Launch-Light-Rider.html.

American Management Association (AMA). (2007). *Creating a sustainable future: A global study of current trends and possibilities 2007–2017*. New York: American Management Association.

Best, J. (n.d.). IBM Watson wowed the tech industry and a corner of US pop culture with its 2011 win against two of Jeopardy's greatest champions. Here's how IBM pulled it off and a look at what Watson's real career is going to be. Retrieved July 20, 2016, from www.techrepublic.com/article/ibm-watson-the-inside-story-of-how-the-jeopardy-winning-supercomputer-was-born-and-what-it-wants-to-do-next/.

Bromwich, J. E. (2017, June 25). Extreme heat scorches Southern Arizona. Retrieved June 25, 2017, from www.nytimes.com/2017/06/25/us/extreme-heat-scorches-southern-arizona.html?mcubz=1.

Business and the Sustainable Development Goals—Paul Polman, Unilever CEO. We Mean Business Coalition. (2016, November 5). Retrieved May 22, 2017, from www.youtube.com/watch?v=GuTPQGPq91M.

Carnegie Mellon University Africa. (n.d.). Retrieved November 22, 2016, from www.cmu.edu/rwanda/.

charity:water. (n.d.). Retrieved June 17, 2016, from www.charitywater.org/about/.

charity:water project partners. (n.d.). Retrieved August 4, 2016, from www.charitywater.org/projects/partners/.

Cho, R. (2013, April 1). Phosphorus: Essential to life—are we running out? http://blogs.ei.columbia.edu/2013/04/01/phosphorus-essential-to-life-are-we-running-out/.

Choi, C. Q. (2016, March 27). New ultrathin solar cells are light enough to sit on a soap bubble. Retrieved July 1, 2016, from www.livescience.com/54192-ultrathin-lightweight-solar-cells.html.

Compact of Mayors. (n.d.). Retrieved July 7, 2016 from www.compactofmayors.org/.

Conversation with Vijay Mahajan. Knowledg@Wharton, edited transcript. (2017, January 26). The growing clout of rural consumers. Retrieved March 10, 2017, from http://knowledge.wharton.upenn.edu/article/why-companies-need-to-understand-rural-markets-in-developing-countries/?utm_source=kw_newsletter&utm_medium=email&utm_campaign=2017-01-26.

Do your best work with Watson. (n.d.). Retrieved July 1, 2016, from www.ibm.com/cognitive/outthink/stories/?S_PKG=&S_TACT=C34403XW&campaign=IBM%20Cognitive_UN&group=Watson%20Cognitive_UN&mkwid=99eb2ee9-c44d-4844-8a49-f9303c5df1c4|447|972128217&ct=C34403XW&iio=CHQ&cmp=C3440&ck=watson%20cognitive&cs=b&ccy=US&cr=google&cm=k&cn=Watson%20Cognitive_UN.

DSM. (n.d.). Retrieved June 29, 2016, from www.dsm.com/corporate/sustainability/nutrition/partnerships.html.

DSM. (n.d.). Retrieved June 29, 2016, from www.dsm.com/corporate/sustainability/our-operations.html.

DSM. (n.d.). Retrieved June 29, 2016, from www.dsm.com/products/ecopaxx/en_US/cases/water-faucet-mixing-valves.html.

Earth Overshoot Day 2017 lands on August 2. (n.d.). The Footprint Network. Retrieved July 21, 2017, from www.footprintnetwork.org/ecological_footprint_nations/ecological_per_capita.html.

Examination stranded sperm whale: Found large quantities of plastic waste in the stomachs—Environment Minister Habeck: "This reminds us that we step up the fight against waste in the sea." (2016, March 23). Retrieved August 19, 2016, from www.nationalpark-wattenmeer.de/sh/misc/untersuchung-der-gestrandeten-pottwale-grosse-mengen-plastikmull-den-magen-gefunden.

Fernholz, T. (2014, February 25). More people around the world have cell phones than ever had landlines. Retrieved August 8, 2016, from http://qz.com/179897/more-people-around-the-world-have-cell-phones-than-ever-had-land-lines/.

Florida, R. (2005, October). The world in numbers. The world is spiky. Globalization has changed the economic playing field, but it hasn't levelled it. Retrieved March 1, 2017, from www.theatlantic.com/past/docs/images/issues/200510/world-is-spiky.pdf.

Food, energy, and water systems (FEWS) are interconnected, interdependent, and complex. (n.d.). Retrieved July 20, 2017, from https://collections.elementascience.org/food-energy-water-systems/.

Gettleman, J. (2013, September 4). The global elite's favorite strongman. Retrieved November 4, 2016, from www.nytimes.com/2013/09/08/magazine/paul-kagame-rwanda.html?_r=0.

Global Transportation Study to Improve City Transport. (n.d.). Retrieved July 10, 2016, from www.xerox.com/en-us/services/transportation-solutions.

Global Wealth Report 2015. Credit Suisse. (2015, October). Retrieved August 1, 2016, from https://publications.credit-suisse.com/tasks/render/file/?fileID=F2425415-DCA7-80B8-EAD989AF9341D47E.

How is the "integrated and indivisible" nature of the Sustainable Development goals being implemented by national governments? (n.d.) Retrieved September 22, 2016, from http://ecoagriculture.org/blog/one-year-in-sdgs-progress/.

Human Development Index. (n.d.). Retrieved August 10, 2016, from http://hdr.undp.org/en/content/human-development-index-hdi.

Humanity's voracious consumption of natural resources unsustainable—UN report. (2011, May 12). Retrieved June 19, 2016, from https://news.un.org/en/story/2011/05/374942-humanitys-voracious-consumption-natural-resources-unsustainable-un-report.

In black phosphorus, engineers look for the future of electronics and optoelectronics in this new 2D material. (2014, July 25). Retrieved August 31, 2016, from http://seas.yale.edu/news-events/news/black-phosphorus-engineers-look-future-electronics-and-optoelectronics-new-2d-mater.

Infertile Crescent, the roasting of the Middle East. (2016, August 6). Retrieved September 22, 2016, from www.economist.com/news/middle-east-and-africa/21703269-more-war-climate-change-making-region-hard-live-infertile.

Julien, M. (2016, June 5). Airbus presents 3D-printed mini aircraft. Retrieved July 10, 2016, from http://phys.org/news/2016-06-airbus-3d-printed-mini-aircraft.html.

Khanna, P. (2016). *Connectography: Mapping the future of global civilization.* New York: Random House.

Khanna, P. (2016, March/April). These twenty five companies are more powerful than many countries, going stateless to maximize profits, multinational companies are vying with governments for global power. Retrieved October 14, 2016, from http://foreignpolicy.com/2016/03/15/these-25-companies-are-more-powerful-than-many-countries-multinational-corporate-wealth-power/.

Latest Resilience News. (n.d.). Retrieved March 5, 2017, from www.100resilientcities.org/.

Leach, A. (2014, January 29). Rwanda's next education: Teacher training and employability. Retrieved November 25, 2016, from www.theguardian.com/global-development-professionals-network/2014/jan/29/rwanda-education-teacher-training-youth-unemployment.

Leggett, M. (2011, May 12). Mankind needs to do more with less, says new UN report. Retrieved June 19, 2016, from www.earthtimes.org/politics/mankind-more-with-less-un-report/833/.

Leleux, B., & van der Kaaij, J. (2014, August). Darwinians at the gate. Retrieved June 26, 2016, from www.imd.org/research/challenges/TC061-14-darwinians-at-the-gate-leleux-vanderkaaij.cfm.

List of mobile phone makers by country. (n.d.). Retrieved August 8, 2016, from https://en.wikipedia.org/wiki/List_of_mobile_phone_makers_by_country.

Local Motors debuts "Olli", the first self-driving vehicle to tap the power of IBM (2016, June 17). Retrieved July 1, 2016, from www.youtube.com/watch?v=K564rXrlZbc.

Military experts: Climate change could lead to humanitarian crisis. (2016, December 1). Retrieved January 27, 2017, from http://eciu.net/press-releases/2016/military-experts-climate-change-could-lead-to-humanitarian-crisis.

Miller, A., & Lim, J. (2015, May 28). Creature feature: Ants don't have traffic jams. Retrieved July 11, 2016, from https://blog.education.nationalgeographic.com/2015/05/28/creature-feature-ants-dont-have-traffic-jams/.

Nicholson, B. (2017, July 15). Drought in high plains the worst some farmers have ever seen. Retrieved July 15, 2017, from www.washingtonpost.com/national/drought-in-high-plains-the-worst-some-farmers-have-ever-seen/2017/07/15/637f3fc0-696b-11e7-94ab-5b1f0ff459df_story.html?tid=ss_tw&utm_campaign=crowdfire&utm_content=crowdfire&utm_medium=social&utm_source=twitter&utm_term=.45c4f67719d3#350509998-tw#1500170171291.

Nickel, R. (2016, September 20). Florida sinkhole to cost Mosaic up to $50 million to fix. Retrieved September 20, 2016, from www.reuters.com/article/us-mosaic-sinkhole-idUSKCN11Q26P.

Nike Reuse-a-shoe FAQS. (n.d.). Retrieved August 18, 2016, from http://help-en-eu.nike.com/app/answers/detail/a_id/39600/p/3897.

Northman, J. (2015, April 16). Feds cancel commercial sardine fishing after stocks crash. Retrieved August 10, 2016, from www.npr.org/sections/thetwo-way/2015/04/16/400177895/feds-place-commercial-sardine-fishing-on-hold-for-more-than-a-year.

On Nauru, a sinking feeling—*New York Times* op-ED by "drowning island" Nauru's president. (n.d.). Retrieved September 13, 2016, from https://brookmeakins.wordpress.com/2011/07/19/on-nauru-a-sinking-feeling-new-york-times-op-ed-by-drowning-island-naurus-president/.

Our Common Journey. (1999). Retrieved June 29, 2016, from www.nap.edu/download/9690, p. 24.

Our Vision and Strategy. (n.d.). Retrieved June 29, 2016, from www.dsm.com/corporate/sustainability/vision-and-strategy.html.

Peace River Natural History. (n.d.). Retrieved September 14, 2016, from www.swfwmd.state.fl.us/education/interactive/peaceriver/natural.php.

Pearce, F. (2011, July 7). Phosphate: A critical resource misused and now running low. Retrieved September 1, 2016, from http://e360.yale.edu/feature/phosphate_a_critical_resource_misused_and_now_running_out/2423/.

Phosphorus. (n.d.). Retrieved September 13, 2016, from http://umm.edu/health/medical/altmed/supplement/phosphorus.

Pinsky, M. L., Jensen, O. P., Ricard, D., & Palumbi, S. R. (2010, October 12). Unexpected patterns of fisheries collapse in the world's oceans. Retrieved August 10, 2016, from www.pnas.org/content/108/20/8317.abstract.

PlasticsEurope and SPE celebrate the excellence of plastics: Winners of the First European Plastics Innovation Awards announced. (n.d.). Retrieved June 29, 2016, from www.plasticseurope.org/information-centre/press-releases/press-releases-2016/plasticseurope-and-spe-celebrate-the-excellence-of-plastics-winners-of-the-first-european-plastics-innovation-awards-announced.aspx.

Pledge 3: Is your country an ecological creditor or debtor? Become a natural resources expert. (n.d.). Retrieved August 8, 2016, from www.overshootday.org/portfolio/creditor-debtor/.

Prahalad, C. K. (2006). *The fortune at the bottom of the pyramid* (paperback ed.). Upper Saddle River, NJ: Wharton School Publishing, pp. 169–185.

Raccagni, S. (2015, July 2). In balance. Ocean, climate, and life—if you get the chance to shape the future, jump on it. Retrieved August 26, 2016, from www.gameplan-a.com/2015/07/ocean-climate-and-life-if-you-get-the-chance-to-shape-the-future-jump-on-it/.

Rare Earth Element. (n.d.). Retrieved August 9, 2016, from https://en.wikipedia.org/wiki/Rare_earth_element#Global_rare_earth_production.

Raworth, K. (n.d.). Can we live inside the doughnut? Why the world needs planetary and social boundaries. Retrieved July 10, 2016, from https://blogs.oxfam.org/en/blog/12-02-13-can-we-live-inside-doughnut-why-world-needs-planetary-and-social-boundaries.

Recycling heroes: The Zabbaleen of Cairo. (2014, March 3). Retrieved July 30, 2016, from www.organicstream.org/2014/03/03/recycling-heroes-the-zabbaleen-of-cairo/.

Rhodes, M. (2016, June 6). adidas spins plastic from the ocean into awesome kicks. Retrieved August 27, 2016, from www.wired.com/2016/06/adidass-newest-shoe-made-recycled-ocean-plastic/.

Rosen, J. W. (2015, April 16). Lake Kivu's great gas gamble. Retrieved November 10, 2016, from www.technologyreview.com/s/536656/lake-kivus-great-gas-gamble/.

Route 66's asphalt to be replaced with light up glass solar panels you can drive on. (2016, June 23). Retrieved July 4, 2016, from http://tribunist.com/technology/route-66s-asphalt-to-be-replaced-with-light-up-glass-solar-panels-you-can-drive-on/.

Running Shoe. (n.d.). Retrieved August 18, 2016, from www.madehow.com/Volume-1/Running-Shoe.html.

Rwanda Summer 2011. (n.d.). Retrieved November 22, 2016, from http://gsl.mit.edu/program/rwanda-summer-2011/.

Sassen, S. (2006). *Territory, authority, rights, from medieval to global assemblages.* Princeton, NJ: Princeton University Press, pp. 408–411.

Science, Technology, and Globalization (STG). (n.d.). Retrieved July 10, 2017, from www.belfercenter.org/project/science-technology-and-globalization/publication.

Shukla, P. R., & Skea, J. (IPCC WG-III Co-chairs). IPCC AR6, the Special Report on 1.5°C and the IAM community. Energy Modelling Forum Snowmass 2016. (2016, July 22). Retrieved February 2, 2017, from www.ipcc-wg3.ac.uk/Presentations/20160722%20Snowmass%20IPCC%20WG%20final.pdf.

Small, A. (2016, September 29). Why GE moved to Boston, according to its CEO. Retrieved September 30, 2016, from www.citylab.com/work/2016/09/why-ge-moved-from-bridgeport-to-boston-atlantic-ideas-forum/502061/.

Smit, S., Remes, J., Manyika, J., Roxburgh, C., & Restrepo, A. (2011). Urban world: Mapping the economic power of cities. Report, McKinsey Global Institute. Retrieved October 23, 2016, from www.mckinsey.com/global-themes/urbanization/urban-world-mapping-the-economic-power-of-cities.

"The Architecture of Collapse" and the rising instability of the global system. (2016, June 23). Retrieved July 1, 2017, from http://knowledge.wharton.upenn. edu/article/160614c_kwradio_guillen/?utm_source=kw_newsletter&utm_ medium=email&utm_campaign=2016-06-23.

The Global Transportation System. (n.d.). Retrieved July 1, 2017, from http:// globaia.org/portfolio/cartography-of-the-anthropocene/.

These African economies have just made entrepreneurship easier. World Bank. (2016, October 25). Retrieved November 25, 2016, from www.cnbcafrica.com/ news/2016/10/25/africa-reforms-to-make-doing-business-easier/.

This American Life. (2003, December 5). Retrieved September 14, 2016, from www. thisamericanlife.org/radio-archives/episode/253/the-middle-of-nowhere?act= 1#play.

Toly, N. J., & Tabory, S. (2016, October 13). 100 top economies: Urban influence and the position of cities in an evolving world order. Retrieved October 23, 2016, from www.thechicagocouncil.org/publication/100-top-economies-urban-influence-and-position-cities-evolving-world-order.

United Nations, General Assembly, Sixty-eighth session. (2013, October 1). Retrieved September 22, 2016, from www.un.org/en/ga/search/view_doc.asp?symbol=A/ 68/L.4.

von Thron, L. A. (2016, June 13). This company uses 3D printing to make foldable performance bikes. Retrieved July 10, 2016, from www.si.com/tech-media/2016/ 06/13/3d-print-foldable-performance-bike.

WatsonPaths. (n.d.). Retrieved July 1, 2016, from www.research.ibm.com/cognitive-computing/watson/watsonpaths.shtml#fbid=8CRgf3T-ykH.

We are happy with our results. (2016, April 26). Geraldine Matchett, DSM CFO. Retrieved June 26, 2016, from http://video.cnbc.com/gallery/?video=3000512686.

Wet Bulb Temperature vs Heat Index. (n.d.). Retrieved August 30, 2016, from www. srh.noaa.gov/tsa/?n=wbgt.

Why cities? Ending climate change begins in the city. (n.d.). Retrieved March 4, 2017, from www.c40.org/ending-climate-change-begins-in-the-city.

World Population Data Sheet 2014. (2014, August). Retrieved January 20, 2017, from www.prb.org/Publications/Datasheets/2014/2014-world-population-data-sheet/ data-sheet.aspx.

World's population increasingly urban with more than half living in urban areas. (2014, 10 July). Retrieved February 3, 2017, from www.un.org/en/development/ desa/news/population/world-urbanization-prospects-2014.html.

Yao, S.-L., Luo, J.-J., Huang, G., & Wang, P. (2017, June 12). Distinct global warming rates tied to multiple ocean surface temperature changes. *Nature Climate Change, 7*, 486–491. doi:10.1038/nclimate3304. Retrieved July 15, 2017, from www.nature. com/nclimate/journal/v7/n7/full/nclimate3304.html.

Sustainability models for collaboration, technology, and community

Linda M. Kelley, Jenny Ambrozek, Victoria G. Axelrod, and William G. Russell

Are people the next artifacts of a throwaway culture?

"The Archaeology of Another Possible Future" is ensconced in a cavernous hall of the former Sprague Electric factory, repurposed to the MassMoCA museum. Artist Liz Glynn has wrenched ordinary discards of our modernity from where they have settled on the sidelines of our lives, invisible to us in the background yet ever-present. Much like bone and shell middens of ancient times piled higher than high by generations of consumers, stacks of wooden shipping pallets distressed from use form hollow pyramids that hold formerly desired treasures. The torn felt of old damper blankets, a cassette recorder set on looped play, now uselessly calling out. Turn around and you are confronted with a metal doorframe, jammed full of old window fans, broken bicycles and scooters, vacuum cleaners, utensils, and all manner of cheap discards—each a marvel of technology in its time.

And then there are the shipping containers, cum office cubicles. Emblazoned with well-known names like Hanjin, and Capital Lease, these world travelers bring us all the hard and soft goods we've been trained to want. Walk through carefully; scattered around the floor are fraying balls of silver wire, like so much electronic tumbleweed that does not turn to dust. Immersion in a sea of artifacts that we normally ignore on an enormous scale can be overwhelming, and it was to some who filled the exhibit opening (October 7, 2017). As art so often does, these constructs of castoffs from our pervasive consumer culture wipe clean the window of our perceptions.

> Glynn asks, what happens to people? How do we reconcile our physical existence in a time when capital is traded in milliseconds via complex algorithms, and when pure ideas and digital currencies create and carry more value than old-line manufacturing or the trading of commodities?
>
> (Posted Exhibit Foreword, MassMoCA, October, 2017)

Yes, the people. It's becoming more and more clear that what happens to the people will be determined by how fully we embrace the principles of sustainability in our values and in our actions.

Inventing our sustainable future

People are nothing if not inventive. From small band beginnings, people have spread around the globe inventing cultures, establishing settlements, and doing business along the way. This overwhelming success, though, has put humanity at a crossroads where sustainability now vies with unsustainability, and frankly the outcome for us is uncertain. In this *Fieldbook* we endeavor to lay out some essential areas where we must generate and grow sustainability's foundations. This chapter builds on work in previous chapters to tease out pathways toward a future where humanity is not only sustained but thrives. We focus on four critical areas that we believe are essential to shifts that will make or break humanity's sustainable future: integrated thinking, collaboration, supportive technology, and transformative business models. It would be a mistake to separate these areas into isolated categories distinct and circumscribed. As with the previous chapter on sustainable globalization, collaboration, supportive technology, and transformative business models are best thought of as lenses where that particular focus highlights and clarifies the importance of what you are seeing to the whole. Because of this, you will find that innovative technologies show up in discussion about collaboration, and stories about community are interwoven with technology and sustainable business.

In everything you read here, look for the interconnections, and look for the white spaces—those spaces where disruption and invention can happen. When something prompts an idea that relates to your business, or your community, pause and make yourself a note. Because of inherent interconnections, the organization of this chapter is more circular than linear. Our objective for the chapter is to inspire people to get in action, leading and collaborating to co-create a sustainable future. Consider for a minute where you believe we are today and how we got ourselves there, because if where we are isn't where we want to be, only we can change it. People are the drivers of sustainability. Business is their engine. Now is the time for us as designers of engines to step up and resolve some of humanity's most pressing problems.

Over the past few years the world has suffered numerous severe environmental events, some of them catastrophic. The best climate science of our time warns that Earth's climate is warming. If climate instability becomes the norm, we will face many risks we haven't experienced before. How are you factoring these kinds of events into your risk assessments and strategic plans? Or are you not? When is the last time you took a real look at your own risk factors? When is the last time you challenged and revalidated assumptions that underlie your business decisions? What about those things you take for granted, the ones that have turned into blind spots that you always skip over? Those are the things that prevent fully recognizing interconnectedness and interdependencies, risks, and also opportunities for building sustainability.

If you haven't owned up to your business risks you can't really own your business. 2017 saw extreme weather across the globe. Each major event left wide-spread destruction in its wake. It's likely that damage costs to Houston from Hurricane Harvey alone will be upward of $100 billion. The common response is yeah, but that stuff isn't going to happen to me. How many homeowners in Santa Rosa, California thought their entire neighborhood would be wiped out overnight by raging fires? How many Napa and Sonoma wineries foresaw the extreme degree to which they were at ruinous risk?

Where have you and your business taken conditions and relationships for granted? How critical are those to your business strategies and operations? Without answers to these questions, you can't make a realistic assessment of where, how, and what your risk exposure is. The good news is that revealing risks also reveals opportunities. Most of us do a decent job of planning for slow, controlled change. These massive environmental events were neither slow in coming nor controlled. Preparation for far-reaching change that happens quickly takes more than the usual planning. It takes a shift in mindset to include responding to rapid change. Much like it is for a top sports player to anticipate a variety of situations, it's important to practice for these different scenarios. You can't learn the mix of skills you'll need on the fly and expect to be as effective as you need to be.

It's not just climate risks though. Resource exploitation over many years has created other problems as well. What if you could no longer rely on having the basics that your business depends on, what then? Water, air, energy are obvious ones. So are food and shelter. What about small conveniences such as pencils? Over 15 billion pencils are produced each year, with about 3.5 billion of those in the US alone. That means that roughly 60,000 hardwood trees are cut down to make pencils.[1] Instead of cutting trees, the body of a pencil could be made from recycled materials, paper for instance or even old denim. The marking part of a pencil is graphite. Almost 80% of the world's graphite supply comes from China, mostly from small, seasonal mines. The easy to reach, close to the surface flake graphite is almost depleted and deep mining will be a lot more costly. Pencils are not the only use for graphite. This soft metal is also used as a lubricant in brake pads. And in batteries, the lithium ion anode requires high quality, pure graphite. Although there is a synthetic version made from petroleum, natural spherical graphite is preferred. 100% of spherical graphite is produced in China. A lot of the graphite could be captured for recycling but very little of it is.

And then there's glass. Basic glass is pretty simple. It's comprised of 70% fine-grained silica sand and soda plus some lime for stability. You can find these ingredients on many of the beaches worldwide. So what could possibly be a problem? Almost impossibly, it seems the world is facing a shortage of sand. The last coastal sand mining operation is scheduled to be shut down in December, 2020. Run by the Mexican multinational building materials company, CEMEX, that mine, in Marina California, has been eating away at the coastline of Monterey Bay for 100 years. On the one hand, sand is sand, but is it? The "right" kind of sand is relatively rare it turns out, and it's been seriously exploited. The shortage is fueled in great part by the growth explosion in Asia, particularly, South Asia, China, and India. Formed by the gradual erosion of rock, the size and shape depend on the conditions of that process. Wind, water, ice break the rock apart over time. Sand aggregate is the main ingredient in both asphalt (94%) and concrete (80%), as well as the base material on which each is laid. "A typical American house requires more than a hundred tons of sand, gravel, and crushed stone for the foundation, basement, garage, and driveway, and more than two hundred tons if you include its share of the street that runs in front of it" (Owen, 2017). Though some construction could use recycled materials, very little does. Concrete waste from construction and demolition in the US comes to about 135 million tons annually.[2] Sand is used for other things as well. It's used in the drilling mud for gas fracking. Foundries use sand for molds. Sand is the second highest in demand raw material worldwide.

Now back to glass. In 2015, production of glass containers and bottles worldwide was 50.63 million metric tons, and that number is expected to rise every year.[3] Beyond that, there's the production of flat glass, fiberglass, and specialty glass. Think of everything that requires glass. Even though there has been a push to recycle glass in recent years, recycling in the US has not improved significantly in the past 20 years. Billions of glass bottles and jars are discarded into landfills every year, over 28 billion in fact.[4]

Pause, take a minute and run through your own list of basics, then consider what it takes for them to get to you so you can use them. What do you do with them after you're finished using them?

Today we have historic opportunities to forsake unsustainable business practices and design smart, responsible ones. Concerned, forward-thinking organizations and companies, large and small are coming together to lead the way to breakthroughs that can create our sustainable future. Recognizing that business can be a force for good, 9,000 companies and 4,000 nonbusinesses have signed the UN Global Compact, committing "to align strategies and operations with universal principles on human rights, labour, environment and anti-corruption, and take actions that advance societal goals."[5] While they are making progress, *The Sustainable Development Goals Report 2017*, makes it clear that they, and all of us as well, must accelerate the work if we are to address climate change, eradicate poverty, and develop thriving societies.[6]

How is it that millions of people aren't already making sustainability the central focus of their personal and business lives? As far back as 1896, when a study by Svante Arrhenius, "On the Influence of Carbonic Acid on the Air upon the Temperature of the Ground" was published, scholarly papers and concerned scientists have been sounding a warning. Yet in 2018, we are depleting natural resources at a dizzying rate while continuing to spew CO_2 and other pollutants into our planet's atmosphere. Even though the general standard of living is increasing for people across the globe, we are also widening the already huge wealth gap between rich and poor. Why would we be risking the sustainability of our human species like this?

Trying to puzzle through this dilemma, two recent articles talking about power and privilege gave some hints at processes worth exploring. Rebecca Solnit writes,

> I always pair privilege with obliviousness; obliviousness is privilege's form of deprivation. When you don't hear others, you don't imagine them, they become unreal, and you are left in the wasteland of a world with only yourself in it, and that surely makes you starving, though you know not for what, if you have ceased to imagine others exist in any true deep way that matters. This is about a need for which we hardly have language or at least not a familiar conversation.
>
> (Solnit, 2017)

In the second article, psychologist Dacher Keltner writes,

> In the behavioral research I've conducted over the past 20 years, I've uncovered a disturbing pattern: While people usually gain power through traits and actions that advance the interests of others, such as empathy, collaboration, openness, fairness, and sharing; when they start to feel powerful or enjoy a position of privilege, those qualities begin to fade. The powerful are more likely than other people to engage in rude, selfish, and unethical behavior. The 19th-century historian and politician Lord Acton got it right: Power *does* tend to corrupt.
>
> (Keltner, 2016)

Keltner goes on to recommend a way to begin to reconnect, to rebuild wholeness: focus on three essential practices—empathy, gratitude, and generosity.

Is it possible that these afflictions that seem to accompany increases in power and privilege, disconnecting people from what really matters, are hobbling people, hindering them from leading from the wholistic, connected foundation that sustainability demands?

Consider your own mental models. Do they include appreciation and gratitude for the bounty of the Earth and the many people who contribute to your quality of life? Do they include empathy for those around you, in your family, in your community, at your work? In the larger world? Do your mental models encourage you to be generous in spirit and deed? Have you thought about the essential roles of these qualities in regard to being a leader of a holistically integrated enterprise that's aligned for sustainability and creating a thriving future? Knowing where we are, where we really are, is the starting point.

Integrated thinking

> Progress is impossible without change, and those who cannot change their minds cannot change anything.
>
> (George Bernard Shaw, 1944)

Why would we head up a section on the future of sustainability and business with integrated thinking? Because achieving sustainability requires that we break down the silos we've created, learn from each other, and translate important learnings across disciplines. Consciously making the change from linear thinking to integrated thinking as your normal, default process is essential to moving beyond sustainability to thriving.

Typically, when we think about something, we focus narrowly ... thoughts about a beautiful sunset, a good movie, or even appreciating the successful launch of a new product. In those moments it's as though each event is a standalone. Thinking about things as separate is fine for casual appreciation but when thinking involves consequential issues that span time and distance, it's important to be aware of the greater context, of systems and inherent unseparateness. The complexities, interconnections, and relationships that operate dynamically within a system and between systems actually comprise the system and give it integrity. Identifying how things are linked—what qualities and conditions are variable and what are fixed, which are strong ties or weak ties, where leverage and inflection points are and how they are triggered, begins to give a sense of the system. Sussing out defining system characteristics and purpose brings into focus context and roots of otherwise seemingly independent instances. Now, we're into unseparate, integrated thinking.

Generalizations arising from one or even a few instances of isolated observations regarding a nonlinear complex system, though, are likely to lead to conclusions that don't hold up over time. "It is impossible, because of the curse of dimensionality, to produce information about a complex system from the reduction of conventional experimental methods in science. Impossible" (Taleb, 2016).

Russell Ackoff (1919–2009), a pioneer in systems thinking, liked to tell a story about building the best car. It goes something like this. There are a lot of good cars out there. Ratings and weightings give some the edge in engine performance, for others it's smooth transmission transitions, or excellent brake system, or highest safety in crashes, or exceptional styling and comfort.

The list could go on. There are many very good cars, but you want to build the best car of all. So you get one of each of these cars, carefully dismantle them and assemble your new car using the best of the best parts from each of these excellent cars. Voilà, you have your new best car! You start it up and … well, it sputters and spurts but won't start. Even with a mechanical system such as a car, excellence requires more than a cobbling together of parts. A system is always more than the sum of its parts.

With living systems, this constitutive quality is even more pronounced. Remember Humpty Dumpty. "All the King's horses and all the King's men couldn't put Humpty together again." If you want to understand a system, it's important to shift your perspective so that you start with acknowledging the existence and influence of the greater whole, even when, especially when, that whole is not readily apparent. Think of the difference between a circle and a polygon. Imagine all you can see is a tiny segment of a circle placed next to a tiny side of a polygon. To your eye, the two images would appear the same. Because they look the same, it's easy to assume they *are* the same. But the only way to get to a circle is to start with a circle. No matter how many tiny sides you give a polygon, it will still be comprised of sides joined by angles. It can never become a circle. While these distinctions are obvious when you think about them, it's also easy and tempting to align our thinking and actions with the first plausible explanation so we can move on to handling the next pressing issue. Plausible is not always the same as actual. The business side of sustainability is one of those areas where it's easy to get lured into taking a "polygon" approach, in effect working piecemeal—small energy-saving projects, community service, paper recycling. All those initiatives are worthwhile and satisfying but each as a standalone is insufficient to move the needle on real, long-term sustainability. To make real progress in the business of sustainability, ground your efforts in a recognition of how they integrate with the whole.

Framing the future: revisiting the strategy of planned obsolescence

> Leaders know the importance of having someone in their lives who will unfailingly and fearlessly tell them the truth.
>
> (Warren Bennis)

Making an excellent, durable product has its perceived upsides and downsides. One upside is having customers who are very pleased with the look and function of the product. A downside has been that the existing customer base is then not highly motivated to replace the product and repeat customer sales decrease or are at least delayed. Looking at this business dilemma from a systems perspective sheds some light on challenges we face today regarding sustainability.

396 Linda M. Kelley et al.

Since the mass production of standardized models, manufacturers have been turning out products in much higher volume than people could do previously. Take automobiles, for instance. Barely over a hundred years ago, in 1913 when assembly line automobile production was in its infancy, Henry Ford made significant improvements that greatly increased throughput. Less than 20 years later, millions of Americans had purchased cars. By the early 1930s, the big three auto makers, Ford, General Motors, and Chrysler, had pretty much saturated the car market. Add to that, The Great Depression had settled in so people's buying power had declined significantly. Not surprisingly, uncertainty and lack of confidence in the market put a damper on spending even with people who could still afford to buy. Everyone used things longer, and made do as long as they could. During those previous 20 growth years, manufacturers hadn't changed automobile technology much at all. So long as the car kept going, there was no need for drivers to purchase new cars, … unless they could be convinced to be dissatisfied with what they owned and motivated to really want that new one. Bernard London, in his 1932 paper, *Ending the Depression Through Planned Obsolescence*, proposed a solution. The intent of the concept of planned obsolescence was to stimulate sales and then build a level of predictable sales into markets, thereby helping to bring America out of its stagnant Depression economy. While the original intentions were laudable, planned obsolescence has become an enduring intentional strategy of business with harmful consequences in today's world. There's more to this story though. Looking from a systems perspective we can see more threads that were pulled in and woven into this economic fabric.

Developing in parallel to manufacturing by mass production and strategic planned obsolescence was the birth of the field of Public Relations. Edward Bernays, a nephew of Sigmund Freud, was a public relations pioneer who made a name in 1917 by helping President Wilson convince the American people to support the war in Europe. Along with journalist Walter Lippmann, Bernays coined the phrase "Make the world safe for democracy." In April of that year, Wilson went before Congress to ask for a declaration of war against Germany. Bernays was working with Wilson's Committee on Public Information (CPI) to shift public opinion out of its long-standing isolationist mindset and into public support for this war, and to get men to enlist and the public to buy war bonds. Bernays' work is notable in this because he went on to write *Propaganda* (1928), in which he promoted the "engineering of consent."

> If we understand the mechanism and motives of the group mind, is it not possible to control and regiment the masses according to our will without their knowing it?
>
> The recent practice of propaganda has proved that it is possible, at least up to a certain point and within certain limits.
>
> (Bernays, 1928, p. 47)

There are some more relevant developments to weave in here. One is the creation of the economic measurements of Gross National Product (GNP) and Gross Domestic Product (GDP). Another is the rise of mass media with increased popularity of glossy magazines, the ubiquity of radio, and the invention of television—all supported financially by advertising.

Though the GNP and GDP measurements are now used as national measures of economic progress worldwide, future Nobel Laureate Simon Kuznets, and his group at the National Bureau of Economic Research (NBER) originated these tools in the early 1930s for a different reason. Looking retrospectively at the US economy back through the 1860s, they laid out categories that could demonstrate economic progress or decline in country year by year. With the country still in the throes of the Depression in the early 1930s, President Roosevelt wanted something well-researched that would indicate to the people not only in the United States, but worldwide, that economic conditions were improving even though people might not yet see it. GNP and GDP were originally developed as tools to support a government marketing campaign.

In the economic readjustments following World War II and the Korean War, these threads came together. By the 1950s they were operating concurrently to accelerate the compelling desirability of a lifestyle of consumption. **Taken together, these initiatives—mass production, public relations as propaganda, planned obsolescence, and measuring Gross Domestic Product transactionally, as income earned minus expenditures within a country, became equated with the notion that "more is better."** Nowhere in this was any regard as to whether these economic activities were beneficial or harmful to society or the environment. So, for instance, the increase in income generated by the treatment of a pandemic or recovery from an environmental disaster registers just as positively as income from a game-changing technology.

Planned obsolescence coupled with economic success measures based on numbers of transactions that are independent of purpose or even quality and conditions of products and services has forced our thinking into this "more is better" box.

Seen from a systems perspective, "more is better" is not merely some catchy slogan. This motto has settled into the foundations of our business economy as a maxim of mythic proportions with a slew of unintended consequences that came about from well-meaning efforts to resolve past pressing problems of economic depression. It's tempting to gloss over all of this or leave it to some future leaders to resolve in order to get on with what's loudly demanding attention today. But we skip shoring up the foundation of business at our peril. The continuous acceleration of consumption-driven business is unsustainable for society and for the environment of a finite planet. Even when we are pushing the limits of the Planetary Boundaries of essential resources, more is better remains a business design feature. Because the genesis of our current condition of unsustainability is at the foundation level, that's where it must be addressed. Once again, we're circling back to the fact that a patch-work of initiatives can't bring about sustainability any more than replacing windows will improve the safety and security of a house if the foundation is cracked and crumbling, no more than a new shiny paint job on a car with a twisted frame makes it safely drivable again. Leaving nonsustainable supports in the foundation of how business should be done ensures that we will be hostages of a past that has us catapulting down the path of unsustainability.

Where does all this leave us? It leaves us with an unprecedented oppor-tunity to create a sustainable, thriving future. When The Club of Rome published this wake-up call to action in 1972, *Limits to Growth* (Meadows & Club of Rome, 1972) painted a bleak picture of the future. An update 30 years later was more hopeful. *Limits to Growth, The 30-Year Update* offers,

> *The necessity of taking the industrial world to its next stage of evolution is **not a disaster—it is an amazing opportunity.*** How to seize the opportunity, how to bring into being a world that is not only sustainable, functional, and equitable but also deeply desirable is a question of leadership and ethics and vision and courage, properties not of computer models but of the human heart and soul.
>
> (Meadows, Randers, & Meadows, 2004)

Pause again and consider what unintended consequences of current initiatives might be forcing your business and industry down an unsustainable path. Investigating from a systems perspective, what are some of the interconnections, variables, risks, opportunities, and possible scenarios that you can anticipate?

Earlier in this chapter we said, "Business is the engine." It's a common enough phrase but is there more to it than meets the eye? If we reach back and reinclude the original sense of "engine," we get a fuller picture of the opportunities business has as the engine. More than merely a mechanical device, in days past the word engine included in its meaning the skillful, clever manner of construction. We might do well to delve back into our col-lective memory to find the roots of many of the forces that have driven us to where we are now. Including a broader sense of meaning is one more tool to awaken awareness of new possible paths forward without demolishing what has already been built. Even though there is an element of intentional design in the building of a business, people not gadgets comprise a business. In that sense, businesses are very much living systems. Business with all its accumulated wealth of skillfulness and cleverness really is the engine of sustainability.

As with "engine," it's worth unpacking the word "sustainability." In ordinary conversation, sustainability has become an almost boring, "oh yeah that" word. When you really consider it though, sustainability is our only viable option for continued existence. Unsustainable is unthinkable. And that's really the problem. No one really believes humans will or even could cease to exist. With all the evidence building that unsustainable is a real possibility for us, why do we continue to act as though this isn't the most urgent concern facing humanity? Joe Overton offered a theory in 1992 to explain how people normalize the previously unacceptable, even unthinkable. With his Window concept, Overton demonstrated given continual bombardment with the unthinkable people become numb from overwhelm and accept any backing off that unthinkable as ok, as acceptable, even a new normal. It's much like the way color vision functions. If you stare at a large red dot for too long, the cones in your eye fatigue out and you can't see red again until your cones recover. With sustainability, like Chicken Little proclaiming the sky is falling, people painted a picture of dire consequences and failing Earth for so long that it has made it difficult to distinguish hype from real danger. A real problem here is that since very few people are offering a way to recover our sensibilities and actually make effective changes, any backing off from a dystopic future is accepted as better than the hopeless despair of widespread catastrophe. More than wrestling with an intellectual exercise, people need to take action and make significant changes. Normalizing the unsustainable is not a viable option for humanity. Back to the work of Rebecca Solnit and Dacher Keltner at the beginning of this chapter, disconnects that promote fantasy can have dangerous consequences, leaving us vulnerable and unprepared. What do we have to do to shore up and rebuild the foundations of business so that we have a sustainable future in which people thrive?

Sustainability isn't really enough. To sustain is to provide sufficient support to keep something going. While sustainable is of critical importance, it's the threshold between survival and thriving. If we stop at sustainability we will have settled for far less than what humanity could be. To move beyond mere sustainability, we need to ask ourselves, "What do I value?" Of all the possibilities, what is of real, enduring value, and why? Considering sustainability to be a baseline, what would it include? What sustains us, our families, our communities, our businesses? Evaluating conditions that establish sustainability isn't an esoteric exercise. We all, everyone on Earth, has skin in this game. Sustainability isn't the start point. Undergirding sustainability is base, core survival. If survival is the essential core, everything else radiates out from this set of core conditions that make human life possible. Sustainability is the threshold where we are able to meet the conditions of survival, and can sustain them so growth and progress are now possible. Beyond the sustainability threshold is a zone of thriving where people can develop smart, efficient, effective, responsible use of resources to better their lives. The outer boundary of a zone of thriving is the limit of the carrying capacity of the system, whether that system is small and local or inclusive of the whole planet Earth. When the use of resources breaches the carrying capacity threshold, the system begins to lose integrity and declines.

Businesses often use the sigmoid function or S-curve for planning and mapping position and trajectory from growth through maturity to decline. This planning usually assumes that the fall from thriving to declining should be a slow, controllable deceleration. If conditions shift unexpectedly, the fall can happen rapidly. Think back to December, 2001. Remember Enron. It imploded within a month of declaring bankruptcy. Enron was a case of human failure and corruption that in very real, consequential systemic ways breached the integrity of the system so that it overwhelmed the carrying capacity for adaptation and removed any possibility of a resilient return. Companies can take severe hits from environmental catastrophes as well. When the earth-quake-caused tsunami hit the west coast of Japan in 2011, it ravaged not only that rural coast but also the Fukushima nuclear plant. As bad as that disaster was, the meltdown effects went far beyond the disastrously damaged plant, rippling through to other businesses as well. Toshiba, a maker of one of the nuclear reactors saw its nuclear business come to a halt. But it didn't stop there. Because a Toshiba chip plant was nearby, that plant was shut down and the company had to delay delivery on orders, stressing the global supply chain that affected many other companies. As a consequence, Apple was missing key components and couldn't deliver on its product orders. In 2010, did Apple consider as part of its strategic business discussions the possibility that it might not be able to deliver a product in the US on account of an environ-mental disaster in Japan? Does that company now include discussions of ser-ious environmental disasters as part of economic risks? Does your company?

We are now living with economic, political, and environmental conditions that are shifting in unexpected, compounding ways. It's just about impos-sible for your business and industry to avoid being affected by many of these changes. While you may not be able to prevent them, you can prepare your-self, your business, and your community to be more resilient.

Visualizing often helps to spark thinking about difficult issues like these. Far from inclusive, the picture below could be thought of as a sculpture in words with hints and highlights to guide your evaluation process. Figure 8.1 shows roughly where things fall into the three zones of surviving, thriving, and declining. For the most part, concept words in the Thriving Zone that are closest to the Survival Zone developed earlier in history than the ones that are further out, often because the benefits of those related closely to continued sustainability.

This picture is best used as a tool for conversation rather than a definitive, comprehensive projection. What goes on in each area? What are the concerns, the pushes and pulls? Influences? Flows? Mixes and mashups? You may think of things that aren't there. Add them. Where in these zones would you place the products and services that you use frequently? What about those that your company uses? And where are your company's primary sources of revenue? What about company intellectual

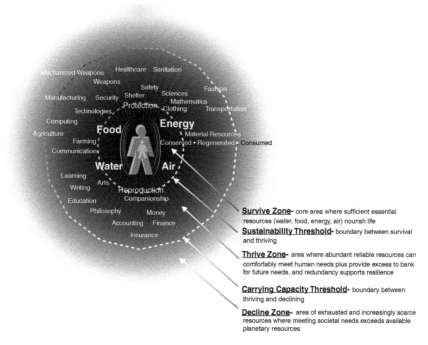

Survive Zone- core area where sufficient essential resources (water, food, energy, air) nourish life

Sustainability Threshold- boundary between survival and thriving

Thrive Zone- area where abundant reliable resources can comfortably meet human needs plus provide excess to bank for future needs, and redundancy supports resilience

Carrying Capacity Threshold- boundary between thriving and declining

Decline Zone- area of exhausted and increasingly scarce resources where meeting societal needs exceeds available planetary resources

Figure 8.1 Human-centered Sustainability Value Zones
Source: Linda M. Kelley, 2017. Used with permission.

property and valuation? On what are you basing those value assessments? How bad could things get if your assumptions behind your assessments are not valid?

What effects, positive or negative, or some of each, do initiatives by your business, and by your industry, have on the quality and condition of the four pillars, the commons, that are core to survival; water, air, food, and energy? Keep in mind that for human life, water, air, food, and energy are not only essential, but also there are no alternatives or substitutes for them. If we degrade our survival environment to the point where it is losing functional integrity, there will be no real support for our continued progress in increasing wellbeing in the thrive zone. If we treat these four essentials for life as commodities rather than commons, it is inevitable that the market-driven quest to derive profits from them will leave some people without adequate access to these essentials. In the past this line of thought might have been dismissed as dealing in hypotheticals or idealizations. Today, evidence is weighing in to support this as being an emerging crisis at the foundational level of our most cherished systems.

Don't think for a moment that these assessments and evaluations are not serious, urgent business issues. As an example, for the past seven years

(2012 through 2018 inclusively) water supply crisis has been one of the World Economic Forum's "Top 5 Global Risks in Terms of Impact." Its *Global Risks Report 2018* (World Economic Forum, 2018) comes out of its annual Global Risks Perception Survey of members of the World Economic Forum's global multi-stakeholder community. Topping the global risks is its sobering assessment that extreme weather events and natural disasters are both very likely to occur and will have major negative impacts. Add to that, in aggregate, the dominant trends it perceives interconnect and converge within 10 years to produce profound social instability. It's the interactions of disruptors on multiple levels across the globe and susceptibility to sudden shocks with uncertainty about spillovers and speed of changes that makes today's risk landscape so much more dangerous than it has been before.

> As the world becomes more complex and interconnected, easily managed incremental change is giving way to the instability of feedback loops, threshold effects and cascading disruptions. Sudden and dramatic breakdowns—future shocks—become more likely.
>
> (World Economic Forum, 2018, p. 33)

No individual person, family, company, or community is capable of tackling these grave risks alone. It will take all of us, working collaboratively to even begin to make needed interventions. Together we need to envision the best while preparing for the worst and building in resilience. For a start, a collective vision is a powerful rallying point.

Leadership, collaboration, and building resilience for our sustainable future

One of the roles of leaders is to hold the vision so others can see it and make it their own. By telling compelling stories, leaders architect participation so that people can collaboratively build bridges from where they are to a future that realizes the vision. Because they are themselves a focal point, respected leaders can change a dominant narrative. Respected leaders of enterprises across the board and across the globe have an opportunity to put forth a business narrative that places human-centered sustainability and thriving at the forefront.

> Always remember, your focus determines your reality. Believe in your vision.
>
> (George Lucas)

We are placing an emphasis on collaboration for a number of reasons. While technology and innovation are extremely important, it is possible to be in business and barely use technology, that's not so for collaboration. Often treated almost as ancillary to "the work," without collaboration there would be no business at all. People comprise companies. People live and work collaboratively. Companies depend on collaboration. Families, towns, and cities depend on collaboration. Collaboration increases innovation and resilience. Collaboration is essential to sustainability. Cities are engaging with this challenge in a big way, and providing opportunities for enterprise in the process.

Cities aren't waiting on national governments or multinational businesses to change the conversation regarding sustainability. Cities are stepping up and leading. Ninety cities comprise the C40, a global network of megacities committed to addressing climate change. Mayor Anne Hidalgo of Paris said in her closing remarks to the 2016 Summit:

> I would like to share with you the words of our friend, Ada Colau, Mayor of Barcelona, who would say, simply but categorically, that "there is no city without citizens." Just like her, I am convinced that true ecology is political, social, economic and cultural. It does not remove the human being from his surroundings, but allows him to progress, saving his environment.[7]

As Mayor Ada Colau of Barcelona stated, "there is no city without citizens," to which we add, there is no business without people. Improving environments so that your business can flourish also sets the stage for other businesses to succeed. Some will become your suppliers, some your collaborators, some your competitors who challenge you to keep improving your business, and the cycle continues. Reducing CO_2 emissions is a good example. If you do what you can alone you have limited impact. If you join together, network together with business associates or neighbors, you can have much greater impact, again, the whole becomes greater than the sum of its parts. Expand your partnerships to include not only other private enterprise but also the public sector.

Inspired to tackle UN Sustainable Development Goal (SDG) #11 that relates to cities and communities, the city of Barcelona deployed Smart Mobility, combining blocks into superblocks, then limiting the use of vehicles to delivery only in that urban neighborhood. The test city for this was the Spanish city of Vitoria-Gasteiz, named European Green Capital in 2012. Smart Mobility reduced the area's emissions and thereby deaths attributed to air pollution, decreased congestion, and revitalized the neighborhood's quality of life. Barcelona now plans on implementing the same pedestrian and bicycle centered Smart Mobility in many more neighborhoods (Bausells, 2016). London, UK, Sydney, AU, and Oslo, Norway are among the cities that have also embarked on Smart Mobility initiatives. Beijing and Delhi may choose to implement this program too. You may have seen photos of people walking in Beijing wearing face masks, walking against a backdrop of sickly yellowed gray where building outlines are barely visible. Sometimes the air has been so toxic that this enormous megacity has shut down for days at a time. What this means is that all out of doors activities, including schools and businesses are closed because the air is too unhealthy to breathe. Estimates are that over a million and a half people in China die of air pollution related diseases each year. Major contributors to this critical problem are smoke from burning coal for energy and exhaust from gasoline and diesel-powered vehicles. Almost a quarter of the emissions comes from transportation. China is setting new, stringent vehicle emissions standards and they know that won't be enough (Dwortzan, 2017). They are mandating that 10% of new car sales be zero emission by 2019, rising to 12% by 2020 (Lambert, 2017), and investigating many other new technologies to fix this air pollution problem.

On December 28, 2017, a little south of Beijing, in Jinan, China opened a kilometer-long solar road, similar to an experimental one in France and to a solar bicycle path in the Netherlands. It's estimated that the Chinese road will be able to generate 1 million kilowatt hours of power annually. The surface of the road is transparent concrete with solar panels underneath. The road will power its streetlights, its tollbooths, roadside billboards, and melt any road snow too. It's likely those activities won't use all the power generated so the rest will be sent into the grid (Hanley, 2017). China has gotten serious about reducing air pollution, but will the efforts be enough, and will the strict rules be enforceable? It's beginning to look like it could happen. For the first time in nine years, Beijing has recorded a dramatic decrease in the levels of hazardous particles in the air.

Shift west to Delhi. On November 8, 2017, earning an air quality index number of 999, this city was the most polluted on Earth—a recognition no city wants. This is not the only instance when Delhi's air quality has been so severely bad that it was serious enough to shut schools. Airlines canceled flights because the visibility was too low to land and take off (Irfan, 2017). While neither of these Asian megacities has yet been able to curb even the well-understood causes of urban air pollution, for each of them reducing carbon emissions is a major initiative. In November, 2017, in New Delhi, the Federation of Indian Chambers of Commerce and Industry hosted its first Smart Mobility Conference to bring together national and local governments, industry, finance, and academia to focus on development and challenges of smart mobility infrastructure for transportation.[8] Around the globe, cross-sector stakeholders are convening to focus on Smart Cities and Smart Mobility. Norway is looking to phase out gasoline and diesel cars completely by 2025. In San Jose, California, the agenda includes the technologies, persistent challenges, and cross-domain solutions offered by big data and analytics, smart traffic control, public-private partnerships, and autonomous vehicles. "The smart transportation market is expected to grow 25% between 2016 and 2021 and will reach $221 billion globally" (Smart Mobility 2018,

2018). In 2015, California enacted a law that requires the State to get 50% of its electricity from renewable sources by 2030. California is on track to meet that goal by 2020, 10 years ahead of schedule (Leary, 2017).

A lot is being written about electric cars, smart cars, and self-driving cars. They certainly are an improvement over creeping through bumper to bumper commuter traffic in gas-burning exhaust-emitting cars, especially if the original energy source is not coal. But if as is now the norm most cars carry only one passenger, or even two, will the impact be sufficient to dramatically reduce overall emissions, and that urban bugaboo, traffic congestion? What about electric two-wheelers? E-bikes and scooters are getting a new look-see. With forward-thinking cities addressing their traffic jam and air quality problems by building elevated bicycle paths, do e-bikes make good economic and environmental sense? Copenhagen, Eindhoven, and Xiamen are all bike-friendly cities where cyclists can commute on elevated tracks above the automobile gridlock and pedestrian traffic. Will London follow suit? London and the other C40 cities have already committed to buying only zero-emission buses by 2025, and having major parts of their cities be zero emission by 2030.

It's not just within cities that people are redesigning transportation. Will Elon Musk's Hyperloop One take off? If it can and does, take off we will. Using maglev technology, Hyperloop is a radical change from the combustion engine plus wheels mode of transportation. Loaded into pods, we'll fly through a vacuum tube at 700 mph, arriving at our destinations in minutes instead of hours! It's not up and running yet and already has some real competition, spurred by Musk's handing Hyperloop off to others to design, build, and operate. Some are even collaborating to advance the basic technology. Partly solar powered, a pod would likely generate more power than it uses. Hyperloop isn't the only maglev city to city transportation in development. Companies are also developing maglev trains with no tubes that would run at about 300 mph. Sounds a lot like sci-fi, yet maglev technology was invented over 200 years ago. Once again, we stand on the shoulders of giants.

Now look from a smaller perspective and you'll see electric bicycles are gaining more serious, widespread interest than they have in a long time, and with good reason. Converts say they have reduced their commute time as well as CO_2 emissions. To manufacture even a compact car produces between 5 and 10 tons of CO_2. Then if the driver has a modest commute of about 10 miles a day, that compact car contributes about 0.7 tons of CO_2 a year just in commuting. An average e-bike by comparison would contribute only about 0.07 tons of CO_2 for that same commute. That's one-tenth of the amount of CO_2.[9] So, the e-bike contributes less CO_2, has a shorter ride time to work during rush hour, and is much less expensive all around. The World Economic Forum puts the cost of an average electric car, including cost to buy plus maintenance as having to work at your job for 40 minutes to pay for each 10 km of driving. An e-bike on the other hand requires only 6 minutes of work to pay for 10 km of riding (Skibsted, 2017). And the bikes are getting design overhauls to be lighter, stronger, and with safe, long-lasting batteries. 3D printed bikes are already coming to market. Already solar cars and solar charging stations are out as prototypes. Lightyear One expects to release its first 10 cars in 2019.[10] Solar power will reduce the impact even further. It only took 20 years for the gasoline-powered car to become a ubiquitous workhorse. How long do you think it will be until today's gas-powered cars become relics displayed next to yesteryear's horse and carriage?

Moving people and goods in and out of cities effectively and efficiently demands innovation. This is a major challenge for the municipalities and a huge opportunity for businesses large and small.

Transportation has surpassed energy as the greatest emitter of CO_2. Cities around the world are stepping up and committing to increase overall sustainability. Air quality is one of their top priorities. Neither cities nor businesses are waiting on national governments to lead the way. How is your organization participating in this big shift? What opportunities do you see for your business and industry?

Design thinking that turns public-private collaborations into transformative community action

> You never change things by fighting the existing reality. To change something, build a new model that makes the existing model obsolete.
>
> (Buckminster Fuller)

One of the fastest-growing cities in China, Chongqing is the Eastern terminus of the New Silk Road. Seven thousand miles to the West, goods traveling along this complex infrastructure of the One Belt Road can arrive in London, UK, having made connections through Central Asia, Tehran, Prague, and Madrid. All along this route, new service and trade markets are developing, very much a modern-day version of the settlements that developed along the original Silk Road. Some are planned sites for infrastructure support, others are free trade zones that are more opportunist and entrepreneurial in nature (Monteleone, 2018).

While cities can be planned, communities form organically. Differences can fuel productive creativity, real innovations that benefit significantly from people engaging with one another. The more unequal a community becomes, the less productive engagement there is among different segments. Income inequality has been growing at a disturbing rate, worldwide, with the US having one of the largest gaps. We read that most of the wealth in the world is held by a small percentage of the population while the rest of the people control very little and the people at the bottom of the economic ladder have an amount so small as to be statistically non-existent.

Historically, this great a differential in equity is not only an economic damper, but also fuels economic and social instability. A full-time worker receiving minimum wage cannot afford to rent a two-bedroom apartment anywhere in the US.[11] Median CEOs' compensation in 2016 was 204 times that of an average wage worker. Top executive compensation is rising significantly while worker wages are not. Many people feel CEOs are taking much more than is fair (Du Boff, 2017). According to current research, people from all walks of life all across the globe believe there should not be such a huge gap between rich and poor.

As worrisome as the gap between rich and poor on an individual level is, the rise of private capital concurrent with the fall in public capital in developed countries is just as ominous. Severely reduced public wealth (assets minus debt) concurrent with great increases in private wealth means that the governments have less capacity to care for the public good, including regulating the economy, managing public health, and maintaining public infrastructure (Alveredo, Chancel, Piketty, Saez, & Zucman, 2017). People, and businesses for that matter, expect that governments will provide for these common goods and services. This is the social contract. In addition to eroding people's quality of life, these very real and growing inequalities destroy trust among people. According to the 2018 Edelman Trust Barometer Global Report, we now have entered a world of distrust. Trust has become more polarized, with the United States exhibiting the most extreme crash, having had a decline in trust of 37% across the four measured institutional categories: NGOs, Business, Government, and Media. Businesses are more trusted than other sectors right now.[12] People are looking to business to lead in committing to make a long-term positive difference in the world. Can business collectively do this? Not just a couple of businesses but business across the board? Will business do this? As powerful and important as business is, business alone cannot make us sustainable. But business must play its part. We agree with what venture capitalist John Doerr said, "If it's business as usual, we're going out of business."[13]

We need to pause here so we can knit in another thread. Hyperpolarization stretches trust to a breaking point. If we gloss over trust (someone's or something's reliability and dependability regarding the area where trust has been given) as though it were a thing, we miss the real dangers and opportunities. When there is trust among people they can disagree, argue with one another but then negotiate and compromise. When trust breaks down, initial anger can turn to resentment, despair, and even betrayal. If distrust devolves into betrayal, it's very difficult to rebuild trust. When distrust between individuals spills over to converge among people and peoples, serious breakdowns ensue. This affects all social realms and has real consequences. The violent dissolution of the former Yugoslavia is an example. Festering structural problems may have been the catalyst for social and economic collapse, but the breakdown of trust induced a fracturing of integrity that had held mixed communities together for generations. Within two years the nation of Yugoslavia degenerated into a collection of ethnic states. Twenty-five years later, while the area is growing economically, it's still in recovery mode. Socially, the Balkans are still readjusting alignments, fracturing primarily along ethnic lines.

Trust and integrity are the foundations of social contracts, and also of the granting of rights, including the right to conduct business by societal governing bodies. This is often lost in the background of everyday life. Breakdowns in trust lead to rifts in integrity that are not always mendable. Building on top of festering rifts never holds up. One way or another they have to be addressed to be healed. How do you identify and handle issues of trust in your personal life and in your professional life? Do you handle those differently? What about in your town or city? Are there ways that distrust among companies in your industry might be inhibiting them from advancing sustainability? How might you contribute to building or rebuilding trust?

In January, 2018, The World Economic Forum held its Annual Meeting in Davos, Switzerland. The focus of the 48th Meeting was "Creating a Shared Future in a Fractured World." Leaders and business gathering to discuss the fracturing of the world should make us all reexamine the real state of our own businesses and the conditions of the societies and environments in which we operate. The sessions were recorded. Here are some of the many relevant topics presented at the WEF Meeting. Each of them was presented as an invitation to further conversation and collaboration.

- Why is Our World Fractured?
- From Growth to Prosperity
- The Remaking of Global Finance
- The Fourth Industrial Revolution
- Future Shock: Cyberwar without Rules
- New Consumption Frontiers
- How Do We Stop at Two Degrees?
- How is Rentier Capitalism Aggravating Inequality?
- On the Menu: Sustainable and Nutritious Food
- The Future of Finite Resources
- Responding to Extreme Environmental Risks
- Rethinking the Modern Consumption Economy
- Visions for a Shared Future
- Creating a Shared Future in a Fractured World[14]

Will these and other thought-provoking sessions about global sustainability and economic enterprise translate into changes that mend these fractures and build a common, thriving future? Will we be inclusive so that everyone has economic sufficiency and opportunities for fulfilment? We don't yet know. Many experts presented compelling ways of rethinking critical aspects of the ways we are doing business. They identified dangers. They described challenges. They proposed opportunities that could increase sustainability, general wellbeing, and business prosperity. As Erik Solheim, Executive Director of the United Nations Environment Programme says in "New Consumption Frontiers," we need a broad theory of change that engages citizens, businesses, and government. In the same session, Feike Sijbesma, CEO of DSM, said that we need to design for recycling, and change financial incentives from owning to paying for use. He added, "You cannot be successful in a world that fails" (Solheim, 2018). You will have to disrupt your own business before someone else does. We agree with Sijbesma on all counts.

Now comes the hard part. Without many of us doing the real work it takes to translate these ideas and examples into company-changing practices, all of these will remain no more than one more set of excellent ideas. As we discussed in Chapter 4, "Managing the change to a sustainable enterprise," even when people really want to change, it takes preparation and planning. If the people, the organizations, and often the industries are not sufficiently prepared, the initiative will fall flat. They must have the capacity for making the changes as well as knowledge and skills. (See Chapter 4, Table 4.1 "Organization Readiness to Undertake System-Level Change," page 187).

A couple of other things come to mind here. One is the centuries-old Japanese practice of kintsugi, of recognizing beauty in broken things and repairing fractured pottery by filling the cracks with gold. The other is two lines of Leonard Cohen's *Anthem* (1992): "There is a crack, a crack in everything. That's how the light gets in."

Businesses are becoming increasingly interdependent globally—customers, resources, knowledge, capital, all flow and intersect. At the same time, the world is becoming increasingly urban. In 1950, 30% of the world's population lived in cities. That's expected to be 60% by 2050. Cities use two-thirds of the consumed energy, and contribute almost three-quarters of the greenhouse gases. Cities also generate more than 80% of global GDP.[15] If the vast majority of GDP is derived from cities, the future success and sustainability of business is intimately and inexorably entwined with city vitality. There is opportunity and challenge in this.

While companies can change their focus or even move locations when changes make business difficult, cities do not have those same choices. They cannot pick up and move. Over their existence, cities that persist do so because they change and adapt and morph and reinvent themselves over and over again, accommodating disruption after disruption. Cities are smart places to start repairing the fractures of this world and create a sustainable shared future.

What makes a city work?

Right now, not all cities, or their people, are fully participating economic engines. Right now, many businesses are not full participants in the vitality of the cities that host and support them.

Whether or not trade was the catalyst for the initial development of cities, it is clear that exchange, trade, value creation, and innovation are what keep cities going. Tools and technologies, clothing, food, and shelter are produced and traded, not just among friends but formally exchanged over time and distance with multiple sets of strangers. Items of value you wanted but couldn't produce were made by someone you didn't know from materials you didn't have available. City marketplaces and storage facilities stretched timeframes of product availability. Because these make it possible for people to get necessities without having to produce all items themselves, people can specialize in other value-added commodities. Specializations and divisions of labor allow people to handle diverse needs and wants. Interactions over desired products increase interactions and spark ideas, suggestions, collaborations. The result is more innovations in technologies and products, services, and delivery. But none of this can keep a metropolis going if the result isn't a sustainable, dynamic, vibrant city.

Collaborating to create value strengthens both cities and companies. Benefiting from their diversity, cities become seats of knowledge; business draws on that knowledge base. Collaboration, competition, exchange, support, artistic expression, and even creative dissonance among people within a city give it vibrancy. A thriving economic life is founded in generative cultures that embolden enterprise and accept some risk-taking. Unfortunately, not all cultures embrace equity and justice, or even include protections for safety of all the populace. As cities grow, they become complex mashups both structurally and socially; if not self-organized at least modified over time by how the people live their lives. Understanding and creative enterprise arise from recurring face-to-face interactions that generate new ideas that segregated or siloed passbys eliminate. How a city handles issues of equity, mobility, separation and integration, and inclusion determines to a great degree how creative and resilient it will be. The same could be said of companies. When you think about it, it's not surprising cities and companies have a number of similar qualities. Both are social constructs. Just for fun, try rereading sentences above, substituting "company" for "city." What do you notice that you hadn't considered before? What will you do with those insights?

People are what make a city great. Towns and cities that have been built according to utopian designs are considered to be cold, unhospitable places, until they are modified, or messed around, by human interactions. Great cities are alive with activity in easily accessible places where people from all walks of life work, play, and interact. In addition to jobs and healthcare, attractive places for gathering, pockets of nature, walkability, and arts all make a positive difference in the quality of life. Cities that work create a cultural and economic life that aligns people's perceptions with a vision and its public narrative in which people can find places for themselves that include opportunities and hope. Those are cities where people want to be. Those are cities that attract talent; they are places where companies want to be.

Reinvigorating public-private collaborations to generate thriving economies

Every developed country has cities that once were industrial engines but suffered from the ebbs and flows of opportunistic economies where bases of manufacturing pulled out of these host communities leaving them decimated—vacant buildings, large numbers of unsold houses, underpopulated schools, supporting businesses devastated, tax rolls wanting, and people unemployed. This uprooting may have brought some gains to those companies, particularly regarding lower labor costs, but there are measurable high costs to these gains if you look from a systems perspective. Sustainability demands taking care of the real costs responsibly because in actuality there are no externalities. Shifting those burdens of cost away from the private profit-making enterprise onto the public agencies responsible for health and wellbeing of people and planet is in effect a transfer of public common wealth into private pockets, even if it isn't currently accounted for in that way. When companies profit from not paying the true environmental and social cost of doing their business, real sustainability remains beyond our collective reach.

In this and previous chapters we've already talked about some of the environmental degradations and toxic waste resulting from extracting resources without taking care of the real costs to the land and the people who live there. Another of the challenges and opportunities we face is to mend the lesions and heal the scars we've left, and move forward equitably. We can no longer afford to waste the potential contributions of people, treating them as necessary collateral damage of profit-seeking. We can no longer afford to sacrifice the health of the planet in order to grow our global economy. Truthfully, we never could but now that we know we're consuming the planet at a wholly unsustainable rate we need to stop, regroup, and invent practices that will repair the damage and sustain us on this marvelous planet. Part of that must be decoupling profit-making from consumption. One place to start is by stopping commodification of life-essential natural resources and of people.

Currently, we are prone to financialize just about everything, including things like water and air. Not only are water and air commonly essential to human life, given the slightest movement they flow. Think about it. In the process of using these resources their molecules don't stay in one place. Obvious, of course. So if they flow in and out, moving all around the globe molecule by molecule regardless of how we try to bound them, how can we assign a financial number to their value? Given their inherent properties, neither water nor air can actually be owned by anyone. By assigning ownership and monetary value to these resources, we prevent accepting the fact that these commons are inherently irreplaceable constituents of the planetary environment. We need to expand our toolbox for evaluations. Using new metrics such as ones discussed in Chapter 6 will help to get more accurate accounts of a business's condition, including nonfinancial measures. Financial considerations including profits are important but if attaining them means sacrificing people and planet, profits are empty numbers.

Another problem, and challenge to sustainability that accompanies ownership, is rights over use and disposal. Using essential commons as owned property that is treated as disposable, and contaminated so that it is unrecoverable for future use, is becoming seen as a moral outrage in some quarters. Technological advances make it increasingly difficult to hide abuses of natural resources and human resources. We will touch on the technology of transparency in a subsequent section. In addition, both companies and communities need to consider the reputational component of resource abuse. Today, people, especially millennials, are holding companies and municipalities to higher standards. The Global Strategy Group's 5th Annual Business and Politics Study says over 80% of the adults they surveyed expected companies to stand up for good, and that the company's bottom line would benefit from those actions.[16] The huge millennial generation is coming into its own. It is diverse, educated, and passionately concerned that a continuation of the current business as usual will rob them of their future.

Indications are that up and coming generations are pressing for what we have wanted but have yet to deliver. According to numerous studies they want such qualities as health, safety, time to spend with family and friends, time with art or nature. They want prosperity and wellbeing, they want to be satisfied that their lives make a positive difference. According to Dan Pink, beyond being able to take care of their basic needs, people want to have 1. Autonomy—the desire to direct their own lives, 2. Mastery—the urge to get better and better at something that matters, and 3. Purpose—the yearning to do what we do in the service of something larger than ourselves.[17] This, in the face of high and rising inequality. There are companies and communities that are determined to turn this challenge into opportunities.

Case 1. Heineken, "How to Brew a Better World"

Linda M. Kelley

Can you run a company adhering to socially and environmentally responsible principles? A number of companies today are saying yes you can, just watch us. Toyota, Nike, Unilever, and Heineken are among the over 9,000 companies that have joined the United Nations Global Compact and committed to support society, operate responsibly, and engage locally.

9,000 is also the number of years that we can trace back the production of fermented beverages. According to "Our 9,000-Year Love Affair With Booze" in *National Geographic*'s February, 2017 magazine, that beverage was rice and honey wine in China. Moving slightly closer to present day, 4,000 years ago the Sumerians were brewing beer. From a grain mush very much resembling a soggy granola of the ancient grain emmer, some crushed barley, and sourdough, a yellowish bubbly dough rises. Wait some days, add some water, and you have the beer. It seems people developed a taste for alcohol even before they began farming. It seems that fermenting makes fruits and grains easier to digest, for us and for a number of our mammalian relatives. Then there's the antiseptic properties of alcohol. Beer may have kept our ancestors healthier.[18]

Heineken, modern-day maker of beer, is committed to making our society and our environment healthier. The company has selected six areas of focus:

Protecting Water Resources—the ultimate shared resource
Reducing CO_2 Emissions—from Barley to the Bar
Sourcing Sustainably—improving farmer livelihoods and raising standards
Responsible Consumption—moderation in drinking
Promoting Health & Safety—zero fatalities
Growing Communities—help local communities prosper.

The company realizes the importance of stable communities to its business so invests in local initiatives and job creation. One example is Project Grow to support a local supply chain of sustainably grown cassava starch in Jamaica. Another is low carbon transport in the Netherlands that's working toward a "green corridor" for delivery. Heineken is a leader in transitioning toward a circular economy in Mexico. Water balancing in southern Spain in partnership with Commonland is an urgent project in a drought-ravaged land where it has improved water filtration, decreased use, and is planting barley in olive groves to increase soil stabilization. The company is committed to increasing diversity, hiring more women to be leaders—40% of the US Heineken workforce is women. It is also working with women leaders and Vital Voices to curb global human trafficking.[19]

A purpose-driven company, as Eileen Fisher says (Chapter 7, pages 331–332), must show up and stand up for its values. Heineken Mexico's CEO, Dolf van den Brink, agrees. "Gender violence is a big issue and a very difficult topic in the Latin world. In Mexico, two out of three women are confronted by violence. What's shocking is that 60% of the population thinks it's okay," he says. Heineken Mexico has taken this on publicly using a commercial for its Tecate brand beer that is perceived to be a very masculine drink. This powerful one-minute video states,

> A man is not defined by his strength, his image, his courage, his anger, his toughness, or his sexual orientation. A man is defined by how he treats a woman. If you're not a man, you don't deserve a Tecate. Don't reach for one. We hope you hate it. You're not one of us. Not one more for you. Tecate. Standing against domestic violence.

Taking a stand is a risk, and this one has sparked controversy for sure. For Heineken Mexico and van den Brink it's living the company's values out loud.

> It allowed us to connect with civil society in a new way and be a part of the solution. We have hundreds of millions of consumers, and a big marketing budget. We can help change negative male-female stereotypes in ways that an NGO does not have the resources to.
>
> (Hurst, 2017)

The ancients were right. Beer really does make life better.

Turning risks into opportunities: bridging the tensions between the ethical and economic considerations

Throughout this book we've tried to balance concerns for economic interests, social concerns, and planetary responsibility: the triple bottom line of people, planet, profits. Not surprisingly tensions arise in trying to manage this dynamic balance. Why should we bother with balancing? Because right now something really important is missing. Point blank, we are not sustainable! In fact, we-the-people are currently unsustainable. The systems we have made, the ones by which we conduct business and account for our outcomes are working perfectly to give us the unsustainable results we've gotten.

If we care about the future, about our future, we all need to show up and reach out to work together and change what we're doing. The UN Global Compact's Global Opportunity Explorer highlights ways people are partnering to manage the paradox that pits ethical against economic. Public-private partnerships are at the forefront. What is often forgotten when we look at this apparent paradox is that companies get their legitimacy and permit to do business by license granted by government. These social operating licenses include responsibilities assigned to public agency and to private enterprise. The fact that accountability for those responsibilities is ignored and the impacts are not measured feeds this paradoxical divide.

> You don't get your social license by going to a government ministry and making an application for one, or simply by paying a fee. It is not a simple case of throwing money at a problem and hoping that it goes away. It requires far more than money to truly become part of the communities in which you operate. Sit down with the local communities and understand

their needs, wants and customs. Tell them what you will do and LIVE UP
TO YOUR PROMISES. Establishing that you are accountable for your actions
is the key to gaining the respect of your stakeholders.
(Pierre Lassonde, President Newmont Mining Corporation, 2003)

Can cities be effective gateways to fruitful, sustainability-aligned public-private partnerships?

What makes a city a gateway city? Are all cities gateways? Could they be? In
Massachusetts gateway city has a specific meaning. The State has designated
25 older cities that once were industrial hubs as gateway cities. It would be
easy to see these cities as gateways to the past, but if you turn your head
and look closer you'll see they are also becoming gateways to our future.
The good news for these cities, and for all cities, is that since they are open
systems with people moving in and out, structures put up and torn down,
and culture adapting, cities are constitutively uncompleted so always open
to redesign.

> Gateway Cities are midsize urban centers that anchor regional econ-
> omies around the state. For generations, these communities were home
> to industry that offered residents good jobs and a "gateway" to the
> American Dream. Over the past several decades, manufacturing jobs
> slowly disappeared. Lacking resources and capacity to rebuild and
> reposition, Gateway Cities have been slow to draw new economy
> investment.
> While Gateway Cities face stubborn social and economic challenges as
> a result, they retain many assets with unrealized potential.[20]

Challenges cities face to become working cities

When cities struggle, people struggle. When people struggle, businesses
struggle. People don't build businesses in isolation. To thrive, people
need companions who work along with them; that's where company
originates. Whether intended or not, people tasked with making decisions
in civil society and in business exercise considerable power over other
people. Milton Friedman pointed this out in *Capitalism and Freedom*. In the
Introduction he wrote, "The power to do good is also the power to do
harm; those who control the power today may not tomorrow; and more
important, what one man regards as good, another may regard as harm"
(Friedman, 2002, p. 3).

Cities and businesses thrive together when each is a reliable, competent
partner. If we expect these partnerships to be dynamically robust and productive, we need to nurture them. Part of that process in gateway cities must

be rebuilding trust. Having those manufacturing bases ripped out of these cities harmed any trust that had built between people and the business sector. Employees assume that there is a social contract even if it is not explicit, and make commitments to buy homes, cars, and other major purchases based on their expectations of employment. While the companies might have moved on, former employees who were left behind felt spurned. If opportunities for new, comparable employment were nowhere to be seen, disappointment easily moves through despair to resignation. When anyone becomes resigned, it's more difficult to recognize opportunities that do appear. When this happens to large numbers of people in a community, reticence permeates the atmosphere. It becomes a nagging sense that hanging back is the safest route to take. That inclination settles unnoticed into the outlooks of the people and the city much like a subtle, faintly noticeable, indistinct scent might. Regaining economic momentum for these cities necessarily involves rebuilding social underpinnings so that trust can regrow and possibilities are transformed.

Living Cities

Community development has a long and global history. According to the definition by the United Nations in 1948, in Article 55 of the Repertory of Practice, "Community development is a process designed to create conditions of economic and social progress for the whole community with its active participation and fullest possible reliance upon the community's initiative" (Head, 1979, p. 101).

The United Nations Development Group (UNDG) "Systems Approach to Capacity Development" lists three levels for coordinated action: Enabling environment (policies, legislation, power relations, social norms); Organizational level (policies, procedures, frameworks); Individual level (skills, knowledge, experience). It considers capacity development to be an essential pillar for effective economic and social development. Successful programs must include addressing community "capacity traps" such as vested interests, ethics and attitudes, power relations, and access.[21]

By 1990, Peter C. Goldmark, President of the Rockefeller Foundation, was becoming increasingly concerned that community development organizations had inadequate support for building capacity so were struggling to fulfill their missions. Goldmark gathered four other foundations and a major insurance company to pool funds that could provide this kind of capacity-building support and be a catalyst for changing practices. Living Cities (originally National Community Development Initiative) has been bringing together financial institutions and foundations with a combination of innovative thinking and capital to harness the collective power of philanthropy ever since. Its goal is to accelerate solutions that dramatically improve economic wellbeing.

The Integration Initiative

The Integration Initiative is one of Living City's signature multi-city initiatives that supports cities to reshape critical programs, policies, and resources allocation so that they may achieve enduring, turnaround changes that positively impact the wellbeing of low-income people. This program supports cross-sector leaders who are taking bold action to remove barriers to transformation so that their cities have thriving, inclusive, resilient economies.[22]

Case 2. The Federal Reserve Bank of Boston

Linda M. Kelley

If you're the Boston Fed, and one of your goals is to maximize employment in Region 1(New England), particularly in low-income communities, what do you do?

In 2008, the Boston Fed engaged leaders across sectors to investigate issues, and potential policy-driven barriers that might negatively affect employment. These actions led them to wonder if it is possible, and if so what might it take, to bring about resurgence in high-need, high-opportunity post-industrial cities after years of population and economic decline? They found that 10 cities out of the 25 they researched nationally were able to make that transition. What made the difference for these 10 cities? "The critical factor was not a city's industry mix, demographic composition, or geographic position. Instead, resurgence resulted from the ability of leaders in those cities to collaborate across sectors around a long-term vision for their success." If the crucial difference between those who were able to rebound economically and those who were not was a strong civic infrastructure, "is there something the Boston Fed can do to help cities strengthen it in a way that extends growth to residents struggling most?"[23]

This quest led the Boston Fed to Living Cities. With the support of Living Cities, the Boston Fed adapted the Integration Initiative for smaller post-industrial New England cities.

The Boston Fed designed the Working Cities Challenge in collaboration with cross-sector partners, including public, private, and philanthropic organizations. Challenge Grants have been awarded through competitions where applicants from eligible cities are evaluated by how well they address the following criteria: leading collaboratively across sectors, engaging community members, using evidence to track progress toward a shared goal, and working to improve the lives of low-income residents by changing systems.

Beginning in Massachusetts where two rounds of grants have now been awarded, the Challenge has expanded to include cities in Rhode Island and Connecticut, with interest in eventually including all the New England States.

Unlike many funders that award grants but have little interaction with grantees between progress reports, the Boston Fed has realized that it has a further supportive role to play. It facilitates a learning community and peer networking among the grantees, and links them to experts who provide insights and best practices to increase the overall success of the programs. One important process to ensure continuation of these initiatives beyond the three-year award period is to incubate and normalize collaborative leadership and embed it deeply within the community.

Case 3. Working Cities Pittsfield: the journey

Linda M. Kelley

The City of Pittsfield, Massachusetts was one of five Round 2 cities to be awarded a Working Cities Challenge Implementation Grant of $475,000 over three years, starting in July, 2016.

Here's why a consortium of organizations in Pittsfield pulled together to apply for the Working Cities Challenge.

Box 8.1   Berkshire Bridges—Working Cities Pittsfield Proposal Summary

Berkshire Bridges—Working Cities Pittsfield
Implementation Grant Narrative
Proposal Summary
OVERVIEW

With the Hoosic Range to the east and Taconic hills to the west, Berkshire County is geographically isolated from the rest of the state and from its NY neighbors. All the nearest urban areas are more than an hour's drive away (40–55 miles), which significantly reduces the feasibility of finding work in an adjacent county. Within the county, extremely limited public transportation makes travel within the city and to other towns challenging. Pittsfield is also the state's smallest Urbanized Area. These two factors have resulted in a culture where the social sector has a history of working together—a strength upon which this project builds. When asked, Pittsfield's residents worry about money and lack adequate housing. They live in unsafe neighborhoods and are troubled about their children's prospects. For many, particularly for people of color, there are additional systemic and perceptual barriers that preclude access to resources that might improve quality of life. We heard repeated reports of a lack of cultural competence during social service interactions—a particularly troubling finding when these services are part of the pipeline to a better life. These stresses have a devastating impact on the lives of individuals and ultimately our city. At the same time, few service providers share their theories of change with the people they seek to help—furthering the potential for disconnects. Pittsfield Bridges: Transformational Movement (PBTM) takes a strength-based view of our community. Programmatic impact, economic development, and widespread transformation can be achieved through multi-faceted collaboration and the active involvement of those who stand to benefit the most from positive changes. Pittsfield's project is already stronger by involving those who are not often invited into the conversation—residents living in under-resourced neighborhoods.

Source: Linda M. Kelley. Not copyrighted.

Partners in the Working Cities Pittsfield coalition include 28 public and private agencies, businesses, community residents and neighborhood groups, local government, service providers, and healthcare providers. All of them really care about this city and want to be idea generators, leadership catalysts, and roll-up-your-sleeves doers to make this city the best place to live and work that it can be. Not surprising, at the first few group meetings, everyone was eager to express their own opinions of what the problems were and offer solutions, each of them sure that they knew how to fix things. Luckily, as conversation sessions progressed, they took a turn-about so that people representing these organizations began to listen more and opine less. These meetings became the seeds for Community Listening Sessions.

The Vision is: All people in Pittsfield experience a just, thriving, and safe community. During the first quarter of 2016, Working Cities Pittsfield hosted 14 Community Conversation and Listening Sessions, with facilitators drawn from the coalition partners. Hundreds of residents participated. Structured much like a World Café and influenced by Appreciative Inquiry, the facilitators asked participants for their help in shaping the focus and priorities of this initiative because the residents were the real experts in these matters. Their ideas, opinions, and voices mattered. Working together, we can do what none of us can do alone. The same five questions were asked at each Session:

1. What are some things you do like about Pittsfield?
2. What would make Pittsfield a better place to live?
3. What is working for you?
4. What is not working for you?
5. How could we break down or remove some of these barriers?

Since the city has experienced significant manufacturing job losses continually over the past 40 years and the unemployment rate is higher than the State average, it wasn't a surprise that people said employment was a concern. Neither were people surprised that inadequate transportation—both routes and hours of operation—was a pervasive impediment not only to employment but also to handling life in general, so was one of the top five concerns. It was a big surprise that inclusion and access was the top concern across the board. Access according to the city's residents was not just about jobs. Residents had trouble finding information about available resources. Once they found the right service, they felt they were not respected by the city's service providers, and in fact they often felt actively disrespected. Because the forms to fill out were not written in a culturally sensitive manner, people struggled to fill them out and sometimes gave up, leaving the offices without getting services to which they were entitled. Hours of service were set to best accommodate service providers, not service seekers. Because the people who needed these services most had less access to transportation or childcare they needed in order to show up at service locations, the process of getting these services was burdensome. This real burden placed on poverty is one of the policy and structural issues under-resourced people must handle every day. It is also an issue that people with sufficient resources seldom consider. When taken as a whole, it became clear that a whole group of people felt marginalized in the city. Because we're human, our experiences bleed through from one venue to another. Rather than risk further disrespect, people who could enjoy and enrich the many, free cultural events this city offers stay away.

WORKING CITIES PITTSFIELD'S ORGANIZATIONAL STRUCTURE

Once Working Cities Pittsfield was awarded the grant, it needed to formalize the Initiative structure. Twelve organizations representative of the coalition self-selected and were approved to become the Steering Committee. Since the Initiative would be managing funds and required office space and support, the coalition voted one of its self-selecting organizations to be the Initiative's backbone organization. That position is held by Central Berkshire Habitat for Humanity. The Steering Committee designated a subset of organizations to comprise the Executive Committee. While the composition of these committees may vary, both of them must include resident representatives. The Executive Director, Working Cities Pittsfield committed to work to break down existing structural and social barriers, and work collaboratively across sectors. The initiative is also determined to create an environment throughout the city where low-income residents, people of color, immigrants, youth, and the elderly are respected, their voices valued, and their engagement in the public sphere is enthusiastically encouraged and supported.

WORKING CITIES WEDNESDAYS

Working Cities Wednesdays are monthly community meetings that the Initiative hosts. They are held in community spaces and switch neighborhood locations so that numbers of people could walk to the meeting. The Initiative provides food and childcare for each meeting. These meetings continue the mood set by the original community listening sessions of remembering assets while tackling problems. Every meeting begins with a quick Round Robin of New & Good, "What new or good has happened to you in the past week?"

The meetings follow an Open Space format with a touch of Deep Democracy where people who have an idea, concern, or problem they're passionate about pitch the group. Those that have traction with some others who have come that evening form a discussion and brainstorming group, huddle and work together for about 30 minutes, and then report out to the whole meeting. There have been a number of benefits from this format. One of these small groups took on a lack of effective traffic management in densely populated neighborhoods, then followed up and petitioned city government together. Another group sparked a new ride-sharing business. Yet another group came together around the problems of homelessness in the city and brainstormed about what they could do to help the government and the service organizations do better. These meetings are well attended because they are not just talking but planting seeds for doing. Without addressing these issues directly, these Wednesday meetings provide supportive speaking opportunities for people who are unaccustomed to publicly voicing their concerns. Lively group discussions also are opportunities for stepping up to lead, stepping back to let someone else lead, engaging support for one's ideas, asking questions when you don't understand, and respectfully listening even when you might disagree. This learning by doing, these engaged conversations that mix people from different economic backgrounds, that surface skills that otherwise go unnoticed gets to the heart of increasing person to person understanding, inclusion, and trust. Bit by bit, people are building new social capital. This is giving the work back to the people in the very best way.

COMMUNITY OUTREACH AND ENGAGEMENT

Always hovering in the background is the question, "A city for whom?" As we've said before, a city that is robust and vibrant is diverse and complex in its makeup and operation. Residents and businesses; businesses and civil society; residents and government; government and business; civil society and residents; government and civil society. Are interactions contentious or respectful? Are people considerate or dismissive? How these elements mix, how mashups happen, how ideas are generated, and turned into policy, how problems are handled, how successes are celebrated matter. The way these engagements happen sets the mood and tone of a city. You can tell viscerally whether a city, or just about any place for that matter, is somewhere you want to be or somewhere you can hardly wait to leave. Do you feel welcome?

Over time, when for whatever reasons spaces that separate diverse sectors become too wide to bridge on a regular basis, cultural awareness and understanding decreases. Two programs of Working Cities Pittsfield are designed to bridge those gaps, facilitate understanding and respect, and increase community engagement. One is cultural competency trainings; the other is having community navigators who are facilitators bridging between different sectors. For more on cultural competency, see the essay in Chapter 2, "Mental models in civil society" (pages 112–115).

THE IMPORTANCE OF CULTURAL COMPETENCY

Why focus on cultural competency? Think of the times in your life that you and your kids, or you and your parents, were speaking with each other but each was actually talking past the other. When did you realize that happened? During the conversation? After you'd walked away? Not until later when something happened and the misunderstanding hit you? Often it's the latter. We're oblivious to miscommunications and lack of understanding until an event shoves it front and center. Now think about how that might get magnified in a city between people who don't have very much opportunity for casual conversation, or in a business where there is little real dialog between executives and line employees. Good cultural competency trainings provide more than information. They provide grounding and space for dialogue that builds understanding, respect, and appreciation among people. If a goal is to have a community or a business, or a service provider where people feel respected, welcomed, and valued, cultural competency training and practice is an important part of the bedrock. What are some outcomes? Increased job opportunities and advancements, and adding diverse representatives from the community to boards and commissions.

Consider the Working Cities case in terms of your business. How engaged are you and your business in the communities where you work? Are you included? Are you being inclusive? Have you taken the time to consider what difference that makes? If you are not reaching out to the community to participate in your business are you missing a valuable perspective that's really hard to see from the inside? What processes might you redesign to be more inclusive? What about holding a monthly, sustainability-themed, 90-minute, open meeting at your company to generate ideas, and give people who wouldn't ordinarily work together an opportunity to come together around a sustainability issue of their choice?

Designing for inclusion is designing for sustainability

When you think about design for inclusion, what comes to mind? Did you think about eyeglasses? Now as much fashion statement as visual aid, eyeglasses have become a $100 billion industry. In the developed world 60% of people use glasses or contact lenses to correct their vision. Do you? Think about life without glasses. Could you or people close to you do their jobs without this vision correction device? Now think of this in terms of inclusion. What if most of these people, say 4 of 10 would not be able to work at their current jobs or levels because they would be disabled without glasses? What would be the social and economic cost of excluding all of us who would be impaired without the aid of corrective lenses? Here are just a few of many well-known glasses wearers: Abraham Lincoln, Thomas A. Edison, Sigmund Freud, Theodore Roosevelt, Winston Churchill, Eleanor Roosevelt, Bill Gates, Steve Jobs. How would our world be different if these people had been excluded, categorized as dimwitted, and marginalized in society because they couldn't see well? What might be the social and economic costs to us now of excluding other groups of people whom we have marginalized?

What would be different if, instead of normalizing the ways we exclude people, we actively worked to include people? Mental models and design work that includes the most furthers sustainability across the board. Once again, this important change is simple to lay out but challenging to make real. We're encouraged to be creative by thinking outside of the box. While that's a fun endeavor, the real challenge is to rethink and design creatively *within* the box. All around the developed world we have well-established cities that are facing enormous challenges and opportunities as they commit to become sustainable—economically, socially, and environmentally. Retrofitting buildings and infrastructure will take extraordinary creative energy. It can't stop there. When they no longer work as well as we need them to, we update the operating system on our computers and smartphones. Historically, the organization and functionality of social systems lag advances in technology. Great discrepancies in economic resources, access to technology, and/or rights and privileges put enormous stress on societies. If these are not addressed at the local level—locale by locale, region by region, business by business, business to business, where hands-on work happens, inequities will eat away at resilience worming through all levels, and make sustainability harder to reach.

Networking: how we get stuff done

One of the goals of The 48th World Economic Forum Annual Meeting is "to rededicate leaders from all walks of life to developing a shared narrative to improve the state of the world."[24]

If you were to tell a new story about business and community that featured inclusion, collaboration, and sustainability, how would it begin? Who would you want to help you tell this story? When you've crafted this new story, how will you share it?

Businesses exist in, and on account of, networks of people who express a need or desire, provide resources, and purchase the products and services offered. Networking is both personal and professional—how you get work done, how you get to work; how you get food and dispose of waste; and how you educate yourself are some of the many networked activities. From a systems perspective, each and every human network is part of a network of networks. Recognizing this fact is essential to sustainability and to thriving. While immediate connections in a network exert the most forceful pushes and pulls, indirect influences are often the ones that shift whole industries and markets. If resource collapse, from any cause, or political upheaval, were to remove a critical connection in a network to which you are indirectly connected, you and your business would still feel the effects. Understanding those kinds of interconnections, especially the more subtle ones, allows businesses to anticipate and prepare for risks that otherwise would seem to come out of the blue.

Your network of networks is a map of power and influence. It looks something like the graphic in Figure 8.2. This busy picture is actually a simplified representation of the real complexity of the networks that include you. Six different networks with you at the center is a good way to start understanding where you stand vis-à-vis how you get things done, and how you influence and are influenced. What do you imagine each of these six networks to be? One might be the company you work for including all the stakeholders with whom you interact in order to get your work done—that means not only your suppliers and customers, but also all the people who provide goods and services that support your work. Another might be all the companies that made the products and provided the services that built the home you live in. Another might be the complex network that brought you your morning coffee.

Make a list, 1 to 6. What networks occur to you on your first pass through this exercise? How is your personal life interconnected with your business life? Who are the doers? Who are the dreamers? Who points out problems? Who points out benefits? Ask friends and colleagues to do this simple exercise, and share results. After considering about 30 examples from friends and colleagues as well as your own, you will begin to glimpse the incredible complexity of 21st-century life. A network of networks resembles the systems of neurons in your body differentiated for your digestive system, your respiratory system, your vision system while still comprising you, much more than it does common business tools such as a Gantt chart or decision tree.

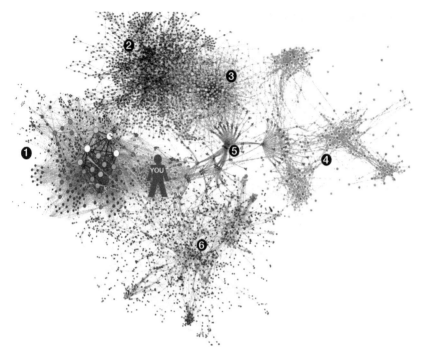

Figure 8.2 Your network of networks
Source: Linda M. Kelley 2017. Used with permission.

After seeing interconnections this way, look back at Figure 8.1 (Human-centered Sustainability Value Zones). If any one of the core survival components shown in the Human Sustainability Valuation Zones picture—air, water, food, energy—were to become unavailable to people in one part of your network of networks, or even of substantially degraded quality, it could easily have a cascading effect through many networks and resulting in multiple overloads and crises that could affect you. Let's look at a simplified example where making a decision that benefits one network may have negative effects on other interconnected networks. Take severe drought where imperative limits are placed on water availability. In that drought area, water has to be rationed. What takes priority? Farmers watering crops or manufacturing plants producing critical equipment? Food vs. technology? How might that play out, and how might it touch some of your own personal and business interests?

These tools are not meant to replace the more straightforward ones you now use for planning. Decision-tree methodology and Johari windows, for instance, are still useful. How useful they are depends more and more on the context within which you use them. The network of networks and the Human Sustainability Valuation Zones are the backdrop to give your more traditional tools wholistic context that enables you to discover important but less obvious opportunities, supports, risks, and challenges relevant to your business.

Case 4. Coca-Cola, an unlikely agent of change

Linda M. Kelley

While it doesn't manufacture critical infrastructure, Coca-Cola manufactures products in demand across the globe. Coca-Cola India is now at the forefront of water sustainability but it wasn't always that way. In the city of Kaladera, in the drought-ravaged area of northern India, Coca-Cola was accused of depleting the groundwater that area farmers had depended on for generations (Singh, 2014). Well bores reached water at 40 feet. By 2003, that had changed drastically. New well bores were going down 120–140 feet and even then, they did not always reach water.

While Coca-Cola India's plant wasn't the only contributor to this water crisis, the plant was clearly a significant drain. The company faced a choice. It could have fought the claims or it could collaborate with the farmers and other community members to build a more sustainable water infrastructure. The company chose to be a good, collaborative partner. Far beyond its legal requirements, Coca-Cola India replenished more water than it used, with the potential of replenishing up to 146% of what it was using. Coca-Cola India prides itself on its collaborative innovation, bringing together civil society and government organizations to work with the company to raise the bar regarding overall sustainability including water best practices (Wells, 2016).

Nestlé is now (in 2018) faced with a similar choice in California. The State Water Resources Control Board has notified Nestlé that as a result of its investigations, it appears the company's Arrowhead Mountain Spring Water is withdrawing far more water from the San Bernardino National Forest watershed than it is permitted to take (Associated Press, 2017). What will Nestlé do? Will it fight the findings or will it choose to collaborate with other community stakeholders in drought-ravaged Southern California to create a sustainable water infrastructure and set new standards for best practices in water sharing and management for the region? The outcome is unknown at the time of this writing. By the time you read this, Nestlé may have made its choice clear. Water issues are challenging, not so much because we lack the technologies to manage them effectively but since we have taken water for granted for so long we tend to discount its paramount value until we begin to run short. Handling the fact that fresh water is no longer available in endless supply requires not only an upgrade in technologies, it also requires a significant culture change. People all around the globe will have to make this change. Already over three-quarters of a billion people do not have adequate access to clean, safe water, and if we don't change our water practices, that number will continue to grow. More and more companies will be faced with these kinds of choices. Changing climate and changing times are bringing new and urgent challenges to us. Water access and safety is one of the most critical.

What major choices are looming for your business? How might those affect you personally and professionally? What considerations will you need to include? Who else will likely be affected by your choices? How are you preparing to handle big choices you may have to make?

Even as a leader, you don't have to go it alone. In fact, you probably shouldn't. Challenging times multiply the benefits leaders and businesses derive from collaborations. As an old Afghan proverb says, "If you think you're leading and no one is following you, then you're only taking a walk."

Collaborate. Get inspired, connect, act!

We've said it before and it bears repeating. No single individual, enterprise, community, or nation has the resources, the capacities, the skills, or the overall means to handle the impacts of changes already in the works by themselves. Individuals and enterprises must collaborate with others to achieve their own objectives while enabling others to achieve theirs. A go-it-alone mentality keeps people blind to externalities that can broadside them. Impacts from changing circumstances affecting the environment, communities, and society at large rumble through all of our networks regardless of whether we are prepared, and whether or not we choose to believe we'll be affected. In a networked world, isolation is a fantasy.

Throughout this chapter we are looking back to look forward. We are interweaving the technological with the social. We are expanding and refurbishing the lens through which we can envision the future. Often here we're taking the long view. That's for a couple of important reasons: (1) it shows that people have been through enormous social, economic, and/or environmental upheavals before, and come out the other side, and (2) it enables us to learn from hard-gained wisdoms from past times to help us cut through the noise of the moment and weigh potential consequences of the serious decisions we must undertake today.

Mapping your networks helps you identify not only the diverse connections of value you operate in but also what your roles and other people's roles are in those relationships. These maps are really visuals of who you depend on for what, and who depends on you. When you don't know something you need to know, to whom do you turn? When you need something you don't have, who do you go to? And vice versa, who turns to you? Where are your important assets, and who (else) controls them? Where is there leverage? Whom do you influence, and who influences you? Where is there reciprocity and where is there not? In these network systems, where are inflection points, spots where even small changes have the potential to disrupt the network(s)?

We sort of know some of these things but usually haven't mapped them out so we can intelligently manage critical relationships.

Sustainable enterprises can learn to architect participation in these globally connected systems by identifying, assessing, and engaging their existing interconnected personal, professional, and business networks. Applying systems thinking and collaborative cultures to an enterprise allows the enterprise to make sense of extremely dynamic and complex real-world events.

Putting networks to work: architecting participation

That value is created through material and human resource exchanges, and human networks and interactions is also not new. The ancient Silk Road was an early value network. Though not yet completed, China is building a New Silk Road with its trillion-dollar investment networked across continents, and is already creating value and driving commerce.

In the 21st century, even local trade has global components. Goods produced on every continent are transported to markets in developed countries; goods and services produced in developed countries are used in developing countries. Customer service and back office processing are often provided via contract by a third party on a different continent from both the customer and the contracting company. Technologically connected people can easily collaborate across distance and time zones. Business is already on a path of transformation where it is co-designing this path with many other organizations, each working to design their own new paths while mutually influencing each other. In this way enterprises are transforming capitalism and globalization. As a result, the world economy is transforming. Although considerable economic effort remains focused on producing goods, increasingly greater value is produced through relationships, knowledge creation, and delivery of services.

How do businesses organize to operate as sustainable enterprises in this connected, 21st-century, global business environment? What are the available tools and technologies to support them? What are the keys to putting human networks to work, architecting, and engaging participation?

Sustainable enterprise depends on understanding organizations as complex network webs. Human networks, built on interactions and knowledge sharing, are not limited to operating only inside organizations. The reach of these networks extends to influence many external organizations as well. Networked enterprises are co-created through relationships with customers, suppliers, partners, competitors, industry groups, and government bodies. Such enterprise network ecosystems are dynamic, reflecting the ability of the computer systems that support knowledge sharing and collaboration to aggregate and diffuse exponentially growing information about business conditions and technology developments.

Organizations as complex network webs

Seeing organizations as systems or networks is a biological rather than a mechanical view of an organization, giving it a "living" rather than a static quality. It also implies that the environment and the entity interact. One influences the other dynamically, which has tremendous relevance for sustainable systems. Death or dysfunction of either has significant consequences for the whole.

Fritjof Capra, a physicist, has written extensively on systems thinking and the importance of seeing organizations as living systems. He provides the following lessons (Capra, 2007) for the management of organizations:

LESSON #1

A living social system is a self-generating network of communications. The aliveness of an organization resides in its informal networks, or communities of practice. Bringing life into human organizations means empowering their communities of practice.

LESSON #2

You can never direct a social system; you can only disturb it. A living network chooses which disturbances to notice and how to respond. A message will get through to people in a community of practice when it is meaningful to them.

LESSON #3

The creativity and adaptability of life expresses itself through the spontaneous emergence of novelty at critical points of instability. Every human organization contains both designed and emergent structures. The challenge is to find the right balance between the creativity of emergence and the stability of design.

LESSON #4

In addition to holding a clear vision, leadership involves facilitating the emergence of novelty by building and nurturing networks of communications; creating a learning culture in which questioning is encouraged and innovation is rewarded; creating a climate of trust and mutual support; and recognizing viable novelty when it emerges, while allowing the freedom to make mistakes.

Today, computer networks track resource flows and show how people are connected. Figure 8.3 depicts a complex web of networks underlying a 21st-century organization. Although engaging employees and mobilizing their talents in a competitive, fast-moving business environment is

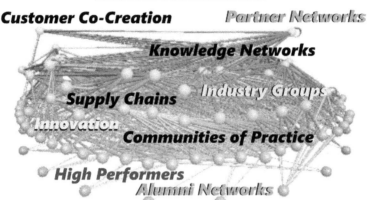

Figure 8.3 Organizations as complex network webs

Source: Adapted by J. Ambrozek from foodwebs.org, 2007, with permission. Image produced with FoodWeb3D, written by R. J. Williams and provided by the Pacific Ecoinformatics and Computational Ecology Lab (www.foodwebs.org, I. Yoon, R. J. Williams, E. Levine, S. Yoon, J. A. Dunne, & N. D. Martinez, 2004).

increasingly critical, it is only part of making enterprises sustainable. Vital too in relationship-focused organizations that have more intentional cores and dynamic peripheries (Gulati & Kletter, 2005) is engaging customers, partners, suppliers, external advisors, and industry groups to co-create the enterprise. For "individuals and groups, networks that span structural holes are associated with creativity and innovation, positive evaluations, early promotion, high compensation and profits" (Burt, 2006, p. 45).

Transorganizational collaboration and stakeholder engagement

Awareness of practices for collaboration and stakeholder engagement is not new; however, their application is still not commonplace. Organizational development publications are a rich resource of practical application and case examples that long predate the Internet. There is, however, still a need for more cross-discipline and transorganizational knowledge sharing. Many technology developers designing the social web or interactive Web tools, and sustainability practitioners seeking to effect change using these tools, are either not familiar with critical collaboration practices or are not practicing them sufficiently to achieve their objectives. Innovation and sustainable solutions emerge from these holistically integrated systems.

Architecting participation

Understanding how an organization operates as a human network ecosystem is a starting point. Architecting interactions and ensuring participation so knowledge is shared and ideas are implemented to create value is required. Paying attention to organizational structures, supporting a collaborative open culture that rewards sharing (Bryan & Joyce, 2007), and a technology platform that enables easy connectedness are all keys.

Personal networks: assets to manage

Sustainable enterprises are organizations that engage. They support employees in being engaged and effective as well. Network analysis helps people and their organizations recognize, understand, and facilitate networks inside and outside enterprise walls to improve strategic and operating effectiveness. The methodology also helps individuals enhance performance by considering the networks in which they participate. Interest in how individuals can network to improve their position has flourished since Mark Granovetter's classic 1973 "Strength of Weak Ties" article alerted people to the value of acquaintances in tasks such as finding jobs. Decades of work by thought leaders including Ron Burt have grown our understanding of how "social capital," the notion that "the people who do better are somehow better connected" (Burt, 2006, p. 32), actually works.

Additional research suggests that

> as much as 90 per cent of the information employees take action on comes from people in their network. As such, the quality and scope of an employee's networks has a substantial impact on his or her ability to solve problems, learn when transitioning into new roles and implement plans of any substance.
>
> (Cross, Thomas, & Light, 2006, p. 2)

Steve Borgatti (2004) summarizes current understanding of human networks:

- human networks are often clumpy—ideas and behavior are more homogeneous within groups;
- weak ties (at least those that are local bridges) connect the clumps;
- cosmopolitans bridge social worlds;
- structural holes increase chances of bridging;
- bridging creates value (slide 9).

Research by Cross et al. (2006) translates the theory into how high performers apply network dynamics by:

- positioning themselves at key points in a network and better leveraging their network when implementing plans;
- investing in relationships and extending expertise to help avoid learning biases and career traps;
- valuing networks and building high-quality relationships, not just big networks.

That people are socially networked today is a given. How people participate in their networks of choice, by connecting and sharing through physical and virtual meeting spaces, people experience the power of bonds with others with whom they share interests and concerns. The more active people are, the more new connections they get, including reconnecting with people from their pasts. Network analysis points out benefits of taking that insight to work, and managing one's network as an asset to bridge groups, grow, and learn. These skills are key to a person's performance. In the process, changing one's pattern of participation can contribute to changing one's organization.

Even if you have done this before, it's likely that the following personal network drawing exercise will give you new insights about your networks.

Personal network drawing exercise[25]

Jenny Ambrozek and Victoria Axelrod

Goal

Examine and learn from one of your personal networks

Tasks

1. **Think** about either your regular job or a project you are currently working on and the people with whom you are involved.
2. **Draw that network** of people with whom you interact by addressing the following questions:
   - Who do you go to for information to get your work done?
   - Who comes to you with questions to get their work done?
   - Who stands in the way of your getting work done?
   - Would you be more efficient if you had more access to some people?
   - Who do you go to for personal support? Professional support?

Use arrows to connect you to people in your network. Show which way the communication flows: toward or away from you. Can be both ways.

Adjust the thickness of the lines to reflect the volume of information flow.

Annotate your drawing using this key to show the nature of the communication flow:

YW: Your work
TW: Their work
RB: Roadblocks
WIHA: Wish I had access
S: Support

3. **Analyze your network.** What defines your network? Are most of the people in your network working for the same company where you work? Or, does your network cross boundaries to include people from different companies? Different industries? Are some of the people you include in your professional network also in your personal network? Consider actions you can take to make your network more efficient.

Add notes to your drawing.

4. **Take action.** Turn your thinking into improving your network and your performance at work. Who has knowledge that would be helpful to you? To what groups are you not connected but should be? Is there a conversation that needs to happen to reduce a roadblock? Reach out and network.

Putting human networks to work

Innovative organizations have always used the power of networks to invent new business models and opportunities that they expect will increase their success and sustainability.

Food revolutions

One of the ways people have always architected participation is around food. Eating together emphasized common needs among us. Breaking bread together, the companionship of sharing meals builds bonds. And so was the origin of company—from the Latin "com" meaning with, together, and "panis" meaning bread. Today the meaning of company has expanded from that original to include the organized connections among people working together. Fascinating that the connection with food is a hidden embedded in every company. An interesting tidbit, but why is it relevant to sustainable enterprise? One of the most critical challenges we face is feeding the billions of people on Earth today, a number that is still rapidly increasing. Zero Hunger is #2 of the 17 United Nations Sustainable Development Goals. According to the most recent report by the Food and Agriculture Organization (FAO) of the United Nations (2016), 815 million people go hungry, including significant numbers of people in developed countries. Add to that, with the global population expected to be close to

10 billion by 2050, we'll need to increase food production by 50%.[26] Food security, nutrition, access to clean water, and basic sanitation go hand in hand. We are not on track to have a world without hunger and malnutrition by 2030. Malnutrition in pregnant mothers increases the risk of preterm births, and subsequently malnutrition of those infants impairs the baby's brain, neurological, and immunological system growth and development (Keunen, van Elburg, van Bel, & Benders, 2014).

Conflict plays a role here also. So does climate change. People living in areas in conflict have less food and fresh water security. When people who have no access to food and water leave an area, they are forced by circumstances to migrate. Food insecurity leads to malnutrition. Migration shifts the burden of providing food and water from the former location to a new location increasing stress all around. Delivering on the challenge of feeding 10 billion people is one of the most pressing and pivotal needs humanity faces today. If we are to do that, we must invent not only new practices but whole new fields of endeavor. It's the ultimate doing well by doing good. This food mandate is part and parcel of human sustainability.

Nutrition is negatively impacted by soil nutrient and microbe depletion, particularly from excessive application of pesticides. Climate change, the droughts, floods, and low-latitude freezes that we're experiencing have the potential of seriously disrupting food supplies. Drought-prone California Central Valley is only one of many major food-producing areas that is extremely vulnerable.

Looking long-term, and from a systems perspective, it's clear that these problems will affect more than just the hundreds of millions directly suffering. Remember also that food and water are life essentials. Without confidence that people have ongoing access to those, the threshold of sustainability is unattainable. Where there are big challenges there are also big opportunity. Looking ahead, the Global Opportunity Report states that health, food, water, and energy are enormous markets of opportunity.[27]

Thinking outside the box, how can your business or organization participate to address this critical need for safe, secure food to nourish the coming 10-billion-person global population? Look to the future, yes, but also look at what you are currently doing that might be negatively impacting food supplies. Are your current supply chains polluting lands that had been productive farmland, like the mining of rare earth metals in Mongolia is doing? Are you using and not recovering phosphorus in manufacturing, making it unrecoverable for growing healthy people and plants? Are you using aquifer water at a rate faster than nature can replenish it? Those are just three examples highlighted earlier in this book. We have prompted you to look at the systems and networks of dependencies and opportunities where you and your business are players. What areas do you see where you are having a positive or negative impact on food supply, directly or indirectly? How might you make changes to what you're doing?

Having reviewed current operations, look to the future. You might want to revisit the six lenses in Chapter 7 and project possible business opportunities you could have related to food and water security. Those lenses are: Economic/financial, Technology, Poverty and inequity, Constraints on growth, Movement of talent, and Geopolitical.

As an inspiration, here are a few ideas and projects other forward-thinking companies are developing. Some of the largest companies in food are beginning to disrupt their own businesses. Cargill and Tyson Foods along with Richard Branson, Bill Gates, Atomico, and DFJ are investing in Memphis Meats. Memphis Meats is producing clean meat without slaughter. Can lab-grown meat taste even better than the pasture-grown variety? They all think so. Today people spend almost $1 trillion on meat, even though eating meat is beyond the reach of many of the world's low-income people. The goal of this company is to produce healthy, clean, nutritious, real meat while being environmentally responsible. It will emit 90% less carbon, use far less land, and consume far less water than conventional meat production does. It has already made beef meatballs, and chicken and duck filets by growing them from cells in its laboratory. Look it up.[28] Follow how it does. Follow the applications of science. Follow the innovations in technology and spinoffs from those. Will this company succeed? Will it be one of the ones creating our food-secure future? Too early to tell. Memphis Meats will have competitors. Follow those businesses too. Are there ways your business might contribute? Does this have the potential to disrupt any of your business? Think outside your box. Reinvent inside your box. Be a player.

Sticking with protein, what about crickets? They are packed with nutrition, and farming them has a very low impact on the environment. Would you eat food made from crickets? Aspire is betting that a whole lot of people will. It is already making cricket flour into snack food such as crackers. They look like ordinary triangle chips. Would you even know if you were eating a cricket cracker? Check it out.[29] Follow its progress. Learn about its technologies. Research its competitors. Is there an opportunity in this market for your business? Think outside the box.

Then there's Beyond Meat making plant-based patties to look and feel like juicy beef burgers. And who would have thought dulse (seaweed) could be made into "bacon?" But scientists at Oregon State University pioneered that, and Seamore Food is one company that is already making nutrient-packed, organic I Sea Bacon and selling it in Europe.[30] What else can be made from marine algae? Kelp forests are already being hurt by higher temperatures and CO_2 in our oceans. Once again, everything interconnects.

Sticking with plants, they're already sticking to the sides of buildings in some cities. Vertical farming. Food out your highrise window. Minimal transportation required. If you don't want your view blocked with your dinner salad, yours can grow on your roof, or your neighbor's roof, or in the old warehouse down the street, or even underground in an abandoned subway tunnel like they are doing in London.[31]

Are you fascinated by 3D printing? What about 3D printed food? Cloé Rutzerveld and Edible Growth see this as the designer sensation of the future. A whole edible ecosystem starts with a 3D printed edible shell containing a growing medium made from mushrooms, into which greens are seeded. The result looks like a beautiful canape with a lattice top and succulent greens peeking out. They haven't stopped there though. Their Digestive Food is a layered sandwich put together so that the carbs that start your digestive process hit your mouth first and the protein in the middle hits later. A sandwich that is designed with digestion in mind. Print dinner in your kitchen just before your guests arrive.[32]

The Japanese are designing food with an aging population in mind. How about taking a whole salmon, grinding it up, retexturing it, and serving it as a delicious salmon filet, with no need to watch for bones.

Almost half the produce grown today is thrown out and never eaten. We cannot afford such wanton waste in the future. In truth, we can't afford it today. Just in case we don't completely solve the problem of producing so much food waste, there are companies that are forming around recycling ugly fruits and vegetables into perfectly good, appealing food products. Industrial agriculture and consumer food waste is a system ripe for disruption. In addition to the high-tech innovations, people are also inventing environmentally supportive ways of growing food, more mindful versions of smaller-scale agroecology supplying regional needs.

IDEO's Design for Food is pioneering entire new food systems to be low or no or recycled food waste, clean, healthy, and sustainable. It's driven not only by technology but also by a new story of what's good to eat.[33]

This is just a tiny sampling of the exciting innovations happening in food. If you pay attention, query your networks, play with your own mashups of currently incongruent technologies and basic human needs, you'll probably come up with new possibilities too. When you do, post your new ventures on the Web so we and others will be inspired by what you do. The technology of sharing and collaboration has taken humanity to new levels.

Possibilities from technology leads us right into a conversation about blockchain.

Trust, transparency, and technology

> Mankind are not held together by lies. Trust is the foundation of society. Where there is no truth, and where there is no trust, there can be no society. Where there is society, there is trust, and where there is trust, there is something upon which it is supported.
>
> (Douglass, 1869)

Trust has reemerged as a critical issue of our time. Trust is essential to cooperation, to community, and to doing business sustainably. Fruitful collaboration that produces mutual benefits hinges on the abilities of participants, many of whom may never meet face-to-face, to be able to trust one another, to share information among the group, to respect each other and appreciate contributions made while valuing differences. The need to trust is built into the fabric of our being. Designed to live in groups and raise our offspring from initial dependency to adulthood, we must trust every step of the way. As we discussed earlier in this chapter though, trust has broken down between key partners, particularly between business and municipalities, citizens and government, and customers and business. Sustainability needs us to repair and rebuild broken trust. Thriveability demands it.

Powerful forces are reshaping the work we do, our workplaces, and our societies. Technological disruptions are rapidly filling the space between where we are today and the future we want. Navigating, harnessing, adapting, and creating with these new technologies will be indispensable skills for every professional. The disruptive potential of Artificial Intelligence (AI) and robotics jump into our newsfeeds every week. Will they change how we live and work? Absolutely! Do we know how, or to what extent? Not really, not yet. Robots attract our interest and scare us at the same time. They're coming but they won't sneak up on us. Some of the other new technologies on the horizon might catch us unaware. Blockchain has that potential.

If blockchain technology isn't on your radar, it should be. If you have heard of blockchain, it's probably in relation to Bitcoin or something about cryptocurrency. Its reach will be much greater than a novelty for financial speculation or microtrading. While those may be interesting developments, they're not even the half of it.

Blockchain and any similar types of open source technologies have the potential to disrupt just about everything from the way we think about things to our expectations of personal and business interactions. If we're not paying attention, we may find ourselves cut out of the loop before we realize what has happened. This is a bold and radical statement to make. There is a chance it won't happen but that chance is slim. Here's what some of the potential of this technology is, what likely areas of disruption are, and some changes that will come of them.

Blockchain technology makes Bitcoin and other cryptocurrencies a reliable medium for exchange because in essence it is a technology for tracking commitments and promises that is verified multiple times by multiple sources so going back and changing what was registered as a previous commitment or entry is almost impossible, and it's all traceable. Think digital ledger. Start with someone requesting a transaction. The request is broadcast through the network and picked up by a number of nodes that validate the request and attach their own digital identification to the resulting block of information. That verified transaction block gets combined with other transaction blocks to create a new combination block that is then added in the chain of already existing blocks. That transaction is completed when picked up by the designated receiver. Here is where the reliability comes in. In order to change the original transaction request, someone would have to be able to change everything that occurred all through the validation and chaining processes and that is so complex in aggregate to make it virtually impossible. While the process is complex, it's also transparent in that many people can see it. This elegant complexity makes blockchain work very well as a medium of exchange of commitments and promises. This kind of exchange is a fundamentally important way of thinking about currency, even now. Money is not really a thing. We no longer exchange salt, or cowry shells, or gold, or silver. Seventy years ago people exchanged paper, promissory notes that represented … promises of exchange of something of value with the exchange delayed by time and physical distance. In recent decades, we moved to electronic representations of promissory notes, so while some of us still hang on to dollar bills and debit or credit cards, the real currency is electronic transactions and transfers mediated by central banks. From here, it isn't a huge jump to cryptocurrency, except blockchain transactions do not require mediation from a central bank. It's peer-to-peer exchange. Here's a potentially huge disruption.

Thought exercise: If use of cryptocurrency outpaces central bank mediated electronic transfers, what does that do to nations? Right now central banks of nations negotiate currency exchange rates. What kind of Wild West might ensue in exchange if the use of central banks dwindled significantly? How would nations' accounting of debt and assets be affected? What about measurements of GDP?

If blockchain is a transaction founded on promises, it will be used for contracting, and in fact already is. In February, 2018, the second Internet of Agreements Conference was held. The theme was Blockchains and World Trade. Some of the session titles were:

* Blockchain, Smart Contracts & Law
* Mattereum: Automating and Enforcing Decentralized Commercial Law for Business on the Blockchain
* Blockchain in the Manufacturing Supply Chain—Implications for Trade and the Global Economy
* The Economic Impact on World Trade of Smart Ledgers.[34]

Cryptospace is fast becoming an indispensable new business space. So far we have blockchain disrupting banking, accounting, contracting, and supply chain. It's an easy jump from those to see how natural resources monitoring (people are already electronically tagging individual fish to track ethical, sustainable catch practices), and the whole of the insurance industry will morph when responsibilities and actions are transparent. Will organizations such as OASIS, Advancing open standards for the information society, take over roles previously performed by government? Let's touch back to governments again here. If transactions take place in cryptospace, with multiple nodes and destinations, and just say credits are left in this virtual space, what happens to government's ability to levy tax? Suddenly the potential disruptions take on enormous proportions.

We need to add in one more thread here, one that has surfaced throughout this chapter. That is trust. In a very real way blockchain types of technologies are certain builders of trust. Betrayal of trust becomes not only difficult, but trackable. This could be very good for collaborations across time and distance where people never meet face-to-face. Physical presence will interact with virtual presences, avatars of people, and again, they already are. Many benefits that we are just beginning to realize will emerge. The cost of this is loss of privacy. Now privacy as people in the United States have come to cherish is a very recent development in human history, only a few hundred years old at most. But if the notion of privacy is blown apart, that will change a number of the social conventions Americans hold dear. What else might this disrupt?

Again, this is only a brief and shallow foray into one of the technology disruptions that are emerging. Use insights from this chapter and the previous ones to hone your awareness. Pay attention to the seemingly insignificant, almost like using peripheral vision to see the Seven Sisters of the Pleiades in the star constellation of Taurus.

Conclusion: white spaces and water coolers

The environment and the economy are both sides of the same coin. You cannot sustain the economy if you don't take care of the environment because we know that the resources that we use, whether it is oil, energy, land ... all of these are the basis in which development happens. And development is what we say generates a good economy and puts money in our pockets. If we cannot sustain the environment, we cannot sustain ourselves.

(Maathai, 2010)

In case you hadn't put it together, many of the examples of collaboration, supportive technology, and transformative business models in this chapter involved one or more of the four survival essentials: water, food, energy, and/or, air. That was deliberate. Some of the most exciting work being done is businesses collaborating with civil society and governments to ensure that these key areas can support thriving metropolises.

We have also interwoven historical perspectives and threads. That's intentional too. Real sustainability demands taking the long view on people, economies, and our planetary environment. Looking back at conditions and threads, decisions and actions that got us to the state we're in is good preparation for honing awareness going forward.

Realities of a future very different from the present, economically, socially, and environmentally, will challenge our notions of control and power in many ways including those conventions regarding people and territory. In fact, it's already happening. Disruptive changes will necessarily recast our ideologies about ownership, intellectual property, and profits. Opportunities for co-creating a future that is equitable and prosperous abound. Who among us will step up to this challenge to be a leader/doer? Will you?

We've used the theme of bridge building for this book. When engineers build a bridge, it's not unusual for them to start from both shores and meet in the middle. For us that image is a good grounding, connecting us to the conditions and resources we have available on one side, and a vision of what it takes to be sustainable on the other side.

Thought exercise: What foundations do we need to lay in order to support the bridge deck on which we will travel? What resources and tools do we already have? What seems to be missing? Might someone else have already developed those? How will you find out? To whom will you reach out?

Humanity really is at a crossroads. Climate change is already exacting a toll on our lives. How best to address this pressing issue of sustainability and sustainable enterprise is an enigmatic question. What we choose is important, of course. How we choose what we choose is also important, and perhaps more so because how we choose will determine the qualities of all the whats that result from those choices. The best advice we can give is choose playfully. This is an unusual phrase to put at the conclusion of a chapter on enterprise, past, present, or future. Perhaps we are and always have been at our heart, as Johan Huizinga says in *Homo Ludens* (1950), players through and through. "In play we move below the level of the serious, as a child does; but we can also move above it—in the realm of the beautiful and the sacred," and, "To dare, to take risks, to bear uncertainty, to endure tension—these are the essence of the play spirit" (pp. 19, 51). In other words, free your mind to play with the question. It is and always has been through playful thoughts, imagining, that we envision a future. It is through play that we engage with others to give that vision substance. Play is how we learn as children when the world is still an unknown and uncertain place to us. Play allows us to experiment, to invent, to be OK not having definitive answers, especially when the outcomes cannot yet be known. Play is underrated and invaluable in today's uncertain world where we must invent sustainable enterprise. To play and be game is to be ready for action, alert, all resources gathered. We need that spirit now as much as anyone ever has.

James P. Carse addresses this in his book *Finite and Infinite Games* (1986). As the conclusion of this book, Carse presents 101 verses. Here are some that relate powerfully to the transformation sustainability demands of us. He starts off with:

1

There are at least two kinds of games. One could be called finite, the other, infinite. A finite game is played for the purpose of winning, an infinite game for the purpose of continuing the play.

2

If a finite game is to be won by someone, it must come to a definite end. It will come to an end when someone has won … It is an invariable principle of all play, finite and infinite, that whoever plays, plays freely. Whoever *must* play, cannot *play*.

Carse goes on to say,

53

I am both the outcome of my past and the transformation of my past. To be related to the past as its outcome is to stand in casual continuity with it … It is the genius in us who knows that the past is most definitely past, and therefore not forever sealed but forever open to creative reinterpretation.

95

A story attains the status of myth when it is retold, and persistently retold, solely for its own sake.

He concludes the book as we conclude this chapter:

100

Infinite players are not actors in any story, but the joyful poets of a story that continues to originate what they cannot finish.

101

THERE IS BUT ONE INFINITE GAME.

We are collectively the authors of a story of sustainability that we continue to originate, one that none of us will finish. To be sustainably engaged in enterprise is to be a key player in human life. How we play together, and what we create together will determine whether or not humanity thrives. Sustainability is not and cannot be a spectator sport. We authors of *The Sustainable Enterprise Fieldbook* do not accept visions of hopelessness or powerlessness to create a thriving future. We are crafting a story of hope and can do. We're shouting it. We're sharing it. We're living it. We are all in. Are you?

Notes

1 "How many trees are used to make pencils each year?" *Pristine Planet.* Retrieved January 3, 2018, from www.pristineplanet.com/eco-info/how-many-trees-are-used-to-make-pencils-each-year.asp.

2 Recyclable. Retrieved November 10, 2017, from www.concretethinker.com/solutions/Recyclable.aspx.

3 Production volume of glass containers and bottles worldwide from 2015 to 2022 (in million metric tons). Retrieved November 12, 2017, from www.statista.com/statistics/700260/glass-bottles-and-containers-production-volume-worldwide/.

4 General recycling facts. Retrieved October 22, 2017, from www.recycleacrossamerica.org/recycling-facts.

5 "The world's largest corporate sustainability initiative." UN Global Compact. Retrieved November 20, 2017, from www.unglobalcompact.org/what-is-gc/mission.

6 The Sustainable Development Goals Report 2017. Retrieved September 14, 2017, from https://unstats.un.org/sdgs/report/2017/.

7 Anne Hidalgo, Summit Closing Speech (December 2, 2016) C40 Blog. Retrieved December 18, 2017, from www.c40.org/blog_posts/anne-hidalgo-summit-closing-speech.

8 Retrieved January 1, 2018, from http://ficci.in/events-page.asp?evid=23185.

9 "Environmental costs of electric bikes vs. cars and motorcycles." *Electric Bike Review*. Retrieved January 21, 2018, from https://electricbikereview.com/guides/environmental-cost-ebikes-vs-cars-motorcycles/.

10 "A fully solar-powered car may be hitting the road by 2019." *Futurism*. Retrieved January 4, 2018, from https://futurism.com/fully-solar-powered-car-hitting-road-2019/.

11 "The struggle is widespread." National Low-Income Housing Coalition. Retrieved February 1, 2018, from http://nlihc.org/oor.

12 2018 Edelman Trust Barometer Global Report. Retrieved January 24, 2018, from http://cms.edelman.com/sites/default/files/2018-01/2018_Edelman_Trust_Barometer_Global_Report_Jan.PDF.

13 John Doerr: Seeking salvation and profit in greentech. TED, May 30, 2007. Retrieved June 4, 2007, from www.youtube.com/watch?v=nuXJFbJNltg.

14 World Economic Forum Annual Meeting. Retrieved January 23, 2018, from www.weforum.org/events/world-economic-forum-annual-meeting-2018/sessions/creating-a-shared-future-in-a-fractured-world.

15 "Urban development." World Bank, January 2, 2018. Retrieved January 30, 2018, from www.worldbank.org/en/topic/urbandevelopment/overview.

16 "A call to action in the Age of Trump." Global Strategy Group. Retrieved February 11, 2018, from www.globalstrategygroup.com/wp-content/uploads/2018/02/BusinessPolitics_2018.pdf.

17 Pink, D. Cocktail Party Summary. Retrieved February 7, 2018, from www.danpink.com/drive-the-summaries/.

18 "Our 9,000-year love affair with booze." *National Geographic* Magazine, February 2017. Retrieved December 26, 2017, from www.nationalgeographic.com/magazine/2017/02/alcohol-discovery-addiction-booze-human-culture/.

19 "Heineken, Brewing a Better World." Retrieved February 9, 2018, from www.theheinekencompany.com/sustainability/brewing-a-better-world.

20 "About gateway cities." *MassINC*. Retrieved January 25, 2018, from https://massinc.org/our-work/policy-center/gateway-cities/about-the-gateway-cities/.

21 UNDG Capacity Development. Retrieved February 12, 2018, from https://web.archive.org/web/20140209130601/http://undg.org/docs/8948/Capacity-Development-UNDG-August-2009.pdf.

22 Integration Initiative. Retrieved February 1, 2018, from www.livingcities.org/work/the-integration-initiative.

23 Working Cities Challenge Overview. Retrieved January 15, 2018, from www.bostonfed.org/workingcities/about/index.htm.

24 "Creating a Shared Future in a Fractured World." WEF Annual Meeting. Retrieved January 20, 2018, from www.weforum.org/events/world-economic-forum-annual-meeting-2018/about.

25 Adapted from an exercise developed by Joe Cloonan, knowledge management research coordinator. First published in *Knowledge Tree* eJournal, 2007.

26 "How close are we to #zero hunger?" FAO. Retrieved, February 15, 2018, from www.fao.org/state-of-food-security-nutrition/en/.

27 Global Opportunity Report 2018. Retrieved February 12, 2018, from www.dnvgl.com/about/sustainability/global-opportunity-report/index.html.

28 Memphis Meats, Our Story. Retrieved February 8, 2018, from www.dnvgl.com/about/sustainability/global-opportunity-report/index.html.

29 Aspire Food Group. Retrieved February 15, 2018, from www.aspirefg.com/.

30 I Sea Bacon. Seamore Food. Retrieved February 3, 2018, from https://seamorefood.com/iseabacon/.

31 "Inside London's first underground farm." *Independent* (February 3, 2017). Retrieved February 15, 2018, from www.independent.co.uk/Business/indyventure/growing-underground-london-farm-food-waste-first-food-miles-a7562151.html.

32 Cloé Rutzerveld Food & Concept Design. Retrieved February 10, 2018, from www.chloerutzerveld.com/#/edible-growth-2014/.

33 "IDEO's approach to designing a better food system." *IDEO*. Retrieved February 3, 2018, from www.ideou.com/blogs/inspiration/ideos-approach-to-designing-a-better-food-system?utm_medium=email&utm_source=mailchimp&utm_campaign=4.1-food-studio-webinar-thanks-2018-jan&mc_cid=4cd9f0f297&mc_eid=26a056d6ab.

34 Internet of agreements. Retrieved February 11, 2018, from www.eventbrite.co.uk/e/the-second-internet-of-agreements-conference-blockchains-and-world-trade-tickets-42355788303.

References

Alveredo, F., Chancel, L., Piketty, T., Saez, E., & Zucman, G. (2017). *World Inequality Report 2018*. Retrieved January 24, 2018, from http://wir2018.wid.world/files/download/wir2018-full-report-english.pdf.

Arrhenius, S. (1896, April). On the influence of carbonic acid in the air upon the temperature of the ground. *Philosophical Magazine and Journal of Science*, Series 5, Volume 41, 237–276. Retrieved February 13, 2018, from www.rsc.org/images/Arrhenius1896_tcm18-173546.pdf.

Associated Press. (2017, December 22). California warns Nestle about millions of gallons of water drawn from San Bernardino National Forest. *Los Angeles Times*. Retrieved December 22, 2017, from http://beta.latimes.com/local/lanow/la-me-nestle-water-20171221-story.html.

Bausells, M. (2016, May 17). Superblocks to the rescue: Barcelona's plan to give the streets back to the residents. *The Guardian*. Retrieved December 20, 2017, from www.theguardian.com/cities/2016/may/17/superblocks-rescue-barcelona-spain-plan-give-streets-back-residents.

Berkshire Bridges—Working Cities Pittsfield Implementation Grant Narrative Proposal Summary Overview. Private papers. Linda M. Kelley 2016.

Bernays, E. (1928). *Propaganda*. New York: H. Liveright.

Borgatti, S. (2004). Burt's "Social origin of good ideas" paper. PowerPoint presentation, MB 814 Fall 2004 Schedule. Retrieved October 9, 2007, from www.analytictech.com/mb814/slides/Burt.pdf.

Bryan, L., & Joyce, C. (2007). *Mobilizing minds: Creating wealth from talent in the 21st century organization*. New York: McGraw-Hill.

Burt, R. S. (2006). Structural holes versus network closure as social capital. In K. S. Cook, R. S. Burt, & N. Lin (Eds.), *Social capital: Theory and research* (pp. 31–56). New Brunswick, NJ: Aldine Transaction, Transaction Publishers. (Original work published 2001).

Capra, F. (2007). Life and leadership: A systems approach (Executive summary). Retrieved December 21, 2007, from www.fritjofcapra.net/management.html.

Carse, J. P. (1986). *Finite and infinite games: A vision of life as play and possibility*. New York: Ballantine Books.

Cross, R., Thomas, R. J., & Light, D. A. (2006). How top talent uses networks and where rising stars get trapped (Research report). Network roundtable at the University of Virginia. Retrieved October 9, 2007, from https://webapp.comm.virginia.edu/NetworkRoundtable/Portals/0/Public/ Research/High_Performer_Networks_and_Traps_Roundtable_Final.pdf.

Douglass, F. (1869, December 7). Our composite nationality. Retrieved February 16, 2018, from http://teachingamericanhistory.org/library/document/our-composite-nationality/.

Du Boff, R. (2017, October 10). What is just when it comes to CEO-to-average worker pay? *Forbes*. Retrieved February 19, 2018, from www.forbes.com/sites/justcapital/2017/10/10/what-is-just-when-it-comes-to-ceo-to-average-worker-pay/2/#64bf2c7d50d4.

Dwortzan, M. (2017, May 17). Tackling air pollution in China. *MIT News*. Retrieved January 2, 2018, from http://news.mit.edu/2017/tackling-air-pollution-in-china-0517.

Friedman, M. (2002). *Capitalism and freedom: Fortieth anniversary edition*. Chicago, IL: University of Chicago Press.

Granovetter, M. S. (1973). The strength of weak ties. *American Journal of Sociology, 78*(6), 1360–1380.

Gulati, R., & Kletter, D. (2005). Shrinking core—expanding periphery: The relational architecture of high performing organizations. *California Management Review, 47*(3), 77–104.

Hanley, S. (2017, December 30). China opens 1-kilometer long solar road. *Clean Technica*. Retrieved January 3, 2018, from https://cleantechnica.com/2017/12/30/china-opens-1-kilometer-long-solar-road/.

Head, W. A. (1979). Community development in post-industrial society: Myth or reality? In D. A. Chekki (Ed.), *Community development: Theory and method of planned change* (pp. 101–113). New Delhi: Vikas Publishing House.

Huizinga, J. (1950). *Homo ludens: A study in the play element in culture.* First Beacon. Paperback edition published 1955. Reprinted by arrangement with Routledge & Kegan Paul, Ltd., London.

Hurst, A. (2017, February 16). How Heineken Mexico's CEO used purpose to unleash the power of his organization. *Fast Company.* Retrieved February 10, 2018, from www.fastcompany.com/3068060/how-heineken-mexicos-ceo-uses-purpose-to-unleash-the-power-of-his-organiz.

Irfan, U. (2017, November 25). How Delhi became the most polluted city on Earth. *Vox.* Retrieved December 31, 2017, from www.vox.com/energy-and-environment/2017/11/22/16666808/india-air-pollution-new-delhi.

Keltner, D. (2016, October). Don't let the power corrupt you. *Harvard Business Review.* Retrieved August 17, 2017, from https://hbr.org/2016/10/dont-let-power-corrupt-you.

Keunen, K., van Elburg, R. M., van Bel, F., & Benders, J. N. L. (2014, October 14). Impact of nutrition on brain development and its neuroprotective implications following preterm birth. *Nature.* Retrieved February 15, 2018, from www.nature.com/articles/pr2014171.

Lambert, F. (2017, September 28). China delays electric car plans by a year—still more ambitious than most countries. *Electrek.* Retrieved January 3, 2018, from https://electrek.co/2017/09/28/china-delays-electric-car-plans-by-a-year/.

Leary, K. (2017, November 17). California may reach its renewable energy goal 10 years early. *Futurism.* Retrieved November 19, 2017, from https://futurism.com/california-reach-renewable-energy-goal-10-years-early/.

London, B. (1932). *Ending the depression through planned obsolescence.* Retrieved December 11, 2017, from https://babel.hathitrust.org/cgi/pt?id=wu.89097035273;view=1up;seq=8.

Maathai, W. (2010, June). Message filmed in Uganda for the G8/G20 Climate Change in Toronto, Canada. Retrieved February 18, 2018, from www.youtube.com/watch?v=ApndDOwO8RA.

Meadows, D., Randers, J., & Meadows, D. (2004). A synopsis, *Limits to Growth*, the 30-year update. White River Junction, VT: Chelsea Green. PDF. Retrieved January 2015, from www.unice.fr.

Meadows, D. H., & Club of Rome. (1972). *Limits to Growth: A report for the Club of Rome's project on the predicament of mankind.* New York: Universe Books.

Monteleone, D. Photographer. (2018, January 8). A new Silk Road. *The New Yorker.* Retrieved January 18, 2018, from www.newyorker.com/magazine/2018/01/08/a-new-silk-road.

Owen, D. (2017, May 29). The world is running out of sand. *The New Yorker.* Retrieved November 10, 2017, from www.newyorker.com/magazine/2017/05/29/the-world-is-running-out-of-sand.

Singh, M. P. (2014, January 23, updated May 13, 2016). At Kaladera farmers battle beverage giant. *The Hindu.* Retrieved December 22, 2017, from www.thehindu.com/news/national/other-states/at-kaladera-farmers-battle-beverage-giant/article5606745.ece.

Skibsted, J. M. (2017, December 21). The small, silent revolution that could change your commute. *World Economic Forum*. Retrieved December 31, 2017, from www. weforum.org/agenda/2017/12/small-silent-commute-revolution/.

Smart Mobility 2018. (2018). *Smart Mobility 2018: Bringing transportation into the 21st century*. Retrieved January 2, 2018, from https://cdait.gatech.edu/sites/default/files/_jw3cnsmartmobility2018main8.pdf.

Solheim, E. (2018, January 24). *New consumption frontiers*. Livestream, January 24, 2018, www.weforum.org/events/world-economic-forum-annual-meeting-2018/sessions/rethinking-waste-as-a-resource.

Solnit, R. (2017, May 30). The loneliness of Donald Trump. *Literary Hub*. Retrieved August 17, 2017, from http://lithub.com/rebecca-solnit-the-loneliness-of-donald-trump/.

Taleb, N. (2016, September 11). Where you cannot generalize from knowledge of the parts. *Medium*. Retrieved August 5, 2017, from https://medium.com/incerto/where-you-cannot-generalize-from-knowledge-of-parts-continuation-to-the-minority-rule-ce96ca3c5739.

United Nations Global Compact. www.unglobalcompact.org/what-is-gc.

Wells, W. (2016, August 25). How Coca-Cola India made water a top priority. *Coca-Cola*. Retrieved December 24, 2017, from www.coca-colacompany.com/stories/how-coca-cola-india-made-water-a-top-priority.

World Economic Forum. (2018). *Global Risks Report 2018*. Retrieved January 17, 2018, from www3.weforum.org/docs/WEF_GRR18_Report.pdf.

Part V

Building new bridges
to the future

A path forward

Building new bridges to the future

*Jeana Wirtenberg, Linda M. Kelley, David Lipsky,
and William G. Russell*

We are at a unique moment in history, where we can and must create a new future for enterprises—indeed for all humanity—to thrive into the future and for perpetuity. It is at once daunting, frightening, overwhelming, and incredibly exciting. Many signals point to things getting worse and worse—as we continue to deplete our natural resources, increase income inequality, value profits over people, destroy biodiversity, and leave less and less for the next generation, and the next. Yet on the positive side, as we have documented throughout this book, we see millions of people on the side of doing what's right, and what's necessary.

It starts with a commitment to work together to accelerate the journey from awareness to understanding and, most important, to action. Factual awareness alone will not slow our regress; global understanding and collective action leading to collective impact will move us in the right direction. This moment, the moment we are all in together, is our greatest opportunity to forge a new path forward.

We have chosen to use the metaphor of building new bridges. We have described many of the stepping stones, accelerators, and pillars that will make these bridges sturdy and passable throughout this book. And we have seen up front many of the barriers keeping us stuck. If only we can release ourselves from the myopia, mental models, and paradigms that keep us so stuck, we firmly believe we can and will move inexorably into a brighter, thriving future for us all.

Let's start with what's keeping us so stuck and how we can move on to get unstuck.

What's keeping us stuck and how do we get unstuck?

Here we distill and discuss 10 restraining forces impeding change, followed by 10 countervailing forces driving positive change, as depicted in Figure 9.1. As we will see, there are big theoretical tensions that must be addressed, and there are more practical ones whose answers require practical research. Our work has amplified the tensions that lie in the different views of the causes

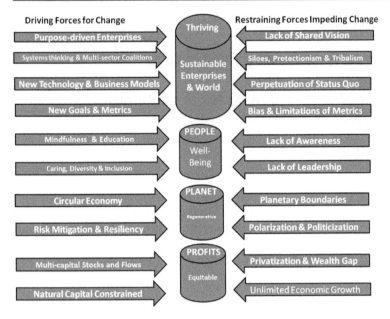

Driving Forces for Change | Restraining Forces Impeding Change

Thriving

Sustainable Enterprises & World

Driving Forces	Restraining Forces
Purpose-driven Enterprises	Lack of Shared Vision
Systems thinking & Multi-sector Coalitions	Siloes, Protectionism & Tribalism
New Technology & Business Models	Perpetuation of Status Quo
New Goals & Metrics	Bias & Limitations of Metrics

PEOPLE
Well-Being

Mindfulness & Education	Lack of Awareness
Caring, Diversity & Inclusion	Lack of Leadership

PLANET
Regenerative

Circular Economy	Planetary Boundaries
Risk Mitigation & Resiliency	Polarization & Politicization

PROFITS
Equitable

Multi-capital Stocks and Flows	Privatization & Wealth Gap
Natural Capital Constrained	Unlimited Economic Growth

Figure 9.1 Driving and restraining forces for change

and cures of sustainability. We are at greatest risk when we think we have the only correct answer for anything. One example of this is the use of biofuels as a solution for reducing the negative environmental impacts of our current fuels, without considering the impact on global food production (Kleiner, 2007). We believe that the opportunities for progress lie in our ability to expose these tensions and come up with solutions that accelerate rather than compromise sustainability.

1. Lack of shared vision

First and foremost what's keeping us stuck is our deep-seated collective fear of the unknown—and the essentially unknowable—future that lies ahead. A significant factor exacerbating this fear is the lack of understanding and alignment around what we're even talking about in our conversations about sustainability. As debates rage on and on, if we stop long enough to *really listen*, we find that we are so often talking past each other, and even taking sides with no common and agreed-upon understanding of our most basic terminology.

Every day we even see sustainability colleagues and advocates arguing over calling this a "green movement," "flourishing," "sustainability," "corporate social responsibility," which to us is like arguing over the color of the deck chairs on the *Titanic*. It's not going to help us survive, but may keep us busy and distracted as we all go down. Fundamentally, we're all talking about the same thing regardless of what we call it, and we choose to focus on the notion of thriving (but would cave in a minute if it meant getting everyone aligned and moving forward!). On a positive note, we are gratified to see how the UN Sustainable Development Goals are gaining strength and momentum as a unifying rallying cry across countries, sectors, and industries.

2. Silos, protectionism, and tribalism

Still a second barrier that's keeping us stuck is the ubiquity of silos. Everywhere we see silos, we lose the opportunity for true collaboration—across functions and disciplines, across generations, across sectors, across industries, across countries, across every kind of artificial fault line we have created to help us stay in our comfort zone. So what's the antidote? We need to step out of our comfort zones, learn to walk in other people's shoes, listen with empathy, caring, and compassion. We need to find ways to let go of "either–or" and move every conversation to the possibilities inherent in "both/and" thinking and ways of being.

3. Perpetuation of status quo

A third factor keeping us stuck is the inertia and perpetuation of the status quo, as we seem to forget that we created these unsustainable systems in the first place, and have the power to change them, if only we have the will. We endlessly complain about the unworkability of the entrenched capital market systems, where profit continues to be king. Despite mountains of evidence that the triple bottom line produces better financial results for companies, we continue to see a preoccupation with the single bottom line. Many large companies act like they are "too big to fail," as we've seen with the rapid descent of GE, which until recently was considered one of the most sustainable companies in the world.

Add to this the short-termism of Wall Street, the narrow view of costs versus total cost of use, and the exclusion of natural capital in our financial evaluations.

As discussed in detail in Chapter 8, built deeply into our systems is entrenched overconsumption and planned obsolescence, two factors that keep us going on the same treadmill of unsustainability.

4. Bias and limitations of metrics

On top of this we have discussed how GDP comes up very short in that it is often measuring the wrong things, and not valuing the right things. Here we surely highlight the fact that externalities are still not counted, so we're not measuring what really counts and the things that will inexorably determine the future of our planet and life as we know it.

5. Lack of awareness

Still another factor that keeps us stuck is the lack of awareness of the general population regarding the current state of affairs as it relates to all aspects of sustainability. One area where this is particularly notable is in the lack of consumer demand for sustainable products. A few years ago I led a major symposium with hundreds of people at the Academy of Management. I'll never forget Jay Barney's comment, after he had just won a lifetime award for his work in Strategy. He looked at the audience and essentially said, although maybe not in so many words, "It's all your fault." What he meant was consumers' choices are shaping what is made and what is not. If consumers choose the sustainable products every day, the rules of supply and demand will help the prices come down, and economies of scale will lead to better outcomes for everyone.

6. Lack of leadership

The leader's role as well as the act of leadership is critical in the shift to sustainability. As we learned in the leadership chapter, Chapter 1, an organization is leaderful when the information flow is open, relationships are healthy, employees are involved in decision-making, and initiative is encouraged. If an employee in the organization, regardless of level, sees something that needs to be done, she or he steps forward to meet the need and is supported in that effort by upper management.

All major change efforts require audacious leaders who have their sights set on future challenges and opportunities. Those at the forefront have to face not only opportunities but also responsibilities. Each of us has enormous potential to contribute to collective sustainability. How will you choose to spend your energy to drive sustainability individually and in the groups and enterprises you belong to? Our hope is that these collective efforts will contribute to a tipping point, and ultimately bring about the global transformation to a sustainable future for us all.

7. Planetary boundaries

As we saw in Chapter 6, humanity is confronting immutable science-based limitations in our ability to support the growing population of 9.5 billion people expected by 2050 and beyond. Just today we saw that "According to UN-endorsed projections, global demand for fresh water will exceed supply by 40% in 2030, thanks to a combination of climate change, human action and population growth."[1] The cities predicted to experience this critical water shortage include: Cape Town, Sao Paulo, Bangalore, Beijing, Cairo, Jakarta, Moscow, Istanbul, Mexico City, London, Tokyo, and Miami.

8. Polarization and politicization

A constraint keeping us stuck is the extreme polarization and politicization of issues that—because they are essential to all people everywhere, should never be politicized. Here we are particularly impressed with social psychologist Jonathan Haidt's (2012) work documenting how the increasing politicization of an entire spectrum of issues (e.g., healthcare, immigration, climate change) dwarfs all other factors combined in explaining the fault lines that draw people to one side or the other, defying all logic and common sense. Haidt argues that it is our righteous certainty that those who see things differently are wrong which stands in the way of mutual understanding. Haidt makes the claim that underlying these divisions is our fundamental need to belong to groups, i.e., our "groupishness." In his groundbreaking final chapter on ideology and civility, Haidt points to the deep-seated values that underlie both sides, arguing that we need the insights of liberals, conservatives, and libertarians to flourish as a nation.

9. Privatization and wealth gap

Limits to growth and the tragedy of the commons are practices that determine who has access to resources. In limits to growth, some resources that people want are scarce so no one can have as much as they would like to have. There just isn't enough. The tragedy of the commons comes about when resources that would be at least marginally sufficient if shared and managed, are grabbed or hoarded by a few people who take excessive amounts, leaving not enough for the rest of the people to use.

With privatization, a few people control who can access desired resources. The owners of those resources tend to retain them and restrict use to people who pay the owners for that use, and as a result, "the rich get richer." Assigning a monetary value to common resources makes increasing prices charged for access the expedient way of limiting access and maintaining control, versus the more sustainable approach involving the dynamic management of those resources for the betterment of all. Only those who can afford to pay the price set by the owner for commonly desired resources (e.g., parklands, museums, water systems) can use them. While we do need to regulate access to scarce, commonly desired or needed resources, we need to create practices that do so equitably. Lack of access is playing out in our healthcare, education, and political systems. These and many other systems will need to set access and use fairly if we are to have a sustainable future. Otherwise these important systems will fail.

10. Unlimited economic growth

This goes along with the mistaken perception that "growth" is a necessity for companies to be successful. As we have discussed many times, it will be critical to decouple the notion of economic growth from the consumption of our precious and finite natural resources.

We could go on and on, but you get the idea. So how do we get out of this conundrum and build new bridges to a better future?

10 driving forces for change

Despite these formidable restraining forces keeping us so stuck, we see much cause for optimism. Ten positive, driving forces for change are briefly described here, each of which could be an entire chapter of our next book! We have loosely juxtaposed these against the related restraining forces in the force field diagram shown in Figure 9.1.

1. Purpose-driven enterprises

The first positive trend we have focused on throughout this book is the pro-liferation of purpose-driven organizations. Young people want to work in these organizations, and the results are paying off for organizations in all sorts of tangible and intangible ways (i.e., in terms of attraction, retention, prod-uctivity, employee engagement). The explosion of the entire field of positive psychology, with its emphasis on finding meaning through work, grati-tude, mindfulness, presence, and compassion breathes positive energy into enterprises which is at once calming, rejuvenating, and energizing.

We need to unlock and unleash the energy, creativity, and talent of people in organizations who seek purpose, passion, challenge, and meaning in their work. Given the statistics on lack of engagement of workers worldwide, we are sitting on a remarkable, underutilized pool of talent that must be applied to designing businesses that can meet the needs of people and increase pros-perity for all.

2. Systems thinking and multi-sector coalitions

As we have seen, systems thinking—also referred to as integrated thinking—is a critically important skill for operating under the kinds of conditions of uncertainty and complexity we see today. This includes understanding how the system works, dealing with ambiguity, understanding the interdependen-cies and interconnections of systems, seeing the big picture and connecting the dots. It also will require working across disciplines, and taking a long-term perspective. Fortunately, because systems thinking is inborn to all human beings, these skills can be rediscovered, upgraded, and honed with practice. On the other hand, since we currently school people in linear, direct cause and effect thinking as the go-to practice for success, the most difficult challenge may be how to make starting from a systems perspective the new normal, and from there tackle any component issues.

One very positive trend for addressing our challenges systemically are the multi-sector coalitions we see proliferating, as discussed in Chapter 8. Public-private partnerships, natural capital coalitions, and the Paris Agreement are all tremendously positive steps giving us hope and accelerating our progress across the bridge to sustainable enterprise.

As discussed in Chapter 2 on Mental Models, as well as in Chapter 1 on Leadership, and Chapter 3 on Strategy, we are largely constrained by our failure to think holistically using systems and integrated thinking. While these skills are not easy, they are learnable. In addition to the tools we have provided in our physical book, and in our *Living Fieldbook*, we call attention to a new way of thinking about learning, which fits the challenges of the future, called Learning 4.0. Here we are inspired by Patricia McLagan's (2017) new book *Unstoppable You* which provides a path forward, tools and exercises, that can help us meet the learning challenges of today and tomorrow head on.

3. New technology and business models

One of the most promising trends we see is the emergence of new economic and business models. Business models that are driving positive change involve the decoupling of growth and prosperity in the capital markets systems, conscious capitalism, B Corporations, social enterprise, the triple bottom line, corporate social responsibility, and corporate citizenship.

A third trend we are bearing witness to every day involves the amazing pace of innovation. We are particularly inspired by the creativity and imagination of young people, such as the four Rutgers students who recently won the Hult Prize of $1 million for their brilliant program to help refugees find work, dignity, and education through solar-powered smart transportation. Innovations in the green economy using not only technology, but biomimicry, to learn from nature and go beyond renewal to regeneration are at once mind-blowing and inspiring.

In Accenture's *Waste to Wealth* book by Lacy and Rutqvist (2015), no fewer than 10 disruptive technologies are cited that are fueling and enhancing the circular economy: mobile technologies, machine-to-machine (M2M) communication, cloud computing, social media, big data analytics, modular design technology, advanced recycling technology, life and material sciences technology, trace and return systems, and 3D printing.

4. New goals and metrics

Our antidote to much of the malaise confronting humanity is to create a shared vision of a possible new future that is better than what we have today. We firmly believe and have seen much evidence that the 17 UN Sustainable Development Goals help to provide such a vision. Every time we have shown the SDGs to audiences as diverse as CEOs of small, medium, and large companies, undergraduate and graduate students, NGOs, and many others, the mood changes and a new spark of possibility lights up the room.

The leading-edge work around new metrics described in Chapter 6 gives us cause for concern if it isn't heeded, as well as optimism if it is. Whether we're looking at the SDGs, CDP, ESG, and tools for measuring profitability from sustainability interventions, there is much cause for hope.

5. Mindfulness and education

Education and training at all levels will inevitably lead to greater awareness, consciousness, and actions around sustainability. In higher education, we see the Principles for Responsible Management Education (PRME) supporting the implementation of the UN SDGs as a huge step forward, gaining momentum, with more than 670 Universities signing on around the world (including Rutgers!). The AIM2Flourish (aim2flourish.com) initiative supports PRME and engages students around the world in identifying positive examples of business doing well and doing good. As these innovations become more visible, they also become more scalable and replicable, fueling positive and sustainable growth both exponentially and organically.

This is buttressed by many other more local associations, such as the New Jersey Higher Education Partnership for Sustainability (NJHEPS), the Association for the Advancement of Sustainability in Higher Education (AASHE), and many others. Exciting programs in K-12 such as the Student Governmental Affairs Program (SGAP) are proliferating. Corporate training and executive education programs are teaching leaders and managers the basics of sustainability-aligned leadership and strategy.

6. Caring, diversity, and inclusion

The sixth positive trend has to do with the increasing attention to diversity and inclusion in businesses around the world, focused on closing the gender gap, reducing racial inequalities, and providing equal opportunities around affordable education to all. Respect for diversity is clearly illustrated in the "Mental models in civil society" case in Chapter 2 (pages 112–115) and is beautifully described in the essay by Shakira Abdul-Ali, "New frameworks for leading sustainable enterprise" in Chapter 1 (pages 69–75), and the Working Cities Challenge in Chapter 8 (pages 418–422).

A related hopeful trend we see is the integration of religious and green faith movements into the conversation on sustainability. The Pope's encyclical, beseeching us to take better care of our planet, inspires millions of people of all faiths to take care of our precious natural resources and our only home on Planet Earth.

Further, we are heartened by the energy of the millennial Y and Z generations we are raising and teaching in the Universities. We see many positive generational shifts, fueled by the war for talent, social media, and their desire for better work-life balance. Seeking social justice, examples abound of young people inventing new ways of working and living that meet the needs of themselves and the generations to come.

7. Circular economy

The seventh positive trend focuses attention on the rapid growth of the circular and sharing economies. Bloomberg's last three sustainability conferences in NYC focused on this topic, highlighting wonderful examples of the sharing economy such as Lyft, Uber, Airbnb, with many more emerging every day. Lacy and Rutqvist's (2015) recent book on turning *Waste to Wealth* gave us the business case to see that this is no longer a pipe dream, but is rapidly becoming the only way to do business in the 21st century. Examples abound of creative and inspiring local economy solutions, along with the development of regenerative products. An entire movement is emerging around resilient cities with successful local economy models throughout the world.

8. Risk mitigation and resiliency

The eighth positive trend comes from myriad examples we see of people stepping up to address climate change through risk mitigation and adaptation. The World Economic Forum's (2018) focus on sustainability-related issues continues to shine a light on how these issues not only affect millions of lives, but trillions of dollars in business hangs in the balance if they are not addressed head on.

9. Multi-capital stocks and flows

The ninth driving force for change has to do with the support for businesses that are not only doing well, but doing good, and even thriving, as we saw in Chapter 3 with BlackRock's groundbreaking support and recent moves to only support businesses that not only have a profit motive but also have a social purpose.

10. Natural capital constrained

The ultimate driving force for change is Mother Nature herself, and the very real restraints and limitations she imposes, including the ecosystem services she provides and its inherent limits. Global warming, climate change, and extreme weather events, including hurricanes, droughts, fires, excessive heat, and frigid cold, and their impact on millions of people and trillions of dollars are begging us to heed Mother Nature's calls for much needed change around the world.

One unifying force that is pulling much of these driving forces for change together is the application of organization development principles and practices to advance sustainability. One particular organization, the OD Collaborative for a Flourishing Future (www.odcfw.org) has dedicated itself to applying systems thinking, question thinking, appreciative inquiry, and dialogic organization development to the most challenging questions facing sustainability practitioners today.

Pillars holding up the new bridges to the future

There are threads that run through the book that hold some keys to accelerating the progress of sustainability. Each of us will have an impact on the world. Will we leave it in a state that is better, worse, or the same as when we found it? What can each of us do to collectively move ourselves toward a more sustainable world? How will we go beyond zero footprint so that collectively we can reverse the effects of our practices and regenerate and replenish the natural resources of our planet? What role can each of us play in creating and implementing the strategies to effect the changes that can be mutually beneficial to our organizations, companies, nations, and the world? These issues are explored in depth in Chapters 3 and 7.

Here we have designed a bridge to the future held up by the eight pillars that represent each of the chapters of our book: Leadership, Mental Models, Strategy, Change, Engagement, Metrics, Sustainable Globalization, and Sustainability Models. The bridge has a three-lane highway to get us across the chasm from the unsustainable, wasteful grey economy on the left, to the sustainable green economy on the right side (see Figure 9.2). To get us started through the toll booth and onto the bridge, we need to have hope (see Box 9.1).

Once on the bridge, we need innovation. As we accelerate, we must behave collaboratively. And most important, we have to be adaptable to discern and continually respond to the feedback signals for resiliency.

Call to action

As Margaret Mead said, "Never doubt that a small group of thoughtful, committed, citizens can change the world. Indeed, it is the only thing that ever has." What is needed more than anything else is not just talk but concerted and intentional action, translating all the wonderful ideas and learning over the last 50 years into meaningful on the ground change. We need to close the "knowing-doing" gap! This process of transitioning from the current unsustainable economy to a new sustainable economy is not an intellectual exercise but one we must learn by doing, by building the bridges as we walk on them. As we learn we will almost certainly change some of our ideas about what we want and can do. Real learning always changes people.

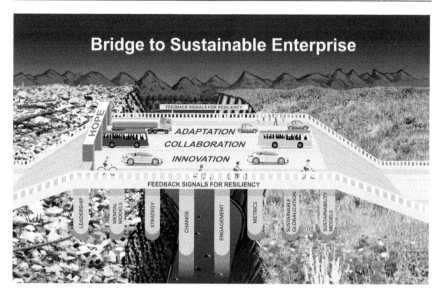

Figure 9.2 Bridge to sustainable enterprise

Accelerators for creating momentum and traction on the new bridge to the future

> ### One-legged man scales 14,408-foot Mt. Rainier
>
> (*New York Times*, July 1982)
> When amputee Don Bennett was asked how he did it, he said one hop at a time!

Climbing mountains or crossing bridges to a thriving future is hard, challenging work. How can we be both optimistic about our outcome and persevere through the reality of the daily hard work needed to achieve it? Crossing this bridge is the ultimate goal, we know we must work and sustain ourselves every day to manage the complex paradoxes, problems, and opportunities of sustainability. To thrive and sustain ourselves on this journey, we have learned that there are some key principles we must focus on including purpose, human connection, responsibility, perseverance, resilience, and learning.

Our purpose of this book is to help forge a path to a better world and a more sustainable, flourishing, and thriving future by supporting employees, managers, and leaders at every level and in every function, sector, and industry. Each day we are challenged to live out this purpose in the work we do to create a thriving world. We have also learned we can be most effective when we create the space, structure, and conversations that will energize ourselves and our readers to take action.

Human connection

Michael Lee Stallard said a connected organization has three key ingredients (Stallard, 2015). Vision + Value + Voice = Connection. Having a clear vision or purpose is the first ingredient. The second is that employees are truly valued, this is evidenced in the organization's design, processes, and policies. The last component is Voice—employees are truly listened to, which influences the organization's focus and decision-making. This is also true for the connected and thriving sustainability movement we are privileged to contribute to. We hope that our book provides the vision, our translation of sustainability thought leaders blended with our own contributions. Valuing our community and listening to their voice comes from what we learned from the thousands of conversations we had in practicing sustainability, resulting in a fieldbook with activities, cases, and tools to continue to keep people connected in our collective journey.

Perseverance

> When we are no longer able to change a situation, we are challenged to change ourselves.
>
> (Viktor E. Frankl, *Man's Search for Meaning*)

This is really hard challenging work! Fulfilling our purpose: to help forge a path to a better world and a more sustainable, flourishing, and thriving future by supporting employees, managers, and leaders at every level and in every function, sector, and industry. This is a big challenging purpose with daunting challenges to traverse the path across the bridge of sustainability. To thrive and sustain ourselves on this journey, how can we be both optimistic about our outcome and persevere through the reality of hard work we need to do to get there? Jim Stockdale, a US military officer held captive as a prisoner of war in Vietnam, had a daunting challenge of surviving over eight long years, always positive he would someday be free. Commander Stockdale was the senior naval officer held captive in Hanoi, North Vietnam and eventual Vice President nominee with Ross Perot in 1992.

> I never doubted not only that I would get out, but also that I would prevail in the end and turn the experience into the defining event of my life, which, in retrospect, I would not trade.

Stockdale used this hope as motivation to do the hard work necessary to improve the lives of his fellow prisoners, such as creating ways for them to communicate and support each other in spite of their isolation and terrible conditions. He also witnessed some prisoners use hope as an excuse for inaction and wait to be freed soon; but sadly, these prisoners most often did not survive.

Our working mantra has become to always be in relentless action towards improving opportunities within our current field of vision while keeping an optimistic eye toward a future where we all thrive! The root of optimist is the word opt, from the Latin, *optare*—to choose, to desire. Choosing is important here. I choose to focus on what I can do. While I'm aware of what I cannot do at this moment, here's what I can do. Imagining Stockdale in solitary confinement along with his fellow prisoners, what could he do (and we suspect he tried a number of things). He could tap once on a wall. The first time might have even happened accidentally. Then someone else realized he also could tap on a wall, and did. There was a connection with someone else. I can do, we can do, and we are connected. Getting a result he (they) desired built hope, as small as it was … and on and on, step by tiny step. I can do this, now I can do this … Were there setbacks? Of course. Most often there are. And again I choose to focus on what I can do. Much to inspire us in moving us toward a sustainable, thriving future. Step by step, I can. When I fall back, I gather myself and start again. I am resilient. I can.

"On Hope for a Sustainable World in 2018"

We couldn't have said it better than our esteemed colleague Eban Goodstein, Executive Director of Bard's MBA in Sustainability, who inspired us when he wrote a wonderful blog "On Hope for a Sustainable World in 2018." We are grateful to be able to reproduce it here in Box 9.1.

Box 9.1   On Hope for a Sustainable World in 2018

BY
EBAN GOODSTEIN
– JANUARY 4, 2018

"In the face of daunting environmental problems and troubling trends in US federal policy, what gives you drive, motivation, and hope, to continue the work?"

This question, recently asked of environmental studies faculty in an online forum by Professor Amy Knisley at Warren Wilson College, resonates with many of us. Here is my response.

I grew up on stories of the holocaust. So, I have always understood that, depending on where and when I happened to be born, I might or might not be hauled out of bed some night at gun point and sent by rail car off with my family to a gas chamber. This is always a possibility.

I also attended one of the first integrated first-grade classes in my little southern town. At the age of six, with an African American teacher and classmates, I was happily unaware that my classroom, two years earlier, was legally white-only.

Humans are animals that have evolved with tremendous capacity for good and evil. There are 7.5 billion of us now, soon to be 10 billion, all aspiring to western living standards, while a tiny elite controls the majority of wealth. Lacking wise governance, we are transforming the planet in ways that will make it hard to sustain that many people, not to mention the ecological systems on which they depend.

That said, in the long run, nature is remarkably resilient. The same is true of human society, if not individual civilizations. And of course, over the very long run, even species diversity will recover. My guess is that 200 or 400 or 600 years from now, there will be fewer humans around, and that natural systems will have the space to recover. How we get to a smaller population matters a lot: we can work towards economic security leading to smaller families—the Japanese or Italian examples. Sustainability means transitioning to a future that is as just and peaceful and respectful of other creatures as we can make it.

For many people, this is the most extraordinary time to ever be alive as a human. More people have more agency to affect the future than ever before. There is much good work to do, many opportunities, and unprecedented tools with which to be creative in the service of a finer world. In western countries, very few of us face dogs or firehoses, torture, prison blacklisting or beatings for doing the work. Given this, existential angst about ultimate dystopic futures seems to me misplaced. Too many people already live in dystopia today, and do not have the agency and opportunity the rest of us have to make things better for people and the planet.

The question of "hope" writ large also seems to me to be misplaced. There will always be people doing terrible things, and there will always be people doing very good things. Whether the moral arc of the universe bends towards justice or chaos depends only on whether enough people work for the good. None of us will ever know the outcome, though each of us can affect the balance.

Source: *Bard EcoReader Blog*, January 4, 2018, www.bard.edu/cep/blog/?p=9943.

Resilience

There are myriad challenges on the bridge to a new future. The one characteristic that will help us make it through, to keep going despite the many obstacles and defeats along the way, is resilience. Resilience gives us the fortitude to bounce back from adversity, to deal with the naysayers and the negativity, and when things inevitably don't go our way, the energy and drive to get up and start moving again.

Technology and innovation

One of the most amazing things we have at our disposal is our imagination. The technological advances of the last few decades are almost beyond comprehension. And the ones ahead—such as augmented reality and autonomous vehicles—to name just two examples, can cause exponential movement when applied to our most intractable problems. But let's be sure to look at the big picture, including the unintended consequences as we move into this new future.

Responsibility

We believe we all have a superordinate moral and civic responsibility to leave the world in at least as good a condition as we found it. Using the original language of the UN Brundtland Commission (World Commission on Environment and Development, 1987), we must "meet the needs of the present without compromising the ability of future generations to meet their own needs." We believe all businesses and all organizations have a moral and an ethical responsibility to—at minimum—do no harm to all their stakeholders, including their employees, customers and ultimate consumers, investors/shareholders, the communities they serve, and the environment. But our bridge to the future requires much more than that. It requires businesses to take positive actions to be restorative, regenerative, and life-affirming to all stakeholders, including and especially the environment.

When organizations, communities, and enterprises start each day, what is their hope for the day, week, year, and decade? Sounds like a funny analogy, but it does get you thinking: What is the collective hope of an enterprise? It is made up and spread across the populations of stakeholders that make up that enterprise. If individuals have been engaged and asked what is most important to them and feel heard, you will achieve results. The "Appreciative Inquiry case study: executive MBA candidates," by Theresa McNichol in Chapter 2 (pages 117–121), gives us tools and processes to bring forth people's deep-seated hopes and dreams.

Learning

Waking up with curiosity and entering every task and conversation with the belief and openness to bringing new ideas and approaches is a measure of our health and progress.

What have we collectively learned about sustainability?

Our intended hopes for our readers are the same hopes we have for ourselves. As a result of writing this book and your reading it, we hope that each of us:

- is energized to make an individual and collective difference towards greater sustainability;
- is prepared to take action on an individual, group, enterprise, and global basis;
- has a clear and realistic understanding of the tensions and challenges we will face;
- has a higher level of comfort to face these challenges and turn them into opportunities by utilizing the tools and learnings from the cases we presented as well as the increased power of connection we now have as part of the larger sustainability network.

So, now what?

We asked ourselves as we sent our final version to our editor. Our answer is it's time to get to work on the big work of sustainability. There is no waiting until you know everything or getting distracted with less important things. Keep moving, one hop at a time on your personal sustainability journey, join our community and drop us a line and let us know how you are progressing.

Note

1 www.bbc.com/news/world-42982959?utm_content=bufferbf274&utm_medium=social&utm_source=twitter.com&utm_campaign=buffer

References

Haidt, J. (2012). *The righteous mind: Why good people are divided by politics and religion*. Gildan Media LLC. Toronto, Canada: Random House of Canada Limited.
Kleiner, K. (2007). The backlash against biofuels. *Nature Reports Climate Change*, 9–11.
Lacy, P., & Rutqvist, J. (2015). *Waste to wealth: Creating advantage in a circular economy*. New York: Palgrave Macmillan.
McLagan, P. (2017). *Unstoppable you*. Alexandria, VA: ATD Press.

Stallard, M. L. (2015). *Connection culture*. Alexandria, VA: ATD Press.

World Commission on Environment and Development (WCED). (1987). *Our common future*. Oxford, UK: Oxford University Press.

World Economic Forum. (2018). *World Economic Forum 2018 Global Risks Report*. Geneva: World Economic Forum.

Index

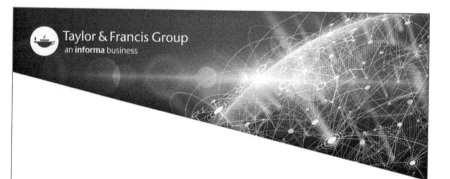